B

Fodor's

D0017237

CROATIA & SLOVENIA

2nd Edition

Where to Stay and Eat
for All Budgets

Must-See Sights
and Local Secrets

Ratings You Can Trust

Fodor's Travel Publications   New York, Toronto, London, Sydney, Auckland
www.fodors.com

FODOR'S CROATIA & SLOVENIA
Editor: Douglas Stallings

Editorial Production: Linda Schmidt
Editorial Contributors: John K. Cox, Jane Foster, Betsy Maury, Paul Olchvary, Marijana Oroz, Evan Rail
Maps & Illustrations: David Lindroth, Ed Jacobus, *cartographers*; Bob Blake and Rebecca Baer, *map editors*
Design: Fabrizio LaRocca, *creative director*; Guido Caroti, Siobhan O'Hare, *art directors*; Tina Malaney, Chie Ushio, Ann McBride, *designers*; Melanie Marin, *senior picture editor;* Moon Sun Kim, *cover designer*
Cover Photo (outdoor café, Vis, Dalmatia): SIME s.a.s/eStock Photo
Production/Manufacturing: Matthew Struble

COPYRIGHT
Copyright © 2008 by Fodor's Travel, a division of Random House, Inc.

Fodor's is a registered trademark of Random House, Inc.

All rights reserved. Published in the United States by Fodor's Travel, a division of Random House, Inc., and simultaneously in Canada by Random House of Canada, Limited, Toronto. Distributed by Random House, Inc., New York.

No maps, illustrations, or other portions of this book may be reproduced in any form without written permission from the publisher.

2nd Edition

ISBN 978–1–4000–1940–3

ISSN 1558–8181

SPECIAL SALES
This book is available at special discounts for bulk purchases for sales promotions or premiums. Special editions, including personalized covers, excerpts of existing books, and corporate imprints, can be created in large quantities for special needs. For more information, write to Special Markets/Premium Sales, 1745 Broadway, MD 6-2, New York, New York 10019, or e-mail specialmarkets@randomhouse.com.

AN IMPORTANT TIP & AN INVITATION
Although all prices, opening times, and other details in this book are based on information supplied to us at press time, changes occur all the time in the travel world, and Fodor's cannot accept responsibility for facts that become outdated or for inadvertent errors or omissions. So **always confirm information when it matters,** especially if you're making a detour to visit a specific place. Your experiences—positive and negative— matter to us. If we have missed or misstated something, **please write to us.** We follow up on all suggestions. Contact the Croatia & Slovenia editor at editors@fodors.com or c/o Fodor's at 1745 Broadway, New York, NY 10019.

PRINTED IN THE UNITED STATES OF AMERICA
10 9 8 7 6 5 4 3 2 1

Be a Fodor's Correspondent

Your opinion matters. It matters to us. It matters to your fellow Fodor's travelers, too. And we'd like to hear it. In fact, we need to hear it.

When you share your experiences and opinions, you become an active member of the Fodor's community. That means we'll not only use your feedback to make our books better, but we'll publish your names and comments whenever possible. Throughout our guides, look for "Word of Mouth," excerpts of your unvarnished feedback.

Here's how you can help improve Fodor's for all of us.

Tell us when we're right. We rely on local writers to give you an insider's perspective. But our writers and staff editors—who are the best in the business—depend on you. Your positive feedback is a vote to renew our recommendations for the next edition.

Tell us when we're wrong. We're proud that we update most of our guides every year. But we're not perfect. Things change. Hotels cut services. Museums change hours. Charming cafés lose charm. If our writer didn't quite capture the essence of a place, tell us how you'd do it differently. If any of our descriptions are inaccurate or inadequate, we'll incorporate your changes in the next edition and will correct factual errors at fodors.com immediately.

Tell us what to include. You probably have had fantastic travel experiences that aren't yet in Fodor's. Why not share them with a community of like-minded travelers? Maybe you chanced upon a beach or bistro or B&B that you don't want to keep to yourself. Tell us why we should include it. And share your discoveries and experiences with everyone directly at fodors.com. Your input may lead us to add a new listing or highlight a place we cover with a "Highly Recommended" star or with our highest rating, "Fodor's Choice."

Give us your opinion instantly at our feedback center at www.fodors.com/feedback. You may also e-mail editors@fodors.com with the subject line "Croatia & Slovenia Editor." Or send your nominations, comments, and complaints by mail to Croatia & Slovenia Editor, Fodor's, 1745 Broadway, New York, NY 10019.

You and travelers like you are the heart of the Fodor's community. Make our community richer by sharing your experiences. Be a Fodor's correspondent.

Happy traveling!

Tim Jarrell, Publisher

CONTENTS

ABOUT THIS BOOK

Our Ratings

Sometimes you find terrific travel experiences and sometimes they just find you. But usually the burden is on you to select the right combination of experiences. That's where our ratings come in.

As travelers we've all discovered a place so wonderful that its worthiness is obvious. And sometimes that place is so unique that superlatives don't do it justice: you just have to be there to know. These sights, properties, and experiences get our highest rating, **Fodor's Choice**, indicated by orange stars throughout this book.

Black stars highlight sights and properties we deem **Highly Recommended**, places that our writers, editors, and readers praise again and again for consistency and excellence.

By default, there's another category: any place we include in this book is by definition worth your time, unless we say otherwise. And we will.

Disagree with any of our choices? Care to nominate a place or suggest that we rate one more highly? Visit our feedback center at www.fodors.com/feedback.

Budget Well

Hotel and restaurant price categories from ¢ to $$$$ are defined in the opening pages of each chapter. For attractions, we always give standard adult admission fees; reductions are usually available for children, students, and senior citizens. Want to pay with plastic? **AE, DC, MC, V** following restaurant and hotel listings indicate whether American Express, Diners Club, MasterCard, and Visa are accepted.

Restaurants

Unless we state otherwise, restaurants are open for lunch and dinner daily. We mention dress only when there's a specific requirement and reservations only when they're essential or not accepted—it's always best to book ahead.

Hotels

Hotels have private bath, phone, TV, and air-conditioning and operate on the European Plan (aka EP, meaning without meals), unless we specify that they use the Continental Plan (CP, with a Continental breakfast), Breakfast Plan (BP, with a full breakfast), or Modified American Plan (MAP, with breakfast and dinner) or are all-inclusive (AI, including all meals and most activi-ties). We always list facilities but not whether you'll be charged an extra fee to use them, so when pricing accommodations, find out what's included.

Many Listings
- ★ Fodor's Choice
- ★ Highly recommended
- ⊠ Physical address
- ✢ Directions
- ⌖ Mailing address
- ☎ Telephone
- ⎙ Fax
- ⊕ On the Web
- ✉ E-mail
- ▣ Admission fee
- ☉ Open/closed times
- Ⓜ Metro stations
- ▭ Credit cards

Hotels & Restaurants
- ⊡ Hotel
- ⇥ Number of rooms
- ⚱ Facilities
- ¶Ⓞ¶ Meal plans
- ✕ Restaurant
- ⇱ Reservations
- ⬍ Smoking
- ⚷ BYOB
- ✕⊡ Hotel with restaurant that warrants a visit

Outdoors
- ⚲ Golf
- ⚑ Camping

Other
- ☿ Family-friendly
- ⇨ See also
- ⊠ Branch address
- ☞ Take note

WHAT'S WHERE

ZAGREB & ENVIRONS 	Croatia's interior capital is provincial, inconveniently located, and not chock-full of unique artistic or architectural wonders. Even the Croatians agree it lacks the stature of Vienna, Prague, or Budapest. That said, travelers will find a charming, well-kept national seat that evokes a distant Habsburg past and a pretty Upper Town lined with lively cafés and restaurants. Northwest of the city is the castle district of the Zagorje. From Zagreb, good roads lead to the coast, where Plitvice National Park—a spectacular series of 16 lakes cascading from one to the other nestled in a wild forest—is about halfway to Zadar.
SLAVONIA 	The least-visited part of Croatia still has much to offer the adventurous traveler. Osijek is filled with churches and Habsburg-era architecture. Bird-watchers may be drawn to the vast wetlands of Kopačice Rit Nature Park. And then there's Vukovar, a sobering reminder that this region is still rebuilding from the war of the early 1990s. Throughout Slavonia, you'll find more charming villages and quiet rural life than almost anywhere else in the country. Come if you want to get away from the hordes of tourists and experience a part of the country that's not often seen.
ISTRIA 	The red-tiled roofs of Venetian Rovinj and the Roman amphitheater at Pula make this region feel more Italian than Croatian. A vibrant café scene and culinary delights like air-dried ham and truffles all add to Istria's *la dolce vita*. Croatia's western peninsula is well situated, especially if you want to combine your trip with a foray into Slovenia or northern Italy. Pula and the western coast are the highlights, but a drive into the interior will reward with pretty medieval villages and vineyards.
KVARNER 	Protected by mountain ranges on three sides, Kvarner enjoys a particularly mild climate. The jewel of the Kvarner is Opatija, with its yellow turn-of-the-20th-century hotels lining the main street and a long promenade along the Adriatic. Opatija in its heyday was a favorite winter getaway for the Habsburgs; today you can still get a whiff of that faded grandeur in some of the hotel dining rooms and patios. Rijeka is more an active port town and less a tourist attraction, where you can experience authentic Croatian atmosphere. And from Rijeka the island of Krk is easily accessible by car via a bridge; Cres and Losinj are reached by ferry.

WHAT'S WHERE

ZADAR & NORTHERN DALMATIA 	Zadar doesn't rival Split or Dubrovnik for ancient ruins, but it's a good base if you want to explore the interior and still get the feeling of the laid-back Dalmatian seaside. If you want an even quieter place, check out nearby Nin. Zadar is about midpoint on the Dalmatian coast. In its own right, Zadar has quite a few good museums and the impressive Church of St. Donat, a 9th-century Byzantine church built on the site of a Roman forum. There's good access to the 89-island Kornati archipelago from nearby Murter, as well as to the fast highway back to Zagreb.
SPLIT & CENTRAL DALMATIA 	Aside from Zagreb, second-city Split has the best transport connections in Croatia. There's an international airport, train and bus stations, and (in the summer, at least) a busy ferry port. If you are looking for someplace less busy, then consider nearby Trogir. The main attraction in Split is Diocletian's over-the-top palace, which dominates the Old Town; it was built in the 4th century to house the retiring Roman emperor, who spared no expense to make it a luxurious home. You're also in a great position to set out island-hopping, either to the pretty island of Vis, the fine pebble beaches of Brač, or the relaxing atmosphere of Hvar.
DUBROVNIK & SOUTHERN DALMATIA 	Few cities in the world impress as Dubrovnik does, with its ancient walls and towers perched above the deep blue waters of the Adriatic. Once the wealthy, semi-independent city-state of Ragusa, Dubrovnik has an interesting history as both a Roman and Slav city. It's a busy place today, so avoid the summer months if you can, when lots of day-trippers clog the Old Town. If you need to escape, strike out for Korčula, which was Marco Polo's birthplace, or quiet Lopud, or even quieter Mljet, which was off-limits to tourists during the Tito years.
SLOVENIA 	With dirt-cheap airfares from London, Ljubljana is a good first stop if you're looking for a gentle entry into the region on the way to Istria and Kvarner. Slovenia itself is the size of New Jersey, so Ljubljana is only a four-hour train ride from Istria's southernmost tip in Pula. The laid-back capital, gracefully situated on the Ljubljanica River, provides a good jumping-off point for exploring the rest of the country: the Julian Alps and lakes to the north, or the Škocjanske or Postojanske caves to the southwest.

Croatia & Slovenia

AUSTRIA

HUNGARY

ITALY

ROMANIA

Ljubljana

SLOVENIJA (SLOVENIA)

Celje

Postojna

Trieste

Portorož

Opatija

Rijeka

Pula

ISTRIA

KVARNER

Krk

Cres

Lošinj

Rab

Pag

NORTHERN DALMATIA

Senj

Karlovac

Zagreb

Varaždin

HRVATSKA (CROATIA)

Virovitica

Daruvar

Osijek

SLAVONIA

Sl. Brod

Bihać

Banja Luka

Doboj

BOSNIA I HERCEGOVINA (BOSNIA AND HERCEGOVINA)

Zenica

Jajce

Sarajevo

Višegrad

Konjic

Mostar

Metković

AP VOJVODINA (VOJVODINA)

Novi Sad

Belgrade

Vršac

Timisoara

Zaječar

Paraćin

SRBIJA (SERBIA)

Kraljevo

Raška

SRBIJA (SERBIA)

Niš

Leskovac

Pirot

Priština

AP KOSOVO (KOSOVO)

CRNA GORA (MONTENEGRO)

Nikšia

Podgorica

Kotor

Herceg-Novi

Dubrovnik

Pelješac

Mljet

Korčula

SOUTHERN DALMATIA

Makarska

Hvar

Brač

Split

Šibenik

Zadar

Dugi Otok

Knin

CENTRAL DALMATIA

Adriatic Sea

ITALY

Danube

Drava

Sava

Sava

Una

Bosna

Drina

Morava

Danube

50 miles

50 kilometers

0

0

QUINTESSENTIAL CROATIA & SLOVENIA

Ljubljana Tržnica

Ljubljanček begin their weekend routine with a trip to the bustling *trnica* (Central Market) located near the Three Bridges. It's a charming European scene of old; students, families, and retired people come to buy their fresh produce, many toting traditional straw baskets and arriving by bicycle. Most people spend the balance of the morning there, buying fresh fruits and vegetables, drinking coffee or even an early schnapps with friends, and then eventually stopping for lunch in the lower level of the fish market for *kalamari na žaru* (grilled calamari) or local trout. The market in Ljubljana couldn't be better situated: on the leafy banks of the Ljubljanica River in an elegant structure purpose-built by local architect Jože Plečnik. The building, combined with some of the highest-quality seasonal produce in Central Europe, makes a Saturday trip to the market a local pleasure not to be missed.

Dalmatian Summer

Although most Zagreb residents go to Kvarner, for many Croatians summer holidays mean Dalmatia. Every family has its favorite spot on the coast, and people remember their blissful childhood holidays in Dalmatia with the most detailed accuracy. Tales of Dingač or Plavac wine, *paski sir* (sheep cheese from the island of Pag), and fresh sea bass enjoyed in a simple seaside restaurant feature heavily in the national memory. Whether a holiday means a wooded campsite in a national park, a sandy beach on Brač, or a small pension on Losinj, summer holidays begin and end for Croatians on their own splendid coast. Roads, accommodations, and ferry travel along the coast have improved over the years, turning Dalmatia into an international tourist destination. After you've relaxed for a week or more, soaking up the sun Dalmatian-style, you'll ask the same question the Croatians do: Why go anywhere else?

If you want to get a sense of contemporary Croatian and Slovenian culture, and indulge in some of its pleasures, start by familiarizing yourself with the rituals of daily life. These are a few highlights—things you can take part in with relative ease.

Naturism

Like it or not, there's a long history of naturism in Croatia, and this country has been one of the most progressive in pioneering the nude resort. Naturist campsites, beaches, and even sailing charters abound in certain parts of the coast (mainly Istria), and hundreds of thousands flock here each year to enjoy some fun in the sun *au naturel.* Naturism in Croatia goes back before World War II, when a leading Viennese naturist developed a beach on the island of Rab. Since then, a thriving culture of naturism has taken root, mainly among European enthusiasts. A glossy brochure published by the Croatian National Tourist Board lists 14 naturist "camps" and "villages" and about as many officially designated "free naturist beaches" on the country's Adriatic coast. Croatians themselves don't seem to make up the bulk of the clientele at naturist resorts, but they graciously make visitors welcome.

Rakija

Get one or two Croatians together, and somebody's bound to introduce *rakija,* a distilled herbal or fruit spirit that makes up an important part of Croatian culture. All across the country business deals are sealed, friendships are cemented, and journeys are begun to the clink of a few shot glasses of the fiery schnapps. Croatians often brew rakija themselves at home, using everything from plums and pears to herbs and juniper berries. In the countryside you can often find roadside stands selling the family blend with pride. Rakija is also enjoyed in Slovenia, where it often begins a meal as an aperitif. If you're game to order one on your travels in the region, start first with the sweeter, fruitier brews (blueberry is a good choice), and then work your way up to the somewhat digestive herbals.

IF YOU LIKE

Pleasures at Sea

Croatia and Slovenia offer prime opportunities to spend time by the clear blue waters of the Adriatic. Each of these unique pleasures is designed to highlight the mysteries of life by the sea. This list of favorites makes for unforgettable vacation memories.

Hvar Town, Central Dalmatia. A favorite destination among the yachting fraternity, Hvar remains completely at ease with its age-old beauty: medieval stone houses are built around a natural harbor and backed by a hilltop fortress.

Strolling around Piran's sea wall at sunset, Istria. It's hard to imagine a more romantic and relaxed setting: the warm sea breezes invigorate as you stroll by the charming marina with the shadow of *Trg Tartini* behind you.

Zlatni Rat, Bol, Central Dalmatia. The spectacular beach on the island of Brač is the jewel of the Adriatic: white, with very fine pebbles, and lapped on three sides by the gentle blue sea.

A walk on the Lungomare in Opatija, Kvarner. Built in 1889, this 12-km (7½-mi) promenade along the sea leads from the fishing village of Volosko, through Opatija—passing in front of old hotels, parks, and gardens and around yacht basins—and all the way past the villages of Ičići and Ika to Lovran in the south.

An excursion to Mljet, Southern Dalmatia. A long, thin island of steep, rocky slopes and dense pine forests, Mljet is one of Croatia's most remote islands. One of Croatia's few sand beaches, Saplunara, is at its southeastern tip, which remains relatively wild and untended.

Soft Adventure

National parks abound in Slovenia and Croatia, with surefire opportunities to commune with the great outdoors. In every season there are peaks to climb, seas to dive in, and white-water rivers to conquer. The thrills are more thrilling in Slovenia. Here are some of our favorite spots for those seeking a bit of soft adventure.

Biking around Lake Bohinj, Slovenia. You can enjoy some easy pedaling along tiny country roads, through dairy farms and villages right out of the 19th century, with the Julian Alps in the background.

Rafting on the Soča River, Slovenia. A rush of adrenaline strikes you as you fly across the bracing blue and green waters that run through unspoiled national forest.

Diving in Kvarner Bay. Diving in the crystal-clear waters of Kvarner Bay—particularly near the islands of Cres and Losinj—is an eye-opening experience. Just remember that the most thrilling sights below the waves are usually wrecks.

Hiking in Risnjak National Park, Kvarner. The thick pine forest, meadows that are stuffed with wildflowers in the spring, and limestone peaks, crevices, and caves cover around 30 square km (18½ square mi).

Boutique Hotels

Slowly but surely local entrepreneurs in Slovenia and Croatia are renovating historic properties and opening boutique hotels. These properties are where you'll find peace and quiet (and usually good food), not to mention owners who are committed to making your stay special.

Hotel Waldinger, Osijek, Slavonia. This intimate hotel is one of the best (and most luxurious) places to sleep in all of Slavonia; it also has an excellent restaurant.

Hotel Vestibul Palace, Split, Central Dalmatia. Luxury and romance are combined in this small boutique hotel within the walls of Diocletian's Palace, as minimalist designer details are played off against exposed Roman stone and brickwork.

Pučić Palace, Dubrovnik, Southern Dalmatia. Showing the new direction of Croatian tourism, this small luxury hotel occupies a romantic baroque palace in Dubrovnik's Old Town.

Dvorac Bezanec, Zagorje, Zagreb & Environs. This lovely old manor house 15 minutes east of Veliki Tabor is a renovated 17th-century castle complete with period furniture and authentic fittings. Enjoy the beautiful landscape of the Zagorje with old-fashioned frills.

Kendov Dvorec, Slovenia. A lovingly restored villa filled with period furnishings in an idyllic rural setting. The owner will go out of her way to cater to your every need.

Roman History

The cultural and historical richness of Croatia make it a destination that satisfies even the most well-traveled visitor. All over the country there are ruins of former civilizations and empires that give you a glimpse of the country's past. A trip to this list of favorites will enrich any vacation to Croatia.

Diocletian's Palace, Split. Roman emperor Diocletian's summer palace, built in the 3rd century AD, is one of the most spectacular sites in all of Croatia. It's unmissable.

The Arena, Pula. Designed to accommodate 22,000 spectators, the Arena is the sixth-largest building of its type in the world (after the Colosseum in Rome and similar arenas in Verona, Catania, Capua, and Arles), and one of the best preserved.

Crkva sv Donata, Zadar. Zadar's star attraction, this huge, cylindrical structure is the most monumental early Byzantine church in Croatia.

Eufrazijeva Basilica (St. Euphrasius Basilica), Poreč. This is among the most perfectly preserved Christian churches in Europe, and one of the most important monuments of Byzantine art on the Adriatic.

Katedrala Sveti Lovrijenac (Cathedral of St. Lawrence), Trogir. A perfect example of the massiveness and power of Romanesque architecture, the most striking detail is the main portal, decorated with minutely carved stonework during the 13th century.

IF YOU LIKE

Summer Nightlife

Seaside nightlife in Croatia and Slovenia generally doesn't disappoint. All over the coast people are enjoying themselves outside most evenings, sipping trendy cocktails, listening to music, or tasting the local wine. Even the smallest village on the coast is littered with outdoor cafés and bars in the summertime. If you find yourself near any of these this summer, join in the fun!

Dubrovnik Summer Festival, Southern Dalmatia. The world-renowned summer festival in Dubrovnik offers quality theatrical performances and classical-music concerts with international performers, all set against the backdrop of the azure Adriatic.

Aquarius, Zagreb. Having climbed out of its post-war depression, Zagreb is once again alive at night. Aquarius is the top spot for dancing until dawn—in the summer and all year-round.

Carpe Diem, Hvar, Central Dalmatia. A harborside cocktail bar with a summer terrace is where Hvar's richest and most glamorous visitors come to see and be seen. Stop in here to see why Hvar has been labeled the next Ibiza.

Monokini, Opatija, Kvarner. Good music, a friendly staff, and Internet access are turning this bar back into one of Kvarner's hot spots.

Ambasada Gavioli, Izola, Slovenia. Gavioli, southwest of the Izola port in the city's industrial area, remains one of the coast's and the country's best clubs. DJs are regularly brought in from around the world to play techno, trance, funk, and fusion.

Going Native

You can find gustatory pleasures at every level in Slovenia and Croatia. Sometimes the ones to seek out are the favorites of the locals, who don't allow restaurants to rest on their laurels. Whether it's a snack at a market stall or a simple seaside restaurant, one of the great pleasures of travel is finding these popular spots. All of these are favorites for their commitment to local, seasonal food.

Slavonska Kuća, Osijek, Slavonia. This small, local restaurant is about as atmospheric as can be. If you stick to the local specialties, you'll enjoy a fine introduction to Slavonian cuisine.

Gostilna As, Ljubljana, Slovenia. One of the most refined restaurants in Ljubljana serves innovative seafood dishes and pasta, and has a first-rate wine list.

Konobe Kod Sipe, Sali, Northern Dalmatia. This rustic favorite is known for serving some of the freshest fish dishes in town. Fishnets hanging from the ceiling's wooden beams plus an outdoor terrace shaded by grapevines add to the homey atmosphere.

Sirius, Losinj, Kvarner. The national press claim that this would be a top contender for best restaurant in the country if it were open year-round, so deserved is its reputation for fresh seafood.

Vodnjanka Restaurant, Vodnjan, Istria. This is the place to go for the most mouthwatering homemade pasta dishes you can imagine, not least *fuži* with wild arugula and prosciutto in cream sauce—delicious.

Wining & Dining

A vacation wouldn't be a vacation if you didn't seek out some of the country's finest dining. All of the following have built their reputation on first-rate cuisine and an impressive wine list to match.

Adio Mare, Korčula, Southern Dalmatia. The menu at this renowned eatery hasn't changed since it opened in 1974: traditional Dalmatian seafood and Balkan meat specialties, prepared over burning coals. Dinner here is unforgettable.

Monte, Rovinj, Istria. An elegant Italian restaurant just below St. Euphemia's offers an excellent repast and quiet surroundings in which to enjoy a long afternoon's lunch.

Katunar, Krk Town, Vrbnik, Kvarner. The wines produced on Krk Island are among the best in Croatia. The torch-lit grill is the place for dinner, but the experience is all about the wine.

Valsabbion, Pula, Istria. This superb restaurant was one of the first in Croatia to specialize in what has come to be known as "slow food," and has been voted the best restaurant in Istria as well as Croatia several times. The menu changes regularly, but you can expect such delights as frogfish in vine leaves or tagliatelle with aromatic herbs and pine nuts.

Paviljon, Zagreb. The Italian-inspired menu of this chic restaurant includes dishes such as tagliatelle with prosciutto and asparagus, crispy roast duck on red cabbage with figs, and oven-roasted monkfish with bread crumbs, pine nuts, and thyme.

Natural Wonders

Croatia and Slovenia are not short on natural wonders. The unusual karst terrain of this region has created caves and waterfalls and made a home for many species of wildlife. Many of the region's best natural areas are now protected as national parks that are accessible throughout the year.

Nacionalni Park Plitvicla Jezera, Velika Poljana, Zagreb & Environs. One of the first-class natural areas in Croatia, this national park has 16 cascading lakes nestled in a protected forest.

Škocjanske Jama, Slovenia. The breathtaking, enormous underground cavern is so deep it looks as if it could hold the skyscrapers of Manhattan.

Kornati National Park, Zadar, Northern Dalmatia. More than 100 remote islands here are privately owned. Although anything but lush today, their almost mythical beauty is ironically synonymous with their barrenness: the bone-white-to-ochre colors present a striking contrast to the azure sea.

Brijuni Archipelago, Istria. Designated a national park in 1983, this group of 14 islands north of Pula has been a vacation retreat par excellence for almost 2,000 years. Yugoslav leader Marshal Josip Broz Tito brought famous guests here from the world over. Today, you can come, too.

Krka National Park, Central Dalmatia. The Krka River and surrounding waterfalls compete with Plitvice for dramatic scenery. The park is home to all sorts of flora and fauna, including a wildlife sanctuary.

GREAT ITINERARIES

SLOVENIA & ISTRIA

Ljubljana makes an excellent starting point if your trip is meant to cover both countries in a week. You'll get the mountains and the seaside, city and countryside, and a first-class Roman ruin. This itinerary is best done by car, but it can be done (perhaps a bit more slowly) by train and bus.

Day 1: Ljubljana

Prešernov trg is a good place to begin a walking tour of Ljubljana. Native son Jože Plečnik designed the Three Bridges, the Dragon Bridge, and the central market hall at Vodnik Square, and you get a good view of them all as they cradle the blue-green Ljubljanica river from here. Stroll through the market hall for a look at the season's best fruits and vegetables. Head into the Old Town and wander along the pretty cobblestone streets up to the castle and admire the view over the city. Head back down and do some shopping at the stylish boutiques around Stari trg. ⇨*Ljubljana in Chapter 8.*

Day 2: Lake Bled & Bohinj

Travel north toward Triglav National Park and stop in Radovljica at the Čebelarski Muzej (Beekeeping Museum) on the way up. Stop for an overnight in picture-perfect Lake Bled and row a boat out to the island church if the weather is nice. Spend the afternoon walking the perimeter of the lake and checking out Vila Bled, one of Tito's former residences. Next morning, explore the equally beautiful but more rustic Lake Bohinj in Triglav National Park. ⇨*Lake Bled & Bohinj in Chapter 8.*

Day 3: Day Trip to Kobarid & Bovec

Head back to Ljubljana via the mountainous Soča Valley and stop first in Kobarid, the site of an award-winning World War

I museum. Try to imagine that you are standing in what was once one of the bloodiest fields of battle between the Italians and Slovenes. From there, move on to Bovec for an afternoon of rafting, fishing, or just admiring the clear, aquamarine waters of the Soča River. Try fresh trout with *tržaška* (garlic and parsley) sauce for lunch at any one of the homey *gostišces*. In good weather, take a hike or bike ride in the area. ⇨*Kobarid & Bovec in Chapter 8.*

Day 4: Day Trip to Škocjanske Jame & Štanjel

Southwestern Slovenia has many stalactite and stalagmite caves to choose from, but our favorite is the UNESCO World Heritage site, Škocjanske Jame. The caves are set deep in the rugged karst and are fed by the river Reka, which is deep upstream, then disappears under the cave and reappears to empty into the Adriatic north of Trieste. Take a drive and stop for lunch in Štanjel. The walled Old Town offers some of the prettiest views of the vineyard-dotted countryside. Head back to Ljubljana for another night. ⇨*Škocjanske Jame & Štanjel in Chapter 8.*

Day 5: Piran & Rovinj

Depart from Ljubljana and head south to the coast, stopping for lunch in Piran. Check out lovely Trg Tartini and the Church of St. George on Cathedral Hill and take in the sweeping view of the Adriatic Sea. Make a quick visit to the Maritime Museum. From here, get in the car and head to Istria. Cross the Croatian border and push on to Rovinj in the afternoon in time to enjoy the sunset over the Brijuni islands that evening. Have dinner at a seaside restaurant, spend the night, and explore the Venetian houses and Church of St. Euphemia in the morn-

ing. ⇨*Piran in Chapter 8 and Rovinj in Chapter 3.*

Day 6: Pula

From Rovinj head south to Pula and spend part of the day exploring the incredible Roman amphitheater. This is one of the best-preserved sites in the Roman world. After walking about the Roman forum and amphitheater as well as the 6th-century Church of Mary Formosa, take a ferry to the Brijuni Islands for the afternoon and see the zoo and tropical gardens that Tito designed. Spend the night in Pula. ⇨*Pula in Chapter 3.*

Day 7: Motovun & Ljubljana

Head back to Slovenia via the Istrian interior. Drive north through Pazin and get out of the car for a quick glance at Pazin Castle. North of Pazin, stop in the hill towns of Motovun or Grožnjan for lunch and breathtaking views. These medieval villages are in the heart of truffle country, so keep your eyes open for some fresh goods to bring home. Continue north toward Ljubljana. ⇨*Motovun in Chapter 3 and Ljubljana in Chapter 8.*

TIPS

■ This itinerary is well served by bus, although you'll have to take a bit more time on the interior stops in both Slovenia (Škocjanske Jame and Štanjel) and Croatia (Motovun and Grožnjan).

■ In July and August the main coastal artery connecting the west coast of Istria is crowded with tour buses and RVs. Consider driving in the evening between destinations.

■ Istria's coast is rocky so don't plan a beach holiday without rubber water shoes and a roll-up cushion for under your beach towel. These items are widely available in tourist shops along the coast, but they cost dearly, so bring your own.

■ Slovenian roads are well paved and maintained. This level of efficiency comes at a price; there are frequent toll stops on all highways throughout the country. Keep some small denominations (1,000, 500, 100 SIT notes and change) with you when driving through Slovenia.

GREAT ITINERARIES

ZAGREB, KVARNER & THE INTERIOR

Croatia's capital, Zagreb, will introduce you to the language and customs of the country quickly. It's a good base if you want to explore a combination of the seaside and the interior. Tourist offices are well equipped with information on the country's national parks, ferry schedules, and sailing charters. Guided tours and accommodations can be arranged from here. Many international airline carriers have connections to Zagreb.

Day 1: Zagreb

Zagreb can best be explored on foot. Begin at the massive Trg Jelačića and check out the statue of Ban Josip Jelačić, hero of Croatian resistance to the Austro-Hungarian empire. It's an imposing figure on an imposing square. From here walk to the funicular and head to the Gornji Grad (Upper Town). Stroll around the castle area and visit the Croatian Historical Museum. You'll get a glimpse of Croatia's recent history, including the controversial nationalism of the 1990s. From here, head back down to the Lower Town and check out Ilica, Zagreb's modern high street. Spend the night here. ⇨Zagreb in Chapter 1.

Day 2: Day Trip to Krumrovec & Varaždin

Strike north to Zagorje and spend the morning seeing Varaždin, Croatia's one-time capital. Along the drive you'll see rolling hills dotted with medieval castles and churches. Varaždin's attraction is its gently restored baroque Old Town, but historically it played an important role as a key defensive outpost for the Habsburgs against the onslaught of marauding Turks. Don't miss the massive fortress (Stari Grad). From here, wind back to Krumrovec, an important historical city of a modern kind. It was here that Josip Broz Tito was born, and although the museum detailing his life seems out of step with Croatia today, it has an interesting collection of Partisan memorabilia. ⇨Krumrovec & Varăzin in Chapter 1.

Day 3: Risnjak National Park

From Zagreb head southwest toward Rijeka, stopping off at Delnice and the Risnjak National Park, gateway to the Gorski Kotor, the unspoiled forested karst. This is a beautiful place for a nature walk to check out all kinds of protected flora and fauna. From here, proceed toward Opatija via Rijeka. ⇨Risnjak National Park in Chapter 4.

Days 4 & 5: Opatija

Plan to spend a couple of relaxing days in Opatija as the highlight of this itinerary. Although the city doesn't offer much in the way of architectural or historical gems, once you see the palm trees lining the streets you'll see this is a place for winding down, Habsburg-style. Choose one of the atmospheric, turn-of-the-century hotels for a little slice of nostalgia and settle in with a good book. Should you visit in winter, you'll find the weather downright Mediterranean. Take time to stroll along the 12-km-long (7½-mi-long) promenade that faces the sea. If you get antsy for more seaside diversity, plan instead one night in Opatija and one night in Cres or Losinj. The islands—with their attractive Venetian town squares—have a different character altogether. ⇨Opatija, Cres & Losinj in Chapter 4.

Day 6: Plitvice National Park

After you've been rejuvenated by a day or two by the sea, you'll be ready for a

change of pace. Head southeast back toward the interior in the direction of Plitvice National Park. Plitvice is a naturally occurring water world, with cascading pools and waterfalls connecting each other. This is one of Croatia's biggest tourist sites and has been for years, so the park is well protected and organized. Consider getting a map and exploring the lakes, which cover about 300 square km (186½ square mi) on your own. The park is well marked, but the guided tours only take you to the highlights. Relax in the evening when the tour buses have gone home and spend the night here at a nearby hotel. ⇨ *Plitvice Lakes in Chapter 1.*

Day 7: Zagreb

Head back toward Zagreb and find lodging in the city center. The next morning, check out the Dolac (market hall) in the Kaptol section of the Upper Town for a look at the city's fresh produce, meats, sausages, and souvenirs. Have a *burek* here and pick up some last-minute trinkets to take home. Stroll back through to the Donji Grad (Lower Town) and visit the Archaeological Museum and Strossmayer Gallery, two of the city's best attractions. *Zagreb in Chapter 1.*

TIPS

■ Consider renting a car for the trip to Krumovec and Varaždin, so that you can drive around the Zagorje. The rolling hills in this area are dotted with baroque castles, country houses, and lovely hilltop churches.

■ The closest ferry crossing from Opatija to Cres and Losinj is at Brestova in Istria. If you plan to make your way there with your car for the day in the height of summer, count on a wait. The ferry operates in the winter as well and is much less crowded then.

■ Don't plan to visit Plitvice National Park without good walking shoes and a rain slicker. Even on the guided tours, a walk through the forest takes you on wooden bridges and paths that can be muddy and damp. The tour can be even sloppier if you explore on your own.

■ Since Plitvice is on the main highway from Zagreb to Zadar and farther down the coast, consider seeing the park on a weekday. Traffic (even with the new highway) can be horrendous on weekends in July and August.

GREAT ITINERARIES

SPLIT, DUBROVNIK & THE DALMATIAN COAST

Both Split and Dubrovnik have international airports, so this itinerary could be reversed if you want to fly into Dubrovnik. Both cities are popular in summer, so be warned: you won't be sightseeing by yourself in August. In some respects, this itinerary can be best enjoyed without a car, as traffic and parking in high season are frazzling aspects of the southern Dalmatian coast. A little advance research about ferry schedules at the time of your travel (ferry and hydrofoil service is significantly reduced in the off-season) can make this a pleasant, mostly seafaring itinerary. Try to start your weeklong trip on a weekday (Monday to Monday, for example) instead of the weekend, so that your weekends are spent on a quiet island instead of in bustling Split or Dubrovnik.

Day 1: Split
Arrive in Split and head to a hotel (which you booked months ago) or take one of the many private rooms available around town. Accommodations in Split can be surprisingly limited. Spend this first day getting your bearings and exploring the Meštrović Gallery and the Archaeological Museum, two of the city's best museums. Save the full day for Diocletian's Palace tomorrow. ⇨ *Split in Chapter 6.*

Day 2: Diocletian's Palace
Get up early and head into the Grad, the Old Town area that once encompassed Diocletian's palace. You'll need a whole day to explore the palace, but the area is best seen on foot. Sit in the open peristyle and admire the imperial quarters, the Cathedral of St. Domnius, and the Egyptian black sphinx. Walk through the Grad area noticing all the different styles and materials used in the construction and renovation of the palace. Head out of the eastern Iron Gate to find a good spot for lunch and then continue along the Riva toward Marjan for a relaxing afternoon by the sea. ⇨ *Split in Chapter 6.*

Day 3: Island-Hopping
Take one of the ferries or catamarans from Split to Brač, Hvar, or Vis, and spend the night in an island paradise. This is the heart of Dalmatia, after all, and these islands are the stuff of glossy tourist brochures. Book your accommodations in advance, or try to book a private room through an agency in Split. In summer, ferries, hydrofoils, and catamarans operate regularly to the islands. Rent a bike or scooter once you've landed and tour the back roads where you can find uncrowded coves and beaches. ⇨ *Brač, Hvar & Vis in Chapter 6.*

Days 4 & 5: Dubrovnik
Get back in the car, or, if traveling without one, take the bus or ferry to Dubrovnik. The arrival by ferry is more dramatic, because you'll see one of the prettiest fortified cities in the world as it was meant to be seen: from the sea. From this view, you can tell why Dubrovnik (formerly Ragusa) was once master of all of Dalmatia. Choose a hotel slightly outside the city walls, as the crowds flock there daily in high season. Have lunch in one of the many fish restaurants near the fish market and enjoy some Dalmatian wine. Save the sightseeing for the late afternoon, when the cruise-ship day-trippers have departed. Stroll along the *placa* in the early evening with the locals, stopping along the way for some Italian-style ice cream. ⇨ *Dubrovnik in Chapter 7.*

Day 6: Elafiti Islands

The great thing about the Elafiti islands is that they're very close to Dubrovnik, so you can easily make a day trip out here if you're pressed for time. A trip out to one of the islands is ideal for a final wind-down before the week's end. Most of the islands have no cars and are sparsely populated, so it's just you and the sparkling Adriatic out there. Logun has the best overnight accommodations if you have an extra day, or for wilderness seekers a trip to farther-flung Mljet is rewarding in its forested beauty and serenity. All the islands have regular service in the summer, and hydrofoils and fast catamarans can get you there in half the time the ferry takes. In winter there is limited boat service from Dubrovnik. ⇨ *Elafiti Islands in Chapter 7.*

Day 7: Split

Day 7 will most likely be a travel day, no matter if you travel by car or ferry. Have one last seafood lunch in a restaurant with a view of the sea, buy a bottle of Dalmatian wine to take home, and vow to come back next year. ⇨ *Split in Chapter 6.*

TIPS

■ Don't take a car to the islands. Ferry reservations for cars must be made well in advance. Once you're there, it's easy enough to get around by bus or rented scooter.

■ Be wary of *soba* (room) offers. Although many are legitimate private rooms, there are unscrupulous vendors out there hard at work in high season. Have a map ready and mark where the accommodation is. Some properties are so far away that your one or two days in Dubrovnik will be spent navigating the local bus routes rather than enjoying the city.

■ Ask your concierge or host for local restaurant recommendations. A fair number are closed for the winter months. In high season (and especially during the Dubrovnik Summer Festival) many of the restaurants along the Prijeko aggressively market themselves to tourists, and a meal here can have less than relaxing aspects (overcharging, gruff service).

WHEN TO GO

The tourist season in Slovenia and Croatia generally runs from April through October, peaking in July and August. The Dalmatian coast is busy all summer long. Early booking is essential in July and August, when most of the summer festivals take place. Roads back from the coast are clogged with returning European tourists on late-summer weekends. Spring and fall can be the best times to visit, when the heat has abated somewhat at the coast and the days are long.

The Slovenian countryside is prettiest in the fall, when the leaves are changing, although the peak season is July and August. The coastal resorts are enjoyable in June or September, when accommodations and parking are more readily available. In a good year, the ski season in Slovenia lasts from mid-December through March. Slovenian ski slopes tend to be less crowded than nearby Austrian or Italian resorts.

Climate
Croatia enjoys a long, hot summer that's usually dry. Southern Dalmatia can still be mild in October, when the first cold snap has already hit in the interior, although swimming then may be only for the brave. Wet winters are the norm for most of the country, making a trip here in January or February somewhat rainy and cold. Winters on the coast are milder but still wet. Kvarner, sheltered on three sides by mountain ranges, has a short, temperate winter and an early spring. It remains mild throughout the summer.

Slovenia's weather is similar to Croatia's, although it's less wet as a rule. Ljubljana, which sits in a basin, is overcast most of the winter, but a quick drive out of town will often reveal sunshine in the rest of the country. The Julian Alps get similar weather

to the Austrian Alps to the north: cold in December and January, sunny in February and March. Summer months are ideal for hiking and biking in the mountains.

The following graphs show the average daily maximum and minimum temperatures for major cities in the region.

Forecasts **Weather Channel Connection** (☎ 900/932–8437 95¢ per minute ⊕ www. weather.com).

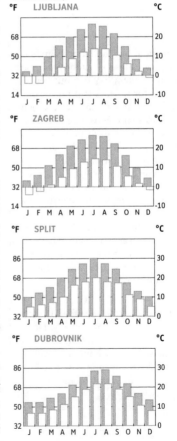

ON THE CALENDAR

		For exact dates and further information about events in Croatia, check the Croatian National Tourist Board Web site (⊕ *www.croatia.hr*). For dates and information about events in Slovenia, the Web site of the Slovenian Tourist Board (⊕ *www.slovenia-tourism.si*) has the details.
WINTER	February	Rijeka stages its own **Karneval,** giving Croatia the second-biggest Carnival celebration in Europe after Venice. **Kurentovanje** in Ptuj, Slovenia, is the largest and most spectacular of numerous Carnival celebrations throughout the country. In an arcane pagan rite, men wearing sheepskin coats ring big cowbells to usher in both spring and fertility.
SPRING	March	The **World Cup Ski-jump Championship** is held at Planica, Kranjska Gora, in Slovenia.
	April	In alternate years Zagreb, Croatia's capital, hosts a **Biennale,** an international festival of contemporary music. It's attended by both the heavy hitters of the classical world as well as groundbreaking pioneers. Check out ⊕ *www.biennale-zagreb.hr* for up-to-date information.
SUMMER	June	**Lent Festival** in Maribor, Slovenia, featuring music and dance events through June and July, opens with the traditional Rafters' Baptism on the River Drava. **Druga Godba,** a one-week festival of alternative and world music, takes place in Ljubljana.
	July	The Roman Arena in Pula makes Istria a stunning venue for the five-day **Pula Film Festival.** Around the same time, the five-day **International Folklore Festival** in Zagreb attracts folklore groups from Eastern Europe and beyond, staging music and dance in traditional costume.
	July and August	Practically every island and city up and down the Dalmatian coast has some kind of music festival in July and August, most taking place in a pretty church or palazzo on the Old Town square. Check with local tourist offices once you arrive for what's going on that week. Croatia's largest and most prestigious cultural event, the **Dubrovnik Summer Festival** (⊕ *www.dubrovnik-festival.hr*), draws international artists and musicians and features drama, ballet, concerts, and opera, all performed on open-air stages within the city fortifications. Similarly, the **Split Summer Festival** hosts opera, theater, and dance events at open-air venues within the walls

of Diocletian's Palace. The **Motovun Film Festival** (⊕*www.motovunfilmfestival.com*) highlights international independent films in a rustic medieval setting.

Slovenia is also abuzz throughout the summer with cultural and music festivals. The **International Jazz Festival** is held in Ljubljana in July, followed by the **International Summer Festival,** running through July and August, incorporating a range of events from classical music recitals to street theater. The **Primorski Summer Festival** of open-air theater and dance is staged in the coastal towns of Piran, Koper, Portorož, and Izola. **Piran Musical Evenings** are held in the cloisters of the Minorite Monastery in Piran, every Friday through July and August. The **Lace-making Festival** is held in Idrija in August, lasting one week.

July–September	In Porec, Croatia, the **Concert Season** in the Basilica of St. Euphrasius features eminent musicians from Croatia and abroad, with sacral and secular music from all periods played inside the magnificent 6th-century basilica.
FALL September	The **Kravji Bal** (Cow Ball) in Bohinj marks the end of summer and the return of Slovenian herdsmen and their cows from the mountain pastures to the valleys.
September and October	The **Varaždin Baroque Evenings** see eminent soloists and orchestras from Croatia and abroad perform baroque-music recitals in the city's most beautiful churches.
October	The **Ceremonial Grape Harvest** on October 1 marks the gathering of grapes from Slovenia's oldest vineyard, in Maribor. In Ljubljana the **LIFFE International Film festival** plays host to independent films.
November	In Zagorje, Croatia, **Martinje (St Martin's Day),** which is November 11, sees the blessing of the season's new wine, accompanied by a hearty goose feast and endless toasts. Slovenia, too, celebrates **St. Martin's Day** on November 11, which sees festivities throughout the country, culminating with the traditional blessing of the season's young wine.

Zagreb & Environs

WORD OF MOUTH

"I have read comments that people do not care for Zagreb and I can see why, if the weather isn't nice. However, on a sunny day, the city of Zagreb would remind you of Vienna or Prague."

—mercy

"I spent two nights at the Plitvice Hotel, which was fine, and absolutely loved the park. The water is a stunning color, the place has more waterfalls than you can imagine, and it's easy to spend an entire day strolling around. Be prepared to take many, many photos."

—thursdaysd

By Paul
Olchváry

ZAGREB HAS EMERGED AS A TOURIST DESTINATION in recent years, and much of its success has to do with the country's spectacular Adriatic coast—beautiful medieval towns, crystal-clear azure waters, and, of course, well-developed tourist resorts. It's all too easy, however, to overlook the fact that much of the country's natural beauty and cultural heritage is rooted in places well inland from the sea. Unless you arrive overland from Slovenia, by boat from Italy, or by one of the few air routes that deliver you straight to the coast, chances are that your first encounter with Croatia will be Zagreb, an eminently strollable city of attractive parks, squares, and museums. Instead of high-tailing it to Dalmatia or Istria, stay a few days to explore the capital's historic center and pastoral environs. You'll be in for a pleasant surprise and will go home with a fuller, more satisfying appreciation of what this alluring country is all about.

Above all, there's Croatia's quietly lovely capital. With its historic center on the northern bank of the Sava River, Zagreb has the walkability of Prague. Spacious, friendly public spaces, grand Austro-Hungarian architecture, and a rich array of churches and museums will lure you down small side streets—as long as it's not raining.

With the exception of the vast plains of Slavonia that stretch to the east (and which are covered in Chapter 2), the rest of the inland region, with Zagreb as its approximate center, can be divided into two parts, north and south. To the north is the hilly, castle-rich Zagorje region; the smaller, often-overlooked and yet likewise appealing Međimurje region; and, just a tram and cable-car ride from the city center, the hiking trails and ski slopes of Sljeme. To the south is the relatively busy route to the coast that includes Karlovac, an important regional center, as well as Croatia's most visited national park, Plitvice Lakes; and a second route along the less traveled banks of the Sava River to Lonjsko Polje, known for its natural beauty, a 16th-century fortress, and historical reminders of Croatia's role in World War II.

EXPLORING ZAGREB & ENVIRONS

ABOUT THE RESTAURANTS

Although there are seafood restaurants in Zagreb and large towns like Varaždin, this inland region is better known for roasted meats accompanied by heavy side dishes such as *zagorski štrukli* (baked cheese dumplings). For dessert, walnut-, jam-, and sweet curd-cheese–filled *palačinke* (crêpes) are on nearly every menu. Balkan-style grilled meats such as *ćevapčići* (grilled spicy cubes of minced meat, often served with raw onions) are popular, and lower in price than more elaborate main courses. The influence of Slavonia to the east and Hungary to the north is evident in the form of paprika-rich (and salt-rich) dishes, whether *fiš paprikas* (made from fish and also called *riblji paprikas*) or various goulashes; likewise, spiced sausages and salamis add further zest. Some restaurants, particularly in Zagreb, and especially those owned and operated by folks from Dalmatia, do excel in fresh seafood straight from the Adriatic. But when it comes to fish, you are likely to find as

ZAGREB & ENVIRONS TOP 5

- With lovely parks, squares, museums, and churches, hoofing it in Croatia's compact capital is an unforgettable experience. If your feet fail, you can always jump on a convenient tram.

- Plitvice Lakes National Park, a UNESCO World Heritage site, is Croatia's most-visited park, with 16 crystal-clear lakes connected by waterfalls and cascades.

- Zagorje's forested hills north of Zagreb are ornamented by some lovely fortresses, built to ward off centuries of onslaughts by various foes.

- Varaždin is the most harmonious and beautifully preserved baroque town in this corner of the continent.

- Here you get the best of both worlds: top-notch seafood *and* Central European meaty, spicy fare. And best of all, prices are fairly reasonable even at the top restaurants.

much or more in the way of freshwater options such as carp, pike, and pike-perch. As on the coast, many restaurants serve pasta dishes and pizzas as budget alternatives, but you'll find noticeably fewer restaurants focusing on Italian-style fare; which is not surprising given that this region's history (and cuisine) was more bound up in centuries past with Austria and Hungary, for example, than with Italy. As for prices, expect to shell out about the same in Zagreb for a main course at a good restaurant as you would on the coast. If you head to Varaždin or a smaller town, however, prices will drop somewhat, though not dramatically. Last but not least, note that some restaurants close for 2 to 4 weeks between late July and August 20, when everyone and his brother and sister are on the coast.

WHAT IT COSTS IN EUROS (€) AND CROATIAN KUNA (KN)					
	¢	$	$$	$$$	$$$$
RESTAURANTS	under 20 Kn	20 Kn–35 Kn	35 Kn–60 Kn	60 Kn–80 Kn	over 80 Kn
HOTELS In euros	under €75	€75–€125	€125–€175	€175–€225	over €225
HOTELS In kuna	under 550 Kn	550 Kn–925 Kn	925 Kn–1,300 Kn	1,300 Kn–1,650 Kn	over 1,650 Kn

Restaurant prices are for a main course at dinner. Hotel prices are for two people in a double room in high season, excluding taxes and service charges.

It's a fact of life that Zagreb doesn't get the same sort of tourist traffic as the coast, so the region's major hotels have gone to great lengths since the end of the Yugoslav war to cater to business travelers. Although this trend has yielded a spate of impressive renovations (some still ongoing or planned as of this writing), it has also driven prices up considerably. Rates of €100 or (much) more for a double room are not uncommon in central Zagreb's largest hotels, though a 10- to 20-minute walk or short tram ride from downtown will bring you to comfortable, modern pensions for considerably less. You have to go to smaller towns or to the countryside to get cheaper options, though some private rooms and agritourism-style accommodations (where the owners often don't speak English, and you don't get such frills as cable TV and air-conditioning) are inexpensive indeed.

TIMING

Although Zagreb and environs is well worth a visit at any time of year, the capital really comes alive in fair weather, which essentially means anytime between early May and mid-September. Since summer is coastal vacation time for so many, July and August are considered low season in the capital, meaning that prices are lower than on the coast. Unless you're in town to do business, avoid visiting during the one-week Zagreb Trade Fair in mid-September, when rooms are harder to come by and may be up to 20% pricier.

ZAGREB

The capital of Croatia, Zagreb has a population of roughly 1 million and is situated at the extreme edge of the Pannonian Plain, between the north bank of the Sava River and the southern slopes of Mt. Medvednica. Its early years are shrouded in mystery, though there are indications of a Neolithic settlement on this site. The Romans are said to have established a municipality of sorts that was destroyed around AD 600, when Croatian tribes moved in.

Like so many other notable European cities, Zagreb started out as a strategic crossroads along an international river route, which was followed much later by north–south and east–west passages by road and rail. For much of its history the city also served as a bastion on a defensive frontier, pounded for half a millennium by thundering hordes of invaders, among them Hungarians, Mongols, and Turks.

From the late Middle Ages until the 19th century, Zagreb was composed of two adjoining but separate towns on the high ground (Gornji Grad): one town was secular, the other expressly religious. In 1242 the secular town, named Gradec (Fortress), was burned to the ground in a wave of destruction by the Tartars, after which it locked itself up behind protective walls and towers. It is from this time that the real Zagreb (meaning Behind the Hill) began to evolve; it was accorded the status of a free royal city in the same year by the Hungarian-Croatian king Bela IV. In the 15th century the ecclesiastical center, named Kaptol (Chapter House), also enclosed itself in defensive walls in response to the threat of a Turkish invasion.

When Zagreb became the capital of Croatia in 1557, the country's parliament began meeting alternately in Gradec and at the Bishop's Palace in Kaptol. When Kaptol and Gradec were finally put under a single city administration in 1850, urban development accelerated. The railway reached Zagreb in 1862, linking the city to Vienna, Trieste, and the Adriatic. It was at this time that Donji Grad (Lower Town) came into

GREAT ITINERARIES

To explore Croatia's interior, begin with Zagreb and work your way outward from there. If you have just a day or two, stick to the capital, but the more time you have beyond that, the more you will want to explore. If you're headed to the coast anyway, you'll pass by Plitvice Lakes National Park; keep that natural wonder on your radar screen for a daytime visit at the very least.

IF YOU HAVE 3 DAYS

Stick to **Zagreb**, with a side trip to its immediate environs. As compact as it is compared to other regional capitals such as Budapest, Croatia's capital nonetheless invites long strolls and more than a fleeting look into at least a few of its museums and parks. This alone can take three days; but you can probably cover most key sights without feeling rushed in two days, leaving a bit of time to spare for a half-day excursion to **Samobor**, for example, or into the hills north of the capital. Renting a car will allow you to cover more of the castles and towns of the

Medvednice hills and the Zagorje region, but even if you have only one full day at your disposal, you can take in a couple of such nearby sites by bus.

IF YOU HAVE 5 DAYS

Start as above, devoting at least two or, better yet, two-and-a-half days to Zagreb, with a half-day excursion to the Medvednice hills on the third day. Visit a castle or two in the Zagorje, such as **Veliki Tabor**, on the fourth day, and spend the night either in the nearby countryside or else in **Varaždin** before making your way back for a fond farewell to Zagreb on the fifth.

IF YOU HAVE 7 DAYS

Do all of the above, but take in both a castle in the Zagorje and an afternoon and evening in Varaždin; throw in a one-night visit to **Plitvice Lakes National Park**, with a daytime stopover in Karlovac on the way. This one-week option will work well if, for example, you wish to spend the second (or first) week on the Adriatic coast.

being. Lying between Gornji Grad and the main train station, it was designed to accommodate new public buildings—the National Theater, the university, and various museums. Built in grandiose style and interspersed by wide, tree-lined boulevards, parks, and gardens, it makes a fitting monument to the Habsburg era.

The Tito years brought a period of increasing industrialization coupled with urban expansion, as the new high-rise residential suburb of Novi Zagreb was constructed south of the Sava. In 1991 the city escaped the war of independence relatively unscathed, but for an attempted rocket attack on the Croatian Parliament building in Gradec. Zagreb did, however, suffer severe economic hardship as the country's industries collapsed, post-Communist corruption set in, and an influx of refugees—mainly Croats from Herzegovina—arrived in search of a better life.

Since 2000 public morale has picked up considerably: trendy street cafés are thriving, numerous smart new stores have opened, and the

IF YOU LIKE

WALKING

Zagreb—a pedestrian-friendly, and just plain friendly city—is a sheer pleasure, what with its rich array of attractive parks and squares as well as its museums and churches. At its center is its spacious main square, Trg Bana Jelačića, whose fine examples of Viennese Secessionist architecture are delightful, and whose constant flow of pedestrian and tram traffic is invigorating. Nearby is Tkalčićeva, the main, bustling pedestrian avenue in the old quarter. Among several churches of note, Crkva Svetog Marka leaves a striking impression with its brilliant, multicolored tile roof. And parks such as Trg Zrinjskog, with its fountains and majestic plane trees, and lovely Maksimir Park on the outskirts of downtown soothe the soul.

NATURAL BEAUTY

Plitvice Lakes National Park is not to be missed. This UNESCO World Heritage Site is Croatia's most-visited park, for good reason. Even if sharing the trail with throngs of other tourists (especially in midsummer) is not your idea of a peaceful escape to nature, the 16 crystal-clear lakes connected by numerous waterfalls and cascades that comprise this natural wonder will leave you in awe.

Besides, it's right on the way to the Dalmatian coast, midway between Zagreb and Zadar.

CASTLES

Centuries of onslaughts by foes such as the Ottomans have left the forested hills to the north of Zagreb that extend to the Slovenian border ornamented by more than a few lovely fortresses, from the 15th-century Veliki Tabor to the neo-Gothic, 19th-century Trakošćan. A one- or two-day drive through this area will also provide some charming villages, including Kumrovec, the birthplace of the late leader of the former Yugoslavia, Josep Broz Tito.

CUISINE

Here you get the best of both worlds. In Zagreb in particular, there are not only plenty of fine restaurants offering the best of Central European meaty fare—from spicy, Balkan-style dishes to paprika-rich cuisine and sausages more characteristic of Slavonia to the east and Hungary to the north—but also some excellent places to get fresh tuna, scampi, and octopus salad even this far from the coast, thanks in part to natives of Dalmatia who have opened a number of top-notch seafood restaurants in recent years.

public gardens are once again carefully tended. However, underlying this apparent affluence, unemployment remains a lingering problem. That said, unlike in Budapest, the much larger capital of neighboring Hungary, obvious signs of economic distress—such as panhandlers and homeless people—are relatively rare, and the casual observer will probably notice a general atmosphere of prosperity (fueled in part by coastal tourism). The prospect of European Union membership for Croatia at some point in the not-too-distant future holds the promise of continued economic vitality.

EXPLORING ZAGREB

The city is clearly divided into two distinct districts: **Gornji Grad** (Upper Town) and **Donji Grad** (Lower Town). Although hilltop Gornji Grad is made up of winding cobbled streets and terra-cotta rooftops sheltering beneath the cathedral and the Croatian Parliament building, Donji Grad is where you'll find the city's most important 19th-century cultural institutions, including the National Theater, the university, and a number of museums, all in an organized grid.

Numbers in the text correspond to numbers in the margin and on the Zagreb map.

GORNJI GRAD (UPPER TOWN)

The romantic hilltop area of Gornji Grad dates back to medieval times, and is undoubtedly the loveliest part of Zagreb.

WHAT TO SEE **Crkva Svete Katerine** *(St. Catherine's Church).* Built for the Jesuit order
⑩ between 1620 and 1632, this church was modeled on Giacomo da
★ Vignola's Il Gesù in Rome. Inside, the vaults are decorated with pink and white stucco and 18th-century illusionist paintings, and the altars are the work of Francesco Robba and 17th-century Croatian artists. ⊠*Katerinin trg, Gornji Grad* ⊟*Free* ☉*Daily 8–8.*

❻ **Crkva Svetog Marka** *(St. Mark's Church).* The original building was
★ erected in the 13th century, and was once the parish church of Gradec. The baroque bell tower was added in the 17th century, while the steeply pitched roof—decorated in brilliant, multicolored tiles arranged to depict the coats of arms of Zagreb on the right and the Kingdom of Croatia, Dalmatia, and Slavonia on the left—was added during reconstruction in the 19th century. ⊠*Markov trg, Gornji Grad* ⊟*Free* ☉*Daily 8–8.*

❷ **Dolac** *(Market).* Farmers from the surrounding countryside set up their stalls here daily, though the market is at its busiest on Friday and Saturday mornings. On the upper level, brightly colored umbrellas shade fresh fruit and vegetables on an open-air piazza, and dairy products and meats are sold in an indoor market below. ⊠*Trg Bana Jelačića, Gornji Grad* ☉ *Weekdays 7–4, weekends 7–noon.*

❾ **Hrvatski Muzej Naivne Umjetnosti** *(Croatian Museum of Naive Art).* This unusual school of painting dates back to the 1930s and features more than 1,600 works of untutored peasant artists, primarily from the village of Hlebine in Slavonia. Canvases by the highly esteemed Ivan Generalić dominate here, though there are also paintings, drawings, sculptures, and prints by other noted members of the movement, plus a section devoted to foreigners working along similar lines. ⊠*Ćirilometodska 3, Gornji Grad* ☎*01/485–1911* ⊕*www.hmnu.org* ⊟*20 Kn* ☉*Tues.–Fri. 10–6, weekends 10–1.*

❺ **Kamenita Vrata** *(Stone Gate).* The original 13th-century city walls had four gates, of which only Kamenita Vrata remains. Deep inside the dark passageway, locals stop to pray before a small shrine adorned with flickering candles. In 1731 a devastating fire consumed all the

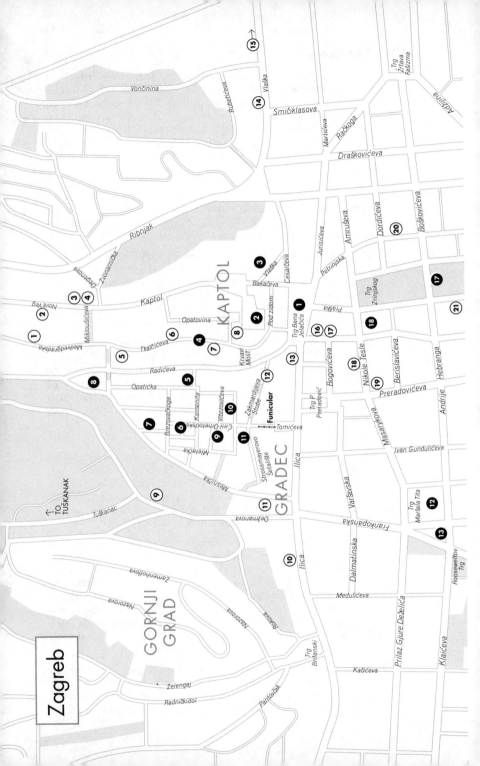

Zagreb

GORNJI GRAD

GRADEC

KAPTOL

Vončinina
Rubetićeva
Vlaška
Smičiklasova
Trg Žrtava Fašizma
Martićeva
Račkoga
Draškovićeva
Augusta
Ribnjak
Zvonarnička
Degenova
Jurišićeva
Amruševa
Đorđićeva
Boškovićeva
Kaptol
Nova ves
Opatovina
Bakačeva
Cesarčeva
Trg Zrinjskog
Petrinjska
Praška
Medvedgradska
Miklošićeva
Tkalčićeva
Pod zidom
Trg Bana Jelačića
Berislavićeva
Hebranga
Radićeva
Krvavi Most
Opatička
Zakmardijeve Stube
Funicular
Bogovićeva
Nikole Tesle
Preradovićeva
Andrije
Brezovačkoga
Kamenita
Vitezovićeva
Ćiril Ometodska
Tomićeva
Trg P Preradović
Masarykova
Ivan Gundulićeva
TO TUŠKANAK
Mesnička
Strossmayerovo Šetalište
Varšavska
Trg Maršala Tita
Tuškanac
Mletačka
Dežmanova
Ilica
Frankopanska
Zamenhoflova
Nazorova
Nazorova
Rokova
Dalmatinska
Roosewelttov Trg
Medulićeva
Klaićeva
Prilaz Giure Deželića
Zelengaj
Trg Britanski
Radničkidol
Pantovčak
Kačićeva

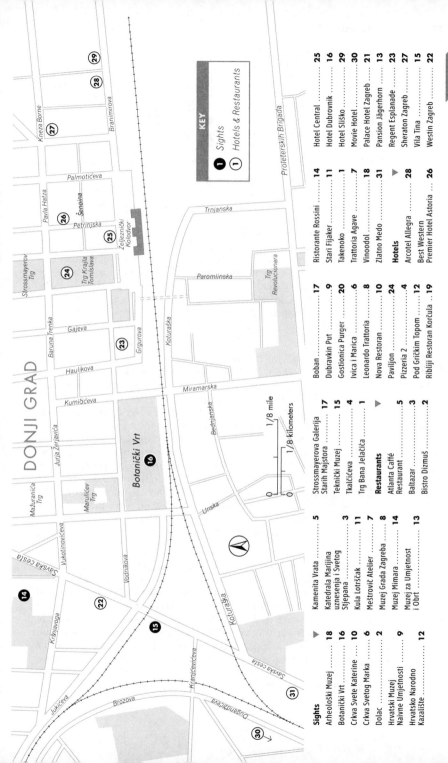

1

DONJI GRAD

Botanički Vrt

KEY

● Sights
① Hotels & Restaurants

0   1/8 mile
0   1/8 kilometers

Sights

Arheološki Muzej	18
Botanički Vrt	16
Crkva Svete Katerine	10
Crkva Svetog Marka	6
Dolac	2
Hrvatski Muzej Naivne Umjetnosti	9
Hrvatsko Narodno Kazalište	12
Kamenita Vrata	5
Katedrala Marijina uznesenja i Svetog Stjepana	3
Kula Lotrščak	11
Meštrović Atelier	7
Muzej Grada Zagreba	8
Muzej Mimara	14
Muzej za Umjetnost i Obrt	13
Strossmayerova Galerija	17
Starih Majstora	15
Tehnički Muzej	4
Tkalčićeva	1
Trg Bana Jelačića	

Restaurants

Atlanta Caffé Restaurant	5
Baltazar	3
Bistro Dizmuš	2
Boban	17
Dubravkin Put	9
Gostionica Purger	20
Ivica i Marica	6
Leonardo Trattoria	8
Nova Restoran	10
Pavilijon	24
Pizzeria 2	4
Pod Gričkim Topom	12
Ribljii Restoran Korčula	19
Ristorante Rossini	14
Stari Fijaker	11
Takenoko	7
Trattoria Agave	18
Vinoodol	31
Zlatno Medo	

Hotels

Arcotel Allegra	28
Best Western Premier Hotel Astoria	26
Hotel Central	25
Hotel Dubrovnik	16
Hotel Sliško	29
Movie Hotel	30
Palace Hotel Zagreb	21
Pansion Jägerhorn	13
Regent Esplanade	23
Sheraton Zagreb	27
Vila Tina	15
Westin Zagreb	22

wooden elements of the gate, except for a painting of the Virgin and Child, which was found in the ashes, remarkably undamaged. Kamenita Vrata has since become a pilgrimage site, as can be seen from the numerous stone plaques saying *hvala* (thank you). ⊠ *Kamenita, Gornji Grad.*

FUEL UP

If you're out and about exploring and your belly starts grumbling, the simplest solution, as elsewhere in Croatia, is to pick up a *burek* (a cheese- or meat-filled pastry) at a *pekarna* (bakery) for a quick, decidedly budget (10 Kn or less), greasy snack.

---

❸ **Katedrala Marijina uznesenja i Svetog Stjepana** *(Cathedral of the Assumption of the Blessed Virgin and St. Stephen).* Built on the site of a former 12th-century cathedral destroyed by the Tartars in 1242, the present structure was constructed between the 13th and 16th centuries. The striking neo-Gothic facade was added by architect Herman Bollé following the earthquake of 1880, its twin steeples being the identifying feature of the city's skyline. Behind the impressive main altar are crypts of Zagreb's archbishops and of Croatian national heroes. The interior is otherwise relatively bare, the main point of interest being the north wall, which bears an inscription of the Ten Commandments in 12th-century Glagolithic script. ⊠ *Kaptol 31, Gornji Grad* 🖾 *Free* 🕑 *Daily 8–8.*

OFF THE BEATEN PATH

Mirogoj Cemetery. A satisfying if somber little outing can be had by catching Bus 106 on Kaptol, in front of the main cathedral (Katedrala Marijina uznesenja i Svetog Stjepana), and riding it about ten minutes to the fifth stop, Arkade. Designed by architect Herman Bollé and opened in 1872, Zagreb's most celebrated cemetery is set on a hillside north of downtown and features an imposing entrance: a long, massive brick wall topped by a row of striking green cupolas. Just behind this is the black-marble grave of Franjo Tuđjman, the man who served as Croatia's first president after the nation declared its independence from the former Yugoslavia. This lovely parklike cemetery, marked by paths lined with towering horse chestnut trees and by more black marble graves than you can count, is the final resting place for those of many creeds, from Roman Catholic and Serbian Orthodox to Jewish and Muslim. The cemetery is open Apr.–Sept., 6 AM–8 PM and Oct.–Mar., 7:30 AM–6 PM.

⓫ **Kula Lotrščak** *(Lotrščak Tower).* Formerly the entrance to the fortified medieval Gradec, Kula Lotrščak now houses a multilevel gallery with occasional exhibits of contemporary art. Each day at noon a small cannon is fired from the top of the tower in memory of the times when it was used to warn of the possibility of an Ottoman attack. You can climb the tower partway via a spiral wooden staircase for a look into the gallery rooms (which occupy several floors) or all the way to the observation deck up top for splendid views of Zagreb and environs. ⊠ *Strossmayer Šetalište, Gornji Grad* 🕾 *01/485–1926* 🖾 *Observation deck 10 Kn; gallery free* 🕑 *Tues.–Fri. 11–7, weekends 2–7.*

❼ Meštrović Atelier *(Meštrović Atelier).*
★ This 17th-century building, with its interior courtyard, served as home and studio to Ivan Meštrović from 1922 until his emigration to the United States in 1942. The building was extensively remodeled according to plans devised by the artist and was turned into a memorial museum with a permanent exhibition of his sculptures and drawings after his death in 1962. (There is a larger collection of his works in the Meštrović Gallery in Split.) ✉ *Mletačka 8, Gornji Grad* ☎ *01/485-1123* 🎫 *20 Kn* ☉ *Tues., Wed., and Fri. 10–6, Thurs. 10–10, weekends 10–2.*

> **CITY VIEWS**
>
> For sublime views east toward the Old Town, with its three prominent church steeples and many red-tile rooftops (including more than a few satellite dishes), stroll through the open wrought-iron gate just to the right of St. Catherine's Church. You'll find yourself on a spacious concrete plaza where you can take in the scene and then catch a flight of steps down past a lively café–bar toward Ilica.

❽ Muzej Grada Zagreba *(Zagreb City Museum).* Well worth a visit for anyone interested in urban design, this museum traces the city's most important historical, economic, political, social, and cultural events from medieval times up to the present day. Exhibits include detailed scale models of how the city has evolved, as well as sections devoted to the old trade guilds, domestic life, and sacred art. ✉ *Opatička 20, Gornji Grad* ☎ *01/485-1361 or 01/485-1362* ⊕ *www.mdc.hr/* 🎫 *20 Kn; free guided tours at 11* AM *weekends* ☉ *Tues.–Fri. 10–6, weekends 10–1.*

❹ Tkalčićeva. This street was once a channel forming the boundary between Kaptol and Gradec, then known as Potok (the brook). Today it is a pretty pedestrian zone lined with 19th-century town houses, many of which have been converted into popular café-bars at street level—attracting a huge cross section of Croatian and international youth from morning until late at night. ✉ *Tkalčićeva north of Krvavi Most, Gornji Grad.*

NEED A BREAK? For morning coffee or an early evening aperitif, stop at Sunčani Sat (✉ *Tkalčićeva 27, Gornji Grad*). Take a comfy wicker chair on the open-air summer terrace and enjoy watching the comings and goings of Zagreb café life. In the evening this space transforms, as with so many others along Tkalčićeva, into a trendy, crowded watering hole.

❶ Trg Bana Jelačića *(Ban Jelačić Square).* Buildings lining the square date from 1827 onward and include several fine examples of Viennese Secessionist architecture. The centerpiece is an equestrian statue of Ban Jelačić, the first Croatian viceroy, erected in 1866. After World War II the Communist government ordered the dismantling and removal of the statue, but it was put back in place in 1991. ✉ *Between Ilica to the west, Praška to the south, and Jurišićeva to the east, Gornji Grad.*

NEED A BREAK?

If you are looking for a quick and inexpensive lunch, consider the groundbreaking Pingvin Sandwich Bar (⊠ *Nikole Tesle 7, Gornji Grad* ☎ *01/481–1446*), a popular stand just a couple of minutes' walk from Trg Bana Jelačića. Try the grilled chicken sandwich or the soy-patty-equipped "veggie burger." Ordering is simple: not only do most clerks speak English, but there are also user-friendly pictures and English translations. The stand is open from 9 AM to 5 AM Monday through Saturday, 9 AM to 3 AM on Sunday.

WHY HIKE WHEN YOU CAN RIDE?

If you're walking along Ilica from the main square, you might wonder about the best route up the hill to Lotršćak Tower and beyond to St. Mark's Church. Well, you can save yourself the steep hike up by catching the funicular, which runs six times an hour, 6 AM to 9 PM, from short Tomićeva ulica (just off Ilica) just a few hundred yards up the hillside. The cost is 3 Kn.

DONJI GRAD (LOWER TOWN)

Donji Grad came into being during the late 19th century. The urban plan, which follows a grid pattern, was drawn up by Milan Lenuci and combines a succession of squares and parks laid out in a "U" shape (known as the Green Horseshoe), all overlooked by the city's main public buildings and cultural institutions.

WHAT TO SEE
❶❽ Arheološki Muzej *(Archaeological Museum).* Museum exhibits focus on prehistoric times to the Tartar invasion. Pride of place is given to the Vučedol Dove, a three-legged ceramic vessel in the form of a bird, dating back to the 4th millennium BC, and a piece of linen bearing the longest known text in ancient Etruscan writing. The courtyard features a collection of stone relics from Roman times. ⊠ *Trg N. Zrinjskog 19, Donji Grad* ☎ *01/487–3101* ⊕ *www.amz.hr* ⊠ *20 Kn* ☉ *Tues.–Fri. 10–5, weekends 10–1.*

❶❻ Botanički Vrt *(Botanical Garden).* Founded in 1889 as research grounds for the faculty of botany at Zagreb University, the garden includes an arboretum with English-style landscaping, a small artificial lake, and an ornamental Japanese bridge. ⊠ *Marulićeva trg 9a, Donji Grad* ⊠ *Free* ☉ *Mon. and Tues. 9–2:30, Wed.–Sun. 9–6.*

❶❷ Hrvatsko Narodno Kazalište *(Croatian National Theater).* The building dates from 1895, designed by the Viennese firm Hellmer and Fellner as part of the preparations for a state visit by Emperor Franz Josef. In front of the theater, set deep in a round concrete basin, is Meštrović's little, eerily lifelike sculpture *Zdenac Života* *(Fountain of Life),* from 1912, which depicts four naked couples writhing uncomfortably in each other's arms around a small pool of water while one lone, likewise naked gentleman stares meditatively into the pool. The only way to see the inside of the theater is to attend a performance. ⊠ *Trg Maršala Tita 15, Donji Grad* ☎ *01/488–8415* ⊕ *www.hnk.hr.*

❶❹ Muzej Mimara *(Mimara Museum).* In a huge gray building that's dull compared to some of those nearby, this vast private collection, includ-

CLOSE UP

Funny Felix

1

Srećko Puntarić celebrated his 30th anniversary in 2005—and much of Croatia knew about it. The event in downtown Zagreb celebrated his distinguished reputation as Croatia's best-loved cartoonist. Popularly known by the alias "Felix" (also the name of his cartoon), this fifty-something, amiable fellow with a boyish face has published 27 books on themes ranging from a history of animals (heavy on dog and cat cartoons) to "computers in the stone age." He has won numerous international awards, and his cartoon in the national newspaper *Večernji* brings a smile to tens of thousands of his compatriots each day. Among the cartoonists who have most inspired Felix is America's Gary Larson, of *Far Side* fame. "There has been no great cartoonist internationally since Larson," he laments, explaining that rampant consumerism in recent years has been much to the detriment of individual creativity. Indeed, Felix's cartoons are vaguely reminiscent of Larson's, what with their simply rendered figures whose faces are grossly out of proportion (Felix specializes in long snouts), and their often absurd situations that are funny even to those who cannot read the Croatian text. (Of course, you might well end up with a different reading of the situation than someone who can attach the words to the pictures.)

Felix does much of his work in what he calls his "cartoon gallery," the Felix Fun Factory. This quiet little shop-cum-workshop, a short tram ride from Zagreb's main square, is indeed one of Europe's few cartoon galleries. Here Felix not only works, but he, his wife, and his son sell postcards, posters, books, and mugs featuring his cartoons—limited-edition products that can be had nowhere else. Felix has, to date, resisted the idea of selling his work to dealers, as he doesn't like the idea of his cartoons being commercialized. He likes the idea that they are available in only *one* place. Although a Felix Web site is in the works at this writing, you'll still be able to buy cartoons and merchandise only in the shop, in person.

Felix began cartooning in 1975 as a student, when, he explains, he undertook "a frontal assault" on a publication by churning out one cartoon after another. His rush of inspiration earned the publication's respect and gained some broader recognition for his work. But cartoons remained a hobby as Felix began a seven-year career as a mechanical engineer. From there he became the advertising designer for a Zagreb-based chocolate company. Eventually, as the books and honors piled up, he quit that job to pursue his passion full-time. "Here in the shop," he says without a trace of vanity, "sometimes I feel like one of those solitary old masters, pursuing his art in isolation from the world."

To get to the Felix Fun Factory and perhaps meet Felix yourself (he generally mans the shop during the second, 4 to 7 shift), take tram 11 or 12 six stops east of Trg Bana Jelačića, almost as far as Maksimir Park, walk back a few yards, and take the first left onto Harambašićeva. The gallery, at No. 10, will soon be on your right. It's open weekdays from 10 to 1 and 4 to 7. You can call the gallery at ☎ 01/231–4915.

ing paintings, sculpture, ceramics, textiles, and rugs, was donated by Ante Topić-Mimara (1898–1987), a Croatian who spent many years abroad where he made his fortune, supposedly as a merchant. On display are canvases attributed to such old masters as Raphael, Rembrandt, and Rubens, as well as more modern works by the likes of Manet, Degas, and Renoir, and ancient artifacts including Egyptian glassware and Chinese porcelain. ⊠ *Rooseveltov trg 5, Donji Grad* 🕾 *01/482–8100* 🖃 *40 Kn* ⊘ *Tues., Wed., Fri., and Sat. 10–5, Thurs. 10–7, Sun. 10–2.*

🔞 **Muzej za Umjetnost i Obrt** *(Arts & Crafts Museum).* Designed in 1888 by Herman Bollé, the architect responsible for the Katedrala Marijina uznesenja i Svetog Stjepana facade, this pleasant museum traces the development of the applied arts from the baroque period up to the 20th century. Exhibits are displayed in chronological order, and although furniture design predominates, there are also sections devoted to sacred art, clocks, and clothing. ⊠ *Trg Maršala Tita 10, Donji Grad* 🕾 *01/488–2111* ⊕ *www.muo.hr* 🖃 *20 Kn* ⊘ *Tues.–Sat. 10–7, Sun. 10–2.*

🔞 **Strossmayerova Galerija Starih Majstora** *(Strossmayer Gallery of Old Masters).* Now under the custody of the Croatian Academy of Sciences and Arts, this impressive gallery was founded in 1884 by Bishop Strossmayer and later expanded to include many private donations. Works by Venetian Renaissance and baroque artists such as Bellini and Carpaccio predominate, but there are also masterpieces by Dutch painters Brueghel and Van Dyck, as well as a delightful Mary Magdalene by El Greco. ⊠ *Trg Zrinjskog 11, Donji Grad* 🕾 *01/481–3344* ⊕ *www.mdc. hr/strossmayer* 🖃 *10 Kn* ⊘ *Tues. 10–1 and 5–7, Wed.–Sun. 10–1.*

NEED A BREAK? The green expanse of Strossmayerov trg with its carefully tended flower beds makes an ideal stopping place for weary feet. At the terrace of the Viennese-style café of the Palace Hotel (⊠ *Strossmayerov trg 10*), you can sip a cappuccino on a vine-enveloped sidewalk terrace across from this leafy square, while sampling from a range of tempting cakes and pastries.

🔞 **Tehnički Muzej** *(Technical Museum).* It may be in a drab box of a building, but this museum is guaranteed to appeal to children and civil engineers alike; try to see it in the afternoon on a weekday or in the late morning on the weekend, when a series of guided visits are offered. The highlight here is the demonstration of some of Nikola Tesla's inventions, which takes place weekdays at 3:30 and weekends at 11:30, but there's also the tour of a lifelike reconstruction of a coal mine at 3 on weekdays and 11 on weekends, and a planetarium visit at 4 on weekdays, noon on weekends. That's not to mention all the various engines on display, as well as a fascinating historical exhibit of firefighting equipment including trucks, ladders, and hoses aplenty. ⊠ *Savska c 18, Donji Grad* 🕾 *01/484–4050* ⊕ *www.mdc.hr/tehnicki* 🖃 *Museum 15 Kn, planetarium 10 Kn extra* ⊘ *Tues.–Fri. 9–5, weekends 9–1.*

OFF THE BEATEN PATH

Maksimir Park. For a peaceful stroll in southeastern Europe's oldest landscaped, English-style park, hop on a tram and go visit Maksimir Park. A short ride east of the center of Zagreb (10 minutes on tram 11 or 12 from Trg Bana Jelačića or 15 minutes on tram 4 or 7 from the train station), this 44½-acre expanse of vine-covered forests and several artificial lakes was a groundbreaker when it opened back in 1794. After getting off the tram, you walk forward a bit and enter on the left, through a prominent gate opposite the city's main soccer stadium, aptly named Stadion Maksimir. A long, wide promenade flanked by benches leads from here to Bellevue Pavilion (1843), perched atop a small hill and featuring a café.

> **SUMMER BREAK**
>
> If you're in town between late July and the third week of August, don't be surprised to find many restaurants closed for two to four weeks while the staff are off at the coast, as is much of Zagreb.

Zoološki Vrt Zagreb. To your right along the way are some small lakes and, beyond, the city's modest zoo, where admission is 20 Kn; it's open daily from 9 AM to 7 PM (last tickets sold at 6). To your left is a playground.

WHERE TO EAT

For budget fare, go up the steps from the main square, Trg Bana Jelačića, and just off the right before you reach the top is a row of bistros where you can get everything from *bureks* (a savory cheese- or meat-filled pastry) to simple pizzas to Balkan-style grilled meats for around half what you'd pay at a modestly priced restaurant. And do remember, though Zagreb is not exactly overflowing with budget sandwich shops, traditional bakeries have long fulfilled that role for locals; at such places, which are on practically every street corner, you can pick up a burek for as little as 10 Kn a piece.

$$$$ ✕**Atlanta Caffè Restaurant.** One of the first restaurants to open among the myriad thriving cafés that line Tkalčićeva, Atlanta boasts a stylish interior with warm terra-cotta walls hung with enormous gilt-framed mirrors. You might begin with the risotto with arugula and prosciutto, followed by steak with truffles, rounded off with tiramisu. ⊠ *Tkalčićeva 65, Gornji Grad* ☎ *01/481–3848* ▤ *AE, DC, MC, V.*

$$$$ ✕**Takenoko.** Don't be deterred by the tiny English-language translations on the menu outside; inside, the menu of this utterly chic, sparkling restaurant is completely readable. You can choose between sushi, both traditional Japanese rolls and American-style varieties; teriyaki; wok dishes; and specialties such as carrot and tofu soup or sea bass in jalapeno-wasabi sauce. Manned by head chefs Moto Mochizuki and Mario Starman, the Takenoko gives meaning to the word "fusion," merging Asian and European cuisine. Black chairs, black place mats, and cherry-toned wood floors set the scene in one of the glittery, glass-walled spaces on the ground floor of the Kaptol Centar facing Tkalćićeva. The drinks menu—including sake, of course—is extensive. ⊠ *Nova Ves 17, Gornji Grad* ☎ *01/486–0530* ▤ *AE, DC, MC, V.*

$$$–$$$$ ✕**Bistro Dizmuš.** Only the somewhat loud pop music detracts from the otherwise intimate atmosphere of this small cellar restaurant with brick-arched ceilings and black-and-white photos adorning the walls. Just beyond Pizzeria 2 and Baltazar, but on the opposite side of the street—a short walk from the Centar Kaptol shopping mall and the forested hills beyond—Bistro Dizmuš has friendly service and hearty, well-prepared food, including a range of grilled meats, squid sautéed in red wine and garlic, cranberry-stuffed chicken in mushroom sauce, and homemade gnocchi. ⊠*Nova Ves 5, Gornji Grad* ☎*01/466–7072* ▭*AE, MC, V.*

$$$–$$$$
Fodor'sChoice
★
✕**Dubravkin Put.** Nestled in a verdant dale in Tuškanac Park, a 15-minute walk from the center in a low-rise building that might be mistaken for a ranch-style house, this prestigious fish restaurant specializes in dishes from the Dubrovnik area, with the house favorites including *buzara* (stew prepared with shellfish and scampi and/or fish) and sea bass fillets in saffron and scampi sauce, as well as appetizers like avocado with scampi, not to mention a few meat delicacies. The dining room is light and airy, with candlelit tables, a wooden floor, palmlike little trees, and colorful abstract art. In warm weather there's outdoor seating on a spacious, leafy terrace, and a playground just outside invites children to scamper about while parents rest on benches. Reservations are recommended, but only on weekdays, as the Dubravkin Put is a popular venue for business dinners. ⊠*Dubravkin put 2, Gornji Grad* ☎*01/483–4975 or 01/483–4970* ▭*AE, DC, MC, V* ⊘*Closed July 20–Aug. 20.*

$$$–$$$$
★
✕**Gostionica Purger.** A flashing neon sign out front seems to suggest you are passing by a diner. Not so. Wildly popular with locals but with a faded, elegant air, this is the sort of restaurant that reminds you of what Zagreb must have been like before the Communists. The food is top-notch, and with animated conversations all around you (at snugly fitting tables—but then this is part of the appeal) and bright yellow walls adorned with historical sketches of Zagreb, this is one fine restaurant. The menu includes everything from goulash with white-wine sauce, on the low end of the price scale, to *domaće krvavice* (black pudding) at the middle, to suckling pig on the spit at the top. ⊠*Petrinjska 33, Donji Grad* ☎*01/481–0713 or 01/481–8631* ▭*AE, DC, MC, V* ⊘*Closed Sun.*

$$$–$$$$
Fodor'sChoice
★
✕**Paviljon.** This chic restaurant—with its round, colonnaded dining room and grand piano—occupies the ground floor of the charming 19th-century Art Pavilion, which faces the train station from across a wide, green mall. The Italian-inspired menu includes dishes such as tagliatelle with zucchini and saffron sauce; lamb cutlets with basmati rice and almonds; and grilled swordfish. The wine list is equally impressive, with a choice of Croatian, Italian, and French vintages. ⊠*Tomislavov trg 22, Donji Grad* ☎*01/481–3066* ▭*AE, DC, MC, V* ⊘*Closed Sun.*

$$$–$$$$
★
✕**Pod Gričkim Topom.** This cozy, endearingly rustic yet elegant restaurant, built into a stone wall on the hillside up a modest flight of steps from the Pansion Jägerhorn, on Ilica, and close to the funicular station in Gornji Grad, affords stunning views over the city rooftops.

Dalmatian cooking predominates, with dishes such as *Jadanske lignje na žaru* (grilled Adriatic squid) and *crni rižoto od sipe* (cuttlefishink risotto) appreciated by locals and visitors alike. ⊠*Zakmardijeve stube 5, Gornji Grad* ☎*01/483–3607* ⟁*Reservations essential* ▭*AE, DC, MC, V.*

$$$–$$$$ ✕**Ribliji Restoran Korčula.** As suggested by the *ribliji* (fish) in its full name, the Korčula is a reliable choice for fresh seafood, including Dalmatian-style cod and tuna with mangold (i.e., Swiss chard). The menu also has a sprinkling of meat dishes, such as stewed beef in wine sauce with dumplings. A five-minute walk from the main square and popular with locals, this cozy restaurant is a moderately appealing place to sit back and fuel up for an hour or two, adorned as it is with black-and-white photos and fishnets hanging from the ceiling. ⊠*Nikole Tesle 17, Donji Grad* ☎*01/487–2159* ▭*AE, DC, MC, V* ⊘*Closed first 3 wks of Aug.*

$$$–$$$$ ✕**Ristorante Rossini.** One of Zagreb's finest Italian restaurants, the Ros-
★ sini sparkles with elegance in its spacious, two-room space a short walk from the main square. You'll feel as if you're in a Zagreb apartment from a bygone age: high ceilings, checkered parquet floors, chandeliers, old architectural sketches and maps adorning the walls—and, yes, white tablecloths and cloth napkins. The menu has a choice selection of highly appealing (and relatively affordable) risottos, including a delicious one with asparagus and pancetta, plus excellent pastas, delectable seafood, and such meatier (and pricier) fare as veal with Gorgonzola and beefsteak with truffles in mushroom sauce. You might get your appetite going with a shot of grappa, of course. ⊠*Vlaška 55, Donji Grad* ☎*01/455–1060* ⟁*Reservations essential* ▭*AE, DC, MC, V* ⊘*Closed Sun. and 3 wks from late July–mid-Aug.*

$$$–$$$$ ✕**Trattoria Agave.** This is the only one among the many dining and drinking venues along bustling Tkačićeva to require a steep walk up a flight of steps—but it's worth it. In warm weather you can stop midway up on a stage-like wooden terrace overlooking the street, or else bask in the homey elegance of one inside room: a wood-beamed ceiling, a parquet floor, and rattan furnishings in between; and large windows likewise providing a good view of the pedestrian thoroughfare below. So sit back, relax, and enjoy one of a range of well-prepared pizzas or pasta; or, if you prefer, steak, poultry dishes, or seafood. ⊠*Tkalčićeva 39, Gornji Grad* ☎*01/482–9826* ▭*AE, MC, V.*

$$–$$$ ✕**Baltazar.** In a courtyard a 10-minute walk uphill beyond the cathe-
★ dral, just beyond Pizzeria 2, Baltazar is best known for classic Balkan dishes such as *ražnjići* (pork on the spit), *ćevapčići* (spiced, ground-meat kebabs), and *zapečeni grah* (oven-baked beans). The interior is elegant, albeit slightly smoky, and the spacious courtyard has leaf-shaded seating. ⊠*Nova Ves 4, Gornji Grad* ☎*01/424–127* ▭*AE, DC, MC, V* ⊘*Closed Sun.*

$$–$$$ ✕**Ivica i Marica.** Celebrated for its delectable cakes made with whole
★ wheat and unrefined brown sugar, Ivica i Marica also serves traditional Croatian pastas, likewise using whole wheat, and hearty meat dishes. Try the tofu-stuffed pepper, homemade ravioli stuffed with spinach and cheese, or Zagorje specialties including *štrukli* (baked cheese dump-

lings). This being in Zagreb, you can also choose grilled seafood or, say, begin with an octopus salad. Waitstaff are decked out in folk costume, and an earnest attempt is made to evoke a folksy atmosphere, with carriage wheels and farm implements hanging from the ceiling. It's a tad touristy, but this charming restaurant, with white tablecloths, sparkling wine glasses, and an upbeat sound track, is still a great place to dine. ⊠ *Tkalčićeva 70, Gornji Grad* ☎ *01/482–8999* ⊟ *AE, DC, MC, V.*

$$–$$$ ✕ **Nova Restoran.** Downtown Zagreb's only full-fledged vegetarian restaurant, the Nova has a wide array of vegan fare made with organic and whole-grain ingredients. It's on the second floor of an apartment building, above the bio&bio health-food store, a few blocks west of the main square, and the dining room is fitted with high-backed chairs in a chic, light-filled interior. ⊠ *Ilica 72, Donji Grad* ☎ *01/481–0059* ⊟ *AE, DC, MC, V* ⊘ *Closed 3 wks from late July–mid-Aug.*

$$–$$$ ✕ **Stari Fijaker.** In this old-fashioned restaurant with vaulted ceilings, wood-paneled walls, and crisp, white table linens the only thing that sometimes mars the ambience is the loud TV set to a pop music channel. The restaurant is just off Ilica, a five-minute walk from the main square on a cobblestone side street. The menu features carefully presented traditional Croatian dishes such as *zagorskajuha* (Zagorje-style potato soup with ham and mushrooms), *pečena teletina* (roast veal), *punjene paprike* (stuffed peppers), and even ostrich steak. ⊠ *Mesnička 6, Donji Grad* ☎ *01/483–3829* ⊟ *AE, DC, MC, V.*

$$–$$$ ✕ **Vinoodol.** A few blocks southwest of the main square, the Vinoodol is
★ an elegant spot locals flock to when they hanker for traditional meaty fare such as veal and lamb, pork with plum sauce, or, for starters, *zagorskajuha* (Zagorje-style potato soup with ham and mushrooms). Enjoy all this in a spacious, shaded courtyard or inside under brick-vaulted ceilings and amid low lighting that contrive to give you an elegant, wine-cellar sensation even though you're not in a cellar at all. ⊠ *Nikole Tesle 10, Donji Grad* ☎ *01/481–1427* ⊟ *AE, DC, MC, V.*

$–$$$ ✕ **Boban.** Just down the street from the Hotel Dubrovnik, Boban is not
★ only a street-level bar but also a restaurant in the large vaulted cellar space below. Specializing in pasta dishes, it is extremely popular with locals, so be prepared to line up for a table, since reservations are not accepted. The owner, Zvonimir Boban, was captain of the Croatian national football team during the 1998 World Cup. ⊠ *Gajeva 9, Donji Grad* ☎ *01/481–1549* ⚠ *Reservations not accepted* ⊟ *AE, DC, MC, V.*

$–$$$ ✕ **Zlatno Medo.** Best known for its excellent beers brewed on the
★ premises, the Zlatno Medo also serves up generous portions of roast meats, goulash, and beans and sausage, accompanied by a range of salads. This cavernous beer hall—replete with long wooden tables, high leather-backed chairs, and wood-beamed ceilings—is close to the Cibona stadium, a good 40-minute walk from the city center. To get here by tram, take either the No. 4 from the train station or the No. 17 from the main square. ⊠ *Savska 56, Donji Grad* ☎ *01/617–7110* ⊟ *AE, DC, MC, V.*

$–$$ ✕ **Leonardo Trattoria.** Sure, it's touristy, and the pop music might be too much for you, but it's undeniably hip, too, and you can eat well for a reasonable price. First you have to get cozy at one of the many tables chock-full of young people squeezed onto the restaurant's 100-foot-long, narrow, wooden platform, which runs right down the middle of the cobblestone pedestrian street between the main cathedral and Tkalčićeva, a one-minute walk from Trg Bana Jelačića. Then you

> **DOUBLY SWEET DREAMS**
>
> Regardless of the price range, Croatian hotels often count two single beds pushed together as a double bed. If it's important to you, be sure to ask if they have rooms with a double mattress.

can choose from a range of risottos, pastas, grilled meats, and more than a dozen types of pizza. Right next door is a similar, albeit slightly less popular restaurant and bar, the Nokturno. ⊠*Skalinska 6, Gornji Grad* ☎*01/487–3005* ▤*AE, DC, MC, V.*

$–$$ ✕**Pizzeria 2.** One of Zagreb's best pizza and pasta joints, this place is popular with the young crowd looking for a budget meal. Wooden tables, vaulted ceilings, and creamy peach walls give you the impression you're in a decked-out cellar, even though it's on the ground floor. The restaurant is near the start of Nova Ves, just beyond Kaptol. ⊠*Nova Ves 2, Gornji Grad* ☎*01/466–8888* ▤*AE, DC, MC, V.*

WHERE TO STAY

Zagreb offers a good choice of large, expensive hotels well geared to the needs of business travelers. This may be in part because tourists tend to frequent the coast, whereas the corporate crowd sticks to the city. However, for summertime vacationers who choose to check out the capital, this is good news: since so much of the country and indeed Europe are on the coast, Zagreb's "low season," when rates are lowest at many hotels, is from early July through late August. Since 2000 several of the capital's major hotels have come under new ownership and been given complete makeovers, guaranteed to appeal to those seeking mid- to upper-range accommodations.

$$$$ ☷**Sheraton Zagreb.** High standards make this modern, six-story hotel on a small side street but just a 10-minute walk from the city center a relative bargain. The main draw for tourists will be the relatively luxurious look and feel; at least you can see what you're paying for here, which isn't always the case when you're down on the coast. Rooms are furnished in classical style, with muted colors and en suite marble bathrooms. Behind the glass facade are excellent sports, business, and entertainment facilities. Pros: top-notch facilities and services, indoor pool, superb dining options. Cons: 30-minute walk from the main square, pricey, not exactly cozy. ⊠*Kneza Borne 2, Donji Grad, 10000* ☎*01/455–3535* 🖷*01/455–3005* ⊕*www.sheraton.com/zagreb* ⤴*312 rooms, 29 suites* ♿*In-room: kitchen (some), refrigerator (some), DVD, Wi-Fi. In-hotel: 2 restaurants, room service, bar, pool, gym, some pets allowed (fee), public Internet, parking (fee), no-smoking rooms* ▤*AE, DC, MC, V* ❑|*BP.*

$$$$ 📺**Westin Zagreb.** After a complete renovation in 2005, this colossal 17-story modern structure between the Mimara Museum and the Botanical Garden—previously the Opera Zagreb—still looks homely on the outside, but on the inside it's a sparkling, five-star affair. Rooms are bright, spacious, and clean, if a bit uninspiring; the signature "Heavenly Beds" are exceptionally comfy. Note that in addition to its 22 suites, the Westin also offers 19 "guest offices," suites with a complete office adjoining the bedroom. Sports and business facilities are first-rate, and a hotel limousine is available for transfers to and from the airport. As of this writing, rooms on the first 11 floors had dial-up Internet access only; those on floors 12 and up had Wi-Fi and Ethernet. Pros: big, comfy rooms, top-notch luxury, excellent amenities and services, superb dining options. Cons: in a boring neighborhood a 45-minute trek from the main square, far from shops and restaurants, in a big, monotonous building. ✉*Kršnjavoga 1, Donji Grad, 10000* 📞*01/489–2000* 📠*01/489–2001* ⊕*www.westin.com/zagreb* 🔌*366 rooms, 22 suites* ♿*In-room: safe, dial-up (some), Wi-Fi (some), Ethernet (some), refrigerator. In-hotel: 2 restaurants, room service, bar, pool, gym, laundry service* ⊟*AE, DC, MC, V* ⦿|*BP.*

$$$–$$$$ 📺**Regent Esplanade.** This beautiful hotel, diagonally across from the
Fodor'sChoice   train station, was built in 1925 for travelers on the original *Ori-*
★   *ent Express.* Louis Armstrong, Elizabeth Taylor, Charles Lindbergh, Orson Welles, Woody Allen, Queen Elizabeth II, and Richard Nixon all stayed here, among other famous names, many of whom left photos for the celebrity wall downstairs. Regular renovations, the last one in 2004, have only enhanced the hotel's luxury and elegance. From its immaculate, Habsburg-era lobby to its dining room replete with huge, resplendent chandeliers, and from its domed ballroom to its spacious outdoor terrace with sweeping views, the Esplanade remains adored by business travelers and tourists alike. The spacious, high-ceilinged rooms and marble bathrooms won't disappoint, and you'll love the special touches like a glass of champagne on check-in and classical music playing in the hallways. Rates for the smallest doubles during Zagreb's low season (early July to late August) are surprisingly affordable. Pros: unmitigated luxury, right by the train station, great fitness center. Cons: pricey and formal (i.e., not a place to shuffle around in your cut-offs), smallish lobby. ✉*Mihanovićeva 1, Donji Grad, 10000* 📞*01/456–6666* 📠*01/456–6050* ⊕*www.regenthotels.com* 🔌*209 rooms, 12 suites* ♿*In-room: safe, DVD (on request), Wi-Fi, Ethernet, refrigerator. In-hotel: 2 restaurants, room service, gym, public Wi-Fi, public Internet, parking (fee)* ⊟*AE, DC, MC, V* ⦿|*EP.*

$$$ 📺**Arcotel Allegra.** Design is the word in this trendy boutique hotel,
★   which opened in 2003 in the same building as the Branimir Center, a bustling little shopping mall. Everything—from the bedspreads and pillowcases, which picture the faces of luminaries like Verdi, Kafka, Frida Kahlo, and Einstein, to the soft, synthetic leather armchairs and "mobile tables," to the deep-blue carpeting showing a map of the world (Zagreb highlighted by a red dot)—is intended to soothe or inspire. All this compliments of Austrian artist, designer, and architect Harald Schreiber. In the Executive rooms (a small supplement to the standard), you get free

newspapers, slippers, bathrobes, and chocolates. The hotel's likewise stylish restaurant is probably the only place in town where you can get such fare as "freshly seared Adriatic Cajun tuna with wasabi dressing and green salad." Pros: near the train station, easy access to the shops and restaurants of the Branimir Center, contemporary and artsy decor. Cons: pricey, 20-minute walk from the main square, no pool. ⊠*Branimirova 29, Donji Grad, 10000* ☎*01/469–6000* 🖷*01/469–6096* ⊕*www.arcotel.at* ⇨*151 rooms* ♿*In-room: safe, DVD, dial-up, refrigerator. In-hotel: restaurant, gym, parking (fee), some pets allowed* ▤*AE, DC, MC, V* ⦿|*BP.*

$$ 🖭**Best Western Premier Hotel Astoria.** The Hotel Astoria reopened with a new name and a luxurious new look in March 2005 after a six-month makeover. Less than five minutes by foot from the train station and 10 minutes from downtown, it offers bright, modern rooms with the silky bedspreads and partly marble bathrooms that meet the requirements of its Premier category. It may be Zagreb's first hotel in which the shutters roll up automatically when you enter your room—do remember that before tearing your clothes off in a fit of passion. The standard rooms are on the small side; the executive rooms, which have king-size beds, are more spacious but also quite a bit more expensive. Pros: good location on a quiet side street midway between the train station and the main square, marble bathrooms with excellent amenities, topnotch 24-hour business center. Cons: smallish rooms, no health facilities or pool. ⊠*Petrinjska 71, Donji Grad, 10000* ☎*01/480–8900 or 01/480–8910* 🖷*01/480–8908 or 01/481–7053* ⊕*www.bestwestern. com* ⇨*100 rooms, 2 suites* ♿*In-room: safe, Ethernet, Wi-Fi, refrigerator. In-hotel: restaurant, bar, room service, laundry service, public Wi-Fi, public Internet, some pets allowed, no-smoking rooms* ▤*AE, DC, MC, V* ⦿|*BP.*

$$ 🖭**Hotel Dubrovnik.** Claiming the most central location in the city, just
★ off Trg Bana Jelačića, Hotel Dubrovnik has been popular with business travelers and tourists alike since opening back in 1929. The garish mirrored-glass facade conceals bright, modern, smallish but perfectly acceptable rooms. Beyond its other amenities, the hotel is also home to one of Zagreb's most popular hangouts, the Cafe Dubrovnik, which has a great view of the main square. Pros: right off the main square, near shops and restaurants, numerous amenities. Cons: smallish rooms, low on historic grandeur. ⊠*Gajeva 1, Donji Grad, 10000* ☎*01/486–3500 or 01/486–3555* 🖷*01/486–3550* ⊕*www.hotel-dubrovnik.hr* ⇨*266 rooms, 8 suites* ♿*In-room: safe, refrigerator, dial-up, room service. In-hotel: restaurant, room service, bar, public Wi-Fi, public Internet, parking (fee), laundry facilities, laundry service, some pets allowed, no-smoking rooms* ▤*AE, DC, MC, V* ⦿|*BP.*

$$ 🖭**Palace Hotel Zagreb.** Built in 1891 as the Schlessinger Palace and con-
★ verted in 1907 to become the city's first hotel, the Palace Hotel offers romantic, old-fashioned comfort. The spacious rooms, which were all completely renovated in 2005 and 2006, have modern beds and furnishings but retain their original art-nouveau look with moldings and long drapes. Golden hues predominate. Overlooking a green square between the train station and the city center—and only a five-minute walk from

either—the Palace is best known by locals for the street-level, Viennese-style café. Pros: great location across from parklike Strossmayerov trg and close to Trg bana J. Jelačića, historical ambience, excellent café, 60% of rooms no-smoking. Cons: no health facilities or pool. ⊠ *Strossmayerov trg 10, Donji Grad, 10000* ☎ *01/489–9618 or 01/492–0530* 🖷 *01/481–1358* ⊕ *www.palace.hr* 🔌 *123 rooms, 5 suites* ♿ *In-room: safe, Ethernet, Wi-Fi, refrigerator. In-hotel: restaurant, room service, laundry service, public Wi-Fi, public Internet, some pets allowed, no-smoking rooms* ⊟ *AE, DC, MC, V* ⦅◯⦆ *BP.*

$ 🖫 **Hotel Central.** On the opposite side of the train station from the Regent Esplanade—and in one boring, concrete block of a building—the Central is convenient rather than quaint. The spacious rooms are simply furnished in shades of blue, and the staff are friendly and efficient. Pros: close to the train station, spacious rooms, friendly service. Cons: rooms facing the street get noise from passing trams, a tad pricey for what you get, few frills, dull-looking building. ⊠ *Branimirova 3, Donji Grad, 10000* ☎ *01/484–1122 or 01/484–0555* 🖷 *01/484–1304* ⊕ *www. hotel-central.hr* 🔌 *76 rooms, 3 suites* ♿ *In-room: Wi-Fi, refrigerator (some). In-hotel: public Internet, bar, laundry service* ⊟ *AE, DC, MC, V* ⦅◯⦆ *BP.*

$ 🖫 **Movie Hotel.** Better known to its adoring British and other European
★ fans as the Movie Hotel & Pub, this is the place to be if you like the idea of falling asleep with a picture of Al Pacino, Sharon Stone, or, say, Brad Pitt, looming on the wall above you. The bright, modern rooms have parquet floors with area rugs, and each room is named after the star whose picture is on the wall over the bed. Downstairs there's a spacious, low-lit Irish pub chock-full of Hollywood pictures on the walls and with old-time tunes playing in the background. There's even a wine gallery in the cellar. A separate building out back has 14 rooms and four apartments at a lower rate, but those rooms lack the Hollywood theme, refrigerators, air-conditioning, safes, and cable TV. Unlike the rooms in the main building, however, the back rooms have one large, queen-size bed as opposed to two single beds pushed together. Pros: atmospheric to a T, spacious rooms, ideal for movie buffs. Cons: 45-minute trek from the main square, few attractions, shops, or restaurants nearby, small bathrooms. ⊠ *Savska cesta 141, Donji Grad, 10000* ☎ *01/600–3600* 🖷 *01/600–3601* ⊕ *www.themoviehotel.com* 🔌 *20 rooms* ♿ *In-room: no a/c (some), DVD (some), safe (some), refrigerator (some), Ethernet. In-hotel: restaurant, bar, no elevator* ⊟ *AE, DC, MC, V* ⦅◯⦆ *BP.*

$ 🖫 **Pansion Jägerhorn** At the far end of a shop-filled courtyard off Zagreb's busiest shopping street, a minute's walk from Trg Bana Jelačića, this friendly pension occupies the building where Zagreb's first restaurant opened back in 1827. Rooms are spacious and bright, with skylights, floral bedspreads (but hard mattresses), and walls adorned with soothing watercolors. You enter through the pension's popular restaurant, which is highly regarded for its wild-game dishes, as you might guess from the stuffed deer, birds, and so forth all over the walls. Pros: central location, good on-site dining, big bright rooms, cash payments yield a 10% discount. Cons: some creaky floors, dark tones, slightly tacky decor in the public areas. ⊠ *Ilica 14, Donji Grad, 10000*

☎01/483–3877 🖷01/483–3573 ⊕*www.hotel-pension-jaegerhorn.
hr* ⟳*11 rooms, 2 suites* ♿*In-room: refrigerator. In-hotel: restaurant,
parking (no fee)* ☰*AE, DC, MC, V* ¶◎*BP.*

$ ☎ **Vila Tina.** If you prefer a quiet environment and don't mind the some-
what tacky look of the lobby (pseudo-classical statuettes, anyone?),
then this family-run hotel may be just for you. It's well outside the
center of town on a peaceful side street near Maksimir Park and a
short walk from forested hills. Each room is individually furnished
with surprising taste, considering the lobby, and with personal touches
like fresh fruit and flowers. There's a good restaurant with a summer
garden. Pros: cozier than big hotels downtown, near Maksimir Park
and hiking opportunities in the hills. Cons: a 90-minute hike from the
main square, few amenities. ✉*Bukovačka c 213, Donji Grad, 10000*
☎*01/244–5138* 🖷*01/244–5204* ⊕*www.vilatina.com.hr* ⟳*14 rooms*
♿*In-room: Wi-Fi, refrigerator. In-hotel: restaurant, public Wi-Fi, public Internet, parking (no fee)* ☰*AE, DC, MC, V* ¶◎*BP.*

¢ ☎ **Hotel Sliško.** This small hotel is just a five-minute walk from the
bus station and a 15-minute walk from the center. Rooms are smart
and functional, and there's a bar and breakfast room. It's normally
fully booked during trade fairs (and rates are 20% more then), so
check for dates well in advance. Cash payments yield a 10% discount.
Pros: reasonably priced, near the bus station, cozier than big downtown hotels. Cons: a 45-minute walk (or 15-minute tram ride) from the
main square, small bathrooms, few frills. ✉*Bunićeva 7, Donji Grad,
10000* ☎*01/619–4210 or 01/618–4777* 🖷*01/619–4223* ⊕*www.
slisko.hr* ⟳*15 rooms, 3 apartments* ♿*In-room: refrigerator, Wi-Fi.
In-hotel: restaurant, bar, public Internet, no elevator* ☰*AE, DC, MC,
V* ¶◎*BP.*

NIGHTLIFE & THE ARTS

Climbing full-steam ahead out of the economic depression caused by
the war, Zagreb now has a lively entertainment scene. Bars, clubs, and
cinemas are predominantly frequented by the city's student population,
whereas the concert hall and theater remain the domain of the older
generation. For information about what's on, pick up a free copy of the
monthly *Events and Performances,* published by the city tourist board.

NIGHTLIFE

BARS & **BP Jazz Club** (✉*Teslina 4, Donji Grad* ☎*01/481–4444* ⊕*www.bpclub.*
NIGHTCLUBS *hr*), the capital's top venue for live jazz, is a smoky basement bar. **Bulldog**
(✉*Bogovićeva 6, Donji Grad* ☎*01/481–7393*) is a popular split-level
café-cum-wine-bar with a large summer terrace. **Jackie Brown** (✉*Nova
Ves 17, Gornji Grad* ☎*01/486–0241*), a sleek-as-can-be cocktail bar, is
just the place to sit back and sip a martini while listening to jazz—after
sushi, say, at the Takenoko *(see Where to Eat)* next door.

Maraschino (✉*Margaretska 1, Donji Grad* ☎*01/481–2612*), named
after Zadar's distinguished cherry liqueur, is a sleek and extremely
popular club that's usually filled to the gills (especially on weekends)
with young people come to listen, and smoke, to loud and funky tunes

by live bands or DJs. **Old Pharmacy**
(✉*Andrije Hebranga 11a, Donji
Grad* ☎*01/492–1912*), a peaceful pub with CNN on television
and a selection of English-language newspapers, also has a nosmoking side room. **Oliver Twist Pub**
(✉*Tkalčićeva 60, Gornji Grad*
☎*01/481–2206*) is definitely not a
bleak house. This is *the* place to be
after dark on Tkalčićeva. Although
in good weather practically all the
(mostly young) patrons are seated
out front, inside is an immaculate
English-style pub whose walls, on
the upper floor, are decorated with
memorabilia associated with different Dickens novels. **Pivnica Medvedgrad** (✉*Savska 56, Donji Grad*
☎*01/617–7110*) is a beer hall and
microbrewery serving the best ale
in town. **Tantra** (✉*Gajeva 2, Donji*

Grad ☎*01/487–2544h*) is a popular place to kick back, drink, and
chat in soft tones while watching the crowds on Trg Bana Jelačića
below. Pillow-equipped white divans and wicker-backed lounge chairs
provide an unbeatable view of Zagreb's main square. To get here, pass
through the narrow arcade between the bookshops yards away from
the square and go up the spiral wooden staircase on the left.

DISCOS **Aquarius** (✉*Aleja Mateja Ljubeka bb, Jarun* ☎*01/364–0231* ⊕*www.
aquarius.hr*) is Zagreb's top club for dancing, especially for disco and
techno music. It overlooks the beach at Malo jezero, the smaller of the
two interconnected lakes comprising Lake Jarun, 4 km (2½ mi) from
the city center. **Saloon** (✉*Tuškanac 1a, Gornji Grad* ☎*01/483–4835*)
is the city's most glamorous club, where you can rub shoulders with
the stars and dance not only to commercial as well as Croatian techno
but also, once a week, to classic rock.

THE ARTS

ARTS For one week in mid-September, the **World Theatre Festival** brings to
FESTIVALS Zagreb theater companies from all over Europe—if not exactly the
world—for one or more performances each evening at various theatrical venues about town. For the best of concerts in the park, keep your
eye out for the free **Promenade Concerts** by Croatian chamber orchestras,
brass bands, and choirs, held every Saturday from 11 AM to 1 PM from
around mid-August to mid-October at the music pavilion set amid the
lovely plane trees and fountains of Zrinjevac Park, on Zrinskog trg.
Adding color to this series are 19th-century-costume contests and displays, an antiques market, a play area and programs for children, rides
in horse-drawn carriages, and even souvenir stands.

FILM **Broadway Tkalča** (⊠*Nova Ves 11, Gornji Grad* ☏*01/466–7686*) is Croatia's first multiplex cinema, in the Centar Kaptol shopping complex, wedged in a serene, parklike atmosphere a 10-minute walk north of the main cathedral, first along Kaptol and then onto Nova Ves. Most foreign films (including those from the United States) are shown in their original language with Croatian subtitles.

MAJOR VENUES The **Hrvatsko Narodno Kazalište** (*Croatian National Theater* ⊠*Trg Maršala Tita 15, Donji Grad* ☏*01/488–8417* ⊕*www.hnk.hr*), a beautiful 19th-century building, hosts classical and contemporary dramas, opera, and ballet performances. **Komedija** (⊠*Kaptol 9, Gornji Grad* ☏*01/481–2179* ⊕*www.komedija.hr*) is a small theater specializing in operettas and Croatian musicals, close to the cathedral. **Koncertna Dvorana Vatroslav Lisinski** (*Vatroslav Lisinski Concert Hall* ⊠*Stjepana Radića 4, Donji Grad* ☏*01/612–1166* ⊕*www.lisinski.hr*), a large, modern complex with two auditoriums, is Zagreb's top venue for orchestral- and classical-music concerts.

SHOPPING

Although Zagreb, for all its other attractions, might not be a shopping mecca, a walk down the bustling Ilica or other nearby streets will take you past plenty of stores chock-full of the latest fashions. Frankopanska particularly is turning into something of a fashion avenue, with labels like Lacoste, Cacharel, and the British design duo Gharari Štrok. Don't pass up the chance to stroll through the beautiful Oktogon shopping arcade. Its long, bright yellow, spacious hall, with elaborate wrought-iron gates at each end and lovely glass ceilings from 1901, connects Ilica 5 with Trg Petra Preradovića and offers more than a few high-class shops along the way.

SHOPPING CENTERS & MARKETS

It's easy to miss downtown's largest shopping mall, the **Importanne Centar** (⊠*Mihanovicéva ul, Donji Grad*), since it's completely underground and not well marked on the street level. Look for the escalators leading down, and once you're inside, good luck finding your way back out. Several blocks north of the cathedral, in a parklike setting between Nova Ves and Tkalčićeva, is the **Centar Kaptol** (⊠*Nova Ves 11, Gornji Grad*), whose stores include Marks & Spencer, Kenzo, and Max & Co. For an authentic Croatian shopping experience, visit the **Dolac open-air market** (⊠*Trg Bana Jelačića, Gornji Grad*), where besides fresh fruit and vegetables there are also a number of arts-and-crafts stalls. It's open weekdays 7 to 4 and weekends until noon.

SPECIALTY STORES

Right next to the Hotel Dubrovnik, near other major bookstores, the **Algoritam** (⊠*1 Gajeva, Donji Grad* ☏*01/488–1555*) has a huge selection of English-language books, including plenty of guides and coffee-table books on Croatia. Ties may not be the most original of gifts, but they are uniquely Croatian. During the 17th century, Croatian mercenaries who fought in France sported narrow, silk neck scarfs, which soon became known to the French as *cravat* (from the Croatian *hrvat*). At **Croata** (⊠*Ilica 5 [within the Oktogon arcade]*, *Donji Grad* ☎*01/481–4600* ⊕*www.croata.hr* ⊠*Kaptol 13, Gornji Grad*) you can buy "original Croatian ties" in presentation boxes, accompanied by a brief history of the tie. **Croatia Records** (⊠*Bogoviceva 5, Donji Grad*) has a good selection of Croatian and international pop and rock music. **Natura Croatica** (⊠*Preradovićeva 8, Donji Grad* ☎*01/485–5076*) offers all manner of Croatian delicacies that use only natural ingredients, from brandies and liqueurs to jams, olive oils, cheeses, truffles, soaps, wild-game jerkies, and pâtés. Housed in a tastefully arranged, vaulted brick cellar, **Vinoteka Bornstein** (⊠*Kaptol 19, Gornji Grad* ☎*01/481–2361*) stocks a wide range of quality Croatian wines, olive oils, and truffle products.

EXCURSIONS NORTH OF ZAGREB

A favorite excursion to the outskirts of Zagreb is to the heights of Sljeme and its observatory. And then there is the peaceful spa town of Stubičke Toplice and, a bit further to the northeast, the Catholic pilgrimage site of Maria Bistrica. Further to the north, beyond the Medvednica Hills, lies a pastoral region known as Zagorje. The scenery is calm and enchanting: redbrick villages, such as Kumrovec, are animated with ducks and chickens, and the hillsides are inlaid with vineyards and orchards. Medieval hilltop castles, including Veliki Tabor and Dvor Trakošćan, survey the surrounding valleys. To the northeast of Zagreb is the charming baroque town of Varaždin. Although Sljeme and Stubičke Toplice are reasonably easy to get to from the capital by bus, having a car at your disposal for a day or two will give you a chance to cover more ground efficiently (e.g., without having to return to Zagreb to board yet another bus).

SLJEME

5 km (3 mi) north of Zagreb by tram and cable car.

A favorite excursion on the outskirts of Zagreb is to the heights of Sljeme, the peak of **Mt. Medvednica,** at 3,363 feet. You can reach it taking Tram 14 (direction Mihaljevac) all the way to the terminal stop, where you should change to Tram 15 (direction Dolje), also to its terminal stop. From there a cable car operates hourly for the 20-minute journey to the top of the mountain for breathtaking views over the surrounding countryside. It's an ideal place for picnicking, but you may wish to save your appetite for dinner at one of the excellent restaurants on the road home.

On the southwest flank of the summit is a reconstructed fortress called **Medvegrad.** The original was built in the 13th century by Bishop Filip of Zagreb, and after a succession of distinguished owners over the next two centuries it was destroyed in an earthquake in 1590. You can wander around the outside (for free), and take in great views of Zagreb. It's a one-hour trek to the fortress from the cable car, or you can reach it more directly by taking Bus 102 from Britansk trg in central Zagreb

Excursions
from Zagreb

(just off Ilica, a 20-minute walk west of Trg Bana Josipa Jelačića) to the "Blue Church" in Šestine, and hiking some 40 minutes uphill from there. Take trail No. 12, which is off the paved road past the church cemetery. ⊠ *Dolje* ☎ *01/458–0394* ⊠ *Cable car 17 Kn round-trip* ⊙ *Daily 8–8.*

WHERE TO EAT

$$$ ✕ **Stari Puntijar.** On the road between Zagreb and Sljeme, Stari Puntijar is renowned for game and traditional 19th-century Zagreb dishes such as *podolac* (ox medallions in cream and saffron), *orehnjaca* (walnut loaf), and *makovnjaca* (poppy-seed cake). The wine list is excellent, and the interior design is marked by trophies, hunting weapons, old paintings, and big chandeliers. ⊠ *Gračanka c 65, Medveščak, Zagreb* ☎ *01/467–5500* ⊟ *AE, DC, MC, V.*

STUBIČKE TOPLICE

37 km (23 mi) north of Zagreb.

Established in 1805 on the foundations of a Roman-era thermal bath and expanded into a full-fledged complex in 1930, this peaceful spa at the northern edge of the Medvednica hills is where the capital's residents go to soak away those nerves and ailments in temps ranging from 45°C to 65°C (113°F to 149°F). Set at the edge of a large park replete with tall spruce trees, the **Matija Gubec** hotel is the place to go to give it a try yourself—though you needn't stay overnight at this complex of six beige, concrete, interconnected ranch-house-like buildings. After paying a small admission fee, you get access to the complex's eight outdoor pools as well as the hotel's indoor pool, sauna, and fitness facility. The rooms (€72) are decent, with cable TV and phones, but otherwise have no frills and no air-conditioning. If you are looking for a bite to eat, Restaurant Bilikum, across the street from the hotel, is a good choice. ⊠ *Viktora Šipeka 31, Stubičke Toplice* ☎ *049/282–501* ⊕ *www.hotel-mgubec.com* ⊠ *45 Kn (40 Kn after 3 PM); sauna only 20 Kn for 20 minutes* ⊙ *Weekdays 7 AM–10 PM, weekends 7 AM–midnight.*

MARIJA BISTRICE

17 km (11 mi) east of Stičke Toplice, 40 km (25 mi) northeast of Zagreb.

Other than its famous pilgrimage site, there's not much of interest in Marija Bistrice. Definitely do this as a day trip, unless you want to spend a night in nearby Stubičke Toplice.

Croatia's preeminent religious pilgrimage site, the **Hodočasnička Crkva Marije Bistricvkve** *(Pilgrimage Church of St. Mary of Bistrica)* is home to the Blessed Virgin of Bistrica, a black, wooden, 15th-century Gothic statue of the Holy Mother associated with miraculous powers (having survived not only the Turkish invasion but a subsequent fire) and set in the main altar. The church, which was proclaimed a Croatian shrine by the nation's parliament in 1715, was rebuilt in neo-Renaissance style in the late 19th century by Hermann Bollé, who also designed the Zagreb cathedral; the shrine complex adjacent to the church was enlarged in time for a 1998 visit by Pope John Paul II, who was in town to beatify Alojzije Stepinac, who became Archbishop of Zagreb in 1937 but was jailed and later placed under house arrest in postwar, Tito-led Yugoslavia. Behind the church is a huge amphitheater that was built for the pope's visit, and from there you can climb up Kalvarija (Calvary Hill) to the stations of the cross, ornamented with sculptures by Croatian artists. ⊠*Trg Ivana Pavla II, Marija Bistrice* ☎*049/469–156 or 049/468–350* ᐧ*Free* ☉*Daily 7:30* AM–6 PM.

NEED A BREAK? If your pilgrimage leaves you famished in a bodily sense, a sure bet for well-prepared grilled meats and seafood is Purga (⊠ *Grančarska 47b, Zlatar Bistrica* ☎*049/461–949* ᐧAE, DC, MC, V) a roadside restaurant 6 km (4 mi) north of Marija Bistrica, which has pleasantly rustic decor with wooden tables and charming seat cushions with an embroidered look, as well as moderate prices.

KUMROVEC

★ *40 km (25 mi) northwest of Zagreb.*

The former Yugoslavia's late president Josip Broz Tito was born here in 1892, and his childhood home has been turned into a small memorial museum. In the courtyard of his birthplace stands an imposing bronze likeness of him by Antun Augustinčić.

☺ The old quarter of Kumrovec, known as **Kumrovec Staro Selo** *(Kumrovec Old Village)*, is an open-air museum with beautifully restored thatched cottages and wooden farm buildings, orchards, and a stream giving a lifelike reconstruction of 19th-century rural life. On weekends craftsmen, including a blacksmith, a candle maker, and others, demonstrate their skills. ⊠*Kumrovec* ☎*049/225–830* ⊕*www.mdc.hr/kumrovec* ᐧ*20 Kn* ☉*Apr.–Sept., daily 9–7; Oct.–Mar., daily 9–4.*

VELIKI TABOR

★ *15 km (9 mi) north of Kumrovec.*

On a lofty hilltop stands the massive fortress of Veliki Tabor. The main pentagonal core of the building dates back to the 12th century, whereas the side towers were added in the 15th century as protection against the Turks. The colonnaded galleries of the interior cast sublime shadows in moonlight. Nine buses daily will get you here from Zagreb's main bus station in 2½ hours for 69 Kn one way; but after getting off you have a 3-km (2-mi) walk still ahead of you. Hence, as is true more generally of site-hopping in the Zagorje region, a rental car may come in handy. ⊠*Desinić* ☎*049/343–052* ⊕*www.veliki-tabor.hr* ᐧ*20 Kn* ☉*Daily 10–6.*

WHERE TO EAT

$$–$$$ ✕**Grešna Gorica.** Visiting this rustic tavern is like stepping into a friend's
★ home. That said, your friend's home is unlikely to have a stuffed fawn
and a pair of *kuna* (martens, the national currency's namesake) on the
wall (this monetary history of kuna dates from the days when the fur
of this large, weasel-like creature was in fact a currency). All produce
used here is supplied by local farmers, and the menu features typical
Zagorje dishes, including *zagorski štrukli* (baked cheese dumplings)
and *pura s mlincima* (turkey with savory pastries). The garden affords
sublime views down onto Veliki Tabor fortress. ⊠*Desinić* ☎*049/343–
001* ▭*No credit cards.*

WHERE TO STAY

$ 🏨**Dvorac Bežanec.** There's a lovely old manor house waiting for you—a
Fodor'sChoice 15-minute drive east of Veliki Tabor—where you can have your spa-
★ cious room with period furniture and breakfast, too, for under €100
a night. Owned by various barons since Count Keglević built it in
the 17th century, Bežanec Castle got a new lease on life as a luxury
hotel in 1990. Part of its charm is its authenticity, and the furnishings,
while in tip-top, dust-free shape, actually feel like the real, 17th-cen-
tury McCoys. Splendid works by various Croatian artists, including a
whole series of superb naive paintings by Slauko Stolmik, line the halls.
With advance notice, the hotel will pick up guests who arrive by bus in
Veliki Tabor. Any activity, from hot-air balloon rides and horseback-
riding instruction to tennis and archery, can be yours, too, for reasonable fees. Sure, there's no air-conditioning—but was there any in the
18th century? Pros: historical ambience, spacious rooms, reasonable
rate. Cons: far from major tourist areas and towns, restaurants, and
shopping; no a/c. ⊠*Valentinovo 55, 49218 Pregrada* ☎*049/376–800*
🖷*049/376–810* ⊕*www.bezanec.hr* ⇌*20 rooms, 5 suites* ♿*In-room:
no a/c, DVD (on request), refrigerator, Wi-Fi, Ethernet. In-hotel: restaurant, room service, tennis court, no elevator, laundry facilities, laundry service, public Wi-Fi, public Internet, parking (no fee), some pets
allowed, no-smoking rooms* ▭*AE, DC, MC, V* ¹◎⎮*EP.*

KRAPINA

⏱ *20 km (12½ mi) east of Veliki Tabor, 66 km (41 mi) north of Zagreb.*

Zagorje's quaint administrative and cultural center is on the tourism
radar screen primarily as home of *krapinski čovjek* (Krapina man)—
no, not the town's one male inhabitant but a Neanderthal of a sort,
whose bones were discovered on a hillside a short walk from the town
center in 1899, in what was a settlement of these early humanlike creatures 30,000 to 40,000 years ago. Indeed, this may be one of the few
places in the world today where you can meet up with a family of such
hominids and even a fearsome bear in the woods—that is, with life-
size statues of Neanderthals going about their daily business (wielding
clubs, throwing rocks, tending fire), at the spot where the discovery
was made.

Displays at the **Museum of Evolution**, which is near the location of the actual discovery, provide insight into who these early Neanderthals were and how they lived, and more broadly into the region's geology and history. ⊠ *Šetalište V Sluge* ☎ *049/371–491* ✉ *15 Kn* ☉ *Apr.– Oct., Tues.–Sun. 9–5; Nov.–Mar., Tues.–Sun. 8–3.*

TRAKOŠĆAN

★ *41 km (25½ mi) west of Varaždin, 36 km (22½ mi) northeast of Veliki Tabor.*

Fodor'sChoice
★
Perched resplendently several hundred feet above the parking lot where the tour buses come and go, the romantic white hilltop **Dvor Trakošćan** *(Trakošćan Castle)* is set amid beautifully landscaped grounds, overlooking a lovely lake circled by a hiking trail. Croatia's most-visited castle took on its present neo-Gothic appearance during the mid-19th century, compliments of Juraj VI Drašković, whose family had already owned the castle for some 300 years and would go on to live there until 1944 (there has been a building here since the 14th century). The inside is as spectacular as the outside, with the wood-paneled rooms— a baroque room, a rococo room, a neoclassical room, and so on— filled with period furnishings and family portraits, giving you some idea of how the wealthy local aristocracy once lived. A restaurant, café, and souvenir shop occupy an uninspiring, Ministry of Culture– owned building at the foot of the hill. ⊠ *Trakošćan* ☎ *042/796–281 or 042/796–422* ⊕ *www.trakoscan.hr* ✉ *20 Kn* ☉ *Apr.–Sept., daily 9–6; Oct.–Mar., daily 9–4.*

VARAŽDIN

70 km (48 mi) northeast of Zagreb.

Situated on a plain just south of the River Drava, Varaždin is the most harmonious and beautifully preserved baroque town in this corner of the continent. A vibrant commercial and cultural center, especially in the 18th century, Varaždin (pop. 50,000) is richly adorned by extraordinary churches and the palaces of the aristocratic families that once lived here. It was Croatia's capital from 1756 until a devastating fire in 1776 prompted a move to Zagreb. First mentioned under the name Garestin in a document by the Hungarian-Croatian king Bela III from 1181, it was declared a free royal town by King Andrew II of Hungary's Arpad dynasty in 1209 and went on to become an important economic, social, administrative, and military center. Near the heart of the city, in a park surrounded by grassy ramparts, the well-preserved castle is the main attraction. A short walk from the castle, on the outskirts of town, is one of Europe's loveliest cemeteries, with immense hedges trimmed and shaped around ornate memorials. Note that Varaždin's main churches are open only around an hour before and after mass, which is generally held several times daily, more often on weekends; the tourist information office can help you contact individual churches to arrange a look inside at other times.

Varaždin's Guitar Great

It's not by chance that Varaždin's distinguished string instrument maker Vladimir Šimunov Proskurnjak, whose studio is in the heart of downtown, at Krančevićeva 5, specializes in guitars. This particular instrument holds a special place in the hearts of the classical-music lovers of Varaždin. Indeed, there was a time when the guitar was among the most popular instruments in Croatia and elsewhere in Europe and earned the respect of the great music critics of the day. That time, in Croatia, peaked in the first half of the nineteenth century. The nation's greatest guitarist of the era, and one of the continent's best, was Varaždin's own Ivan Padovec. Born in 1800, Ivan was often ill as a child and extremely nearsighted. To make matters worse, at the age of 10 he was left half blind when a stone thrown at him by another boy hit his left eye. Since his physical limitations meant he could not become a priest, as his parents had hoped, Padovec trained to become a teacher. However, he chose quite another path.

By the age of 19 Ivan Padovec had not only taught himself to play the guitar, he was indeed able to support himself by giving lessons to friends. Before long he decided to devote his life to music. Within five years, Padovec had a reputation not only as a virtuoso guitarist but also as a talented composer. By 1827 he was giving concerts from Zagreb and Varaždin to Zadar, Rijeka, and Trieste, and before long he'd earned the respect of even the court in Vienna. While living in the Austrian capital from 1829 to 1837, Padovec gave concerts throughout Europe, though weakening eyesight eventually forced a return to his native Varaždin. After a concert in Zagreb in 1840, one critic wrote, "[Padovec] showed that even on such an instrument it was possible to play tenderly and skillfully, thus surpassing everyone else." In addition to writing more than 200 compositions, he authored an influential book on guitar instruction and invented a 10-string guitar. Completely blind by 1848, Padovec retreated to his sister's house in Varaždin, unable to compose or teach. In 1871 he gave his final performance at the city theater. A life of music reaped little financial compensation for Padovec, and he died in poverty on November 4, 1873. Appropriately, Varaždin's tourist office is located in the house where he was born, at Ivana Padovca 3.

WHAT TO SEE

Fodor'sChoice
★
Today a historical museum, Varaždin's main attraction is the massive **Stari Grad** *(Castle)*, which assumed its present form in the 16th century as a state-of-the-art defense fortification against the Turks, complete with moats, dikes, and bastions with low, round defense towers connected by galleries with openings for firearms. In the ensuing centuries it was often reconstructed by the families that owned it; for more than three centuries, until its 1925 purchase by the city, it belonged to the Erdödy clan. From the 12th century up until 1925, the castle served as the seat of the county prefect. You enter through the 16th-century tower gatehouse, which has a wooden drawbridge, to arrive in the internal courtyard with three levels of arcaded galleries. Indoors, there's an extensive display of antique furniture, with pieces laid out in chrono-

1

logical order and each room representing a specific period. Even if you don't go inside, do take a stroll around the perimeter, along a path that takes you between the outer wall and a ditch that used to be the moat. ✉*Strossmayerovo Šetalište 7* ☎*042/210–399* ⊕*www.varaz din.hr* 💶*15 Kn* 🕐*Oct.–Apr., Tues.–Fri. 10–3, weekends 10–1.*

> **THIRSTY?**
>
> But not in the mood to sit down at a café or search for bottled water? Well, if you're on Trg M. Stančića, near the tourist office, look for the nice old water pump, the ideal thing to fill your water bottle.

NEED A BREAK?

For a bite of Varaždin's specialty bakery product, a *klipić* (a salted, finger-shaped bread), stop by one of the bakeries at the city's open-air food market (✉*Trg Bana Jelačića*), which is open Monday through Saturday from 7 AM to 2 PM.

Consecrated to Varaždin's patron saint in 1761 on the site of an older church, the **Župna Crkva Sv. Nikole** *(Parish Church of St. Nicholas)* is a baroque structure that is more attractive on the outside than the inside. Note the false yet imposing white columns in the facade; the red-tiled, conical steeple; and the sculpture at the foot of the steeple of a firefighting St. Florian pouring a bucket of water onto a church, presumably an allusion to the fire that devastated Varaždin in 1776. ✉*Trg slobode 11.*

The **Uršulinska Crkva Rođenja Isusovog** *(Ursuline Church of the Birth of Christ)*, a single-nave, pale-pink baroque church with a particularly colorful, late-baroque altar, was consecrated in 1712 by the Ursuline sisters, who came to Varaždin from Bratislava nine years earlier at the invitation of the Drašković family. Its charming, strikingly slender tower was added in 1726. ✉*Uršulinska 3.*

Consecrated in 1650 on the site of a medieval predecessor, the pale yellow **Franjevačka Crkva** *(Franciscan Church)* has the highest tower in Varaždin, at almost 180 feet. Right out front is a statue of 10th-century Croatian bishop Grgur Ninski, who is memorialized in a feverish pose; this is a replica of the original, which is in Split; another such replica can be seen in Nin. ✉*Franjevački trg 8.*

Housed in the Herzer Palace, the **Entomološka Zbirka** *(Entomological Collection)* museum has a fascinating presentation of some 1,000 different insects. ✉*Franjevački trg 6* ☎*042/210–474* 💶*20 Kn* 🕐*May–Sept., Tues.–Sun. 10–6; Oct.–Apr., Tues.–Fri. 10–5, weekends 10–1.*

The 16th-century **Lisakova kula** *(Lisak Tower)* is the only part of Varaždin's northern town wall that has been preserved. The wall formed part of the onetime city fortress, but most of it was razed in the early 19th century. Unfortunately, you can't enter the tower. ✉*Trg Bana Jelačića.*

The **Galerija Starih i Novih Majstora** *(Gallery of Old and Modern Masters)* is housed in the striking, 18th-century rococo Palača Sermage (Sermage Palace)—characterized by cinnamon-colored, black-framed geometric medallions decorating its facade and an impressive wrought-iron terrace. The museum has a rich array of traditional paintings by Croatian and other European artists. ⊠ *Trg M. Stančića 3* ☎ *042/214-172* ☜ *20 Kn* ☉ *May–Sept., Tues.–Sun. 10–6; Oct.–Apr., Tues.–Fri. 10–5, weekends 10–1.*

Gradska Vijećnica *(City Hall),* one of Europe's oldest city halls, is still in use. This imposing landmark has been the seat of Varaždin's public administration since December 14, 1523. Restored after the great fire of 1776, it received a thorough external makeover in 1793. From April through October you can stop by on a Saturday morning between 11 and noon to watch the changing of the guard, a 250-year-old tradition that lives on. ⊠ *Trg Krajla Tomislava.*

Palača Varaždinske Županije *(Varaždin County Hall)* rivals City Hall (on nearby Trg Krajla Tomislava) in terms of sheer visual appeal, what with its flamingo-pink facade across from the Franciscan Church, even if it is more than two centuries younger than City Hall. Opened in 1772, it boasted a late-baroque pediment for four years only, until the fire of 1776 did away with that, and saw it bestowed with a triangular, neoclassical one. ⊠ *Franjevački trg.*

★ Built in 1773 and thoroughly relandscaped in 1905 by Hermann Haller, a self-taught landscape architect who revolutionized traditional notions of what graveyards should look like, Varaždin's **Gradsko Groblje** *(Town Cemetery)* is as pleasant a place for a restful stroll as it may be, when the time comes, to be laid to rest in. Replete with flower beds and rows of tall cedars and linden trees flanking ornate memorials and laid out in geometric patterns, the cemetery sublimely manifests Haller's conviction that each plot should be a "serene, hidden place only hinting at its true purpose, with no clue as to whether its occupant is rich or poor, since all are tended equally, surrounded by every kind of flower ... producing perfect harmony for the visitor." Haller himself, who ran the cemetery from 1905 to 1946, is buried here in a rather conspicuous mausoleum. You can reach the cemetery by walking about 10 minutes east of the castle along Hallerova aleja. ⊠ *Hercega* ☉ *May–Sept., daily 7 AM–9 PM; Oct. and Mar.–Apr., daily 7 AM–8 PM, Nov.–Feb., daily 7 AM–5 PM.*

WHERE TO EAT

$$–$$$ ✕ **Restoran Zlatna Guska.** In a lovely, vaulted brick cellar with walls orna-
★ mented by coats of arms, the Golden Goose Restaurant makes a good stopping-off point for a quick lunch or a relaxed dinner over a bottle of local wine. Here you'll find not only a whole array of soups hard to get elsewhere, such as cream of nettle, but an impressive salad bar and vegetarian fare such as fried cauliflower in mushroom sauce with sesame seeds. They also serve plenty of seafood and meat. The wood-covered menu has helpful photos of imaginatively named main dishes—"Last Meal of Inquisition Victims" (a soup, actually), "Daggers of Count Brandenburg" (skewered meat with pasta and vegetables), and "Countess Juliana Drašković's Flower" (a pair of crepes filled with fruit and

topped with powdered sugar and whipped cream)—itself almost worth the trip. ⊠*J. Habdelića 4* ☎*042/213–393* ⊟*AE, MC, V.*

$–$$ ✕**Gostionica Grenadir.** Fish is king in this elegant, spacious, red-carpeted cellar restaurant near Trg M. Stančića. Well-prepared dishes include sea bass and trout, but also a good selection of meats and poultry. ⊠*Kranjčevićeva 12* ☎*042/211–131* ⊟*AE, DC, MC, V.*

$ ✕**Pizzeria Angelus.** Whether Varaždin's best pizza is here or at the more
★ laid-back and affordable Domenico *(see below)* is debatable, but here you can have your pie by candlelight, with soothing background music under brick-arched ceilings to boot. Across the street from a peaceful shaded park, a five-minute walk from the center of town, the Angelus has a huge menu that also includes plenty of pastas and other, meatier (and more pricey) fare, not to mention a half dozen creative salads and lots of beer (including Guinness and Kilkeny). The desserts may sound scrumptious, by the way, but the peaches capelleti, for one, is in the plural only because the single peach at its center—in a bath of cherry sauce and soft, sweet curd and ice cream—has been sparingly sliced in half. ⊠*Alojzija Stepinca 3* ☎*042/303–868* ⊟*AE, DC, MC, V.*

$ ✕**Pizzeria Domenico.** This little gem of a place is hidden away at the end
★ of a cobblestone alleyway off one of Varaždin's main squares. With red-checkered tablecloths and a spacious, airy inner room—with little windows that look out onto a peaceful courtyard on the other side—it's a justifiably popular place for pizza. ⊠*Trg Slobode 7* ☎*042/212–017* ⊟*AE, DC, MC, V.*

WHERE TO STAY

Hotel options were limited in Varaždin until 2006—with just one large hotel, the characterless Hotel Turist, and a couple of pension-style accommodations. But that changed in 2007 with the opening of the Hotel Varaždin and the Hotel Istra. Prices even at the newer Varaždin hotels are refreshingly lower than in Zagreb.

$ ⌸**Hotel Istra.** Varaždin's one and only centrally located accommoda-tion, the Istra, opened in July 2007, has 11 simply furnished but sleek, pricey rooms with small windows that don't offer much of a view. The silky peach bedspreads offer a nice contrast against the dark blue or gray carpeting. Pros: near attractions, shops, and restaurants, all rooms have bathtubs. Cons: pricey, hallways are hot in warm weather, small windows, few frills. ⊠*Kukuljevićeva 6, 42000* ☎*042/659–659* ☎*042/659–660* ⇙*11 rooms* ⌂*In-room: refrigerator, Ethernet. In-hotel: restaurant, no elevator* ⊟*AE, DC, MC, V* ⏧|*BP.*

$ ⌸**Hotel Varaždin.** This hotel is in an early-20th-century building across
★ the street from the train station and a 15-minute walk from down-town. It opened in 2007 just a month after its less-appealing competi-tor, the Istra (which is, however, in the town center). The rooms are modern and bright with gray carpeting and a beige armchair; some have a large single bed, others twin beds. The bathrooms are small, with showers only; but some of the showers play music and have mas-sage shower-head attachments. The hotel's cellar restaurant is attrac-tive, with arched-brick ceilings. Pros: convenient if you come by train, attractive breakfast room, all rooms are no-smoking. Cons: a hefty

walk from the town center, small bathrooms, few frills. ✉*Kolodvorska 19, 42000* ☎*042/290–720* 📠*042/201–915* ⊕*www.hotelvarazdin. com* ⟳*27 rooms* ⚴*In-room: refrigerator, Ethernet. In-hotel: restaurant, bar, parking (no fee), no elevator, no-smoking rooms* ☰*AE, DC, MC, V* ⦿*BP.*

¢ 🔢 **Pension Garestin.** A few hundred yards down the road from the Pension Maltar and a bit farther from the town center, this small hotel occupies an elegant, onetime single-family house. There are 13 simply furnished rooms, with ochre carpeting, sturdy if scratched desks, and small windows under a pitched roof. Some have two twin beds, others a single, large bed. There's also a spacious, old-fashioned restaurant. Pros: reasonably priced, comfy basic rooms, pleasant outdoor dining terrace. Cons: small bathrooms, small windows, no Internet access, few frills. ✉*Zagrebačka 34, 42000* ☎*042/214–314* ⊕*www.gastrocom. hr* ⟳*13 rooms* ⚴*In-room: refrigerator. In-hotel: restaurant, bar, parking (no fee)* ☰*AE, DC, MC, V* ⦿*BP.*

¢ 🔢 **Pension Maltar.** A short walk from the town center, this small pension has clean, no-frills, but spacious rooms that are quite acceptable for a short stay. Rooms with double beds are the same price as those with twins, and many include a couch, too. The café is rather smoky. The pension also rents rooms for longer stays in a separate building near the train station. Pros: good price, friendly service, a five-minute walk to the town center. Cons: smoky café, no Internet access. ✉*F. Prešernova ul 1, 42000* ☎*042/311–100* 📠*042/211–190* ⊕*www.maltar.hr* ⟳*25 rooms, 3 suites* ⚴*In-room: safe (some), refrigerator (some). In-hotel: room service, laundry facilities, laundry service, parking (no fee), no elevator, some pets allowed, no-smoking rooms* ☰*AE, DC, MC, V* ⦿*BP.*

NIGHTLIFE & THE ARTS

Throughout the month of December, the town celebrates **Advent in Varaždin,** when the streets and squares come alive with the Christmas spirit. Ornaments and sweets are on sale, there's outdoor skating, and, yes, Santa Claus wanders about handing out gifts to kids. For three weeks from mid-September to early October, the **Varaždin Baroque Evenings** take the form of classical-music concerts in various churches, palaces, and other venues throughout town. This is one of the most important cultural events in north Croatia. For 10 days from late August to early September, the **Špancirfest** (translated in tourist brochures as "Street Walkers' Festival"), on various squares in the center of town, features a colorful array of free, open-air theatrical and acrobatic performances, live music from classical to rock, traditional and modern dance, arts-and-crafts exhibits, and more. **Aquamarin** (✉*Gajeva 1* ☎*042/311–868*) is one of several bustling, ho-hum cafés on or near capacious Trg Krajla Tomislava, the site of City Hall; it is the only one that offers Internet access. Trg M. Stančića, by the tourist office, is another good place to sit back at one of the cafés and enjoy some drinks. For a beer or two between walls adorned with pictures of famous revolutionaries from Elvis to Che Guevara, not to mention glass-encased electric guitars, stop by the **Rock Art Café** (✉*P. Preradovića* ☎*042/321–123*), which has frequent live-music evenings September through April.

ČAKOVEC & THE MEÐIMURJE

15 km (9½ mi) northeast of Varaždin.

At the northernmost tip of Croatia, between the Drava river to the south and the Mura river to the north, the Meðimurje region looks small on the map, but it possesses

> **DON'T BRING MOM**
>
> For your fill of martial arts, horror, and sci-fi flicks, check out the **Trash Film Festival,** a three-day event Varaždin hosts annually in various locations in mid-October.

a distinctive character that makes it ripe for at least a day's worth of exploration. Long off the radar screens of Croatia-bound visitors, the Meðimurje is also one of the country's newest up-and-coming inland tourist destinations: its largest town, Čakovec, is the most important cultural center between Varaždin and Hungary and Slovenia to the north (many Zagreb–Budapest trains stop there). Its many small villages are the home of rich wine-making and embroidery traditions, and there is even a locally cherished spa town, Toplice Sveti Martin, in the very north close to the Mura river. Back in the 13th century, Count Dimitrius Chaky, court magistrate of the Croatian-Hungarian king Bela IV, had a wooden defense tower erected in the central part of the Meðimurje that eventually became known as Chaktornya (Chak's Tower). It was around this tower and other, nearby fortifications that Čakovec saw a period of intense economic and cultural development, from the mid-16th century to the late 17th century—under the influential Zrinski family. After a failed rebellion by the Zrinskis and the Frankopans against the Viennese court, the Viennese imperial army plundered the tower for building materials; and the last Zrinski died in 1691. A disastrous earthquake in 1738 saw the old, Gothic architecture give way to the baroque. Meðimurje's last feudal proprietors were the Feštetić counts, who lived here from 1791 to 1923—a period during which the region came under the administrative control of Hungary and then Croatia and Hungary once again (until 1918). Toward the close of the 19th century the region was linked inextricably to the railroad network of the Austro-Hungarian empire, setting the stage for intense economic development.

Set in the middle of a large shaded park right beside the main square is Čakovec's key landmark, the massive four-story **Stari grad Zrinskih** *(Zrinski Castle)*. Built over the course of a century from around 1550 by Nikola Šubic Zrinski, in an Italian-Renaissance style, it was the Zrinski family nest until the late 17th century. The fortress's foremost present-day attraction, the **Muzej Meðimurje** *(Museum of Meðimurje)*, can be reached through the courtyard. Though it receives too few visitors to have regular opening hours, a staff member will be happy to let you in. Just climb the steps to the hallway of offices on the second floor to find someone. If you kindly overlook the lack of English-language text, you will be treated on this floor to an intriguing, life-size look at a year in the life of a peasant family, from season to season as you proceed through the rooms. Move up a floor for a chronological display of the region's history, from the Stone Age to the recent past. Also on this floor are individual rooms dedicated to the Zrinski family (this one does have English text); lovely, period furniture; displays of printing machinery; an old pharmacy; a fascinating collection of 19th- and 20th-century bric-a-brac; and, last but not least, a three-room gallery of impressive modern art by various painters. (⊠*R. Boškovića 7* ☎*01/313–285 or 01/313–499* 🎟*15 Kn* ☉*Tues.–Fri. 10–3, weekends 10–1*)

Čakovec's main square, Trg Republike, is a mostly bland, modern affair—with the striking exception of **Trgovački Kasino** *(Commercial Casino).* Odd that the key gathering place of the town's early-20th-century rising bourgeois class should have survived the communist era intact, but here it has stood since 1903, wearing its Hungarian art nouveau style very much on its sleeve: red brick interspersed with a white stucco background, squares and circles across the bottom, curved lines formed by the brickwork working their way to the top. Back in its heyday, this was much more than a casino in the gambling sense of the word: in addition to a card room and a game parlor, it housed a ladies' salon, a reading room, and a dance hall. It was mostly a trade-union headquarters in the post–World War II era—and so it is today, rendering the inside off-limits to the public. Just off the main square, by the way, is Krajla Tomislava, the town's one and only major pedestrian shopping street. ⊠*Trg Republike* ☎*No phone.*

★ **Župna crkva franjevački samostan svetog Nikole** *(Parish Church and the Fransiscan Monastery of St. Nicolas).* Čakovec's key ecclesiastical landmark was built between 1707 and 1728 on the site of a wooden monastery that burned down in 1699. The bell tower was added in the 1750s. Inside is a late-baroque altar decorated with elaborate statues; and on the outside is a facade from the turn of the 20th century (while Hungary ruled the region), with reliefs of several great Hungarian kings from ages past. ⊠*Krajla Tomislava* ☎*040/312–806* ☉*Daily 8–8.*

OFF THE BEATEN PATH

Štrigova. Please don't take literally the unfortunately translated sign outside one of Međimurje's most important ecclesiastical landmarks: "Saint Jerome's Church is a zero category monument of culture." Of course, in this case the "zero" means "top"; for this church (plus a well-developed local wine industry) is what ensures the otherwise sleepy, out-of-the-way village of Štrigova its place on the tourism map. In a bucolic hilly setting near the Slovenian border, 15 km (9½ mi) northwest of Čakovec, Štrigova is indeed best known for **Crkva sv. Jeromnima** *(St. Jerome's Church)* and as the largest producer of Međimurje wines. Whether you arrive by bus (45-minute runs from Čakovec daily) or car, the first thing you are likely to notice is the striking yellow-and-white double steeple of the church, which is perched sublimely on a hillside just above the village center. Completed in 1749 on the site of a 15th-century chapel that was destroyed in the region's 1738 earthquake, the church is dedicated to the village's most famous son: St. Jerome (340–420), known for translating the Bible from Greek and Hebrew into Latin. Note the painting of a bearded St. Jerome on the facade, framed by two little windows made to look like red hearts. The church is most famous, actually, for its lovely wall and ceiling frescoes by the famous baroque artist, Ivan Ranger the Baptist (1700–1753). The main steeple was completed only in 1761, and the church also has two

1

smaller steeples. The church is usually closed, but you can call the local parish to arrange a look inside. Just down the hill from the church, in the village center, is Štrigova's one and only restaurant, the agreeable **Restoran Stridan.** While you can get to Štrigova easily enough by one of several daily buses from Čakovec, it's good to have a car if you want to drop by the smaller village of Železna Gora, some 5 km south of Štrigova, along a country road to Čakovec. Here—well, 2½ km south of the village center—you will find the best restaurant in these parts, **Restoran Dvorac Terbotz.** *Štrigova Parish Office* ☎*040/851–039.*

WHERE TO EAT

$$–$$$$ ✕**Restoran Dvorac Terbotz.** In the village of Železna Gora some 5 km
★   (3 mi) south of Štrigova, along a country road to Čakovec, stands the best restaurant in these parts. At the Dvorac Terbotz you can dine on everything from poultry to pork to wild game to seafood, in a lovely country house with wood-beamed ceilings. A spacious terrace overlooks the area's sweeping vineyards, and on a breezy day you'll hear the clackety-clack of the windmill just outside. ⊠ *Železna Gora 113, Železna Gora* ☎*040/857–444* ▤*AE, DC, MC, V.*

$$–$$$$ ✕**Restoran Katarina.** You needn't venture far from Čakovec's main
★   square, Trg Republike, for some fairly fine dining—on foot it's just a minute to this comely cellar restaurant in an antique building that now functions mostly as a shopping center. Replete with brick-arched ceilings, pink cloth napkins, an extensive wine list, and pop music that mars the elegance, the Katarina has a big menu, but specializes in pork, poultry, and beef dishes. The popular Katarina Platter, for example, is a sizeable two-person affair including pork stuffed with tomatoes and Gorgonzola cheese, turkey stuffed with cranberries and walnuts, and mixed veggies on the side. And then there's beef with truffles or, say, the goose liver pâté with mushroom sauce. ⊠ *Matice hrvatske 6* ☎*01/311–990* ▤*AE, DC, MC, V.*

$$ ✕**Restoran Stridan.** Štrigova's one and only restaurant serves up decently prepared traditional fare, with an emphasis on grilled meats and local wines, amid rustic decor. ⊠ *Štrigova 31, Štrigova* ☎*040/851–202* ▤*No credit cards.*

WHERE TO STAY

You can stay in Varaždin and venture into Međimurje for a day trip, but Čakovec does have a couple of decent lodging options, one of which is a short walk from the main square.

¢   🖭**Hotel Aurora.** A short walk from both the bus station and the main square, this uninspiring modern building has a chic, light-filled interior whose simple furnished rooms have dark blue carpeting, soothing pinkish walls, and a sofa and coffee table in each. Pros: close to the bus station and the main square, large common areas and breakfast room, reasonable rate. Cons: small, hard-to-reach windows; no no-smoking rooms; along a bland, busy road; few frills. ⊠ *Franje Punčeca 2, 40000* ☎*040/310–700* 🖷*040/310–787* ⊕*www.hotel-aurora.hr* ✎*10 rooms* ⟐ *In-room: refrigerator, Ethernet, no a/c (some). In-hotel: bar, no elevator.* ▤*AE, DC, MC, V* ▮◧*BP.*

SOUTH OF ZAGREB TOWARD THE COAST

SAMOBOR

20 km (12½ mi) west of Zagreb.

That Samobor has been one of the capital's top weekend haunts since
before the turn of the 20th century without really being on the way to
anything else in Croatia testifies to its abounding cultural and natural charms. Close to the Slovenian border, this picturesque medieval
town on the eastern slopes of the lushly forested Samoborsko Gorje
was chartered by the Hungarian-Croatian king Bela IV in 1242. The
town and environs are popular with hikers, with trails leading into the
hillside right from the center of town. Perched there, a 30-minute walk
from town—and visible in all its sublimity from the main square—are
the ruins of a 13th-century castle. And what would a visit to Samobor be without a stroll along Gradna, the peaceful stream that runs
through town?

After an energetic hike, you may wish to fortify yourself with a glass
of locally made *bermet,* a vermouthlike drink whose secret recipe was
apparently brought here by French forces during their occupation of
1809 to 1813.

By far, Samobor's most famous event is its carnival, the *Samobor fašnik*
(⊕ *www.fasnik.com*), which draws many thousands of visitors to town
for several days beginning the weekend before Lent to catch the daz-
zling sight of its parades, with floats and masked revelers.

The rectangular main square is called **Trg Krajla Tomislava.** Its largely
baroque look is positively lovely, all the more so because some building
facades show a bit or more of art nouveau influence. In particular, the
pharmacy building at No. 11 has two angels presiding, appropriately,
on top. Also overlooking the square is a 17th-century parish church.

May 2003 saw Croatia's first private museum open in a quiet street
just above Trg Krajla Tomislava. **Museum Marton** was created to house
a private collection of furniture, paintings, glass- and metalware, porcelain, and clocks previously on loan to the Zagreb Museum of Arts &
Crafts. ⊠ *Jurjevska 7* 🕿 *01/332–6426* ⊕ *www.muzej-marton.hr* 🕿 *15
Kn* ⊙ *Weekends 10–1.*

⬛ NEED A
BREAK?
If you need a dose of sugar to perk you up, try some *samoborska kremšnita*, a
mouthwatering block of vanilla custard between layers of flaky pastry that,
served warm, can be tasted at its best at the otherwise small and smoky café
U Prolazu (⊠ *Trg Krajla Tomislava 6*).

In the lovely, streamside park by the square is the **Samobor Museum,**
which tells the story of the town's past. ⊠ *Livadićeva 7* 🕿 *01/336–
1014* 🕿 *5 Kn* ⊙ *Tues.–Fri. 8–3; weekends 9–1.*

1

WHERE TO EAT

$$–$$$ ✕**Pri Saroj Vuri.** Small yet ever so cozy, its walls decorated with old
★ clocks (as per its name in Croatian) and paintings by noted Croatian
artists, this lovely old villa a few minutes' walk from the main square
is the best place in town to try such meaty fare as *teleća koljenica*
(knuckle of veal) and *češnjovke* (smoked sausage cooked in sour cabbage). Unfortunately, the latter is available only late in the year, after
the hogs are butchered and the sausage smoked. Round off with a glass
of bermet, served with lemon and ice. ✉*Giznik 2* ☎*01/336–0548*
🚪*AE, DC, MC, V.*

WHERE TO STAY

¢ 🏨**Hotel Livadic.** If you want to spend more than a half-day in Samobor,
you could do much worse than this elegant and pleasant hotel right on
the main square. Although the rooms vary in size, they're all spacious,
and the pine floors impart a soothing scent while the silky bedspreads
and golden-framed mirrors help create a luxurious historical ambience.
Some rooms have showers only. Downstairs is a splendid and spacious, if smoky, café. Pros: centrally located, redolent of history. Cons:
rooms vary in size, downstairs café is smoky, few frills. ✉*Trg Krajla
Tomislava 5, 10430* ☎*01/336–5850 or 01/336–5851* 🖨*01/336–5851*
⊕*www.hotel-livadic.hr* ➶*23 rooms* ⚘*In-room: no a/c (some), refrigerator. In hotel: public Internet, no elevator* 🚪*AE, MC, V* 🍴*BP.*

KARLOVAC

40 km (25 mi) south of Zagreb.

Many tourists have tasted the beer, but few stop by for a taste of the
city. Karlovac is, however, much more than just home to one of Croatia's most popular brews, Karlovačko. Founded all at once on July 13,
1579, by the Austrians as a fortress intended to ward off the Turks,
Karlovac is today that big dot on the map between Zagreb and the
coast that visitors to the country more often than not pass by. Well,
anyone intrigued by the question of how a onetime fortress—still much
in evidence—can develop into an urban center will want to stop here
for at least a half day and, perhaps, spend a night on the way to or from
the coast. Once you pass through the city's industrial-looking suburbs,
there is a redolent historical center awaiting you, one rendered that
much more atmospheric because it is wedged between two of Croatia's
most important rivers, the Kupa and the Korana. The city's Renaissance-era urban nucleus is popularly known as the Zvijezda (Star),
since its military planners were moved to shape it as a six-pointed
star—as is evident from the surrounding moat, which is today a pleasant, if sunken, green space that is even home to a basketball court.
Eventually, this center's military nature gave way to civilian life, and it
took on the baroque look more evident today. Though the town walls
were razed in the 19th century, their shape is still discernible.

At the center of this old part of town, which you access over any of
several bridges over the moat, is the main square, **Trg Bana Josip Jelačić,**
one side of which, alas, features a great big empty building with some

missing windows. At the center of this otherwise largely barren square is an old well dating to 1869; long filled in, it is ornamented with allegorical imagery.

WHERE TO EAT

$$–$$$ **Ribarska kuča Mirnah.** Off on its own, overlooking the quietly flowing Korana River on the edge of the town center, this restaurant, which has a terrace for outdoor dining, makes the best of the view. The seafood here—whether squid, octopus, sea bass, or freshwater varieties such as carp, pike-perch, catfish, pike, or trout—is abundant and excellent. Round off your meal with a jam- or walnut-filled palačinke and reflect on what went through the mind of whoever designed the funky, hectagonal tubing of the ceiling lights. ✉ *Rakovačko šetalište* ☎ *047/654–172* 💳 *AE, DC, MC, V.*

$$ **Restoran Kerempuh.** Cozy and friendly, with hip music that's just a bit too loud, the Kerempuh is on a side street a few minutes' walk from the historic center. The offerings include decent meat and poultry (including grilled rabbit) and a few odd fish dishes at rustic wooden tables and benches. ✉ *V. Nazora 4* ☎ *042/614–366* 💳 *AE, DC, MC, V.*

WHERE TO STAY

$ ★ **Hotel Korana Srakovčić.** Deep within a tree-shaded park a few minutes' walk from the Old Town, this luxury hotel overlooks a peaceful stretch of its namesake, the Korana River. The hotel was built in 2003 as a re-creation of the 19th-century Park Hotel, which had long fallen into disrepair. Catering mostly to businesspeople, it has bright, modern, spacious rooms with maroon bedspreads and bright yellow walls. Its main restaurant, the Dobra, has a terrace with a soothing river view. For 26 kunas extra you can get a room with a balcony. Pros: luxurious, spacious rooms, in a tranquil park, two restaurants, indoor pool, excellent business facilities. Cons: pricey, 25-minute walk from the town center. ✉ *Perivoj Josipa Vrbanića 8, 47000* ☎ *047/609–090* 📠 *047/609–091* 🌐 *www.hotelkorana.hr* *15 rooms, 3 suites* *In-room: safe, DVD, Wi-Fi, refrigerator. In-hotel: 2 restaurants, bar, pool, laundry service, room service, parking (no fee), public Wi-Fi, public Internet, no elevator* 💳 *AE, DC, MC, V* *BP.*

¢ **Hotel Carlstadt.** At the center of Karlovac's business district, a couple of minutes' walk from the Old Town, the Carlstadt—the town's original name under Austrian rule—offers simply furnished, modern rooms. Though somewhat cramped, they are otherwise fine, considering the relatively affordable price. Pros: centrally located, modest prices. Cons: some rooms get street noise, few frills. ✉ *Vraniczanyeva 2, 47000* ☎📠 *047/611–111* 🌐 *www.carlstadt.hr* *37 rooms, 3 suites* *In-room: dial-up, refrigerator. In-hotel: restaurant, bar, parking (no fee), public Internet, laundry service, no elevator* 💳 *AE, DC, MC, V* *BP.*

CLOSE UP

Bloody Easter

It's called "Bloody Easter" for a good reason. Sunday, April 2, 1991, has gone down in Croatian history as the day Croatia suffered its first casualties—and its first fatality—in its war of independence from the former Yugoslavia. And the unlikely setting was none other than one of Europe's most visited natural wonders, Plitvice Lakes National Park.

Two days earlier, Croatian Ministry of Interior commando units—under the direction of General Josip Lucić, later to become head of the Croatian Armed Forces—were dispatched to Plitvice to restore order after the region had been occupied by Serbs led by Milan Martić, who aimed to annex the park to Serbian Krajina. The commandos were ambushed en route, near the group of hotels at Entrance 2. One member of the team, Josip Jović, was killed and seven of his comrades were wounded. As recorded in the annals of Croatian history, nine of the "terrorists" were arrested, and order was restored. For a time.

The region, which had long been home to many Serbs, was occupied by Serb forces for the next four years. The national park became a military encampment, and soldiers threatened to blow up the fragile travertine dams separating the lakes. UNESCO sent missions to prevent war from wreaking such havoc on a natural wonder. In the end, with the exception of the park's red-deer population, which fell dramatically during the occupation—the park's natural beauty pulled through intact. Only the human infrastructure was damaged, including the hotels. By 1999, four years after Croatian forces reoccupied the park and painstakingly cleared the area of mines, the last of the three hotels reopened, and the park was back in business.

Today a memorial in the park—behind the bus stop at Entrance 2 on the southbound side of the road—marks the life and death of Josip Jović, the first fatality in what was to be a long and bloody war.

NACIONALNI PARK PLITVIČKA JEZERA

Fodor'sChoice *135 km (84 mi) southwest of Zagreb.*
★

Triple America's five Great Lakes, shrink them each to manageable size (i.e., 536 acres in all), give them a good cleaning until they look virtually blue, envelop them in lush green forest with steep hillsides and cliffs all around, and link not just two but all of them with a pint-sized Niagara Falls. The result? **Nacionalni Park Plitvička Jezera** *(Plitvice Lakes National Park)*, a UNESCO World Heritage Site and Croatia's top inland natural wonder. And it's not even out of the way. The park is right on the main highway (E71) from Zagreb to Split, but it's certainly worth the three-hour trip from the capital regardless. This 8,000-acre park is home to 16 beautiful, emerald lakes connected by a series of cascading waterfalls, stretching 8 km (5 mi) through a valley flanked by high, forested hills home to deer, bears, wolves, and wild boar. Thousands of years of sedimentation of calcium, magnesium carbonate, algae, and moss have yielded the natural barriers between the lakes; and since the process is ongoing, new barriers, curtains, stalactites, channels, and cascades are constantly forming and the existing ones changing. The deposited sedimentation, or tufa, also coats the beds and edges of the lakes, creating their sparkling, azure look. Today a series of wooden bridges and waterside paths leads through the park. The only downside: as lovely as it is, all of Europe wants to see it, so the trails can get crowded from June through September. That said, there's not a bit of litter along the way—a testament either to respectful visitors or to a conscientious park staff, or both. No camping, no bushwhacking, no picking plants. And no swimming! This is a place to visit, for a day or two, but not to touch. It is, however, well worth the 110 Kn entrance fee.

There are two entrances just off the main road about an hour's walk apart, aptly named Entrances 1 and 2. The park's pricey hotels are near Entrance 2, the first entrance you'll encounter if arriving by bus from the coast. However, Entrance 1—the first entrance if you arrive from Zagreb—is typically the start of most one-day excursions, if only because it's within a 20-minute walk of Veliki slap, the big waterfall (256 feet high). Hiking the entire loop that winds its way around the lakes takes 6 to 8 hours, but there are other hikes, ranging from 2 to 4 hours. All involve a combination of hiking and being ferried across the larger of the park's lakes by national park service boats.

There are cafés near both entrances, but avoid them for anything but coffee, as the sandwiches and strudels leave much to be desired. Instead, buy some of the huge, heavenly strudels sold by locals at nearby stands, where great big blocks of cheese are also on sale. At the boat landing near Entrance 2, by the way, you can rent gorgeous wooden rowboats for 50 Kn per hour. ⊠ *Velika Poljana* ☎ *053/751–014 or 053/751–015* ⊕ *www.np-plitvicka-jezera.hr* ✉ *110 Kn for a one-day pass* ☉ *May– Sept., daily 8–7; Oct.–Apr., daily 9–4.*

WHERE TO EAT

Although there's a restaurant near the hotels at Entrance 2, it has the same uninspiring look and feel as the hotels, and few people flock to it. You're much better off heading over to the excellent restaurant at Entrance 1—unless of course the food store near Entrance 2 provides you enough in the way of staples for all the hiking you'll be up to.

$$$–$$$$ ✕ **Restoran Lička Kuća.** With unadorned log walls, wood-beam ceilings,
★ white-curtained windows, lively Croatian folk music playing, and an open kitchen with an open hearth, this is exactly what a restaurant in a great national park should be. Fill up on hearty *lička juha* (a creamy soup of lamb, vegetables, and eggs), followed by boiled lamb with vegetables, suckling pig, or a peasant platter (a wide array of meats—from beef to turkey, pork chops to sausage and bacon). Meat and poultry are the focus, here; grilled trout is the only fish on the menu. Finish off with an apple (or cheese) strudel. The place is buzzing with tourists, but it's the only decent restaurant for miles around. ⊠ *Across from Entrance 1, Velika Poljana* ☎ *053/751–023* ▭ *AE, MC, V.*

WHERE TO STAY

None of the park's state-run, communist-era hotels is much to write home about—and they were damaged extensively by Serb forces during the early 1990s. However, the main advantage of staying in a park hotel is that you'll be right in the center of all the hiking action. The hotels are particularly convenient if you arrive without your own car.

As an alternative, there are lots of private rooms in the immediate vicinity, where doubles go for around 240 Kn, a bargain compared to the hotels. We recommend checking out the tiny village of Mukinje, about a 15-minute hike south of Entrance 2. A bit farther south is the village of Jezerce, which also has rooms. (Note that the bus does not stop at either Mukinje or Jezerce, but it's a pleasant walk to both.) You can also get a private room in the rather faceless, one-road village of Rastovača, just off the main road a few hundred yards north of Entrance 1 (where the bus stops). Practically every one of the village's newish-looking houses has rooms for rent, and they're generally bright, clean, and modern. A national park service booth (☎053/751–278) at Entrance 2 provides help with bookings in July and August, and will provide contacts the rest of the year. A bit farther afield, the village of Rakovica, 12 km (7½ mi) north of the park, usually has more vacancies in high season and is a good option if you have a car. The tourist office in Rakovica (☎047/784–450) can help with bookings. Last but not least, bear in mind that there's no place to store your bags in the park during the day if you arrive by bus and plan to head on to the coast or to Zagreb later in the day—so unless you're ready to cart your bags for hours along the park's steep trails or are traveling light, plan on an overnight stay.

$ ⬚**Hotel Jezero.** Yards away from two other, lower priced, fewer-frills hotels (the Plitvice and the Bellevue), this long, three-story, wood-paneled building looks almost like a U.S.–style motel. The rooms are simply furnished and a bit worn, but clean, and offer cheap plastic chairs on the unappealing terraces (not all rooms have terraces). It's not a great value, but quite all right for a one-night stay. Some rooms have only showers; all have a somewhat smoky scent. Pros: centrally located (near trails, gift shops, and so on), the best of the park's three hotel options, a decent array of services and amenities. Cons: pricey, slightly worn rooms, so bustling with tourists that communing with nature might be difficult. ✉*Near Entrance 2, Velika Poljana, 53231* ☎*053/751–400* 🖷*053/751–600* ⊕*www.np-plitvicka-jezera.hr* ⤳*222 rooms, 7 suites* &*In-room: refrigerator, no a/c. In-hotel: restaurant, bar, gym* ▭*AE, DC, MC, V* ⦿*BP.*

LONJSKO POLJE

An excursion southeast of Zagreb to the Lonjsko Polje region along the Sava River will bring you to an area that is rarely seen by most visitors. Along Croatia's extensive border with Bosnia Herzegovina are two sights of pronounced historical interest, and one—Lonjsko Polje

Nature Park—with special appeal to lovers of big birds, along with plenty of pretty wooden architecture in and around the sleepy villages along the way.

SISAK

75 km (47 mi) southeast of Zagreb via the Autocesta Expressway.

The unassuming little town of Sisak was the site of one of the more important battles in Croatia's history.

A bit to the south of the town center—3 km (2 mi) to be exact, where the rivers Kupa and Sava meet—stands the once-mighty **Sisak Fortress** (built 1544–50), with one prominent bastion at each point of its famously triangular form and a hugely significant past. It was here, on June 22, 1593, that the Habsburgs, in the company of Croats and Slovenes, pulled off a monumental victory over the fearsome Ottoman Turks, a triumph that figured prominently in halting the Turks' advance toward Zagreb and farther into Western Europe.

Today the locals celebrate the victory over the Turks with their annual **Knightly Tournament** on a weekend in early June. A whole lot of folks in medieval garb will entertain you with archery and equestrian contests, not to mention balloon rides, souvenirs, and plenty of food and drink. Check with the Sisak tourist-information office for details on this free event.

ČIGOĆ

28 km (17½ mi) southeast of Sisak.

The charming village of Čigoć is officially known as the "European Village of Storks" because it draws so many of the migrating birds each spring, and a testament is its annual Stork Festival in late June. That said, people live here, too, as attested to by the wooden, thatched-roof houses that are likewise a sight to behold. But several hundred of the birds while away much of the summer here before most embark on the long journey to southern Africa.

The **Čigoć Information Center** (⊠ *Cigoć 26* ☎*044/715–115 or 098/222–085 [ask for Davor Anzil]*), in a traditional house of Posavina oak, on the main road that runs through the village center, is the top regional source for all you need to know about storks, the Stork Festival, and last but not least, Lonjsko Polje Nature Park. It's open daily 8–4, and park maps are available for purchase.

JASENOVAC

35 km (22 mi) southeast of Čigoć.

Where the Sava marks Croatia's remaining long stretch of east–west border with Bosnia until it arrives in Serbia more than 150 km (94 mi) away, is Jasenovac, the site of Croatia's most notorious World War II

1

labor camps. Current estimates are that somewhere between 56,000 and 97,000 people—mostly Serbs, it is believed, along with Jews, Gypsies, and Croatian antifascists—perished at this string of five camps on the banks of the Sava River between 1941 and 1945 from exhaustion, illness, cold weather, and murder.

Though the camp was razed after the war, a memorial park was eventually established at the site, along with a **museum** featuring photographs and other documentation of what happened. ⊠*Braće Radić 147* ☎*044/672–033* ⊕*www.jusp-jasenovac.hr* ✉*Free* ⊗*Weekdays 7–3.*

In addition to the labor-camp memorial, Jasenovac is, by contrast, happily home to the headquarters of **Lonjsko Polje Nature Park** (⊠*Trg Krajla Petra Svačića* ☎*044/672–080* ⊕*www.pp-lonjsko-polje.hr*). One of the largest floodplains in the Danubian basin, this unique ecological and cultural landscape of 20,506 acres along the Sava River was accorded park status in 1990 and is included on UNESCO's roster of World Heritage sites. It has numerous rare and endangered plant and animal species, from white-tailed eagles and saker falcons to otters and the Danube salmon—and, as much in evidence in Čigoć, to storks. Its 4,858 acres of pastureland is also home to Croatia's highest concentration of indigenous breeds of livestock. Traditional village architecture—in particular, houses made of posavina oak— further contributes to the region's appeal. The park office provides park maps and other information on where to go and what to see; and, yes, issues park entrance passes (25 Kn). The easiest way to access the park is by car: while driving from Zagreb, exit the motorway at Popovača and take the road to the right through the villages of Potok and Stružec toward Sisak.

ZAGREB & ENVIRONS ESSENTIALS

AIR TRAVEL
There are no direct flights between the United States and Zagreb, but Croatia Airlines and several major European carriers fly to Zagreb from Amsterdam, Brussels, Frankfurt, London, Paris, Vienna, and other cities. Croatia Airlines operates at least two flights daily to Split (45 minutes) and three flights daily to Dubrovnik (55 minutes). Through the summer there are also daily service to Prague (1 hour, 30 minutes) and flights several times a week to Warsaw (1 hour, 40 minutes).

CARRIERS **Airlines & Contacts Adria** (☎*01/481–0011*). **Air France** (☎*01/483–7105*). **Alitalia** (☎*01/480–5555*). **Austrian Airlines** (☎*01/626–5900*). **British Airways** (☎*01/456–2506*). **Croatia Airlines** (☎*01/481–9633*). **CŠA** (☎*01/487–3301*). **Delta Airlines** (☎*01/487–8760*). **KLM–Northwest** (☎*01/487–8600*). **LOT** (☎*01/480–5555*). **Lufthansa** (☎*01/487–3123 or 060/505–505*) **Malev** (☎*01/483–6935*).

AIRPORTS & TRANSFERS
Zagreb Airport (ZAG) is in Pleso, 17 km (10 mi) southeast of the city. Information **Zagreb Pleso Airport** (☎*01/626–5222 general information, 01/456–2229 lost and found* ⊕*www.zagreb-airport.hr*).

A regular shuttle bus runs from the airport to the main bus station every 30 minutes from 7 AM to 8 PM and from the main bus station to the airport from 6 AM to 7:30 PM. A one-way ticket costs 30 Kn, and the trip takes 30 minutes. By taxi, expect to pay 150 Kn to 200 Kn to make the same journey; the trip will be slightly faster, about 20 minutes.

Information **Airport bus** (☎ *01/615–7992*).

BUS TRAVEL

Frequent regular coach service to destinations all over mainland Croatia departs from the capital. The traveling time is 6 hours from Zagreb to Split and 10½ hours from Zagreb to Dubrovnik. There are also daily international bus lines to Slovenia (Ljubljana), Hungary (Barcs and Nagykanisza), Yugoslavia (Belgrade), Austria (Graz), Germany (Munich, Stuttgart, Frankfurt, Dortmund, Cologne, and Düsseldorf), and Switzerland (Zurich). Timetable information is available from the main bus station, a 20-minute walk from the center.

About 10 buses run daily between Zagreb and Karlovac in just under an hour and for a one-way fare of around 30 Kn.

Samobor is a 50-minute bus ride from Zagreb; buses between Zagreb and Samobor run every 30 minutes or so weekdays, roughly every hour on weekends; the fare is 20 Kn each way, and Samobor's little bus station is about 100 yards north of the main square.

Most buses between Zagreb and Split will stop at both entrances to Plitvice Lakes National Park; the fare is around 70 Kn one way between Zagreb and Plitvice.

A small handful of buses daily go on from Sisak on narrow, two-lane roads to the charming village of Čigoć.

Information **Zagreb Bus Station** (✉ *Av M Držića, Donji Grad* ☎ *060/313– 333, 01/600–8607, or 01/600–8605* ⊕ *www.akz.hr*). **Čakovec Bus Station** (✉ *Masarykova 26* ☎ *040/313–947*). **Karlovac Bus Station** (✉ *Prilaz V. Holjevca 2* ☎ *060/338–833*). **Varaždin Bus Station** (✉ *Zrinskih Frankopan bb* ☎ *042/407–888*).

BUS & TRAM TRAVEL WITHIN ZAGREB

An extensive network of city buses and trams—in the center of town, almost exclusively trams—runs both during the day (4 AM–11:45 PM) and at night (11:35 PM to 3:45 AM). Tickets cost 6.50 Kn if you buy them from a newspaper kiosk, or 8 Kn from the driver. A full-day ticket (18 Kn) available at some kiosks is valid until 4 AM the next morning. As an alternative, for 90 Kn you can buy the Zagreb Card, which covers public transport within the city limits for three days and offers substantial discounts at various museums and other cultural venues. After you board the bus or tram, you must validate your ticket with a time stamp; tickets are good for 1½ hours and are transferable in the same direction. If you are caught without a valid ticket, you will be fined 150 Kn payable on the spot.

Information **ZET** (*Zagreb Transport Authority* ☎ *01/660–0442* ⊕ *www.zet.hr*).

CAR RENTALS

Prices vary, and you will probably pay less if you rent from a local company that's not part of an international chain; it's best to shop around. A small car (e.g., Opel Corsa or Fiat Uno) costs at least 400 Kn per day or 2,100 Kn per week. A slightly larger car (e.g., Opel Astra or Fiat Punto) costs more like 550 Kn per day or 2,700 Kn per week. A large car (e.g., Opal Astra Automatic) costs closer to 800 Kn per day or 4,200 Kn per week; automatic transmission is rarely available on smaller cars. These prices include CDW (collision damage waiver) and TP (theft protection) but not PAI (personal accident insurance), and allow for unlimited mileage. If you drive one way (say, from Zagreb to Dubrovnik), there is an additional drop-off charge, but it depends on the type of car and the number of days you are renting.

Information An Nova (✉ *Prilaz Rudolfa Frizira bbDonji Grad, Zagreb* ☎ *01/456– 2531* ⊕ *www.an-nova.hr)*. **Avis** (✉ *Sheraton Zagreb, Kneza Borne 2, Donji Grad, Zagreb* ☎ *062/222–226 central reservations line, or 01/467–6111* ⊕ *www.avis. com.hr* ✉ *Zagreb Airport, Pleso* ☎ *01/626–5840)*. **Budget** (✉ *Sheraton Zagreb, Kneza Borne 2, Donji Grad, Zagreb* ☎ *01/455–6936* ⊕ *www.budget.hr* ✉ *Zagreb Airport, Pleso* ☎ *01/626–5854)*. **Dollar Rent A Car & Thrifty Car Rental** (✉ *Sub Rosa, Donji Grad, Zagreb* ☎ *01/483–6466 or 021/399–000* ⊕ *www.subrosa.hr* ✉ *Zagreb Airport, Pleso* ☎ *01/626–5333)*. **Europcar** (✉ *Pierottijeva 5, Donji Grad, Zagreb* ☎ *01/483–6045* ⊕ *www.europcar.com* ✉ *Zagreb Airport, Pleso* ☎ *01/626–5333)*. **Hertz** (✉ *Ulica grada Vukovara 274, Donji Grad, Zagreb* ☎ *062/727–277 central reservations line, or 01/618–8500 main office in Zagreb* ⊕ *www.hertz.hr* ✉ *Zagreb Airport, Pleso* ☎ *01/456–2635)*. **National** (✉ *Westin Zagreb, Kršnjavoja 1, Donji Grad, Zagreb* ☎ *0800/443–322 central reservations line, or 01/481–1764 [desk at the Westin Zagreb hotel]* ⊕ *www.nationalcar.hr* ✉ *Zagreb Airport, Pleso* ☎ *0800/443–322 or 01/621–5924)*. **Sixt** (✉ *Trg Krešimira Ćosića 9, Donji Grad, Zagreb* ☎ *01/301–5303* ⊕ *www.e-sixt.com* ✉ *Zagreb Airport, Pleso* ☎ *01/621–9900)*.

CAR TRAVEL

While staying in the capital you are certainly better off without a car. But if you wish to visit the nearby hills of Zagorje, or go farther afield to the Međimurje region, a vehicle is helpful unless you want to be riding to a different attraction by bus each day.

INTERNET

Zagreb has about half a dozen Internet cafés within a short walk of the main square. Our favorite is the reasonably priced and spacious Sublink Internet Centar, set far back in a courtyard in a onetime apartment and with plenty of machines. Here you can surf the Net for 0.245 Kn per minute, which adds up to 14.70 Kn per hour. There are a couple of log-on venues along Tkalčića, but prices tend to be higher.

Information Art Internet Caffee (✉ *Tkalčića 18, Gornji Grad, Zagreb* ☎ *01/481– 1050)*. **Surf Internet Point** (✉ *Tkalčića 13/II, 2nd fl., Gornji Grad, Zagreb* ☎ *01/169-8586)*. **Sublink Internet Centar** (✉ *Teslina 12, Donji Grad, Zagreb* ☎ *01/481-1329)*.

MAIL & SHIPPING

Zagreb's Central Post Office is one block east of Trg Bana Jelačića.

Information **Main Post Office** (✉ *Jurišićeva 13, Donji Grad, Zagreb* ☎ *01/481–1090*). **24-hour Post Office** (✉ *Branimirova 4, next to the train station, Donji Grad, Zagreb* ☎ *01/498–1300*).

TAXIS

You can find taxi ranks in front of the bus and train stations, near the main square, and in front of the larger hotels. It is also possible to order a radio taxi. All drivers are bound by law to run a meter, starting at 19 Kn and increasing by 7 Kn per kilometer. Each piece of luggage incurs a further 3 Kn. The night tariff is 20% more and is in effect from 10 PM to 5 AM; the same tariff applies to Sunday and holidays.

Information **Radio Taxi** (☎ *01/660–0671 or 01/660–1235* ⊕ *www.radio-taksi-zagreb.hr*).

TOURS

The tourist-information center closest to the Zagreb train station organizes amusing and informative guided tours of the city. Every day of the week the Ibus travel agency offers combination bus-and-walking guided tours of the city center for between 165 Kn and 225 Kn a person (minimum five people); call a day in advance to reserve. It also provides tours of attractions farther afield, including Veliki Tabor, Trakošćan and Varaždin, and Plitvice Lakes National Park. For a state-of-the-art experience, you can try the Segway CityTour from mid-April through mid-October. The 80-minute "Welcome Tour" takes place daily at 11 AM and costs 233 Kn per person; the 130-minute "All Around Tour" takes place daily at 5 PM and costs 333 Kn per person (minimum two people for all tours). Show up 15 minutes before departure at the main entrance of the Regent Esplanade Hotel *(see Where to Stay)*.

Information **Ibus** (✉ *Kranjčevićeva 29 [in the Hotel Laguna], Donji Grad, Zagreb* ☎ *01/369–4333 or 01/364–8633* ⊕ *www.ibus.hr*). **Segway CityTour** (✉ *Antuna Štrbana 6 [Segway dealer and main office; tours meet in front of the Regent Esplanade Hotel], Donji Grad, Zagreb* ☎ *01/301–0390* ⊕ *www.segway.hr*). **Zagreb Tourist Information** (✉ *Trg Nikole Šubića Zrinskoga 14, Donji Grad, Zagreb* ☎ *01/492–1645*).

TRAIN TRAVEL

Zagreb's main train station lies in Donji Grad, a 10-minute walk from the center. There are daily international lines to and from Budapest (Hungary), Belgrade (Yugoslavia), Munich (Germany), Vienna (Austria), and Venice (Italy).

From Zagreb there are four trains daily to Split in Dalmatia (8 hours) and five trains daily to Rijeka in Kvarner (3½ hours). The easiest way to get to Varaždin from Zagreb is by rail, with some 15 trains daily. Travel time is about 2½ hours and costs 53 Kn each way. About 10 trains run daily between Zagreb and Karlovac (with a like number of buses), in just under an hour and for a one-way fare of 28 Kn. If you don't have wheels, your best bet reaching Sisak is by rail, with 15 trains daily from Zagreb that take just over an hour.

Information **Zagreb Train Station** (✉ *Trg Kralja Tomislava, Donji Grad, Zagreb* ☎ *060/333-444 domestic train information [nationwide number], 01/481-1892 international train information [nationwide number]* ⊕ *www.hznet.hr*). **Čakovec Train Station** (✉ *Kolodvorska 2*). **Karlovac Train Station** (✉ *Vilima Reinera 3*). **Varaždin Train Station** (✉ *Frana Supila*).

VISITOR INFORMATION

Zagreb's main tourist-information center overlooks the main square, Trg Bana Jelačića. It's open weekdays 8:30 AM to 8 PM, Saturday 9 to 5, and Sunday 10 to 2. A smaller office is a tad closer to the train station and open weekdays 9 to 5. The Croatian Angels information hotline, sponsored by the Croatian National Tourist Board, can be called from anywhere in the country for any advice at all.

Information **Čakovec Tourist Information** (✉ *Kralja Tomislava 1, Čakovec* ☎ *040/313-319*). **Croatian Angels** (☎ *062/999-999* ⊕ *www.croatia.hr*). **Jasenovac Tourist Information** (✉ *Trg Petra Svačića 3, Jasenovac* ☎ *044/672-490*). **Karlovac Tourist Information** (✉ *Ul Petra Zrinskog 3, Karlovac* ☎ *047/615-115*). **Kumrovec Tourist Information** (✉ *C Lijepe naše 6a, Kumrovec* ☎ *049/502-044* ⊕ *www.kumrovec.hr*). **Marija Bistrica Tourist Information** (✉ *Zagrebacka, Marija Bistrice* ☎ *049/468-380*). **Plitvice Lakes National Park Tourist Information** (✉ *Plitvička jezera, at Entrance 1, Velika Poljana* ☎ *053/776-798* ⊕ *www.np-plitvicka-jezera.hr*). **Samobor Tourist Information** (✉ *Trg Krajla Tomislava 5, Samobor* ☎ *01/336-004*). **Sisak Tourist Information** (✉ *Rimska, Sisak* ☎ *044/522-655* ⊕ *www.sisakturist.com*). **Stubičke Toplice Tourist Information** (✉ *Viktora Šipeka 24, Stubičke Toplice* ☎ *042/282-727 or 042/210-985* ⊕ *www.tourism-varazdin.hr*). **Varaždin Tourist Information** (✉ *Ivana Padovca 3, Varaždin* ☎ *042/210-987 or 042/210-985* ⊕ *www.tourism-varazdin.hr*). **Zagreb Tourist Information** (✉ *Trg Bana Jelačića 11, Donji Grad, Zagreb* ☎ *01/481-4051 or 01/481-4052* ⊕ *www.zagreb-touristinfo.hr* ✉ *Trg Nikole Šubića Zrinskog 14, Donji Grad, Zagreb* ☎ *01/492-1645*).

Slavonia

By Paul
Olchváry

A COUNTRY'S BREADBASKET IS, OF COURSE, often flat, and so it is also a place visitors tend to pass through rather than go to (or never pass through in the first place). Regrettably, it can also be a place where wars rage most intensely. All this is true of Slavonia, the sweeping agricultural plain of eastern Croatia, which shares a border not only with Hungary to the north but also with Serbia to the east and Bosnia and Herzegovina to the south. Long a vital transport route—not least, between Zagreb and Belgrade—Slavonia today is still recovering from the aftermath of the Yugoslav war of the early 1990s. Most famously, the baroque town of Vukovar, whose siege and utter destruction in 1991 was viewed on televisions around the world, made it clear that the former Yugoslavia was indeed at war, and earned Croatia international sympathy. Despite some remaining hurdles and the unalterable fact that the coast is far away (along with most tourists), much of Slavonia today looks and feels almost as rejuvenated as the rest of Croatia. The region's sleepy towns and rural surroundings—from cornfields to forest-covered hills—have a distinctive low-key charm that can only be called Slavonian.

Slavonia has been inhabited since ancient times, and the Romans had a settlement called Mursa on the outskirts of present-day Osijek. Though its flatness is broken in places—by the Papuk Hills in the center and around the celebrated wine region of Ilok in the east—the region's largely lowland terrain has been inhabited and traversed through the ages by more ethnicities than practically any other region of Croatia. It has been home to Croats, Serbs, Hungarians, Germans, Turks, and others. Though settled by Slavic tribes in the 7th century and later an integral part of the Hungarian-Croat kingdom, Slavonia experienced a major change of culture with Sultan Sülejman the Magnificent's march toward Hungary and Austria in 1526. For almost 150 years much of the region became an Ottoman stronghold. Such places as Osijek and Požega flourished not as part of Christian Europe, but rather as full-fledged, mosque-filled Turkish towns. The Turkish retreat in the late 17th century brought with it an era of Austrian influence, with Osijek, now with a vastly different look, still the region's economic, administrative, and cultural capital. Though damaged in the Yugoslav war, Osijek pulled through in much better shape than Vukovar, and since the late 1990s it has made considerable headway in re-establishing itself as a center of regional culture. North of Osijek is the Baranja, a marshy, particularly fertile corner of northeastern Slavonia that straddles the gentle, vineyard-rich hills of southern Hungary to the north.

EXPLORING SLAVONIA

ABOUT THE RESTAURANTS
With paprika-rich Hungary not far away, you'll often see dishes characterized by an unmistakable, bright-red zest. As in Vienna and Budapest, vegetables are typically prepared in a flour-thickened sauce. Though far from the Adriatic, Slavonia counts fish among its staples—namely, freshwater varieties including carp, pike, catfish, and pike-perch. You'll often find the scrumptious, spicy-hot, paprika-flavored fish stew known

SLAVONIA TOP 5

■ Strolling around Osijek, Slavonia's largest town, packs a lot of charm into a compact space, from attractive churches and parks to Trvđa, the Old Town redolent of ages past.

■ Bjelovar and Požega, two small towns between Zagreb and Osijek, are the picture of charm, with pretty squares and lovely churches.

■ Base yourself in or near Osijek, and head out with your binoculars to serenely beautiful Kopački Rit Nature Park, one of the last great wetlands along the Danube, for excellent bird-watching.

■ From Đakovo's magnificent cathedral to the centuries-old churches of Osijek and Požega, Slavonia has a rich ecclesiastical heritage.

■ This once-lovely baroque town of Vukovar is a testament to the destruction wrought by the Yugoslav war and to the quiet strength of Croatia's rejuvenation.

as *riblji paprikaš* or *fiš paprikaš*. Meat is also a key part of the dining picture. Regular menu staples include *čobanac,* a stew of pork and another type of meat, bathed in paprika sauce and served with spaetzle; chicken paprikash; *sarma* (pork-stuffed cabbage leaves); pork-stuffed paprika; and, last but not least, paprika-flavored sausages and blood sausages. As for wines, look for dry whites, in particular those from Ilok, such as fraševina, riesling, and traminac. And then there is the ubiquitous *rakija* (fruit brandy). Dining out is a tad less expensive than in Zagreb and on the Adriatic coast, with substantial main courses from around 30 Kn to 40 Kn.

ABOUT THE HOTELS

Although business travelers have been streaming into Osijek in larger numbers in recent years, tourists have been few. Thus, Osijek offers a small selection of hotels plus a few smaller, pension-style accommodations with practically no private rooms or apartments. At least everything available is in the heart of town and costs less than comparable accommodations in Zagreb or on the coast. When traveling outside of Osijek, bear in mind that, unlike in more tourist-trodden reaches of the country, such frills as air-conditioning and cable TV are not necessarily givens. The region is still recovering from war, and renovations are proceeding at a slower pace.

WHAT IT COSTS IN EUROS (€) AND CROATIAN KUNA (KN)				
¢	$	$$	$$$	$$$$
RESTAURANTS	under 20 Kn	20 Kn–35 Kn	35 Kn–60 Kn	60 Kn–80 Kn	over 80 Kn
HOTELS In euros	under €75	€75–€125	€125–€175	€175–€225	over €225
HOTELS In kuna	under 550 Kn	550 Kn–925 Kn	925 Kn–1,300 Kn	1,300 Kn–1,650 Kn	over 1,650 Kn

Restaurant prices are for a main course at dinner. Hotel prices are for two people in a double room in high season, excluding taxes and service charges.

TIMING

Slavonia can get hot in summer, and there's no sea to cool off in, so you may want to save this region for spring, late summer, or early fall. Indeed, given that hundreds of thousands of birds gather at the Kopački Rit Nature Park in April, May, and early June and again around September and into October, a visit during such a time would be optimal. The last weekend of September sees one of the region's largest annual cultural events, the Đakovački Vezovi (Đakovo Embroidery) festival. Of course, regardless of when you come to Croatia, a couple of days in Slavonia are always worthwhile.

OSIJEK

280 km (175 mi) east of Zagreb.

Far from where sea-spirited tourists typically tread—and surrounded on all sides by cornfields—Osijek is an often overlooked treasure trove of cultural and architectural attractions. Although it came out of the Yugoslav war the worse for wear, a revival has been going on here ever since. Eastern Croatia's largest city (pop. 115,000) and the economic, administrative, and cultural capital of Slavonia, it rests on the south bank of the Drava River, 22 km (14 mi) west of that river's confluence with the Danube, a short drive from the Hungarian border to the north and the Republic of Serbia and Montenegro to the east.

EXPLORING OSIJEK

Osijek is, in a sense, three towns in one. By the mid-12th century it was a prosperous market town in the Hungarian-Croatian kingdom, occupying the area of present-day **Trvđa,** which functions today as more of a cloistered and somewhat sleepy historical and cultural center. After more than 150 years of Ottoman occupation in the 16th and 17th centuries, Osijek was a flowering Turkish town, mosques and all. At 11 AM on September 26, 1687, that era ended, with the flight of the last Turkish soldier. (As a continuing legacy of this watershed event, the church bells of Osijek undertake a celebratory ringing each and every Friday at 11 AM.) Osijek henceforth became a military garrison under the Austrians, who turned it into a walled fortress in the late 17th century. The **Gornji Grad** (Upper Town) was developed by the Austrians during this period; today it's the city's commercial and administrative center. A few years later the **Donji Grad** (Lower Town) rose to the east on the site of the ancient Roman settlement Mursa; today, it's relatively residential.

The view north across the Drava is bucolic. Across from Gornji Grad, for example, you'll see not a suburb but a striking expanse of countryside—cornfields, cottonwood groves, and the like. The region remained undeveloped because it was relatively low and marshy; more recently, the Yugoslav war turned it into a battleground, and it is still littered with land mines, whose ongoing removal is vital to the nation's continuing economic development.

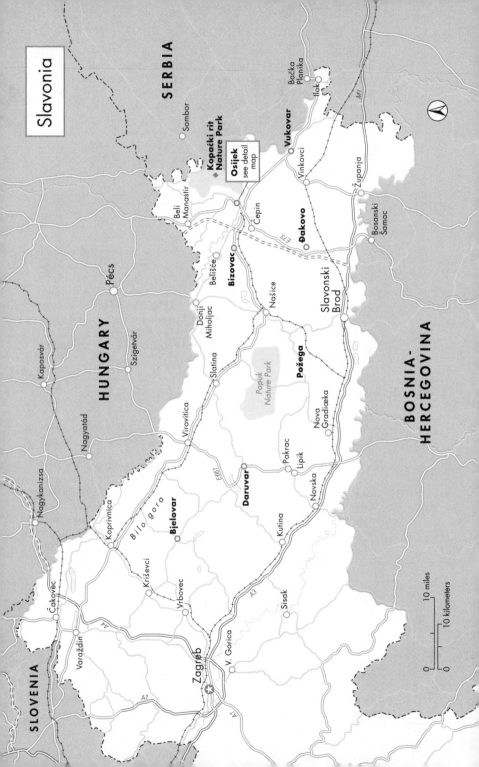

Slavonia

SERBIA

Sombor

Bačka
Planika

Ilok

M1

Kopački rit
Nature Park

Vukovar

Osijek
see detail
map

Vinkovci

Županja

Beli
Manastir

Čepin

Đakovo

E73

Bosanski
Šamac

Belišće

Bizovac

Našice

Slavonski
Brod

Pécs

Donji
Miholjac

Papuk
Nature Park

Požega

HUNGARY

Szigetvár

Slatina

Nova
Gradiška

BOSNIA-
HERCEGOVINA

Kaposvár

Virovitica

E661

Pakrac

Lipik

Nagyatád

Novska

Bilo gora

Daruvar

Nagykanizsa

Koprivnica

Bjelovar

Kutina

Sisak

Križevci

Vrbovec

A3

Čakovec

SLOVENIA

Varaždin

A4

Zagreb

V. Gorica

A2

A1

10 miles

10 kilometers

GREAT ITINERARIES

IF YOU HAVE 3 DAYS
Spend two days in **Osijek**, with either a short visit to nearby **Kopački Rit Nature Park**, or—if a spa stirs your fancy more than a bird sanctuary—a morning or afternoon of soaking in the thermal saline water at **Bizovac**. If time allows, drop by **Đakovo**, which is only a bit farther away but whose cathedral is well worth a look; and if you're driving and heading back toward Zagreb, do stop for lunch or for the night in either **Požega** (first choice) or **Bjelovar** (second choice).

IF YOU HAVE 5 DAYS
Begin with the above, by all means including **Đakovo** and at least a half day in either **Požega** or **Bjelovar**, as well as a meal or two plus a couple hours' walk in **Vukovar**. If **Kopački Rit** soothes you, you may want to spend more time there, opting for a longer excursion and perhaps a stroll around the village of **Kopač** and a meal at its excellent Zelena Žaba restaurant.

Although it is certainly possible to walk everywhere in Osijek, hopping aboard one of the trams that wind their way around the city will save you lots of time—given the huge park between the two main parts of town. To get between Gornji Grad and Trvđa, take Tram No. 1; to get between the train station and Gornji Grad, it's Tram No. 2. Fares are 7 Kn for a one-way ticket, 18 Kn for a day pass, payable to the driver. If you are caught without a valid ticket, you will be fined 150 Kn on the spot.

Numbers in the margins correspond to numbers on the Osijek map.

WHAT TO SEE

❼ Evangelička Crkva *(Lutheran Church)*. Some churches go to great lengths to stand out from the pack, as evidenced by the small Lutheran Church, whose blue-brick doorway and window arches offer a striking contrast to its otherwise redbrick facade. Ivan Domes's design must surely have raised some eyebrows when the church opened its doors in 1905. ⊠ *Lorenza Jägera ul, Gornji Grad* ☯ *Open only during services.*

❽ Kino Urania *(Urania Cinema)*. Built in 1912, this historic movie theater was based on drawings by famed Osijek architect Viktor Axmann. This one-of-a-kind beige cinema looks a tad like a church, displaying a heady mix of art nouveau and modernist influences. ⊠ *V. Hengla 1, Gornji Grad* ☎ *031/211–560.*

❾ Muzej Slovonije *(Museum of Slavonia)*. Slavonia's oldest museum was established in 1877 and moved to this location on the eastern side of Trg Svetog Trojstrva in 1946. Although most of the myriad objects on display are accompanied by little explanatory text in any language, they give a lasting impression of the region's folklore, culture, and natural history. You'll see a little bit of everything, from stuffed animals to old coins, from pottery to swords and halberds, from a collection of 16th- to 19th-century locks and keys to timepieces and typewriters. A key attraction is in the courtyard: a sarcophagus and other sculptural fragments from Mursa, the Roman settlement that was situated in pres-

IF YOU LIKE

STROLLING AROUND OSIJEK

Set in its somewhat sleepy splendor on the south bank of the Drava river, Slavonia's economic, administrative, and cultural capital is especially pleasant to explore on foot. The magnificent, neo-Gothic Župna Crkva Sv. Petra i Pavla is the main attraction in Gornji Grad, and a 15-minute walk or short tram ride away—past a lovely, spacious park, Perivoj Krajla Tomislava—is the historic, baroque district of Trvđa.

BIRD-WATCHING

Embracing more than 74,100 acres just north of the Drava, where that fast river flows eastward into the Danube, this vast natural area is covered with immense reed beds as well as willow, poplar, and oak forests and crisscrossed by ridges, ponds, shallow lakes, and marshes. More than 285 bird species can be spotted here. The park plays host to several endangered species, including the white-tailed sea eagle, the black stork, and the European otter.

VUKOVAR RENEWAL

Though more of an experience than a pleasure, perhaps, this once lovely baroque town on the Danube offers the chance to see for yourself—rather than just on TV—the destruction wrought by war. More of a pleasure, actually, is noticing how Vukovar has begun to make

itself lovely again. In the years since 1991—when the city came under siege and thousands of its inhabitants died or went missing—great headway has been made to rebuild the city as faithfully as possible. At the same time, vital new public spaces are beginning to blossom.

ĐAKOVO CATHEDRAL

Đakovo's influential 19th-century bishop, Josip Juraj Strossmayer, commissioned this magnificent structure, which was designed by architect Frederick Schmidt. The structure towers outside and is beautifully decorated inside. If you're a fan of churches, this is one you won't want to miss.

SMALL-TOWN CHARM

Once known as the "Athens of Slovenia" for its cultural dynamism, Požega today may resemble a frontier town as you approach its outskirts—but you'll soon discover a charming historic center marked by the Trg Sv. Trojstva (Holy Trinity Square). The town has several notable churches, including the main attraction, the Gothic, 14th-century Crkva Sv. Lovre (Church of St. Lawrence). If Požega seems too far out of the way to fit your itinerary, small-town charm can also be had in Bjelovar, whose capacious, parklike main square in particular is something to behold.

ent-day Donji Grad. Should you find the front door locked during open hours, press the buzzer to be let in. ⊠ *Trg Svetog Trojstrva 6, Trvđa* ☎ *031/250–730* ⊕ *www.mdc.hr/osijek* ☎ *15 Kn* ☉ *Tues.–Sun. 10–1.*

❾ **Perivoj Krajla Tomislava** *(King Tomislav Gardens).* One of Osijek's most soothing spots, the King Tomislav Gardens is a spacious, forested oasis along the Drava that was laid out in the 18th century. It separates historic Trvđa from Gornji Grad, the more bustling, commercial heart of town. Today the park is home to playgrounds, a tennis court, and a rowing club.

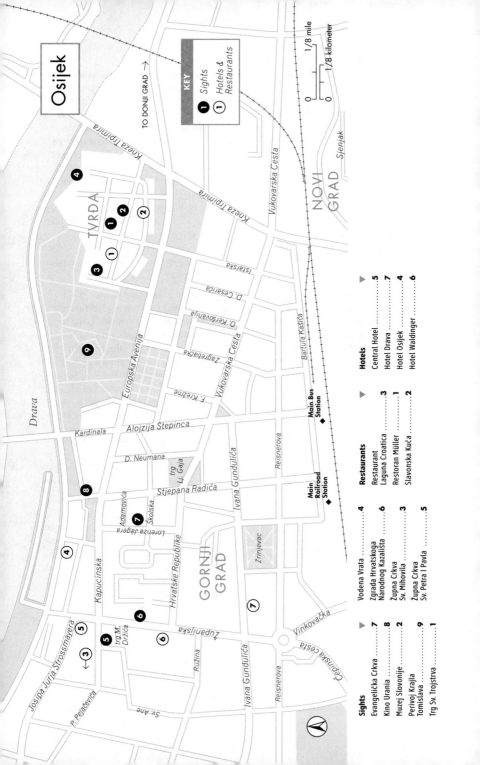

Osijek

KEY
- **1** Sights
- **(1)** Hotels & Restaurants

0 — 1/8 mile
0 — 1/8 kilometer

TO DONJI GRAD →

TVRDA

NOVI GRAD

Sienjak

Drava

GORNJI GRAD

Main Railroad Station ◆

Main Bus Station ◆

Sights
▶
Evangelička Crkva **7**
Kino Urania **8**
Muzej Slovonije **2**
Perivoj Kralja
Tomislava **9**
Trg Sv. Trojstrva **1**

Vodena Vrata **4**
Zgrada Hrvatskoga
Narodnog Kazališta **6**
Župna Crkva
Sv. Mihovila **3**
Župna Crkva
Sv. Petra I Pavla **5**

Restaurants
▶
Restaurant
Laguna Croatica **3**
Restoran Müller **1**
Slavonska Kuća **2**

Hotels
▶
Central Hotel **5**
Hotel Drava **7**
Hotel Osijek **4**
Hotel Waldinger **6**

A Bridge Is Born

When Sultan Sülejman the Magnificent decided in autumn of 1525 to attack Hungary, Osijek's fate was settled. Emissaries from Osijek, aiming to save their town, met the Ottomans on August 8, 1526, to hand over the town keys. Less than two weeks later an Ottoman army crossed into Osijek over a pontoon bridge across the Drava. From this point on, Osijek became a key element in the Ottoman's movement north toward Buda and east, toward Vienna. Indeed, far from suffering devastation, the town thrived.

Many an Ottoman war campaign proceeded through Osijek on its way west. However, there was the lingering problem of getting a mammoth army across the Drava and the swamps to the north. The answer: a bridge such as the world had never seen.

With the labor of 25,000 people, Sülejman's Bridge—all 8 km (5 mi) of it—was completed on July 19, 1566. Not only did it span the Drava; it also worked its way in gentle curves across that river's tributaries and across marshes to the town of Darda to the

north. The bridge became known as a world wonder; it was depicted and written about by painters and other travelers who came here from afar. Thanks to Sülejman's Bridge, Osijek's strategic and commercial importance as a vital link in the communication route between Constantinople and Budapest blossomed all the more. Osijek, whose inhabitants at the time comprised mostly Turkish settlers and a smaller number of locals who'd converted to Islam, developed rapidly as the most important town in Turkish Slavonia.

Not until the defeat of the Ottoman army by Vienna in 1683 did the Turkish grip on the region begin to weaken. The following year, with the area under attack, Sülejman's Bridge was partly burned. But before long the Turks restored it. But after the last Turkish solider left Osijek in 1687, ongoing wars sealed its fate: it was eventually destroyed beyond repair. Today it lives on only in the history books and in paintings, one of which is on display at Osijek's Muzej Slovonije (Museum of Slavonia).

❶ Trg Svetog Trojstrva *(Holy Trinity Square).* Chief among the architectural highlights on Trvđa's main square is the plague pillar at its center. The Zavjetni stup svetog trojstva (Votive Pillar of the Holy Trinity) is one of Osijek's finest baroque monuments. Erected in 1729–30 by the widow of General Maksimilijan Petraš, who died of the plague in 1728, it has an elaborate pinnacle and four pedestals at its base bearing the statues of various saints, including St. Sebastian. Overlooking the northwest side of the square is the yellow Zgrada Glavne straže (Building of the Main Guard), built in 1729 with the observation post jutting out of its roof and capped by a Venetian-Moorish dome. On the square's western side is the grand Zgrada glavne komande (High Command Building), erected originally as a single-story building between 1724 and 1726 on the order of Prince Eugene of Savoy, with a Renaissance facade and a dual-columned, baroque entrance; a second floor was added in 1765.

❹ Vodena Vrata *(Water Gate).* Facing the Drava River, the gate, which was once known by the Latin appellation Porta Aquatica, is the only remaining gate in the original fortress wall, most of which was razed in the 1920s. Flanked by columns, this arched entrance to the fortress was built as part of a major construction project that also included several bastions and was completed by 1715.

❻ **Zgrada Hrvatskoga Narodnog Kazališta** *(Croatian National Theater).* The building that has housed the theater since 1907 is an imposing ochre structure whose Venetian-Moorish style renders it the most striking of a string of classical facades along Županijska ulica. Not open for tours, the theater can only be seen if you take in a performance. ✉ *Županijska ul 9, Gornji Grad* ☎ *031/220–700.*

❸ **Župna Crkva Sveta Mihovila** *(St. Michael's Parish Church).* Near the site of the onetime Kasim-Pasha Mosque, this mustard-yellow church has a single nave with two bulb-topped bell towers on each side of its facade. It was built by the Jesuits over 30 years beginning in 1725. In accord with the late-baroque style in fashion in continental Croatia at the time, the interior displays a conspicuous absence of paintings. Unfortunately, it's often closed except during services and weddings. ✉ *Trg Jurja Križanića, Trvđa* ⊙ *Open only during services.*

NEED A BREAK? Offering old-world elegance, the Kavana Waldinger (✉ *Hotel Waldinger,* *Županijska 8* ☎ *031/250–470*) is, hands down, Osijek's finest café. Locals flock here all day until closing time at 11 PM to indulge in coffee, beer, and other drinks, plus exquisite pralines and heavenly kolači *(cakes)* topped with chocolate, sliced almonds, and fig.

❺ **Župna Crkva Sv. Petra i Pavla** *(Parish Church of Saints Peter and Paul).* Discounting the modern sky-high Hotel Osijek—several blocks away, thankfully—the majestic, redbrick, neo-Gothic, single-naved church is the highlight of Osijek's downtown skyline. At 292 feet, its steeple is the second highest in Croatia. Built between 1894 and 1898 on the site of a former church of the same name by the architects Franz Langenberg of Germany and Robert Jordan of Austria, and on the initiative of the famous Đakovo-based bishop Josip Juraj Strossmayer, it has no less than five neo-Gothic altars, an unusually frescoed ceiling replete with individual praying figures human and divine, and stained-glass windows. The colorful but rather bland wall frescoes do not testify to much in the way of divine inspiration. ✉ *Trg Ante Starčevića, Gornji Grad* ⊙ *Daily 8–8.*

NEED A BREAK? A 20-minute walk across Osijek's pedestrian bridge over the Drava, and across from Trvđa, is Copacabana Rekreacijski Centar (*Copacabana Recreation Center* ✉ *Along the Drava River* ☎ *No phone*), a pleasant and spacious, unfenced—and free—aquatic-recreation complex that includes pools, a waterslide, a restaurant, and plenty of willow trees. Impossible to miss if you stroll along this section of the river, it operates from mid-June through mid-September, daily from 8 to at least 7 PM (sometimes as late as 11 PM).

OFF THE BEATEN PATH

Zavičajni muzej Našice *(Našice Regional Museum).* On the northern slopes of the Krndija hills, the sleepy village of Našice (pop. 8,000) is home to a resplendent ochre palace once owned by the Pejačević family. Surrounded by a lovely and spacious English-style landscaped garden, this massive baroque building, which dates to 1811, is today the site of the Našice Regional Museum, which has impressive exhibits on the history of Našice and surroundings from ancient times to World War II, as well as four attractive memorial rooms dedicated to distinguished Croatian artists, including Dora Pejačević, Croatia's first female composer. The historical collection includes everything from displays of ancient archaeological frag-

WAR-WEARY FACADES

Although Osijek came out of the Yugoslav war in far better shape than Vukovar, one thing you can't help noticing during a stroll about town are all those pockmarked buildings: the result of shrapnel from the intensive shelling the city suffered over several months starting in September 1991. Hundreds of civilians died and several thousand were injured. On the brighter side, a conversation begun in a local cellar during the shelling spawned the Osijek-based Center for Peace, Nonviolence, and Human Rights, which has since focused on conflict resolution in the region and beyond.

ments and 16th-century coins to the bygone equipment of the local fire brigade and an ethnographic exhibit with a typical room from a turn-of-the-20th-century peasant home, not to mention plenty of interesting historical photographs. There are several trains and buses each day to Našice from Osijek (45–60 minutes, 30 Kn). By car from Zagreb, the fastest way to get here is via the E7 motorway through southern Slavonia; exit at Slavonski Brod and drive north on local route 53 to Našice—from where, in turn, you can easily get to Osijek in around a half hour along the east-west route that traverses northern Slavonia. ⊠ *Pejacevicev trg 5* ✛ *Off the east-west M3 motorway, 51 km (32 mi) southwest of Osijek* ☎ *031/613–414* ⊕ *www.mdc.hr/nasice/en* ☞ *12 Kn* ⊙ *Tues.–Thurs. 8–6, Mon. and Fri. 8–3, Sat. 9–noon.*

WHERE TO EAT

$$–$$$$
Fodor's Choice
★

✕ **Restoran Müller.** This is one of Osijek's finest restaurants, where not only regional specialties but also coastal as well as continental cuisine are prepared and served with great care and complemented by the finest wines. Whether you're up for grilled calamari, Slavonian *fiš paprikaš* or *čobanac*, or beefsteak Wellington, you will leave this elegant and intimately lighted room well satisfied. The mustachioed owner, Želko Kolar, a dapper gentleman who talks proudly of the large wine cellar downstairs, makes it a matter of policy that only he and his son deal with guests. At the time of this writing, the only foreign-language menu was in German. ⊠ *Trg Jurja Križanića 9, Trvđa* ☎ *031/204–270* ▭ *AE, DC, MC, V.*

$$–$$$

✕ **Restaurant Laguna Croatica.** With an arched brick ceiling above, the cellar dining room of this restaurant is a pleasant place to indulge in a

2

hearty meat or freshwater fish dish—whether *ćevapčići* (grilled spicy cubes of minced meat served with raw onions), grilled turkey, beef, or breaded carp. You might try the Slavonian steak—grilled veal shank stuffed with ham and cheese—and wash it down with a glass of plavac mali wine. The restaurant is a 10-minute walk west of downtown. ✉*Dubrovačka 13, Gornji Grad* ☎*031/369–203* ▭*AE, DC, MC, V.*

$$

Fodor's Choice

★

✕**Slavonska Kuća.** Just a couple of blocks from Trvđa's main square, this small one-room eatery is about as atmospheric as can be, with rustic wooden benches, walls adorned with bric-a-brac, including a fishing net, and folksy Croatian background music. Choose between regional fare like *riblji paprikaš* (elsewhere called *fiš paprikas*) and *perkelt* (meat in paprika sauce). For dessert, try the *palačinke* (crepes). As of this writing, the menu was in Croatian only, but the waiters here all know some English. ✉*Kamila Firingera 26, Trvđa* ☎*031/369–955* ▭*AE, DC, MC, V.*

WHERE TO STAY

If you'd prefer to save money by staying in a private room rather than a hotel, and don't mind being 6 km (4 mi) north of town, in the village of Bilje, the friendly folks at **OK Tours** (✉*Trg Slobode 8, Osijek* ☎*031/212–815*) will arrange this for you. Figure on at least 160 Kn per person. Getting to Bilje is straightforward: there are around 10 buses daily, roughly once an hour until around 10:20 PM, so this option won't allow much of a nightlife in Osijek unless you have a car. At around 13 Kn one way (payable to the driver), at least the price of the ticket is reasonable.

$$–$$$

★

⊞**Hotel Osijek.** This skyline-dominating, steel-and-glass edifice is the city's one ultra-contemporary luxury hotel. The three types of rooms include the classic, a bit on the small side and with showers only; the more generously sized superior; and the deluxe, with a small sitting area. In addition there are seven suites, which the hotel calls "apartments," with separate living rooms in various sizes. The gym, on the top floor, affords a great view of the town and river below, and the Slavonian plains beyond. The hotel restaurant, Zimska Luka, in an airy room overlooking the Drava, is one of Osijek's most distinguished places to savor not only regional specialties but wild game and a broad selection of international cuisine. Pros: great views, centrally located, excellent services and amenities, fine in-house dining, a lovely, light-filled café. Cons: impersonal, many rooms smallish. ✉*Šamačka 4, Gornji Grad, 31000* ☎*031/230–333* 🖶*031/230–444* ⊕*www.hotelosijek.hr* ⬎*140 rooms, 7 suites* ⚐*In-room: safe, refrigerator, Wi-Fi, Ethernet. In-hotel: restaurant, bar, gym, parking (no fee), laundry service, laundry facilities, public Wi-Fi, public Internet, some pets allowed, no-smoking rooms* ▭*AE, DC, MC, V* ⦿|*BP.*

$$

Fodor's Choice

★

⊞**Hotel Waldinger.** Opened in 2004 in a 19th-century art nouveau building on one of central Osijek's main thoroughfares, the Waldinger—named after famous local painter Adolf Waldinger—offers luxury on a par with the Hotel Osijek, but on a smaller, cozier scale and with a period look and feel. Standard doubles have a jetted tub in the bathroom, whereas the suite's jetted tub is right in the bedroom. The small, lovely restaurant, accessible through the courtyard, is as exquisite as the hotel, offering delicately prepared Slavonian specialties as well as a choice selection of wine. Try the sumptuous and subtly spiced beef with fried vegetables. Behind the main building, in a bucolic square complete with a little pond, is an older, one-story pension with seven bright, spacious rooms. Removed from the moderate bustle of the city, they go for just for 440 Kn. Pros: unmitigated luxury, superior in-house restaurant, lavish breakfast. Cons: pricey (for Slavonia), rooms on top floor have smallish windows hard to look out of, no public Internet. ⊠ *Županijska 8, Gornji Grad, 31000* ☎*031/250–450* 🖷*031/250–453* ⊕*www.waldinger.hr* ↪*15 rooms, 1 suite* ⅃*In-room: safe, refrigerator, Ethernet, Wi-Fi. In-hotel: restaurant, gym, parking (no fee), room service, public Wi-Fi, no elevator* ☰*AE, DC, MC, V* †⊙|*BP.*

¢ 🏨 **Central Hotel.** While it could use some sprucing up, Osijek's oldest continuously operated hotel, opened in 1889, is still alive and well today. A spiral staircase with a (frayed) red carpet and wrought-iron railing leads to spacious, elegant rooms with armchairs and sofas. Some rooms have balconies, and all the bathrooms have bidets. Request a large double with a king-size bed and a view of the main square for no extra cost; most of the doubles are a bit smaller, with twin beds. The entrance is off an arcade on Trg Ante Starčevića, near the towering Parish Church of Saints Peter and Paul. Across the arcade is the hotel's Viennese-style café, replete with red-velvet chairs. Pros: old-world elegance at a decent price, splendid views of main square from many rooms, elegant bathrooms. Cons: some rooms may get noise from the main square, some rooms have a smoky-musty smell on entering, no no-smoking rooms, no Internet access, few frills. ⊠*Trg Ante Starčevića 6, Gornji Grad, 31000* ☎*031/283–399* 🖷*031/283–891* ⊕*www.hotel-central-os.hr* ↪*39 rooms* ⅃*In-room: no a/c, safe, refrigerator. In-hotel: restaurant, laundry service, no elevator* ☰*AE, DC, MC, V* †⊙|*BP.*

¢ 🏨 **Hotel Drava.** Osijek's newest hotel opened in 2007, bestowing the city with a fine little place to stay if you can't find a room at any of downtown's other, more attractive hotels. A bland two-story building set in a large, enclosed, redbrick parking lot, the Drava has 11 red-carpeted, simple, but satisfactory rooms. Pros: bright, modern rooms, sleek, light-filled dining room, just a 15-minute walk from the center. Cons: not right in the center, bland views; few frills, no Internet access. ⊠*I. F. Gundulića 25a, Gornji Grad, 31000* ☎*031/250–500* 🖷*031/250–503* ⊕*www.hotel-drava.com* ↪*10 rooms, 1 suite* ⅃*In-room: refrigerator. In-hotel: laundry service, no elevator, parking (no fee)* ☰*AE, DC, MC, V* †⊙|*BP.*

NIGHTLIFE & THE ARTS

NIGHTLIFE

Though one of Osijek's most popular dance clubs is in the heart of quiet, historic Trvđa, most of the city's nightlife is east of the Hotel Osijek on Šetalište Kardinal Franje Šepera—the promenade along the city harbor (Zimska Luka) in Gornji Grad. In fair weather you can easily lose yourself in crowds of nighttime revelers. Just doors away from the San Francisco Coffee House, the **Amsterdam Pub** (⊠ *Radićeva 18, Gornji Grad* ☎*No phone*) is a classic little cellar bar, where a youngish crowd squeezes into a small, low-lit room amid wood furnishings and under brick-arched ceilings. Right next door to the Slavonska Kuča restaurant, the aptly named **Club Sound** (⊠*Kamila Firingera 24, Trvđa* ☎*031/201–057*) is an inviting place to dance the night away, with a mix of R&B, pop, and commercial hits. Theme parties are often held on Friday, Saturday, and Tuesday nights in the cool back room equipped with flashing lights. Beyond the name and the cool print of the Golden Gate Bridge on the wall, the smoky, popular **San Francisco Coffee House** (⊠*Radićeva 12, Gornji Grad* ☎*099/212–8032*) has little to do with modern-day San Francisco, unless you count the vaguely Starbucks-like look of the main room and the English-language magazines on hand for you to browse. This is the place to milk a mocha or latte while discussing life. Right on the Old Town's main square, the ever-popular **St. Patrick's Pub** (⊠*Kuhačeva 15, south side of Trg Svetog Trojstva, Trvđa* ☎*031/205–202*) is a paean to all things English, including Jack the Ripper, but the prevailing interior-decorating theme is soccer.

THE ARTS

The **Zgrada Hrvatskoga Narodnog Kazališta** (*Croatian National Theater* ⊠*Županijska ul 9, Gornji Grad* ☎*031/220–700*) is Osijek's venue for a fairly broad array of Croatian and international plays from September through May. The **Children's Theater** (⊠*Trg bana J. Jelačića 19, Gornji Grad* ☎*031/501–485*) is the place to go for a good puppet show.

SHOPPING

Although Osijek has few quality opportunities, bustling Županijska, leading up to Trg Ante Starčevića, is the best stretch of street in town to see what's for sale. **Rukotvorine** (⊠*Županijska 15, Gornji Grad* ☎*031/212–217*) has a rich array of top-notch Slavonian embroidery and handicrafts in its small store across the street from the Hotel Waldinger. If you haven't yet acquired your all-original Croatian silk tie in Zagreb at one of the capital's attractive boutiques in the same chain, you can do so at **Croata** (⊠*Županijska 2, Gornji Grad* ☎*031/200–260*).

BIZOVAC

★ *18 km (11 mi) west of Osijek.*

Rising up out of the Slavonian plains 2 km (1 mi) outside the pretty little town of Bizovac is a vast, weirdly modern building complex with an unmistakably sci-fi look to it. Lavishly ornamented with an intricate network of pipes along part of its exterior, this is **Bizovačke toplice,** Slavonia's largest spa, which sprang up here in 1990—a year before war visited the region. Inside are Europe's only thermal salt springs, which issue from a depth of almost 2,000 meters with a salinity approaching that of the Adriatic. Exceptionally rich in minerals and up to 96°C (205°F) at its source, this water can be yours within the aptly named **Aquapolis Water City**, which consists of four indoor and two outdoor pools containing thermal water and three other pools for just plain swimming or fun. Though frequent trains make the 20-minute trip between Osijek and Bizovac, the 25-minute walk from the railway station over rural roads can hardly compete with the convenience of a 30-minute bus trip that drops you off at the hospital right across the road from the spa. ⊠*Sunčana 39* ☎*031/685–100* ⊕*www.bizovacke-toplice.hr* ⚏*30 Kn* ⊘*Mon.–Thurs. 8–8, Fri.–Sun. 8–8 and 9–midnight.*

WHERE TO STAY & EAT

You could choose to spend the night—490 Kn for a no-frills, simply furnished double room (including breakfast) at Aquapolis Water City's **Termia Hotel**—and if you do, you'll have complimentary access to the spa.

$–$$ ✕**Nacionalni Restaurant.** Technically separate from the hotel but accessible via a convoluted route from the reception desk, the restaurant is the one fine-dining venue in the Aquapolis Water City complex. With main courses ranging from simple pastas to scrumptious pike-perch, catfish, carp, or pork-rich house specialties, this brick-walled cellar restaurant is the spa's best bet for a good meal. ⊠*Sunčana 39* ☎*031/685–252* ⊟*AE, MC, V.*

KOPAČKI RIT NATURE PARK

★ *10 km (6 mi) northeast of Osijek.*

More than 80% of the historical wetlands along the Danube has been lost since the late 19th century. One of the largest remaining areas is now preserved in Kopački Rit Nature Park, a place of serene beauty that makes for a deeply satisfying visit whether or not you're partial to birds. Embracing more than 74,100 acres immediately north of the Drava, where the fast river flows eastward into the Danube, the park is covered with immense reed beds as well as willow, poplar, and oak forests and crisscrossed by ridges, ponds, shallow lakes, and marshes. Its exact aquatic contours vary a tad each year, depending on the degree to which the Danube backs up under pressure from the Drava and floods over the area. More than 285 bird species, 400 varieties of plants, and dozens of species of butterflies, mammals, and fish live in Kopački Rit. A vital spawning ground for Danube river fish, the park is also a breeding area for numerous endangered species—including the white-tailed sea eagle, the black stork, and the European otter. Egrets, herons, and cormorants are abundant, as are red deer, roe deer, and wild boar. In winter, Kopački Rit plays host to thousands of migrating geese and ducks. Although efforts have been underway since 1999 to make Kopački Rit a full-fledged national park, the going has been

CLOSE UP

Off Limits

When a young Hungarian went hang gliding in July 2005 and drifted unwittingly over the Croatian border, he landed in a field north of Osijek, brushed himself off, and was preparing to walk out when a local woman yelled, "No!" The man—who had landed in the middle of a minefield—had to stay put until a helicopter plucked him out.

Though ongoing efforts have gone far toward resolving the situation, Croatia is still littered with mines left over from the 1990s Yugoslav war. Out of some 2 million such devices, it is believed that over 200,000 are still out there. Between 1998 and early 2007, 273 people fell victim to leftover mines, 101 of whom have died. Mines have also inflicted great harm to wildlife, including in such protected natural areas as Kopački Rit Nature Park, near Osijek, and Plitvice Lakes National Park, between Zagreb and the Dalmatian coast. Happily, Plitvice Lakes has been back in business in recent years as a top tourist destination, and the treasured wine region

around Ilok, southeast of Vukovar, has been cleared of its mines. Twelve of the country's 21 counties, including several in Slavonia, still have minefields. It is estimated that there are more than 40,000 mines in Osječko-Baranjska County alone, with almost 5% of its land off-limits to people and to development. Nearly 60% of the contaminated land is forest, but 27% is arable. Almost half of the county's 42 municipalities are affected. Croatia's government established the Croatian Mine Action Centre (CROMAC) in 1998 to coordinate the removal of these mines, and aims to de-mine its territory by 2009.

Before venturing off a road or path into field or forest, check for the skull-and-crossbones signs that warn of minefields; as of this writing, there were still around 13,000 such signs around the country. Even in the absence of signs, ask qualified locals whether an area is safe. For more information, visit the Web site of the Croatian Mine Action Centre at *www.hcr.hr.*

slow on this front—in no small part because the necessary restrictions on hunting in such a game-rich area make the issue politically sensitive. The best times of year to visit are during spring and autumn bird migrations, when there are often several hundred thousand birds in the park. Should you come in warm weather, be prepared to be feasted on by mosquitoes. Although the park administration building is in Bilje, the information office at the park entrance in Kopač serves visitors. A short nature trail leads to the landing where boat excursions set out daily into the marshy heart of the park along a channel to Kopačevo Jezero, the largest lake. English-language excursions are available if there is sufficient demand. Although walking or driving past the visitor center into the park is easily accomplished for free, technically speaking you are supposed to have an access card, available at the information center for 10 Kn. For 70 Kn (50 Kn in low season), you also get a one-hour boat ride followed by a guided walk of at least one hour along a dike to the park's northern reaches. In 1991, Kopački Rit became a no-man's-land along the front line of the Yugoslav war. For the next six years the natural area and the human communities around it were ravaged, not least by thousands of land mines, which have not only brought great danger to humans but have drastically reduced populations of large mammals such as deer and wild boar. Though major de-mining efforts have been underway since Croatia's reintegration of the Baranja region in 1997, about one-tenth of the surface area of Kopački Rit is still inaccessible due to minefields. A prized hunting and fishing area for centuries—and in particular during the Austro-Hungarian Empire—Kopački Rit also has a rich cultural-historical heritage. **Dvorac Tikveš** (⊠ *15 km [9 mi] north of Bilje*), a historic villa with a rich history dating back to the Austro-Hungarian monarchy, also served as a hunting lodge for Yugoslav leader Josep Broz Tito. The complex includes a restaurant and research laboratories for visiting scientists. Getting to Kopački Rit from Osijek is simple if you have a car—just follow the signs once you're in Bilje. If you go by bus, it's a pain in the neck unless you are not at all pressed for time: be prepared to follow the signs on foot for some 4 km (2½ mi) along rural roads after the bus drops you off in Bilje. ⊠ *Information Center near Kopaceva* ☎ *031/752–321 or 031/752–320* ⊕ *www.kopacki-rit.com* ✎ *10 Kn; one-hour boat ride plus guided tour, 70 Kn Apr., May, Sept. and Oct., or 50 Kn June–Aug. and Nov.–Mar.* ☉ *May–Sept., daily 8–5; Oct.–Apr., daily 8–4.*

WHERE TO EAT

$$ ✕ **Zelena Žaba.** Also known locally by its Hungarian name, Zöld Béka,
★ the Green Frog restaurant is an absolutely delightful village restaurant, with a quiet, willow-fringed marsh behind the building that you can look out upon from the back room. Its hunting-cum-fishing theme is expressed in the form of rifles, antlers, an oar, and fishnets on the walls. Try house specialties such as *žabliji kraci* (frogs' legs) and *riblji perkelt* (fish in a thick paprika sauce), not to mention other favorites such as roast pike. For dessert, there's nothing like *palačinke* filled with walnuts or jam. ⊠ *Ribarska ul 3, Kopač* ☎ *031/752–212* ▭ *AE, DC, MC, V.*

$-$$ ✕ **Restoran Kod Varge.** On Bilje's main road a few hundred yards before the major intersection (if you're coming from Osijek and going toward Kopački Rit), this charming restaurant offers such hearty regional fare as *ribli paprikaš*, a spicy-hot paprika-flavored fish stew that is rather salty, too. If you're not troubled by the discordant but somehow appealing blend of folksy Croatian music in the background, not to mention a TV in the corner of the room that plays whatever happens to be on, you'll enjoy your meal here. ⊠ *Ul Kralja Zvonimira 37a, Bilje* ☎ *031/750–120* ▭ *AE, DC, MC, V.*

VUKOVAR

35 km (22 mi) southeast of Osijek.

Tourists don't exactly flock to this once-lovely baroque city that was reduced to rubble in 1991 in one of the most notorious events of the Yugoslav war. On May 2, 1991, 12 Croatian policemen were ambushed and killed in the suburb of Borovo. By September, Croat refugees had fled from outlying areas to the city center, which came under siege by the JNA (Yugoslav People's Army). After weeks of heavy bombardment that left the city in ruins, Vukovar fell on November 18. Of the thousands of Croatian residents who were captured—many had fled to the hospital, where they were awaiting the arrival of the Red Cross—a substantial number wound up in a mass grave outside the village of Ovčara, 7 km (4½ mi) to the southeast. All told, some 2,000 Croatians perished in the siege of Vukovar, with roughly the same number still reported as missing. As of this writing, two Serbs were on trial in The Hague for allegedly carrying out the massacre of those who'd fled to the city hospital. Vukovar was named after the ancient Vučedol culture that inhabited a site 5 km (3 mi) downstream along the Danube from the present-day city some 5,000 years ago. The area near the present-day town was later the site of a Roman settlement, and by the 11th century a community existed at the town's present location; this settlement became the seat of Vukovo County in the 13th century. After Turkish rule (1526–1687), almost all of Vukovar and environs was bought by the counts of Eltz, a German family that strongly influenced the development of the town for the next two centuries and whose palace, severely damaged in the 1991 siege, is home to the local museum. In a poignant reminder of what happened here not long ago, the visitor cannot help but notice a steady, somber stream of pedestrian traffic to one of present-day Vukovar's most conspicuous sites: a tall, simple concrete cross situated at the tip of a narrow causeway overlooking the Danube. While this war memorial honors all victims on both sides, with inscriptions in both Cyrillic and Roman letters, within eyeshot of here is another conspicuous sight that presumably does not win the hearts of local Serbs—a bust of the late Croatian leader Franjo Tuđman on a square bearing his name.

Vukovar is as much the scene of urban renewal as it is of destruction. A steady influx of European Union reconstruction funds has been changing the face of the city; Vukovar may very well be Croatia's only town with an ulica Europske Unije (European Union Street). Although at least half of all structures are damaged to some degree, new houses and ongoing construction are much in evidence; and you have the sense that most of those heavily damaged buildings that *are* still standing are there precisely because their reconstruction is planned at some point. As a walk around the town center in later afternoon or early evening will amply show, public life is again taking shape here, and new public spaces are gaining vitality and purpose—even if the underlying tensions between the town's Serbian and Croatian residents remain.

In the 18th-century palace Dvorac Eltz, which was severely damaged in the siege of Vukovar, the **Gradski Muzej Vukovar** (*Vukovar Town Museum*) is back in business, albeit feebly, since the 2001 signing of an agreement for the return of its collection, which was expropriated by the Serbs in 1991. Unfortunately, most of the collection is still stored away. As of this writing, the museum was hosting temporary, varied exhibitions of art. Plans call for the eventual renovation of the build-

Young Love

There's an intriguing legend associated with an unassuming, 18th-century baroque chapel off to the side of downtown, at the corner of Kneza Trpimira and Vukovarska Cesta, which these days has a fuel station as its neighbor. It was built in memory of a young man put to death for a murder that, apparently, he didn't commit. Arrested after a killing within the town walls in Trvđa, the young lad, a commoner, denied involvement but could not provide an alibi. After his execution, however, a young woman of gen-teel stock explained that he couldn't possibly have been the killer—as they'd been together on the night of the murder, a fact that he had apparently kept from airing so as to save the girl's honor. Her mother had the chapel built in memory of the unfortunate young man. For more authoritative versions of this and other colorful stories of Osijek, check with the tourist-information office, or with Professor Grgur Ivanković at the Museum of Slavonia (☎031/208–501).

ing—which from the outside still looks so war-torn that you wonder how the few rooms inside can remain intact. A portion of the building will be left as is, as a poignant reminder of the siege of Vukovar. ⊠ *Županijska 2* ☎*032/441–270* 💶*10 Kn* 🕓*Mon.–Sat. 10–3.*

Vukovar's main ecclesiastical attraction, on a hill a bit to the southeast of the town center, is the 18th-century **Franjevački Samostan** *(Franciscan Monastery),* which was pieced back together again after being ravaged in the war. ⊠*Samostanska ul* ☎*032/441–381* 🕓 *Weekdays 8–noon and 2–4, Sat. 8–noon.*

NEED A BREAK? Yards away from the pedestrian bridge and across from the Velepromet supermarket, the hip little café-cum-bar Caffe El Maritimo (⊠*Trg Matije Gupca 21* ☎*No phone*) is an inviting place either for a daytime coffee or an evening beer. Its opening in 2005 suggests that Vukovar's social scene is slowly blossoming anew after the ruin wrought by war.

WHERE TO EAT

$–$$$ ✕**Arka.** Opened in 2006, the Arka's popularity with locals has much to do with where it is: inside a multipurpose boat docked permanently on the Danube behind the Dunav Hotel. The vessel also has a covered terrace furnished with reed armchairs, where you can dine in good weather; and the lower decks include both a bar and a dance club. Fortunately, the menu is also quite good, with grilled meats, Wiener schnitzel, poultry, and steak, not to mention scrumptious desserts like *palačinke* (crepes). ⊠ *Trg Republike Hrvatske bb* ☎*032/450–465* 🚫*AE, DC, MC, V.*

$–$$ ✕**Vrške.** This apricot-color restaurant with a charming farmhouse look rests on an islet that is reached by a pedestrian bridge behind the Hotel Lav. Its spacious, thatched-roof terrace overlooks the Danube, and beside it is a pavilion where live music is played; the interior features reed walls and wood-beamed ceilings. Carp, catfish, pike-perch, and other freshwater fish are the favorites here, whether grilled, fried, or in a thick, vegetable-rich sauce; they are typically complemented by French fries. You can get a huge, four-person bowl of paprika-rich *riblji paprikaš* (fish stew). Combine this with some Ilok wine and a *palačinke s marmeladom* (jam-filled crepe). ⊠*Parobrodska 3* ☎*032/441–788* ▭*AE, DC, MC, V.*

WHERE TO STAY

$ 🏨**Hotel Lav.** Strange as it may seem to have a luxury hotel pop up in the middle of Vukovar, that's just what happened in 2005 when the Hotel Lav—a sparkling white building with a glass front—reopened its doors after a complete reconstruction, primarily with business travelers in mind. The spacious rooms, with bright-yellow silky bedspreads and an unmistakably modern look, are nonetheless decorated with pictures of the "old" Vukovar; the suites include jetted tubs. As of this writing, plans call for an indoor pool here by 2008. The huge, bombed-out building next door used to be Vukovar's main shopping center, and it is slated for eventual reconstruction. Pros: the only bright, modern hotel in town, centrally located, pool planned for 2008. Cons: pricey, no Danube views. ⊠*J. J. Strossmayera 18, across from the tourist-information office, 32000* ☎*032/445–100* 📠*032/445–110* ⊕*www. hotel-lav.hr* ⇄*39 rooms, 4 suites* �*In-room: safe, refrigerator, Ethernet. In-hotel: restaurant, public Wi-Fi, public Internet* ▭*AE, DC, MC, V* ⦿*BP.*

¢ 🏨**Dunav Hotel.** The worn-looking Dunav has no frills, but is an acceptable—if somber—place to stay. The rooms on the fifth floor have relatively new bathrooms and are just 30 Kn more than the rooms on the first four floors, which are shabbier. The top two floors are empty. Ask for a room with a river view. Danubium Tours, a local agency that offers various guided tours of Vukovar and environs, is headquartered at the hotel. Pros: good views, relatively good rate. Cons: in need of sprucing up, little English spoken, no Internet access, few frills. ⊠*Trg Republike 1, 32000* ☎*032/441–285* 📠*032/441–762* ✐*hotel-dunav@ uupik.htnet.hr* ⇄*58 rooms* �*In-room: no a/c. In-hotel: restaurant, bar* ▭*AE, DC, MC, V* ⦿*BP.*

ĐAKOVO

38 km (24 mi) southeast of Osijek.

Đakovo is a peaceful little town, where the din of bicycles and the dribbling of basketballs on a Sunday afternoon outdoes the roar of cars. The relatively bustling pedestrian main street is ulica Hrv. Velikana, whose far end has a little parish church that was built rather cleverly from a former 16th-century mosque. The best time to be in town—though a difficult time to book a room on short notice—is the last weekend in September, during the annual Đakovački Vezovi (Đakovo Embroidery Festival), which sees a whole array of song-and-dance performances, an all-around party atmosphere, and, above all, a folklore show replete with traditional embroidered costumes, folk dancing, and folk singing—and even a show by the famous Lipizzaner horses, who train in town. You can get to Ðakovo from Osijek in about 40 minutes by one of several daily trains for roughly 20 Kn one way. The Ðakovo train station is 1 km (½ mi) east of the center, at the opposite end of Kralja Tomislava.

Fodor'sChoice In Ðakovo's town center is the majestic redbrick, neo-Gothic **Ðakovačka**
★ **Katedrala** *(Ðakovo Cathedral)*, which was commissioned by the Bishop of Ðakovo, Josip Juraj Strossmayer (1815–1905), and designed by architect Frederick Schmidt. Consecrated in 1882 after two decades of construction, the three-nave structure is distinguished by two steeples towering to 274 feet, by beehivelike cones on either side of the entrance, and by a pinnacled cupola. The inside walls feature colorful biblical scenes—some representing the life of St. Peter, the cathedral's patron saint—painted over 12 years by the father and son team of Alexander and Ljudevit Seitz. The striking blue ceiling is dotted with gold stars; and the floor is paved with impressive red, yellow, and black checkered tile. ⊠ *Trg Strossmayera* ☎ *031/811–784* ⊗ *Daily 8–noon and 3–6.*

Just north of the cathedral is the **Spomen-muzej Biskupa Josipa Jurja Strossmayera** *(Strossmayer Museum* ⊠ *Luke Botića 2* ☎ *No phone* ⌨ *10 Kn* ⊗ *Tues.–Fri. 8–7, Sat. 8–2),* which presents the life of the influential bishop by displaying some of his effects and writings.

Close to the train station, a 10-minute walk from the cathedral and the town center if you follow ulica Matije Gupca but still very much in town, you will notice the unmistakable smell of horse. That is because you are approaching the **Lipizzaner stud farm,** where several dozen of these prized white horses are trained. Although there are generally no scheduled events here except during the Ðakovo Embroidery Festival, you will probably be allowed in to take a glimpse of the horses while training if you stop by in the morning. ⊠ *Augusta Šenoe 45* ☎ *031/813–286.*

WHERE TO EAT

$–$$$ ✕ **Gradski Podrum.** The Ðakovo Lion's Club meets under the vaulted brick ceiling of this cellar restaurant once a month, amid several fine paintings and two not-so-fine, tacky ones. The menu, which focuses on grilled, Balkan-style meats as well as poultry and a scrumptious variety of *palačinke* filled with jam, walnuts, chocolate sauce, or sweet curd-cheese, is only in Croatian and in German. ⊠ *Ulica Hrv. Velikana 9* ☎ *031/813–199* ▭ *AE, DC, MC, V.*

WHERE TO STAY

¢ ⊡ **Croatia-Tourist.** Ðakovo does not have much in the way of accommodation, but this homey if uninspiringly named hotel offers a handful of bright, comfy rooms, some of which are fancier than others. All have delightful white closets built into the walls on each side of the bed, but there is otherwise a dearth of frills (such as cable TV or air-conditioning). The hotel's spacious restaurant is among the best in town, with a decent range of fish and meat specialties, as well as fried frogs' legs and even fried brains. For dessert, try a walnut-filled *palačinke* topped off with chocolate sauce. Pros: good price, attractive rooms, near the cathedral. Cons: 25-minute walk from train station. ⊠*P. Preradovića 25, 31400* ☎*031/813–391* 🖷*031/814–063* ☎*8 rooms* ⌂*In-room: no a/c, safe, no TV. In-hotel: restaurant, no elevator* ⊟*AE, DC, MC, V* 🍴*BP.*

POŽEGA

66 km (41 mi) southeast of Bjelovar, 150 km (94 mi) southeast of Zagreb, 96 km (60 mi) southwest of Osijek.

As you cannot fail to notice on the huge, user-friendly maps posted about town, Požega's *industrijska zona* (industrial zone) is about the same size as the adjacent town center. And yet Požega (pop. 21,000)—in the center of the fertile, vineyard-rich Požega Valley, which the ancient Romans knew as "Vallis Aurea," or Golden Valley—is the prettiest city in central Slavonia. Požega was first mentioned in historical documents in 1227, but not much remains on the ground of that early era of local history. Stari Grad, a 13th-century fortress, today exists only as a small, thickly wooded hilltop park right beside the town center. As evident from the litter scattered here and there, and by young lovers you pass on benches in the woods, some folks are given to partying and necking in this otherwise pleasant park—within easy view of the rear windows of a nearby monastery. During the 150-year-long period of Ottoman rule that began in 1537, Požega become central Slavonia's most important administrative and military center. With the expulsion of the Turks in 1688, a new era of Habsburg control ensued. In 1739 the town was ravaged by a plague that killed 798 citizens. But by the mid-18th century it had become a vibrant university center, and the town core was fast on its way to assuming its present appearance. By the 19th century Požega's cultural dynamism had earned it a reputation as the "Athens of Slavonia." In 1847 it became the first city to officially adopt the Croatian language. The construction of the central Slavonian railway, which began in 1894, was vital to the local economy as the 20th century arrived. As with much of Slavonia's interior, reaching Požega is easiest by car. By train, it takes about three hours to get here from Osijek (53 Kn), with a transfer in Našice.

Trg Sv. Trojstva *(Holy Trinity Square)* is Požega's most celebrated public space, though the large parking lot at its center undermines its beauty a bit. Notice the striking baroque archways on the late-18th-century building that houses City Hall. The votive pillar is from 1749, built in memory of 798 local residents who perished in a plague a decade earlier. An inscription explains that the pillar was sculpted by one Gabriel Granici at a cost of 2,000 eggs and 300 forints. He didn't eat the eggs or give them to his relatives, though: he used them to cement the pillar's marble sand.

Opposite the votive pillar, the **Franjevački Samostan i Crkva Duha Sve-toga** *(Franciscan Monastery and Church of the Holy Spirit)* was built in the late 19th century on the foundations of a 13th-century Gothic church ravaged by the Turks. Inside are impressive baroque altars and paintings, and a crypt (under the sanctuary) where a number of prominent local citizens—judges, political leaders, and nobility—are buried, including friar Luka Ibrišimović, credited with liberating the Požega area from the Turks. The monastery has a library of some 15,000 books, many of them rare historic volumes. ⊠ *Trg Sv. Trojstva* 🕾 *No phone* ⊙ *Weekdays 9:30–11:30 and 5–6, Sat. 9–11:30.*

At the corner of the main square, in an imposing 18th-century building, is the **Gradski muzej** *(City Museum)*, whose collection of some 30,000 items comprises almost 20 display rooms on three floors covering regional archaeology, history, art, and ethnography from prehistoric times to the present day. You'll find paintings by regional artists, including family portraits by the renowned 19th-century painter Gustav Poša, and early-20th-century work by Miroslav Kraljević. There are also regional folk costumes and embroidery; ancient pottery and jewelry; artifacts from the Roman occupation of the region; and, yes, plenty of rocks, minerals, and fossils to wonder at, too. ⊠ *Matice Hrvatske 1* 🕾 *034/312–946* 🖃 *10 Kn* ⊙ *Weekdays 10–noon, weekends by appointment.*

The town's main ecclesiastical attraction, the Gothic **Crkva Sv. Lovre** *(Church of St. Lawrence)*, was built in the 14th century on the foundations of an even older church; until the Jesuits arrived in town in the late 17th century, it was dedicated to St. Mary. Impressive medieval frescoes adorn on its south wall, and in the sanctuary you can see a Renaissance tabernacle. ⊠ *A. Kanižlića* 🕾 *No phone* ⊙ *Daily 8–1.*

On a capacious shaded square in the town center is one of Slavonia's loveliest baroque churches, **Župa Sv. Terezije Aliviske** *(Church of St. Theresa of Avila)*. Completed in 1763, it is marked by a single nave and two side chapels; and unusually, it has series of double volutes (spirals) on each side of its otherwise largely ordinary, yellow facade. The interior is dominated by a grand altar blending baroque and rococo elements, and rococo pews carved from oak as well as impressive wall and ceiling frescoes made in 1898 and 1899 by the famous Croatian painters Celestin Medović and Oton Iveković—including Medović's striking scene on the sanctuary ceiling of St. Theresa ascending to heaven. The six stained-glass windows were added in the late 19th century. ⊠ *Trg Sv. Terezije 13* 🕾 *No phone* ⊙ *Weekdays 8:30–12:30 and 5–6:15, Sat. 8:30–12:30.*

WHERE TO EAT

$–$$ ✕**Pizza Zrinski Bar.** This restaurant stands out a bit from the many others in the town center for its ample outdoor seating and cozy rustic interior. You can choose between some 20 appealing pizzas plus a small selection of the usual Croatian pastas, grilled meats, and salads. The interior has wooden benches and tables, but the bar is the focal point (hence the name). On a nice day the tables out front make for a pleasant place to fuel up before heading on. ⊠*Mesnička 5* ☎*034/313–222* ⊟*AE, DC, MC, V.*

$–$$ ✕**Restoran Obrtnički Dom.** Just down the road from the Vila Stanišic, the Obrtnički Dom gives you a choice between a somewhat spuriously elegant interior with folksy Croatian tunes for background music or, in fair weather, outdoor seating in wicker chairs facing a shaded park. The simple fare ranges from grilled meats to grilled carp. ⊠*Dr. Franje Tuđmana 9* ☎*034/271–213* ⊟*AE, DC, MC, V.*

WHERE TO STAY

¢ ⛏**Vila Stanišic.** The simple rooms in this modern boutique hotel are smallish, but otherwise have what it takes for a good night's sleep: pleasant peach-hued walls; either a king-size bed (half the rooms) or two twin beds; and extra furniture including a desk and at least one armchair. Most of the bathrooms have showers only, so if you want a tub, be sure to request it. Also, only two rooms have refrigerators, but you probably won't need one. The in-house restaurant offers reasonable (entrées 45 Kn–75 Kn), traditional fare like grilled meats and grilled carp, plus delectable palačinke (crepes) with walnut stuffing and bathed in whipped-egg-and-wine sauce. Locals come here to drink (in a civilized manner) and smoke. The hotel is just a 10-minute walk from the train station. Pros: between the train station and the town center, on-site dining. Cons: the restaurant doubles as a bar and can get smoky, smallish rooms, few frills. ⊠*Dr. F. Tuđmana 10, 34000* ☎*034/312–168* 📠*034/272–608* ✉*leonardo.perinovic@zg.hinet.hr* 🛏*18 rooms* &*In-room: dial-up, refrigerator (some). In-hotel: restaurant, room service* ⊟*AE, DC, MC, V* ⦿|*BP.*

BJELOVAR

74 km (46 mi) east of Zagreb, 180 km (112 mi) west of Osijek.

Bjelovar (pop. 42,000) is the first major town you encounter east of Zagreb in what can already be considered Slavonia; a stopover here of either several hours or a night before you head on toward Osijek is well worth the easy detour. Situated on a low plateau, Bjelovar has long been one of Croatia's leading centers of agriculture, livestock breeding, and lumber.

Bjelovar was first mentioned as a settlement in records dating back to the 15th century, and it has an attractive historic center with one of Croatia's loveliest town squares, Trg Eugenia Kvaternika. Once a pasture, the square is today sublimely shaded by tall horse chestnut, plane, and pine trees, and its lovingly tended flower beds and charming bandstand—surrounded by statues of four saints dating from the 1770s—make it all the more inviting. Last but not least, it's home to a small but moving memorial to more than 100 residents of Slavonia who died in the Yugoslav war.

Morning is the best time to visit the main square, when the outdoor market, **Šetalište Dr. Ivše Lebovića**—one of Croatia's largest and liveliest—really comes alive with tables full of fruits, vegetables, and flowers. ⊠ *Trg Eugenia Kvaternika* ☎ *No phone* ☉ *Mon.–Sat. 7–4, Sun. 7–1.*

On the south side of the main square is the town's key ecclesiastical landmark, the **Crkva svetog Terezija Avilske** *(Church of Saint Theresa of Avila)*, completed in 1772. Its yellow, baroque facade blends several eras of architecture and is adorned by white false columns and volutes (spirals). ⊠ *Trg Eugenia Kvaternika* ☎ *No phone* ☉ *Weekdays 8–noon and 2–4, Sat. 8–noon.*

WHERE TO EAT

$$ ✕ **Bjelovar.** This aptly named, low-lit restaurant is just a five-minute walk from the main square. Sit down under a brick-arched ceiling amid walls adorned by sepia-toned photos of old Bjelovar, and choose between 30 types of pizza, plus grilled meats, steaks, and salads. ⊠ *Augusta Šenoe 19* ☎ *043/242–186* ☰ *AE, DC, MC, V.*

$$ ✕ **Golub.** Deep in a plane-tree-shaded courtyard, a 10-minute walk
★ from the main square, is the restaurant locals go to for fine dining. The lighting is low and pleasant, and the decor is a conscientious mix of chic and rustic. On the menu you'll find everything from soups and salads to grilled meats, pastas, steaks, and wild game. The extensive wine list includes choice options from all over Croatia and abroad. ⊠ *Franjevačka 6* ☎ *043/244–620* ☰ *AE, DC, MC, V.*

WHERE TO STAY

$ ⌂ **Hotel Central.** True, you might not be inspired to write home about this slightly worn, concrete, boxlike place, which could use a bit of sprucing up, but it's the only reliable lodging option in the heart of town. The simply furnished, red-carpeted, wood-floored rooms are pleasant enough for a good night's sleep, and the service is friendly. Pros: right by the main square, reasonable rates, friendly service. Cons: a bit worn, no a/c, tiny elevator. ⊠ *Vatroslava Lisinskog, 2, 43000* ☎ *043/242–473* ⊜ *043/243–133* ✍ *turist@bj.htnet.hr* ⌨ *46 rooms* ⌂ *In-room: refrigerator, no a/c. In-hotel: restaurant, public Internet, parking (no fee)* ☰ *AE, DC, MC, V* ⦿ *BP.*

FESTIVALS

Bjelovar hosts an annual Terezijana Theresa's Days festival in June. The main event, alongside various musical and other performances, is a stage presentation of Maria Theresa's visit to town.

**OFF THE
BEATEN
PATH**

Daruvar. The ancient Romans called the town of Daruvar (pop. 9,815) Aquae Balissae—and they knew a good spa site when they saw one. On the forested slopes of the Papuk Hills, 40 km (25 mi) southeast of Bjelovar and just west of Papuk National Park, Daruvar is Slavonia's prettiest place to sit and soak. Though a pain in the neck to reach by public transport, it is a more atmospheric complex of baths than the comparatively bland, modern facility in Bizovac, much farther to the east (and a lot closer to Osijek). The present-day face of Daruvar's center—including an imposing two-story baroque manor house—took shape from 1760 to 1777 within the estate of Count Antun Jankovič. Among other buildings with which the family endowed Daruvar are the key structures of its spa, **Daruvarske Toplice,** (⊠ *Julijev park, Daruvar 43500* ☏ *043/623–623 or 043/623–000*) which they had built between 1810 and 1818 on the foundations of the very baths the Romans once enjoyed. Celebrated for its mildly alkaline water, which is said to be good for treating various ailments, the bath complex also includes a large park full of rare old trees. The spa is open daily 7 AM to 9 PM. Beyond having two 18th-century baroque churches also worth a look, Daruvar and some nearby villages carry the unusual distinction of being home to Croatia's large population of ethnic Czechs—many of whom still speak their native tongue and observe Czech customs. In this light, it is not surprising that Daruvar is also the home of a major brewery that produces Staročeško pivo *(Old Bohemian Beer)* —based on an old Czech recipe, of course. There are around five buses daily that make the one-hour trip from Bjelovar and Virovitica, but if you have a car available, that is by far the more convenient option. *Daruvar Tourist Information* ⊠ *Julijev park 1, Daruvar* ☏ *043/623–000.*

SLAVONIA ESSENTIALS

BUS TRAVEL
Numerous daily buses connect Osijek and the rest of Slavonia, including Vukovar and Đakovo. However, a train may get you where you're going faster or at a more convenient time, so it's a good idea to check at the railway station next door before hopping on board the bus. Timetables are posted in the Osijek Bus Station. Around 10 buses daily (on weekends; more buses weekdays) make the 45-minute trip between Osijek and Vukovar, for 28 Kn one way. You can get to Đakovo from Osijek in about 40 minutes by bus for about 20 Kn one way. The bus station is closer to the town center than the train station.

Information **Bjelovar Bus Station** (⊠ *Tomaša G. Masaryka [at the corner of Matice Hrvatske] Bjelovar* ☏ *043/241–269*). **Osijek Bus Station** (⊠ *Bartula Kašića, by trg L. Ružičke, Osijek* ☏ *060/334–4466*). **Požega Bus Station** (⊠ *Industrijska 2, Požega* ☏ *034/273–13*). **Vukovar Bus Station** (⊠ *Olajnica, Vukovar* ☏ *032/441–829 or 060/337–799*).

CAR RENTALS
Although you certainly don't need a car to get from Zagreb to Osijek and then around Osijek itself, having wheels will make it a whole lot easier to shuttle around Slavonia's other towns, which are scattered far and wide. You might consider taking a train to Osijek and then renting a car here for a day or two; small cars go for around 400 Kn per day, including taxes, insurance, and unlimited mileage.

Information Budget (✉ *Kapucinska 39, Osijek* ☎ *053/1211-500*). **Euro-Buba** (✉ *Hravtske Republike 43/1, Osijek* ☎ *031/214-753*). **Hertz** (✉ *Gundulićeva 32, Osijek* ☎ *031/200-422*).

INTERNET

One of Slavonia's few Internet cafés—and Osijek's only one as of this writing—is the aptly named VIP Internet Caffe. It's more a bar, actually, with a spacious terrace out front and a handful of computers just inside that you can use for 14 Kn/hour.

Information VIP Internet Caffe (✉ *L. Jägera, Osijek* ☎ *031/212-313*).

POST OFFICE

Information Osijek Post Office (✉ *K. A. Stepinca 17, Osijek* ☎ *031/253-868*).

TRAIN TRAVEL

Six trains run daily between Zagreb and Osijek (around 110 Kn one way), one of these being an express, three-hour run; most take four to five hours. The route cuts right through the heart of Slavonia, giving you a real sense of the sweeping vistas of Croatia's breadbasket.

Information Bjelovar Train Station (✉ *Tomislavov trg, Bjelovar* ☎ *043/241-263* or *060/333-444*). **Osijek Train Station** (✉ *Trg L. Ružičke, Osijek* ☎ *060/333-444*). **Požega Train Station** (✉ *Cirakijeva, Požega* ☎ *034/273-911* or *060/333-444*).

VISITOR INFORMATION

Information The Web sites of the tourist boards responsible for **Osijek-Baranja County** (⊕ *www.tzosbarzup.hr*) and **Vukovar-Srijem County** (⊕ *www.tzvsz.hr*) have information on towns within their purview without individual sites.

Bizovac Tourist Information (✉ *Krajla Tomislava 138, Bizovac* ☎ *031/675-770*). **Bjelovar Tourist Information** (✉ *Trg Eugenia Kvaternika 4, Bjelovar* ☎ *043/243-944*). **Daruvar Tourist Information** (✉ *Julijey park 1, Daruvar* ☎ *043/623-000*). **Đakovo Tourist Information** (✉ *Krajla Tomislava 3, Đakovo* ☎ *031/812-319* ⊕ *www.tz-djakovo.hr*).

Osijek Tourist Information (✉ *Županijska 2, Osijek* ☎ *031/203-755* ⊕ *www.osijek.hr*). **Park Prirode Papuk** (*Papuk Nature Park*) headquarters (✉ *Trg Gospe Voćinske bb, Papuk* ☎ *033/565-269* ⊕ *www.pp-papuk.hr*).

Vukovar Tourist Information (✉ *J. J. Strossmayera 15, Vukovar* ☎ *032/442-889*).

Istria

WORD OF MOUTH

"I would spend a minimum of 3 days in Istria, with Rovinj as the perfect place to rest your bags, take day trips from, and have wonderful dinners in."
—LAZnSTEVEgo2HR

"We stayed in Rovinj and did day trips by bus to Pula and Porec. Don't stay in Pula. Rovinj and Porec are much more charming."
—christycruz

Updated by
Betsy Maury

THE WORD CONJURES SOMETHING MAGICAL as it rolls off the tongue: *Istria*. Beyond sounding poetic, however, the name of this region of Croatia is derived from the name of the Illyrian people who occupied the area well before the Romans first arrived in the 3rd century BC—namely, the Histrians, whose chief architectural legacy comprised numerous hilltop fortresses. In the northwest corner of Croatia bordering Slovenia, the triangular-shaped Istrian peninsula looks rather like a bunch of grapes—and, given its strong viticultural heritage, some might say this is not a coincidence.

Much of Europe's history has passed through Istria for more than a thousand years, not least the history associated with three great civilizations—the Roman, the Germanic, and the Slavic. Centuries of Venetian rule later reinforced by years of Italian occupation between the world wars have left a sizable Italian minority here, and Italian influence is apparent in the architecture, the cuisine, and the local dialect. Here, even the effects of the concrete-box style of communist-era architecture seem relatively minimal compared to the overall sense of a much deeper past suggested by the rich mix of architectural styles—from a whole array of well-preserved Roman ruins to early-Christian churches, Byzantine mosaics, and Romanesque basilicas; from breathtakingly well-preserved medieval towns, towers, and town walls to baroque palaces and Austro-Hungarian fortifications.

The region's principal city and port, Pula, is on the tip of the peninsula and is best known for its remarkably preserved 1,900-year-old Roman amphitheater and Forum as well as the Triumphal Arch of the Sergians. Close by, the beautifully nurtured island retreat of Brijuni National Park can be visited in a day. Towns along the west coast have an unmistakable Venetian flavor left by more than 500 years of Venetian occupation (1238–1797). Poreč and Rovinj, Croatia's two most popular seaside resorts, are both endowed with graceful campanili, loggias, and reliefs of the winged lion of St. Mark, patron saint of Venice. Although the effects of package tourism have long encroached—to varying degrees—on the immediate outskirts of various towns, most notably Poreč among Istria's largest coastal destinations, Rovinj, though likewise brimming with tourists in high season, retains more of its ravishing historic beauty and redolence than almost any other town on the Adriatic. A side trip to the romantic hill towns of Motovun and Grožnjan will prove unforgettable, whether as a brief excursion from the sea in the warmer months or as a more substantial autumn journey. This inland area is particularly rich in truffles and mushrooms, and from mid-September to late October these local delicacies are celebrated with a series of gastronomic festivals.

EXPLORING ISTRIA

ABOUT THE RESTAURANTS

Food in Istria is more sophisticated and varied than in the rest of Croatia. Culinary tourism is one of the region's biggest draws, and you will get (for a price) a markedly better meal here than elsewhere in the coun-

ISTRIA TOP 5

■ Take a walk through the Roman Area in Pula, where you will find one of the world's biggest and best-preserved amphitheaters (in fact, the sixth-largest in the world).

■ Have dinner at one of Rovinj's elegant seaside restaurants (Blu and Monte are among the city's finest dining establishments).

■ A scenic drive through the medieval towns of Grožnjan and Motovun in the hilly interior is not to be missed; these are villages that time seems to have forgotten.

■ Enjoy a tour of the amazing 6th-century Byzantine mosaics at St. Euphrasius Basilica in Poreč; St. Euphrasius is one of the best-preserved early-Christian churches in Europe.

■ As in Italy, gelato is available everywhere in dozens of flavors all over Istria. Grab a cone and enjoy the early evening passeggiata, a stroll through any town square in the evening, just like a local.

3

try. The quaysides and old town squares have a plethora of touristy restaurants, and many new exceptional places have opened in recent years, helping to set the standard for the country's gastronomical identity. Istrian food today means fresh and simple seafood dishes, locally made *fuži* (egg noodles), elegant truffle sauces and flavors, and earthy *pršut* (air-dried local ham), alongside the familiar Italian staples of pizza and pasta. Seafood is usually grilled, baked in sea salt, or served *crudo* (raw) with a dash of local olive oil. Truffles are the superstars of the interior villages and work their way onto autumn menus in pastas, game dishes, and on beds of homemade polenta. Keep your eyes peeled for traditional favorites like *supa*, a brew of red wine, sugar, olive oil, pepper, and warm, toasted bread; and *meneštra*, an Istrian minestrone soup, both popular in winter. All these gourmet aspirations mean that dining in Istria can be costly relative to much of inland Croatia. Average prices for main courses start at 40 Kn for pasta and pizza, and move up to 80 Kn, or even twice that, for seafood (much of which is priced by the kilogram) and certain beef dishes. For a quick and cheap, albeit greasy, lunch, you can buy a *burek* (a curd-cheese or meat-filled pastry) in a bakery for around 10 Kn apiece.

ABOUT THE HOTELS
In Istria, as in most other reaches of the Croatian coast, it's basically a question of whether to stay at the big, impersonal resorts on the beach, with a full range of services and activities available, or at smaller, boutique, sometimes family-run hotels. Either way it's imperative to book ahead, as most places—big and small—book up fast for the summer months. Bear in mind that most hotels and pensions impose a surcharge—usually 20%—for stays of fewer than three nights in high season, since they cater primarily to tourists who stay a week or two. Hotels listed here are geared for the traveler who is looking to stay in Istria for fewer than seven nights in the same city. If you plan to stay in Poreč, Pula, Rovinj, or Labin for longer than that, a package tour

company like the U.K.-based **Inghams** (☎020/8780–4400 ⊕*www.ing-hams.co.uk*) or **Thomson** (☎0870/156–0079 ⊕*www.thomson.co.uk*) arranges excellent half- or full-board packages with airfare from the United Kingdom for the best per-night rates available. As a budget alternative to staying in a hotel, various tourist agencies can help you book a room for around 250 Kn or more for two people, though prices may edge upward later in the day, when it is presumed that tourists are more desperate.

WHAT IT COSTS IN EUROS (€) AND CROATIAN KUNA (KN)					
	¢	$	$$	$$$	$$$$
RESTAURANTS	under 20 Kn	20 Kn–35 Kn	35 Kn–60 Kn	60 Kn–80 Kn	over 80 Kn
HOTELS In euros	under €75	€75–€125	€125–€175	€175–€225	over €225
HOTELS In kuna	under 550 Kn	550 Kn–925 Kn	925 Kn–1,300 Kn	1,300 Kn–1,650 Kn	over 1,650 Kn

Restaurant prices are for a main course at dinner. Hotel prices are for two people in a double room in high season, excluding taxes and service charges.

TIMING
If you are partial to sun and the idea of swimming in the warm, blue-green waters of the Adriatic, and you don't mind crowds and a bit of extra expense, by all means visit Istria in summer. Otherwise, this tourism-trampled region might be best saved for spring or fall (the water stays warm well into September), when you might save as much as 15% to 20% on lodging. The season in Istria for many restaurants and bars is Easter through the first week in November. You won't find much going on at all in January.

PULA

292 km (182½ mi) southwest of Zagreb.

Today an industrial port town and Istria's chief administrative center (pop. 86,000), as well as a major tourist destination, Pula became a Roman colony in the 1st century BC. This came about a century after the decisive defeat by the Romans, in 177 BC, of the nearby Histrian stronghold of Nesactium, prompting the Histrian king Epulon to plunge a sword into his chest lest he fall into the hands of the victors, who indeed conquered all of Istria. Remains from Pula's ancient past have survived up to the present day: as you drive in on the coastal route toward its choice setting on a bay near the southern tip of the Istrian peninsula, the monumental Roman amphitheater blocks out the sky on your left. Under Venetian rule (1331–1797), Pula was architecturally neglected, even substantially dismantled. Many structures from the Roman era were pulled down, and stones and columns were carted off across the sea to Italy to be used for new buildings there. Pula's second great period of development took place in the late 19th century, under the Habsburgs, when it served as the chief base for the Imperial Austro-Hungarian Navy. Today it's as much working city as tourist

GREAT ITINERARIES

IF YOU HAVE 3 DAYS

There is so much to see in Istria that three days is a must, though it may seem like a rush if that's all the time you have. Start in Pula, as suggested below, if you are coming from Zagreb; if from the north (from Slovenia or Italy), start with Rovinj instead. Either way, by all means do visit Rovinj. If you are interested in Istria's ecclesiastical heritage, you may want to prioritize Poreč over Pula; if Roman ruins are more your thing, by all means focus on Pula, whose architecture also gives you more of a sense of Istria's Austro-Hungarian past. On the first day, start off in **Pula**. Visit the Arena and at least take a stroll to the Forum. By all means spend the night here. A short drive or bus ride toward the Verudela or Stoja resort area gets you to eminently swimmable, if rocky, stretches of shoreline. The next morning, head off to **Rovinj**. Visit the 18th-century baroque Crkva Sv Eufemije, and just revel in strolling about the most beautiful town on the Istrian coast. On the third day, spend some more time in or around Rovinj, whether strolling the Old Town or taking a dip in the sea. If you're up to it, particularly if you have a car, move on to **Poreč** to see the Eufrazijeva Basilica.

IF YOU HAVE 5 DAYS

Spend your first day as above, but consider adding an excursion from Pula to **Vodnjan** or **Brijuni National Park,** depending on whether you're more interested in Vodnjan's countryside, medieval atmosphere, mummies, and food, or in Brijuni's natural splendors and luxurious, seaside ambience. Move on to **Rovinj** by the evening of Day 2 or the morning of Day 3, spending at least a full day or more there. On Day 4, it's on to **Poreč.** Perhaps go inland and spend the night in **Motovun.** On Day 5, if you're driving, take a look at **Grožnjan** as well before heading back. If you're getting around by bus, it's time to head back to a major town on the coast. Indeed, why not spend a few more hours in Rovinj or Pula before bidding adieu to Istria?

IF YOU HAVE 7 DAYS

Spend your first five days as above, but be sure to supplement your time in Rovinj, Pula, and Porec with a lunch in **Labin,** on the east coast of Istria; if you're driving from Zagreb do it on the way to the more important towns; if you're driving through the countryside that takes you through both **Motovun** and **Grožnjan,** spend a night in or near Motovun. Before going inland, you may want to pay a visit to Vrsar and the Limski kanal or, instead, Baradine Cave. If you have a car, you can do so as you go inland or on your way back to the coast; if traveling by bus, you can get to these places most easily on a group excursion from Poreč or Rovinj. You may want to visit **Novigrad,** too, especially if you're driving, but save Umag for a 10-day trip. Spend Day 6 in Grožnjan then go back to Porec or, better yet, Rovinj for the night. On Day 7, proceed to **Pula,** with a stop in **Labin** if you haven't been there yet and will be going farther east. Perhaps spend your final night in Labin as well.

3

IF YOU LIKE

OLD-WORLD CHARM

Rovinj is itself a complete pleasure. Istria's star attraction occupies a fantastic setting, with centuries-old red-roofed houses clustered around the hill of a former island, and is crowned by the monumental baroque Crkva Sv Eufemije (Church of St. Euphemia). It's a ravishing place that draws artists, writers, musicians, and actors. Throughout the summer, the winding cobbled streets are crowded with vacationers from all reaches of Europe.

ARCHITECTURE

A visit to Istria without a look at the magnificent Roman Arena—the sixth-largest structure of its type in the world—and Pula's Forum would be almost beside the point. You needn't go to Italy to revel in what the Romans left behind. Pula, which like other major towns on the coast was in Venetian hands for centuries, also served for decades as the Aus-tro-Hungarian Empire's chief naval base. As Istria's largest city and chief administrative center, it saw a spate of relatively bland, concrete-box-style construction during the communist era as part of Yugoslavia. However, Pula—as much as any other place in the peninsula—displays a richly layered architectural heritage unique to Istria.

CHURCHES

From Poreč's magnificent Eufrazijeva Basilica—among the most perfectly preserved Christian churches in Europe and one of the most important monuments of Byzantine art on the Adriatic—to Rovinj's Crkva Sv Eufemije, to Pula's Katedrala svete Marije, Istria has a wealth of religious sites that are among the most important not only in the Mediter-ranean but the world. Through them, you also gain a special appreciation for the rich span of the region's history, from Roman times through Venetian rule and beyond.

HILL TOWNS

Instead of searching for imaginary castles from *The Lord of the Rings* in the wilds of New Zealand, you can visit such magical, strikingly preserved, onetime fortress towns as Motovun and Grožnjan and smaller gems like Buje and Gračišće.

FOOD & WINE

In that order, Istria is the home of one of the Adriatic's most alluring gastronomic traditions. Here you can have not only a whole host of dishes complemented by the much sought-after truffle, but also such Istrian specialties as sheep's cheese, *pršut* (air-dried ham), wild asparagus, and *supa* (a brew of red wine, sugar, olive oil, pepper, and warm, toasted bread), and also such meaty-spicy fare as *čevapčići*.

town, where Roman ruins and Austro-Hungarian architecture serve as backdrop for the bustle of everyday life amid a bit of communist-era soot and socialist realism, too. James Joyce lived here for a short time, in 1904–05, before fleeing what he dismissed as a cultural backwater for Trieste. What's more, there are some outstanding restaurants and a number of pleasant family-run hotels, not to mention the nearby resort area of Verudela, where seaside tourism thrives in all its sooth-ing, sunny sameness.

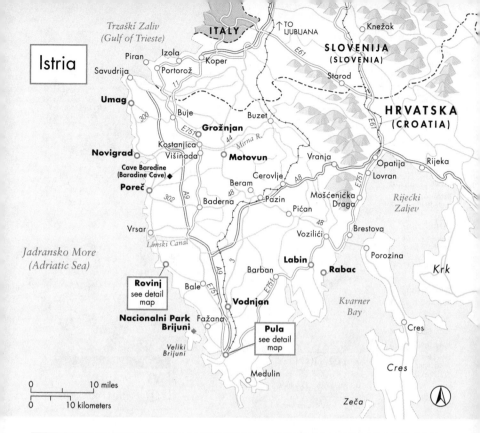

EXPLORING PULA

Pula's compact commercial and administrative center is situated on a small, semicircular protrusion of land in the Puljski Zaljev (Bay of Pula), which faces west into the Adriatic. Several ringlike streets radiate inward from the port, culminating in the small, fortress-capped hill at the center of this semicircle. Most of the cultural and historical sites are along this web of streets to the south, west, and north of the hill, with the huge Roman amphitheater on the northeastern fringes of this zone (accessible via Giardini and then Istarska ulica, on the landward side of the hill, a couple of blocks in from the bay); the bus station is another few minutes' walk from there. Meanwhile, a long walk (or a short drive) south of the city center are suburbs that culminate with the Verudela and Stoja peninsulas, home to bustling tourist resorts, beaches, and some excellent restaurants.

Numbers in the text correspond to numbers in the margin and on the Pula map.

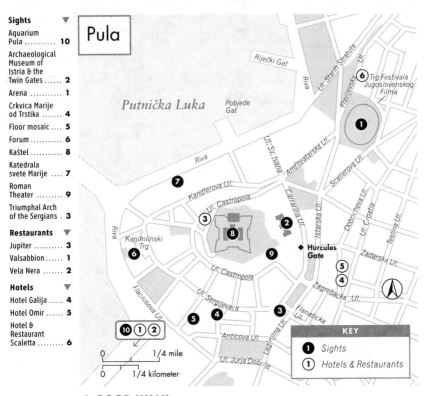

A GOOD WALK

The most convenient spot to begin a walk in Pula is the most visible, at the **Arena ❶**, a five-minute stroll from the bus station and easily accessible by car. By taking Istarska ulica toward the Giardini, you will be heading into Pula's Old Town and central, bustling pedestrian street, Sigirijeva ulica. Before you even reach the Giardini, though, you will pass by a small, shaded park to your right, a nice place to rest after exploring the amphitheater. From here you can either proceed along the Giardini, or else cross the street on the other side of the park to the **Archaeological Museum of Istria & the Twin Gates ❷**. This marks the entrance to the east slope of the fortress hill—which you can cross in about 15 minutes as a shortcut (timewise, if not in terms of exertion) to the Forum on the other side, and thus avoid or postpone the crowds on the Giardini and Sigirijeva ulica. If you continue on Istarska ulica, however, after one more block you'll reach the start of the Giardini, Pula's liveliest one-block stretch of road, whether by day or night—chock-full of outdoor cafés set back from the street by an impressively broad, shaded sidewalk. Two blocks on, you'll see the **Triumphal Arch of the Sergians ❸** to your right. Just after the arch, on the right, is Pula's very own statue of James Joyce, sitting, cane in one hand and elbow on a café table, staring contemplatively skyward; a nearby wall plaque marks the onetime language school where he taught for six months

A Wreck of a Vacation

On August 14, 1908, the *Baron Gautsch*, a passenger ferry owned by Austria's royal family, was on its way from Kotor to Trieste when it collided with an undersea mine and sank 12½ km (8 mi) from Rovinj, claiming 240 lives.

One person's tragedy often becomes—years, decades, or centuries later—another's vacation. This certainly holds true as regards the longstanding tradition of diving to shipwrecks, of which Istria's coastal waters hold several good examples. Almost 100 years later, the 85-meter-long, 12-meter-wide *Baron Gautsch* is considered one of the most beautiful dive sites in the world. With its upper deck at a depth of 28 meters, its lower deck at 36 meters, and its bottom at 42 meters, the site—now home to plenty of flora and fauna, including a whole lot of lobsters—caters to advanced divers while stirring the imaginations of many others.

From shipwrecks to caves and cliffs to coral reefs, Croatia has more than 85 officially registered dive sites. There are around a dozen other shipwrecks off the Istrian coast that make for popular dives. Near Novigrad lies the *Corleanus*, a suspected British spy ship that sank in 1945 after hitting a mine. And then there are the war ships *Dezza*, *Rossarol*, and *Flamingo*, as well as the ships *Draga*, *Varese*, *Tihany*, *Rimorchiatore*, *Istra*, *Relitto Nuovo*, *Josephine*, and *John Gilmoure*. Of course, Croatia's waters abound in shipwrecks well beyond Istria. For example, the waters off Krk Island are the resting place of the *Peltasis*, sunk in 1968 after smashing into rocks during a storm. At a depth of 7 to 32 meters, the ship is accessible to divers of all abilities.

Diving in Croatia is permitted to those in possession of a valid diving license issued by the Hrvatski ronilacki savez (Croatian Diving Association), which is good for one year and can be purchased for 100 Kn at authorized diving centers and clubs all along the coast. This permit allows you to dive only under the supervision of a diving center instructor. To dive alone, you must take this permit to a local Harbor Master's Office and pay a hefty 2,400 Kn. Permits are issued to those who hold a license or certificate from an internationally recognized diving school—including but not limited to the BSAC (British Sub-Aqua Club), CMAS (Conféderation Mondiale des Activités Subaquatiques), and IANTD (International Association of Nitrox and Technical Divers).

Although diving in Istria is possible year-round, optimal sea temperatures are to be enjoyed from May to November. Locations must be marked by orange or red buoys or flags (and, at night, fitted with a yellow or white light visible from 300 meters); the maximum allowable diving depth, when using a compressed-air cylinder, is 40 meters. Diving is prohibited in protected areas, including Brijuni National Park and Krka National Park.

Dive centers can be found in all the major destinations in Istria, including Poreč and Rovinj.

3

from October 1904. Proceeding along Sigirijeva ulica, you are now in the heart of Pula's Old Town. After four blocks there will be a parklike open space to your left. Turn left here for a detour to the 6th-century **Crkvica Marije od Trstika 4** and, nearby, an immaculately preserved 2nd-century **floor mosaic 5**. Back on Sigirijeva ulica, after two more blocks you are at the ancient Roman **6 Forum**. From here you can go on to Kandlerova ulica, which leads to **Katedrala svete Marije 7**. A right here—uphill, that is—will take you to the **8 Kaštel** and, on the way down the other side of the hill, to the **Roman Theater 9** and back to the Twin Gates.

TIMING

A leisurely stroll that covers Pula's key attractions and includes a stop for coffee and a snack will take two or three hours (depending in part on whether you also climb the fortress hill). Add to this a bona fide meal and a substantial visit to a museum or two, for example, and you're looking at all morning or all afternoon. But to really do Pula in a relaxing fashion (and perhaps stroll outside the center as well), a full day would be ideal.

WHAT TO SEE

10 Aquarium Pula. Pula's newest attraction opened in 2004 on the ground floor of the onetime Austro-Hungarian fortress in the resort complex of Verudela, a few kilometers from the city center. The aquarium was originally Croatia's first sea-turtle rescue center, which opened two years earlier. Its five rooms offer a colorful look at hundreds of sea creatures from the Adriatic's underwater world, and include a "touching pool" that allows you to touch a dogfish, turtle, sea urchin, crab, or sea squirt during limited periods of time. There are also exhibits of fishermen's traditional equipment and of underwater photography, and children's playgroups are regularly organized on the terrace out front. For an extra fee, a three-hour boat tour on nearby waters offers an educational program on the ins and outs of oceanography. ⊠ *Verudela* ☎ *052/381–402* ⊕ *www.aquarium.hr* 🖼 *25 Kn, boat tour 200 Kn* ☉ *May–Sept., daily 9–9; Oct.–Apr., weekends 11–5.*

2 Archaeological Museum of Istria & the Twin Gates. On passing through or past the 2nd-century gates, whose paired arches account for the name Porta Gemina (Twin Gates), you will find yourself amid a potpourri of Roman ruins on the shaded grounds of Pula's most intriguing museum, home to around 300,000 artifacts from prehistoric, Roman, and medieval times. ⊠ *Carrarina 3* ☎ *052/218–603* 🖼 *20 Kn* ☉ *May–Sept., Mon.–Sat. 9–8, Sun. 10–3; Oct.–Apr., weekdays 9–2.*

1 Arena *(Roman Amphitheater).* Designed to accommodate 22,000 spectators, Pula's arena is the sixth-largest building of its type in the world (after the Colosseum in Rome and similar arenas in Verona, Catania, Capua, and Arles). Construction was completed in the 1st century AD under the reign of Emperor Vespasian, and the Romans staged gladiator games here until such bloodthirsty sports were forbidden during the 5th century. During the 16th century, the Venetians planned to move the Arena stone by stone to Venice, where it was to be recon-

Fodor'sChoice
★

structed in its original form. The plan failed, and it has remained more or less intact, except for the original tiers of stone seats and numerous columns that were hauled away for other buildings. Today it is used for summer concerts (by musicians including Sting, James Brown, and Jose Carreras), opera performances, and the annual film festival in late July. The underground halls house a museum with large wooden oil presses and amphorae. ⊠ *Amfiteaterska ul* ☎ *052/219–028* 🖃 *30 Kn* ⊙ *May–Sept., daily 8–9; Oct.–Apr., daily 9–5.*

OFF THE
BEATEN
PATH

City Cemetery. For a peaceful and reflective stroll where few tourists tread, but without leaving the heart of Pula, walk over to the traffic circle just to the east of the Arena, where Flavijevska ulica meets ulica 43 Istarkse Divizije. Take the latter road to the left, and then the first road to your left. After a five-minute walk uphill you will arrive at Pula's hushed city cemetery, whose long rows flanked by tall cypresses, graves adorned with pictures of the departed, and view of Pula and the harbor below add up to a sublime and poignant atmosphere. From the cemetery, you can also see the nearby ruins of a centuries-old, albeit little-visited fortress (full of loose brickwork that makes for a risky walk if you opt to enter); a hiking trail will take you into a lovely pine forest just beyond the cemetery.

➍ **Crkvica Marije od Trstika** *(Chapel of St. Mary of Formosa).* In a green space between Sigirijeva ulica and the port, this now humble-looking stone structure was once part of a magnificent basilica built in the 6th century by Bishop Maximilian of Istria, during the reign of the Byzantine emperor Justinian. Fragments of the luxurious mosaics that once adorned it can be seen at the Archaeological Museum of Istria. Although the chapel itself is usually closed to visitors, it's occasionally used as a gallery space, which will give you a chance to take a peek at the interior. ⊠ *Between Sigirijeva ul and Flaciusova ul (left off Sigirijeva ul two blocks before the Forum).*

➎ **Floor mosaic.** The central scene of this large and lovely mosaic—which otherwise features geometric patterns and plants aplenty—is of the punishment of Dirce, who, as per the Greek legend, lies under the enraged bull to whose horns she is about to be fastened. Unearthed after World War II bombing, the mosaic, which was once part of a Roman house, can be viewed for free by looking down through a grating beside an uninspiring apartment building, a stone's throw from the Chapel of St. Mary of Formosa. ⊠ *Between Sigirijeva ul and Flaciusova ul (left off Sigirijeva ul two blocks before the Forum).*

➏ **Forum.** Still Pula's most important public meeting place after 2,000 years, the ancient Roman forum is today a spacious paved piazza ringed with cafés. There were once three temples here, of which only one remains. The perfectly preserved **Augustov Hram** *(Temple of Augustus* 🖃 *8 Kn* ⊙ *Weekdays 9–8:30, Sat. 2:30–8:30))* was built in the 1st century AD on the north side of the square. Next to it stands the **Gradska Palača** (Town Hall), which was erected during the 13th century using part of the Roman Temple of Diana as the back wall. The Renaissance arcade was added later.

NEED A
BREAK?
Stop at the chic but unpretentious Café Galerija Cvajner (⊠ *Forum 2*) for morning coffee or an evening aperitif. Inside, contemporary art and minimalist furniture play off against frescoes uncovered during restoration, and outdoor tables offer great views onto the Forum square.

❽ Kaštel *(Fortress).* Whether from the cathedral or elsewhere along Kandlerova ulica, a walk up the hill will lead you within minutes to the 17th-century Venetian fortress, the Kaštel, that towers over Pula's city center and houses the **Historical Museum of Istria.** Though the museum has a somewhat lackluster collection, including scale-model ships as well as Habsburg-era relics, it does carry the value-added benefit of allowing you to wander around its ramparts. But simply walking around its perimeter also ensures fine views of the city's shipyard below and, if you look to the north, the steeple of Vodnjan's church 12 km (7½ mi) away. ⊠ *Kaštel, off Kandlerova ul* ☎ *052/211–740 or 052/211–566* ☜ *15 Kn* ☉ *May–Sept., weekdays 8–7; Oct.–Apr., weekdays 9–5.*

❼ Katedrala svete Marije *(Cathedral of the Assumption of the Blessed Virgin Mary).* Built originally in the 4th century by the town's defense walls and facing the sea, Pula's star ecclesiastical attraction—more often called simply St. Mary's Cathedral—was transformed in the second half of the 5th century into a three-nave basilica. Extensive reconstruction that began in the 18th century was completed in 1924, with the adjacent campanile constructed in the 19th century from stones taken from the Arena. Note that the Roman-era mosaic on the floor of the central nave bears a 5th-century donor's inscription. ⊠ *Kandlerova ul* ☎ *No phone* ☜ *5 Kn* ☉ *Daily 9:30–7.*

❾ Roman Theater. If you make your way down from the Fortress along the eastern slope of the hill, toward the Archaeological Museum and the Twin Gates, you will pass right through the redolent ruins of the 2nd-century Roman Theater, a quiet, sublime spot to rest and reflect. ⊠ *Fortress Hill.*

❸ Triumphal Arch of the Sergians. Built by Salvia Postuma Sergia in 30 BC as a monument to three members of her family who excelled in battle and otherwise, this striking monument features some elaborate reliefs that inspired even Michelangelo to draw it during a 16th-century visit to Pula. The surrounding city gate and walls were removed in the 19th century to allow the city's expansion beyond the Old Town. ⊠ *Trg Portarata, between Giardini and ul Sergijevaca.*

NEED A
BREAK?
For a lively and aromatic atmosphere in which to have a shot of espresso, buy a banana, or just wander about gazing at food stands, do check out Pula's market square, Narodni trg. On one side of its stately, two-story market building—whose iron-and-glass construction was state-of-the-art when it opened to great fanfare in 1903—you'll find fruit and vegetable stands, and on the other side, cafés; inside are a fish market (downstairs) and fast-food eateries (second floor).

WHERE TO EAT

$$$$ ✕🏠 **Valsabbion.** This superb restaurant and hotel is 3 km (2 mi) from
Fodor'sChoice the city center, overlooking the sea. It was one of the first restaurants in
★ Croatia to specialize in what has come to be known as "slow food" (the
owner prefers the term "creative cuisine"). Many consider it the best
restaurant in Istria, if not all of Croatia. The menu changes regularly
depending on available produce, but you can expect such goodies as
frogfish in vine leaves or tagliatelle with aromatic herbs and pine nuts.
The lavender *semifreddo*—vanilla ice cream, pine nuts, and warm fig
sauce complemented by two long, delicate sticks of dark chocolate,
all served artistically on several plates arranged on a large mirror—is
simply divine. For all its unimpeachable elegance, the interior also feels
open and friendly. The small hotel is likewise top-notch, with 10 rooms
(at around €175) furnished in pine with cheerful colored linens, fresh
fruit, and flowers. There's a small swimming pool on the top floor
and a range of beauty treatments and aerobics courses. ✉*Pješčana
uvala IX/26* ☎052/218–033 ⊕*www.valsabbion.net* ⚖*Reservations
essential* ☰*AE, DC, MC, V* ⊗*Closed Jan.*

$$$–$$$$ ✕**Vela Nera.** In hot competition with Valsabbion—only a few hundred
★ yards away—Vela Nera is likewise located 3 km (2 mi) from the city
center, just above a yacht marina. Favorite dishes include pasta with
lobster and truffles, fish baked in a salt crust, and an ever-changing
range of creative seafood specialties. The quality of the wines matches
that of the cuisine, and the spacious, light-filled dining room makes
for a pleasant atmosphere in which to savor it all. ✉*Pješčana uvala*
☎*052/219–209* ⊕*www.velanera.hr* ⚖*Reservations essential* ☰*AE,
DC, MC, V.*

$$ ✕**Jupiter.** In a quiet street a couple of blocks' walk above the Forum,
this is Pula's premier place for budget, Italian-style fare. Try any of
its 18 types of pizza as you sip a glass of house red wine at one of the
rustic wooden tables on the rear terrace. There's a cozy little table in a
nook on your way up the stairs. ✉*Castrapola 38* ☎*052/214–333 or
052/222–002* ☰*AE, DC, MC, V.*

WHERE TO STAY

One reliable bet for private rooms is **Kompas Travel** (✉*Starih Statuta
4, 52100* ☎*052/212–511* 🖨*052/211–592* ✉*kompas.headquarters@
kompas-travel.com*), which also has offices in Rovinj and Poreč as well
as other towns in Istria and elsewhere in Croatia, and which, like other
similar agencies, also offers daytime excursions to Istria's top, out-of-
the-way exploring sites.

$ 🏠 **Hotel Omir.** A block from the newer Hotel Galija and likewise close
to Giardini, this small hotel offers rooms that, though cramped, have
vestibules that compensate. The dark hues are a touch somber. Pros:
central location, pet-friendly. Cons: street-side parking near the hotel
is hard to find, breakfast is very basic. ✉*Serđa Dobrića ul 6, 52100*
☎*052/218–186* ☎🖨*052/213–944* ⊕*www.hotel-omir.com* ⤢19

rooms ⟐ *In-room: no a/c (some), refrigerator. In-hotel: restaurant, some pets allowed* ⊟ *AE, DC, MC, V* ⦶*BP.*

$
★   ▦ **Hotel & Restaurant Scaletta.** Ideally situated close to the Arena, this small, family-run hotel occupies a tastefully refurbished old town house. The interior is decorated in cheerful yellows and greens, with simple modern furniture. The restaurant offers a small but select menu with exquisite dishes such as filet mignon in bread crumbs with dates and croquettes, and the Scaletta Pavilion, across the road, serves pizza, grilled meats, and fish dishes. Pros: friendly B&B atmosphere, good restaurant. Cons: popular but small, so books up early. ⊠*Flavijevska 26, 52100* ☎*052/541–599 or 052/541–025* 🖷*052/540–285* ⊕*www. hotel-scaletta.com* ⟿*12 rooms* ⟐*In-room: safe, refrigerator. In-hotel: restaurant, no elevator* ⊟*AE, DC, MC, V* ⦶*BP.*

¢–$ ▦ **Hotel Galija.** Expanded from a restaurant into a hotel in 2002, this family-run establishment is centrally located in a bright yellow building on a quiet street just two blocks from Giardini and the Sergian Gate. The rooms are bright, spacious, and clean; nine are in the main building, with another seven plus five suites in a building right across the street. Pros: prime downtown location, parking garage nearby. Cons: some say hotel's hot water isn't sufficient. ⊠*Epulonova 3, 52100* ☎*052/383–802* 🖷*052/383–804* ⊕*www.hotel-galija-pula.com* ⟿*16 rooms, 6 suites* ⟐*In-room: safe, refrigerator. In-hotel: restaurant, no elevator, parking (fee)* ⊟*AE, DC, MC, V* ⦶*BP.*

NIGHTLIFE & THE ARTS

BARS & CLUBS

Club life in Pula tends to begin in early April and continue through late October or early November. Pubs are open year-round.

★   With an intimate rustic atmosphere marked by low lighting and wooden booths with cushioned seats, the **Bounty Pub** (⊠*Veronska 8, near Narodni trg* ☎*052/218–088*) is a comfy place for a beer or, if you prefer, a coffee. The seating outside is on a stylish wooden platform. Just outside Pula in the resort area of Verudela (follow the signs once you're there), **Disco Club Oasis** (⊠*Verudela* ☎*052/218–603 or 052/218–609*) is *the* place to go to dance it up on weekends from April through early November. Conveniently located in the city center, with posters announcing its various musical events ubiquitous about town, **Club Uljanik** (⊠*Jura Dobrile ul 2* ☎*052/217–117*) is an exceedingly popular counterculture haven with "DJ nights" all year and live music on its spacious terrace.

ARTS FESTIVALS

Being the most prominent place in town, the Arena hosts a fair share of the city's core art events. The decades-old annual **Pula Film Festival** (⊕*www.pulafilmfestival.hr*) around the third week of July before the Motovun Film Festival *(see Nightlife & the Arts in Motovun)* features both Croatian and, in recent years, an increasing number of international works. The **Histria Festival** (⊕*www.histriafestival. com*) an annual summer music festival that runs from June through

August, has all types of performances, from opera and ballet to popular-music concerts that draw famous stars such as Sting, who has been here several times.

SPORTS & THE OUTDOORS

Unlike some smaller towns farther up the coast, such as Rovinj, downtown Pula is a bit too much of a port and industrial center to allow for a dip in the sea in between visits to cultural attractions. Now for the good news: the **beaches** aren't far away. A short drive or bus ride to the Verudela or Stoja resort areas, each around 4 km (2½ mi) south of downtown along the coast, will provide the clear water (and rocky shores) Croatia has in no short supply. You might also try the long stretch of relatively isolated beach between the two, on the Lungomare. If you have a car or a bicycle, this lovely little stretch of undeveloped coast is close to town and popular with locals as well as tourists. Head south about 2 km (1½ mi) along the main road out of Pula and follow the signs to the right toward Stoja, a resort-cum-camping area. Once there, proceed left and then back north along the pine-fringed coastal road Lungomare as it makes its way to the Verudela resort area.

If you have a car at your disposal, drive 10 km (6¼ mi) southwest of central Pula to the Premantura peninsula. The relatively remote shoreline there, at the very southern tip of Istria, is even more scenic, punctuated by cliffs and caves, and the crowds are mercifully thinner.

SHOPPING

Pula is no shopping mecca, but it does have a handful of stores with quality goods from Istria and other Croatian delicacies, wines, crafts, and more. On Monday evenings in July (from 8 to midnight) and August (from 7 to midnight) the Forum hosts an open-air fair of Istrian handicrafts. A walk through the Triumphal Gate of the Sergians onto bustling Sergijevaca ulica will show you much of what the city has available, shopping-wise; the stores listed below are on the fringe of this central business zone.

Aromatica (⊠ *Laginjina 4, just beyond Garibaldi* ☎*No phone*) is the place to browse for a whole array of natural—fennel, rosemary, pine, and sage—"Adriatic" oils, bath salts, perfumes, and soaps. **Saxa** (⊠ *Kandlerova 28, across from the Cathedral of the Assumption of the Virgin Mary* ☎*052/212–063*) is yet another spot to get those Istrian wines, olive oils, honey, and, yes, truffles. As suggested by its name, **Zigante Tartufi** (⊠ *Smareglina 7* ☎*052/214–855* ⊕*www.zigantetartufi. com*) has everything truffle-related (or that might complement truffles on the table) that you can imagine, from a golf-ball sized box of minced truffles (black or white) to sheep cheese with truffles, as well as olive oil, honey, and herb-flavored brandies. This outlet is part of a family-owned chain throughout Istria (others are in Buje, Buzet, Livade, Grožnjan, and Motovun).

VODNJAN

★ *12 km (7½ mi) north of Pula.*

Vodnjan may look a bit run-down at first glance, but there are three good reasons to come here: its saintly mummies; its quiet, narrow, centuries-old streets populated by a higher percentage of Italian speakers than you'll find almost anywhere else in Istria; and the Vodnjanka Restaurant's scrumptious fare. There are 10 buses daily between Pula and Vodnjan, at 12 Kn each way, payable directly to the driver.

☺ From the tourist office on the main square, stroll down ulica Castello to **Crkva svetog Blaža** *(St. Blaise's Church)*, an 18th-century structure built in the style of Palladio that not only has the highest campanile in all of Istria but is also the unlikely home of the mummies or mummified body parts of six saints impressively preserved without embalming. Though some see divine intervention behind their state of preservation, the degree to which these saints are really intact—they are definitely chipping away at the edges, it must be said—is open to question. Among the best-preserved of the saints are St. Nicoloza of Koper and Leon Bembo the Blessed. Nicoloza, whose relatively elastic skin and overall postmortem presentableness have given her the distinction of being among the best-preserved human bodies in Europe, was born in Istria in the 15th century and developed a reputation for holiness as a nun in Venice and elsewhere; she's the one with the garland of flowers still on her head. Leon Bembo the Blessed was a 12th-century Venetian priest who was tortured to the point of disfigurement in religious riots while ambassador to Syria, and spent his final years back in Venice in monastic contemplation. And then there is St. Sebastian, a Roman officer-turned-Christian who was whipped and strangled around AD 288 in Rome after initially surviving torture by arrows. The head, spinal column, neck muscles, and related parts of this very famous saint are on display here. As for St. Barbara, from 3rd-century Nicomeda (in present-day Turkey), only her leg remains; she so disagreed with her father's pagan, slave-keeping lifestyle that he personally killed her with a sword, though legend has it that he was then promptly struck by lightning and turned to ashes. Admittance to the mummy room, behind the main altar, includes an English-language recording that sums up the saints' lives and roads to mummihood. ☒ *Župni ured Sv Blaža* ☎ *052/511–420* ☒ *40 Kn for both mummies and museum, 30 Kn for just one* ☉ *July–Sept., daily 9–7; Oct.–June only when you can find someone to take your money and let you in.*

WHERE TO EAT

$$$ ✕ **Vodnjanka.** This restaurant is the place to go for the most mouthwa-
★ tering homemade pasta dishes you can imagine, not least *fuži* with wild arugula and prosciutto in cream sauce, which is simply unforgettable. The outer of two small rooms features bizarre but fantastic wall art by sculptor/painter Lilia Batel: 3-D reliefs with sponge-based puppets caricaturing real locals as they gaze out their windows, sit at the bar, and so on. The inner room, with its six tables and framed family-style

photographs, is positively homey. Though there's no English-language menu, navigating the Italian and German menus isn't at all hard, and the staff, including the friendly owner, Svjetlana Celija, can help you in English. In the summer, be sure to make a reservation for dinner. ⊠ *Istarska, right across from where the Pula bus lets you off and about where you board for the return trip* ☎ *052/511–435* ☐ *AE, MC, V.*

$–$$ ✕ **Pansion-Restaurant San Rocco.** For a good budget meal—pizza in particular—this is your best bet in Vodnjan. The pension is in the heart of town, a few blocks from the main square. You can also stay in one of the eight clean but no-frills rooms. ⊠ *Sv Rocco 15* ☎ *052/511–011* ☐ *No credit cards.*

NACIONALNI PARK BRIJUNI

Fodor'sChoice
★

Ferry from Fažana, which is 15 km (9 mi) northwest of Pula.

When Austrian industrialist Paul Kupelwieser set off for Brijuni by boat from Fažana in 1885 with a bottle of wine, roast chicken, bread, and peaches (and a couple of brawny locals to row him and his son there), the archipelago had long been a haven for the Austro-Hungarian military and for malaria. Kupelwieser was to change all that. In 1893 he bought the 14 islands and islets, eradicated the disease with the help of doctors, and fashioned parks from Mediterranean scrub. Thus arose a vacation retreat par excellence—not for rich Romans, as had been the case here 17 centuries earlier, but for fin de siècle Viennese and other European high-society sorts. Archduke Franz Ferdinand summered here, as did such literary lights as Thomas Mann and Arthur Schnitzler; James Joyce came here to celebrate his 23rd birthday. Two world wars ensued, however, and the islands' fate faded as they changed hands—coming under Italian rule and, later, Yugoslavian. From 1949 to 1979 the largest island, Veli Brijun, was the official summer residence of Marshal Josip Broz Tito, Yugoslavia's "president for life." Here he retreated to work, rest, and pursue his hobbies. World leaders, film and opera stars, artists, and writers were his frequent guests; and it was here that, together with Nasser of Egypt and Nehru of India, Tito forged the Brioni Declaration, uniting the so-called nonaligned nations (countries adhering to neither NATO nor the Warsaw Pact). The archipelago was designated a national park in 1983 and opened to the public. These days, **Fažana** itself seems to exist mainly as a low-key access point to Brijuni, but it too has a rich past. The archipelago's development in the late 19th century yielded a spate of construction in Fažana, including several hotels, a toffee factory, a liquor plant, a fish-processing facility, and a shipyard. Today Fažana seems to offer little more than the usual collection of touristy restaurants along its small harbor; since tourists tend to pass through on their way to Brijuni, however, the town is at least refreshingly quiet compared to some other tourist-traveled spots along Istria's west coast. Its main cultural attractions—all just a short walk from the harbor—are the 15th-century **Church of Saints Kosmas and Damian,** whose bell may be in need of oiling, as it sounds like a fork striking a plate; and the smaller but older 14th-century **Church of**

Our Lady of Mount Carmel, which you enter through an atmospheric loggia and whose ceiling features several layers of fascinating 15th-century Renaissance frescoes. But you are presumably here to visit the archipelago. Before doing so, call or e-mail the Brijuni National Park office in Fažana at least one day in advance to make a reservation; you can also do so in person, but especially in midsummer there is a substantial risk that there won't be space. (Though various private tourist agencies in Fažana and Pula offer excursions, they do not generally measure up, either cost-wise or quality-wise, to making your arrangements directly with the national park. Indeed, some of the tourist agencies simply reserve you a spot on the "official" tour, adding their own commission when doing so.) To get here, take the National Park ferry from Fažana, which takes about 15 minutes. The entire tour of the park takes about four hours. Your first view of the park is of a low-lying island with a dense canopy of evergreens over blue waters. Ashore on Veli Brijun, the largest island, a **tourist train** takes you past villas in the seaside forest and relics from the Roman and Byzantine eras. The network of roads on this 6½-km-long (4-mi-long) island was laid down by the Romans, and stretches of original Roman stonework remain. Rows of cypresses shade herds of deer, and peacocks strut along pathways. The train stops at the **Safari Park,** a piece of Africa transplanted to the Adriatic, its zebras, antelopes, llamas, and elephants all gifts from visitors from faraway lands. In the **museum,** an archaeological exhibition traces life on Brijuni through the centuries, and a photography exhibition, "Tito on Brijuni," focuses on Tito and his guests.

Those who have made the rounds of Kupelwieser's golf course—the oldest golf course in Croatia—report that it is more a historic experience than anything else, since it looks much the same as it did when built in 1923, with "natural," sandy tees and deer grazing where there is grass; it's blessed by an absence of fertilizers. Even if isn't quite up to snuff by modern golfing standards, how often do you find a course that allows you to take a dip in the sea between holes? ⊠ *Brijunska 10, Fažana* ☎ *052/525–883 or 052/525–882* ✎ *izleti@brijuni.htnet. hr* ⊕ *www.brijuni.hr* 🎫 *180 Kn* ☉ *Apr.–Oct., eight tours daily; Nov.–Mar., four tours daily; reservations required.*

WHERE TO STAY

You can save money by booking a room in Fažana and taking a day trip to the islands. **Stefani Trade** (⊠ *Župni trg 3, Fažana* ☎🖶 *052/521–910* 🖶 *098/980–7820*), an accommodations and travel agency in Fažana, can help you arrange a place to stay, not to mention tours around the region.

$$ 🏨 **Neptun-Istria Hotel.** The most luxurious of three hotels adjacent to
★ each other on Veli Brijun has bright, spacious rooms. The rates include unlimited passages on the National Park boats between the islands and the mainland. But you must leave your bikes, boats, and pets on the mainland. A daily surcharge for a room with a sea view is 100 Kn, and secure parking in Fažana is 60 Kn per day. Pros: location can't be beat. Cons: outdated interior design, pricey for the level of service. ⊠ *Javna*

Ustanova Nacionalni Park Brijuni, 52214 ☎*052/525–807* 🖷*052/521–367* ⊕*www.brijuni.hr* 📞*88 rooms* &*In-room: safe, refrigerator. In-hotel: restaurant, room service* ☰*AE, DC, MC, V* ⦿❘*BP.*

ROVINJ

Fodor'sChoice
★

35 km (22 mi) northwest of Pula.

It is hard to imagine how Rovinj could be more beautiful than it is. In a fantastic setting, with centuries-old red-roofed houses clustered around the hill of a former island, Istria's cultural mecca is crowned by the monumental baroque Crkva Sv Eufemije (Church of St. Euphemia), which has a typical Venetian bell tower topped by a gleaming bronze figure of St. Euphemia. Far below, a wide harbor crowded with pleasure boats is rimmed with bright awnings and colorful café umbrellas. Artists, writers, musicians, and actors have long gravitated to this ravishing place to carve out apartments in historic houses. Throughout the summer, the winding cobbled streets are crowded with vacationers from all reaches of Europe, who are more often than not staying in nearby resort developments. South of the harbor lies the beautiful landscaped park of Zlatni Rt, planted with avenues of cedars, oaks, and cypresses and offering numerous secluded coves for bathing.

EXPLORING ROVINJ

Practically all of Rovinj's key cultural and commercial attractions are packed into the compact, onetime island and present-day peninsula that juts like the tip of a hitchhiker's thumb westward into the sea. The main square, Trg M. Tita, is at the southern juncture of this little peninsula with the mainland; from there you can either cut straight up the center of the peninsula (i.e., west) along Grisia toward the cathedral or walk around the outer edge of the peninsula, or you can go south along the harbor to some fine restaurants and the beaches of Zlatni Rt beyond.

Numbers in the text correspond to numbers in the margin and on the Rovinj map.

WHAT TO SEE

❹ **Akvarij** *(Aquarium).* The Rovinj aquarium displays tanks of Adriatic marine fauna and flora. It opened in 1891, making it one of the oldest institutions of its type in Europe. It's housed within the Ruđer Bošković Institute's Center for Maritime Research. ⊠*Obala Giordana Paliage 5* ☎*052/804–702* 🎟*10 Kn* ⊗*May–Sept., daily 9–9; Oct.–Apr., by appointment only.*

❸ **Church of St. Tommaso** Today a public art gallery, this small, bright yellow church dates to the Middle Ages but was rebuilt in 1722. It's on your way back down the hill from the main cathedral, and right after you pass by it, you will pass under a lovely, arched hall some 50 feet long, its ceiling replete with wooden beams. Be careful here, as signs warn of loose brickwork above. ⊠*Begovita ul via del Monte* ☎*No phone* 🎟*Free* ⊗*Tues.–Sun. 6 AM–10 PM.*

NEED A
BREAK?

The Adriatic may not be quite as warm as the Caribbean, but at the Havana Club (✉ *Obala Alda Negria*)—a spacious, tropical-themed cocktail bar-cum-café right on the harbor—you can sip a piña colada or, if you dare, a Sex on the Beach (vodka, peach and melon juices, plus "sex mix"). There are also nonalcoholic cocktails, including, of course, Safe Sex on the Beach, as well as iced tea and coffee. Kick back and relax in a wicker chair under one of five huge, bamboo umbrellas while listening to reggae. That's not to mention the Cuban cigars you can puff for anywhere between 34 Kn and 228 Kn. Ah, the life!

2 Crkva Sv Eufemije *(Church of St. Euphemia).* Inside the 18th-century

Fodor'sChoice   baroque church, the remains of Rovinj's patron saint are said to lie
★   within a 6th-century sarcophagus. Born near Constantinople, Euphemia was martyred in her youth, on September 16 in AD 304, under the reign of Emperor Diocletian. The marble sarcophagus containing her remains mysteriously vanished in AD 800 when it was at risk of destruction by iconoclasts—and, legend has it, it somehow floated out to sea and washed up in faraway Rovinj! (Note the wall engraving just to the right of the entrance of St. Euphemia holding Rovinj in her arms.) Not surprisingly, Euphemia has long been among the most popular names

in Istria for girls, and on September 16 of each year many people gather to pray by her tomb. In the church there's a great big mural on the wall in the sarcophagus room portraying Euphemia being picked at by two lions who, legend has it, didn't eat her, after all; she ended up being tied to a killer wheel. As at other churches in Croatia, a sign at the entrance makes it clear that no short-shorts or miniskirts (or dogs, or ice-cream cones, or lit cigarettes) are allowed inside. Judging from the scanty dress of some folks streaming inside in the summer heat, such rules can be bent, but you won't be let up the campanile unless you abide. ⊠ *Grisia* ☎ *052/815–615* ✉ *Church and sarcophagus room free, campanile 10 Kn* ☉ *Daily 10–noon and 4–7.*

> ### SWIMMING IN ROVINJ
>
> Swimming in the sea in Rovinj is a rocky business. There are no sandy beaches in the town itself; most of the swimming is done off the rocks or cement slabs (with ladders in some places) that jut into the sea. Head out to Črveni Otok (Red Island) or Sveti Katarina (St. Catherine) for a pebble beach and a place to lay your towel, but don't forget to bring some rubber water sandals, as entering the water there, as in the rest of Istria, is a bit rough on your feet.

① **Trg M. Tita.** Standing on the Old Town's main square, you can't help but notice the **Balbi Arch,** which at one time was the gate to Rovinj's fish market. Notice the Venetian lion on one side and the Turkish head on the other. At the top, between the two Balbi coats of arms, is a Latin epigraph that used to be on a neighboring building and refers to the 1680 construction of the public granary. Also quite prominent on the square is the city's pinkish-orange **watchtower,** whose base houses the tourist office. Although it looks Venetian, the tower was erected in 1907. That said, the winged-lion relief on one side is indeed from the 16th century.

OFF THE BEATEN PATH

Dvivigrad. When its residents abandoned Dvivigrad suddenly in the mid-17th-century—fleeing the combined misfortune of plague and attacks by Uskok raiders—and established nearby Kanfanar, surely they didn't foresee that more than three centuries later tourists would delight in what they left behind. In any case, if exploring ruins is your (or your child's) thing, this is the place for you. Along an isolated road 23 km (14 mi) east of Rovinj, outside the sleepy town of Kanfanar (a short detour if you're headed north toward Poreč, Motovun, or Grožnjan), this huge maze of dirt paths surrounded by high stone walls makes for an adventuresome, imagination-stirring walk. Indeed, just enough restoration has been done to let your imagination "reconstruct" the rest: some of the walls, which rise to around 20 feet (with signs warning of loose brickwork) are vine-covered, and much of the place is overgrown with vegetation. Nor is there a single explanatory sign, in any language. All this combines to give you the sense that you are discovering this eerie ghost town of a fortress city, even if a few other tourists are also wandering about. The battlements are impressively intact, and toward the center of the fortress you will find the remains of Crkva uznesenja (St. Sophia's Church), replete with depressions in the ground that contained the crypts of very important persons. To get here, take the main road east out of Rovinj toward Kanfanar, 23 km (14 mi) away. Just before you cross the railroad tracks and enter Kanfanar, you'll see a sign pointing to Dvivigrad, which is to your left; from the sign the ruins are about 4 km (2½ mi) down an isolated, scrub-lined road.

WHERE TO EAT

$$$$
Fodor'sChoice
★
✕**Blu.** Three km (2 mi) north of Rovinj's old town, perched on the sea in the Borik section of town, Blu is the epitome of Istrian seaside elegance. The cozy dining room has a wall of windows to the sea, a couple of stone terraces, tables on an ivy-covered patio, and a spectacular canopied table at the breakwater's edge. There's simply no bad table here. One terrace juts out into the sea, where you're so close you can look at the crustaceans on the sea floor in between courses. Expect refined seafood dishes that showcase the bounty of the Adriatic waters; for example, tagliatelle with crayfish and baby zucchini, or monkfish carpaccio. It's hard to beat this class act for a quiet, romantic dinner. ✉ *Val de Lesso 952210* ☎*052/511–265* ⊕*www.blu.hr* ⟺*Reservations essential* ☰*AE, DC, MC, V* ⊘*Closed Nov.–Easter.*

$$$$
✕**Enoteca Al Gastaldo.** Walls lined with wine bottles and tables lit by candles create a warm and intimate atmosphere in this sophisticated eatery, hidden away in the Old Town a couple of blocks back from the harbor. Indulge in spaghetti with either truffles or crab, fresh fish prepared over an open fire, and a colorful rocket (arugula) and radicchio salad. Round off with a glass of local *rakija*. ✉*Iza Kasarne 1452210* ☎*052/814–109 or 098/224–707* ☰*No credit cards.*

$$$$
Fodor'sChoice
★
✕**Monte.** Upscale Italian-Istrian dishes like crisp medallions of monkfish with caviar are what you'll find at this lovely restaurant not far from Grisia. Crisp white tablecloths on wrought-iron patio tables dot the shady terrace, where you can sip glasses of local *malvazija* and while away the afternoon in peace and quiet, a surprise given the restaurant's location just below St. Euphemia's. The menu changes often, but usually includes *mare crudo,* an eye-popping feast of super-fresh seafood carpaccio. If the branzino with lobster roulade is available when you visit, don't miss it. The place is known locally as Casa Đekić after the family that owns it. ✉*Montalbano 7552210* ☎*052/830–203* ⟺*Reservations essential* ☰*AE, MC, V* ⊘*Closed Nov.–Easter.*

$$$–$$$$
✕**Amfora.** Location, location, location is the thing to remember at this elegant but pricey fish restaurant right on the harbor near the Old Town. With helpful photos of menu items outside, this spacious, light-filled, and air-conditioned restaurant is a sure bet for grilled fish specialties such as *bakalar* (oven-baked cod in salt crust) and Istrian dishes like steak with truffle sauce. Blue tones and damask chairs combine with a waterfall to give that extra-special touch. ✉*Obala Alda Rismonda 33* ☎*052/816–663* ☰*AE, DC, MC, V* ⊘*Closed Jan. and Feb.*

$$–$$$
✕**Kantinon.** Wine cellar or steak house? That is the question. Regardless of the answer, the food and milieu are equally pleasant. Red-checkered curtains, stone floors, long wooden tables, and high vaulted ceilings befitting a wine-cellar restaurant combine scrumptiously with standard

but good grilled fish and such meat specialties as veal in artichoke sauce. ⊠ *Obala A. Rismonda 6* ☎ *052/816–075* ▭ *AE, DC, MC, V.*

$$-$$$ ✕**Pizzeria Da Sergio.** With 40-plus varieties of pies and pasta dishes, there's plenty to choose from at this conveniently located venue along the narrow road leading up to the main cathedral. Inside it's pleasantly cool, even on a hot day. One of four ornamental plates on the wall to your right as you enter reads, in Hungarian, LONG LIVE THE GIRLS OF TRANSYLVANIA! A gift from one of Croatia's many Hungarian visitors, perhaps? ⊠ *Grisia 11, on the way up to the main cathedral* ☎ *052/816–949* ▭ *AE, DC, MC, V.*

$$-$$$ ✕**Veli Jože.** This popular *konoba* lies close to the seafront, at the foot of the Old Town. Specialties include *bakalar na bijelo* (dried cod in white wine with onion and potatoes), *fuži* (pasta) with goulash, and roast lamb with potatoes. The house wine is excellent, but the rock music doesn't quite match the traditional decor that includes antlers, old photos, and nautical instruments. ⊠ *Sv Križa 1* ☎ *052/816–337* ▭ *AE, DC, MC, V.*

WHERE TO STAY

One reliable bet for private rooms is **Kompas Travel** (⊠ *Obala M. Tita 5, Rovinj 52210* ☎ *052/813–211* 🖶 *052/813–478* ✐ *kompas.headquarters@kompas-travel.com*), which has offices in Pula and Poreč, as well as other towns in Istria and elsewhere in Croatia. Like other similar agencies, the company can also arrange daytime excursions to Istria's out-of-the-way exploring sites.

$$$ 🏨**Villa Angelo d'Oro.** Rovinj's first boutique hotel is housed in a beautifully restored 16th-century building in the heart of the Old Town. The smallish rooms are individually furnished with antiques, and a few have balconies with breathtaking vistas. The sometimes indifferent service and dated rooms don't quite meet the aspirations of the place, but breakfast is served on a glorious roof terrace, and there's a well-regarded restaurant on the ground floor. Pros: beautiful Venetian building with wrought-iron and stone details. Cons: rooms are old-fashioned and service is sporadic. ⊠ *V Švalbe 38–42, 52210* ☎ *052/840–502* 🖶 *052/840–112* ⊕ *www.rovinj.at* ⇆ *22 rooms, 1 suite* ♿ *In-hotel: restaurant, room service* ▭ *AE, DC, MC, V* ⦿ *BP.*

$$-$$$ 🏨**Hotel Villa Valdibora.** The Valdibora is a cross between a villa rental and a small luxury hotel, as all four apartments have kitchens, yet the rooms are cleaned daily and breakfast is included in the price. Though pricey, the apartments are spacious (they can accommodate up to four people) and fitted out with computers and sparkling bathrooms. Rustic–chic wooden tables and upholstered day beds are set against exposed-brick walls. The location can't be beat either, just a stone's throw away from the Church of St. Euphemia. Pros: kitchens are well equipped with appliances like toasters and coffeemakers, rental bikes are on-site. Cons: narrow, one-way streets make reaching the hotel by car tricky. ⊠ *Chiurca Silvana 8, 52210* ☎ *052/845–040* ⊕ *www.valdibora.com* ⇆ *4 apartments* ♿ *In room: safe, Ethernet, refrigerator* ▭ *AE, DC, MC, V* ⦿ *BP.*

$$ ⚏Hotel Adriatic. Founded in 1912, this harborside hotel is the oldest
★ (still functioning) one in town, and its attractive, Habsburg-era facade shows its age. A comprehensive renovation in the late 1980s yielded bright, clean, and fairly spacious rooms with soft blue hues. Not only do the harborside rooms offer a spectacular, soothing view of the sea but also an oh-so-pleasant Adriatic aroma. The service is friendly, but as at many a hotel in Croatia's resort areas, there is a 20% surcharge for stays of fewer than four nights. Pros: first-class view of Old Town square and harbor, breakfast is served on the terrace. Cons: no elevator, parking garage is a short walk away, rooms facing the square are noisy. ⊠P. Budicin, 52210 ☎0800–8858 toll-free within Croatia or 052/815–088 ⎙052/813–573 ⊕www.maistra.hr ⇦27 rooms ♿In-room: safe, refrigerator. In-hotel: 2 restaurants, no elevator ⊟AE, DC, MC, V ⑩BP.

NIGHTLIFE & THE ARTS

Every few days from late July to early September at 9 PM the Church of St. Euphemia and other major churches in Rovinj play host to classical-music recitals and concerts as part of the city's **Summer Festival.**

★   In a residential district a 15-minute walk southeast of the town center, the **Monvi** (⊠Luje Adamovića ☎052/545–117) is the most popular place in Rovinj to dance the night away, in part because it is, as of this writing, reportedly the only place to do so. The musical focus is house, and there's a spacious outdoor terrace open in summer. To get here, follow Mattea Benussia from the bus station to Fontana, which then becomes Zagrebačka, and then go slightly right after a block onto Luje Adamovića. **Puntulina Wine & Cocktail Bar** (⊠Sv Križ 38 ☎No phone) may have a hard time deciding what it is, but take the steps down to its terrace, where you can enjoy a glass of Istrian or other Croatian wine—all in a pleasant atmosphere yards from the sea, with light pop music setting the tone. And, yes, you can take a few more steps down if you wish, to the rocks, and take a dip before or after being served—for this is where Rovinj's free, public swimming area begins. It's not especially a "night" spot, so you may wish to confine your wine-sipping to daylight hours. Will it be on the rocks? Yes? Then it'll be either the setting or a cocktail at the **Valentino** (⊠Santa Croce 28 ☎052/830–683), situated idyllically on the rocks across from Katarina Island, with the sea illuminated by the club's theatrical lighting. When the weather turns foul, the crowds squeeze into the small, altarlike interior. It's closed from November through March.

The **Zanzibar** (⊠P. Budicina ☎052/813–206) might not be the place to let it all hang out, but it is trendy—even tropical—and a bit upscale. It's also closed from November through March.

SPORTS & THE OUTDOORS

As elsewhere along the coast, the Rovinj area has its share of places to dive, and several diving centers to go along with them—most of which will take you by boat for supervised dives to shipwrecks and other fascinating spots, not least the famous wreck of the *Baron Gautsch,* an Austrian passenger ferry that sank in 1908 just 13 km (8 mi) from Rovinj. **Diver Sport Center** (⊠ *T. N. Villas Rubin* ☎*052/816–648* ⊕*www.diver.hr*) offers three- to four-hour boat trips with supervised dives for between €20 and €35 (equipment rental 30 Kn more), as well as courses ranging from a three-day program for beginners to various advanced, specialized courses for much more. **Scuba-Rovinj** (⊠*Braće Brajković* ☎*052/813–290 or 098/219–203* ⊕*www.scuba.hr*), has the same sort of dive programs as Diver Sport Center for similar prices.

SHOPPING

Rovinj is worth visiting for its beauty, not its boutiques. The souvenir market is nothing to write home about, but there are at least a couple of shops with fine Istrian and/or Croatian products worth checking out. Between the main square and the souvenir market, **Istria Terra Magica** (⊠*Giuseppea 7* ☎*No phone*) advertises itself as an "authentic Istrian shop," and its quality selection of wines, olive oils, vases, and framed, glass-encased sailing ships does seem to stand out among the many more tacky souvenir shops in town. **Art Studio** (⊠*Grisia 48, on your left on the way up the hill soon before the main cathedral* ☎*098/274–665*) is one cliché of a name, to be sure, but one gem of a little shop. Zagreb jewelry maker (and documentary filmmaker) Radovan Sredić spends his summers here selling lovely jewelry that he creates by hand from rare, natural materials, mostly from Asia.

EN ROUTE

Getting to Poreč is easier straight from Pula than from Rovinj, as you simply take the main inland highway north for 42 km (26 mi) and then follow the signs before turning west onto the secondary road that leads you another 13 km (8 mi) to Poreč—a 60- to 90-minute drive in all, depending on the traffic and how much pressure you apply to that pedal. If you go from Rovinj, you must skirt the Limski kanal. Ten km (6 mi) north of Rovinj you'll pass right by the Matošević vineyard in Sv. Lovreč. **Wine Cellar Krunčići** (⊠*Krunčići 2* ☎*052/448–588* ⊕*www.matosevic.com*) is a first-class spot to get a tour of some Istrian vineyards and taste the local wine. Tastings are held on a stone patio attached to a farmhouse, and the owner, Ivica Matošević, is usually on hand to tell you about his vintages including the Alba wine, an Istrian malvazija considered one of the region's best. Call ahead to arrange tastings. There are a couple of apartments to rent if the tastings last into the evening.

POREČ

55 km (34 mi) northwest of Pula.

A chic, bustling little city founded as a Roman castrum (fort) in the 2nd century BC and swarming with tourists more than 2,000 years later, Poreč may not be quite as lovely as Rovinj—nor does it enjoy the benefits of a hilltop panorama—but it is nonetheless a pretty sea of red-tile roofs on a peninsula jutting out to sea. Within the historic center, the network of streets still follows the original urban layout. Dekumanova, the Roman *decumanus* (the main traverse street), has maintained its character as the principal thoroughfare. Today it is a worn flagstone passage lined with Romanesque and Gothic mansions and patrician palaces, some of which now house cafés and restaurants. Close by lies the magnificent UNESCO-listed Eufrazijeva Basilica (St. Euphrasius Basilica), Istria's prime ecclesiastical attraction and one of the coast's major artistic showpieces. Although the town itself is small, Poreč has an ample capacity for overnight stays, thanks to the vast hotel complexes of Plava and Zelena Laguna, situated along the pine-rimmed shoreline an unappealingly short distance from the center. Although you can cover the main sights in two or three hours, Poreč surely merits a one-night stay, or more if you figure in a day trip to a nearby attraction such as the Baradine Cave or the Limski kanal.

WHAT TO SEE

You may want to begin exploring Poreč at the helpful **Tourist Information Center Poreč,** which not only supplies a detailed brochure-cum-map and offers 15 minutes of free Internet access, but is also just yards away from the main square. ⊠ *Zagrebačka 9* ☎ *052/451–293 or 052/451–458* ⊙ *Apr.–Oct., daily 8 AM–10 PM; Nov.–Mar., weekdays 8–3.*

Fodor'sChoice ★ The magnificent **Eufrazijeva Basilica** *(St. Euphrasius Basilica)* is among the most perfectly preserved early-Christian churches in Europe, and one of the most important monuments of Byzantine art on the Adriatic. It was built by Bishop Euphrasius in the middle of the 6th century and consists of a delightful atrium, a church decorated with stunning mosaics, an octagonal baptistery, a 16th-century bell tower you can climb (for a modest fee), and a 17th-century Bishop's Palace whose foundations date to the 5th century and whose basement contains an exhibit of stone monuments and of mosaics previously on the basilica floor. The church interior is dominated by biblical mosaics above, behind, and around the main apse. In the apsidal semidome, the Virgin holding the Christ child is seated in a celestial sphere on a golden throne, flanked by angels in flowing white robes. On the right side there are three martyrs, the patrons of Poreč; the mosaic on the left shows Bishop Euphrasius holding a model of the church, slightly askew. High above the main apse, just below the beamed ceiling, Christ holds an open book in his hands while apostles approach on both sides. Other luminous, shimmeringly intense mosaics portray further ecclesiastical themes. ⊠ *Eufrazijeva* ⊠ *Basilica free; bell tower 10 Kn; Bishop's Palace 12 Kn* ☎ *No phone* ⊙ *Basilica daily 7–7; bell tower daily 7–6:30; Bishop's Palace daily 7–6:30.*

Trg Marafor. This square toward the tip of the peninsula was the site of Poreč's Roman forum, whose original stonework is visible in spots amid the present-day pavement. Beside it is a park containing the ruins of Roman temples dedicated to the gods Mars and Neptune.

NEED A BREAK?

Do not be deterred by the cannon facing you as you enter this 15th-century tower that now houses the Torre Rotonda caffé bar (⊠ *Narodni trg 3a* ☎ *052/98–255–731*). Climb up a spiral staircase to a second floor replete with several intimate nooks, or go one more flight to the roof for an unbeatable view of Poreč and its harbor. Sip that coffee or drink at a fake-marbletop table while light pop music plays in the background.

Since its opening in 2005, crowds have been flocking to **Aquarium Poreč**, which is just yards from the main square, Trg Slobode. Come if you'd like to catch a glimpse of the underwater world of some 40 species from sea horses to sea urchins, from small sharks to arm's-length octopi and foot-long crabs. ⊠ *F. Glavinića 4* ☎ *052/428–720* ⊕ *www.aquarium-porec.com* ⊠ *Apr.–Oct., 25 Kn; Nov.–Mar., 15 Kn* ☉ *Apr.–Oct., daily 9–9; Nov.–Mar., daily 10–5.*

On the main pedestrian thoroughfare through town, between the aquarium and the basilica, is Istria's oldest museum, the **Zavičajni muzej** *(Regional Museum)*, which opened in 1884 in the 18th-century baroque Sinčić Palace. Presenting the history of Poreč and environs from ancient times through the 20th century, it features 2,000 exhibits, with highlights that include Roman tombstones, mosaics, and other archaeological fragments from antiquity, 16th-century portraits, and exhibits of baroque furniture; there's also a wonderful historical library with first editions of Diderot's 18th-century encyclopedia. ⊠ *Decumanus 9* ☎ *052/431–585* ⊠ *10 Kn* ☉ *July and Aug., daily 10–1 and 5–8; Sept.–June, daily 10–1.*

OUTSIDE OF TOWN

Far from sun and sea though it may be, the **Baradine Cave** has long been one of the Poreč area's top natural attractions. About 8 km (5 mi) northeast of town, near Nova Vas, this wonderful world of five limestone halls includes not only miniature transparent crabs and insects but, of course, stalactites, stalagmites, and dripstone formations—from "curtains" 10 yards long to "statues" resembling the Virgin Mary, the Leaning Tower of Pisa, and the body of the 13th-century shepherdess Milka, who supposedly lost her way down here while looking for her lover Gabriel (who met the same fate). One of the halls includes a hatch some 70 yards deep that leads to underground lakes. Groups leave every half hour on a 40-minute guided tour. You can also partake of either a brief round of "speleoclimbing" that allows you to try out caving techniques with equipment and under the watchful eye of a professional spelunker; or a more involved, five-hour "speleo-adventure" that gives you even more technical training (plus a certificate at the end) as you explore various other caves nearby. Those without car transport may wish to contact one of the various private agencies in Poreč and other nearby towns that offer excursions to Baradine Cave. ⊠ *Nova Vas* ☎ *098/224–350* ⊕ *www.baredine.com* ⊠ *Cave tour 25 Kn, speleoclimbing 40 Kn, speleo-adventure 350 Kn* ☉ *July and Aug., daily 9:30–6:30; May, June, and Sept., daily 10–5; Apr. and Oct., daily 10–4; Nov.–Mar., by appointment or occasionally on Sun. and holidays.*

3

There's even a bit of Norwegian-style fjord in Croatia. The **Limski kanal** is a 13-km-long (8-mi-long) karst canyon, whose emerald-green waters are flanked by forested valley walls that rise gradually to heights of more than 300 feet inland. The canyon was formed in the last Ice Age, and it is Croatia's most fertile breeding area for mussels and oysters—hence, you'll find some excellent seafood restaurants in the village of Sveti Lovreč (if you are passing through the town, try the Viking or the Fjord restaurants). Tours are available from both Poreč and Rovinj with various agencies and independent operators, whose stands and boats are impossible to miss. A reservation a day or two in advance can't hurt, though, particularly in midsummer. Kompas offices in either Poreč or Rovinj can arrange tours, as can Excursions Delfin and Excursions Maris, both in Rovinj *(see Travel Agencies in Istria Essentials, below)*; expect to pay approximately 80 Kn for the four-hour tour or 150 Kn for a daylong tour that includes a "fish picnic." ⊠*Sveti Loreč.*

Although the Limski kanal is a bit closer to Rovinj (which is to the south), one advantage of approaching from Poreč (to the north) is the opportunity to visit **Vrsar**, a pretty, medieval hilltop town just 13 km (8 mi) to the south and situated near the fjord's northern juncture with the sea (and yet another place you can catch a tour of the fjord). Famous since Roman times for its high-quality stone, which helped build Venice, Vrsar is home to the 13th-century Romanesque church St. Marija Od Mora (St. Mary of the Sea), which has three naves. In his memoirs, the Venetian adventurer Casanova fondly recalled the local red wine, refošk. Just a couple of miles south, by the way, is Croatia's oldest and largest naturist resort, FKK Park Koversada *(see Barely Vacationing box, below)*.

WHERE TO EAT

$$$$ ✕**Dvi Murve.** Since this restaurant is in a suburb on the edge of town, you'll need to drive to it unless you're up for a long walk. The acclaimed menu includes bass baked in a salt crust: the waiter delivers the salt-encrusted catch flaming to the table, where he deftly extinguishes the fire with a white cloth, removes the salt crust, skin and all, and serves you the steaming white flesh. The garnish, Swiss chard and boiled potatoes, is included in the price, which is by the kilogram and averages out to about 250 Kn for the popular meal for two. But there are also such meat specialties as beefsteak *dvi murve* (with a cream, mushroom, and ham sauce). The interior is very traditional, such as you would find in any Istrian *konoba*; outside is a large summer terrace shaded by two mulberry trees, after which the restaurant is named. Getting here is a bit tricky: go about 2½ km (1½ mi) on the main road north toward Novigrad, then straight where a fork in the road bears left. From there, follow the signs a short distance. ⊠*Grožnjanska 17, Vranići* ☎*052/434–115* ▭*AE, DC, MC, V.*

$$$$ ✕**Sv Nikola Restaurant.** Those with a discriminating palate and a not so
★ discriminating pocketbook should try this restaurant, opened in 2004. Service is included in the price, which is a good thing, since the price is

CLOSE UP

Barely Vacationing

It's just like any other campground on the Croatian coast. People pitch tents, sit around tables talking and sipping coffee or wine beside their RVs. There's just one difference: here, practically everyone is naked. This is Koversada, the largest naturist retreat in Croatia and, in fact, in all of Europe, with a daily capacity of some 12,000 visitors, space for some 1,700 campsites, and 215 rooms in attractive villa-like buildings—not to mention eight tennis courts, Ping Pong tables, a miniature golf course, and a supermarket (*some* clothing obligatory inside).

In 1961 Koversada—situated just outside the picturesque little town of Vrsar, 13 km (8 mi) south of Poreč—ushered in a new commercial craze for Croatian tourism. By some estimates, today more than 100,000 people a year stay in the country's naturist resorts, and tens of thousands more shed their clothes at less official secluded stretches of the coastline. Together, this represents roughly 15% of the country's annual tourist population. As accepting and encouraging as Croatians and their government have long been of this phenomenon, however, Croatians make up only a handful of these naturists, but they are there as well. The history of naturism in Croatia goes back to before World War II. In 1934 a leading Viennese naturist established a naturist beach on the island of Rab, and in 1936 the authorities there famously allowed England's King Edward VIII and his lover, Mrs. Wallis Simpson, to skinny dip in the sea. Apparently the experience was a happy one for them, as the king abdicated later that year and married Simpson the following year.

A glossy brochure published by the Croatian National Tourist Board lists 14 naturist "camps" and "villages" and about as many officially designated "free naturist beaches" on the country's Adriatic coast—14 of them in Istria, eight in the Kvarner region, a couple in northern and central Dalmatia, and a handful around Split and Dubrovnik. Many such areas are marked with signs reading FKK—short for *Freikorperkultur,* a German term that translates as "Free Body Culture."

Traditions vary somewhat from place to place, of course, but at Koversada, as at most such campgrounds-cum-resorts, the theme is family-oriented naturism. Men traveling alone are usually admitted to naturist resorts in Croatia only if they can show an International Naturist Federation (INF) card. Men traveling together are likewise well advised to carry such cards.

The camping and accommodation rates at naturist facilities are, surprisingly, not all that much more than at their clothes-minded counterparts. At Koversada, for example, you pay €6.60 per person plus €9.70 per pitched tent—i.e., €22.90 in all for two. A room is €48 per person, breakfast and dinner included (€3 less without dinner). You can contact Koversada directly at **FKK Park Koversada** (✉ *Vrsar 52540* ☎ *052/441–371 or 052/441–123* 🖷 *052/441–761*). The owner of Koversada is **Adria Resorts** (✉ *V. Nazora 6, Rovinj 52210* ☎ *052/441–222, 052/800–250, 0800–8868 toll-free within Croatia* 🖷 *052/441–122 or 052/800–215* 🌐 *www.maistra.hr*).

nothing to sneeze at in this sparkling, air-conditioned venue right across from the harbor. The menu offers such delicacies as fish fillet in *malvazija* (white) wine sauce; meat carpaccio with truffles, Parmesan, and wild arugula; and beefsteak Decumanus (with pine nuts, goose-liver pâté, and black truffles). You can set forth on this culinary adventure with a plate of raw clams and oysters from Istria's west coast or Istrian prosciutto. As good as the food may be, though, the elegant, spotless interior isn't exactly brimming with character. ⊠*Obala maršala Tita 23* ☎*052/451–018* ♨*Reservations essential* ⊟*AE, DC, MC, V.*

$$–$$$ ✕**Peterokutna Kula.** A 15th-century pentagonal tower in the heart of the Old Town has been cleverly renovated to accommodate this sophisticated restaurant on a series of floors and terraces, including the roof. House specialties include spaghetti with lobster and steak with truffles. Finish your meal with a glass of *šlivovica* (plum rakija). When deciding on your tip, do remember that the waitstaff must trudge up and down all those steps all day. ⊠*Decumanus 1* ☎*052/451–378* ⊟*No credit cards.*

$$ ✕**Pizzeria Nono.** Right across the street from the main tourist office (where you can check your e-mail for free), the Nono is teeming with folks saying "yes, yes!" to scrumptious budget fare from pizzas and salads to such seafood standards as grilled squid. ⊠*Zagrebačka 4* ☎*052/453–088* ⊟*AE, DC, MC, V.*

WHERE TO STAY

One reliable bet for private rooms is **Kompas Travel** (⊠*Obala M. Tita 16, 52440 Poreč* ☎*052/451–100* 🖷*052/451–114* ✉*kompas.headquarters@kompas-travel.com*), which also has offices in Pula and Rovinj as well as other towns in Istria and elsewhere in Croatia, and which, like other similar agencies, also offers daytime excursions to Istria's top, out-of-the-way exploring sites.

$$ ☷**Hotel Laguna Galijot.** This large, modern hotel sits on a small peninsula surrounded by pines in the Plava Laguna resort complex, 2 km (1 mi) south of the Old Town. Most rooms have balconies and sea views. Excellent sports facilities make this ideal for families on a longer stay and those in search of an active holiday. You'll pay extra for a room with a sea view. Pros: activities and entertainment for families. Cons: no sandy beaches nearby, Poreč is a 20-minute walk away. ⊠*Plava Laguna, 52440* ☎*052/451–877* 🖷*052/452–399* ⊕*www.plavalaguna. hr* ⬆*103 rooms* ⚬*In room: refrigerator. In-hotel: 2 restaurants, bar, tennis court, pool, diving, bicycles, parking (fee), some pets allowed* ⊟*AE, MC, V* ⊙*Closed Oct.–Apr.* ⦿*MAP.*

$ ☷**Hotel Neptun.** On the seafront promenade, where Poreč's oldest hotels are found, the Neptune was renovated in 2000 to provide smart, functional accommodations right in the center of town. Still, the rooms—most of which have a sea view—are smallish and somber-hued, and the mattresses are hard. The chic, air-conditioned restaurant includes one *big* salad bar. Stays of under three nights are subject to a 20% surcharge, and there's a small premium on rooms with a view. Pros: easy access to the Old Town and the sea, parking in front of hotel. Cons: no air-conditioning in the rooms, noise from the promenade reaches the rooms. ⊠*Obala M. Tita 15, 52440* ☎*052/400–800 or 052/408–000* 🖷*052/451–440* ⊕*www.riviera.hr* ⌁*145 rooms* ♿*In-room: no a/c. In-hotel: restaurant, room service, bar, parking (no fee)* ⊟*AE, DC, MC, V* ⦿*MAP.*

$ 🖳**Hotel Poreč.** Not beautiful on the outside, this hotel is well situated between the Old Town and the nearby beaches, yards from the bus station and a supermarket. It's also quite okay on the inside and has friendly service to boot. The rooms are clean and modern, if small-ish, but they do have balconies; the furniture has pine veneer, and the beds are a bit wobbly. Stays of under three nights are subject to a 20% surcharge; an extra daily supplement gets you dinner, too. Pros: convenient location, nearby parking on street. Cons: close to a noisy nightclub, no-frills breakfast. ⊠*R. Končara 1, 52440* ☎☎*052/451–811* 🖷*052/451–730* ⊕*www.hotelporec.com* ⌁*54 rooms* ♿*In-room: safe, refrigerator. In-hotel: restaurant, bar* ⊟*AE, DC, MC, V* ⦿*BP.*

NIGHTLIFE & THE ARTS

Fodor'sChoice
★ Live performances of Croatian jazz can be heard once a week in July and August, usually on Wednesday evening, behind the 18th-century baroque palace housing the Zavičajni muzej (Regional Museum), at Decumanus 9. Throughout August, Poreč's annual **Street Art Festival** enlivens the Old Town's streets and squares with musical, theatrical, art, multimedia, and acrobatic events. In the Plava Laguna resort area just south of town, **Club Plava** (⊠*Plava Laguna* ☎*091/202–0399*) is yet another great place to live it up once the sun sets. An open-air disco set shoreside in the pines about 1 km (½ mi) south of the center of town, on the path to the Plava Laguna resort area, the **Colonia Beach Club** (⊠*Šetalište A. Štifanića* ☎*091/4430–3222*) is a perennial favorite (especially after midnight) with a young, trendy, international crowd for late-night revelry, with live rock and jazz provided by groups from all over Croatia and beyond.

SPORTS & THE OUTDOORS

BEACHES

Walk 10 minutes south of Poreč along the shore, past the marina, and you'll meet with the thoroughly swimmable, if typically rocky, pine-fringed beaches of the Plava Laguna resort area. Keep walking until you're about 5 km (3 mi) south, and you'll be right in the center of the Zelena Laguna, which, though more concrete than rock, is one of the best-equipped tourist resorts on the Adriatic coast. Every day in the summer months (from May through September), two charming little "tourist trains," tiny open-walled buses, run hourly from 9 AM to midnight between the town center and the Zelena Laguna resort, as well as the Hotel Luna to the north—costing you 25 Kn but saving you the walk and providing you a virtual rail experience in a part of Istria otherwise without. Those who prefer traversing the brief distance by sea can do so by way of a ship that runs from 8:30 AM to midnight daily, likewise May through September, between Zelena Laguna and the center, making a couple of stops at other resort areas in between. Tickets can be purchased on board.

DIVING

Divers—aspiring or advanced—may want to contact the **Starfish Diving Center** (✉ *Autocamp Porto Sole, Vrsar* ✛ *13 km [8 mi] south of Poreč* ☎ *052/442–119 or 098/334–816* ⊕ *www.starfish.hr*) for daily diving tours to local shipwrecks, reefs, and caves or a four-day beginners' course that yields an international diving certification.

NOVIGRAD

15 km (9½ mi) northwest of Poreč.

Imagine a mini Rovinj of sorts, not quite so well preserved, it's true, and without the hill. This is Novigrad—a pretty little peninsula town that was the seat of a bishopric for more than 1,300 years, from 520 to 1831, and, like Rovinj, was at one time an island (before being connected with the mainland in the 18th century). With its medieval structure still impressively intact, along with its Old Town wall, it merits a substantial visit and perhaps a one-night stay as you make your way up and down the coast or before heading inland toward the hill towns of Grožnjan and Motovun. At first glance, as you enter town on an uninspiring main road bordered by communist-era, concrete-box apartment buildings, you might wonder if it was worth coming this far. Drive on (or let the bus take you), for you then arrive at a little gem: to your right is a pint-sized, protected harbor, the Old Town is in front of you, and to your left is a peaceful park that even has a water fountain (good news for those tired of constantly buying bottles of spring water to stave off the summer heat). The bustling, harborside square has one of Istria's few Middle Eastern sandwich eateries—a great place for a bite if you're on a budget. A nearby ice-cream stand is manned by enterprising, acrobatic young men who wow the crowds repeatedly by hurling scoops 50 or more feet into the air to open-mouthed colleagues who then discreetly spit them into napkins, garnering much applause (and generating long lines).

The 13th-century **Crkva svetog Pelagija** (Church of St. Pelagius), built on a 6th-century foundation and containing some elaborate baroque artwork, stands near the tip of the peninsula with its towering late-19th-century campanile. As in Rovinj, the main church faces the sea, and the statue atop the campanile doubled as a weather vane for the benefit of sailors.

On nearby Veliki trg is Novigrad's pale-red **city hall,** topped by a watch-tower and contrasting sharply with the yellow building beside it. Here and there, Gothic elements are in evidence on the medieval architecture about town (e.g., two windows on a 15th-century building at Velika ulica 33).

WHERE TO EAT

$$$$ ✗**Damir e Ormela.** Tucked away in a quiet side street, this superb (and
★ pricey) little family-run establishment is a secret wonder you may want
to share only with your fellow *gourmands* who appreciate Japanese-
style raw-fish specialties. Indeed, it may be the one restaurant in Istria
where fish—the fresh catch of the day, that is—is brought to the table
this way and served with such care. The service is elegant and friendly.
Although the main reason to dine here is the raw fish, you can also
delight in fried or grilled seafood and *tagliatte* (tagliatelle), not to mention some fine pastries. There's no English menu, but things are somehow clear enough, and the owners' daughter, who is often on hand,
speaks English. ✉*Ul. Zidine 5* ☎*052/758–134* ⚓*Reservations essential* ☰*AE, DC, MC, V.*

$$ ✗**Restaurant "MD" Novigrad.** A few hundred yards before you enter
Novigrad's Old Town, this exceedingly popular place, which has a very
pleasant garden terrace with a stone wall and a red-tile roof, is the best
spot in town to have your fill of hearty food. It's a sure bet for such
meat staples as *čevapčiči.* Finish off with a *palačinke* (crepe). ✉*Murvi
8* ☎*052/757–147* ☰*AE, DC, MC, V.*

$$ ✗**Vecchio Mulino.** The Old Mill pizzeria may look touristy—it is, after
all, centrally located right by the harbor, and it is packed—but it's also
good, and the raised terrace gives you the feeling of being a bit above
the fray. This is the place for pizza, spaghetti, salads, *čevapčiči,* and
tiramisu. ✉*Mlinska ul 8* ☎*052/726–300* ☰*AE, DC, MC, V.*

WHERE TO STAY

Though hotels are also available in a resort area southeast of town, the
in-town alternatives are more attractive and quite reasonably priced
by Istrian standards. For private rooms, check with the tourist agency
Rakam Trade (✉*Mlinska ul 45* ☎*098/366–407* ☎*052/757–047*
⊕*www.rakam-trade.hr*).

$$$$ ⬛**Nautica Hotel.** Sparkling marble bathrooms and plasma-screen TVs in
every room promise comfort of the highest order in this modern hotel a
few steps from the harbor in Novigrad. Vintage cruise-ship details like
portholes and nautical maps decorate the rooms and make you feel like
you're traveling first class on the Titanic. The hotel's restaurant has a
view of the harbor and a spacious patio to enjoy in summer months.
The pool and spa facilities are top-notch. Pros: soundproof rooms,
hearty breakfast. Cons: nautical theme a bit over-the-top, wireless sig-
nal in rooms is weak. ✉*Sv. Anton 15, 52446* ☎*052/600–400* ⊕*www.
nauticahotels.com* ⮑*38 rooms, 4 apartments* ⚐*In room: Wi-Fi, safe,
refrigerator. In hotel: restaurant, bar, pool, spa* ☰*AE, DC, MC, V.*

$$ ⬛**Hotel San Rocco.** Nine km (6 mi) up the road from Novigrad (on the
★ road to Buje), the Hotel San Rocco is a real change of pace from the
coast. Among rolling hills surrounded by olive trees and vineyards,
this upscale boutique hotel makes an impressive entrée to the Istrian
interior. It's in a renovated farmhouse with exposed stone walls and
wide wooden ceiling beams. Rooms are decorated with warm colors

and rich fabrics, and the outdoor pool and patio area has stunning views of the hilly towns nearby. Pros: excellent (though pricey) restaurant on-site, magnificent views. Cons: not regularly accessible by public transportation, terrace is within earshot of busy road. ✉ *Srednja ul 2, Brtonigla–Verteneglio52474* ☎ *052/725–000* ⊕ *www.san-rocco. hr* ✈ *12 rooms* ⚲ *In room: safe, Ethernet, refrigerator. In hotel: pool* ⊟ *AE, DC, MC, V* |○| *BP.*

$ ⊡ **Hotel Cittar.** The facade of this hotel is part of the medieval Old Town wall. Inside, a glass-covered vestibule imaginatively separates the wall from the hotel lobby. The rooms, while smallish, are bright, modern, and clean, with pine floors and silky bedspreads, and the service is very friendly. Pros: central location, pleasant patio and breakfast room. Cons: somewhat sterile modern interior. ✉ *Prolaz Venecija 1, 52466* ☎ *052/757–737 or 052/757–229* ☐ *052/757–340* ⊕ *www.cittar.hr* ✈ *40 rooms* ⚲ *In-hotel: restaurant, tennis courts. In-room: refrigerator* ⊟ *AE, DC, MC, V* |○| *BP.*

¢   ⊡ **Torci 18.** This family-run hotel offers modern rooms at good rates, plus one of Novigrad's best-reputed restaurants. Just inside the city walls, it's around the block from the sea, where you can take a dip at your leisure. Pros: the restaurant serves the family's own wine and olive oil. Cons: hotel only has 12 rooms, so books up fast, simple decor. ✉ *Ul Torci 43, 52466* ☎ *052/757–799* ☐ *052/757–174* ⊕ *www.torci18.hr* ✈ *12 rooms* ⚲ *In-hotel: restaurant* ⊟ *AE, DC, MC, V* |○| *BP.*

EN ROUTE   As you head north to Umag or northeast toward the interior hill towns remember that you're driving through some of Istria's most fertile olive oil territory. The tourist offices in Novigrad and Umag can give you a map outlining an olive-oil route with directions to several production facilities that offer tastings.

UMAG

14 km (8¾ mi) northwest of Novigrad.

Yet another onetime island, the peninsula town of Umag draws the fewest tourists of any of the major towns along Istria's western coast, even if it has more than its share of the usual beach resorts nearby. Perhaps it's the frustration with waiters who, while twiddling their thumbs in front of their restaurants, call out to every passing tourist, "Italiano? Deutsch? English?" and, less often, "Français?"

And yet Umag is a nice enough place to stroll for a couple of hours if you are passing this way, even if you might not be moved to stay for the night. Although the town grew up under the rule of Rome, practically none of its ancient roots are apparent in what remains of the historic core, which dates to the Middle Ages.

A spacious main square, **Trg Slobode** (Piazza Liberta—i.e., Freedom Square) is a jarring architectural mix from the medieval to the 20th-century mundane. It's where you'll find the towering **Church of the Assumption of the Virgin Mary & St. Pelegrin,** which was reconsecrated in 1760 after extensive reconstruction to repair the 14th-century original, which suffered damage in a fierce storm in 1651. Among its main attractions are a wooden, 14th-century Venetian triptych and a 16th-century painting depicting the resurrected Christ.

Just off Trg Slobode is the town's best-preserved historic street, **Riječka ulica,** where the souvenir vendors tend to congregate. The palm-lined main road leading through town from the coastal road to the square is a pleasant, comparatively modern, somewhat bustling thoroughfare. Along it you'll pass a large open square to your left that is home to both the tourist office and Istria's newest aquarium. A bit farther down, the **Church of St. Roche,** a lovely little stone structure, was erected in 1514 to mark the end of a plague outbreak some years earlier.

Aquarium Umag is modeled after its counterparts in Pula and Poreč. This aquarium opened in summer 2005 to bring the nearby world of Adriatic sea life closer to home—in the form of dozens of species from sea horses to starfish, morays to rays, and corals to crabs. ⊠*Svibnja ul 1* ☎*052/721–041* ✉*Apr.–Oct., 25 Kn, Nov.–Mar., 20 Kn* ☉*Apr.–Oct., daily 9–9; Nov.–Mar., daily 10–5.*

WHERE TO EAT

$$-$$$ ✕**Restaurant Konoba.** With a tad more ambience than the more touristy restaurants beside it, this spot on a quiet, seaside promenade right behind the cathedral is a decent place to have your fill. The one-room, rustic interior can get sultry in midsummer, but you can always sit outside. The fare—including standard, grilled fish dishes—is well prepared. If you order water (i.e., spring water), be sure to ask for a small bottle, unless you want a *big* one for 40 Kn. Good to bear in mind when ordering water elsewhere, too. ⊠*Ul Pod urom 7* ☎*052/751–423* ▭*AE, DC, MC, V.*

EN ROUTE Istria's interior hilltop villages have been much celebrated in recent years, both for their beauty and their gastronomical traditions. We recommend renting a car, even for a day, for a drive into the interior in the late afternoon, when fewer tour buses are likely to be on the road. Aside from Motovun and Grožnjan, Buje and Momjan to the northwest, Buzet and Hum to the east, and Gračišće to the south are all picturesque villages with their own medieval churches, old clock towers, and small-town restaurants.

MOTOVUN

Fodor'sChoice *30 km (19 mi) east of Poreč.*
★

It is an understatement to say that a day exploring the undulating green countryside and medieval hill towns of inland Istria makes a pleasant contrast to life on the coast. Motovun, for one, is a ravishing place. The king of Istria's medieval hill towns, with a double ring of defensive walls as well as towers and gates, may even evoke a scene straight from *Lord of the Rings*. Motovun is *the* place to visit if you opt to travel inland for a day or two from the sea. Be warned though, the town sees lots of tour buses. That said, a walk around the ramparts offers views across the oak forests and vineyards of the Mirna Valley. Just outside the village wall stands a church built according to plans by Palladio. In late July Motovun transforms for about five days into one of Croatia's liveliest (and most crowded) destinations—for the famed **Motovun Film Festival.**

WHERE TO EAT

$$$–$$$$ ✕ **Barbacan.** On the narrow cobblestone road you traverse into the Old Town—just before you pass through the city gate—this popular restaurant, whose rustic interior, complete with pots and pans on the walls, makes you feel as if you're in an Istrian farmhouse, is the best place in town for fresh seafood (no small accomplishment so far from the sea). The menu also has delectable truffle fare, from polenta (corn porridge) with black truffles and sheep's cheese, to Istrian beef with black truffles and truffle pâté. ⊠*Barbacan 1* ☎*052/681–791* ▤*AE, DC, MC, V.*

$$$ ✕ **Restaurant Enoteka & Zigante Tartufi.** This family-run restaurant-cum–truffle shop 3 km (2 mi) from Motovun is not simply a gift shop (as with other branches of the chain). Here, you can feast on such delectables as gilthead carpaccio with white truffles (gilthead being a type of sea bream) or crepes filled with white-chocolate mousse and black truffles. The place is rustic yet elegant, and, above all, captivating, what with low lighting cast by wrought-iron, streetlamp-style lights, stone walls, and wooden beams overhead. ⊠*Livade 7, Livade* ☎*052/664–030* ▤*AE, DC, MC, V.*

$$–$$$ ✕ **Restaurant Mčotić.** If you love truffles, whether with pasta or steak, this is a fine place to eat. Unquestionably an acquired taste, these earthy delicacies are gathered each autumn in the nearby Mirna Valley. Mčotić has a large summer terrace and occupies one of the most prominent buildings of the new Motovun, at the main intersection just below the Old Town. ⊠*Zadrugarska 19* ☎*052/681–758* ▤*AE, DC, MC, V.*

WHERE TO STAY

$ ☷ **Hotel Kaštel.** Just outside the Motovun town walls—but nonetheless nestled in a cloistered niche atop the hill—this peaceful, old-fashioned hotel makes an ideal retreat if you prefer green hills to sea and islands. Out front there's a small garden and pretty summer terrace. For just €10 more, dinner is also included. Pros: breathtaking panoramic views. Cons: uphill walk to the hotel. ⊠*Šetalište V. Nazora 7, 52424* ☎*052/681–607 or 052/681–735* ☎*052/681–652* ⊕*www.hotel-kastel-motovun.hr* ⥹*30 rooms* ⌂*In-hotel: restaurant, some pets allowed* ▤*AE, DC, MC, V* ⚏*BP.*

EN ROUTE As you near Grožnjan, you can take a small detour for a stop in the hilltop village of Buje. Drive up the hill through this quiet, lovely town, and take a stroll around its hushed little square shaded by plane trees, under which is a statue of a goat that seems to be reaching in vain for the leaves inches above its head. The pale yellow Church of the Madonna of Mercy is around the corner.

A Scent to Swoon Over

A ball-shaped candy often coated with cocoa? (That's what *Webster's* says about the truffle.) Think again. Such truffles are a dime a dozen compared to the real thing—namely, the sort of record-breaking, 1,310-kilogram (2,882-pound) truffle Giancarlo Zigante unearthed on November 2, 1999, with the help of his sharp-nosed dog in the village of Livade, near Motovun. What he found was—as attested to by the 100 guests he served in an effort to promote the cause of the Istrian truffle—the most delicious fungus you are likely to find.

For one thing, truffles grow underground, in a symbiotic relationship with the roots of oaks and certain other trees. As such, they cannot readily be seen. It is their scent that gives them away—a swoon-inducing scent. Sows were once the truffle hunter's favored companion, as truffles smell a lot like male hogs. (To be fair, the earthy aroma and pungent taste of truffles, which has also been likened to garlic, is prized by gourmands the world over.) These days, dogs are the truffle hunter's best friend.

For another thing, truffles are extremely rare. Most efforts to grow them domestically have failed, not least because you first need to grow a forest full of trees whose roots are just right for truffles. The white truffle, prized for its superior scent—the "white diamond," it's often called—sells for upwards of $1,000 a pound. This was the sort unearthed by Zigante, whose family owns a chain of truffle-oriented shops in Istria. In addition to the white truffle, Istria is also home to three sorts of black truffle, which sell for a mere $300 to $500 a pound.

In Istria truffles have been extracted since ancient times. Even Roman emperors and Austro-Hungarian aristocrats had a taste for truffles, not least because of the aphrodisiac qualities attributed to them. Truffles were once consumed and gathered like potatoes—that's how plentiful they were. That was in the 1800s. No longer, of course. Still, their fine shavings impart an unforgettable, earthy aroma and an irresistibly pungent, vaguely garlicky taste to pastas, salads, omelets, beef specialties, sauces, and more.

Economics and truffle scarcity being what they are, the Istrian truffle has become a hot commodity indeed. These days, for example, much of what is sold by Italy as Italian white truffles actually comes from Croatia—not least, from the moist woods around Motovun, near the river Mirna.

If you'd like to join a truffle hunt, reserve a spot on a brief truffle-hunting excursion that departs from Livade at 5 PM daily throughout the year (assuming two or more people sign up in advance) that includes an introductory drink, 1½ hours in the woods with trained truffle-sniffing dogs, and a hearty dinner. An experienced local organizer is **Activatravel Istra** (✉ *Scalierova 1, Pula* ☎ *052/215–497* 🖷 *052/211–889* 💲 *€60 per person for two people, €50 per person for three people, €45 per person for four people [maximum]*). The peak season for white truffles stretches from October through December, with January to September being more amenable to black truffles.

GROŽNJAN

★ *10 km (7 mi) east of Motovun.*

Close to Motovun and a reasonable drive from Poreč, Novigrad, or Umag, Grožnjan is also among Istria's preeminent hill towns, with a Renaissance loggia adjoining the town gate. Much visited by busloads of summer tourists, it is quite empty the rest of the year. In 1358, after at least 250 years in existence as a walled city, Grožnjan came under Venetian rule and remained so for more than 400 years. Though most of its population left after World War II, when decades of Italian rule came to an end and it officially became part of Yugoslavia, from the mid-1960s the government encouraged artists and musicians to settle here. This explains the number of painting and sculpture galleries you will encounter in this otherwise unassuming village. During the summer, an international federation of young musicians meets for training and workshops, presenting concerts beneath the stars through July and August.

Walk straight ahead from the small parking area just outside Grožnjan and you will come to the **Crkva sveta Voida i Modesta** *(Church of St. Vitus and St. Modestus)*. Reconstructed in baroque style from an earlier, 14th-century church, it stands on a relatively unassuming, parklike space a bit removed from the gallery scene, with panoramic views of the surrounding countryside and plateaus of Istria all the way to the sea. Conveniently, there's an ATM right beside the church.

Grožnjan may be small and out of the way, but enough tourists visit to merit yet another outlet in the Zigante family's **Enoteka & Zigante Tartufi** chain. Half of the shop sells truffles and everything truffle-related you can imagine, as well as local products from aromatic herb brandies to honey to dried boletus, whereas the other side is a sparkling, impeccably intimate wine bar. It is attached to the town's loggia, which means you can sit and sip inside or outside, as you prefer. ⊠ *Ul Gorjan 5* ☎ *Store 052/776–099, wine bar 052/721–998.*

NEED A BREAK? | If you are looking for a more substantial meal in Grožnjan, visit the chic if a bit smoky Bastia Konoba (⊠ *Trg Ferruccia Poiania 2* ☎ *052/776–370*), which is right on the main square. You can have a full meal in style for around 140 Kn, not including wine.

For a bit of wine tasting with Istrian prosciutto and similar hearty fare to accompany the elixir, stop by at **Vina Dešković**. The house-cum–wine cellar is on a lonely country road about 10 minutes outside Grožnjan by car. You can get not only a tasty selection of five Istrian wines—for example, malvazija among the whites and teran among the reds—but also a selection of hearty snacks from its simple menu and even a breathtaking view of the tiny village of Kostanjica several hundred yards away. Though the friendly family members here speak little English, communication need not be a barrier to a pleasant experience; you need to be able to say little more than "vino" and "prosciutto." Figure on at least 50 Kn per person for food and a glass of wine. Since finding your way there through the hills outside Grožnjan is much easier said than done, do check with the town's tourist-information office for directions here and/or to similar wine-tasting opportunities nearby. You will want to have a designated driver, by the way. ⊠ *Kostanjica 58, Kostanjica* ☎ *052/776–315, 052/776–316, or 091/516–5371.*

EASTERN ISTRIA: LABIN & RABAC

Labin is 44 km (28 mi) northeast of Pula.

Few travelers take time to explore Istria's often-overlooked eastern coast. Although the region's mostly mountainous terrain offers a relative dearth of large towns abounding in historical sights and easy-to-access, swimmable stretches of sea, the region does contain one notable exception: Labin.

Perched in all its compact medieval redolence atop a hill a short drive or walk from the sea, **Labin** is Croatia's former coal-mining capital and the birthplace of Matthias Flacius Illyricus, a Reformation-era collaborator of Martin Luther. Its narrow, historic streets are well deserving of a good walk, followed, if time allows, by a dip in the sea at Rabac, the relatively crowded and less inspiring complex of hotels and beaches 3 km (2 mi) away. From Labin's endearing little main square, **Titov trg,** with its 16th-century loggia and bastion, it's an easy stroll to Šetališste San Marco, a semicircular promenade with a spectacular view of the sea. Walk to the end, past a half dozen or so busts of historical luminaries, and take a sharp left up the cobblestone road. By following the spray-painted PANORAMA signs on the stone walls, you will soon reach the top of the hill, where (for 5 Kn) you can climb another 98½ feet up for an even better view from the town's onetime fortress, the **Fortica.** From here Labin's relatively bustling commercial center, which seemed nonexistent a few minutes ago, comes fully into view below, as do the dry, craggy hills of inland Istria. Making your way down the other side of the hill back toward the main square, you will pass by Labin's other major attractions, not least the **Crkva rođenja blažene djevice Marije** (Church of the Birth of the Virgin Mary). With a facade featuring a 14th-century rose window and a 17th-century Venetian lion of the sort you will encounter elsewhere in Istria, the church was thoroughly renovated in 1993 to repair serious damage from mining under the Old Town in the 1960s. That said, its mix of architectural styles essentially dates from a late-16th century renovation, though its foundations may date to the 11th century—and, farther back, to an earlier church built here by the Avars in AD 611.

As for **Rabac** (buses hourly from Labin for 1 Kn), your first thought on arriving may be: Why come all the way to Europe for a place that looks much like a generic beach resort anywhere? Its series of huge, honeycomb-shaped, Italian-owned hotel monstrosities with names like Narcis, Casino, and Mimosa are truly the last place the writer of these lines, for one, would want to stay. But wait. Make a *right* on entering town rather than a left, then walk down the hill by road or the steps

CLOSE UP

Agritourism in Istria

Given the vast tourism infrastructure you see along the Istrian coast, not to mention the number of picturesque swimming coves that dot the coastline, you might be forgiven for thinking that the hinterlands—whether Motovun or Grožnjan or beyond—are nice places to visit for the day or for the evening, but that the coast is the place to be when night falls. In fact, Istria has been at the forefront of Croatia's efforts to expand tourism into the countryside with a program to promote "agritourism," where visitors stay at family farms. Farm vacations come in many shapes and sizes in Istria. Many are more like estates and deliver something along the lines of a gourmet vacation with just enough of a rustic touch to remind you that you are not vacationing at a resort. **Stancija 1904,** a turn-of-the-century villa that has been lovingly restored, is an excellent place to stay—and a good example of what you're likely to find if you venture into the agritourism section of the Istria brochure. A stay here gets you in tune with the countryside, breathing fresh air and seeing the stars at night. The agri part of the tourism here is a high-

light; plenty of what you eat comes from the family garden, prepared by Draženka, the friendly cook and hostess. The grounds are laced with stone walkways, and leafy trees provide shady corners for you to grab a lawn chair and doze in. Quiet it is—and in that sense, you are a world away from the crowds back on the coast. You'll awake to a cock crowing and see the family dog chasing rabbits around the yard. There are three immaculately furnished apartments, each with a private terrace, for €96 per day, plus a full-fledged, two-story house for rent for €280 per day. Breakfast is an additional €10 per person; three times a week you can also get dinner for another €20. The owners' meticulous attention to every detail of your surroundings ensures that not a doorknob is left with so much as a smudge of grease or dirt. The farm is in the tiny village of Smoljanci, just beyond the picturesque Renaissance-era town of Svetvinčenat (5 km [3 mi] from Kanfanar, which is near Dvivigrad). ⊠ *Smoljanci 2–3, Svetvinčenat 52342* ☎ *052/560–022 or 098/738– 974* 🖶 *052/560–028* ⊕ *www.stancija. com* 🖃 *AE, DC, MC, V.*

to the harbor. Once you reach the harbor, go *left* and then along the harborside promenade, rather than right. Doing so will reveal a side of Rabac that, although still somewhat touristy, also retains something of the idyllic—with its quiet harbor replete with small yachts, motorboats, and other pleasure craft, not to mention dozens of tiny, harborside coves you can walk down into for a quick dip via short flights of concrete steps. Although you can rent a plastic beach chair, making yourself comfortable on the smooth, roundish stones isn't nearly as difficult as it sounds; and even in midsummer, you can usually find yourself a rock to sprawl out on.

WHERE TO EAT

$$$ ✕ **Due Fratelli.** Owned by a family that also has a fishing boat down on
Fodor'sChoice the bay, this restaurant has plenty of fresh, delicious seafood specialties
★ on offer in addition to a good selection of meat and poultry dishes. Get-
ting to this well-reputed restaurant, whose decor is pleasantly folksy
and which has a cool, shaded terrace with a lush wall of pink flow-
ers and grapevines out front, is easy if you're driving; keep your eyes
peeled along the winding road downhill from Labin to Rabac for the
restaurant's little sign to the left as the road curves right. If you're on
foot, the walk is a bit of a haul. ⊠*Montozi 6, Labin* ☎*052/853–577*
⌑*Reservations essential* ▭*AE, DC, MC, V.*

WHERE TO STAY

$$ 🔲 **Villa Annette.** Although you'll pass by quite a few ugly hotels on the
★ way, once you arrive at Villa Annette, perched on top of a cliff over-
looking Rabac harbor, you'll be happy you persevered. All the rooms at
this boutique hotel are suites with large balconies and stunning views.
Plush leather sofas and chairs sit next to modern beds covered with
neutral-color cotton spreads, giving the rooms a minimalist but luxurious feel. Rooms can accommodate 2 to 6 people in style. An extra
€30 gets you dinner, a four-course affair served by the pool in summer
months. Getting to Villa Annette is easiest by car; the walk up to it is
long and steep. Pros: spacious rooms with undisturbed views. Cons: not
easily accessible without a car, Rabac is an unattractive town. ⊠*Raška
24, 52221* ☎*052/884–222* ⊕*www.villaannette.hr* ⌁*12 suites* ⌂*In
room: safe, refrigerator, Ethernet. In hotel: restaurant, parking, pool*
▭*AE, DC, MC, V* ⦿*BP.*

$–$$ 🔲 **Hotel Amfora.** The Amfora has an enviable location above the Rabac
harbor. The hotel's immediate surroundings are quiet and spacious, but
restaurants, bars, shops, and beaches are no more than a 10-minute
walk away. Sea-view rooms overlook the bay of Kvarner and on clear
days the islands of Cres and Losinj. Rooms are a bit dated, though
comfortable enough with very good air conditioning. The helpful
staff remains cheerful even in high season. Pros: central location but
removed from noisy town square, large pool complex. Cons: no elevator, not much nightlife nearby. ⊠*Rabac bb, 52221* ☎*052/872–222*
⊕*www.hotel-amfora.com* ⌁*52 rooms* ⌂*In room: safe, refrigerator.
In hotel: restaurant, bar, parking (no fee), no elevator* ▭*AE, DC, MC,
V* ⦿*BP.*

ISTRIA ESSENTIALS

AIR TRAVEL

Croatia Airlines operates flights to Pula from Zagreb. Ryanair has service three times a week from Dublin and London Stansted to Pula, and daily service from London Stansted to Trieste, Italy. EasyJet flies from Bristol and London Luton to nearby Rijeka from May until mid-September.

Information **EasyJet** (⊕ *www.easyjet.com*). **Ryanair** (⊕ *www.ryanair.com*). **Croatia Airlines** (⊕ *www.croatiaairlines.hr*).

BOAT & FERRY TRAVEL

In summer the Italian company Adriatica runs a catamaran service from Trieste and Grado (in Italy) to Rovinj and Brijuni. In Rovinj, tickets for the catamaran are available from Eurostar Travel. The Adriatica agent in Trieste is Samer & Co.

Information **Adriatica** (⊕ *www.adriatica.it*). **Eurostar Travel** (⊠ *Obala P. Budičina 1, Rovinj* ☎ *052/813-144*). **Samer & Co.** (⊠ *Piazza dell'Unità d'Italia 7, Trieste, Italy* ☎ *040/6702-7211*).

BUS TRAVEL

There are domestic connections all over mainland Croatia to and from Pula, Poreč, and Rovinj, and local services between these towns and smaller inland destinations such as Motovun and Vodnjan. International buses offer daily connections to Italy (Trieste) and Slovenia (Ljubljana, Koper, Piran, and Portorož). Timetables are available at all bus stations. However, as elsewhere in Croatia, the sheer number of different companies offering bus service out of each station can be confusing; so it's best to confirm at the information window what you might find posted on the wall.

Information **Poreč Bus Station** (⊠ *Rade Končara 1, Poreč* ☎ *052/432-153*). **Pula Bus Station** (⊠ *Trg 1 Istarske Brigade, Pula* ☎ *052/500-040*). **Rovinj Bus Station** (⊠ *Mattea Benussia, by trg na Lokvi, Rovinj* ☎ *052/811-453*).

CAR TRAVEL

While visiting Pula, Rovinj, and Poreč a car may be more of a hindrance than an asset: all three towns are served by good bus connections, and having your own vehicle only causes parking problems. The best way to see the Istrian interior, however, is by car. The "sight" to see is the countryside itself and the small villages that dot it, so renting a car even for a day will give you much more satisfaction than trying to arrange a bus trip to one or another hill town. (And bus connections to the interior are infrequent.) If you are traveling from Zagreb, you can, of course, rent there, but major agencies have offices in Pula, and other towns along the coast all have one or more local agencies that generally offer better rates than the major chains without sacrificing quality of service; however, they may be less equipped than the major chains to take reservations by phone. (Some, such as Vetura and Manuel, also rent bicycles and scooters [i.e., mopeds].) Lastly, bear in mind that finding an available car on short notice in midsummer can be tricky regardless of the agency involved.

Novigrad **Avis** (⊠ *S Dobrića 1, Novigrad* ☎ *052/223-739*).

Poreč **Europcar** (⊠ *Hotel Poreč, Poreč* ☎ *052/433-413*). **Avis** (⊠ *S Dobrića 1, Poreč* ☎ *052/223-739*). **Budget** (⊠ *Obala M. Tita, Poreč* ☎ *052/451-188*). **Vetura** (⊠ *Trg Joakima Rakovca 2, Poreč* ☎ *052/434-700* ⊠ *Zelena Laguna, Poreč* ☎ *052/451-391 or 052/451-395*).

Pula **Europcar** (⊠ *Pula Airport, Pula* ☎ *052/530-351*). **Avis** (⊠ *S Dobrića 1, Pula* ☎ *052/223-739*). **Budget** (⊠ *ACI marina, Riva 1, Pula* ☎ *052/218-252*). **Hertz** (⊠ *Hotel Histria, Verudela, Pula* ☎ *052/210-868*). **Manuel** (⊠ *Giardini 10, Pula* ☎ *052/211-858 or 098/367-637*). **Vetura** (⊠ *Verudela, Pula* ☎ *091/535-8755, 091/535-8755 for airport office*).

Rabac **Vetura** (⊠ *Obala M. Tita, Rabac* ☎ *052/872-129 or 091/557-5113*).

Rovinj **Avis** (⊠ *S Dobrića 1, Rovinj* ☎ *052/223-739*). **Lucky Way** (⊠ *Nazorova, Rovinj* ☎ *052/811-503*). **Unirent** (⊠ *Istarska, Rovinj* ☎ *098/230-302*). **Vetura** (⊠ *Nazorova, Rovinj* ☎ *052/815-209*).

Umag **Interauto** (⊠ *Trgovačka 3, Umag* ☎ *052/741-483, 052/741-358, or 098/214-208*). **Vetura** (⊠ *Trgovačka 4, Umag* ☎ *052/742-700*).

INTERNET
All the major towns along the Istrian coast have a few Internet cafés, some with Wi-Fi. Expect to pay at least 10 Kn for 20 minutes, or 30 Kn per hour. The Tourist Information Office in Poreč offers 15 minutes of free Internet use, more if no one is waiting in line *(see Visitor Information, below)*.

Information **Enigma Internet Center** (⊠ *Kandlerova 19, Pula* ☎ *052/381-615*). **Planet Tourist Agency** (⊠ *Sv Križ 1, Rovinj* ☎ *052/840-494*).

TRAIN TRAVEL
Istria is not well connected to the rest of Croatia by rail. To get to Zagreb or Split you need to transit through Rijeka. However, there is a line running north from Pula to Ljubljana in Slovenia.

Information **Pula Train Station** (⊠ *Kolodvorksa, Pula* ☎ *052/541-733*).

TRAVEL AGENCIES
Kompas-Istria can arrange private accommodations, as well as tours to the Limski kanal from either Poreč or Rovinj. Excursions Delfin also arranges tours to the Limski kanal, as do several other local companies and independent operators who happen to own boats and post flyers about their towns.

Information **Excursions Delfin** (⊠ *Zagrebačka 5, Rovinj* ☎ *091/514-2169 or 091/520-5309*). **Kompas-Istria** (⊠ *Obala M. Tita 16, Poreč* ☎ *052/451-1000* ⊠ *Obala M. Tita 5, Rovinj* ☎ *52/813-211* ⊠ *Starih Statuta 2, Pula* ☎ *052/212-511* ⊠ *Gradska Vrata 11, Novigrad* ☎ *052/726-383* ⊠ *Trgovačka 13, Umag* ☎ *052/741-613*).

TOUR COMPANIES

Guided cycling tours of Istria can be arranged by Saddle Skedaddle, a U.K.-based cycling outfit. Gourmet tours, including wine-tasting tours of Istria, can be arranged through My Croatia. Arblaster and Clarke offers gourmet tours including a truffle hunt in the fall in Istria.

Information **Saddle Skeddadle** (☎ *0191/265–1110* ⊕ *www.skedaddle.co.uk*). **My Croatia** (☎ *0118/961–1554* ⊕ *www.mycroatia.co.uk*). **Arblaster & Clarke** (☎ *0173/026–3111* ⊕ *www.winetours.co.uk*).

VILLA RENTALS

Villa rentals are popular in Istria, where many properties—from one-bedroom apartments to houses for 16—have been brought up to a high standard in recent years. The medieval villages of the hilly interior are scenic, and offer sweeping (and almost uninterrupted) views of vineyards and olive groves. Hunkering down in a stone farmhouse and exploring the rest of the peninsula from there is certainly a leisurely way to appreciate Istria. Sadly, the region's been a bit oversold as "the new Tuscany" by tourism specialists, and while comfortable villas with pools are available, often they're as expensive as their equivalent in France or Italy but not quite as well-appointed or charming. On the upside though, Istria is still not nearly as crowded as other parts of Europe, so you won't have to share your view with the hordes. The following companies specialize in villa rentals in Istria.

Information **Vintage Travel** (☎ *0845/344–0460* ⊕ *www.vintagetravel.co.uk*). **Home Away** (☎ *512/493–0375* ⊕ *www.homeaway.com*). **Hidden Croatia** (☎ *0800/021–7771* ⊕ *www.hiddencroatia.com*). **Adriatica.net** (✉ *Slavonska u. 26, Zagreb* ☎ *01/241–5611* ⊕ *www.adriatica.net*).

VISITOR INFORMATION

Although the official tourist offices listed below can provide you with every bit of information imaginable, they generally leave the booking of rooms and excursions to private tourist agencies. The office in Poreč does offer 15 minutes of free Internet surfing, which may be enough for you to check your e-mail.

Contacts **Brijuni Tourist Information** (✉ *Fažana* ☎ *052/525–888* ⊕ *www. brijuni.hr*). **Grožnjan Tourist Information** (✉ *Umberto Gorjan 3, Grožnjan* ☎ *052/776–131*). **Istria Tourist Board** (⊕ *www.istra.hr*). **Labin & Rabac Tourist Information** (✉ *A. Negri 20, Labin* ☎ *052/855–560* or *052/852–399* ⊕ *www. istra.com/rabac*). **Motovun Tourist Information** (✉ *Šetalište V. Nazora 1, Motovun* ☎ *052/681–642*). **Novigrad Tourist Information** (✉ *Porpolella 1, Novigrad* ☎ *052/757–075* ⊕ *www.istra.com/novigrad*). **Poreč Tourist Information** (✉ *Zagrebačka 9, Poreč* ☎ *052/451–293* ⊕ *www.istra.com/porec*). **Pula Tourist Information** (✉ *Forum 3, Pula* ☎ *052/219–197* ⊕ *www.pulainfo.hr*). **Rovinj Tourist Information** (✉ *Pino Budičin 12, Rovinj* ☎ *052/811–566* ⊕ *www.istra. com/rovinj*). **Umag Tourist Information** (✉ *Trgovačka 6, Umag* ☎ *052/741–363* ⊕ *www.istra.com/umag*). **Vodnjan Tourist Information** (✉ *Narodni trg 3, Vodnjan* ☎ *052/511–672* ⊕ *www.vodnjan.hr*).

Kvarner

WORD OF MOUTH

"Definitely walk the Promenade [in Opatija] . . . and enjoy the amazing views. Take advantage of the numerous ice cream stands along the way."

—Debs

"We absolutely loved Rab Town on Rab Island!! We would not have even given it a second thought but our friends from Germany said that we had to go there. Rab Town is beautiful and there are several nice restaurants and bars. There isn't a lot to do, but you are on holiday so what the heck!

—eurotraveller

Updated by
Betsy Maury

THE KVARNER GULF IS A LARGE, DEEP BAY with the Istrian peninsula to the north and Dalmatia to the south. Four major islands, Cres, Krk, Lošinj, and Rab, along with numerous smaller specks of land, fill the heart of the bay and can be viewed from the gentle resort towns strung around the coastal arc. The lush, rolling hills of this coastal strip wind their way around the gulf from Opatija. East of Rijeka, the scenic Magistrala costal highway cuts into the solid rock of the foothills on its way to the southern tip of Croatia.

The wild Gorski Kotar mountain nature park is on the mainland northeast of Rijeka. Across the narrow range sits the inland part of Primorsko-goranska županija (Primorje-Gorski Kotar county), a region of small towns and agricultural land on the edge of the Pannonian Basin, through which you pass if you are traveling overland to Zagreb. Although the entire northern stretch of the Croatian coast exhibits a strong Italian influence, thanks to centuries of control from across the Adriatic, most of the mainland resorts developed during Habsburg rule. Robust and sophisticated Austro-Hungarian architecture and infrastructure predominate in these towns.

In contrast, the islands tend toward the cozier, less aspirational features of Italy. Dwellings are simpler, often of stone, and set in less geometric layouts. The elder population may struggle with any language other than Italian, and that includes Croatian.

Krk, entered via a short bridge from the eastern shore of the gulf region, reflects the mainland's arid nature more than its brethren. On Cres the northern stretches are a twisted knot of forest peaks and rocky crags, while gentler, cultivated slopes appear toward the center. Pine forests marching down to the shores provide welcome shade in the middle of the day. On the island's southern end, hollows have filled up to make freshwater lakes that provide the island's drinking water, counterbalancing the salty sea that licks at the land just a hill crest away. At the foot of Cres, a hop across a narrow stretch of the Adriatic brings you to Lošinj. This lush, Mediterranean oasis owes much of its charm to the gardens and villas that were built here during the seafaring heydays of the 19th century. As you approach from the north, the silhouette of Rab resembles the humped back of a diving sea monster. The high north of the island is dry and barren, almost a desert of rock and scrub, whereas the lower southern hemisphere is lush and fertile.

EXPLORING KVARNER

The Kvarner's principal city, Rijeka, is a somewhat dilapidated port (although the 21st century has seen it making a reasonably committed effort at a comeback), with good road and rail connections to Zagreb. Genteel Opatija was founded by the Habsburgs in the mid-19th century as Croatia's first seaside resort. The regional airport is found on the island of Krk.

KVARNER TOP 5

- Opatija's Lungomare waterfront path. The Lungomare is an ideal place for a leisurely stroll anywhere between Opatija and Volosko; the path is over 7 mi long.

- Baška beach on Krk island. For a day of seaside family fun—windsurfing, sandy expanses, and ice-cream stands galore—take a trip to this great beach on the southern end of the island.

- Eco-Center Caput Insulae-Beli. You'll get a look at the rare grif-fin vultures of Cres island and find out about other bird-watching opportunities.

- The Great Bell Tower in Rab Town. The view from the top of the town's tallest and most beautiful tower (there are four) is of a perfectly preserved medieval square.

- The picturesque harbor of Lošinj. Watch yachts come in and dock in front of stately 19th-century villas on both sides of the marina.

ABOUT THE RESTAURANTS

Without wanting to force square pegs into round holes, there are essentially four types of restaurants in Kvarner, if not the whole of the country. Unsurprisingly, many of them fall heavily under the influence of the Italian *tricolore*. In place of faith, hope, and charity, expect white pasta, green salads, and red pizza. The many pizza and pasta spots tend to be the cheaper and more casual alternatives.

Possibly the most delightful Croatian establishment is the *konoba*. Originally, the konoba was a humble cottage or shed, where fishermen would gather after returning to shore and might toast to surviving another day's trip out to sea by raising a few glasses, followed by a sample of their catch cooked to soak up the booze. These rustically styled fish restaurants have cropped up everywhere in the last few years. Especially on the islands, you'll see quite a few originals around.

Few dishes come specifically from Kvarner, but several parts of the region carry a healthy reputation for certain produce. In Rijeka try *jota,* a thick soup with sauerkraut or pickled beets with meat. *Maneštra* is the local version of minestrone, but made only with beans instead of pasta. The Gorski kotar region serves a mean polenta made with potatoes, local cheese, blood sausage, and game. On Krk try *Krk–Šurlice,* the local version of pasta; handmade on a spindle, it's often served with wild-game goulash. Cres has a fierce rivalry with the northern Dalmatian island of Pag regarding who serves the best lamb in Croatia. Calamari cooked in herbs and wine is a good bet on Lošinj. In Kvarner, *mrkač* is the local word for octopus; it's *hobotnice* in the rest of the country. If you order white fish, either grilled (*na žaru*) or cooked in white wine (*na buzara*), you'll be charged by the kilogram, whereas squid and shrimp come in regular portions, often offered cooked in the same manner. The classic accompaniment to fish is chard (*blitva*) and potatoes (*krumpir*). Many choices will come smothered in olive oil and garlic; you'll likely be told that this is what keeps the population so healthy. Krk and Sušak are home to the most highly regarded wines from the region, with the dry white *Vrbnička žlahtina* a strong candidate for "best." *Rakija* (fruit brandies) are, of course, the common end to a meal and the start of a long night.

ABOUT THE HOTELS

Opatija, Krk, and Lošinj have a healthy selection of quality hotels, but outside these (relatively) major resorts, hotels become a rarer commodity. Much more common is renting a house or apartment. There are multitudes of these holiday homes available across the region, and local tourist offices and many agencies can assist in booking. If you want to save money, consider renting a room in a private home. At major transport hubs you'll often be accosted by elderly ladies attempting to entice you to their spare room. (They shout out, "Soba!," meaning "room.") Having a map in hand to understand exactly the location of the room being offered is wise, since out-of-town rooms often mean navigating the public transport system late in the evening or shelling out for a taxi ride.

■ TIP➔ It can be close to impossible to get accommodations for fewer than two consecutive nights in high season, so plan to stay at least that long in each place you overnight.

WHAT IT COSTS IN EUROS (€) AND CROATIAN KUNA (KN)					
	¢	$	$$	$$$	$$$$
RESTAURANTS	under 20 Kn	20 Kn–35 Kn	35 Kn–60 Kn	60 Kn–80 Kn	over 80 Kn
HOTELS In euros	under €75	€75–€125	€125–€175	€175–€225	over €225
HOTELS In kuna	under 550 Kn	550 Kn–925 Kn	925 Kn–1,300 Kn	1,300 Kn–1,650 Kn	over 1,650 Kn

Restaurant prices are for a main course at dinner. Hotel prices are for two people in a double room in high season, excluding taxes and service charges.

TIMING

⚠ The Kvarner region gets very busy in high summer, so don't even dream of heading, for instance, to Opatija or Krk in August without accommodations lined up. Late May through early June and September are ideal times to visit, since you can expect good weather, warm seas, and open facilities. Early May and October are good if you're looking for peace and quiet, but remember that few tourist-related activities are on offer and you still need to book accommodations in advance.

RIJEKA

182 km (114 mi) southwest of Zagreb.

Water is the essence of Kvarner, and the region's largest city expresses this simply. Whether in Croatian or Italian (Fiume) the translation of the name to English is the same: *river*. Although the history of Croatia's third city goes back to the days of Imperial Rome, modern Rijeka evolved under the rule of Austria-Hungary. The historic core retains vestiges of the old Habsburg monarchy from the time when Rijeka

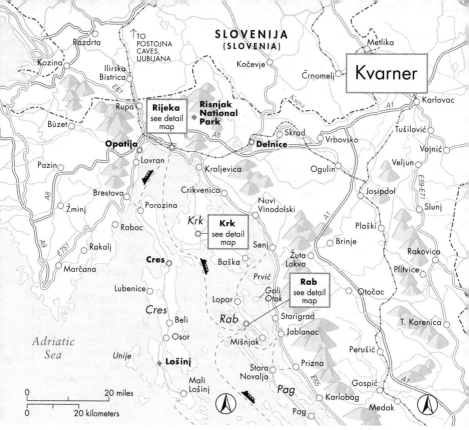

Rijeka
see detail
map

Krk
see detail
map

Rab
see detail
map

Kvarner

SLOVENIJA
(SLOVENIA)

Risnjak
National
Park

Adriatic
Sea

Cres

Cres

Krk

Rab

Pag

Lošinj

0   20 miles

0   20 kilometers

Razdrta
TO
POSTOJNA
CAVES,
LJUBLJANA
Kozina
Ilirska
Bistrica
Rupa
Rijeka
Opatija
Bùzet
Pazin
Lovran
Brestova
Žminj
Porozina
Rabac
Rakalj
Marčana
Lubenice
Beli
Osor
Unije
Mali
Lošinj
Kočevje
Metlika
Črnomelj
Karlovac
Tušilović
Vojnić
Skrad
Vrbovsko
Delnice
Kraljevica
Ogulin
Veljun
Crikvenica
Josipdol
Slunj
Novi
Vinodolski
Plaški
Rakovica
Senj
Žuta
Lokva
Brinje
Plitvice
Baška
Prvić
Goli
Otok
Lopar
Starigrad
Otočac
T. Korenica
Jablanac
Mišnjak
Perušić
Stara
Novalja
Prizna
Gospić
Karlobag
Medak
Pag

served as the empire's outlet to the Adriatic. During the 1960s, under
Yugoslavia, the suburbs expanded rapidly. Rijeka is the country's largest port, with a huge shipyard, massive dry-dock facilities, refineries,
and other heavy industries offering large-scale employment. Since the
break-up of Yugoslavia however, Rijeka's role as a shipping town has
declined significantly. Much business shifted north to the smaller Slovene ports during the crippling wars of the 1990s, and although some
has returned, the volume remains less than half that seen in 1980.

At the city's core sits Korzo, a pedestrian street of shops and cafés running parallel with the harbor and just to the south of where the land
begins to rise toward the peaks of the mountains that back the bay.
The high ground ensures that the suburbs stretch out to the east and
the west, with little space to expand to the north. The general rule is
that Rijeka is more of a transit town than a holiday destination, and
it's not known for its points of interest, apart from the hilltop fortress
of Trsat. However, the city is well worth investigating more thoroughly
than most would have you believe.

Many visitors stay in the nearby seaside resort of Opatija, and locals
will often head that way in their free time as well. That said, Rijeka is
a perfectly pleasant small city (approximately 200,000 people call it
home); if it did not command the wonderful bay that it does, it would

GREAT ITINERARIES

IF YOU HAVE 3 DAYS
With only three days, start off on **Krk** to enjoy a little island life, heading straight to the action on Baška beach. From here, either choose another town like Malinska or Krk Town, or make your way to **Rijeka**, visiting the fruit and vegetable market and possibly taking in a cultural exhibit or two. On the final day, scoot farther west for some classic seaside resorting in **Opatija**, and don't miss an afternoon stroll along the Lungomare.

IF YOU HAVE 5 DAYS
Begin your trip either in Opatija or Krk, reversing the three-day itinerary to suit your fancy, and add a visit to the relatively wild island of **Cres**. Ferries connect northern Cres (Porozina) to Brestova west of Opatija and central Cres (Merag) with Krk at Valbiska. A day divided between swimming at the beaches and relaxing in

a café or ice-cream parlor in Cres Town can be enhanced by a second day exploring the more remote areas of the island, taking in some of the smaller villages or the rugged north.

IF YOU HAVE 7 DAYS
With a full week, explore the upscale marina at **Mali Lošinj** for one day (reachable by bus from Cres Town). You'll have to work your way back to Rijeka or Krk at this point to get to Rab, as ferries don't connect Cres and Lošinj to Rab. On your way, spend an extra day on the Opatija Riviera, taking in the pretty towns of **Lovran** and **Ičići**. From Rijeka jump on a bus or, in summer, a catamaran and head south to sample some of the region's only sandy beaches on the beautifully lush island of **Rab**. Spend at least a day admiring the medieval churches and campaniles of **Rab Town**.

also be unremarkable. This makes it one of the more authentically Croatian spots in the region in summer. Those looking to avoid the hordes could do much worse than to stay in Rijeka—albeit with very few options for accommodation—and use the excellent network of ferries to explore the rest of Kvarner.

Rijeka is the home port of Jadrolinija, the coast's major ferry company. Local ferries connect with all the Kvarner islands and will take you farther afield as well. If you're planning on heading south and would rather dodge the slow and dangerous roads that head that way, then let the boat take the strain. Ferries leaving Rijeka weave through islands all the way down to Dubrovnik, stopping at most major points on the way. Sunsets, sunrises, plus a mingling of stars and shore-anchored town lights in between, help transport one further than just the few hundred kilometers to the other end of the country.

Rijeka is linked with Zagreb by the new E65 motorway, which is clean and fast, though tolls add up on the journey. To reach the Dalmatian coast from Rijeka, you'll have to backtrack 75 km (47 mi) away from the coast and get on the motorway heading south toward Split and Dubrovnik. Rijeka is also the start of the Jadranska Magistrala (the coastal highway), which follows the coast south, all the way to the Montenegro border. Alternately offering startling views from on high

IF YOU LIKE

CLEAR WATER

Given the geography of the region, it's thoroughly predictable that the stars of Kvarner are the beaches that line the Adriatic. For the most part they are covered with stone, which may not be so forgiving on the body when lying upon them, nor on the feet when traversing, but you can thank the mineral shores for the stunning aquamarine purity of the water. Diving below the gentle waves is a great attraction, as is hoisting sail to allow the wind to propel you across them.

HIKING

The wonderful climate, plentiful sunshine, and fresh sea breezes should give thanks to the mountains that plunge toward the waters around the whole Kvarner bay. Nature lovers will enjoy hiking here, dropping into remote villages to refuel and sample a pace of life rarely found in 21st-century Europe.

RESORT TOWNS

Kvarner offers the visitor perhaps the greatest variety of cultural and architectural styles in Croatia. The mainland, thanks to its popularity with former rulers, features resort towns built on the grand scale of the Austrian Empire, particularly on the Opatija Riviera. Although many are somewhat faded in spots—and must compete with the "modifications" of Communist-era planners—their original intention to serve the upper echelons of late-19th-century society from Central Europe still manages to impress.

THE QUIET ISLANDS

The islands, meanwhile, are bastions of Mediterranean culture, and Italian in particular. Aside from certain tourist-heavy locations (e.g., parts of Krk), one can still lap up the joys of rustic southern Europe, including stone cottages and peaceful village harbors, in relative authenticity.

or the illusion that one could simply reach out to disturb the crystal surface of the sea with a hand trailing from the car, this is one of the most beautiful trips in Europe. However, with sharp drop-offs, series upon series of sharp curves, numerous slow-moving trucks, and many hot-headed car drivers, it's also one of the most dangerous roads on the continent.

EXPLORING RIJEKA

Numbers in the text correspond to numbers in the margin and on the Rijeka map.

The *Turisticka magistrala* (Tourist Route) will guide you on foot around Rijeka's main sights, many of which are labeled with plaques. The **Rijeka Tourism Association** (✉ *Užarska 14* ☎*051/315–710* ⊕*www. tz-rijeka.hr*) can provide you with an official guide.

❶ ★ City Market. A set of five turn-of-the-20th-century halls host the city's main market, one of the liveliest spots in Rijeka on a weekday or Saturday morning. Get here before midday to enjoy the trading in full cry. The original constructions from the 1880s have suffered a little from later additions, but the fish market, the last to be built, is a wonderful

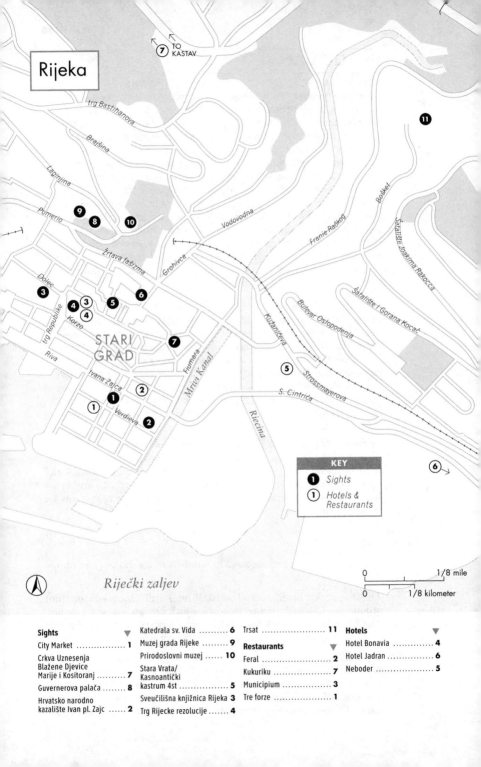

Rijeka

7 TO KASTAV

trg Bastihanova

Brajšina

Lagnjina

Pomerio

9 **8** **10**

Vodovodna

Žrtava fašizma

Grohivca

11

Franje Račkog

Bošket

Šatalište Joakima Rakocca

Dolec

3

trg Republike

Korzo

4 **3**

4

5

6

STARI GRAD

7

Riva

Ivana Zajca

Fiumara

Mrtvi Kanal

Kružnićeva

Bulevar Oslopodenja

Šatalište I Gorana Kocať

2

1

Verdieva

2

Riečina

S. Cintrića

Strossmayerova

5

6

KEY

1 *Sights*

(1) *Hotels & Restaurants*

0 ———————— 1/8 mile
0 ———————— 1/8 kilometer

Riječki zaljev

example of art nouveau design. The castings by well-known Venetian artist Urbano Bottasso ape the fish and crustaceans being sold below. The streets surrounding the market are filled with no-frills eateries that are good for a quick lunch. It's a good bet that their offerings will be fresh. ⊠ *Verdijeva.*

❼ **Crkva Uznesenja Blažene Djevice Marije i Kositoranj** *(Church of St. Mary of the Assumption)*. Formerly the city's main church and dating back to the Middle Ages, St. Mary's is still known to locals as the "big church." However, many additions and changes now obscure much of the original architecture. The relatively recent updates have not imposed severe geometry, though: the bell tower remains leaning to one side by 40 centimeters or so. Presently undergoing renovation, the interior is stuffed with baroque stuccowork. We advise examining it during the spectacle of mass. ⊠ *Pavla Rittera Vitezovica 3* ☏ *051/214–177* ⊙ *Daily 8–noon and 4:30–6:30.*

❽ **Guvernerova palača** *(The Governor's Palace)*. High on a hill, the palace affords a grand view over the harbor from all the front windows, from its gardens, and from the approach. Built in 1893 by Alajos Hauszmann, who also worked on Budapest's castle and Palace of Justice for the then-governor of Hungary, the building itself is no eyesore either. The large columned facade communicates the self-confidence of the robust Habsburg empire, as do the numerous statues placed throughout its grounds. The **Maritime & Historical Museum of the Croatian Littoral,** which investigates the Kvarner's seafaring traditions and the region's cultural heritage from both the Mediterranean and Central Europe, is housed here. You can also admire the rest of the interior while viewing a temporary exhibition in the atrium or attending a meeting or concert in the impressive Marble Hall. ⊠ *Muzejski trg 1* ☏ *051/213–578* ⊕ *www.ppmhp.hr* 🗪 *10 Kn* ⊙ *Tues.–Fri. 9–8, Sat. 9–1.*

❷ **Hrvatsko narodno kazalište Ivan pl. Zajc** *(Croatian National Theatre Ivan Zajc)*. Designed by specialist Viennese architects Fellner and Helmer, Rijeka's National Theatre introduced the city to the lightbulb in 1885. In high summer the theater plays host to a Festival of Summer Nights, held beneath wonderful ceiling paintings by Gustav Klimt and emerging from behind a stage curtain decorated by an artist from the island of Krk. However, you'll have to buy a ticket to a performance to see the inside of the theater. ⊠ *Verdijeva ul 5a* ☏ *051/355–900.*

❻ **Katedrala sv. Vida** *(St. Vitus's Cathedral)*. Unusual in this part of the world, the church centers on a rotunda, although numerous additions and mixtures of style blunt its effect on the onlooker. Fine baroque statues are sheltered by baroque and Gothic construction. Founded by the Jesuits in 1638, the cathedral was named for Rijeka's patron saint. An 18th-century gallery was reportedly built to protect young novice monks from the tempting sights presented when the local lovelies attended services. At the main entrance you can find a cannonball in the wall, apparently sent from a British ship during the Napoleonic wars. ⊠ *Grivica 11* ☏ *051/330–897.*

⑨ Muzej grada Rijeke *(The Museum of the City of Rijeka).* Found in a cube-shaped building on the grounds of the Governor's Palace, the museum has eleven collections but does not have a permanent exhibit. There's always a mix of military artifacts along with cultural and scientific displays. Temporary exhibits can be interesting. ⊠*Muzejski trg 1/1* ☎*051/336–711* ☎*10 Kn* ☉*Weekdays 10–1.*

⑩ Prirodoslovni muzej *(Natural History Museum).* Exploring the geology
★ and biology of the region invariably involves holding a sizable chunk of marine life up to the eyes. The shark and ray display here is predictably popular, starring a brigade of stuffed sharks swimming in strict formation while suspended from the ceiling. A multimedia center based on an aquarium adds to the extensive collection of nonmammalian species, which boasts 90,000 specimens in total, but includes rocks, plants, and other less animated elements of the locality. The botanical garden contributes more exotic plants to the array from the museum's grounds. Considering the fearsome appearance of some of the more fascinating inhabitants of the museum, it may be worth considering putting off a visit here until the end of your stay on the coast, lest your imagination get the better of you while bathing off the beaches. ⊠*Lorenzov prolaz 1* ☎*051/553–669* ⊕*www.prirodoslovni.com* ☎*10 Kn* ☉*Mon.–Sat. 9–7, Sun. 9–3.*

⑤ Stara Vrata/Kasnoantički kastrum 4st *(The Roman Gate and Remains of the 4th-Century Roman Praetorium).* Enter this patch of ground from Trg Ivana Koblera by passing through the oldest structure in the city. The enormous stone arch is partly engulfed by additions from more recent times, but it was from this site many centuries ago that the chain of mountain fortresses in the region was commanded by the Romans. These days, the Roman elite's enthusiasm for comfort is catered to with a handful of park benches amidst what is left of the ancient walls and columns. ⊠*Trg Ivana Koblera.*

③ Sveučilišna knjižnica Rijeka *(University Library).* Formerly a school, the University Library now houses a permanent exhibition about the Glagolitic script. Stone tablets written in the ancient Slavic script, including the important Baška tablet from Krk, are the stars. Books, paintings, masonry, and frescoes are also displayed. Call in advance to view the exhibition. ⊠*Dolac 1* ☎*051/336–129* ☎*Free* ☉*Mon. and Thurs. 2–7, Tues., Wed., and Fri. 10–2.*

④ Trg Rijecke rezolucije *(Rijeka Resolution Square).* The buildings housing the **municipal palace** were originally part of an Augustinian monastery, and they connect to St. Jerome's Church. Named for the resolution that was drawn up here in 1905—and which contributed to the formation of Yugoslavia—the square's lemon-meringue buildings cluster around the foot of the city **flagpole**, erected on a high base in the 16th century and featuring a likeness of the city's patron saint, St. Vitus, holding a scale model of Rijeka protectively in his hand.

⑪ Trsat *(Trsat Castle).* The medieval castle was built on the foundations
Fodor'sChoice of a prehistoric fort. In the early 1800s it was bought by an Austrian
★ general of Irish descent, who converted it into a kind of pre-Disney-

land confection that even includes a Greek temple with Doric columns. Today it hosts a popular café, offering some stunning views of the Kvarner Bay; throughout the summer, open-air theater performances and concerts take place here. Across the street, the pilgrimage church of **Sveta Marija** (St. Mary) was constructed in 1453 to commemorate the Miracle of Trsat, when angels carrying the humble house of the Virgin Mary are said to have landed here. Although the angels later moved the house to Loreto in Italy, Trsat has remained a place of pilgrimage. The pilgrimage path up to Trsat begins in the city center, close to Titov trg, at a bridge across the Rječina. It passes through a stone gateway, then makes a long, steep climb up 538 steps. Local bus 1 will get you here, too. ⊠*Frankopanski trg* ☎*No phone* ☏*10 Kn* ☉*Apr.–Oct., Tues.–Sun. 9* AM*–11* PM*; Feb., Mar., Nov., and Dec., Tues.–Sun. 9–3.*

4

OFF THE BEATEN PATH

Kastav. One of the finest spots from which to admire the splendors of the Kvarner Bay is Kastav, 11 km (7 mi) northwest of Rijeka. Originally a medieval fortress comprising nine defensive towers, the hilltop village sits at 1,237 feet in elevation and is home to 900-some people. Without the crowds of Rijeka, you, along with city residents that spend their leisure time here, can concentrate more properly on the quality of your relaxation. The local vintage, Kastavska Belica, is a decent white wine that is gulped merrily at Kastav Cultural Summer, a festival that celebrates the feast day of patron St. Helena (as featured on the coat of arms) on May 22. Having been home to wealthy and powerful clans in times past, the tiny town has many splendid—if not officially noted—buildings from throughout the ages.

WHERE TO EAT

$$$–$$$$ ✕**Kukuriku.** Here's one house in Kastav that is definitely worth a visit. Having been in the same family for over a century, this wonderful restaurant has walked off with many an award for select offerings from the inland menu of Croatia, including turkey hearts cooked in fruit brandy and lamb medallions in basil and olive oil. You are advised to wander onto the terrace, and to take the time to appreciate the chic, modern form of the dishes that still maintain traditions of taste and texture. ⊠*Trg Katka Laginje 1a, Kastav* ☎*051/691–417* ▤*AE, DC, MC, V* ☉*Closed Mon.*

$$$–$$$$
★ ✕**Municipium.** Classic dining in a fine old house, this is Croatian cuisine, both fish and meat, at its finest. An extensive wine list concentrates on home produce, with a good range of Istrian and Dalmatian vintages available. Tried-and-true coastal specialties such as octopus salad and *črni rižot* (black cuttlefish risotto) are expertly prepared. It's perhaps as upmarket as one can get in Rijeka. ⊠*Trg riječke rezolucije 5* ☎*051/213–000* ▤*AE, DC, MC, V* ☉*Closed Sun.*

$$–$$$$ ✕**Feral.** This excellent seafood restaurant lies on a side road close to the main bus station. House specialties are *crni rižot* (cuttlefish-ink risotto), seafood tagliatelle, and *fuži* (homemade pasta) with asparagus and scampi. ⊠*Matije Gupca 5b* ☎*051/212–274* ▤*AE, DC, MC, V* ☉*Closed Sun.*

$–$$ ✕**Tre forze.** Fish for breakfast anyone? A fairly new, family-run restaurant down by the market is stuffed with solid wood tables and chairs and a no-nonsense approach to hearty and tasty fresh food. All homemade and respectful of the seasons, the menu is handy for a filling lunch when visiting the market or before embarking at the nearby ferry terminal. ✉ *Verdieva 19a* ☎ *051/312–056* ◷ *No dinner Sun.*

WHERE TO STAY

The selection of hotels in Rijeka reflects the city's status as a simple transit town. To book a private room, contact the **Rijeka Tourism Association** (✉ *Užarska 14* ☎ *051/315–710* ⊕ *www.tz-rijeka.hr*).

$–$$ ⌂**Hotel Bonavia.** In the city center, one block back from the Korzo,
★   this modern, luxury high-rise has comfortable rooms with specially designed furnishings and original oil paintings. Rooms on the top two floors have balconies and views of Kvarner Bay. The restaurant has a sophisticated dining room with tables in the garden throughout summer. A limousine and chauffeur are at guests' disposal. Pros: spacious rooms, top-notch service, excellent pastries in café. Cons: parking is in a garage a short walk away instead of on-site. ✉ *Dolac 4, 51000* ☎ *051/357–100* 🖷 *051/335–969* ⊕ *www.bonavia.hr* ⇲ *114 rooms, 7 suites* ♿ *In-room: safe, refrigerator, Ethernet. In-hotel: restaurant, room service, bars, gym, parking (fee)* ▭ *AE, DC, MC, V* ⚐ *BP.*

$ ⌂**Hotel Jadran.** It's a good 15-minute walk (or 10-minute bus ride) from central Rijeka to this pleasant hotel right on the water, but views of the Gulf of Kvarner don't come much better than this. Spacious balconies let you enjoy the sound of the sea lapping the breakfront, and hearty breakfasts set you up for further travel onto the islands. Pros: substantial breakfast, unfettered sea views. Cons: a bit out of town to take in any nightlife, walk into town is along a busy street. ✉ *Šetalište XIII divizije 46, 51000* ☎ *051/216–000* ⊕ *www.jadran-hoteli.hr* ⇲ *60 rooms* ♿ *In room: safe, refrigerator, Ethernet. In hotel: restaurant, parking (no fee)* ▭ *AE, DC, MC, V* ⚐ *CP.*

$ ⌂**Neboder.** While by no means luxurious, a room in the upper portions of this white skyscraper offers decent views of the city, and the hotel is in the very center of Rijeka near all of the city's attractions. Pros: central location, helpful staff. Cons: rooms are dated with a budget feel. ✉ *Strossmayerova 1, 51000* ☎ *051/373–538* 🖷 *051/373–551* ⇲ *32 rooms* ♿ *In-hotel: restaurant, bar, parking (fee)* ▭ *AE, DC, MC, V* ⚐ *CP.*

NIGHTLIFE & THE ARTS

Beginning in June, the six-week annual **Rijeka's Summer Nights** (⊕ *www.rijeckeljetnenoci.com*) festival ensures that venues, streets, and squares are filled with cultural performances. You can experience classical music and theater as well as contemporary music and performance art. In late winter the streets of the city are taken over by crazy antics and costumes during the **Rijeka Festival.**

★ **El Rio** (✉ *Jadranski trg 4c* ☎ *051/214–220*) plays host to Rijeka's younger crowd with karaoke and theme nights. **Karolina** (✉ *Gat Karoline Riječke* ☎ *051/330–909*), an upmarket greenhouse right on the quayside, serves cocktails and wine to the smart set as they watch the tide flow in and out of the bay. The center of alternative culture in the city, **Palach** (✉ *Kružna ul 6* ☎ *051/215–063*) is a somewhat grotty space filled with exhibitions, performance, live music, and DJs on a regular basis. For those who might remember summer nights sitting on a terrace, drinking, dancing, chatting, and actually being able to hear what others are saying, the **River Pub** (✉ *Frana Supila 12* ☎ *051/213–406*) is the place to make it all come back.

SHOPPING

Appearance is of great importance to Croatians, and the local ladies will invariably be exhibiting style and glamour even as they sip coffee or shop for vegetables on any given weekday morning. To serve this fashion-hungry crowd, many hip little boutiques offer the latest styles in imported clothing and shoes (mostly from Italy). Prices are generally higher than what you'd pay in Italy, so unless you're caught short needing some posh clothes, it's better for your wallet to do your high-fashion shopping elsewhere. The Korzo, a pedestrian strip that strides through the center of Rijeka, is the best place to go should you be unable to contain your shopping urges.

Fresh local produce, fish, cheeses, olive oils, wines, and *rakijas* (fruit brandy) are the items that should be on your Kvarner shopping list. The best place to buy these is the City Market on Verdijeva. Although there are "professional" traders present, many of the stallholders are still locals, who bring their home-produced wares to sell. Noisy and colorful, Rijeka's central market is the place to haggle over fresh produce, swap gossip, and, of course, drink coffee. Pick up a picnic lunch of cheeses, salads, fruit, and nuts here, then pop into one of the multitude of bakeries for freshly baked *burek* (cheese and meat pies) to complete the feast. Although a little tricky to transport, homemade olive oil, apple-cider vinegar, and *rakija*—usually sold in recycled bottles—are good buys as well. Smaller containers of dried herbal tea leaves and spices like rosemary and oregano are a good alternative if your luggage is already tightly packed.

All things that glitter or smash easily are available at the **Mala galerija** (✉ *Užarska 25* ☎ *051/335–403* ⊕ *www.mala-galerija.hr*). Although not entirely exclusive to Rijeka (you'll find similar, if more ostentatious, artifacts in Venice), the *Morčić* is the figurehead of a Moor wearing a white turban and is associated with the luck that all seafarers rely on. This small shop has many items bearing the "little Moor." It's closed on Sunday.

SPORTS & THE OUTDOORS

FISHING

The Croatian coast is well known for its population of bluefin tuna. You need a fishing license to hunt for any marine life using a line or gun. Prices start from 60 Kn per day. In Rijeka licenses are available from the local office of the **Ministry of Agriculture, Forestry & Water Management** (⊠ *Demetrova 3* 🕾 *051/214–877*).

HIKING & CLIMBING

The mountains around Rijeka—and indeed throughout the Kvarner—are riddled with tracks with international signs. Many lovely starting spots can be reached by car. Relatively small and hospitable, close to civilization, and tucked beneath gentle skies, these mountains pose few dangers. However, if you do face an emergency, contact **Mountain Rescue Service** (🕾 *92 for the local police, 985 for the information center*).

★ **Ad natura** (⊠ *Mate Sušnja 12, Rijeka* 🕾 *091/590–7065*) can help out if you want to do some exploring on two wheels, on foot, underground, on horseback, or above the clouds in Mount Učka Nature Park. At the **Kvarner County Mountaineering Association** (⊠ *Korzo 40/I* 🕾 *051/331–212*) you can find information about routes and mountain huts for overnight tramps. But be prompt; they're only open on Tuesday and Friday evenings between 6 and 8 PM.

BEACHES

Since it serves as the country's largest port, there aren't too many beautiful beaches in the middle of Rijeka. However, you don't imagine locals stay here the whole summer without having a few spots they try to keep secret from the tourists, do you? Favorite beaches easily accessible from the city include the **Bivio Cove**, near Kantrida to the west. In the opposite direction around the coast, **Uvala Žurkovo**, at Kostrena, is wonderful. Within the city itself, the popular place is Pecine to the east, where you can swim off rocky beaches and admire the local villas.

RISNJAK NATIONAL PARK

37 km (23 mi) northeast of Rijeka.

The northern outpost of the forested and karst-peaked Gorski kotar region, Veliki Risnjak is the major peak in this national park, peering over Rijeka from 5,013 feet. The thick pine-forest meadows that are stuffed with wild flowers in the spring, and limestone peaks, crevices, and caves cover around 30 square km (12 square mi).

In winter you'll find a healthy contingent of skiers desperately trying to avoid a trip up to Austria to sample the real thing. In summer, however, as the sun and the tourists beat down upon the coast, this is perhaps the best place to be. The cooling mountain air—the average temperature in these heights in July is around 12°C (53°F)—is a bonus to Risnjak's virtually deserted landscape.

You'll be free to commune with the locals, which include deer, bear, wildcat, and lynx (*ris*), from which the park takes its name. Geologic and botanical features are occasionally explained by English-language information points over which you may stumble on one of the more popular walking routes. Marked trails can occupy you for an hour's evening stroll to a full seven-day trek on the monstrous Rijeka Mountain Transversal from one side of Gorski kotar to the other. Hiking huts are strung across the peaks to accommodate such ambitious expeditions. More information regarding these multiday hiking trips is available from the Kvarner County Mountaineering Association *(see Hiking & Climbing in Sports & the Outdoors, above)*. For those of a gentler disposition, there's a month-long dandelion-picking contest in May.

The park information office is in the village of Crni lug, at the eastern entrance to the park; in the off-season, from October through April, you can pick up information at the reception desk of the Motel Risnjak (open 7 AM–10 PM). You can easily explore the gentler trails on day trips from either Rijeka or Delnice. Paths from the villages of Razloge and Kupari lead up to the source of the wild Kupa River, which can then be followed down the slopes through the "Valley of the Butterflies." ⊠ *Bijela vodica 48, Crni lug* ☎ *051/836–133* ⊕ *www.risnjak.hr* ▨ *Free* ⊙ *Park information office May–Sept., daily 9–5.*

OPATIJA

15 km (9 mi) west of Rijeka.

In the late 19th century, Opatija (Abbazia in Italian) was among the most elegant and fashionable resorts in Europe. Its history dates from the 1840s, when villas were built for members of minor royalty. In 1882 the start of rail service from Vienna and Budapest, along with an aggressive publicity campaign, put Abbazia on the tourist map as a spa of the first magnitude. With the high mineral content of the sea water, iodine in the air, and an annual average of 2,230 hours of sunshine, it qualified as a top-rated climatic health resort, and emerged as a favorite wintering spot for Central European nobility and high society.

A hint of the formality that shrouded Opatija in its heyday still survives; the narrow pines and grand buildings remind one of the Italian lakes. This means that many visitors from all over Europe continue to head to the Opatija Riviera in the summer. At the same time, this stretch of coast has not gone unnoticed by the locals. Until recent years the town was a weekend haunt for some younger, motorized Rijeka citizens. Thanks to these driving forces, the upmarket hotel guests still share the resort with some of the region's more upwardly mobile restaurants. However, their number is dwindling, while the town's once admirable nightlife has packed up and headed back to the cooler parts of Rijeka, leaving Opatija to wealthy and more elderly visitors from the surrounding countries. These guests seem more eager to sip the waters than wine and spirits.

The main street, ulica Maršala Tita, runs parallel to the coast for the length of town, and you can go from one end of town to the other on foot in about half an hour, passing numerous terrace cafés along the way. The best seafood restaurants are in the neighboring fishing village of Volosko, a 15-minute walk along the seafront. The mild climate year-round and resulting subtropical vegetation, frequently sunny skies, and shelter from cold north winds provided by Mt. Učka give Opatija pleasant weather for much of the year. In summer, fresh sea breezes tend to dispel any oppressive heat, making the city an ideal seaside resort.

WHAT TO SEE

★ If you enjoy walking by the sea, set off along the magnificent paved, waterfront **Lungomare**. Built in 1889, this 12-km (7½-mi) path leads from the fishing village of Volosko, through Opatija—passing in front of old hotels, parks, and gardens and around yacht basins—and all the way past the villages of Ičići and Ika to Lovran in the south. In the middle you'll find the popular town beach that fronts the center of Opatija. Close to many cafés, ice-cream shops, and other essentials, the beach also has a couple of protected sections of water for safe swimming. These would be handy for kids if it weren't for the fact that the concrete sides and underwater steps feature extremely sharp stones that can slice skin quite nastily if met with sufficient force. ✉ *Obalno Šetalište Franza Josefa.*

The grounds of **Park Angiolina** are a wonderful spread of palm-punctuated lawns with a botanical garden. The vegetation is strikingly lush, including cacti, bamboo, and magnolias, plus neatly kept beds of colorful flowers and sweet-scented shrubs. Indeed, Opatija as a whole is a town saturated with botanical splendor. Iginio Scarpa, a Rijekan aristocrat and the first settler in Opatija, began importing exotic plants, and the tradition has survived into the present. The camellia is the symbol of the city. ✉ *Between Maršala Tita and the seafront* 🎟 *Free* 🕐 *Tues.–Sun. sunrise–sunset.*

OFF THE BEATEN PATH

Lovran. Just 5 km (3 mi) southwest of Opatija, the lovely town of Lovran is home to good swimming coves, Habsburg villas, and paths up to Učka Nature Park. Massive chestnut trees dot the medieval town, giving shady relief from the sun on long summer days. If the crowds of Opatija leave you no place for peace and quiet, walk along the Lungomare through Ičići and Ika (or take bus No. 32) to Lovran, where you can take in the sea air that lured Austrian royalty to winter here. If you find yourself on the Opatija Riviera in October, don't miss Lovran's **Marunada**, or chestnut festival. The **Lovran Tourist Office** (✉ *Šetalište Maršala Tita 63* ☎ *051/291–740* ⊕ *www.tz-lovran.hr*) can help you find a room in one of the town's many lovely restored villas.

From gentle hiking to mountain biking, climbing and paragliding, all are available in the 160 square km (62 square mi) of **Mount Učka Nature Park**, a series of peaks that help shelter the Liburnia Riviera (which is actually the official name for the stretch of coast centered on Opatija) and the islands from weather systems to the north. Paths toward the summit of the range start from all the resorts along the coast. A climb up to the highest peak, Vojak (4,596 feet), with a fine stone lookout tower at its summit, can be well worth it, particularly on a clear day. The view offers a cheap (but somewhat distant) tour of the islands of Kvarner Bay, the Italian Alps, and perhaps even an indistinct version of Venice. Most routes up to the heights lead through forest, so you can make the trek in summer without overheating. Along the way you'll find natural springs from which to quench your thirst, along with lakes, ponds, tumbling waterfalls (in the wetter months), impressive natural stone columns and several hundred caves. The local inhabitants include deer, wild boar, and, in the northernmost sections of the park, bears. Humans have been living in these hills for centuries also, rearing cattle, farming, and working the forest; you'll come across numerous tiny villages and historic sites if you roam far enough. If you're running short of time, there are many mountain-biking tracks throughout the park offering the chance to expand your lungs on the way up and test your nerve rattling back down to the coast. ⊠ *Liganj 42, Lovran* ☎ *051/293–753* ⊕ *www.pp-ucka.hr.*

WHERE TO EAT

$$$$ ✕ **Le Mandrac.** This upscale seafood restaurant has a glassed-in terrace
Fodor's Choice for winter dining, something of a novelty here by the sea. The splashy
★ menu—somewhere between traditional and avant-garde—changes with the seasons and the whims of the proprietors. Voted the second-best restaurant in the country by a national newspaper, Le Mandrac is Kvarner's bid to put itself on the gastronomical map. Expect dishes like prawn ravioli in tomato and cardamom sauce and octopus salad with pumpkin pesto. ⊠ *Supilova obala 12, Volosko* ☎ *051/701–357* ⊟ *AE, DC, MC, V.*

$$$–$$$$ ✕ **Plavi Podrum** Although this is one of the more traditional fish restaurants in Volosko, don't be fooled into thinking it's not classy. The owner has been "Sommelier of the Year" twice in this young century. All the usuals are cooked excellently here for you, but *jaja od hobotnice* ("octopus egg") is a house special featuring squid, octopus, caviar, mustard, and fresh spinach. The terrace is a little more relaxed than inside. ⊠ *Obala Frana Supila 12, Volosko* ☎ *051/701–223* ⊟ *AE, DC, MC, V.*

$–$$$ ✕ **Istranka.** With a delightful covered terrace flanked by a twisting tree, this small restaurant is the best option for those who are not the greatest fans of seafood (although if that's you, what you're doing in Kvarner is a mystery). Taking its influence from the neighboring region of Istria, the menu concentrates more on landlubber food: hams, cheeses, and of course, the famous Istrian truffle! ⊠ *Bože Milanoviča 2* ☎ *051/271–835* ⊟ *AE, MC, V.*

WHERE TO STAY

$$–$$$ ⊡**Milenij Hotel Opatija.** On the coastal promenade, this bright pink villa is part old and part new. Rooms are furnished accordingly, with either Louis XV–style antiques heavily striped in silk or modern designer pieces. There's a pleasant terrace café overlooking the sea, as well as outstanding beauty, fitness, and business facilities. Pros: slippers and robes in the rooms, an excellent restaurant. Cons: small pool with few lounge chairs, fee parking. ⊠ *Maršala Tita 109, 51410* ☎*051/202–000* 🖶*051/271–812* ⊕*www.ugohoteli.hr* ⌨*129 rooms* ⌂*In-room: dial-up, refrigerator. In-hotel: restaurant, room service, bar, pool, gym, parking (fee)* ⊟*AE, DC, MC, V* ⑲*BP.*

$–$$ ⊡**Astoria Design Hotel.** Sleek flat-screen TVs and Wi-Fi in every room aren't what you'd expect in a hotel in this price category in a city popular with Austrian pensioners. The modern interior here is more South Beach than "faded grandeur," and with perks like these the Astoria is justifiably popular with the young international jet set. Big breakfasts are served in the cheery dining room. Pros: boutique touches like flat-screen TVs and deluxe toiletries. Cons: superior rooms are on the small side. ⊠ *Maršala Tita 174, 51410* ☎*051/706–350* ⊕*www.hotel-astoria.hr* ⌨*51 rooms* ⌂*In room: safe, Wi-Fi. In hotel: restaurant, bar* ⊟*MC, V* ⑲*BP.*

$–$$ ⊡**Grand Hotel Kvarner-Amalia.** The former summer residence of European royalty, Kvarner's oldest hotel first opened its doors to guests in 1884. More suited to sedentary tourists than business travelers, it's a grand neoclassical-style building with peaceful gardens and a terrace overlooking the sea, close to Villa Angelina. The Crystal Ballroom is used for the annual Miss Croatia contest. Pros: Habsburg-era grandeur, spacious patio overlooking the sea. Cons: outdated furnishings and spotty air-conditioning in some rooms. ⊠ *Park Tomašica 1–4, 51410* ☎*051/271–233* 🖶*051/271–202* ⊕*www.liburnia.hr* ⌨*86 rooms* ⌂*In room: refrigerator. In-hotel: restaurant, room service, bar, pool, beachfront, parking (fee)* ⊟*AE, DC, MC, V* ⑲*BP.*

¢–$
★ ⊡**Hotel Opatija.** A prime location, elegant surroundings, and helpful service are rare at this price level; to have them all, along with something left over in your wallet, is extraordinary. Part of the Vienna International chain, this huge villa at the top of a park in the center of town is perfectly situated. It was originally a spa and sanatorium when it was built in the late 19th century. Now guests relax on the terrace, which with almost comfortable, postmodern sofas, is a delight. There is a €10 per-night supplement for the use of air-conditioning. Pros: close to the train station, well-maintained garden in front of hotel. Cons: hilltop location makes it challenging to get there on foot. ⊠ *Gortanov trg 2/1, 51410* ☎*051/271–388* 🖶*051/271–317* ⊕*www.hotel-opatija.com* ⌨*216 rooms* ⌂*In-room: refrigerator, no a/c (some). In-hotel: restaurant, room service, bar, pool, parking (fee), public Internet* ⊟*AE, DC, MC, V.*

NIGHTLIFE & THE ARTS

There was a time when folk from Rijeka used Opatija as their playground; then, the town offered superb nightlife options. These days, however, the big city along the coast is reclaiming its post as the cultural hot spot of the region, and Opatija has been busy transforming itself back into Central and Eastern Europe's health resort. The wealthy, older Italians and Austrians who dominate here have done little to inspire energetic evenings.

★ **Hemingway** (⊠*Zert 2* ☎*051/272–887* ⊕*www.hemingway.hr*), a Croatian chain of cocktail bars for the upwardly mobile, is spreading across the country, and tends to thrust its nose in the air wherever it goes. Pack your wallet with at least one gold card if you're planning on gaining entry to *the* elite bar in this most elite of resorts. Wood is big here, and it gives a warmer feel than might be expected among the dressed-up clientele. The two floors offer a rainbow of cocktail choices on three terraces, including one up on the roof that spies down on the small harbor. Right on the main road that winds through town along the seafront, **Monokini** (⊠*Maršala Tita 96* ☎*051/703–888*) has a shaded, street-side terrace with plenty of comfortable seating, whereas inside all is funky and modern. You'll find good music, a friendly staff, loads of computers for Internet access, good drinks and cocktails, and an atmosphere that invites locals to meet up here for a chat. A city museum is slated to fill the gorgeous pink **Villa Angiolina** (⊠*Park Angiolina 1* ☎*051/711–124*) in the botanical gardens. The neoclassical design both inside and out includes superb mosaic floors and frescoes. The appeal of the building and grounds makes the local artists that display here brave souls indeed. At this writing, the gallery is open from 8 AM to 3 PM from June through September.

SPORTS & THE OUTDOORS

Mount Učka Nature Park, accessible from virtually any point along the coast, offers the easiest opportunity for active exploring, including mountain-bike and hiking trails up through the forested slopes. **Ad Natura,** in nearby Rijeka, can help you explore.

ADVENTURE SPORTS

★ **Ad natura** (⊠*Mate Sušnja 12, Rijeka* ☎*091/590–7065*) in nearby Rijeka can help out if you want to do some exploring on two wheels, on foot, underground, on horseback, or above the clouds in Mount Učka Nature Park.

CRES

Brestova is 20 km (12 mi) south of Opatija, then a 20-minute ferry ride.

Twisting down the entire length of the Kvarner Bay on its eastern side is Cres, whose latest claim to fame is that it is the largest of all Croatian islands. For many years, squat neighbor Krk was awarded this distinction, but recent recalculations have rectified a long-standing error. Ferries to Cres take about 20 minutes, embarking from Brestova, which is on the mainland south of Opatija, to Porozina; another ferry goes from Valbiska on Krk to Merag, on the east side of Cres.

Cres has been known as one of the most unspoiled islands in the Adriatic for a long time. More difficult to get to than Krk or Rab, and with a wilder and more rugged topography, Cres is quite frankly a delight. Its natural stretches are punctuated with olive groves and tiny towns and villages that remain authentic for the most part. Even in the capital, Cres Town, you'll find older inhabitants who struggle to speak Croatian, having been brought up under the much stronger Italian influence.

WHAT TO SEE

Fodor'sChoice
★
The northern end of the island is mountainous and forested, harboring wildlife such as the rare griffin vulture. **Eco-Center Caput Insulae–Beli** is run by the organization that helps protect these (in truth, pretty ugly) beasts, as well as the environment and heritage of the island. Two small exhibitions concentrate on the biodiversity and the history of northern Cres, and the center can also give you information on bird-watching and eco-trails. ⊠*Beli 4, Beli* ☎*051/840–525* ⊕*www.caput-insulae.com.*

Cres Town is found tucked into a well-protected bay, midway down the island. Set around a lovely little fishing harbor, the town is small but perfectly formed, with numerous Gothic and Renaissance churches, monasteries, and palaces. For the most part these are in the Old Town, which sits protected by winged Venetian lions atop three 16th-century gates, the only remains of a defensive wall. Developed under Venetian rule, the present-day Renaissance appearance of the town is due to a reconstruction in 1552.

The **town beach,** at Kovačine campsite, holds a Blue Flag award for cleanliness. To get there, follow the path around the harbor from the main road and keep going for at least 15 minutes along the promenade, where you'll find spots to jump into the water and the odd café or restaurant to keep you fueled. Although the seaside here is man-made, for the most part it somehow doesn't detract too much from the experience. Across the bay from Cres, the village of **Valun** has a nice beach. The town's claim to fame is the "Valun Tablet," a gravestone that is the oldest known example of Glagolitic script. The tablet is now kept in the parish church, right on the waterfront. Get to Valun by car or by taking the wooden boat that sits just outside the Cres Harbor wall; it's easily spotted from the main square. The **Alan Excursion Boat** (✉ *Cres Harbor* ☎ *051/571–070*) is a wooden sailing ship offering differing routes around the island's coast. A trip to Valun costs 80 Kn, with an additional 50 Kn if you'd like a meal on your journey. The ship offers regularly scheduled sailings.

One of the most tempting beaches on the island is on the western coast of Cres at the foot of a steep cliff, at the top of which is the tiny village of **Lubenice,** which offers great views out to sea and up the western coast. This picturesque collection of houses that surround the 15th-century Church of St. Anthony the Hermit has been clinging to its outcrop for around 4,000 years. The hamlet is popular among arty types and hosts exhibitions and music performances in the summer. From the beach below, a short walk through vineyards will bring you to Žanja Cove, which has a blue grotto, a cave at water level that enjoys brilliant blue light as strong sunlight filters through the azure water.

At the southwestern tip of Cres is the town of **Osor,** whose strategic position on the channel between the island and Lošinj ensured that wealth flowed into the town from trade ships. A tour of the town makes for a pleasant afternoon. Reflecting its former status, there's even a cathedral, and many important archaeological sites have been discovered in the vicinity. The **Osor Archaeological Collection** houses booty from throughout the ages, including artifacts from across the Roman empire. ✉ *Gradska vijecnica* ☎ *051/237–346* ⊟ *8 Kn* ☉ *Apr.–Sept., daily 10–noon and 7–9; Oct.–Mar. by appointment only.*

WHERE TO EAT

$$–$$$$ ✕ **Hibernica.** A nice little terrace right by the bell tower in the heart of
★ the stone hilltop town is the perfect location for a light lunch of *pršut* (prosciutto), cheese, olives, and a glass of local wine. ✉ *Lubenice 17, Lubenice* ☎ *051/840–422* ⊟ *No credit cards* ☉ *Closed Oct.–Apr.*

$$–$$$$ ✕ **Konoba Bonifačić.** The subtitle on the road signs reads *nonina kuhinja* (granny's cooking), and you were a spoiled child indeed if your grandma turned out dishes of this standard for you. The shady garden in the heart of ancient Osor is a perfect setting in which to enjoy the typical plates of the Konoba: meat, seafood, pasta, and salads. ✉ *Osor 64, Osor* ☎ *051/237–413* ⊟ *AE, DC, V.*

$$–$$$$ ✕ **Konoba Toš.** The terrace of this little konoba celebrates the famous Valun Tablet, which was discovered just up the road. If you can't get to the real thing, then spend your time perusing the replica inscriptions in the walls here. The lamb *ispod peke,* which means it stews for hours under a metal top resembling nothing more than the lid of a garbage can, is superb, although you have to order it a day in advance. ✉ *Valun* ☎ *051/525–084* ⊟ *AE, DC, V* ☉ *Closed Oct.–Apr.*

$$–$$$$ ✕ **Riva.** The colorful square on the edge of Cres Town harbor is lined with many restaurants serving seafood, pasta, and risotto. Riva is an excellent choice, although many of the alternative options are perfectly decent also. Tables edge out onto the flagstones of the square, meaning the steady stream of strollers through the town will eye your plate

with appreciative glances. A good selection of shellfish is up for grabs, including the seafood spaghetti, which is wonderful. It's a good idea to reserve a table in the evening. ⊠ *Riva creskih kapetana 13, Cres Town* ☎*051/571–107* ⊟*No credit cards.*

WHERE TO STAY

Reflecting its splendid, undeveloped nature, Cres offers very few hotels, though there are plenty of apartments and guest rooms available for rent on the island. A good place to start a search for private accommodation is **Autotrans Rijeka Office Cres** (⊠*Zazid 4, Cres Town* ☎*051/572–050* ⊕*www.autotrans.hr*), whose Web site offers a long list of options and who will look after all details. Note that the office is only open from May through September.

$–$$ ⛉**Zlatni lav.** A delightful 20-minute drive south from Cres Town, in the small, west coast resort of Martinšćica, Zlatni lav is a large, new building. Rooms look across 100 meters of land to the Adriatic. The clean lines of the interior are granted a little more character by nicely designed features such as funky modernist stairs, but keep a close eye on younger children in their vicinity. Pros: spectacular views, high-quality fittings in public spaces and bathrooms. Cons: far from any nightlife. ⊠*Martinšćica 18d, Martinšćica, 51556* ☎*051/574–020* 🖨*051/574–034* ⊕*www.hotel-zlatni-lav.com* ⇥*25 rooms, 5 suites* ⚷*In-room: refrigerator. In-hotel: restaurant, bar, parking (no fee)* ⊟*AE, DC, MC, V* ⊚|*BP.*

$ ⛉**Hotel Kimen.** Submerged in a shady pine forest just a stone's throw from the town beach and a 10-minute walk from the center, Kimen's six stories provide the only hotel accommodation in Cres Town. Built in the 1970s, Kimen is not the most glamorous hotel, but its clean, straight lines are perfectly functional. The location does much to compensate for any small annoyances, but you'll hardly need to spend any time actually at the hotel anyway. Pros: enviable position on an attractive cove. Cons: outdated furnishings. ⊠*Melin 1, Cres Town 51557* ☎*051/573–305* 🖨*051/573–002* ⊕*www.hotel-kimen.com* ⇥*212 rooms* ⚷*In-room: no a/c, no TV (some). In-hotel: restaurant, bar, some pets allowed, parking (no fee)* ⊟*AE, DC, MC, V* ⊚|*BP.*

NIGHTLIFE & THE ARTS

The half-dozen or so bars around the main harbor are great for casual drinking and chatting while you sit outside on balmy evenings listening to the chinking chains of boats. Head inside for quicker quaffing and shouting above Croatian high-energy pop music, where you'll share the space with German yachtsmen. If you're looking for livelier options, unfortunately you're on entirely the wrong piece of land for that sort of nonsense.

SPORTS & THE OUTDOORS

CYCLING

Camp Kovačine (✉ *Melin 1, Cres Town* ☎ *051/573–150* ⊕ *www.camp-kovacine.com*) is nicely set out under shady pines and right on the main town beach. The staff can rent you bikes and boats, organize diving trips, beach volleyball, and even paragliding.

DIVING

If you prefer to explore underneath the waves, **Diving Cres** (✉ *Cres Town* ☎ *051/571–706*) can be found on the town beach, about a 10-minute walk from the harbor. A single orientation dive can be tried for €5.

LOŠINJ

4

Mali Losinj is 26 km (16 mi) from Cres Town.

As you approach the southern tip of Cres, you'll see the steep slopes of Televrina Mountain on nearby Losinj. Sheltered from poor weather by the Alps and closer ranges such as the Velebit, the excellent climate prompted the creation of a health resort here in 1892.

Blink and you might miss the bridge that connects Cres to Lošinj, unless you happen to arrive when the span is raised to allow a ship through the narrow channel that splits the two islands. In fact, until Roman times the two islands were one, connected near Osor. Mother Nature's inconsiderate arrangement did much to frustrate trade ships; entire vessels would be hauled across the few feet of land that blocked the route here rather than sail around the southern tip of the Apsyrdites archipelago. Eventually, some bright spark decided to cut the present-day channel, opening the shipping lanes. Lošinj is an elongated, low-lying island covered with a pine forest. Viewed from the hills of Cres, the slim green outline of the main island and its surrounding islets, with a backbone of hills in the middle, resembles a long frog splayed out in the water, basking in the sun and contrasting beautifully with the water. Lošinj's past and present are very much connected to the shipping industry. The sea captains who populated the towns of Veli and Mali Lošinj when the island reached its golden age in the 19th century are very much responsible for bringing exotic plant life here from around the world and for building the fine villas that have made this a colorful destination for vacationers, who contribute much more to the island's economy today. The smaller islands that make up the Apsyrdites archipelago include Unije, Sušak, and Ilovik—all of which are large enough to provide some type of accommodation—and even smaller islands such as Vele and Male Srakane, Orjule, Oruda, and Sveti Petar, which can be reached by tourist boats from the resorts on Lošinj.

WHAT TO SEE

With 6,500 inhabitants sheltered around an inlet, **Mali Lošinj** is the largest island settlement in the Adriatic. In the 19th century Mali and Veli Lošinj experienced a golden age, when many wealthy sea captains lived on the island. Brightening the waterfront, the mansions and villas they constructed contribute greatly to the towns' appeal. A long tradition of tourism means that you'll find a healthy selection to choose from. A number of attractive churches will catch your gaze as you wander around town. Somewhat scruffy and announcing its presence with a tall, square tower that tapers to a spike at the summit, the 15th-century **St. Martin's Church** was the original centerpiece around which the town was built. The cemetery it lords over amalgamates much of the history of the town. If you wish to dig a bit deeper, **The Church of the Little Lady** hosts many fine examples of religious art.

NEED A BREAK? The road that runs along the Mali Lošinj harbor leads to Čikat Bay, a pine-covered area dotted with impressive Habsburg-era villas and pebbled beach coves. Nearby hotels and campsites, plus good parking, lots of cafés, and ice-cream stands make these beaches popular. There's a gracious promenade along the bay that's perfect for strolling, a windsurfing school for the adventurous, and paddleboat rentals.

The sea captains of **Veli Lošinj** evidently preferred to escape their working environment during their time off, and thus built their villas away from the waterfront, surrounding themselves with exotic plants brought back from their travels. Archduke Karl Stephen built a winter residence in Veli Lošinj; it's now a sanatorium surrounded by wonderful gardens, again with a range of exotic plants, and an arboretum. It's possible to stay in the sanatorium, even for the healthy, but we can't recommend the option until some serious cash is invested in reconstructing it. A short walk beyond the main harbor is the little fishing cove of Rovenska. Beyond, there's a pebble beach and some nice restaurants. The breakwater was established by Habsburg archduke Maximilian. Walking in the other direction brings you to a great rocky Blue Flag beach, where water-sports equipment can be rented in the Hotel Punta complex.

The intimate harbor is the centerpiece of Veli Lošinj, at the entrance to which is the delightful **Church of St. Anthony the Hermit,** with a separate bell tower in pink and cream stone. Built on the site of a former church in 1774, the church has always had a congregation of seafarers, who have filled it with religious art and altars from spots such as Venice. ⊠ *On the Veli Lošinj waterfront* ☎ *No phone* ☉ *June–Sept., daily 10–noon and 7–9. Mass Sun. and holidays at 10.* Opposite the harbor, but now hidden by a row of houses, are the battlements of a defensive tower, which dates from 1455. The squat construction, known ☾ as the **Venetian Tower,** now houses an art gallery with a collection of ★ European art from the 17th and 18th centuries, as well as displays on town history and a copy of a Greek statue of Apoximen, which was discovered on the seabed in 1999. ⊠ *Kaštel 2* ☎ *051/231–173* 🕾 *8 Kn* ☉ *June–Sept., daily 10–noon and 7–9 PM.*

A community of around 150 bottlenose dolphins makes its home just off the coast of Lošinj. Locals claim that its choice of habitat here proves how clean the waters are in the area. The nonprofit **Lošinj Marine Education Centre** will tell you all about the bottlenose dolphins cruising

Fodor'sChoice ★

When It All Gets Too Much

If the pace of life on the major islands is too hectic, knock your engine down to quarter-speed and head out to one of the tiny islands that pepper the seas around the coast of Lošinj. The island of **Unije** is by far the largest, managing to fit in a population of 81, although many of them are summer-only residents. The tiny town of the same name has a handful of restaurants settled around a large pebble bay, although exploring the northern coasts, by foot or by boat, should reveal many private swimming spots. **Ilovik** is the southernmost island of the group. Its nickname, "Island of Flowers," is accurate; oleanders and roses surround almost every home. Watch yachts at close quarters cutting through the channel between Ilovik and the islet of Sveti Petar, on which there was once a convent. The graveyard remains, and burial processions by fishing boat still take place. Parzine, on the southeastern coast, has a large sandy beach.

If you're from New Jersey, you may have a good chance of being related to one of the 188 people living on **Sušak** since many folk from here have settled in the Garden State. Sušak, flung farther out into the sea than any of the other islands, is a very different beast. First, while the rest of the Kvarner is composed of limestone karst, Sušak consists entirely of sand, so its coast is far gentler both in elevation and indentation. Not wanting to be outdone, the population retains a distinctive character and culture. Their dialect is difficult for other Croats to follow, while it's not uncommon to spot women in full folk costume. The only wheeled transport on the island are wheelbarrows.

just off the coast. Excellent displays and videos take you right into their underwater world. This is fascinating stuff for kids and adults alike. You may even end up adopting your own dolphin, although you can't take it home with you. For a mere 200 Kn you'll receive a bundle of stuff such as certificates and T-shirts and, of course, that warm fuzzy feeling of doing something good for the world. The best bit is that you'll be able to visit your newfound family member in his or her natural environment every time you swing through town. (He or she will laugh at you, of course.) ⊠ *Kaštel 24, Veli Lošinj* ☎ *051/604–666* 💰 *200 Kn.*

NEED A BREAK?

After a few days of dipping your toes in the water and basking in the sun, you might be itching for a diversionary outing. The Miomirisni otočki vrt *(Garden of Fine Scents)* is a pleasant place to spend the afternoon—rain or shine—sitting on the terrace admiring the sea of lavender on the hilltop. Donkeys, rabbits, and ponies prance around delighting visitors, especially children. A small shop in a wooden building sells organic products like soaps, candles, and of course, lavender oil. ⊠ *Ulica braće Vidulić* ☎ *098/326-519* ⊗ *June and Sept., daily 10 AM–noon; July and Aug., daily 6 PM–9 PM. Closed Oct.-May.*

WHERE TO EAT

$$$$ ✕ **Baracuda.** Many of the yachts that line the harbor unload their
★ human cargo at this small restaurant that enjoys a big reputation for
fresh fish dinners. Tuna carpaccio, shark on the grill, and lobster *na
buzaru* (cooked with wine) are all great. The occasional land-based
course, such as pork medallions with asparagus, invades the lively and
leafy terrace from time to time. Baracuda's size, matched with its good
name, make an early arrival or a reservation advisable. ⊠ *Priko 31,
Mali Lošinj* ☎ *051/233–309* ⊟ *No credit cards* ☉ *Closed Oct.–Apr.*

$$$$ ✕ **Bora Bar.** Creative Italian dishes like tuna carpaccio with celery root
Fodor'sChoice and truffles are what you'll find at this friendly restaurant in the Roven-
★ ska bay. The place bills itself as a "tartuferia," and in case your trip to
Croatia didn't include a visit to Istria to taste the truffles, this is a good
place to try the local delicacy. The dynamic owners—part Croatian,
part expat—bring a very local *joie de vivre* to the place and check up
on you to see you're enjoying your meal. Breakfast is from 10 to noon
and there's Wi-Fi. ⊠ *Rovenska, Veli Lošinj* ☎ *051/867–544* ⊟ *MC, V*
☉ *Closed Oct.–Easter.*

$$$$ ✕ **Sirius.** This is definitely the place to go on Lošinj if you want a clas-
★ sic, high-quality Croatian seafood meal. The national press claim that
it would be considered one of the best eateries in the whole country if
it were open year-round. The terrace, looking onto the lazy little harbor
that was once Veli Lošinj's fishing harbor, has a smart nautical theme
with navy tablecloths and striped seats. The dining room is patrolled
by a friendly and efficient crew, and the reputation for fresh seafood is
well deserved. ⊠ *Rovenska 4, Veli Lošinj* ☎ *051/236–399* ⊟ *AE, DC,
MC, V* ☉ *Closed Oct.–Apr.*

$$$–$$$$ ✕ **Konoba Lanterna.** From this former lighthouse, which is in a work-
ing-class district by the seashore, you'll see (and hear) boats being
mended. The tiny stone building has the feel of an old pub inside, and
the simple terrace seems far away from the packed quayside tourist
restaurants in the main Losinj square. Tangled nets, small fishing boats
and buoys provide the scenery, with the occasional diving seagull for
excitement. At lunchtime you are likely to be joining a crowd of mostly
elderly gents from the neighborhood. But who cares that the clientele
isn't so glamorous when you can enjoy tasty traditional food such as
baked fish, or sausages cooked in wine? ⊠ *Sveti Martin 71, Mali Lošinj*
☎ *051/233–625* ⊟ *AE, DC, MC, V* ☉ *Closed Oct.–Apr.*

WHERE TO STAY

$$$$ ⊡ **Hotel Apoksiomen.** Named after a Greek statue that was recovered
★ from the seabed near Mali Lošinj in 1999, this renovated magnolia-
shaded villa imposes itself on the seafront close to the main square in
Mali Lošinj and offers a good example of how to run a small, family-
run establishment. Spic and span, the inside shines almost too brightly
with polished marble. Rooms are comfortable and protected from noise
on the busy seafront side by double-glazed windows, though the decor
may seem a bit pedestrian compared with the promise of the exterior.
The staff is efficient and ever eager to please. Free parking is 100 meters

from the hotel, and guests get a card that allows them to drive into the center of town. Pros: free parking in the heart of town, delicious pastries at the café. Cons: rooms don't match the gorgeous hotel exterior. ⊠*Riva Lošinjskih kapetana 1, Mali Lošinj 51550* ☎*051/520–820* 🖶*051/520–830* ⊕*www.apoksiomen.com* 🖙*24 rooms, 1 suite* ♿*In-room: refrigerator, safe, dial-up. In-hotel: parking (no fee)* ⊟*AE, DC, MC, V* ⊗*Closed Oct.–Apr.* ⦿I*BP.*

$–$$ 🖳 **Villa Favorita/Residence Villa Jelena.** This lovely, historically pro-
*Fodor's*Choice tected Austro-Hungarian villa has been beautifully renovated and
★ furnished in traditional style, with wooden floors in the restaurant and rooms. Rooms offer almost anything you might want; those in Jelena are simpler but still excellent. Luxuriating in its own gardens, the Villa and accompanying residence are protected from the hoi polloi by impressive wrought-iron fences, literally a stone's throw from the Veli Žal beach in Sunčana Uvala, a large bay, five minutes' drive from the center of Mali Lošinj. This rocky Blue Flag beach is shaded by pine trees that bring relief on hot summer afternoons. This complex is the best on the island for those who demand proximity to a family seaside facility. The restaurant with its lovely terrace overlooks the seawater swimming pool in the gardens. Pros: first-rate property in a prime location, well-tended gardens with chairs to enjoy them. Cons: near a crowded family-friendly beach. ⊠*Sunčana uvala, Mali Lošinj 51553* ☎*051/520–640 or 051/520– 641* 🖶*051/232–853* ⊕*www.villafavorita.hr* 🖙*8 rooms* ♿*In-room: refrigerator, safe, Ethernet. In-hotel: restaurant, pool, beachfront, parking (no fee)* ⊟*AE, DC, MC, V* ⊗*Closed Oct.–Apr.* ⦿I*BP.*

$ 🖳 **Hotel Punta.** Punta is a cheaper option in Veli Lošinj that still offers a Blue Flag beach and a wellness center. Attractive, colored blocks line the seashore in a style that complements the old architecture of the island surprisingly well. Best (but most expensive) are the modern apartments filled with modern furnishings that open onto large balconies. Cool blue hotel rooms are simpler (and older) but perfectly acceptable, again offering balconies and sea views for the most part. A fish restaurant is on a terrace just above the beach, and a swimming pool is nearby; the terrace becomes a disco with live music in the evening and hosts children's activities during the day. The wellness center—with full facilities—is possibly the best feature, especially given Veli Lošinj's tradition as a convalescent center. Note that the rates for a stay of fewer than three nights are 20% higher. Pros: terrace restaurant, near both the sea and the town of Veli Lošinj. Cons: small pool complex. ⊠*Veli Lošinj 51550* ☎*051/662–000* 🖶*51/236–301* ⊕*www. jadranka.hr* 🖙*181 rooms, 53 apartments* ♿*In-room: kitchen (some), refrigerator (some). In-hotel: 2 restaurants, bar, tennis courts, pools, gym, spa, beachfront, diving, bicycles, children's programs (ages 4–12), parking (no fee)* ⊟*AE, DC, MC, V* ⊗*Closed Oct.–Apr.* ⦿I*BP.*

4

NIGHTLIFE & THE ARTS

Both Mali and Vela Lošinj offer a healthy selection of bars, where you can sit outside on warm evenings, sip drinks, and chat. Those looking for brighter lights better move on to Krk or the mainland.

SPORTS & THE OUTDOORS

BIKING

Sanmar Tourist Agency (✉ *Priko 24, Mali Lošinj* ☎ *051/238–293*) rents bikes for 100 Kn per day.

DIVING & SAILING

Diver Sport Center (✉ *Uvala Čikat 13, Mali Lošinj* ☎ *051/233–900* ⊕ *www.diver.hr*) offers a three-day course (three hours per day, but no certification) for €170, but an orientation dive costs a whopping €60. The same center offers two- to seven-day cruises on a wooden ship with seven air-conditioned cabins starting at €240 per person for a weekend.

FLIGHTSEEING

To put it all in perspective, from **Airport Lošinj** (✉ *Privlaka 19, Mali Lošinj* ☎ *051/235–148* ⊕ *www.airportmalilosinj.hr*), you can take a panoramic flight over the archipelago (15 minutes for €52), or if you're in a hurry you can take a taxi flight to destinations across Croatia or even Italy (Rome costs €910 plus V.A.T.) or Germany (Munich costs €1,390 plus V.A.T.), among others. Most useful of the lot may be a quick lift to spend the day on the tiny island of Unije; flights to the small island leave at 8:15 AM and 1:50 PM Monday, Wednesday, and Friday, and cost 120 Kn per person. The airport is open from March through October.

KRK

Krk Town is 53 km (33 mi) southeast of Rijeka.

It's no surprise—since Krk is one of the largest Croatian islands, hosts the regional airport, and is connected to the mainland by a bridge—that the robust island is one of the most developed in the country. The dusty edges and agricultural interior get very busy during the high season, and if you visit then you will likely find yourself in traffic jams along the snaking routes between the resort towns. Add the sight of the oil refinery on the mainland near the bridge and the terminal for tankers near Omišalj on the northern coast of the island, and you may think twice about heading here. The sights aren't exactly what you'd call picturesque. Don't be put off so easily. Krk still offers many of the same delights found in the rest of the region: great beaches, interesting history, and pretty old towns. Although other islands may offer a slower pace, Krk compensates by offering more facilities and convenience. With numerous accommodation options and more entertainments, it may very well be the best choice for families that have easily bored children in tow.

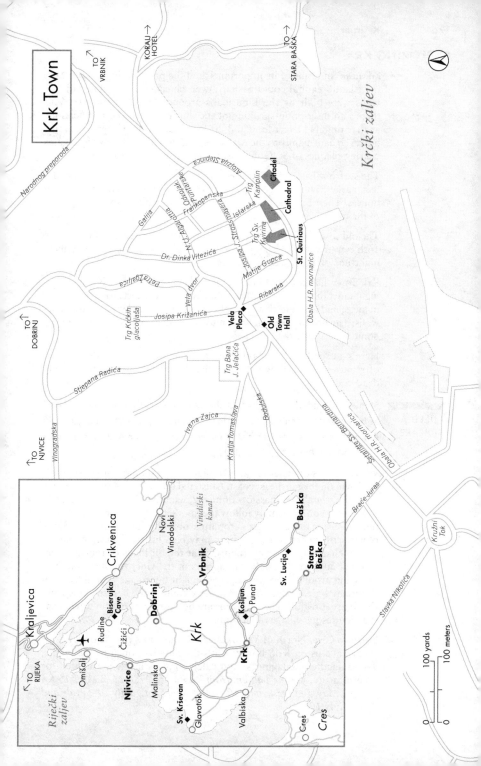

EXPLORING KRK

Krk Town. In terms of its importance and the pride of the 3,000 locals, the island's capital could perhaps even be called a city. The old city walls were built by the Liburnians around the 1st century BC, and there's an inscription speaking of the dimensions of the fortifications at that time (111 feet long and 20 feet high). The present-day walls, however, date mainly to the Middle Ages. The city walls have four gates bearing plaques of St. Quirinius, the protector of the town.

The seafront has a pleasant green area that takes you past cafés and a fish market. The main square, **Vela Placa,** is just behind the first row of houses. There's a beach underneath the town walls with a lovely view of the town.

The **old town hall** on Vela Placa was built by the Venetians in the late 16th century. Its clock shows all 24 hours: daytime on the upper part, nighttime on the lower.

Krk Town has two well-known visual anchors. The first is the imposing **citadel** that sits on Trg Kamplin. Summer concerts, theater performances, and a jazz festival are held on the square and within the citadel walls. The bell tower of **St. Quirinius** is the other, with its angular onion dome typical of Krk.

Here's a useful tip: streets that are thoroughfares have a straight line of stones running down the middle; those without are most likely dead ends.

NEED A BREAK? Stanic is a wonderful gallery chockablock with works by local artists, as well as books and souvenirs. If you're not into shopping, you can simply remain downstairs at the café–bar, or the many other watering holes around Vela Placa. ⊠ *Vela Placa* ☎ *051/220–052.*

Vrbnik. Lovers of majestic views or high-diving should head to the cliff-top town on the northeast coast. Clustered on a hilltop 48 meters above a small harbor, it's a mass of confusing, winding streets. Happily, as in Krk Town, you can simply follow the lines set in the streets. The bumpy terrain means that staircases crop up around most corners. One of the oldest settlements on Krk, Vrbnik may be a little ramshackle, but it's utterly charming, That's certainly what the busloads of tourists seem to think anyway. Vrbnik's fragrance is of the vine; you'll see old barrels lying around everywhere. These might once have been filled with Žlahtina, a great white wine that some claim is the best to come from the Kvarner region. The vineyards are but a short hop from town, near the picturesque village of Dobrinj.

★ **Biserujka Cave.** North of Vrbnik, near Rudine, this cave is only one of many caverns on Krk; however, it's the only one open to the public. The stalactites, stalagmites, and calcine pillars inside are lighted for your pleasure. ⊠ *One-half km from Rudine* ☎ *098/326–203* 💲 *15 Kn* ⊗ *Apr., May, and Oct., daily 10–3; June and Sept., daily 10–5; July and Aug., daily 10–7.*

★ **Baška.** On the southern end of the island, this town has a great beach as well as the conveniences of civilization. However, this naturally means that you must sometimes fight to find a spot in season. The 2-km (1-mi) beach is fronted by houses (and hotels at the southern end), which are often painted in bright colors and adorned with interesting nooks and stairways, all lending a fun and slightly eccentric air to the town. Cute backstreets behind the houses offer a selection of thirsty cafés and ice-cream shops. Driving into Baška, you'll pass through Jurandvor and then find yourself in Baščanska draga. While on this road, take the chance to visit the **Church of St. Lucy,** which has achieved cultlike status since the discovery of the glagolithic Baška Tablet on its grounds in 1851. ⊠*Jurandvor* ☎*051/860–184* 🖼*12 Kn* ☉*Daily.*

☾ **Stara Baška.** If you're looking for a more secluded spot, head to this town that sits just above the beaches that trim a wide cove and peninsula. The road here is a single track through the tiny village, so you may find yourself performing intricate maneuvers in your car should you be unlucky enough to meet the local water truck that keeps the houses supplied.

OFF THE BEATEN PATH

Goli Otok. Like Communist history? Consider a day trip to this uninhabited former Yugoslavian prison island just off the coast of Rab. Goli Otok means "naked island" and was so named for the lack of vegetation and habitable conditions on the island. After Tito broke ranks with Stalin in 1948, the island became infamous as a place where Yugoslav political prisoners sympathetic to the Soviet Communist agenda were imprisoned. Men were incarcerated here while women were taken to nearby Grgur island. The treatment of these prisoners is wholly unknown, as very few prisoners lived to tell of their experiences, but a stone quarry indicates that prisoners were forced to do hard labor quarrying stone. Conditions on Goli Otok were harsh, with blistering temperatures in the summer, and brutal Bora winds ripping across the barren island in the winter. Any mention of Goli Otok was strictly forbidden in Yugoslavia until after Tito's death. The prison was completely abandoned in 1989, but prison barracks remain there. You can make a short trip to this legendary gulag by taxi boat with one of the many charter companies in Baška or Punat on Krk island. The charge is around €50.

WHERE TO EAT

In the summer you'll be sharing tables with busloads of tourists at many of Krk's best restaurants, all of which tend to be outside the capital. However, Krk Town has many restaurants that will serve you perfectly reasonable renditions of less ambitious fare, such as fish, pasta, and pizza.

$$–$$$$
★ ✕**Katunar.** The large, modern building is surrounded by vineyards on the approach to Vrbnik, and you come here as much for the wine as the food. Wines produced around Vrbnik are considered some of the best in Croatia. You can try *Vrbnicka žlahtina* here. *Biser mora* (sea pearl) is a light, semi-sparkling white, perfect for summer drinking. *Nigra* (a

brand of syrah) is a full-bodied red wine ideal for easy drinking, while *porin* is dry and sparkling. All are well priced here, cheaper than in shops. The restaurant offers both wine and rakija tasting, including brandy made from figs, which is very sweet. There's a shop and grill restaurant outside for visitors, which is an excellent choice at night, when it is lighted by flaming torches. Call ahead to arrange a tour and a gastronomic accompaniment to your boozing. ⊠ *Sv. Nedilja, Vrbnik* ☎ *051/857–393* ⊟ *AE, DC, MC, V.*

$$–$$$$ ✕ **Nada.** Considered top-notch by many islanders and Croatians who know their stuff, the tiny downstairs konoba provides an authentic Croatian atmosphere. The large restaurant upstairs has much more space, although it's still quite cozy and traditional, and has a terrace with spectacular sea views. This is a great place to try Kvarner specialties. Of course, it's extremely popular, so definitely make a reservation if you choose to wade through the tour-bus crowds. ⊠ *Glavača 22, Vrbnik* ☎ *051/857–065* ⊟ *AE, DC, MC, V* ⊘ *Closed Oct.–Apr.*

$$–$$$$ ✕ **Rivica** One of the best-known restaurants in the region, Rivica has a
★ long tradition but lacks any sense of glitz. Try the *grdobina* (monkfish, which is cooked in local wine) while you sit on the terrace shaded from the sun. Should you demand that your dinner be extra special, ask the staff to recommend what's fresh in that day. ⊠ *Ribarska obala 13, Njivice* ☎ *051/846–101* ⊟ *AE, DC, MC, V* ⊘ *Closed Oct.–Apr.*

WHERE TO STAY

$$ ⌨ **Koralj.** For long days on the beach and all conveniences on tap, the
☾ Koralj is a decent choice, though it's on the edge of Krk Town, so if you plan busy evenings you may want to find somewhere closer to the center. Perched in the trees just above a tidy beach, the rooms are on the small side, but comfortable. Apartment suites on the ground floor have their own terraces, although promises of beach access mean little when there are no stairs between your terrace and the beach. Be aware of the extras that will be tacked onto the bill (balcony, insurance, etc.). There is a lot of entertainment for the kids. Pros: great for families with kids, peaceful location amid pine trees. Cons: nickel and diming by the management for extra services; access to the beach from the rooms is complicated. ⊠ *Ul. Vlade Tomašiča, Krk Town 51500* ☎ *051/655–400* 🖷 *051/655–410* ⊕ *www.zlatni-otok.hr* ⇗ *170 rooms, 20 apartments* ⌂ *In-room: no a/c, dial-up. In-hotel: restaurant, bar, gym, beachfront, children's programs (ages 4–12), laundry service, public Internet* ⊟ *AE, DC, MC, V* ⊘ *Closed Dec.–Feb.* ⏇ *CP.*

$ ⌨ **The Blue House.** As the island is heavily developed, hotels on Krk tend to be big and somewhat impersonal. For a little more soul, a private apartment is the best bet. This pastel-painted house offers a choice of three apartments, all with terraces looking out to Soline Bay, famous for its healthy mud (so expect to see people smothering themselves in the stuff on the beach). Down a rutted road amid trees that reach down toward the water, the apartments are artistically adventurous with bright colors dominating the sparingly furnished (in a good way) rooms. Dobrinj is possibly the most delightful old town in the region.

Pros: peaceful environment and cheery decorations. Cons: not much in the way of extra facilities or services. ⊠*Cizici 338 b, Dobrinj, 51500* ☎*051/853–126* ⊕*www.cizici.com* ⋗*3 apartments* ⚥*In-room: kitchen* ⊟*No credit cards* ⊘*Closed Nov.–Apr.*

$ ▦ **Corinthia I.** This cheaper option in the busy Baška resort area might be better suited for families. Rooms at this large complex may not offer the most charm and character—unless you're enamored of standard late-1980s-style furnishings—but they keep the rain off your head; those facing the sea offer a wonderful view of austere hills plunging into aquamarine waters. Make sure you get a room with a balcony. If you can do without air-conditioning (not ideal in July or August) and an Internet connection in your room, then staying in the other parts of the complex (Corinthia II and III) can save you around 20% per person on accommodation costs. Villa Corinthia apartments are the top-of-the-line for the complex, with new bathrooms and modern furniture. Pros: prime location on Baška beach, large indoor/outdoor pool and spa complex. Cons: rooms in the Corinthia III are in need of renovation. ⊠*Emila Geistlicha 34, Baška 51523* ☎*051/656–111* ⚏*051/856–584* ⊕*www.hotelibaska.hr* ⋗*105 rooms, 13 suites* ⚥*In-room: refrigerator, safe, dial-up. In-hotel: restaurant, bar, pool, public Wi-Fi* ⊟*AE, D, MC, V* ⊘*Closed Dec.–Mar.* ⦿|*CP.*

¢–$ ▦ **Hotel Adria Malinska.** Rooms here are much nicer than you'd expect
★   in this category, with spotless bathrooms, sea views, and comfortable beds. The furnishings are nothing to write home about and there's no air-conditioning, but if you can snag a room with a balcony, you'll spend most of your time sitting there watching the Malinska promenade and the colorful harbor below. A small pebble beach is a stone's throw away. Pros: spiffy bathrooms and pleasant terrace overlooking the harbor. Cons: not much going on in Malinska at night. ⊠*Obala 40, Malinska, 51513* ☎*051/859–131* ⊕*www.hotel-adria.com.hr* ⋗*37 rooms* ⚥*In room: safe. In hotel: restaurant* ⊟*AE, MC, V* ⦿|*BP.*

NIGHTLIFE

Krk Town and Baška are the places to head for relatively low-key drinks in the evening. The center of the capital and the stretch of town above the beach at Baška offer numerous bars with music and tables out under the stars. A firm family favorite, Krk is definitely not the place for cutting-edge nightlife. However, if you really can't live without getting your club fix, there are a couple of large venues offering house DJs. Note that clubs are open only in the summer months. **Cocktail Bar Volsonis** (⊠ *Vela Placa 8, Krk Town* ☎*051/220–052*) is one of the livelier nightspots in Krk Town. It's suitably, although somewhat mysteriously, symbolized by the remains of a wonderful sacrificial altar to love-goddess Venus down in the basement. **Discotheque Crossroad** (⊠*Sveti Vid, Malinska* ☎*No phone* ⊕*www.crossroad-discotheque.com*) hosts such shenanigans as foam parties as well as international DJs and live bands. Check the Web site for a schedule of events. It's open June through September.

SPORTS & THE OUTDOORS

BICYCLING

You can bike around the island for transportation or exercise. The best place to rent a bicycle is at the **Hotel Punat** (✉ *Obala 94, Punat* ☎ *051/854–024*).

DIVING

The most interesting sights in Kvarner Bay are usually wrecks. At **Divesport** (✉ *Dunat, Kornic* ☎ *051/867–303* ⊕ *www.divesport.de*) on the Bay of Punta, a one-day diving course sets you back €26, including all the equipment you need.

HIKING

There are many marked paths in the area around Baška. For a longer hike, consider visiting the splendid remote villages at Vela and Mala Luka; take this path as part of a group, and be aware that the section of the trail through the canyon may flood if there's rain. For some nice hikes around Baška, consider the path from Baška to Mjesec Hill (5½ km [3 mi]/2 hours). Offering spectacular views over the bay, this easy route passes by St. John's Church, where you can take a breather while you contemplate higher things. The route from Baška to Jurandvor (5 km [3 mi]/2 hours) takes you through the Baška Valley and leaves you with a visit to the Church of St. Lucy, home of the Baška Tablet. The short hike between Baška and Stara Baška will give you a little exercise; a delightful stretch of small, quiet beaches is the reward for a short hike. For more hiking information, contact the **Krk Tourist Office** (✉ *Trg Sv. Kvirina 1, Krk Town* ☎ *051/221–359* ⊕ *www.krk.hr*).

WATERSKIING

Always fancied spraying majestic jets of water across the aquamarine seas, but sorting out a boat and someone to drive just seems too much trouble? Well, the answer lies with **Cable Krk** (✉ *Punat* ☎ *091/262–7302* ⊕ *www.waterski-krk.com*), on a calm bay just outside the resort of Punat, between Krk Town and Stara Baška. A large wooden pier with a bar and restaurant to entertain your companions is the gateway to a cableway, which is not much different than a drag-lift at a ski resort. The cable pulls you around a short course, with tuition on hand to help you get your sea legs. Four circuits cost 30 Kn.

DELNICE

45 km (28 mi) east of Rijeka.

Delnice, which sits on the road between Rijeka and Zagreb, is itself not much to write home about. However, it makes a good base for exploring the mountains of the Gorski kotar region that sits above Kvarner Bay. This is the place to head for hiking trails that swing away from civilization and other humans. It's also a convenient stopover should you not be in too much of a hurry to get back to Zagreb and your transport home. Take a day or two to swap the brilliant blue domination and ramshackle culture of the coast for the bright green mountains and hearty way of life in Gorski kotar.

4

WHERE TO EAT

$$–$$$$ ✕**Volta.** The small town of Fužine is very close to Delnice and is well known for its pine-bordered lake. *Volta,* which means vaults, tells you exactly what to expect from this vaulted, cellar-style dining room, fronted by a conservatory. The publike simple interior is a cut above most of the restaurants in the Gorski kotar, which tend to be a little old-fashioned. Try the pasta with truffles or snail risotto; the house specialty is horse meat, from which they even produce *čevapčići* (spiced meat rolled into sausage shapes and grilled), but you don't have to go there. A long list of Croatian wines rounds things off. ✉*Franja Račkog 8, Fužine* ☎*051/830–030 or 051/830–035* ▤*AE, DC, MC, V.*

WHERE TO STAY

$ ⛰**Hotel Risnjak.** This modern hunting lodge is unlikely to have seen too many genuine mountain men. Still, rooms are nicely appointed, displaying the more robust character of inland Croatia despite being situated just a short hop over the mountaintops from the Adriatic. The on-site restaurant serves hearty local fare. Pros: good restaurant, friendly service. Cons: basic amenities. ✉*Lujzinska 36, Delnice 51300* ☎*051/508–160* 🖶*051/508–170* ➴*20 rooms* ♿*In-hotel: restaurant, bar, gym, laundry service* ▤*AE, DC, MC, V* ⊙*CP.*

SPORTS & THE OUTDOORS

HIKING
Delnice is a good base for hiking around Risnjak and the Gorski kotar range, which have many marked walking and hiking paths.

RAFTING & CANOEING
The Kupa River either meanders or rushes down through the mountains toward the coast. You can join expeditions organized by **Outdoor Centar Kupa** (✉*Zrinska 13, Brod na Kupi* ☎*051/837–139* ⊕*www.foris.hr*), which start out at 10 AM or 3 PM from a point near Delnice and tackle the rough or the smooth sections of the river. The company also runs canyoning trips, in case you want to omit the boat portion of the exercise.

RAB

Jablanac is 100 km (62½ mi) south of Rijeka; then take the ferry 1½ nautical mi to Mišnjak, 9 km (6 mi) from the town of Rab.

Rab presents an utterly schizophrenic landscape. When you drive southward, down the Magistrala, you see that the island resembles the humped back of a diving sea monster. Once you've mounted this beast, via a short ferry ride from Jablanac to Mišnjak, you travel along the center of its back, which is almost entirely bald to the north, letting all its hair hang out to the south. The high northern coast, which bears the brunt of the northern Bora winds, is dry, rocky, and barren. Crouching below this crusty ledge, the southern half of the island could hardly differ more, and has possibly the lushest terrain found on any Croatian island. Low, green hills dip into the seas, while the ancient Dundo forest grows so voraciously that it's almost impossible to walk in.

EXPLORING RAB

Numbers in the text correspond to numbers in the margin and on the Rab map.

Barbat. The first town you'll come to on the southern coast of Rab after leaving Mišnjak feels more like a collection of houses, shops, and restaurants spread across the green slopes, despite being the site of a Benedictine abbey dating back to the 11th century. Nowadays, you'll find many modern houses, surrounded by terraces and colorful gardens, offering rooms and apartments at good rates. For a short stay of a just a handful of days, this could be a good place to plant yourself. The strip of path that constitutes a promenade ambles, rather than parades, past cafés, bars, and restaurants on one side and a narrow beach facing the green hillock that is the islet of Dolin across a channel on the other. Between Barbat and the ferry port on Puderica Beach, all-night parties are usually on the bill for those with the energy.

Fodor'sChoice
★ **Rab Town.** Sitting on a narrow peninsula halfway up the island's southern coast, the compact, well-preserved medieval village is best known for its distinctive skyline of four elegant bell towers, and its many churches. Author Rebecca West, who traveled through Yugoslavia in the 1930s, called Rab Town "one of the most beautiful cities of the world" in her masterpiece, *Black Lamb and Grey Falcon.* Closed to traffic, the narrow cobbled streets of the Old Town, which are lined with Romanesque churches and patrician palaces, can be explored in an hour's leisurely stroll. The urban layout is simple: three longitudinal streets run parallel to the waterfront promenade and are linked together by steep passages traversing the hillside. The lower street is Donja ulica, the middle street Srednja ulica, and the upper street Gornji ulica.

The oldest part of Rab Town is **Kaldanac,** the very tip of the narrow peninsula that juts into the sea. From here the ancient city grew in the 15th century to include Varoš, farther north, and later was widened and fortified by walls during a brief Venetian rule.

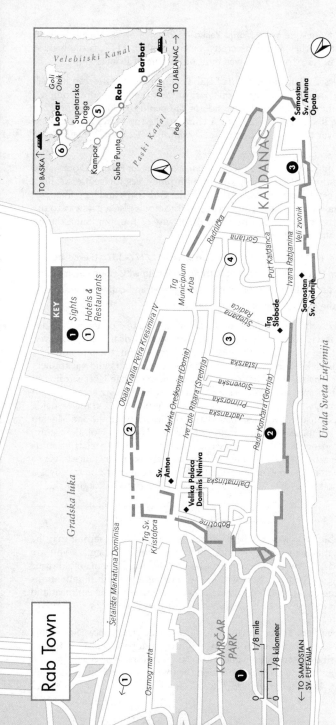

Rab Town

KEY
- ① Sights
- ① Hotels & Restaurants

Gradska luka

Šetalište Markatuna Dominisa

Osmog marta

Trg Sv. Kristofora

Obala Kralja Petra Kresimira IV

Marka Oreškovića (Donja)

Ive Lole Ribara (Srednja)

Rade Končara (Gornja)

Sv. Anton

Velika Palača Dominis Nimiva

Bobotine

Dalmatinska

Jadranska

Primorska

Slovenska

Istarska

Stjepana Radića

Trg Municipium Arba

Trg Slobode

Radnička

Gorliana

Put Kaldanca

Ivana Rabjanina

Veli zvonik

Samostan Sv. Andrije

Samostan Sv. Antuna Opata

KALDANAC

Uvala Sveta Eufemija

KOMRČAR PARK

← TO SAMOSTAN SV. EUFEMIJA

0   1/8 mile
0   1/8 kilometer

Velebitski Kanal

Goli Otok

Lopar

Supetarska Draga

Kampor

Suha Punta

Rab

Dolin

Barbat

Paški Kanal

Pag

TO BASKA ↑

TO JABLANAC →

⑤ ⑥

Sights ▶
Komrčar Park **1**
Sveta Marija Velika **3**
Velizvonik **2**

Hotels & Restaurants ▶
Arbiana Hotel **2**
Hotel Imperial **1**
Hotel Village San Marino ...**6**
Konoba Rab **3**
Konoba Santa Maria **4**
Zlatni Zlatag **5**

4

❸ The Romanesque **Sveta Marija Velika** *(Cathedral of St. Mary)*, built in the 12th century and consecrated by the pope in 1177, is the biggest church in Rab Town, and was built on the site of Roman ruins.

❷ The tallest and most beautiful of Rab's campaniles, the freestanding **Veli Zvonik** *(Great Bell Tower)* forms part of the former cathedral complex and dominates the southwest side of the peninsula. Built in the 12th century, it stands 85 feet high. A climb to the top offers breathtaking views over the town and sea. ⊠ *Gornja ulica* ⬚5 Kn ☉ *Daily 10–1 and 5–8.*

❶ On the edge of town, the green expanse of **Komrčar Park,** laid out in the 19th century, offers avenues lined with pine trees for gentle strolling and access down to the sea. Although the Old Town and its immediate surroundings are Rab's chief treasures, the city is also a gateway to the great stretches of beach that rim the towns of Kampor, Suha Punta, Lopar, and neighboring islands.

NEED A BREAK? Paradiso Gallery (⊠ *Stjepana Radiča 2* ☎ *051/777-157*), tucked behind the town lodge, has a wonderful atrium brimming with stone columns and palms; it's ideal for a quick lunch or just a seat and coffee. Alternatively, peruse the gallery, or stock up on local wine.

Lopar. Traveling to the far end of Rab brings you to a perfectly pleasant tourist town that has a couple of interesting historical sights; however, the real draw is mainly the beaches. In high season, though, you'll be lucky to make it to the beach, as you meet many cars and vacationers from nearby resorts. The search for a quieter spot can be rewarding in itself; the Lopar headland is covered with paths crossing areas of scrub and forest, where you can get to all kinds of beaches. On the east side of the peninsula is **Rajska Plaža** (Paradise Beach), with the San Marino tourist complex and the location of the first Naturist Holiday Camp, which opened in 1934. The beach is sandy, but the water is frustratingly shallow: you have to walk for what feels like many miles to get to deep water. This means it's great for kids, of course. If Lopar proves a little too busy, you can always jump onto a ferry to Baška on Krk.

WHERE TO EAT

$$$-$$$$ ✕ **Konoba Santa Maria.** Although the medieval-palace setting may be a little much for some, it does offer spectacular seating, as you are perched in front of and upon massive wooden furniture in an old stone building in the heart of town. In the evening, the torch illuminations allow the background to take a backseat. Come for excellent meat and seafood dishes. ⊠ *Dinka Dokule 6, Rab Town* ☎ *051/724–196* ⊟ *AE, DC, MC, V.*

$$-$$$ ✕ **Konoba Rab.** Tucked away in a narrow side street between Srednja ulica and Gornja ulica in Rab Town, this konoba is warm and inviting, with exposed-stone walls and rustic furniture. Barbecued fish and meat are the house specialties, along with a good choice of pastas and risottos. ⊠ *Kneza Branimira 3, Rab Town* ☎ *051/725–666* ⊟ *AE, DC, MC, V.*

$$-$$$ ✕**Zlatni Zlatag.** In Supertarska Draga, 10 km (6½ mi) from Rab Town,
★ this restaurant is frequently mentioned as the best on the island. Nestled in a small bay and backed by Mediterranean woods, the restaurant and its summer terrace offer wonderful views of the sea. *Škampi i školjke Sv. Kristofor* (scampi and shells baked in béchamel sauce) is a favorite offering. The family that runs "Golden Sunset"—and with the west-facing terrace, this is exactly what you'll see at the appropriate time—is well known for supporting Rab's traditional cuisine. Tradition is met with a smart and modern air-conditioned interior. ⊠*Supertarska Draga 379, Supertarska Draga* ☎*051/775–150* ▤*AE, DC, MC, V* ⊘*Closed Jan.*

WHERE TO STAY

You'll see plenty of private rooms advertised on the Internet, as well as signs on the side of the road. If you want to seek out private accommodations, perhaps the best place to start is the Web site of the tourist office in the closest main town. Costs vary wildly, but private rooms are almost always a cheaper alternative to hotels.

$$ ⌂**Arbiana Hotel.** It's hard to imagine a more romantic setting than this
★ harborside inn in a perfectly restored medieval villa with balconies overlooking Rab marina and the hills of Barbat in the distance. Rooms are decorated in warm tones and rich fabrics, and have squeaky-clean bathrooms stocked with fluffy bathrobes. Breakfast is served in the restaurant's leafy garden partially enclosed by the old city walls. Pros: boutique-hotel feel, personal service. Cons: no pool or beach access, not all rooms have balconies. ⊠*Obala Petra Kresimira 12, 51280* ☎*051/775–900* ⊕*www.arbianahotel.com* ⤴*28 rooms* ⌂*In room: Wi-Fi, safe, refrigerator. In hotel: restaurant, bar* ▤*AE, DC, MC, V* ⦿*BP.*

$ ⌂**Hotel Imperial.** On the edge of the Old Town amid the greenery of Komrčar Park, this peaceful 1930s-era resort hotel has excellent sports facilities and a beach. Suffering a little from a lack of investment, the Imperial clearly displays its socialist-era past. However, the setting, an admirable villa in a richly scented forest park, just a stone's throw from the center of Rab Town, atones for many sins. Certainly not glamorous, it's functional and trying hard. Rooms are modern and comfortable, offering either seaside or park views. Pros: good location in a wooded park near Rab Town. Cons: a little run-down, dated furnishings. ⊠*Palit, Rab Town 51280* ☎*051/724–184* ⊟*051/724–117* ⊕*www.imperial.hr* ⤴*134 rooms* ⌂*In-room: refrigerator. In-hotel: restaurant, room service, bar, tennis courts, gym, beachfront* ▤*AE, DC, MC, V* ⊘*Closed Jan.–Mar.* ⦿*CP.*

$ ⌂**Hotel Village San Marino.** A complex of five hotels stretches across
Ⓒ the peninsula at this family-friendly resort wrapping around the gentle Paradise Beach. The focus here is on activities, ensuring that the kids are never at a loss for something to do. Expect the appropriate crowds in high season. Pros: access to Paradise Beach couldn't be better, good value. Cons: sprawling complex lacks personality, rooms are on the small side and lack luxuries. ⊠*Lopar, 51281* ☎*051/775–*

144 ☎*051/775–128* ⊕*www.imperial.hr* ♿*In-room: no TV. In-hotel: restaurant, bar, tennis courts, pool, beachfront* ⊟*AE, DC, MC, V* ⊘*Closed Nov.–Mar.* ⦿*CP.*

NIGHTLIFE

For such a small town, Rab has a surprisingly lively nightlife, although it's certainly not extreme by any stretch of the imagination. Trg Municipium Arbe on the waterfront is lined with bars and can get noisy as the night progresses; they're mostly anchored by troops of waiters with some attitude as well as a habit of setting drinks on fire when they're not throwing them around. All-night house parties are found at Santos Beach Club on Puderica Beach, 2 km (1 mi) from Barbat toward the ferry terminal. Buses to Puderica leave Rab Town every hour from 10 AM onward.

★ **Café Bar Amadeus** (✉*Biskupa Draga 25, Rab Town* ☎*No phone*) is a hilariously tiny bar, short on luxury but with no lack of entertainment, stuffed as it is with local fishermen pogoing to 1980s Croatian hard rock. Those after a little glitz to show off their suntan can head to the center of Rab Town nightlife at **San Antonio** (✉*Trg Municipium Arba 4, Rab Town* ☎*051/724–145*). The club is open until 4 AM.

SPORTS & THE OUTDOORS

BOATING

Travel Agency Kristofor (✉*Poslovni centar, Mali Palit, Rab Town* ☎*051/725–543* ⊕*www.kristofor.hr*) can satisfy most of your wishes, including motorboat rentals so you can explore the coast and use it as your own private diving board. Prices start at €50–€77 per day, depending on the power.

DIVING

At **Aqua Sport** (✉*Supetarska Draga 331, Supetarska Draga* ☎*051/776–145*) a single dive costs €40, a full diving course €290. In addition, you can dive at various sites from their boat, and your nondiving companions are welcome to go along for the ride.

KVARNER ESSENTIALS

AIR TRAVEL

Rijeka's airport is located on Omišalj on Krk Island, with regular bus service provided by Autotrans to downtown Rijeka and the beach towns on Krk island as well as to Mali Lošinj and Cres (though not to Rab). The airport is served by EasyJet from the United Kingdom (Bristol and London), Norwegian Air Shuttle from Oslo, Croatian Airlines from Zagreb, as well as charter-flight companies from several cities in Germany. These charter companies usually sell air tickets only in combination with holiday packages, and flights cannot be booked separately.

Information **Rijeka Airport** (⊠ *Hamec 10* 🕾 *051/842–132* ⊕ *www.rijeka-airport.hr)*.

Autotrans (⊕ *www.autotrans.hr)*.**Croatia Airlines** (🕾 *reservations: 01/487–2727* ⊕ *www.croatiaairlines.com)*.**EasyJet** (⊕ *www.easyjet.com)*. **Norwegian Air Shuttle** (⊕ *www.norwegian.no)*.

BOAT & FERRY TRAVEL

During high season (July through August), Jadrolinija ferries travel between Dubrovnik and Rijeka (journey time approximately 20 hours), stopping at Zadar, Split, Stari Grad (island of Hvar), Korčula, and Sobra (island of Mljet) en route. During the rest of the year, the service is less frequent. The fare between Dubrovnik and Rijeka is €127 for a reclining seat in your own two-berth cabin with bathroom and TV. The cheapest way to go with no booked seat at all is €36. In good weather you'll find the rear decks of the ship smothered with passengers camping out beneath the stars, which lends the journey a special atmosphere. Prices vary according to the season, with rates falling as much as 30% in low season. Cars cost €92. Round-trip tickets save 20%. Hourly on the half-hour, ferries leave Brestova, which is south of Opatija, heading to Cres; these ferries arrive at Porozina. Ferries also leave Valibska on Krk to dock at Merag on Cres. Each brief hop across the channel sets you back €1.75 per person, €12.16 if you have a car.

Every day in high season, ferries leave Rijeka at 5 PM to call at Ilovik, Sušak, Unije, Cres, and Mali Lošinj; the entire trip from Rijeka to Mali Lošinj takes around four hours. Meanwhile, a catamaran service heads out to Rab at 4 PM, drops into the northern Dalmatian island of Pag, and then pulls into Mali Lošinj about two-and-a-half-hours later. Six times per day from 6 AM to 6 PM, ferries head out from Baška on Krk toward Lopar on Rab. The trip costs €4.18, €25.27 for a car. Tourist boats and water taxis offering transport on shorter stretches are also abundant at many resorts.

Information **Jadrolinija** (🕾 *051/211–444* ⊕ *www.jadrolinija.hr)*.

BUS TRAVEL

There's daily international bus service to Rijeka from Italy (Trieste), Slovenia (Ljubljana and Nova Gorica), and Germany (Dortmund, Frankfurt, Munich, and Stuttgart). You can also reach destinations all over mainland Croatia from Rijeka and Opatija. Timetable information is available from the Rijeka Bus Terminal.

Buses travel from Rijeka to all the major towns on the mainland and the islands at least once a day. If you're traveling independently, you'll find that buses to the various islands are roughly scheduled to tie in with ferry services.

Information Autotrans (✉ Žabica 1, Rijeka ☎ 051/660-300 ⊕ www.autotrans. hr). Rijeka Bus Termina (✉ Žabica 1, Rijeka ☎ 051/211-222).

CAR TRAVEL

Although local buses and ferries are an excellent, stress-free method of touring the region (buses are scheduled in tandem with the docking of ferries, so don't fear that you'll be left stranded at an empty dock), touring the Kvarner by car does offer the opportunity to nose your way around some of the smaller and more remote villages on the islands and up in the mountains. In addition, despite a poor safety record and heavy traffic in high season, there are few roads more scenic than the Magistrala. A car is also useful if you plan to leave Kvarner and head for Istria (passing through the Učka Tunnel).

Car Rentals Avis (✉ Riva 22, Rijeka ☎ 051/337-917). Europcar (✉ Rijeka Airport, Omišalj ☎ 051/430-3038).

INTERNET

Internet cafés are common at the resorts on both the mainland and the islands. That said, they may not contain many terminals, so you may find yourself with plenty of time to relax, sip a coffee, and enjoy the wait to spend your 20 to 30 Kn per hour.

Information Ecom Club (✉ Ivana Zajca 24A, Rijeka ☎ 051/333-070). Grafit Dizajn Studio (✉ Bočac 46, Mali Lošinj ☎ 051/233-495 ⊕ www.grafit-studio.hr) charges 25 Kn per hour.Inter Club Cont (✉ Šetalište A. Kacica Miošica 1, Rijeka ☎ 051/371-630 ⊕ www.interclub-cont.com) charges 12 Kn for 15 mins. Internet Krk sistemi (✉ Šetalište sv. Bernardina 3, Krk Town ☎ 051/222-999 ⊕ www. krksistemi.hr). Monokini (✉ Maršala Tita 96, Opatija ☎ 051/703-888). Turisticka agencija Croatia (✉ Cons 10, Cres Town ☎ 051/573-053). VIP Internet Corner (✉ Hotel Padova, Banjol, Rab Town ☎ 051/724-54).

MAIL & SHIPPING

Opening times listed are for the main tourist season; hours will be reduced from November through April. All are closed on Sunday unless otherwise indicated.

Information Rijeka Post Office (✉ Korzo 13, Rijeka ☎ 051/200-111) is open Mon.–Sat. 7 AM–9 PM, Sun. 7–2. Opatija Post Office (✉ Maršala Tita 145, Opatija ☎ 051/271-732) is open weekdays 7:30 AM–9 PM, and Sat. 8–noon and 6–9 PM. Cres Post Office (✉ Cons 3, Cres Town ☎ 051/571-155) is open Mon.–Sat. 8 AM–noon and 6–9 PM. Krk Post Office (✉ Bodulska, Krk Town ☎ 051/221-017) is open weekdays 7:30 AM–9 PM, Sat. 8–noon and 6–9 PM. Lošinj Post Office (✉ Vladimira Gortana 4, Mali Lošinj ☎ 051/231-239) is open weekdays 7:30 AM–9 PM, Sat. 8–noon and 6–9 PM. Rab (✉ Palit 67, Rab Town ☎ 051/724-555) is open weekdays 7:30 AM–9 PM, Sat. 8–noon and 6–9 PM.

MONEY MATTERS

On the islands, bank branches can be found in the respective capitals. ATMs are numerous and easily found in many locations, save the smallest villages.

Information **Hypo Alpe Adria** ($\boxtimes$ *Jadranski trg 3, Rijeka* $\textcircled{\scriptsize\textbf} 051/660-444$). **Privredna banka Zagreb** ($\boxtimes$ *Maršala Tita 136/4, Opatija* $\textcircled{\scriptsize\textbf} 051/751-322$). **Volksbank** ($\boxtimes$ *Medulićeva 8, Rijeka* $\textcircled{\scriptsize\textbf} 051/317-630$).

TRAIN TRAVEL

There are five trains daily from Rijeka to Zagreb (journey time is approximately 3½ hours), three trains daily to Split (16 hours) and two trains daily to Ljubljana (2½ hours).

Information **Rijeka Train Station** ($\boxtimes$ *Krešimirova 5, Rijeka* $\textcircled{\scriptsize\textbf} 051/213-333$). **Hrvatske Željeznice (Croatian Railways)** ($\textcircled{\scriptsize\textbf} 060/333-444$ ⊕ *www.hznet.hr*).

VISITOR INFORMATION

Contacts **Cres Tourist Information** ($\boxtimes$ *Cons 10, Cres Town* $\textcircled{\scriptsize\textbf} 051/571-535$ ⊕ *www.tzg-cres.hr*). **Krk Tourist Information** ($\boxtimes$ *Vela placa 1/1, Krk Town* $\textcircled{\scriptsize\textbf} 051/221-414$ ⊕ *www.tz-krk.hr*). **Lošinj Tourist Information** ($\boxtimes$ *Riva lošinjskih kapetana 29, Mali Lošinj* $\textcircled{\scriptsize\textbf} 051/231-884$ ⊕ *www.tz-malilosinj.hr*). **Opatija Tourist Information** ($\boxtimes$ *Vladimira Nazora 3, Opatija* $\textcircled{\scriptsize\textbf} 051/271-710$ ⊕ *www.opatija-tourism.hr*). **Rab Tourist Information** ($\boxtimes$ *Donja ul. 2, Rab Town* $\textcircled{\scriptsize\textbf} 051/724-064$ ⊕ *www.tzg-rab.hr*). **Rijeka Tourist Information** ($\boxtimes$ *Uzarska 14, Rijeka* $\textcircled{\scriptsize\textbf} 051/315-710$ ⊕ *www.tz-rijeka.hr*).

Zadar & Northern Dalmatia

WORD OF MOUTH

"Zadar is very small, but 2 days will give you time to really enjoy what is a town on the rebound in so many ways."

—yorkshire

"[We stopped for a day] at Paklenica National Park. This is rock climbers paradise! It was fun to watch. We hiked for a couple of hours, had lunch, then drove up to Opatija."

—issy

By Paul
Olchváry

WHERE EXACTLY DOES NORTHERN DALMATIA BEGIN? Zadar may be the region's cultural and urban capital—it is, after all, the first sizeable city you encounter in Dalmatia on your way south from Zagreb or Rijeka—but it is not where the region begins, either culturally or geographically. Look instead to the southern reaches of the Velebit mountains, where that coastal range gives way to the flat, sandy coastline of Nin and environs. Practically speaking, though, you enter Dalmatia proper when you cross the long, bright-red span of the Maslenica Bridge going south on the route from Zagreb to Zadar.

Though it's easy enough to drive on straight to Zadar, you won't regret stopping for a visit in Nin. While today it's an unassuming little town with well-preserved 17th-century architecture, more than 1,000 years ago—and for centuries afterward—it was one of the most important Croatian towns of all.

Much of the region is not on the mainland at all but rather comprises the Zadar archipelago, including Pag Island, and, farther south, the Adriatic's largest archipelago, Kornati National Park. Farther inland, only miles from the coast, is a sweeping expanse of countryside still visibly recovering from the Yugoslav war of the 1990s, where tourists rarely tread. Benkovac, the region's center, is home to an imposing 16th-century fort; nearby are the massive ruins of the ancient city of Asseria. Zadar itself, with its mix of Roman, Venetian, communist-era, and modern architecture, has a bustling and beautiful historic center and is also the main point of access by ferry to the islands, which include the beautiful Telašćica Nature Park.

EXPLORING NORTHERN DALMATIA

If you're driving or bussing it from the north, you can stop for an excursion to Pag Island and at Paklenica National Park before arriving in Zadar. The pretty little town of Nin, meanwhile, is just a half-hour north of Zadar and most easily done as a day trip (or even a half-day trip). Though many daily ferries can take you to the Zadar archipelago, Sali (two hours from Zadar by ferry) is a good place to base yourself for a night or two if you want to explore the outer reaches and have the best access to Telašćica Nature Park. A drive or bus trip to Murter will get you within a short boat ride of the spectacular Kornati National Park.

ABOUT THE RESTAURANTS
Fresh seafood is the cuisine of choice in Northern Dalmatia, as it is elsewhere on Croatia's coast. Beyond standard coastal fare, look for Dalmatian specialties including Pag Island lamb and Paški sir (Pag cheese); prosciutto and šokol (smoked pork neck) from Posedarjedried; and sheep's cheese and peppery meat dishes from inner Dalmatia. And of course, there's Zadar's famous Maraschino liqueur—compliments of the area's uniquely zesty cherry and the Maraška company—whose facility is just across the town's pedestrian bridge and whose brand name graces the bottles of the best maraschino.

NORTHERN DALMATIA TOP 5

■ From the Crkva sv. Donata, Croatia's most monumental surviving early Byzantine church, to Katedrala sv. Stošije, Dalmatia's largest basilica, ecclesiastical marvels abound.

■ The barren but beautiful Kornati Islands, Telašćica Nature Park, and the Zadar archipelago are ripe for exploration, as is Pag Island to the north.

■ Comprising 35 pipes under the quay, Zadar's incredible Sea Organ yields a never-ending concert that delights listeners with the music of the sea itself.

■ With its extraordinary karst features towering over the sea at the southern end of the Velebit range, Paklenica National Park is easily accessible from Zadar.

■ North of Zadar—around Nin and, farther afield, on Pag Island—are some of Croatia's sandiest, and shallowest, beaches.

ABOUT THE HOTELS

As elsewhere along practically every populated area of the Croatian coast, package-hotel resorts are easy to find, in particular in the Borik complex on the northern outskirts of Zadar. Top-notch pensions and intimate, elegant small hotels are in somewhat short supply, though a whole host of private rooms and apartments can be found, often for half the price of larger, more established accommodations, either through the local tourist-information office or through private travel agencies. And, as is the practice in other parts of Croatia, short stays (i.e., fewer than three days) often mean a surcharge of around 20%.

WHAT IT COSTS IN EUROS (€) AND CROATIAN KUNA (KN)					
	¢	$	$$	$$$	$$$$
RESTAURANTS	under 20 Kn	20 Kn–35 Kn	35 Kn–60 Kn	60 Kn–80 Kn	over 80 Kn
HOTELS In euros	under €75	€75–€125	€125–€175	€175–€225	over €225
HOTELS In kuna	under 550 Kn	550 Kn–925 Kn	925 Kn–1,300 Kn	1,300 Kn–1,650 Kn	over 1,650 Kn

Restaurant prices are for a main course at dinner. Hotel prices are for two people in a double room in high season, excluding taxes and service charges.

TIMING

If you don't mind crowds, midsummer is a good time to visit Northern Dalmatia—when the Adriatic is at its optimal temperature for beach-going, and you can also delight in the varied music, dance, and drama of the Zadar Summer Theatre (late June to early August), the Full Moon Festival (late July) in and around Zadar, the Pag Carnival (late July or early August), and Sali's annual Saljske užance, which features raucous, horn-blown "donkey music" and donkey races (early August). However, if you don't mind missing out on midsummer culture and crowds, late spring to early autumn is preferable—when you can relax on relatively quiet beaches and enjoy discounts of up to 20% on accommodations relative to high season prices.

GREAT ITINERARIES

Unless you stop at Paklenica National Park, head straight for Zadar and work outward from there, depending on how much time you have. It's easier to take day trips to visit the closer parts of the Zadar archipelago, as well as Nin. To see the farther reaches of the archipelago, stay over in Sali. Keep Benkovac and environs in mind if you have some time to spare and might appreciate a look at the relatively tourist-free interior, including the ruins of the ancient city of Asseria.

IF YOU HAVE 3 DAYS

Plan on two nights in **Zadar** with excursions to the city of **Nin** and also to Ugljan Island, which is in the **Zadar archipelago.** For your final day and night, go either to **Sali** to see **Telaščica Nature Park** or, if you're hankering for mountains, spend one night in Starigrad and see **Paklevica National Park** (unless you've already stopped there on the way south or might do so on your return north).

IF YOU HAVE 5 DAYS

Spend your first three days as outlined in the three-day itinerary, but spend the third night in Zadar. Then spend one night in Starigrad or environs to devote some quality time to Paklevica National Park, and do a loop that includes a night on Pag Island, too.

IF YOU HAVE 7 DAYS

Follow the itinerary above, adding a trip to **Murter** and perhaps inland, to Benkovac or, if you have a car, to the nearby ruins of the ancient city of Asseria *(see ⇨CloseUp: "Benkovac, Truly Off the Beaten Path").*

5

ZADAR

347 km (217 mi) southwest of Zagreb.

Dalmatia's capital for more than 1,000 years, Zadar is all too often passed over by travelers on their way to Split or Dubrovnik. What they miss out on is a city of more than 73,000 that is remarkably lovely and lively despite—and, in some measure, because of—its tumultuous history. The Old Town, separated from the rest of the city on a peninsula some 4 km (2½ mi) long and just 1,640 feet wide, is bustling and beautiful: the marble pedestrian streets are replete with Roman ruins, medieval churches, palaces, museums, archives, and libraries. Parts of the new town are comparatively dreary, a testament to what a world war followed by decades of communism, not to mention a civil war, can do to the architecture of a city that is 3,000 years old.

A settlement had already existed on the site of the present-day city for some 2,000 years when Rome finally conquered Zadar in the 1st century BC; the foundations of the forum can be seen today. Before the Romans came the Liburnians had made it a key center for trade with the Greeks and Romans for 800 years. In the 3rd century BC the Romans began to seriously pester the Liburnians, but required two centuries to bring the area under their control. During the Byzantine era, Zadar became the capital of Dalmatia, and this period saw the construction of its most famous church, the 9th-century St. Donat's Basilica. It remained

IF YOU LIKE ...

ZADAR'S CHURCHES

Even discounting its size and the fact that 60% of the Zadar was destroyed in World War II, Zadar has an astonishing number of churches of key significance to Croatia and, more broadly, to Europe—from the Crkva sv. Donata, the country's most monumental surviving early Byzantine church, to Katedrala sv. Stošije, Dalmatia's largest basilica.

ISLANDS

Much of Northern Dalmatia—and certainly the natural wonders associated with it—consists of huge archipelagos, from the more than 100 barren but beautiful Kornati Islands in the south to the Telašćica Nature Park, the splendorous, indented bay at the southern end of the Zadar archipelago's largest island, Dugi Otok. A visit to one of these places—whether a quick ferry ride to the island of Ugljan, right across from Zadar; a day or a night or more in Sali or Murter; a more substantial excursion by boat to the heart of one or both of these parks; and/or an all-out *Robinson turizm* stay in a stone cottage on one of the Kornati Islands—will prove unforgettable.

INLAND BEAUTY

Their names may sound similar, but in fact they're some distance apart, and technically, neither one is in Northern Dalmatia. But both Paklenica National Park—with its extraordinary karst features towering over the sea at the southern end of the Velebit range—and Plitvice National Park *(see ⇨Chapter 1, Zagreb & Environs)*—that most famous of all Croatia's parks, with its crystal-clear connected lakes and waterfalls, enveloped by rich forests and teeming with wildlife—are both easily accessible from Zadar.

NIN, PAG & THEIR BEACHES

Today an unassuming little town with a 17th-century historic face, Nin was once one of the most important Dalmatian towns of all. Beyond this rich legacy, for miles around the town you will find the only major stretch of sandy beaches on this part of the Croatian coast—some of the best swimming in all of Dalmatia. Though farther from Zadar, Pag has even more in the way of sandy, sheltered beaches, as well as Pag Town with its attractive historic center.

the region's foremost city through the ensuing centuries. The city then experienced successive onslaughts and occupations—both long and short—by the Osogoths, the Croatian-Hungarian kings, the Venetians, the Turks, the Habsburgs, the French, the Habsburgs again, and finally the Italians before becoming part of Yugoslavia and, in 1991, the independent republic of Croatia.

Zadar was for centuries an Italian-speaking city, and Italian is still spoken widely, especially by older people. Indeed, it was ceded to Italy in 1921 under the Treaty of Rapallo (and reverted to its Italian name of Zara). However its occupation by the Germans from 1943 led to intense bombing by the Allies during World War II, which left most of the city in ruins. Zadar became part of Tito's Yugoslavia in 1947, prompting many Italian residents to leave. Zadar's most recent ravages occurred during a three-month siege by Serb forces and months more of bombardment during the Croatian-Serbian war between 1991 and

Northern
Dalmatia

Krk
Cres
TO
RIJEKA
Baška
Lopar
Rab
Cres
Unije
Lošinj
Mali
Lošinj
Novalja
Pag
Island
Pag
Prízna
Žuta Lokva
Otočac
Starigrad
Rakovica
Drežnik-
Grad
Plitvice
BOSNIA-
HERCEGOVINA
Bihać
HRVATSKA
(CROATIA)
Korenica
Perušić
Gospić
Karlobag
Medak
Barić-
Draga
Starigrad-
Paklenica
Rok
Udbina
Bruvno
Paklenica
National
Park

Zadar
see detail
map

Nin
Posedarje
Obrovač
Novigrad

Adriatic Sea

Dugi
Otok
Ugljan
Zadar
Archipelago
Sukošan
Zemunik
Benkovac

KEY
⊢━━⊣ Rail Lines
🚢 Ferry

Sali
Telašćica
Nature Park
Kornat
Pašman
Biograd
Vrana
Vransko
jezero
Pirovac
Murter
Tijesno
Vodice
Kornati
National
Park

Bribir
Skradin
Lozovac
Šibenik

0   30 miles
0   30 kilometers

TO
SPLIT
Primošten

1995. But you'd be hard-pressed to find outward signs of this today in what is a city to behold.

Numbers in the margins correspond to numbers on the Zadar map.

A GOOD WALK

Zadar's main tourist-information office not only provides friendly service but is also ideally located yards from one of the Old Town's two main squares, **Narodni trg ❶**, so it makes sense to begin your walk here. For the shortest route to the city's most prominent churches and the adjacent Roman forum (or what remains of it), take Mihe Klaića one block west past the tourist office, and turn right on Plemića Borelli. These narrow, marble streets are full of cafés, jewelers, perfumeries, shoe stores, fashion (often lingerie) boutiques, and ATMs. Continue straight as the road becomes Madijevaca, which takes you to **Crkva sv. Marije ❷**, which has a good exhibition of religious art, and the pleasantly modern building of the **Archaeological Museum ❸**, both on your right. If you continue on, you will pass a row of souvenir stands to your left and arrive at the wide, mostly empty space of the **Forum ❹**; just to the right is the monumental, cylindrical presence of **Crkva sv. Donata ❺**. To the left side of Crkva sv. Donata, you'll notice a lone column—what

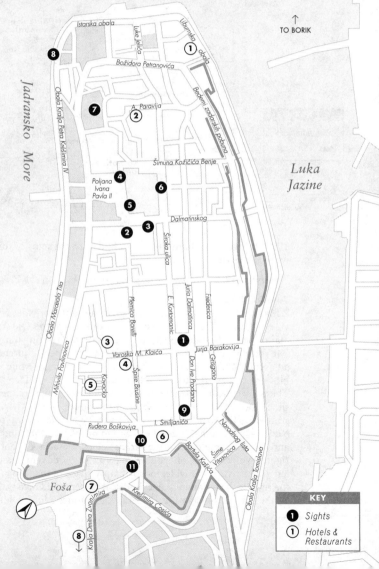

Zadar

0 ____ 1/4 mile

0 ____ 1/4 kilometer

Zadarski Kanal

Borik

Zadarski Kanal

↑ TO BORIK

Jadransko More

Luka Jazine

Foša

KEY

① *Sights*

① *Hotels & Restaurants*

CLOSE UP

Zadar's Court Phenomenon

In June 2005, team Zadar beat Cibona Zagreb to win the Croatian basketball league's championship for the first time in 19 years. The city was delirious with joy. Basketball has long rivaled soccer in Croatia for sheer popularity, and in Zadar this is especially the case. Its team was among the best in the former Yugoslavia, alongside Cibona Zagreb and Split's team, then called Jugoplastika Split. To see one reason for yourself, walk south from the foot of the pedestrian bridge in the Old Town about 10 minutes along Obala Kralja Tomislava to the grassy area on your left (where the bay reaches an end) and consider the huge statue of Zadar's preeminent basketball hero as he towers even higher than the 6 feet, 11 inches he was in real life, captured meditatively with ball in hand. His name is Krešimir Ćosić. (Appropriately, the statue is across the street from Zadar's basketball auditorium.) Born in Zagreb but raised in Zadar, Ćosić enrolled at Brigham Young University in Utah in 1970 after leading Yugoslavia to a silver medal in basketball in 1968. His decision opened the way for other foreign

players to likewise hone their skills in America on the collegiate level. In both 1972 and 1973, Ćosić—who led BYU in scoring for two years in a row—won All-America honors, the first foreign player to do so. In 1973 he achieved the added distinction of being drafted by both the NBA's Los Angeles Lakers and the ABA's Carolina Cougars—and saying "no thanks." He went back home, where he continued to shine on court. Ćosić played on three more Yugoslav Olympic teams, in 1972, 1976, and finally, 1980, when he led his team to a gold medal in Moscow. He played not only for leading Croatian teams but also for the two-time Italian champions, Virtus Bologna. With the close of his playing days he turned to coaching and led the Yugoslav team to a silver medal in the 1988 Seoul Olympics. He later became the third foreign player elected to the Basketball Hall of Fame in Springfield, Massachusetts. Eventually Ćosić stepped away from the court to serve as a diplomat for his newly independent country in Washington, D.C. He died on May 25, 1995, after a long illness, at the young age of 46.

5

remains of the much larger complex of the onetime Forum, dismantled over the centuries for such lofty purposes as cathedral-building.

Follow Simuna K. Benje, and turn left onto Široka ulica. As you proceed, the side of **Katedrala sv. Stošije ❻**, on your left, may well be manned by a small army of older peasant ladies hawking embroideries. Soon you are on Trg Sv. Stošije, the square in front of Dalmatia's largest basilica, which is also home to a couple of nice cafés. Go straight on J. Bjankinija into a compact, tree-shaded little park with 10 busts of serious-looking notables from centuries past. From here it's a one-minute stroll west to the seaside promenade commonly referred to as the Riva, toward the tip of the peninsula. Pass by the **Franjevački samostan i Crkva sv. Franje Asiškog ❼** on the way. Out on the Riva, meanwhile, not only can you take in the view of the hilly islands opposite Zadar and of cruise liners and yachts floating by, but also of what impressed Alfred Hitchcock as one of the world's most beautiful sunsets during his visit to Zadar in May 1964 (so says a large tourist-information sign posted along the Riva). What is more, along with so many other visitors of all ages and temperaments, you can now stand or sit in quiet awe as the wondrous **Sea Organ** ❽ soothes you with nature's very own "music." Hands down, this is the best place in the city for a romantic evening stroll. Take Široka ulica back to Narodni trg; the street is drabber, but the shopping opportunities much greater. Along the way, a detour two blocks to the left (east) will get you to the Old Town's main food market. The market naturally leads you to Jurja Barakovića, which culminates in the Bridge Gate in the city wall. Beyond this gate is Zadar's famous pedestrian bridge, which you can cross into the newer, less sparkling part of town. However, if you backtrack along Jurja Barakovića for two short blocks, you'll find yourself back at Narodni trg. This time, go south, along either Don Ive Prodana or E. Kotromanić, one block to **Crkva sv. Šimuna** ❾. Just beyond the church to the right is the **Square of Five Wells** ❿. The Roman-looking column you pass on the way was erected in 1729, using fragments of the column of the Roman temple on the Forum. From the square you can make your way down to the **Kopneva Vrata** ⓫ and tranquil Foša harbor.

TIMING
A couple of museums close in the early afternoon before reopening in the evening, so start early if museums are high on your agenda. This will allow for some down time in the afternoon, a swim on Ugljan Island, or a quick trip to Nin. In any case, figure on six hours or more of strolling, museum-visiting, and dining in the heart of Zadar.

WHAT TO SEE

There are helpful interpretive signs in English all around the Old Town, so you certainly won't feel lost when trying to make sense of the wide variety of architectural sites you might otherwise pass by with only a cursory look.

❸ **Archaeological Museum.** Founded in 1832, Zadar's archaeological museum is one of the oldest museums in this part of Europe. It occupies a plain but pleasant modern building beside the convent complex of Crkva sv. Marije. It is home to numerous artifacts from Zadar's past, from prehistoric times to the first Croatian settlements. Head upstairs to move back in time. The third floor focuses on ceramics, weaponry, and other items the seafaring Liburnians brought home from Greece and Italy, whereas the second floor covers the classical period, including a model of the Forum square as it would have looked back then; a smaller exhibit addresses the development of Christianity in Northern Dalmatia and contains rare artifacts from the invasion of the Goths. On the first floor you'll find an exhibit from the early Middle Ages, taking you to the 12th century. ⊠ *Trg Opatice Čike 1* ☎ *023/250–542* ⊕ *www.donat.com/arh* ⌨ *10 Kn* ☉ *Mon.–Sat. 9–noon and 5–8, Sun. 9–noon.*

⑤ Crkva sv. Donata *(St. Donat's Church).* Zadar's star attraction, this huge,
Fodor's Choice cylindrical structure is the most monumental early Byzantine church
★ in Croatia. Originally called Church of the Holy Trinity, and probably inspired by plans set forth in a book by the Byzantine emperor
Constantine Porphyrogenet, *On Ruling the Empire,* centuries later
it was rededicated to St. Donat, who was bishop here from 801 to
814. Legend has it that Donat, an Irishman, was the one who had
it built, using stone from the adjacent Forum. The stark, round interior features a circular center surrounded by an annular passageway;
a sanctuary consisting of three apses attached to the lofty mantle of
the church walls, set off from the center by two columns; and a gallery
reached by a circular stairway. Although the church no longer hosts
services, its fine acoustics make it a regular concert venue. During the
off-season (November to March), when the church is closed, someone
at the Archaeological Museum next door may have a key to let you
in. ⌂ *Šimuna Kožičića Benje* ☎ *023/250–516* 🖙 *10 Kn* ⊙ *May–Sept.,
9 AM–9 PM; Apr. and Oct., 9 AM–1 PM.*

② Crkva sv. Marije *(St. Mary's Church).* Legend has it that a local noble-
woman founded a Benedictine convent on this site in 1066, and the
adjoining St. Mary's Church in 1091. Rebuilt in the 16th century, the
church was supposed to incorporate a new, Renaissance look into the
remnants of its earlier style: its rounded gables remained, continuing
to express a certain Dalmatian touch; early Romanesque frescoes are
still evident amid the largely baroque interior; and your eyes will discover 18th-century rococo above the original columns without being
any worse for the effect. Most noteworthy for modern-day visitors,
however, is the adjoining convent complex, two wings of which house
one of Zadar's most treasured museums. The **Permanent Exhibition
of Religious Art,** whose highlight is commonly called "The Gold and
Silver of Zadar," is a remarkable collection of work from centuries
past by local gold- and silversmiths (including Italians and Venetians
who lived here), from reliquaries for saints and crucifixes, to vestments interwoven with gold and silver thread. ⌂ *Poljana Opatice Čike*
☎ *023/211–545* 🖙 *Museum 20 Kn* ⊙ *Museum Mon.–Sat. 10–1 and
6–8, Sun. 10–1.*

⑨ Crkva sv. Šimuna *(St. Simeon's Church).* Built in the 5th century as a
three-nave basilica, it was later reconstructed in Gothic style, and again
in baroque style, though the terra-cotta and white exterior pales in
comparison to some of the city's other churches. St. Simeon's Church
is best known for housing the gilded silver sarcophagus of Zadar's
most popular patron saint. The chest, which depicts intricately detailed
scenes from St. Simeon's life and the city's history, was commissioned in
1381 by Elizabeth, wife of Croat-Hungarian King Ludwig I of Anjou,
and made by Francesco De Sesto of Milan, one of Zadar's best silversmiths. As for St. Simeon, legend has it that his body wound up here
while being transported from the Holy Land to Venice by a merchant
who got caught in a storm, took refuge here, fell ill, and died—but not
before drawing attention to the saintliness of the body he'd brought
with him. Palm trees outside the church lend the site a pleasant, Medi-

5

terranean touch. ⊠*Crkva sv. Šime* ☎*023/211–705* 🖵*Free* ☉*Week-days 9–noon and 3–5, Sat. 9–noon. Masses 8* AM *weekdays, 8:30* AM *and 10* AM *weekends.*

❹ Forum. Established in the 1st century BC by the first emperor Augustus, the Roman Forum is, more than 2,000 years later, pretty much a wide empty space with some scattered ruins. However, since it was rediscovered in the 1930s and restored to its present condition in the 1960s, the Forum has been one of Zadar's most important public spaces. A raised area on the western flank indicates the site of a onetime temple dedicated to Jupiter, Juno, and Minerva, and if you look closely you will notice what remains of its altars that served as venues for blood sacrifices. The only surviving column was used in the Middle Ages as a "Pillar of Shame," to which wayward individuals were chained. Fragments of a second column were removed from the Forum in 1729 and put back together again near the Square of Five Wells, where the column still stands today.

❼ Franjevački samostan i Crkva sv. Franje Asiškog *(St. Francis Church & Franciscan Monastery).* Dalmatia's oldest Gothic church, consecrated in 1280, is a stellar example of a so-called Gothic monastic church, characterized by a single nave with a raised shrine. Although the church underwent extensive reconstruction in the 18th century, behind the main altar is a shrine dating to 1672; inside the shrine you can see choir stalls in the floral Gothic style that date to 1394. In 1358 a peace treaty was signed in this very sacristy under which the Venetian Republic ended centuries of attack and handed Zadar over to the protection of the Croat-Hungarian kingdom. You can walk around the atmospheric inner courtyard for free, by the way, but you must pay a fee to enter the church itself. From mid-October through March or April, the church may keep irregular hours. ⊠*Samostan sv. Franje* ☎*023/250–468* 🖵*10 Kn* ☉*May–Sept., daily 9:30–3; Oct.–Apr., daily 7–noon and 4–5.*

❻ Katedrala sv. Stošije *(St. Anastasia's Cathedral).* Dalmatia's largest basil-★ ica was shaped into its magnificent Romanesque form in the 12th and 13th centuries from an earlier church; though it was damaged severely during World War II, it was later reconstructed. The front portal is adorned with striking Gothic reliefs and a dedication to the archbishop Ivan from the year 1324. The interior includes not only a high, spacious nave but also a Gothic, stone ciborium from 1332 covering the 9th-century altar; intricately carved 15th-century choir stalls by the Venetian artist Matej Morozon; and, in the sacristy, an early Christian mosaic. St. Anastasia is buried in the altar's left apse; according to legend, she was the wife of a patrician in Rome but was eventually burned at the stake. Bishop Donat of Zadar obtained the remains in 804 from Byzantine Emperor Niceforos. The late-19th-century belfry, which is separate from the main church building, offers a sweeping view to those who climb to the top for a fee, but even the 20 steps up to the ticket desk rewards you with a decent view of the square below. ⊠*Trg Svete Stos* ☎*023/251–708* 🖵*Church free; belfry 10 Kn* ☉*Belfry weekdays 8* AM*–10* PM*, Sat. 8–3.*

NEED A BREAK?

Hidden away on a quiet square between St. Anastasia's Church and the Franciscan Monastery, Caffe Bar No. 7 (⊠ *Braće Bersa 1* ☎ *023/235–419*) is a soothing place to sit and sip (anything from coffee to beer). It also goes by the name Internet Cafe No. 7, as there are two computers in the back room that you can use for ½ Kn per minute. The spacious, shaded terrace out front has high wicker chairs beside marble-top tables with wrought-iron legs.

⑪ Kopneva Vrata *(The Land Gate).* A walk around the walls of Zadar's Old Town is a walk around what was, once, the largest city-fortress in the Venetian Republic. One of the finest Venetian-era monuments in Dalmatia, the Land Gate was built in 1543 by the small Foša harbor as the main entrance to the city. It takes the form of a triumphal arch, with a large, central passage for vehicles and two side entrances for pedestrians, and is decorated with reliefs of St. Chrysogonus (Zadar's main patron saint) on his horse, and the shield of St. Mark (the coat of arms of the Venetian Republic).

❶ Narodni trg *(People's Square).* One of the Old Town's two main public spaces, the ever bustling Narodni trg is home of the Gradska Straža (City Sentinel), which was designed by a Venetian architect in late-Renaissance style with a large, central clock tower. The sentinel's stone barrier and railing, complete with holes for cannons, were added later. This impressive tower once housed the ethnographic section of the National Museum and is today a venue for various regular cultural exhibits.

❽ Sea Organ. In 2004 Zadar was provided with a round-the-clock tourist

FodorśChoice ★ attraction unlike any other in the world (as of this writing). Comprising 35 pipes under the quay stretching along a 230-foot stretch of Zadar's atmospheric Riva promenade, the Sea Organ yields a never-ending (and ever free) concert that delights one and all. Designed by architect Nikola Bašić with the help of other experts, the organ's sound resembles a whale song, but it is in fact the sea itself. It's hard not to be in awe as the sound of the sea undulates in rhythm and volume with the waves. ⊠ *Obala kralja Petra Krešimira IV, toward the end of the western tip of the peninsula.*

⑩ Square of Five Wells. The square is the site of a large cistern built by the Venetians in the 1570s to help Zadar endure sieges by the Turks. The cistern itself has five wells that still look quite serviceable, even though they have long been sealed shut. Much later, in 1829, Baron Franz Ludwig von Welden, a passionate botanist, established a park above an adjacent pentagonal bastion that was also built to keep the Turks at bay.

WHERE TO EAT

$$$$ ★ ✕**Foša.** One key reason to eat at the Foša, whose name includes the tag "Riblji [Fish] restaurant," is the choice setting just outside the city walls a stone's throw from the Kopneva Vrata. And then there's the excellent seafood, of course. Whether you opt to sit at a white-table-cloth-and-candle adorned table inside or on the hugely appealing out-

CLOSE UP

New Wave Music, Really

In 2005 Zadar was presented with a round-the-clock art installation unlike any other in the world. The first of a series of planned seaside projects aimed at enhancing Zadar's allure as a port of call for cruises, the Sea Organ has quickly become one of the city's key public (and tourist) attractions. It's visited by as many people as visit the city's venerable churches—or more. Comprising 35 polyethylene pipes of varying lengths, diameters, and tilts under the quay along a 230-foot stretch of Zadar's already atmospheric Riva promenade, it provides a never-ending (and ever free) concert that delights and soothes one and all, of all ages.

Designed by architect Nikola Bašić with the help of a craftsman from Murter and organ builders from Zagreb, this one-of-a-kind pipe organ sounds a bit like a whale's hushed cooing, but it is in fact the sea itself. Each pipe ends in a whistle that churns out five tones in seven chords, through openings on the quayside above it. This explains all those people—many of whom might otherwise not be inclined to attend ordinary concerts—bending down to place their ears against the concrete, positively entranced. Even when the sea seems otherwise still, the music plays. This is a continuous concert produced by nature itself, in unrepeatable variations. It's hard not to be in awe as the sound of the sea undulates in rhythm and volume with the waves—just wait and listen after a big boat goes by! After a while, sitting there on the simple, elegant stone steps that have been built on the quayside to allow you to savor the experience, you may find yourself wondering why there isn't a sea organ in every coastal city in the world.

door terrace overlooking quiet little Foša harbor, your palate is likely to be pleased—whether on account of a staple like grilled squid or, say, Dalmatian-style tuna with Swiss chard. ⊠ *Kralja Dimitra Zvibimira 2* 🕾 *023/314–421* ⊟ *MC, V.*

$$$–$$$$ ✗ **Konoba Martinac.** Notwithstanding the fishnet overhead, the spacious courtyard seating here offers little shade on a hot day, so you might want to make yourself at home at one of the four wooden tables in the smallish interior amid stone walls and sea-themed decor, including miniature sailing ships above an old fireplace. Regardless of where you sit at this cozy, family-owned restaurant, in a narrow side street near the St. Francis Church, you can delight in excellent seafood as well as meat dishes suitable for landlubbers. While there's great standard fare such as *čevapčići* (grilled spicy cubes of minced meat, often served with raw onions), the lamb is top-notch, as is the veal with tuna and caper sauce. ⊠ *Aleksandra Paravije 7* 🕾 *091/794–5350* ⊟ *No credit cards.*

$$$–$$$$ ✗ **Restoran Kornat.** Just outside the city walls on the tip of the peninsula, the Kornat offers fine dining, even if the space is a tad dull despite (or because of) all the sparkling elegance, marked by warm yellow hues that extend also to the cloth napkins. On the ground floor of a four-story concrete-box building, the restaurant serves original, first-rate cuisine, including delightful lamb with rosemary in red-wine sauce and a monkfish fillet with truffle sauce. Desserts include melon with champagne.

There's also an extensive wine list, from the best of Croatian elixirs to the smoothest shiraz. ⊠*Liburnska obala 6* ☏*023/254–501* ▤*AE, DC, MC, V.*

$$–$$$$ ✗**Konoba Skoblar.** Near the Square of Five Wells, this restaurant, with its spacious outdoor terrace shaded by a huge awning and two likewise huge plane trees, is a lovely place to have a meal, whether you opt for grilled or boiled squid or scampi, veal in lemon sauce, or just a simple seafood salad consisting of anything from marinated anchovies to marinated salmon. As an added

plus, during the dog days of summer on the Adriatic the interior is air-conditioned; and there's live music on most weekend evenings. ⊠*Trg Petra Zoranića* ☏*023/213–236* ▤*AE, DC, MC, V.*

$$–$$$ ✗**Na po ure.** On a side street just a block from Narodni Trg is an irre-★ sistible little konoba-style eatery with sea-blue ceiling arches, natural stone walls, and blue-and-white checkered tablecloths. The place is small and smoky, and it's often crowded at lunchtime—but for good reason. The likewise small menu features a choice selection of grilled meats and seafood, shark being a specialty. Folksy background music sets the scene, and you can wash down your food with a glass of wine straight from the barrel. ⊠*Špire Brusine 8* ☏*023/312–004* ▤*AE, DC, MC, V.*

$$–$$$ ✗**Niko.** Just across from a public beach and near the Borik resort com-
Fodor'sChoice plex, this distinguished restaurant has been serving up a delicious array
★ of seafood, beef, veal, pork, and pasta dishes since 1963. You can choose between such lower-end fare as spaghetti with scampi or more expensive delights like scampi on the skewer. That's not to mention the mouthwatering banana splits. Upstairs are 11 spacious, elegant, peach-toned, pricey rooms, at €130 (in cash; or €150 by card) for a double with breakfast. ⊠*Obala Kneza Domagoja 9* ☏*023/337–888* ▤*AE, DC, MC, V.*

$$ ✗**Trattoria Canzona Pizzeria.** This delightful and popular restaurant is hidden away in the Old Town's atmospheric Varoš district. Here you can choose between more than 20 delicious pizzas as well as a host of pasta dishes, or else go for shark in white-wine sauce, leaving room for tiramisu at the end. The interior is a seamless blend of rustic and hip, the brick walls of the inner room adorned with fake windows that give the space an open, airy feel. "Integral flour"—an option for every pizza on the menu—is, simply, whole wheat. ⊠*Stomorica 8* ☏*023/212–081* ▤*AE, DC, MC, V.*

WHERE TO STAY

There are very few hotels in or near Zadar's Old Town—the pension-style Venera used to be the only option until construction started on the Bastion Hotel, due to open in spring 2008 on Trg Tri Bunara. As you leave the center, you'll find either fairly expensive, top-end hotels or relatively simple, budget places, but not much in the middle price ranges. In midsummer, you can step off the ferry from Pula at midnight and be reasonably assured that some relatively trustworthy person—more likely than not a pensioner who speaks more Italian than English—will offer you a room in a centrally located apartment for around 300 Kn for 2 people. But your best bet is to book a room—for a slightly higher cost—through one of the following travel agencies, which also offer excursions to nearby islands and national parks:

Kompas (⊠ *Poljana Natka Nodila 9* ☎ *023/254–304* 🖶 *023/254–305*). **Miatrade** (⊠ *Vrata sv. Krsevana* ☎ *023/254–300 or 023/254–400*). **Terra Travel Agency** (⊠ *Matije Gupca 2a* ☎ *023/337–294*).

$$$$ 🔟 **Hotel Adriana Select.** Flanked beachside by a grove of tall pines, and
★   encircled by a security fence (more to keep nonguests from enjoying the hotel's outdoor pool than for the sake of safety), this is an appealing place to stay even if the long, narrow lobby does resemble an airport terminal. Indeed, it is the only hotel in the Austrian-owned Falken-steiner complex here in outer Zadar's Borik resort area to look more like a tropical villa than a package resort. Bright and modern, with warm hues, the spacious rooms (some with a sea view for only slightly more) have pine floors and large bathrooms complete with tubs. Pros: bright, spacious rooms, lovely private beach, substantial discounts for stays of three nights or more. Cons: pricey, in a huge, somewhat characterless complex, far from the town center. ⊠ *Majstora Radovana 7, Borik, 23000* ☎ *023/206–100* 🖶 *023/332–065* ⊕ *www.falkensteiner. com* ⤳ *48 rooms* ⅋ *In-room: safe, DVD, refrigerator, Ethernet, Wi-Fi. In-hotel: restaurant, pools, gym, public Wi-Fi, public Internet* ⊟ *AE, DC, MC, V* 🔘 *MAP.*

$$$ 🔟 **Hotel President.** The name is stuffy and so is the place, but if you're looking for cloistered luxury, you will find it here, albeit on a bland suburban street. Though a place where an unannounced sneeze or a cough may be bad etiquette, the hotel does sparkle. The rooms have a silky look and feel, not to mention cherrywood Biedermeier-style furniture—and it's just a 10-minute walk from Borik's public beach. The Vivaldi Restaurant, whose thick curtains are drawn even by day, offers an original variety of fish and game dishes, albeit at high prices, and a huge wine list in an atmosphere of refined elegance, its walls adorned with tasteful oil paintings. Pros: unmitigated luxury, fine dining, close to a public beach. Cons: pricey, stuffy, far from the town center. ⊠ *Vladana Desnice 16, Borik 23000* ☎ *023/333–696* 🖶 *023/333–595* ⊕ *www.hotel-president.hr* ⤳ *27 rooms* ⅋ *In-room: safe, DVD, Ethernet, refrigerator. In-hotel: restaurant, bar, public Wi-Fi, public Internet, no elevator* ⊟ *AE, DC, MC, V* 🔘 *BP.*

$$ 🔟 **Hotel Kolovare.** One of the few large hotels close to the Old Town, the Kolovare looks as if it was built in a bygone era by an army of colossal communist bees—what else could explain its homely concrete-box facade pockmarked with darkish sunken windows? On the inside, things are much better, with four floors of bright, yellow-hued, simply furnished rooms. Pros: in a quiet, elegant neighborhood just 15 minutes' walk from the Old Town, right by a public beach, two outdoor pools (including one for kids), all rooms have balconies. Cons: pricey, not much character, no no-smoking rooms. ⊠*Šima Ljubića 4A, 23000* ☎*023/203–200* 📠*023/203–300* ⊕*www.hotel-kolovare-zadar.htnet.hr* 🛏*203 rooms, 12 suites* ♿*In-room: refrigerator, Ethernet. In-hotel: restaurant, bar, pools, gym, tennis court, public Wi-Fi* ⊟*AE, DC, MC, V.*

¢ 🔅**Hotel Venera.** One of only two hotels in the Old Town, this small, friendly lodging is tucked away in a quiet side street a few minutes' walk from Narodni trg. The modest-size rooms are done in soothing blue tones with carpeting and closets of varying size. Though there's no breakfast, you're very near many pretty cafés. Pros: centrally located, good price, on quiet side street, friendly service. Cons: no frills, no breakfast, no Internet access. ⊠*Ul Šima Ljubića 4A, 23000* ☎*023/214–098 or 098/330–958* ⊕*www.hotel-venera-zd.hr* 🛏*12 rooms* ♿*In-room: no a/c, no phone, no elevator* ⊟*No credit cards.*

¢ 🔅**Pension Albin.** On the narrow, busy, road that leads from the city
Fodor's Choice center to the Borik resort area, the Pension Albin is one of Zadar's
★ best places to stay and even eat. The jovial owner, Albin Jurin, is a celebrated local chef who opened this welcoming and elegant hotel-cum-restaurant in the mid-1980s. In summer his friendly grandson, an English-speaking university student, is also on hand to help manage the place. Despite the somewhat tacky facade and the communist-era look of the main lobby, the wood-floored rooms are bright and modern. Those in the newer building are more spacious, and have balconies and cheery, floral curtains to boot; rooms facing the sea have superb views. A lovely little pool is shaded by a lush wall of kiwi leaves behind the older building. You can savor some of the best cuisine in town at the hotel's restaurant. Pros: quality dining, outdoor pool, friendly service, great views from some rooms. Cons: a 45-minute walk from the Old Town, 15 minutes from the sea, smallish bathrooms, few frills, limited Internet access. ⊠*Put Dikla 47, 23000* ☎*023/331–137* 📠*023/332–172* ⊕*www.albin.hr* 🛏*34 rooms* ♿*In-room: safe, refrigerator, DVD, dial-up. In-hotel: restaurant, pool, no elevator* ⊟*AE, DC, MC, V* ⏷*BP.*

NIGHTLIFE & THE ARTS

SUMMER FESTIVALS

Keep your eyes skyward around late July, for the night of the full moon in high summer marks the **Full Moon Festival,** when Zadar's parklike seaside promenade, the Riva, is lit up by torches and candlelight, fishing boats sell their catch, and nightlong konobas pop up to provide you with drinks, figs, and cheese. This is not to mention dance and musical performances in a generally cozy atmosphere that unfolds not only in Zadar but in many of the region's island communities.

Despite its name, **Musical Evenings in Saint Donat,** not all the monthlong series of concerts and recitals beginning in early July are held in the splendid St. Donat's Church. From late June to early August the annual **Zadar Summer Theatre** festival sees a whole range of music, dance, and drama performed in various squares, churches, and other buildings about town. Particular years are devoted to certain themes (in 2005 it was contemporary music—from jazz to blues to flamenco—and dance). Talk about eclectic. The **Zadar snova** *(Zadar of Dreams)* festival, in the second week of August, welcomes everything from contemporary dance and films to comic-strip exhibits and workshops, to theatrical events, to a rich array of music, and more. ⊠*Zadar Theater House, Široka ul 8.*

BARS & CLUBS

Viaz (⊠*Široka ul 3* ☎*023/314–926)* is an ultramodern, hip-as-can-be café-cum-nightspot with bright yellow and orange chairs and cool ceiling lights that would fit Manhattan, San Francisco, or London like a kid glove. This is apparently one new face of Zadar. Sip and socialize while watching the crowds stream by on bustling Široka ulica. Cloistered in a walled garden right atop the city walls, **The Garden** (⊠*Bedemi Zadarskih Pobuna* ☎*023/250–631* ⊕*www.thegardenzadar.com)* is a minimalist and exceedingly popular place to drink, soak in the sun and the views, play a game of chess, and even dance to the jazz, Latin, and down-tempo electronica. It's open daily from 10 AM to 1:30 AM.

Adorned in futuristic Batman style, **Gotham** (⊠*Marka Oreškovića 1, next to the Nova Banka tower north of the Old Town* ☎*023/200–289* ⊕*www.gotham.hr)* is part café (sometimes with live jazz), part cinema, and even a cool-as-can-be dance club with theme parties manned in summer by international DJs, live music from Latin to hip-hop, and go-go dancers. It's open from midnight through 6 AM Sunday through Tuesday. Befitting its classical name, the **City Club Forum** (⊠*Marka Marulića* ☎*No phone)* is a smallish, colosseum-shaped space with three bars, a hedonistic, fall-of-Rome atmosphere, and music ranging from commercial pop to R&B. It's only open Friday and Saturday from 11 PM; ladies get in for free until 1 AM.

SPORTS & THE OUTDOORS

BEACHES

As in many another coastal city, you can feel free to take a short dip off the quay in the Old Town—the most atmospheric place to do so being the **Riva** promenade and especially the tip of the peninsula directly over the Sea Organ, as nature's music accompanies your strokes. But for a more tranquil swim, head to the **Kolovare** district, just southeast of the Old Town, with its long stretch of park-flanked beach punctuated here and there by restaurants and cafés. This is not to mention the resort complex in **Borik,** where relatively shallow waters and a sandy bottom may be more amenable to kids. Last but not least, by driving or bussing it 30 minutes north along the coast you can reach the famously sandy beaches of **Zaton** and **Nin.** For true peace and quiet, though, your best bet is an excursion by ferry and then on foot, by bicycle, or in a rental car out to some more isolated stretch of beach on an island of the Zadar archipelago.

BICYCLING

Being relatively flat, with lots of relatively quiet thoroughfares both in the Old Town and on the outskirts of the city, Zadar is indeed a bicycle-friendly place. You can rent a bike at **Eurobike** (✉ *Obala kneza Branimira 6c* ☎ *023/241–243*).

DIVING

Since diving on your own is possible only with two pricey permits, it is advisable to take that deep dip through a diving center (i.e., with the supervision of a licensed instructor). Just one of the many such centers in Zadar and on the surrounding coast and islands is **Zadar Sub** (✉ *Dubrovačka 20a* ☎ *023/214–848*).

SHOPPING

As hip as it otherwise is, Zadar is low on high fashion and has few outlets for quality souvenirs (as opposed to the usual kitsch, which there is plenty of). That said, those interested will be happy to know that jewelry stores are in no short supply. Also, one of the first shopping opportunities you will pass if you enter the Old Town via the main pedestrian bridge is a large enclosed hall with an antiques market inside; keep your eyes open for the open doorway to your right on Jurja Barakovića, just before you reach H. Vukšića Hrvatinića (9–2 and 5–10 daily). It's not by chance that the light-filled, massive stone structure on

★ the northern end of the Old Town is called **Arsenal** (✉ *Trg Tri Bunara 1* ☎ *023/253–820* ⊕ *www.arsenalzadar.com*) and resembles one, too. That's exactly what it was back in the 16th century, while the Venetians were in town and had military might on their minds. By the late-20th century it was a carpet warehouse. Since reopening in 2005, it has been a shopping and entertainment center. The first floor has a bar and a stage for concerts, plus various stores selling wine, music, clothing, and Croatian jewelry. There's also an Internet access point, and on the second floor are a café and a visual arts gallery.

★ **Galerija Morsky** (✉ *Plemića Borelli 3* ☎ *091/780–6101*) sells fine paintings by local artists. Music fans will want to check out **Naima** (✉ *Varoška 1* ☎ *023/315–816*), which has a decent stock of Croatian folk tunes and Dalmatian men's choral music. **Mondo Media** (✉ *Široka ul, at the corner of ul Dalmatinskog Sabora across from the Konzum food store* ☎ *023/251–358*) focuses on Croatian as well as international popular music. **Studio Lik** (✉ *Don Ive Prodana 7* ☎ *023/317–766*) allows you to buy Pag lace without ever setting foot on Pag Island; and it also sells textiles, ceramics, glassware, and more from elsewhere in Croatia. **Suvenirica-Galerija More** (✉ *Široka ul* ☎ *023/211–624*) has a quality selection of Dalmatian edibles, wine jugs, and handicrafts.

NIN

14 km (9 mi) north of Zadar.

On a tiny, 1,640-foot-wide island in a shallow, sandy lagoon that affords a spectacular view of the Velebit range to the northeast, Nin is connected to the mainland by two small bridges. The peaceful town of 1,700, a compact gem whose present-day size and unassuming attitude belie a stormy history, is well worth a visit, whether on the way to Zadar or as a day trip from there, assuming that the beautiful sand beaches stretching for miles around Nin don't inspire you to stay a bit longer.

Nin was a major settlement of the Liburnians, an Illyrian people who also settled Zadar, hundreds of years before the Romans came, conquered, and named it Aenona. A vital harbor for centuries, it was the first seat of Croatia's royalty, and was long the region's episcopal see, whose bishop was responsible for the conversion to Christianity of all Croatian territory. In 1382 the Venetians seized it and prospered from the trade in salt, livestock, and agriculture. However, the Venetian-Turkish wars eventually brought devastating onslaughts, including Nin's destruction in 1571; later, the Candian Wars of 1645–69 led to the decimation of Nin and the surrounding area yet again.

Aside from its historic buildings and monuments that testify to a rich past, Nin's draw also includes the only sandy beaches on this stretch of the Adriatic, not to mention the area's medicinal seaside mud. Since the sea here is shallow, water temperatures are warmer than in the rest of the Adriatic; moreover, the water is more saline, accounting for Nin's major export product—salt. But what would a Croatian coastal town be without the usual resort complex on its fringes? Holiday Village Zaton is a 15-minute walk from the Old Town.

If you're coming from Zadar, soon before you reach Nin proper, look to your left (your right if headed back toward Zadar) to see the squat, stony, 12th-century form of **St. Nicholas's Church** on a hillock out in the middle of a field, looking rather like a cake ornament, with a lone Scotch pine at the foot of the little hill keeping it company, as it were. You can enter Nin via one of two small bridges—the most likely of the two being the charming, pedestrian **Donja most** (Lower Bridge), only yards from the tourist-information office, which provides a helpful map that folds small enough to fit in your palm. If you're coming by car, you can park in a lot on the right just beyond the office and then cross the bridge, or else find a semi-legal spot along the road roughly opposite the lot, which plenty of enterprising visitors prefer.

Croatia's oldest church, the 8th-century **Crkva sv. Križa** (*Church of the Holy Cross*) is also known locally as the "world's smallest cathedral." Indeed, the unadorned, three-naved whitewashed structure—which has a solid, cylindrical top and a few tall, Romanesque windows (too high to peek inside)—has an unmistakable monumental quality to it even though it's no larger than a small house. There's little to see inside, though it is sometimes open, erratically, in summer; check with the tourist office or the Archaeological Museum. ⊠*Petra Zoranića.*

Nin's shallow coast and centuries of sand deposits preserved numerous remains from prehistory to the Middle Ages under the sea. The **Arheološki muzej** *(Archaeological Museum)* has a rich collection for a town of this size, including replicas of two small, late-11th-century fishing boats discovered only in 1966 and carefully removed from the sea in 1974. One of these boats has been completely reconstructed, the other only to the extent to which it had been preserved underwater. The main themes in each room are elucidated in clear English translations. ⊠*Trg Krajlevac 8* ☎*023/264–160* ᗅ*10 Kn* ☉*Tues.–Sun. 9* AM–*10* PM.

The 18th-century **Crkva sv. Anselma** *(St. Anselmo's Church)*, dedicated to a 1st-century martyr believed to have been Nin's first bishop, was built on the site of Nin's former, 9th-century cathedral, the first cathedral of the medieval Croatian principality. To the right of the altar is a 15th-century statue of the Madonna of Zečevo, inspired by the appearance of the Virgin Mary to a woman on a nearby island. Though the church is plain—the ceiling is adorned with only a nice chandelier and a smoke detector—the foundations of the onetime cathedral are still much in evidence. Beside the church is the belfry, and next door is the treasury, which houses a stunning little collection of reliquaries containing various body parts of St. Anselmo. ⊠*Branimirova, near Višeslavov trg* ᗅ*10 Kn* ☉*Treasury: May–Sept., Mon.–Sat. 10–noon and 5:30–9:30.*

Around the corner from the Archaeological Museum are the ruins of the large **Temple of Diana,** one of the few remaining testaments in Nin to the Roman era. ⊠*Sv. Mihovila.*

WHERE TO STAY & EAT

Though Holiday Village Zaton has its share of the usual, package-tourist accommodations, in Nin proper there's not much hotel-wise but for the **Perin Dvor** (⊠*Petar Surić, 23232* ☎*023/264–307*), a popular restaurant offering decent fare that also has five clean, comfortable kitchenette-equipped suites. You can rent one for €60 a night, but don't expect to be greeted by an English speaker. For a private room or apartment, check with the travel agency next door to the tourist-information office.

$$–$$$ ✕**Konoba Branimir.** Strategically located yards away from the Church of the Holy Cross—indeed you might enter the restaurant by mistake, thinking you are proceeding to the churchyard from a back entrance—this is the most pleasant place to dine in Nin. The well-prepared fare ranges from fresh seafood to meats, and desserts such as pancakes with fig marmalade. Note that the spaghetti, though listed as a children's meal, makes for a hearty "light" (and budget) meal even for an adult. ⊠*Višeslavov trg 2* ☎*023/264–866* ⊟*AE, DC, MC, V.*

Benkovac: Truly Off the Beaten Path

It's a hot August day, and our rickety bus is *not* one of those modern, air-conditioned wonders that ply the bustling coast we're about to leave. Unlike those packed coaches, however, our bus—which has just 12 passengers—leaves on time; for there is no one else waiting to get on.

We are headed to Benkovac, 37 km (23 mi) east of Zadar, away from the sea. Not far at all geographically, this town—so prominent on the map, and indeed a main transit point to points farther inland—is far indeed economically and psychologically. Soon after you leave Zadar, the coastal construction boom fades away; house after house is missing its roof, a legacy of the war that ravaged the region until 1995. For a while, the Velebit range forms a striking view many miles to the left, but then the mountains vanish and the horizon is flat in all directions.

There's next to no tourism in Benkovac. The only hotel in town—a concrete box called the Hotel Asseria (named after an ancient city whose ruins lie nearby)—is hardly a place for a cozy stay. The town was abandoned by most of its Serb population by the mid-1990s, and it's strangely empty on a summer day. Despite its spare feel, Benkovac's small business district is attractive, and the town is so close to Zadar that it's easily done as a day trip. You'll certainly leave Croatia with a richer impression of its diversity and of the reality of so many small inland towns away from the tourist path.

Among the bright spots in this region is the family-owned **Markica farm** (⊠ *Jošani, near Galova* ☎ *023/392-222*), less than 4 km (2½ mi) from the airplane crossing. At this farm you can sample all sorts of scrumptious homemade fare, and children can play with farm animals, including a donkey and ostriches. Unless you're passing by, anyway, call before going out there; as of this writing, the English-speaking family member to ask for is Marina.

Benkovac's early-16th-century fortress, the **Kaštel** (⊠ *Obitelji Benkovića 9, Benkovac* ☎ *023/681-055* ⊕ *www.benkovac.com*), houses the local museum. This austere structure, built by the Benkovič family (after which the town probably takes its name), towers prominently on a hill a short walk above a charming town center that is home to a few pleasant if unassuming cafés and pizzerias. It's open weekdays, from 8 to 3. Admission is 10 Kn.

Near Benkovac are the massive ruins of **Asseria,** an ancient city. First settled around 6 BC by Liburnians, who built it into one of their most important towns before the Romans came, Asseria—which is nearly 1,640 feet long and roughly a third as wide, and is situated 6 km (3¾ mi) east of Benkovac, near the village of Podgrađe—was inhabited for more than 1,000 years before crumbling away along with the Roman empire.

For more information on the city and Asseria, contact the **Benkovac Tourist Association** (⊠ *Šetalište Kneza Branimira 12, Benkovac* ☎ *023/684-880*). But you may need to brush up on your Croatian before calling or dropping by, since English is not likely to be spoken here.

SPORTS & THE OUTDOORS

☾ With its long sandy **beaches,** the coastline in and around Nin, and Pag Island just to north, is widely regarded as the most beautiful—and most swimmable—in Dalmatia. The Holiday Village Zaton resort complex, a 15-minute walk from Nin, is home to **Scuba Adriatic** (✉ *Holiday Village Zaton* ☎ *023/280–350*), which offers diving excursions for advanced and beginning divers, formal diving instruction, as well as a two-hour "Discovery Diving" course.

SALI & TELAŠČICA NATURE PARK

Sali is approximately 30 km (19 mi) south of Zadar; Telaščica Nature Park is 10 km (6 mi) south of Sali.

The largest and most westerly island of the Zadar archipelago, facing the open sea, Dugi Otok culminates at its southern end with a spectacular nature preserve in and around Telaščica Bay, the town of **Sali** being the ideal access point. Situated toward the southeastern tip of the 52-km (32-mi) long island, which is no more than 4 km (2½ mi) wide, Sali is Dugi Otok's largest settlement—with around half of the island's 1,800 inhabitants, the rest of whom reside mostly in its 10 other villages—but it's an awfully peaceful little place you arrive in after the two-hour ferry ride from Zadar. Once an out-of-the-way fishing village, Sali draws tourists these days due to its location in and near such natural splendors. It is home to several old churches, including the 12th-century **St. Mary's church,** whose baroque altar was carved in Venice. Adding to the village's appeal is its annual **Saljske užance** (Donkey Festival) during the first full weekend in August, which includes an evening ritual during which lantern-lit boats enter Sali harbor and there are donkey races and *tovareća muzika* (donkey music) produced by locals blowing or braying raucously into horns. Spending at least a night or two here can provide a relatively peaceful, nature-filled respite from the rigors of tourism on the mainland or, for that matter, on more tourist-trodden reaches of the Zadar archipelago.

★ **Telaščica Nature Park** encompasses Telaščica Bay, which cuts 7 km (4½ mi) into the southern tip of Dugi Otok with an inner coastline so indented that it is really a series of smaller bays and a handful of islands. Flanked by high vertical cliffs facing the open sea to the west, with low, peaceful bays on the other side, it has a variety of vegetation. Relatively lush alpine forests and flower-filled fields as well as vineyards, olive groves, and onetime cultivated fields give way, as you move south, to bare rocky ground of the sort that predominates on the Kornati Islands, whose northern boundary begins where Telaščica Nature Park ends. Aside from Telaščica's other attractions, most of which are accessible only by boat, one of the park's key highlights—accessible by land on a 20-minute drive from Sali—is the salt lake **Jezero mir,** which was formed when a karst depression was filled by the sea. Small boats (generally with 8 to 12 passengers) bound for both Telaščica Nature Park and the northern fringes of Kornati National Park leave the east side of Sali's harbor (i.e., where the Zadar ferry arrives) at 9 or 9:30 each morning and return by 6 or 6:30 in the evening. Expect to pay 200 Kn per person, sometimes less. The best way to arrange this is in person—by going to the harborside square near the post office around 8 PM on the day before you wish to leave (which means at least a one-night stay in Sali), when boat captains gather there looking for passengers for the next day's excursion. However, the tourist-information office in Sali can put you in touch with operators by phone as well. ⊠*Put Danijela Grbina, Sali* ☎*023/377–096* ⊕*www.telascica.hr.*

The **Zadar archipelago** is so close and yet so far away. Ugljan and Pašman are just two of the myriad islands comprising the lacelike islands, and yet they are among the largest and the easiest to reach from Zadar. More than 15 ferries a day run the 5 km (3 mi) distance between Zadar and Ugljan, a 19-km-long (12-mi-long) island whose narrow width of just a couple of kilometers runs parallel to the mainland, with its midway point across from Zadar *(see* ⇨Boat & Ferry Travel *in* Zadar & Northern Dalmatia Essentials, *below)*. From the ferry landing on Ugljan, your best bet may be to head north along the seafront 10 minutes on foot to the heart of **Preko**, a fine access point to several worthwhile destinations (very) near and (not too) far. Going south will get you in roughly the same time to the unassuming fishing village of Kali. From Preko's harbor you can walk about 1 km (½ mi) farther north to a shallow bay locals like to swim in; or better yet, take a taxi-boat to **Galevac**, a charming wooded islet less than 100 yards from Preko that not only has splendid swimming but also a 15th-century Franciscan monastery set in a lush green park. And then there's the **Tvrđava sv. Mihovila** (Fortress of St. Michael), a 13th-century landmark atop a hill roughly an hour's walk west of town. Though largely in ruins, the fortress offers spectacular views not only of nearby Zadar, to the west, but on a cloudless day the Italian coast as well. Meanwhile, 10 km (6 mi) farther north is the quiet village of **Ugljan**, accessible from the ferry port by a handful of buses daily. For a somewhat sleepier island experience, hop aboard one of eight buses daily from Preko to the village of **Pašman**. Continuing on, you can eventually get to Tkon, Pašman island's largest village, from which some 10 ferries daily can get you back to the mainland south of Zadar.

WHERE TO EAT

$$–$$$ ✕**Konobe Kod Sipe.** There are plenty of tourist places harborside in
★   Sali, but if you want to have a hearty meal well above the harborside fray, you'll have to climb some steps. Start at the steps between the Suvenirica Porat store and the Gelateri Contes café, near the tip of the harbor, and walk up more than 100 of them, passing two pretty little churches on your left along the way. After the second church, follow the KONOBA signs to this popular restaurant that serves everything from grilled calamari and pork chops to cuttlefish spaghetti and "octopus under a baking lid." The rustic decor is pleasingly punctuated by a barrel theme, with both the chairs and the tables on barrels, and the usual fishnets hanging from the ceiling's wooden beams. The outdoor terrace

is shaded by grapevines (and, yes, some fishnet) and has an enticing open hearth. All this, in a villagelike atmosphere where tourists rarely tread. ⊠ *Ulica sv. Marije, Sali* ☎ *023/377–137* ▤ *No credit cards.*

WHERE TO STAY

The tourist-information office *(see* ⇨ *Visitor Information in Zadar & Northern Dalmatia Essentials, below)* can put you in touch with locals who rent private rooms, at around 220 Kn per night in high season. Large hotels will generally accept payment in either euros or kunas.

$ ★ **▥ Sali Hotel.** A 10-minute walk from the harbor on the quiet waters of Sašćica, the next bay north, this low-key hotel occupies a pair of two-story, concrete-boxish buildings perched on a lovely, pine-covered hill leading down to a beach on a pristine bay worlds away from the hub-bub of busier coastal resorts. The rooms are clean, comfy, and pleasantly *(very)* blue, even if they do smell a bit of cigarette smoke. Pros: lovely setting on private beach, diving center yards away. Cons: rooms have smoky smell, hotel bland and boxlike on the outside, few frills. ⊠ *Adresa, Sali 23281* ☎ *023/377–049* ▤ *023/377–078* ⊕ *www.hotel-sali.hr* ↩ *52 rooms* ⎐ *In-room: safe, refrigerator. In-hotel: restaurant, public Internet, no elevator* ▤ *AE, DC, MC, V* ⦿ *BP.*

SPORTS & THE OUTDOORS

"Diving is not about sitting around on land, sipping wine, and watching the sea," says the chief instructor of Sali's **Diving Center** (⊠ *Adresa, just below the Sali Hotel, Sali* ☎ *023/377–128* ⊕ *www.dive-kroatien. de),* as several clients huddle nearby sipping coffee and watching the sea—true, it's cold and rainy just now. This German-owned firm, which operates out of a compact cabin on the pine-covered hillside below the Sali Hotel, offers everything from a 30-minute resort course to a five-day certification course, in English if you prefer. Diving can be done both from shore or farther afield from a boat, whether on Sašćica Bay itself or farther out, in Teščica Nature Park or on the fringes of Kornati National Park.

MURTER & THE KORNATI ISLANDS

70 km (44 mi) south of Zadar.

Built near the ruins of the 1st-century Roman settlement of Colentum, **Murter** has that unmistakable tourism-driven hustle and bustle in mid-summer that Sali doesn't—both because it is the key gateway to one of Croatia's chief offshore natural splendors, Kornati National Park, and because it is easily accessible by road from Zadar. However you go to Murter, you'll pass through Biograd-Na-Moru, a relatively big, bustling—but thoroughly tourist-trampled—town, where the resorts have long come to predominate in what was once a charming place; Biogrand-Na-Moru also serves as another access point for ferries to the Kornati Islands.

Murter, a town of 2,000 on the island of the same name that lies just off the mainland, is accessible by road from the main coastal route that runs south from Zadar toward Split. As important as tourism is to its present-day economy, boatbuilding has, not surprisingly, long been vital to Murter as well. This is not to mention its olive oil, which was once so famous that it made its way to the imperial table in Vienna.

Fodor'sChoice

★

The largest archipelago in the Adriatic, **Kornati National Park** comprises more than 100 islands that are privately owned, mostly by residents of Murter, who purchased them more than a century ago from Zadar aristocrats. The new owners burned the forests to make room for sheep, which in turn ate much of the remaining vegetation. Although anything but lush today, the islands' almost mythical beauty is ironically synonymous with their barrenness: their bone-white-to-ochre colors represent a striking contrast to the azure sea. However, owners tend vineyards and orchards on some, and there are quite a few small buildings scattered about, mostly stone cottages—many of them on **Kornat**, which is by far the largest island, at 35-km long (22-mi long) and less than a tenth as wide. Indeed, some of these cottages are available for so-called *Robinson turizm* (ask at the Murter tourist office, or enquire around town). In 1980 the archipelago became a national park. It was reportedly during a visit to Kornati in 1936 that King Edward of England decided between love for his throne and love for Wallis Simpson, the married woman who was to become his wife a year later. ⊠*Butina 2* ☎*022/435–740* ⊕*www. kornati.hr* 🖳*50 Kn if paid in advance, 60 Kn inside the park.*

WHERE TO EAT

$$$–$$$$

★

✕**Tic-Tac.** The chef likes putting seafood in wine sauce here, to gratifyingly delicious effect. In this elegant little restaurant near the main square, with tables lining the length of the narrow, historic alleyway where you'll also find the main entrance, you can begin with an appetizer such as mussels in wine sauce and move on to monkfish tail in wine sauce or grilled scampi in wine sauce. Whatever you get, accompany it with a glass of Graševina, the house white. ⊠*Hrokešina 5* ☎*022/435–230* ▤*AE, DC, MC, V.*

WHERE TO STAY

Coronata Tourist Service (⊠*Žrtava ratova 17* ☎*022/435–089* 🖷*022/ 435–555* ⊕*www.coronata.hr*) or **KornatTurist** (⊠*Hrvatskih vladara 2* ☎*022/435–854* 🖷*022/435–853* ⊕*www.kornatturist.hr*).

$$

🛏**Hotel Colentum.** Situated in a pine forest, the Colentum, about five minutes from the town center, offers simply furnished, bright, modern, blue-themed rooms that are a tad cramped, but whose balconies enhance your sense of space just enough. Pay 15 Kn extra per person for a sea view. Oh yes, there's a naturist beach just 1 km (½ mi) away, if you feel like breaking free. Pros: lovely forest setting, bright modern rooms, balconies. Cons: rooms are small, pricey, few frills, limited Internet access. ⊠*Put Slanica, 22243* ☎*022/431–100* 🖷*022/434–255*

⊕www.hotel-colentum.hr ⟿78 rooms ⟟In-room: safe, refrigerator, Ethernet. In-hotel: restaurant, tennis courts, no elevator ⊟AE, DC, MC, V ⊺◯⫾BP.

SPORTS & THE OUTDOORS

DIVING

Whether for exploring shipwrecks or reefs or underwater cliffs, Kornati National Park is among Croatia's most popular diving destinations. That said, you can't dive alone here, only through a qualified diving center. The permit for diving in the park is 150 Kn, which includes the park entrance fee. **Aquanaut Diving Center** (⊠ *Luke, near intersection of Kornatski, across from supermarket* ☎022/434–988 ⊕*www.diving-murter.com*) offers a small menu of choice courses and excursions (to more than 100 sites), including a daylong boat trip that includes two dives and a stopover in the Kornati Islands. **Najada Diving** (⊠ *Luke 57, on the jetty behind the supermarket* ☎022/436–630 ⊕*www.najada. com*) offers supervised shore dives as well as half-day group excursions that include two dives. Among the highlights on its menu of excursions to more than 30 sites is a visit to the wreck of the World War II cargo ship *Francesca*.

TOURS TO KORNATI NATIONAL PARK

All-day excursions generally include two substantial stops, one for a swim and another for a picnic, and include the park entrance fee of 50 Kn; trips usually cost around 230 Kn per person. In Murter, **Atlas** (⊠*Hrvatskih vladara 8* ☎022/434–999) is one prominent contact to arrange such a fun-filled day. If you prefer to save yourself the long and meandering drive to Murter, or don't have wheels to begin with, you can catch a tour on one of several boats that ply the waters straight from Zadar, for a daylong excursion price of around 270 Kn per person. One good option is the boat **Plava Laguna** (☎098/875–746 or 023/334–68), which departs from the Borik marina at 8 AM daily and returns by around 6 PM.

PAKLENICA NATIONAL PARK

50 km (31 mi) northeast of Zadar.

For mountain scenery at its most spectacular and mountain tourism at its most advanced, you need go no further from Zadar than Paklenica National Park. The Velebit mountain range stretches along the Croatian coast for more than 100 km (62 mi), but nowhere does it pack in as much to see and do as in this relatively small, 96-square-km (37-square-mi) park at the southern terminus of the range. Here, less than an hour from Zadar, is a wealth of extraordinary karst features from fissures, crooks, and cliffs to pits and caves. The park comprises two limestone gorges, Velika Paklenica (which ends, near the sea, at the park entrance in Starigrad) and Mala Paklenica, a few kilometers to the south; trails through the former gorge are better marked (and more tourist-trodden).

All that dry rockiness visible from the seaward side of the range turns resplendently green as you cross over the mountains to the landward side. Named after the sap of the black pine, *paklina*, which was used long ago to prime boats, the park is in fact two-thirds forest, with beech and the indigenous black pine a key part of this picture; the remaining vegetation includes cliff-bound habitats featuring several types of bluebells, and rocky areas abounding in sage and heather. The park is also home to 4,000 different species of fauna, including butterflies that have long vanished elsewhere in Europe. It is also the only mainland nesting ground in Croatia for the stately griffin vulture.

The park has more than 150 km (94 mi) of trails, from relatively easy ones leading from the **Velike Paklenica Canyon** (from the entrance in Starigrad) to the 1,640-foot-long complex of caverns called Manita Peć cave, to mountain huts situated strategically along the way to the Velebit's highest peaks, Vaganski Vrh (5,768 feet) and Sveto brdo (5,751 feet). The most prominent of the park's large and spectacular caves, **Manita Peć** is accessible on foot from the park entrance in Starigrad; you can enter for a modest additional fee, but buy your ticket at the park entrance. Rock climbing is also a popular activity in the park. Meanwhile, mills and mountain villages scattered throughout Paklenica evoke the life of mountain folk from the not too distant past.

About a half mile down the park access road in Starigrad, you pass through the mostly abandoned hamlet of **Marasovići,** from which it's a few hundreds yards more downhill to the small building where you buy your tickets and enter the park (from this point on, only on foot). From here it's 45 minutes uphill to a side path to Anića kuk, a craggy peak, and from there it's not far to Manita Peć. However, if you don't have time or inclination for a substantial hike into the mountains, you will be happy to know that even the 45-minute walk to the entrance gate and back from the main road affords spectacular, close-up views of the Velebit range's craggy ridgeline and the gorge entrance. Also, be forewarned that if you are looking to escape the crowds, you will be hard-pressed to do so here in midsummer unless you head well into the mountains or, perhaps, opt for the park's less-frequented entrance at Mala Paklenica; more likely than not, you will be sharing the sublimities of nature with thousands of other seaside revelers taking a brief respite from the coast.

Although the park headquarters is on the main coastal road in the middle of Starigrad, fees are payable where you actually enter the park on the access road. Beyond the basic park admission and the supplemental fee to enter Manita Peć cave, the park offers every imaginable service and presentation that might encourage you to part with your kunas, from half-day group tours (350 Kn) and full-day tours (700 Kn) to presentations every half hour from 11 to noon and 4 to 7 on the park's birds of prey and on falconry. ⊠ *Dr. Franje Tuđmana 14a, Starigrad* ☎ *013/369–202* ⊕ *www.paklenica.hr* ✉ *30 Kn; Manita Peć cave 10 Kn* ♡ *Park: July and Aug., daily 7 AM–9 PM; Apr.–June, Sept., and Oct., daily 8 AM–noon and 4–8 PM. Cave: daily 10–1.*

WHERE TO EAT

$$ ✕ **Restaurant Miramar.** From the outside, Miramar looks much like the other restaurants along Starigrad's main thoroughfare. But here you get the added plus of hearty Dalmatian and even Bosnian specialties, not to mention huge servings. While Croatian pop music plays in the background and locals sit across the room quietly drinking beer, you can feast on Mućkalica, for example—a scrumptious dish consisting of slices of pork with pepper and onions in a thick, peppery sauce, served on a bed of rice. ⊠ *Sv. Jurja 23, Starigrad* ☎ *023/369–017* 🗖 *AE, DC, MC, V.*

WHERE TO STAY

For private rooms in Starigrad or nearby (around €30 high season, €20 the rest of the year), check with the tourist-information office or, better yet, the friendly travel agency **Koma-Maras** (⊠ *Dr. Franje Tuđmana 14, Starigrad 23244* ☎ *023/359–206* 🖷 *023/359–207*), where communication in English goes more smoothly. It's located in a little shopping center on your left as you go north, immediately before the INA fuel station.

$ 🖵 **Hotel Alan.** Once inside this high-rise hotel, which experienced a thorough makeover in 2004, you might easily forget that you are, in fact, in a concrete box that still looks rather like a college dormitory. It's part of a complex that also includes 28 apartments in adjacent, low-rise buildings and a small campground as well as a public beach and an outdoor pool. Hotel Alan offers rooms that, though a bit cramped, are nonetheless bright and modern, with soothing pastel bedspreads. Rooms on the upper floors, at least, carry the added pleasure of stunning views of the sea on one side and mountains on the other. As an added plus, every Thursday the hotel hosts Karaoke Night. There's a 10% discount if you stay more than one night. Pros: great views, beach and pool, bright and modern interiors. Cons: bland high-rise look on the outside, pricey, smallish rooms. ⊠ *Dr. Franje Tuđmana 14, Starigrad 23244* ☎ *023/209–050* 🖷 *023/369–203* ⊕ *www.hotel-alan.hr* ⇨ *138 rooms* ⚲ *In-room: safe, refrigerator, Wi-Fi. In-hotel: restaurant, bar, pool, gym, sauna, beachfront, public Internet* 🗖 *AE, DC, MC, V* ¶◎*BP.*

¢ 🖵 **Hotel Rajna.** On an isolated stretch of the main road just before you
★ enter Starigrad from the south—and close to the national park access road—this friendly little hotel is a bit concrete-boxish in appearance. However, for years now it has been offering not only a splendid view of the mountains to the east and clean, spacious (though not quite sparkling and modern) rooms, but also a restaurant with carefully prepared, scrumptious seafood fare. Note that a stay of two nights or more yields a 30% discount. Pros: pleasantly isolated spot near park-access road, fine mountain views, good on-site dining, friendly service. Cons: 15-minute walk from the village center, bland on the outside, rooms a tad worn. ⊠ *Dr. Franje Tuđmana, Starigrad 23244* ☎ *023/359–121* 🖷 *023/369–888* ⊕ *www.hotel-rajna.com* ⇨ *10 rooms* ⚲ *In-room: refrigerator, dial-up. In-hotel: restaurant, laundry service, public Internet, no elevator, parking (no fee), some pets allowed* 🗖 *AE, DC, MC, V* ¶◎*BP.*

5

SPORTS & THE OUTDOORS

TOURS

Koma-Maras (✉ *Dr. Franje Tuđmana 14, Starigrad* ☎ *023/359–206* 🖷 *023/359–207*) rents bicycles and sells tickets for various excursions in the national park as well as tickets for daylong boat trips up the lovely Zrmanja River gorge and its waterfalls, which are near Obrovac, toward the southern end of the Velebit range; the boat tours cost about 250 Kn per person. There's an ATM by the agency entrance.

PAG ISLAND

48 km (30 mi) north of Zadar.

Telling an urbane resident of architecturally well-endowed Zadar that you are headed to Pag Island for a night or two will make them think you want to wallow on a sandy beach all day and party all night. Indeed, Pag Island has developed a reputation in recent years as a place to sunbathe and live it up rather than visit historic sites. The town of Novalje, in the north, has quite a summertime population of easy-livin' revelers. But to be fair, this narrow island, one of Croatia's longest, stretching 63 km (40 mi) north to south, has long been famous for other reasons, among them its cheese, salt, and, not least, its lace. Moreover, Pag Town in particular has an attractive historic center, a surprising contrast to the modern, resortish feel of its outskirts, and a contrast to the breathtaking natural barrenness of so much of the island.

Inaccessible for centuries except by sea, Pag Island saw a dramatic boost in tourism starting in 1968 with the completion of the Paškog mosta (Pag Bridge), which linked it with the mainland and the Zagreb-Split motorway. The first thing you notice on crossing over the bridge onto the island is that practically all vegetation disappears. You are on a moonlike landscape of whitewashed rocks scattered with clumps of green hanging on for dear life. But, sure enough, soon you also notice the sheep so instrumental in producing both Pag cheese—that strong, hard, Parmesan-like product that results from the sheep munching all day long on the island's salty herbs—and, yes, Pag lamb. Then, five minutes or so apart, you pass through a couple of small villages and, finally, the huge salt flats stretching out along the road right before you pull into Pag Town.

Lest you think the modern vacation homes lining the bay are all there is to **Pag Town,** park your car (or get off the bus) for a walk into the historic center, whose narrow streets provide not only a rich sense of centuries past but also a refuge of shade on a hot summer day. Pag Town was founded in 1443, when Juraj Dalmatinac of Šibenik, best known for designing Šibenik's magnificent cathedral, was commissioned by the Venetians to build a fortified island capital to replace its predecessor, which was ravaged by invaders in 1395. Today a few odd stretches remain of the 7-meter-high wall Dalmatinac built around the town, and a walk around the center reveals several Renaissance buildings and palaces from his era as well as baroque balconies and stone coats of arms from the 15th to 18th centuries. Pag Town's compact main square, **Trg Krajla Petra Krešimira IV,** is home to three of the town's key landmarks, two of them original buildings designed in the mid-14th century by Juraj Dalmatinac. Most notably, there is **Crkva Sveta Marija** *(St. Mary's Church)* (☎ *No phone*), a three-nave basilica whose simple front is decorated with a Gothic portal, an appropriately lacelike Renaissance rosette, and unfinished figures of saints. A relief over the entrance depicts the Virgin Mary protecting the townsfolk of Pag. Begun in 1466 under Dalmatinac's direction, it was completed only decades later, after his death. Inside, note the elaborate, 18th-century

PAG CHEESE

Thanks to its many sheep, Pag Island is known as the home of one of Croatia's most esteemed cheeses—*Paški sir* (Pag cheese). You can buy some for 150 Kn per kilogram, or 15 Kn for a decagram, which is a small piece indeed. If that sounds expensive, just try ordering a bit as an appetizer in a restaurant, where it's more than twice as much. You can easily find it on sale in private homes on some of the narrow streets off the main square. Celebrated local complements to the cheese include the local lamb, an herb brandy called travarica, and Pag prosciutto.

baroque altars, and the wood beams visible on the original stone walls. The church is open daily 9–noon and 5–7. Across the square is the imposing **Knežev dvor** *(Duke's Palace)* (☎ *No phone*) with its magnificent, richly detailed portal. Until recently it housed a grocery store and a café; as of this writing it was closed for renovation, but was expected to reopen by sometime in 2008—not that the inside is the main attraction anymore. Right next to the tourist-information office, the **Galerija Paške Čipke** *(Pag Lace Gallery)* (☎ *No phone* ⌖ *Free*)displays beautiful examples of the island's most famous nonedible product. The gallery is open mid-June through mid-September, daily 9–1. A mere 20-minute walk south of the present town center lie the ruins of the previous, 9th-century town, **Stari grad** (Old Town). You can wander around for free, taking in the Romanesque-style Crkva svete Marije (St. Mary's Church), first mentioned in historical records in 1192; the ruins of a Franciscan monastery; and a legendary, centuries-old well whose filling up with water after a drought was credited to the intervention of the Holy Virgin. On August 15, one of only two days St. Mary's Church is open to the public (the other is September 8), a procession of locals carries a statue of the Virgin Mary from here to the church of the same name on present-day Pag's main square. On September 8 they return. To get to Stari grad, walk across the bridge and keep left on Put Starog Grada, the road that runs south along the bay. The bay stretches far, with sandy, shallow beaches aplenty—making Pag Island a great place to sunbathe and swim for a day or two, especially with children. The best and biggest beaches, amid pretty groves of pine and Dalmatian oak, are in Novalja.

CLOSE UP

White Gold

There was a time when paške čipke was passed off abroad as Greek, Austrian, or Italian. Those days are long over. Today an officially recognized "authentic Croatian product" that is sometimes called "white gold," Pag lace is the iconic souvenir to take home with you from a visit to Pag Island—unless you are confident that a hulking block of Pag cheese won't spoil. An integral component of the colorful folk costumes locals wear during festivals, this celebrated white lace is featured most saliently as the huge peaked head ornament ladies don on such occasions, which resembles a fastidiously folded, ultra-starched white cloth napkin.

Originating in the ancient Greek city of Mycenae, the Pag lace-making tradition endured for centuries before being popularized far and wide as a Pag product beginning in the late-19th century. A lace-making school was founded in Pag Town in 1906, drawing orders from royalty from distant lands. In 1938 Pag lace makers participated in the world exhibition in New York.

Pag lace differs from other types of lace in two key respects: a thin thread and exceptional durability. Using an ordinary mending needle against a solid background, and usually proceeding without a plan, the maker begins by creating a circle within which she (or he) makes tiny holes close together; the thread is then pulled through them. The completed lace has a starched quality and can even be washed without losing its firmness. It is best presented on a dark background and framed.

Since the process is painstaking, Pag lace is not cheap: a typical small piece of around 20 centimeters in diameter costs at least 200 Kn from a maker or perhaps double that from a shop. You needn't venture farther than the main square and surrounding narrow streets of Pag Town to find a seller—whether an old lady or an equally enthusiastic child. Of course, you can also try Pag Town's very own **Galerija Paške Čipke** *(Pag Lace Gallery)* (⊠ *Trg Krajla Petra Krešimira IV, Pag Town* ☎ *No phone* 🖃 *Free*), open mid-June through mid-September, daily 9–1, or else any of several local shops that you are certain to encounter near the main square in Pag Town. In Zadar, try **Studio Lik** (⊠ *Don Ive Prodana 7* ☎ *023/317–766*).

WHERE TO EAT

$$–$$$$ ✕**Restaurant Tamaris.** The courtyard seating here has lots of shade from the grapevine overhead, and the inside has elegant, pink-clothed tables. A large menu has everything from the usual grilled meats to squid stuffed with prosciutto, cheese, and Dalmatian-style Swiss chard, to a handful of "Grandma's recipes" such as old-style Pag lamb. An extensive wine list seals the deal. ⊠ *Križevačka bb* ☎ *023/612–277* 🖃 *AE, DC, MC, V.*

$$–$$$$ ✕**Smokva.** Reopened in 2007 after lengthy restoration, this restaurant
★ has the most comfy outdoor seating of any in Pag Town. The huge shaded terrace out front is cloistered from the outside world by an iron gate and rendered all the more pleasing by a lovely fig tree. Inside,

the rustic stone walls and wood-beamed ceilings are equally charming. Once you're settled in, you can choose from an impressive range of well-prepared grilled meats, poultry, steak, seafood, and scrumptious desserts from palačinkes to tiramisu. ✉ *Caskin put bb* ☎ *023/611–015* ▤ *AE, DC, MC, V.*

$$$ ✕ **Konoba Boduto.** The menu may be small at this family-owned spot, but it manages to squeeze in everything from staple pastas and risottos to grilled meats and steak—and the service is friendly. You can enjoy this combination under the courtyard's grapevine or next to the interior's stone walls, with Croatian pop for background music. ✉ *Vangrada 19* ☎ *023/611–689* ▤ *AE, DC, MC, V.*

WHERE TO STAY

$$ ⊡ **Hotel Meridijan.** Pag's newest hotel opened in 2006, bestowing the town with yet another bland hotel facade. But in contrast with the nearby Hotel Pagus and its more modern room decor, the Meridijan is a cozier place, with Biedermeier-style furniture and abstract paintings. All rooms have balconies and sofas, with sea views from the top floor. For a fee, guests can use the health facilities of the Hotel Pagus. Pros: all rooms are no-smoking, balconies, large bathrooms, outdoor pool. Cons: pricey. ✉ *Ante Starčevića bb, 23250* ☎ *023/492–200* 🖷 *023/492–222* ⊕ *www.hotel-meridijan.com* ↩ *37 rooms, 6 suites* ♿ *In-room: safe, refrigerator. In-hotel: restaurant, bars, room service, pool, laundry service, parking (fee), public Wi-Fi, public Internet* ▤ *DC, MC, V* ⦿*BP.*

$ ⊡ **Hotel Pagus.** It's bland on the outside but pleasant on the inside, with spacious rooms decorated in a bright, modern style. Peach carpets complement the striped, silky bedspreads, and each room has a sofa bed, armchair, and table (with ashtray). Pros: spacious rooms, balconies, private beachfront. Cons: no no-smoking rooms, a bit bland overall. ✉ *Ante Starčevića 1, 23250* ☎ *023/611–310* 🖷 *023/611–101* ↩ *120 rooms* ♿ *In-room: refrigerator, Ethernet. In-hotel: 2 restaurants, bar, pools, gym* ▤ *AE, DC, MC, V* ⦿*BP.*

¢ ⊡ **Hotel Tony.** Set apart from the touristy fray closer to town, the Hotel Tony has simply furnished, spacious, shower-equipped rooms with balconies. Pros: large rooms, good views, shaded garden, relatively good rate. Cons: 25-minute walk from the town center, smallish bathrooms. ✉ *Dubrovačka 39, 23250* ☎ *023/611–370* ⊕ *www.hotel-tony.com* ↩ *20 rooms* ♿ *In-room: refrigerator, Wi-Fi. In-hotel: restaurant, bar, public Wi-Fi, some pets allowed* ▤ *AE, DC, MC, V* ⦿*BP.*

FESTIVALS

In late July or early August, Pag Town hosts the **Pag Carnival**, featuring a range of music on and around the main square, dance and folk-song performances—and, not least, the annual reenactment of a 16th-century folk drama, Paška robinja "Slave Girl of Pag," which tells the story of buying back an enslaved girl, the granddaughter of the ruler Ban Derenčin, who was defeated by the Turks.

5

SPORTS & THE OUTDOORS

BEACHES

Deciding where to swim once you reach Pag Town is a no-brainer; you can pick practically anywhere in the huge, sheltered bay that stretches out from the short bridge in the town center. If you have kids, all that sand and shallow water is an added plus, compared to Zadar and so many other stretches of Croatia's often deep, rocky coast. Most of the 27 km (17 mi) of public beaches in the bay are accessible by car. For even better swimming, if that is possible, try heading north to Novalja and environs. The tourist-information office has a free map showing the locations of the best beaches.

BICYCLING

Pag Island's historic sites may be limited and its vegetation may be sparse, but its 115 km (72 mi) of bicycle routes—many of them traversing the island's barren, rocky hills, on what used to be shepherds' paths—are not. The tourist-information office has a free map showing suggested routes. Pag Town is a logical starting point, from which you can head up to Novalja (or beyond, to the tip of the island) and back in a day; or head in the other direction, stopping for a look at the ruins of Starigrad and the salt flats. In Pag Town you can rent a bike at the **Scuba Centar Pag** (⊠ *Branimirova obala 10* ☎ *098/209–144*), which also organizes diving excursions for 350 Kn.

ZADAR & NORTHERN DALMATIA ESSENTIALS

AIR TRAVEL

Zadar's airport is in Zemunik Donji, 9 km (5½ mi) southeast of the city. Croatia Airlines, which offers service between Zadar and Zagreb as well as Paris and other European cities, runs buses (20 Kn one way) between the airport, the city bus station, and the harborside near the ferry port on the Old Town's peninsula.

Information **Croatian Airlines** (⊠ *Poljana Natka Nodila 7* ☎ *023/250–101 or 062/777–777*).

BOAT & FERRY TRAVEL

Jadrolinija's local ferries (*trajektne linije*) and passenger boats (*brodske linije*) run daily routes that connect Zadar not only with the surrounding islands but also with Rijeka. Do check also with Miatours, which offers alternative service to the islands and also between Zadar and Ancona, Italy. Twice a day most days of the week there is ferry service between Pula and Zadar; at eight hours and at a cost of only 123 Kn it's a decent alternative to the bus, though a downside is that the ferry from Pula arrives in Zadar at midnight. The offices are by the Harbor Gate in the city walls, across from the ferry port.

Both Jadrolinija and Miatours run ferry routes from the port of Zadar, just outside the city walls on the western side of the Old Town, to Sali. The trip, which takes about two hours and costs from 30 Kn (Miatours) to 38 Kn (Jadrolinija), takes you initially south in the Zadarski kanal, then through a narrow strait between Ugljan and Pašman islands before proceeding to the island of Dugi Otok, where you stop briefly in Zaglav before heading on to Sali. If you don't want to base yourself in Murter, you can take a cruise straight from the Borik marina just outside Zadar all the way to Kornati National Park, that almost mythical archipelago even further south. The *Blue Lagoon,* which holds 90 passengers, will take you on a full-day journey (8 AM to 6 PM) to the national park, including stops on the islands of Mana and Kornat.

Information Jadrolinija (✉ *Liburnska obala 7* ☎ *023/254–800 or 023/250–996* ⊕ *www.jadrolinija.hr*). **Miatours** (✉ *Vrata sv. Krševana 7* ☎ *023/254–300*).

BUS TRAVEL

Though sometimes crowded in midsummer, Zadar's bus station will almost certainly figure prominently in your travel plans unless you're driving or flying directly here. The trip to or from Zagreb takes around four and a half hours, for around 105 Kn. Timetables are available at the station. The luggage room (*garderobe*) is open from 6 AM to 10 PM, and costs 1.20 Kn per hour.

Getting to Nin from Zadar is easy by bus. The half-hour trip follows the coastal road north; the fare is 11 Kn one way, with buses running daily out of Zadar's station every 45 minutes or so. By bus, getting to Murter—to its tiny main square, Trg Rudina, which is where you're dropped off and get back on—from Zadar is certainly doable, if a bit complicated. You can transfer either at Šibenik or at Vodice; although the former option looks longer on the map, given the crowded confusion at Vodice's small station, Šibenik—around 12 buses daily from Zadar—may be a less trying experience (and a surer way of getting a seat) even if it might take a bit longer; about 9 buses go on from Sibenik to Murter (via Vodice). Travel time via Šibenik is 2½ hours or more (i.e., 90 minutes from Zadar to Šibenik, up to an hour of waiting time, then another 45 minutes to Murter via Vodice). The total cost: around 70 Kn via Šibenik and around 50 Kn if you go straight to Vodice (travel time is under two hours, and an even harder-to-predict wait time, since the bus from Šibenik might be contending with heavy traffic). Numerous buses ply the one-hour route daily between Zadar and Starigrad for access to Paklenica National Park. The one-way cost to or from Starigrad—via the Zadar–Rijeka bus—is between 25 Kn and 34 Kn, depending on the company. There are two stops in Starigrad; the national park information office is between the two, and the access road to the park is near the first stop (if you're coming from Zadar).

Around half a dozen buses daily ply the one-hour route from Zadar to Pag Town, on Pag Island (35 Kn).

Last but not least, the easiest way to get either from the bus station to Zadar's town center, or from the center to the Borik complex (with its beaches, hotels, and restaurants) on the northern outskirts, is by any of several, user-friendly local buses. You can buy tickets at news kiosks for 6.50 Kn (single ride) or for 8 Kn from the driver; be sure to validate your ticket on boarding by inserting it into the stamping device.

Information Zadar Bus Station (✉ *Ante Starčević 2* ☎ *023/211-555*).

CAR TRAVEL

With the completion of the Mala Kapela tunnel in June 2005, the A1 motorway between Zagreb and Dalmatia has become a complete, uninterrupted whole. Zadar is the first major stop on the highway, which proceeds south toward Split. Barring traffic congestion, especially on weekends, the trip between Zagreb and Zadar is doable in 2½ hours. That said, you can also easily get to Zadar by bus, whether from Zagreb, Rijeka, or Split, and rent a car there if necessary. As the Zadar bus station can be a chaotic place at times, especially in midsummer, you might want to rent a car for some excursions—to Murter, for example, which otherwise involves a somewhat complicated, time-consuming trip to or toward Šibenik with a transfer. But you'll be just fine without a car in and immediately around Zadar, as bus service is both good and affordable. How to get to Pag Island? By the Pag Bridge route, Pag Town (at the island's center) is within a one-hour drive from Zadar. One good option is to take two nights and take in Paklenica National Park, then drive another 25 minutes or so north along the coastal road toward Rab Island and Rijeka, and take the ferry from the village of Prizna—roughly midway between Rijeka and Zadar, just south of Rab Island—to Žigljen, in the north of the island (14 Kn per person, 89 Kn for a car); or do the same in reverse.

Information Avis (✉ *Zračna luka Zemunik, Zadar* ☎ *023/205-862*). **Budget** (✉ *Obala kneza Branimira 1, Zadar* ☎ *023/313-681*). **Hertz** (✉ *Vrata sv. Krševana [downtown] and at Zadar Airport, Zadar* ☎ *023/254-301 [same number for both locations]*). **National** (✉ *Bože Peričića 2, Zadar* ☎ *091/320-0121*). **Uni rent** (✉ *Poljana N. Nodila 9, Zadar* ☎ *023/250-111*).

INTERNET

Zadar is Northern Dalmatia's only sizeable city, and the only place you can find more than a handful of options for Internet access. As of this writing, the Old Town itself had only a couple of good options—most notably, the Internet Corner (9 AM–10 PM), just a couple of blocks from Narodni Trg. And just outside the Old Town is the aptly named Internet (10 AM–10 PM); take a left immediately after crossing the pedestrian bridge into the newer part of town, and then turn into the first street on your right.

Information Caffe bar Bua (✉ *Kralja Tomislava 5, Pag* ☎ *092/137-199*). **Internet** (✉ *Rikarda Katalinića Jeretova 5, Zadar* ☎ *023/309-160*). **Lanarchy Internet Corner** (✉ *Varoška 3, Zadar* ☎ *023/311-265*).

TRAIN TRAVEL

It's possible to travel between Zadar and Zagreb by train. Five trains run daily from Zadar to Knin (in just over two hours with almost 20 stops in between), and from Knin you can transfer within an hour to a train that gets you to Zagreb in roughly four hours—that's around seven hours in all from Zadar to Zagreb, for about 130 Kn one way. Unless you want to see some relatively war-wearied parts of the interior, though, you'll do well to simply hop aboard one of the many daily Zagreb-bound buses at Zadar's bus station, which get you to the capital in less time and for less money (around 100 Kn). Trains also run between Knin and Split, and service and travel times are improving yearly on all these routes.

Information **Zadar Train Station** (⊠ *Ante Starčevica 4, Zadar* ☎ *060/333–444*).

VISITOR INFORMATION

If there's no English speaker at the office you happen to contact, try the Zadar County Tourist Information office or the city of Zadar's corresponding office.

Contacts **Murter Tourist Information** (⊠ *Rudina, Murter* ☎ *022/434–995 or 022/434–950* ⊕ *www.tzo-murter.hr*). **Nin Tourist Information** (⊠ *Trg braće Radića 3, Nin* ☎ *023/264–280* ⊕ *www.nin.hr*). **Pag Tourist Information** (⊠ *Od Špitala 2, Pag* ☎ *023/611–301* ⊕ *www.pag-tourism.hr*). **Sali Tourist Information** (⊠ *Western side of Sali harbor, Sali* ☎ *023/377–094*). **Starigrad Tourist Information** (⊠ *Trg Tome Marašovića 1, Starigrad* ☎ *023/369–245* ⊕ *www.stari-grad-faros. hr*). **Zadar County Tourist Information** (⊠ *Sv. Leopolda B. Mandića 1, Zadar* ☎ *023/315–107 or 023/315–316* ⊕ *www.zadar.hr*). **Zadar Tourist Information** (⊠ *Mihe Klaića, 2 yards from Narodni trg, Zadar* ☎ *023/316–166 or 023/212–412* ⊕ *www.zadar.hr*).

5

Split & Central Dalmatia

WORD OF MOUTH

"Split and Trogir are only ½-hour apart by car … but I would say that it doesn't matter so much where you're actually staying. Trogir is closer to the Split airport, if that makes a difference."

—Travel3D

"Be sure to be able to visit Diocletian's palace around dawn, before the tourist bric-brac is set up. Then you can visualize the audacity and majesty of the Roman shell, which for me rivals the Roman colleseum for thrill factor."

—viking

"We loved Hvar, the area around the harbor is delightful. We stayed about a 15 minute walk to town, would stay closer next time!"

—sasi

By Jane Foster

CENTRAL DALMATIA IS MORE MOUNTAINOUS, wild, and unexploited than the northern coastal regions. And while tourist facilities may be less sophisticated than in Istria and Kvarner, Dalmatia's rugged limestone peaks, emerald-blue waters, countless islands, and magnificent coastal towns offer an unrefined Mediterranean charm all of their own.

The region's capital (and Croatia's second-largest city) is the busy port of Split, with its historic center protected by the sturdy walls of an imperial Roman palace. From here you can take an overnight ferry service to Ancona, Italy, plus regular ferry and catamaran services to the outlying islands. Split is also Central Dalmatia's main base for yacht-charter companies.

A 90-minute drive up the coast, northwest of Split, lies Šibenik, home to a splendid Gothic-Renaissance cathedral. Once an important industrial center, since the war for independence Šibenik has fallen into economic decline, but it still makes a good base for visiting Krka National Park, a chain of thundering waterfalls surrounded by dense woodland, and the peaceful riverside town of Skradin. Moving back from Šibenik toward Split, Trogir is a gem of medieval stone architecture, built on a tiny island connected to the mainland by a bridge. And a 30-minute drive down the coast from Split brings one to Omiš and the mouth of the River Cetina, forming a steep-sided valley renowned for such adventure sports as rafting and rock climbing (called free climbing in Croatia). However, for many people what makes Central Dalmatia so special are the islands. The nearest, Brač, is home to Croatia's most photographed beach, the stunning Zlatni Rat (Golden Cape). The nearby village of Bol, backed by the soaring limestone heights of Vidova Gora, has modern hotel accommodations and excellent sports facilities. West of Brač lies Šolta. Although there is little of cultural interest here, those lucky enough to be sailing along the south side of the island will find several idyllic bays that are accessible only by sea. South of Brač rises the island of Hvar, home to Central Dalmatia's most exclusive destination, Hvar Town, with its 16th-century Venetian buildings ringing three sides of the harbor, its magnificent main square overlooked by a baroque cathedral, and the entire scene presided over by a proud hilltop castle. Farther out to sea still lies wild, windswept Vis, Croatia's most distant inhabited island. There are only two real settlements: Vis Town and Komiža, the latter making the best starting point for a day trip to Modra Spilja (Blue Cave) on the island of Biševo. Back on the mainland, a two-hour drive down the coast south of Split brings you to Makarska, a popular seaside resort built around a bay filled with fishing boats and backed by the rugged silhouette of the Biokovo Mountains, with Croatia's third-highest peak, Sveti Jure (5,780 feet); the peak offers stunning views over the entire region.

Lastovo, Croatia's second–most distant inhabited island (after Vis), remains firmly off the beaten track, its fertile green valleys overlooked by the crumbling stone buildings of Lastovo Town. Although it is part of Southern Dalmatia, it is not connected to the region by boat, the islanders having chosen to establish ferry and catamaran services to Split.

6

EXPLORING CENTRAL DALMATIA

ABOUT THE RESTAURANTS

Eateries fall into two main categories: you can eat in a *restoran* (restaurant) or *konoba* (tavern). Restaurants are more formal affairs, catering mainly to tourists and offering Croatian cuisine plus a choice of popular international dishes. In contrast, a konoba serves typical regional dishes; many offer a *merenda* (cut-price lunch), and at those you are likely to see locals as well as tourists. Central Dalmatian specialties are mainly seafood-based. *Rižot* (risotto) reflects the region's historic ties with Venice, as does *brodet* (fish stewed in a rich tomato, onion, and wine sauce). Fish are divided into two categories: "white" fish, including *brancin* (branzino, or sea bass) and *san pjero* (John Dory), being the more expensive, while "blue" fish, including *srdele* (sardines) and *skuša* (mackerel) are cheaper but less frequently on offer. In restaurants, be aware that fresh fish is priced by the kilogram, so prices vary dramatically depending on how big your fish is.

ABOUT THE HOTELS

Central Dalmatia's best and most expensive hotels are in Hvar Town on the island of Hvar. The region's socialist-era resort hotels are gradually being privatized and refurbished, and a number of small family-run hotels have opened as well. However, many visitors still prefer to rent a private room or apartment, a solution that offers value for money, direct contact with the locals, and (if you are lucky) an authentic stone cottage opening onto a terrace lined with potted geraniums and a blissful sea view. The season runs from Easter to late October, and peaks during July and August, when prices rise significantly and when it may be difficult to find a place to sleep if you have not booked in advance.

WHAT IT COSTS IN EUROS (€) AND CROATIAN KUNA (KN)				
¢	$	$$	$$$	$$$$
RESTAURANTS	under 20 Kn	20 Kn–35 Kn	35 Kn–60 Kn	60 Kn–80 Kn	over 80 Kn
HOTELS In euros	under €75	€75–€125	€125–€175	€175–€225	over €225
HOTELS In kuna	under 550 Kn	550 Kn–925 Kn	925 Kn–1,300 Kn	1,300 Kn–1,650 Kn	over 1,650 Kn

Restaurant prices are for a main course at dinner. Hotel prices are for two people in a double room in high season, excluding taxes and service charges.

TIMING

High season runs from July through August, when the region is inundated with foreign tourists, predominantly Italians. During this period prices rise significantly, it's difficult to find a place to sleep if you haven't reserved in advance, restaurant staff are overworked, and beaches are crowded. On top of everything, it can be very hot. On the positive side, some museums and churches have extended opening hours, the season's open-air bars and clubs bring nightlife to the fore, and there are several cultural festivals with performances starring international musicians, dancers, and actors.

Low season runs from November through April, when many hotels and restaurants close completely, the exception being over the New Year's period, when some of the more sophisticated establishments (for example in Hvar Town) open their doors for the holidays. At this time of year the weather is unreliable, but if you're lucky you could find yourself drinking morning coffee in the sunshine below a deep blue sky, albeit against a backdrop of snowcapped mountains.

However, for most people the best time to visit is midseason, May through June and September through October. During these periods you'll miss the crowds, the weather should be sunny and dry, and the sea will be warm enough to swim in; the region's hotels and restaurants will be open, but their pace slow enough to lend an air of true relaxation.

SPLIT

Split is 365 km (228 mi) south of Zagreb.

Split's ancient core is so spectacular and unusual that a visit is more than worth your time. The heart of the city lies within the walls of Roman emperor Diocletian's retirement palace, which was built in the 3rd century AD. Diocletian, born in the nearby Roman settlement of Salona in AD 245, achieved a brilliant career as a soldier and became

CENTRAL DALMATIA TOP 5

■ Explore Diocletian's Palace, a massive 3rd-century AD Roman edifice that now shelters Split's Old Town within its walls. This is a don't-miss attraction if you are traveling to Split.

■ Spend a night in one of Hvar Town's hip new design hotels. The best of these is the Hotel Riva; though very expensive, it's in a prime seafront location and looks great.

■ Plunge into the sea after sunbathing on Zlatni Rat on the island of Brač. Though composed of tiny

pebbles rather than sand, it's one of Dalmatia's best beaches and a prime windsurfing spot.

■ Sail into Komiža harbor on Vis island, aboard a yacht after a long day on the water, perhaps having visited Modra Spilja (the Blue Cave) on the nearby island of Biševo.

■ Climb Biokovo Mountain. You'll be awed by the panoramic view at the top.

emperor at the age of 40. In 295 he ordered this vast palace to be built in his native Dalmatia, and when it was completed he stepped down from the throne and retired to his beloved homeland. Upon his death, he was laid to rest in an octagonal mausoleum, around which Split's magnificent cathedral was built.

In 615, when Salona was sacked by barbarian tribes, those fortunate enough to escape found refuge within the stout palace walls and divided up the vast imperial apartments into more modest living quarters. Thus, the palace developed into an urban center, and by the 11th century the settlement had expanded beyond the ancient walls.

Under the rule of Venice (1420–1797), Split—as a gateway to the Balkan interior—became one of the Adriatic's main trading ports, and the city's splendid Renaissance palaces bear witness to the affluence of those times. When the Habsburgs took control during the 19th century, an overland connection to Central Europe was established by the construction of the Split–Zagreb–Vienna railway line.

After World War II, the Tito years saw a period of rapid urban expansion: industrialization accelerated and the suburbs extended to accommodate high-rise apartment blocks. Today the historic center of Split is included on UNESCO's list of World Heritage Sites.

EXPLORING SPLIT

The Old Town (often referred to as the Grad), where most of the architectural monuments are found, lies within the walls of Diocletian's Palace, which fronts on the seafront promenade, known to locals as the Riva. West of the center, Varoš is a conglomeration of stone fishermen's cottages built into a hillside, behind which rises Marjan, a 3½-km-long (2-mi-long) peninsula covered with pinewoods. Southeast of the center, the ferry port, bus station, and train station are grouped close together on Obala Kneza Domagoja.

GREAT ITINERARIES

Central Dalmatia warrants weeks of discovery; even many locals admit that they haven't even seen it all. However, if your time is limited, the itineraries listed below aim to give you a taste of the major attractions.

IF YOU HAVE 3 DAYS

Devote Day 1 to **Split,** exploring the historic monuments within the walls of Diocletian's Palace and attending an open-air opera performance if the Split Summer Festival is in progress. On the next day, take an early morning ferry to Supetar on the island of Brač, then a local bus to **Bol,** for an afternoon bathing on Croatia's finest beach, Zlatni Rat. Catch the late-afternoon catamaran to Jelsa on the island of Hvar, then a local bus to **Hvar Town,** the region's hippest island resort, where you should sleep. Next morning, either check out Hvar's Venetian-style architecture or take a taxi boat to Pakleni Otoci for a swim. Catch the late-afternoon ferry back to Split for your final night.

IF YOU HAVE 5 DAYS

Spend your first day in Split. On the next morning, drive or take a local bus to **Trogir,** a compact settlement of stone houses built on an island linked to the mainland by a bridge, then proceed up the coast for an afternoon in **Šibenik,** where the most-visited monument is the Gothic–Renaissance cathedral. Spend the night in either Šibenik or **Skradin.** Give Day 3 to the waterfalls and dense woodland of **Krka National Park,** returning to Split for the night. Days 4 and 5 should be dedicated to the islands of **Brač** and **Hvar** *(see above),* returning to Split for the final night.

IF YOU HAVE 7 DAYS

Spend your first day in Split, the second and third days in Trogir, Šibenik, Skradin, and Krka National Park, as outlined above, returning to Split on the third night. Days 4 and 5 can then be given over to the islands of Brač and Hvar *(as described above),* returning to Split for the fifth night. On the next morning, either drive or take a local bus down the coast to **Omiš,** from which you can set off up the **Cetina Valley** and participate in adventure sports (by prior arrangement). In the evening continue down the coast to **Makarska,** where you should sleep. The final day you can explore Makarska and its beaches, or venture up Biokovo Mountain for spectacular views over the entire region. Return to Split for your last night.

Numbers in the text correspond to numbers in the margin and on the Split map.

WHAT TO SEE

❶ Dioklecijanova Palača *(Diocletian's Palace).* The original palace was a ★ combination of a luxurious villa and a Roman garrison, based on the ground plan of an irregular rectangle. Each of the four walls bore a main gate, the largest and most important being the northern *Zlatna Vrata* (Golden Gate), opening onto the road to the Roman settlement of Salona. The entrance from the western wall was the *Željezna Vrata* (Iron Gate), and the entrance through the east wall was the *Srebrena Vrata* (Silver Gate). The *Mjedna Vrata* (Bronze Gate) in the south wall faced directly onto the sea, and during Roman times boats would have

IF YOU LIKE

HISTORIC MONUMENTS

The shores of Central Dalmatia abound with spectacular architecture, bearing witness to its rich and complex history. There are three UNESCO World Heritage Sites in the region: Diocletian's Roman Palace in Split; the old town of Trogir with its 13th-century Romanesque cathedral; and in Šibenik the 16th-century Gothic–Renaissance cathedral. Fortunately, many historic centers have been listed and protected, saving them from the ravages of modern development.

ISLAND RETREATS

Everyone loves the romantic image of escaping to an island, and in Central Dalmatia there are plenty to choose from. The two that stand out are Hvar and Vis. Hvar is probably Croatia's hippest island, pulling gossip column–worthy celebrities, would-be artists, politicians, and nudists. The main resort, Hvar Town, seems to have it all: beautifully preserved Venetian-style architecture, stylish modern hotels, classy seafood restaurants, and a sophisticated nightlife. In contrast, distant Vis remains free of commercial development. Closed to foreigners until 1989 (during the Tito years it was a Yugoslav naval base), it is now very "in" with the yachting crowd, who appreciate its unspoiled nature, tumbledown stone cottages, and rustic eateries.

BEACHES

The best beaches and the cleanest water for swimming are on the islands. Croatia's most stunning beach has to be Zlatni Rat, a cape made up of fine shingle, close to the village of Bol on the island of Brač. If you want to enjoy it at its best, try to avoid peak season, when it becomes very crowded. Close to Hvar Town lie the Pakleni Otoci (Pakleni Islands), a group of tiny, unpopulated islets with pine woods and indented coasts offering secluded pebble beaches for bathing. Taxi boats relay visitors back and forth from Hvar Town to the most accessible spots.

SAILING

Central Dalmatia is probably Croatia's top region for sailing, thanks to the myriad islands and well-equipped marinas. Split is the main charter base, with dozens of companies keeping boats there. Other well-equipped marinas in the region can be found in Trogir, Skradin, and Vodice on the mainland, and Palmižana, Vrboska, and Milna on the islands.

ADVENTURE SPORTS

In the Cetina Valley, near Omiš, the River Cetina has cut a high-sided canyon between the mountains of Mosor and Biokovo, with a series of rapids sided by sheer-faced cliffs, making this one of the country's major spots for rafting and rock climbing. A short distance farther down the coast, Biokovo Mountain, behind Makarska, is a nature park and home to rare animals such as chamois goats and mouflon sheep, which thrive on the scanty pastures and bare limestone rocks. On the island of Brač, Zlatna Rat offers good conditions for windsurfing, whereas the mountain of Vidova Gora is popular for hiking and mountain biking.

docked here. The city celebrated the palace's 1,700th birthday in 2005. ✉ *Obala Hrvatskog Narodnog Preporoda, Grad.*

❹ Etnografski Muzej *(Ethnographic Museum).* Occupying this splendid new location within the walls of Diocletian's Palace, the Ethnographic Museum relocated from the former Town Hall on Narodni trg in 2005. The museum displays traditional Dalmatian folk costumes and local antique furniture. ✉ *Severova 1, Grad* ☎ *021/343–108* ⊕ *www.etnografski-muzej-split.hr* 🎟 *10 Kn* ⊗ *June, weekdays, 9–2 and 5–8, Sat. 9–1; July and Aug., weekdays 9–9, Sat. 9–1; Sept.–May, weekdays 9–2, Sat. 9–1.*

⓬ Galerija Meštrović *(Mesßtrović Gallery).* A modern villa surrounded by
★ extensive gardens, this building designed by Ivan Meštrović was his summer residence during the 1920s and '30s. Some 200 of his sculptural works in wood, marble, stone, and bronze are on display, both indoors and out. Entrance to the Galerija Meštrović is also valid for the nearby **Kaštelet** (✉ *Šetalište Ivana Meštrovića 39*), housing a chapel containing a cycle of New Testament bas-relief wood carvings that many consider Meštrović's finest work. ✉ *Šetalište Ivana Meštrovića 46, Meje* ☎ *021/340–800* ⊕ *www.mdc.hr* 🎟 *15 Kn* ⊗ *May–Sept., Tues.–Sun. 9–9; Oct.–Apr., Tues.–Sat. 9–4, Sun. 10–3.*

❼ Galerija Vidović *(Vidović Gallery).* Emanuel Vidović (1870–1953) is acknowledged as Split's greatest painter. Here you can see 74 of his works, donated to the city by his family. Large, bold canvasses depict local landmarks cast in hazy light, while the sketches done outdoors before returning to his studio to paint are more playful and colorful. ✉ *Poljana Kraljice Jelene bb, Grad* ☎ *021/360–155* 🎟 *10 Kn* ⊗ *June–Sept., Tues.–Fri. 9–9, weekends 10–1; Oct.–May, Tues.–Fri. 9–4, weekends 10–1.*

❽ Gradski Muzej *(City Museum).* Split's city museum is worth a quick look both to marvel at the collection of medieval weaponry and to see the interior of this splendid 15th-century town house. The dining room, on the first floor, is furnished just as it would have been when the Papalić family owned the house, giving some idea of how the aristocracy of that time lived. ✉ *Papaličeva 1, Grad* ☎ *021/341–240* ⊕ *www.mgst.net* 🎟 *10 Kn* ⊗ *Nov.–May, Tues.–Fri. 10–5, weekends 10–noon; June–Oct., daily 9–noon and 5–8.*

❻ Jupiterov Hram *(Jupiter's Temple).* This Roman temple was converted into a baptistery during the Middle Ages. The entrance is guarded by the mate (unfortunately damaged) of the black-granite sphinx that stands in front of the cathedral. Inside, beneath the coffered barrel vault and ornamented cornice, the 11th-century baptismal font is adorned with a stone relief showing a medieval Croatian king on his throne. Directly behind it, the bronze statue of St. John the Baptist is the work of Meštrović. ✉ *Kraj Sv Ivana, Grad* 🎟 *5 Kn* ⊗ *May–Oct., daily 8–6.*

❺ Katedrala Sveti Dujam *(Cathedral of St. Dominius).* The main body of the cathedral is the 3rd-century octagonal mausoleum designed as a

6

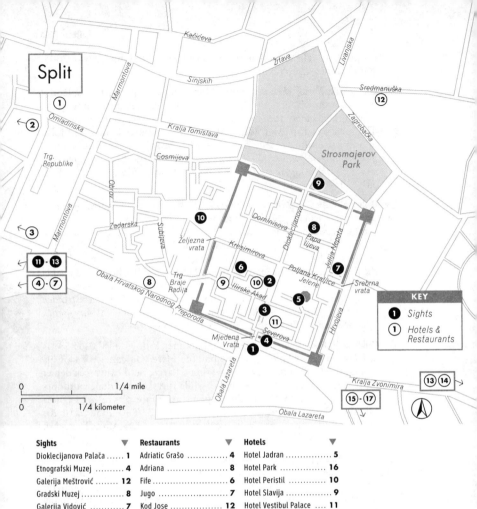

Split

shrine to Emperor Diocletian. During the 7th century, refugees from Salona converted it into an early Christian church, ironically dedicating it to Sv Duje (St. Domnius), after Bishop Domnius of Salona, one of the many Christians martyred during the late emperor's persecution campaign. The cathedral's monumental main door is ornamented with magnificent carved wooden reliefs, the work of Andrija Buvina of Split, portraying 28 scenes from the life of Christ and dated 1214. Inside, the hexagonal Romanesque stone pulpit, with richly carved decoration, is from the 13th century. The high altar, surmounted by a late-Gothic canopy, was executed by Bonino of Milan in 1427. Nearby is the 15th-century canopied Gothic altar of Anastasius by Juraj Dalmatinac. The elegant 200-foot Romanesque-Gothic bell tower was constructed in stages between the 12th and 16th centuries. ⊠*Peristil, Grad* 🏛*Cathedral free, bell tower 5 Kn* ⊙*Sept.–June, daily 8–noon and 4:30–7; July and Aug., daily 8–8.*

⑬ Marjan *(Marjan Hill).* Situated on a hilly peninsula, this much-loved park is planted with pine trees and Mediterranean shrubs and has been a protected nature reserve since 1964. A network of paths crisscrosses the grounds, offering stunning views over the sea and islands. ⊠*Marjan.*

NEED A BREAK?	Having reached this point, you're undoubtedly in need of refreshment. Sit on a sofa at Vidilica (⊠ *Nazorov Prilaz, Marjan*), a lounge-style café terrace, and order a long, cold drink. Then sit back and enjoy the breathtaking view.

⑪ Muzej Hrvatskih Arheološki Spomenika *(Museum of Croatian Archaeological Monuments).* This modern building displays early Croatian religious art from the 7th through the 12th centuries. The most interesting exhibits are fine stone carvings decorated with plaitwork designs, surprisingly similar to the geometric patterns typical of Celtic art. In the garden you can see several stećci, monolithic stone tombs dating back to the cult of the Bogomils (an anti-imperial sect that developed in the Balkans during the 10th century). ⊠*Šetalište Ivana Meštrovića, Meje* ☎*021/358–420* ⊕*www.mhas-split.hr* 🏛*10 Kn* ⊙ *Weekdays 9:30–4, Sat. 9:30–1.*

⑩ Narodni trg *(People's Square).* A pedestrianized expanse paved with gleaming white marble, this is contemporary Split's main square. Although religious activity has to this day centered on Peristil, Narodni trg became the focus of civic life during the 14th century. In the 15th century the Venetians constructed several important public buildings here: the Town Hall (housing a contemporary art gallery, with erratic opening hours), plus the Rector's Palace and a theater, the latter two sadly demolished by the Habsburgs in the 19th century. The Austrians, for their part, added a Secessionist building at the west end of the square. ⊠*Grad.*

❷ Peristil *(Peristyle).* From Roman times up to the present day, the main public meeting place within the palace walls, this spacious central courtyard is flanked by marble columns topped with Corinthian capitals and richly ornamented cornices linked by arches. There are six columns on both the east and west sides, and four more at the south end, which mark the monumental entrance to the Vestibul. During the Split Summer Festival, Peristil becomes an open-air stage hosting evening opera performances. ⊠ *Grad.*

❸ **Vestibul.** The cupola of this domed space would once have been decorated with marble and mosaics. Today there's only a round hole in the top of the dome, but it produces a stunning effect: the dark interior, the blue sky above, and the tip of the cathedral's bell tower framed in the opening. ⊠ *Peristil, Grad.*

NEED A BREAK? The summer terrace at the Luxor Café (⊠ *Peristil, Grad*) makes a perfect place to sit over coffee or a glass of local wine and absorb the 2,000 years of magnificent architecture that surround you. You'll even find cushions so you can sit comfortably on the stone steps if all the tables are full.

❾ **Zlatna Vrata** *(Golden Gate).* Formerly the main entrance into the palace, Zlatna Vrata, on the north side of the palace, is the most monumental of the four gates. Just outside the Zlatna Vrata stands Meštrović's gigantic bronze **statue of Grgur Ninski** (Bishop Gregory of Nin). During the 9th century, the bishop campaigned for the use of the Slav language in the Croatian Church, as opposed to Latin, thus infuriating Rome. This statue was created in 1929 and placed on Peristil to mark the 1,000th anniversary of the Split Synod, then moved here in 1957. Note the big toe on the left foot, which is considered by locals to be a good luck charm and has been worn gold through constant touching. ⊠ *Dioklecijanova, Grad.*

WHERE TO EAT

Split does have some good restaurants, though they're not always easy to find. As in any city of fishermen and sailors, seafood predominates here. In most restaurants, fresh fish is normally prepared over a charcoal fire and served with *blitva sa krumpirom* (Swiss chard and potato with garlic and olive oil). For a cheaper option, bear in mind that the pizza in Split is almost as good as (and sometimes even better than) that in Italy. Last but not least, complement your meal with a bottle of Dalmatian wine.

$$$–$$$$ ✕**Adriatic Grašo.** Above the ACI marina, close to the gardens of Sveti Stipan, this seafood restaurant has a light and airy minimalist interior with a glazed frontage, and a summer terrace where you can watch the yachts sail in and out of port. In the vein of "slow food" (a reaction against fast food that started in Italy in the late 1980s), the kitchen gives great care to seasonal ingredients and presentation. The owner, Zoran Grašo, is a retired basketball player, so you may spot some well-known sporting stars from time to time among the diners. ⊠ *Uvala Baluni, Zvončac* ☎ *021/398–560* ▭ *AE, DC, MC, V.*

$$$–$$$$ ✕**Konoba Varoš.** The dining-room walls are hung with seascapes and fishing nets, and the waiters wear traditional Dalmatian waistcoats. The place can seem a little dour at lunchtime, but mellows when the candles are lighted during the evening. The fresh fish and *pržene lig-*

CLOSE UP

Imperial Quirks

Many powerful state leaders tend toward eccentricity, and Roman emperor Diocletian was no exception. Born to a humble family in Dalmatia, he went on to govern the empire for 20 years, proving to be an astute and innovative leader. However, he was also something of a megalomaniac. Believing himself to be Jupiter's representative on Earth, he set about persecuting Christians, ordering religious scriptures to be burnt, churches destroyed, and thousands of believers executed. He dressed in robes of satin and gold, along with a crown embedded with pearls and shoes studded with precious stones. His imperial apartments were guarded by eunuchs, and anyone who came into his presence was obliged to fall prostrate on the ground out of respect. The best-known of his many massive building schemes is the Baths of Diocletian in Rome, a vast complex of marble and mosaics, constructed by 10,000 Christian prisoners for the pleasure of some 3,000 bathers.

nje (fried squid) are excellent, and there's also a reasonable choice of Croatian meat dishes. It's a five-minute walk west of the center, at the bottom of Varoš. ⊠*Ban Mladenova 7, Varoš* ☎*021/396–138* ⊟*AE, DC, MC, V.*

$$$–$$$$ ✕**Šumica.** The first thing you'll notice upon arrival at Šumica, which is set in the shade of pine trees overlooking Bačvice Bay, is the number of black BMWs in the parking lot. The atmosphere in the dining room, which tends to be overly formal, is more than compensated for by the fresh sea breezes on the summer terrace. The house specialty is tagliatelle with salmon and scampi. ⊠*Put Firula 6, Bačvice* ☎*021/389–895* ⊟*AE, DC, MC, V.*

$$–$$$ ✕**Adriana.** Overlooking the seafront promenade, Adriana is a perfect spot for people-watching day and night. It can get a little rowdy, with loud music and large groups, but the food is remarkably good, with good grilled meat dishes such as *čevapčići* (kebabs), *pohani sir* (fried cheese), salads, and pizzas. ⊠*Obala Hrvatskog Narodnog preporoda 6, Grad* ☎*021/340–000* ⊟*AE, DC, MC, V.*

$$–$$$ ✕**Jugo.** In a modern white building with floor-to-ceiling glass windows and a large roof terrace above the ACI marina, Jugo offers great views back to town across the bay, with rows of sailing boats in the foreground. The menu includes Dalmatian seafood specialties and barbecued meats, with pizza as a cheap option. ⊠*Uvala Baluni bb, Zvončac* ☎*021/398–300* ⊟*AE, DC, MC, V.*

$$–$$$ ✕**Kod Jose.** This typical Dalmatian *konoba* is relaxed and romantic, with exposed stone walls and heavy wooden furniture set off by candlelight. The waiters are wonderfully discreet, and the *rižot frutta di mare* (seafood risotto) delicious. You'll find it just outside the palace walls, a five-minute walk from Zlatna Vrata (Golden Gate)—it's slightly hidden away, so many tourists miss it. ⊠*Sredmanuška 4, Manuš* ☎*021/347–397* ⊟*AE, DC, MC, V.*

$$–$$$ ✕**Šperun.** This cozy, homey eatery has just eight tables in its dining room (four more are on the sidewalk). It is decorated with antiques and brightly colored modern oil paintings. The Italo-Dalmatian menu features pasta dishes, seafood risottos, and old-fashioned local fish specialties such as *bakalar* (salt cod cooked in a rich tomato and onion sauce) and *brudet* (fish stew). ⊠*Šperun 3, Varoš* ☎*021/346–999* ⊟*No credit cards.*

$$–$$$ ✕**Stellon.** With tables on a roof terrace affording sunset views over Bačvice Bay, this restaurant-cum-pizzeria serves an eclectic array of Italian-inspired cuisine including pasta and risotto dishes, excellent steaks, fish, colorful salads, plus first-rate pizza as a cheap option. It's owned by a former Croatian national team football player, Goran Vučević, and is seriously popular with locals and visitors alike. ⊠*Kupalište Bačvice bb, Bačvica* ☎*021/489–200* ⊟*AE, DC, MC, V.*

$–$$ ✕**Pizzeria Galija.** The best pizzas in town, as well as delicious pasta dishes and a range of colorful salads, are to be found in this centrally located pizzeria, which is close to the fish market. A favorite with locals, its dining room is bustling and informal, with heavy wooden tables and benches, and a large brick oven; draft beer and wine are sold by the glass. The owner, Željko Jerkov, is a retired Olympic gold medal–winning basketball player. ⊠*Tončićeva 12, Grad* ☎*021/347–932* ⊟*No credit cards.*

$ ✕**Fife.** With a small terrace out front overlooking the wooden fishing boats of Matejuška harbor, Fife is a firm favorite with local fishermen. Come summer, it's also popular with tourists, who come here for the reasonably priced, down-to-earth Dalmatian cooking. There's no menu, and the dishes on offer change daily depending on what the owner finds at the morning market. If it's busy, you may be asked to share a table with other guests. ⊠*Trubičeva Obala 11, Matejuška* ☎*021/345–223* ⊟*No credit cards.*

WHERE TO STAY

In the past, Split was overlooked as a sightseeing destination and considered a mere transit point to the islands. As a result, it still suffers from a shortage of good places to stay. However, there are now three recommendable hotels within the palace walls, plus several pleasant, reasonably priced hotels within walking distance from the Old Town.

$$$$ ⊞ **Hotel Vestibul Palace.** Split's first boutique hotel opened in June 2005.
Fodor's Choice Within the palace walls and accessed through the ancient vestibule, the
★ interior of this building has been carefully renovated to expose Roman stone- and brickwork, which have been cleverly combined with more modern, minimalist designer details. A bar and restaurant can be found on the ground floor, and seven rooms are upstairs, complete with subtle lighting and plasma TVs. A new Villa Dobrić annex opened near Trg Braće Radića in spring 2007, with an additional two suites, two rooms, and a bar with a terrace out front. Pros: inside the palace walls, beautiful interior, small (so guests receive individual attention). Cons: expensive, often fully booked, no sports facilities. ⊠*Iza Vestibula 4, Grad, 21000* ☎*021/329–329* 🖶*020/329–333* ⊕*www.vestibulpalace.com* ➬*7 rooms, 4 suites* ♿*In-room: safe, refrigerator, dial-up. In-hotel: restaurant, room service, bar, laundry service, no elevator* ⊟*AE, DC, MC, V* ⭐|*BP.*

$$$$ ⬚ **Le Meridien Lav.** A world unto its own, this vast, self-contained complex lies 5 mi (8 km) south of Split. Set in landscaped gardens with a half mile of beach, it reopened in December 2006 after a $100-million renovation, making it Split's first five-star hotel. The modern, sleek, minimalist interior was designed by Italian architect Lorenzo Bellini. The spacious guest rooms and suites have floor-to-ceiling windows and are decorated in beige with splashes of scarlet-red and petrol-blue, and most of the light-wood-paneled bathrooms have a separate tub and shower. Sports facilities include a palm-lined infinity pool overlooking the sea, a private marina with berths for 60 yachts, scuba diving, waterskiing, windsurfing, tennis courts, and the luxurious Diocletian Spa & Wellness Center. There is also a vast casino with 20 gaming tables and 140 slot machines. Pros: beautifully designed modern interior, excellent sports facilities, luxurious spa. Cons: far from the center of Split (5 mi), expensive, large (so the hotel can seem somewhat impersonal). ✉ *Grljevačka 2A, Podstrana, 21312* ☎*021/500–500* ⊕*www.starwoodhotels.com* ☏*364 rooms, 17 suites* ♿*In-room: safe, refrigerator, Ethernet. In-hotel: 3 restaurants, room service, bars, tennis courts, pools, gym, spa, beachfront, diving, water sports* ▭*AE, DC, MC, V* ⴹ*BP.*

$$ ⬚ **Hotel Park.** Smart and reliable, Hotel Park reopened in 2001 after extensive renovation work. The building dates back to 1921 and lies 10 minutes east of the city walls, overlooking Bačvice Bay. The rooms are modern and neatly furnished, and a pleasant restaurant terrace with palms offers views over the sea. Pros: close to both Old Town and beach, breakfast is served on a lovely open-air terrace. Cons: no sports facilities, rather small rooms, parking can be difficult. ✉*Hatzeov Perivoj 3, Bačvice, 21000* ☎*021/406–400* ☐*021/406–401* ⊕*www.hotelpark-split.hr* ☏*54 rooms, 3 suites* ♿*In-room: dial-up, refrigerator. In-hotel: restaurant, room service, bar, laundry service, no elevator* ▭*AE, DC, MC, V* ⴹ*BP.*

$$
★ ⬚ **Hotel Peristil.** Offering visitors one of only three chances to wake up within the palace walls, Hotel Peristil lies behind the cathedral, just inside Srebrena Vrata, the city gate leading to the open-air market. The 12 rooms are comfortable and well equipped, and most have wooden floors. The Tiffany restaurant has open-air dining on a pleasant, shady terrace out front. Many guests are impressed by the friendliness and helpfulness of the staff. Pros: inside the palace walls, small (so guests receive individual attention), lovely open-air restaurant terrace. Cons: small and often fully booked, nearby parking difficult, limited facilities. ✉*Poljana Kraljice Jelena 5, Grad, 21000* ☎*021/329–070* ☐*021/329–088* ⊕*www.hotelperistil.com* ☏*12 rooms* ♿*In-room: safe, refrigerator, dial-up. In-hotel: restaurant, no elevator* ▭*AE, DC, MC, V* ⴹ*BP.*

$ ⬚ **Hotel Jadran.** This small 1970s-style hotel lies close to the ACI marina and the gardens of Sveti Stipan, overlooking Zvončac Bay. A pleasant 15-minute walk along the seafront brings you to the city center. All the rooms are decorated in blue and white and have balconies with either a sea view or a park view. There are decent sports facilities: the Croatian national water-polo team, winners of the 2007 World Cup, train here. Pros: proximity to sea, decent sports facilities, friendly staff. Cons: dated 1970s interior, very basic rooms, unremarkable restaurant. ⊠*Sustipanjska put 23, Zvončac, 21000* ☎*021/398–622* 🖷*021/398– 586* ⊕*www.hoteljadran.hr* ⇴*30 rooms, 2 suites* ⧖*In-hotel: restaurant, bar, pool, gym, no elevator* ☰*AE, DC, MC, V* ⦿|*BP.*

$ 🛏 **Hotel Slavija.** Split's first hotel when it opened in 1900, Slavija occupies an 18th-century building within the palace walls. Fully renovated in 2004, the 25 rooms are basic but comfortable, and the ones at the top have terraces affording views over the city's terra-cotta roofs. Some travelers may find the noise from the surrounding open-air bars excessive. Breakfast is served in the bar area, but there is no restaurant as such. Pros: inside the palace walls, nightlife nearby, several four-bed family rooms. Cons: noise from surrounding bars can be a problem at night, basic rooms, limited facilities. ⊠*Buvinina 2, Grad, 21000* ☎*021/323–840* 🖷*021/323– 868* ⊕*www.hotelslavija.com* ⇴*25 rooms* ⧖*In-room: dial-up. Inhotel: bar, no elevator* ☰*AE, DC, MC, V* ⦿|*BP.*

$ 🛏 **Villa Diana.** On a peaceful side street just a five-minute walk east of the Old Town, Villa Diana is a traditional Dalmatian stone building with green wooden shutters. The five spacious rooms and one suite (which is in the attic and has a Jacuzzi tub) are simply furnished with either wood or tiled floors; rooms have wrought-iron beds. The ground-floor restaurant, with exposed stone walls and modern wooden furniture, serves local specialties, notably seafood. Pros: close to Old Town, pleasant traditional interior but modern facilities, small (so guests receive individual attention). Cons: often fully booked, parking can be difficult. ⊠*Kuzmanića 3, Radunica, 21000* ☎*021/482–460* 🖷*021/482–460* ⊕*www.villadiana.hr* ⇴*5 rooms, 1 suite* ⧖*In-room: refrigerator. Inhotel: restaurant, no elevator* ☰*AE, DC, MC, V* ⦿|*BP.*

NIGHTLIFE & THE ARTS

Split is much more lively at night during the summer season, when bars stay open late, discos hold open-air parties by the sea, and the Split Summer Festival offers a respectable program of opera and classical-music concerts.

NIGHTLIFE

Through summer, many bars have extended licenses and stay open until 2 AM. The clubbing scene is rather tame, but the local twentysomethings frequent the discos listed below. In August, rock musicians from Croatia and the other countries of the former Yugoslavia perform open-air concerts. There's no particular source of information about what's on, but you'll see posters around town if anything special is planned.

BARS   In a narrow side street off Trg Braće Radića (better known to locals as Voćni trg), **Galerija Plavca** (⊠*Kaštelanova 12, Grad* ☎*No phone*) is a laid-back café-bar with outdoor seating in a pleasant courtyard, plus occasional art and photography exhibitions. With a colorful, bohemian interior and a courtyard garden lit with flaming torches, **Ghetto**

Klub (⊠ *Dosud 10, Grad* ☎ *No phone*) pulls in the cool, young, artsy crowd and hosts occasional exhibitions and concerts. Hidden away on a small piazza in the Old Town, **Jazz** (⊠ *Poljana Grgur Ninski, Grad* ☎ *No phone*) offers outdoor tables and an artsy, intellectual clientele. Close to Zlatna Vrata, **Teak** (⊠ *Majstora Jurja 11, Grad* ☎ *No phone*) is a small café with an exposed-stonework-and-wood interior plus tables outside through summer. It's popular with highbrow locals, who come here to leaf through the piles of international newspapers and magazines. One of several amusing but vaguely pretentious bars overlooking Bačvice Bay, **Tropic Club Equador** (⊠ *Kupalište Bačvice, Bačvice* ☎ *021/323–574*) serves pricey cocktails to a background of Caribbean music and fake palms.

DISCOS In an underground space below the bars overlooking Bačvice Bay, **Discovery** (⊠ *Kupalište Bačvice, Bačvice* ☎ *021/488–556*) plays a mix of mainstream, techno, disco, and rock. At **Metropolis** (⊠ *Matice Hrvatska 1, Trstenik* ☎ *021/305–110*) a program of theme nights and special performances attracts a mixed crowd of all ages. Commercial techno music predominates, with a smattering of rock and pop. Croatian singers perform at **Shakespeare** (⊠ *Uvala Zenta 3, Zenta* ☎ *021/519–492*) on weekends, backed up by a selection of commercial techno and disco dance music played by DJs.

THE ARTS

Kino Bačvice (⊠ *Put Firula, Bačvice*) is an open-air summer cinema in the pine woods above Bačvice Bay. Predominantly English-language films are shown in original version with subtitles. Running from mid-July to mid-August, the **Split Summer Festival** (⊠ *Trg Gaje Bulata 1, Grad* ☎ *021/363–014* ⊕ *www.splitsko-ljeto.hr*) includes a variety of open-air opera, classical-music concerts, and theatrical performances, the highlight being *Aïda* on Peristil.

SPORTS & THE OUTDOORS

BEACHES
The best beach is **Uvala Bačvica** (Bačvice Bay), a 10-minute walk east of the Old Town, where you will find showers, beach chairs, and umbrellas to rent, plus numerous cafés and bars offering refreshments.

SAILING
Well connected to the rest of Europe by plane and ferry—and within just a few hours' sailing of several of the Adriatic's most beautiful islands—Split is the center of the yacht-charter business in Dalmatia. *For a listing of Split-based charter companies, see* ⇨ *Sailing & Cruising the Croatian Coast in Understanding Croatia at the end of this book.* The 364-berth **ACI marina** (⊠ *Uvala Baluni, Zvončac* ☎ *021/398–548*) is southwest of the city center. It stays open all year, and is a base for dozens of charter companies organizing sailing on the Adriatic.

WHITE-WATER RAFTING

Atlas Travel Agency (✉*Nepotova 4* 🕾*021/343–055* ⊕*www.atlas-cro-atia.com*) organizes one-day guided rafting expeditions on the River Cetina, with the transfer from Split and back included in the deal.

SHOPPING

Dalmatian women—and those from Split in particular—are renowned for their elegant sense of style. Despite a poor local economy, you'll find countless exclusive little boutiques selling women's clothes and shoes imported from Italy. However, the city's most memorable shopping venue remains the *pazar*, the colorful open-air market held each morning just outside the palace walls. When looking for gifts, bear in mind that Dalmatia produces some excellent wines, which you can buy either in Split or while visiting the islands.

Aromatica (✉*Dobrić 12, Grad* 🕾*021/344–061*) stocks its own brand of deliciously scented soaps, shampoos, body creams, and massage oils made from local herbs. If you buy a selection, they will also gift-wrap them for you. **Croata** (✉*Mihovilova Širina 7, Grad* 🕾*021/346–336*), overlooking Trg Brace Radića, close to the seafront, specializes in "original Croatian ties" in presentation boxes. **Vinoteka Bouquet** (✉*Obala Hrvatskog Narodnog Preporoda 3, Grad* 🕾*021/348–031*) is a small shop selling a select choice of Croatian regional wines, plus some truffle products and olive oils. **Vinoteka Terra** (✉*Prilaz Braće Kaliterna 6, Bačvice* 🕾*021/314–800*) is a stone cellar under the same management as Vinoteka Bouquet, where you can taste wines, accompanied by savory appetizers, before purchasing bottles.

ŠIBENIK

75 km (47 mi) northwest of Split.

Šibenik's main monument, its Gothic-Renaissance cathedral, built of pale-gray Dalmatian stone and designated a UNESCO World Heritage Site, stands on a raised piazza close to the seafront promenade. From here a network of narrow, cobbled streets leads through the medieval quarter of tightly packed, terra-cotta–roof houses, and up to the ruins of a 16th-century hilltop fortress. The city has never been a real tourist destination. Before the Croatian war for independence, it was a relatively prosperous industrial center, but when the factories closed, Šibenik sank into an economic depression. However, the cathedral more than warrants a look, and it makes a decent base for visiting the waterfalls of Krka National Park.

★ Šibenik's finest piece of architecture, the **Katedrala Sv Jakova** *(Cathedral of St. Jacob)*, was built in several distinct stages and styles between 1431 and 1536. The lower level is the work of Venetian architects who contributed the finely carved Venetian-Gothic portals, whereas the rest of the building follows plans drawn up by local architect Juraj Dalmatinac, who proposed the Renaissance cupola. Note the frieze running around the outer wall, with 74 faces carved in stone, depicting the locals from that time. The cathedral's best-loved feature, the tiny baptistery with minutely chiseled stone decorations, was designed by Dalmatinac but executed by Andrija Aleši. As you leave, take a look at the bronze statue just outside the main door: that's Dalmatinac himself, by Croatia's greatest 20th-century sculptor, Ivan Meštrović. ✉ *Trg Republike Hrvatske* 🖃 *Free* ☉ *Daily 9–7.*

WHERE TO EAT

$$–$$$ ✗ **Gradska Vijećnica.** On the main square, this 16th-century Venetian building was originally the town hall. Croatian dishes top the menu, with several Italian and vegetarian options, and the house specialty is *paprika punjena sirom* (peppers stuffed with cheese). The best tables are under the arched portico out front, overlooking the cathedral. There's occasional live jazz in the evenings. ✉ *Trg Republike Hrvatske 1, 22000* ☎ *022/213–605* 🖃 *AE, DC, MC, V.*

$$–$$$ ✗ **Uzorita.** Since 1898, customers have frequented tables in Uzorita's wooden-beamed dining room and vine-covered courtyard garden. The emphasis is on seafood, notably shellfish. The signature dish is *arambasici od plodova mora u morskim algama* (seaweed rolls stuffed with seafood), a creative take on traditional Croatian *sarma* (cabbage leaves filled with rice and mince). Uzorita is a 20-minute walk northeast of the town center. ✉ *Bana Josipa Jelačića 58, 22000* ☎ *022/213–660* 🖃 *AE, DC, MC, V.*

WHERE TO STAY

$ 🏨 **Hotel Jadran.** On the seafront promenade, just a two-minute walk from the cathedral, the Jadran is a white, 1970s-era, five-story hotel that was fully renovated in spring 2005. The furnishings are simple but smart, and the café terrace looks onto the sailboats moored up along the quay. Pros: excellent location on the Old Town seafront, pleasant open-air terrace for breakfast. Cons: basic rooms, limited facilities. ✉ *Obala Dr Franje Tuđjmana 52, 22000* ☎ *022/242–000* 📠 *022/212–480* ⊕ *www.rivijera.hr* 🛏 *57 rooms* 🔑 *In-room: no a/c, refrigerator. In-hotel: restaurant, bar* 🖃 *AE, DC, MC, V* ⦿ *BP.*

$ 🏨 **The Konoba.** In the medieval, pedestrian-only Old Town, this B&B occupies two traditional stone buildings. The five rooms, three with en suite bathrooms, have wooden floors and are furnished with antiques, and some—but not all—have exposed stone walls. There's a large roof terrace offering views over the Old Town and across the bay. Pros: in the Old Town, small (so guests receive individual attention from the owner), excellent breakfast. Cons: often fully booked, finding nearby parking is difficult, no credit cards. ✉ *Andrije Kačića 8, 22000* ☎ *022/214–397* ⊕ *www.bbdalmatia.com* 🛏 *5 rooms* 🔑 *In-room: no a/c, safe, kitchen (some), refrigerator* 🖃 *No credit cards* ⦿ *BP.*

6

PRVIĆ

Prvić lies 4.5 nautical mi west of Šibenik by ferry.

Beyond Šibenk Bay lie the scattered islands of the Šibenik archipelago, four of which—Zlarin, Prvić, Kaprije, and Žirje—are accessible by ferry from Šibenik. For a quick taste of island life, the nearest, Zlarin and Prvić, can be visited as day trips, but if you intend to stay overnight, Prvić is the better equipped, with a lovely, small hotel, rooms to rent, and half a dozen rustic eateries. Tiny, car-free Prvić is just 2 mi long (3 km long) and has a year-round population of 540. Its two villages, Prvić Luka and Šepurine, are made up of centuries-old traditional stone cottages and connected by a lovely footpath leading through a stand of pine trees that takes about 15 minutes to walk. Though some of the locals work in Šibenik, others still live by cultivating figs, olives, and vines and by fishing. There are no large beaches, but plenty of small, secluded pebble coves with crystal-clean water, perfect for swimming. Through high season, there are four ferries per day from Šibenik, calling at Zlarin (30 minutes), Prvić Luka (45 minutes), Šepurine (1 hour), and Vodice (1 hour 10 minutes). All four then return to Šibenik, doing the same journey in reverse. Alternatively, you can take a water taxi from the Šibenik seafront to Prvic'c Luka (expect to pay a hefty 1,200 Kn, as opposed to the ferry, which charges 10 Kn).

WHERE TO EAT

$$–$$$ ✕**Konoba Nanini.** This down-to-earth, family-run eatery occupying an old stone building furnished with heavy wooden tables offers a decent selection of Dalmatian dishes, with an emphasis on fresh seafood. It stays open all year and is a popular spot for local wedding receptions. ✉*Prvić Luka bb* ☎*020/759–170* ▤*AE, DC, MC, V.*

WHERE TO STAY

$ ⚏**Hotel Maestral.** On the seafront in Prvić Luka, this 19th-century
★ stone building was once the village school. After a careful restoration, it reopened as a boutique hotel in 2004. The rooms have dark wooden floors, modern minimalist furniture, and some exposed stone walls. Most also offer a sea view. On the ground floor, the Val Restaurant serves Dalmatian cuisine on a delightful waterside terrace. The owners organize excursions to neighboring islands and to the Krka and Kornati national parks, and the hotel stays open all year. Pros: delightful island location, small (so guests receive individual attention), good restaurant. Cons: if you miss the ferry, you could end up stranded, often fully booked, limited nightlife possibilities. ✉*Prvić Luka bb, 22333* ☎*022/448–300* 🖷*022/448–301* ⊕*www.hotelmaestral.com* 🛏*11 rooms, 1 suite* ♿*In-room: Wi-Fi. In-hotel: restaurant, no elevator, public Wi-Fi, some pets allowed* ▤*AE, DC, MC, V* ❙⦿❙*BP.*

SPORTS & THE OUTDOORS

Swim Trek (⌖ *3–7 Sunnyhill Rd., London SW16 2UG* ☎ *[44] 20/8696–6231* ⊕ *www.swimtrek.com*) is a Britain-based agency, whose motto is "Ferries are for wimps—let's swim." The company offers a challenging and unusual one-week holiday, including swimming around the islands of the Šibenik archipelago. Participants cover an average of 4 km (2½ mi) per day, including the stretch between the islands of Zlarin and Prvić. Overnight accommodation is in the Hotel Maestral in Prvić Luka.

KRKA NATIONAL PARK

★ *Skradin is 16 km (10 mi) north of Šibenik.*

The Krka River cuts its way through a gorge shaded by limestone cliffs and dense woodland, tumbling down toward the Adriatic in a series of spectacular pools and waterfalls. The most beautiful stretch has been designated as **Nacionalni Park Krka** *(Krka National Park)*. There are several entrances into the park, but the easiest and most impressive route of arrival is to drive from Šibenik to the town of Skradin, then take a 25-minute boat ride up the Krka River on a national-park ferry (price included in entrance fee). This will bring you to the park entrance close to Skradinski Buk. Within the park there are a couple of snack bars, plus wooden tables and benches for picnics. However, for a full-blown meal your best bet is to return to riverside Skradin, which is itself well worth a look. The town dates back to Roman times, though its recent history is also significant. During the Croatian war for independence it was on the front line, being on the edge of the Serb-held Krajina. Serbs and Croats had lived together peacefully for centuries, as can be seen from Skradin's two church spires, one Catholic the other Orthodox. But in August 1995 most of the Serbs fled when the Croatian army sprung the surprise *Oluja* (Operation Storm), and they are only now beginning to return. On a happier note, Skradin is popular with sailors, thanks to its marina, and is also home to several good seafood restaurants, where you can order the highly esteemed local shellfish.

A series of seven waterfalls is the main draw here, the most spectacular being Skradinski Buk, where 17 cascades fall 40 meters into an emerald-green pool, perfect for bathing. Moving upriver, a trail of wooden walkways and bridges crisscrosses its way through the woods and along the waterside to the next falls, Roški Slap, passing the tiny island of Visovac, home to a Franciscan monastery, en route. It's possible to visit the monastery by boat. The national park office is in Šibenik. ⌖ *Trg Ivana Pavla II 5, Šibenik* ☎ *022/201-777* ⊕ *www.npkrka.hr* 💰 *80 Kn (June–Sept.), 65 Kn (Oct. and Mar.–May), 25 Kn (Nov.–Feb.)* 🕐 *May–Oct., daily 8–8; Nov.–Apr., daily 9–5.*

WHERE TO EAT

$$–$$$ ✕ **Zlatne Školjke.** A favorite among the yachting crowd, due in part to its location close to ACI marina, Zlatne Školjke occupies a natural stone building with a terrace overlooking the water. Popular dishes include *crni rižot* (black risotto made with cuttlefish), *špageti s plodovima mora* (seafood pasta), and *riba na žaru* (barbecued fresh fish). ✉ *Grgura Ninskog 9, Skradin* 📞 *021/771–022* 🟰 *AE, DC, MC, V.*

WHERE TO STAY

$ ▥ **Hotel Skradinski Buk.** A friendly, family-run hotel in a refurbished stone town house in the center of Skradin is also the only hotel in town. It has comfortable rooms and a restaurant with a pleasant terrace out front. The hotel stays open year-round. Pros: great location in pretty village close to the entrance of Krka National Park, friendly staff, good breakfast. Cons: only hotel in town and often fully booked, limited nightlife in Skradin. ✉ *Burinovac, Skradin 22222* 📞 *022/771–771* 🖷 *022/771–770* 🌐 *www.skradinskibuk.hr* ⟳ *24 rooms, 4 suites* ⟐ *In-room: dial-up, refrigerator. In-hotel: restaurant, bar, no elevator* 🟰 *AE, DC, MC, V* ⦿ *BP.*

SPORTS & THE OUTDOORS

Skradin, approached by boat through the Šibenik Channel, is a favorite retreat for those **sailing** on the Adriatic. It's also a popular place to leave boats (especially wooden ones) for the winter, as the water is less saline here, thanks to the fresh water running down from the Krka River. The 153-berth **ACI Marina** (✉ *Skradin* 📞 *022/771–365* 🌐 *www.aci-club.hr*) stays open year-round.

SHOPPING

While in Skradin, pay a visit to **Vinarija Bedrica** (✉ *Fra Luje Maruna 14, Skradin* 📞 *022/771–095*), an old-fashioned family-run wine cellar where you can taste and buy bottles of locally produced wine and rakija.

TROGIR

27 km (17 mi) west of Split.

On a small island no more than a few city blocks in length, the beautifully preserved medieval town of Trogir is connected to the mainland by one bridge and tied to the outlying island of Čiovo by a second. The settlement dates back to the 3rd century BC, when it was colonized by the Greeks, who named it Tragurion. It later flourished as a Roman port. With the fall of the Western Roman Empire, it became part of Byzantium and then followed the shifting allegiances of the Adriatic. In 1420 the Venetians moved in and stayed until 1797. Today it is a UNESCO World Heritage Site, and survives principally from tourism. You can explore the city in about an hour. A labyrinth of narrow, cobbled streets centers on Narodni trg, the main square, where the most notable buildings are located: the 15th-century loggia and clock tower, the Venetian-Gothic Čipko Palace, and the splendid cathedral, with its elegant bell tower. The south-facing seafront promenade is lined with cafés, ice-cream parlors, and restaurants, and there are also several small, old-fashioned hotels that offer a reasonable alternative to accommodations in Split.

Fodor's Choice
★ The remarkable **Katedrala Sveti Lovrijenac** *(Cathedral of St. Lawrence)*, completed in 1250, is a perfect example of the massiveness and power of Romanesque architecture. The most striking detail is the main (west) portal, adorned with superb Romanesque sculpture by the Croatian master Radovan. The great door, flanked by a pair of imperious lions that form pedestals for figures of Adam and Eve, is framed by a fascinating series illustrating the daily life of peasants in a kind of Middle Ages comic strip. In the dimly lit Romanesque interior, the 15th-century chapel of Sveti Ivan Orsini (St. John Orsini) of Trogir features statues of saints and apostles in niches facing the sarcophagus, on which lies the figure of St. John. The bell tower, built in successive stages—the first two stories Gothic, the third Renaissance—offers stunning views across the ancient rooftops. ⊠ *Trg Ivana Pavla II* 🕮 *Cathedral free, bell tower 5 Kn* ⏱ *June–Oct., daily 8–7; Nov.–May, daily 8–noon and 4:30–7.*

WHERE TO EAT

$$–$$$ ✕ **Čelica.** An old wooden car ferry, anchored next to Čiovo bridge, is the home of this unusual eatery. The owner is a fisherman who catches what is on offer. The former captain's bridge is now a bar, and the car platform and cargo hold have been converted to serve as the dining space. The house specialty is *riblja juha* (fish soup). The bridge is a five-minute walk from the Old Town. ⊠ *Čiovo Bridge* 🕮 *021/882–344* ▭ *AE, DC, MC, V* ⏱ *No lunch Nov.–Mar.*

$–$$$ ✕ **Restaurant Fontana.** On the seafront overlooking the Trogir Channel, this highly esteemed restaurant and pizzeria has a vast waterside terrace. Fresh fish and seafood top the menu, but can be pricey, whereas pizza makes a cheap alternative. ⊠ *Obrov 1* 🕮 *021/885–744* ▭ *AE, DC, MC, V.*

$ ✕ **Škrapa.** More down-to-earth than the expensive seafood restaurants that line the seafront, this eatery is much loved by locals and visitors alike, who come here to feast on platters of fried seafood, with no more elaborate accompaniment than a sprinkle of salt and a dash of lemon. ⊠ *Hrvatskih Mučanika 9* 🕮 *021/885–313* ▭ *No credit cards* ⏱ *Closed Sun. Oct.–Apr.*

WHERE TO STAY

$ 🏨 **Hotel Fontana.** In the Old Town overlooking the Trogir Channel, this old building has been tastefully refurbished to form a small hotel above a popular restaurant. Most of the rooms have Jacuzzis. Pros: location on seafront promenade in the Old Town, friendly staff, breakfast served on the seafront terrace. Cons: some rooms rather small, furnishings basic and modern (less atmospheric than some of Trogir's more old-fashioned hotels). ⊠*Obrov 1, 21220* ☎*021/885–744* 🖷*021/885–755* ⊕*www.fontana-trogir.com* ⤳*13 rooms, 1 suite* ♿*In-room: kitchen (some), refrigerator. In-hotel: restaurant, room service, bar, no elevator, parking (no fee)* ⊟*AE, DC, MC, V* ⏁*BP.*

$ 🏨**Hotel Pašike.** In the Old Town, in a typical Dalmatian stone building, this small hotel has seven rooms with heavy wooden antique furniture and modern en suite bathrooms, plus one apartment with a hydro-massage tub. The adjoining Konoba Pašike serves barbecued Dalmatian meat and fish dishes at outdoor tables, with occasional live Dalmatian music. A nice touch, the Pašike offers free transfers to and from the airport. Pros: location in the Old Town, cozy and atmospheric rooms but modern facilities, friendly and helpful staff. Cons: some rooms are dark, lack of elevator could pose a problem for some visitors, reception is sometimes left unattended. ⊠*Sinjska bb, 21220* ☎*021/885–185* 🖷*021/797–729* ⊕*www.hotelpasike.com* ⤳*7 rooms, 1 suite* ♿*In-room: safe, kitchen (some), refrigerator, dial-up. In-hotel: restaurant, no elevator* ⊟*AE, DC, MC, V* ⏁*BP.*

$ 🏨**Tragos.** Occupying an 18th-century baroque palace in the heart of the Old Town, two blocks from the cathedral, Tragos has 12 simply furnished, modern rooms, decorated in warm hues of cream, yellow, and orange, each with a modern, spacious tiled bathroom. Restaurant Tragos serves local specialties such as *pasticada* (beef stewed in sweet wine and served with gnocchi) and brudet at tables in the courtyard garden. Pros: located in Old Town, friendly and helpful staff, good restaurant. Cons: rooms can be noisy from downstairs restaurant, no elevator could be a problem for some visitors. ⊠*Budislavićeva 3, 21220* ☎*021/884–729* 🖷*021/884–731* ⊕*www.tragos.hr* ⤳*12 rooms* ♿*In-room: dial-up. In-hotel: restaurant, no elevator, parking (no fee)* ⊟*AE, DC, MC, V* ⏁*BP.*

$ 🏨**Villa Sikaa Hotel.** This 18th-century villa has been converted into a small, family-run hotel overlooking the Trogir Channel. All rooms have wooden floors and shiny, newly tiled bathrooms. Two computers with Internet access are available in the bar, and it is possible to rent bicycles. Pros: seafront location offers great views of Trogir's Old Town, friendly and helpful staff, beautiful old building with modern facilities. Cons: front rooms can be noisy (loud music and motorbikes), two hotels are in the same building (which can be confusing), parking can be difficult. ⊠*Obala kralja Zvonimira 13, 21220* ☎*021/881–223* 🖷*021/885–149* ⊕*www.vila-sikaa-r.com* ⤳*8 rooms, 2 suites* ♿*In-room: refrigerator. In-hotel: restaurant, bar, bicycles, public Internet, no elevator* ⊟*AE, DC, MC, V* ⏁*BP.*

SPORTS & THE OUTDOORS

Several charter companies have their boats based in Trogir, making the town a key destination for those sailing on the Adriatic. The 180-berth **ACI Marina** (⊠*Trogir* ☎*021/881–544* ⊕*www.aci-club.hr*) is open year-round.

OMIŠ & THE CETINA VALLEY

28 km (17½ mi) southeast of Split.

An easy day trip from Split, Omiš is a pleasant seaside town with a colorful open-air market and a conglomeration of old stone houses backed by a small hilltop fortress. What makes it special is its location at the mouth of a dramatic gorge, where the Cetina River meets the sea. It is also the venue of the Dalmatian Klapa Festival, which attracts singers from all over Croatia. The Cetina River carves a spectacular gorge with the fertile, green **Cetina Valley** at the bottom, surrounded by sheer limestone cliffs. As the river tumbles its way down toward the sea over a series of rapids, it has become a popular and challenging site for rafting and rock climbing. An asphalt road follows the course of the river upstream from Omiš, leading to a couple of pleasant waterside restaurants.

WHERE TO EAT

$$–$$$ ✗**Radmanove Mlinice.** This renovated water mill is well known for miles around for its fresh *pastrva* (trout) and *janjetina* (roast lamb) served at tables under the trees in a picturesque riverside garden. It lies 6 km (4 mi) from Omiš, up the Cetina Valley. ⊠ *Cetina Valley regional road, in the direction of Zadvarje* ☎*021/862–073* ▭*AE, DC, MC, V* ⊙ *Closed Nov.–Mar.*

$$–$$$ ✗**Restoran Kaštil Slanica.** With a large riverside terrace and an indoor dining space, Kaštil Slanica serves freshwater specialties such as frogs' legs and trout, plus freshly baked bread. The signature dish is *brudet od jegulja* (eel stewed in tomato and white wine, served with polenta). It lies 4 km (2½ mi) upstream from Omiš. ⊠ *Slanica* ☎*021/861–783* ▭*AE, DC, MC, V.*

WHERE TO STAY

$ ⌂**Hotel Settlement Brzet.** Totally refurbished in 2004, the Brzet overlooks a pebble beach and is backed by a pine forest. The hotel offers basic accommodation within a 15-minute walk from the Omiš town center. It stays open all year and is a few minutes'—less than 1 km—walk from the town center. Pros: seafront location with a small beach, all rooms have balconies and sea views. Cons: rooms rather basic, Omiš offers limited nightlife. ⊠ *Brzet 13, Omiš 21310* ☎*021/756–880* ⊠*021/756–900* ⊕*www.ruzmarin.hr* ⊷*88 rooms* ⌂ *In-room: refrigerator. In-hotel: restaurant, bar, beachfront, bicycles, laundry service, no elevator* ▭*AE, DC, MC, V* ⦿*BP.*

$ ⌂**Hotel Villa Dvor.** Built into a sheer cliff face overlooking the River Cetina, and reached via a challenging flight of 96 stone steps (the friendly staff will help carry your bags), Villa Dvor has 23 comfortable rooms offering sea, mountain, or river views. Out front, the Poljica restaurant terrace looks onto the river canyon, and there's also a small outdoor whirlpool. The eco-friendly owner has ingeniously devised a way of using the river to power the hotel's heating and air-conditioning systems. The hotel boat shuttles guests down the river to the local beaches. Pros: hillside location offers a great view across river to Old Town and sea, friendly and helpful staff, all rooms are no-smoking. Cons: difficult access with a steep flight of steps, no elevator inside the hotel, Omiš offers limited nightlife. ✉ *Mosorska Cesta 13, Omiš 21310* ☎ *021/863–444* ✉ *021/863–452* ⊕ *www.hotel-vil-ladvor.hr* ⟳ *23 rooms* ↻ *In-room: refrigerator, dial-up. In-hotel: restaurant, no elevator, no-smoking rooms* ☰ *AE, DC, MC, V* ↻|*BP*.

KLAPA

When visiting towns and villages along the Dalmatian coast, you may be lucky enough to come across a group of locals giving an impromptu *klapa* (Dalmatian plain-song) performance. Traditionally, klapa groups are formed by men, who sing occasionally and for pleasure, the classic themes being love, family life, and local gossip. Each July the town of Omiš hosts a three-week Klapa Festival.

THE ARTS

The **Dalmatian Klapa Festival** (✉ *Ivana Katušića 5, Omiš* ☎ *021/861– 015*) features traditional Croatian harmony singing from various regions along the coast. It lasts three weeks each summer, usually starting in late June, during which performances are staged in the parish church and on the main square.

SPORTS & THE OUTDOORS

The Cetina Valley has become a destination for both white-water rafters and rock climbers, who appreciate the sheer limestone cliffs of the canyon. Several small adventure-tour companies can arrange Cetina Valley trips. There's also a company in Split that organizes one-day rafting trips on the Cetina (*see* ⇨ *White-Water Rafting in Sports & the Outdoors in Split, above*).

Active Holidays (✉ *Knezova Kačić, Omiš* ☎ *021/861–829* ⊕ *www. activeholidays-croatia.com*) offers rafting and rock climbing in the Cetina Valley, as well as windsurfing at nearby Ruskamen beach.

BRAČ

9 nautical mi south of Split by ferry.

Close at hand and well-connected to Split by ferry and catamaran services, the island of Brač can be visited in an easy day trip, though you may want to stay a night or two. With extensive tourist development along the coast and a stark, wild interior, the island is best known for its stunning beach. It is also a prime windsurfing spot. The top resort area is **Bol**. To get there, either catch an early morning Jadrolinija ferry from Split to Supetar (9 nautical mi) and then take a bus across the island to the south coast, or catch the midafternoon Jadrolinija catamaran from Split to Bol (24 nautical mi), which then continues to Jelsa on the island of Hvar.

☾ A spectacular beach, **Zlatni Rat** *(Golden Cape)*, in the south-coast fish-
★ ing village of Bol, is the main attraction on Brač. A tree-lined coastal
promenade leads from the village to an extraordinary geographical
cape composed of tiny pebbles, which juts out ¾ km (1/3 mi) to sea,
moving and changing shape slightly from season to season depending
on the winds. This is Croatia's prime site for windsurfing and an ideal
beach for kids, as the water is shallow and the seabed is easy on their
feet. ⊠*Bol ✢1 km (2 mi) west of town center.*

With its beautiful gardens overlooking the sea, the **Dominikanski Samostan** *(Dominican Monastery)*, on the western edge of Bol, was founded
in 1457. The monastery church is home to a valuable 16th-century
painting by the Venetian Tintoretto, and the small museum displays
ancient Greek coins and amphorae found on the nearby islands of Hvar
and Vis. ⊠*Bol bb, Bol* ☎*021/778–000* 🖭*10 Kn* ⊙*May–Sept., daily
10–noon and 5–8.*

In a fine baroque building on Bol's seafront, the **Galerija Branislav
Dešković** *(Branislav Dešković Gallery)* displays over 300 paintings and
sculpture by 20th-century Croatian artists who have been inspired by
the sea and landscapes of Dalmatia. ⊠*Porat bolskih pomoraca bb, Bol*
☎*021/635–270* 🖭*10 Kn* ⊙*June–Sept., daily 6* PM*–11* PM*; Oct.–May,
weekdays 9* AM*–1* PM*.*

The village of Bol is backed by the highest peak on all the Croatian
islands, **Vidova Gora.** From here, at a height of 2,552 feet above sea
level, the Adriatic sea and the islands of Hvar and Vis spread out before
you like a map. It's possible to reach the top following a clearly marked
footpath from Bol, but be sure to wear good hiking boots, take plenty
of water, and expect to walk at least two and a half hours to reach the
summit. Alternatively, Big Blue *(see* ⇨ *Sports & the Outdoors, below)*
organizes mountain-biking trips (for experienced mountain bikers) on
Vidova Gora, with the option of a minibus ride part way. ⊠*Bol ✢4
km (2½ mi) north of the town center.*

Local travel agencies arrange boat trips to the 16th-century **Pustinja
Blaca** *(Blaca Hermitage)* built into a cliff face overlooking the sea, 13
km (8 mi) west of Bol. From the bay below the complex, it's a 2-km
(1-mi) hike uphill. Inside, visitors can see a fine collection of period
furniture and old clocks. In its heyday, the hermitage had a printing
press, a school, and an observatory. There are no longer any monks
living there. ⊠*Blaca Bay.*

WHERE TO EAT

$$–$$$ ✗**Gušt.** Possibly the most authentic eatery in Bol, Gušt serves tradi-
tional Dalmatian dishes and homemade rakija at heavy wooden tables
and benches in a whitewashed dining room decorated with an eccentric array of old local paintings and fishing tools. Ceiling fans keep the
interior cool and airy, and there are several tables out on the terrace.
⊠*Frane Radić 14, Bol* ☎*021/635–911* ⊟*AE, DC, MC, V* ⊙*Closed
Nov.–Mar.*

> **BRAČ MARBLE**
>
> The island of Brač is well known for its fine white marble, quarried in the village of Pučišća, on the north coast. Through the centuries, it has been used for world-famous buildings, including Diocletian's Place in Split, the U.S. White House, and the Parliament building in Budapest. Today it is used by sculptors and for the reconstruction of historic monuments.

$$–$$$ ✕ **Konoba Mlin.** This old stone mill, which originally used to make flour for the town's bread and is now a cultural monument, has been refurbished to form a summer restaurant. There's a wide choice of barbecued meat and fish dishes. A terrace with tables overlooks the sea. ✉*Ante Starčević 11* ☎*021/635–376* ▭*AE, DC, MC, V* ⊙*Closed Oct.–May.*

$$–$$$ ✕ **Konoba Tomić.** High up in the hills, on the road to Supertar, 12 km (8 mi) outside Bol, this agritourism center occupies an 800-year-old family house. Everything on offer is produced by the owners, including the wine, the freshly baked bread, and the vegetables from the garden. Traditional farm implements such as an old winepress, large wooden barrels, and a grindstone for milling wheat set the atmosphere in the stone-walled dining room. House specialties include pasta fažol (pasta with beans) and delicious meals prepared under a *peka* (a domed lid), notably lamb and octopus. ✉*Gornji Humac bb, Bol* ☎*021/647–242* ⊙*Closed Nov.–Apr.*

$$–$$$ ✕ **Ribarska Kučica.** On the waterside footpath near the Dominican monastery, with romantic nighttime views over the open sea, this friendly eatery serves delicious seafood dishes, with pizza or pasta as a cheaper option. Look for the delicious gnocchi with Gorgonzola and prosciutto. The same owners run Gušt in the Old Town. ✉*Ante Starčević bb, Bol* ☎*021/635–033* ⊙*Closed Oct.–May.*

WHERE TO STAY

$$$ **Hotel Riu Borak.** Set amid pine trees on the path to Zlatni Rat beach—and just a 10-minute walk from Bol's Old Town—Hotel Riu Borak occupies a modern, three-story white building with a restaurant terrace and a pool out front. Standard double rooms lie within the main building, while the more spacious suites (with a living room and sofa bed, making them ideal for families) occupy pavilions behind the hotel. Guests are welcome to use the Croatia Wellness & Spa in the nearby Hotel Elaphusa. Pros: proximity to Zlatni Rat beach, good sports facilities, family rooms available for those with kids. Cons: large and slightly impersonal, popular with large tour groups. ✉*Bračka Cesta 13, 21420* ☎*021/306–202* 📠*021/306–215* 🌐*www.bluesunhotels.com* *186 rooms, 48 suites* *In-room: safe, refrigerator. In-hotel: 2 restaurants, bars, pool, diving, water sports, bicycles, public Internet* ▭*AE, DC, MC, V* ⊙*Closed Nov.–Apr.* 🍽*BP.*

$$ ★ **Hotel Kaštil.** This harborside stone building has been tastefully refurbished without becoming overly design-conscious. Interior walls are predominantly white, with occasional splashes of vivid yellow or red, and the furnishings are minimalist. There's a street-level pizze-

ria and the popular Varadero cocktail bar with wicker sofas, plus an upper-level restaurant with a romantic terrace looking down onto the water. Pros: location in center of village of Bol, overlooks harbor and has nice views, attractive and modern interior. Cons: can be noisy at night (ground-floor bar), often fully booked, Bol can be very touristy. ⊠*Frane Radića 1, 21420* ☎*021/635–995* ᐩ*021/635–997* ⊕*www. kastil.hr* ⇨*32 rooms* ⚿*In-room: safe, refrigerator. In-hotel: restaurant, bar, no elevator* ▤*AE, DC, MC, V* ☯*Closed Nov.–Feb.* ⅏*BP.*

$ ᐃ **Villa Giardino.** Set in lovely leafy gardens with Mediterranean plantings and an English lawn, this hotel is right in the center of Bol, a five-minute walk from the harbor. The structure is a white three-story building with green wooden window shutters. Rooms are furnished with antiques and have ceiling fans but no air-conditioning. The owner, who is a sculptor, is keen to share his homemade rakija with guests. Sauna and massage are also available. Pros: renowned for friendly and helpful owners, small (guests receive individual attention), breakfast served in lovely garden. Cons: often fully booked, limited facilities, Bol can be very touristy. ⊠*Novi Put 2, 21420* ☎*021/635–900* ᐩ*021/635–566* ✑*villa.giardino@st.t-com.hr* ⇨*5 rooms* ⚿*In-room: safe, no a/c. In-hotel: bar, laundry service, no elevator* ☯*Closed Nov.–Apr.* ⅏*BP.*

SPORTS & THE OUTDOORS

The obvious spot for swimming and sunning is the glorious **Zlatni Rat** beach, complete with a café and snack bar, plus paddleboats and Jet Skis for rent through peak season. Be aware that to the west of Zlatni Rat lies a small beach reserved for nudists. Regular taxi-boats run from the Old Town harbor to Zlatni Rat beach, if the 20-minute walk is too much.

For windsurfing and scuba-diving training and equipment rentals, the best established local company is **Big Blue** (⊠*Podan Glavice 2, Bol* ☎*021/635–614* ⊕*www.big-blue-sport.hr*), which also rents sea kayaks and mountain bikes, and organizes cycling trips on Vidova Gora and Blaca Monastery.

HVAR

FodorsChoice
★

Hvar Town is 23 nautical mi south of Split by ferry.

The island of Hvar bills itself as the "sunniest island in the Adriatic." Not only does it have the figures to back up this claim—an annual average of 2,724 hours of sunshine with a maximum of two foggy days a year—but it also makes visitors a sporting proposition, offering them a money-back guarantee if there is ever a foggy day (which has been known to happen).

EXPLORING HVAR

Hvar is both the name of the island and the name of the capital, near the island's western tip. Little **Hvar Town** rises like an amphitheater from its harbor, backed by a hilltop fortress and protected from the open sea by a scattering of small islands known as Pakleni Otoci. Along the palm-lined quay, a string of cafés and restaurants is shaded by colorful awnings and umbrellas. A few steps away, the magnificent main square, **Trg Sveti Stjepan,** the largest piazza in Dalmatia, is backed by the 16th-century **Katedrala Sveti Stjepan** (Cathedral of St. Stephen). Other notable sights include the kazalište (a theater) and the Franjevački Samostan (Franciscan Monastery). Hvar Town is currently a very "in" spot, so expect it to be crowded and expensive through peak season. Visitors have included King Abdullah of Jordan and his wife, Queen Rania, Italian clothing entrepreneur Luciano Benetton, and local tennis champion Goran Ivanišević. The easiest way to reach Hvar Town is to catch a midafternoon Jadrolinija catamaran from Split, which stops at Hvar Town (23 nautical mi) before continuing to the South Dalmatian islands of Korčula and Lastovo. Alternatively, take an early morning Jadrolinija ferry from Split to Stari Grad (23 nautical mi) and then catch a local bus across the island.

> **A WORD ABOUT WINE**
>
> The island of Hvar makes some of Croatia's top wines. On the south coast, the steep, rugged, seaward-facing slopes between the villages of Sveti Nedelja and Ivan Dolac produce full-bodied reds, made predominantly from the *plavac mali* grape. In contrast, the vineyards in the flat valley between Stari Grad and Jelsa on the north side produce whites, such as the greenish-yellow Bogdanuša.

① On the upper floor of the Arsenal, the **Kazalište** *(Theater)* opened in 1612, making it the oldest institution of its kind in Croatia and one of the first in Europe. The Arsenal building, where Venetian ships en route to the Orient once docked for repairs, dates back to the 13th century but was reconstructed after damage during a Turkish invasion in 1571. It was closed for renovation in 2007 but, at this writing, was expected to reopen for summer 2008. ✉ *Trg Sv Stjepana, Hvar Town* 🎫 *15 Kn* ⊙ *May–Oct., daily 9–1 and 5–9; Nov.–Apr., daily 10–noon.*

② East of town, along the quay past the Arsenal, lies the **Franjevački samostan** *(Franciscan monastery).* Within its walls, a pretty 15th-century Renaissance cloister leads to the former refectory, now housing a small museum with several notable artworks. ✉ *Obala Ivana Lučića Lavčevića, Hvar Town* 🎫 *15 Kn* ⊙ *May–Oct., daily 10–noon and 5–7.*

Jelsa. In this village on the northern coast of the island, you'll see many structures from the Renaissance and baroque periods, though **St. Mary's Church** dates back to the early 1300s. A **tower** built by the ancient Greeks overlooks the harbor; it dates to the 3rd or 4th century BC. About 1 km (½ mi) east of the modern town is the older **Grad,** the original fortified area that was protected by the fortress called

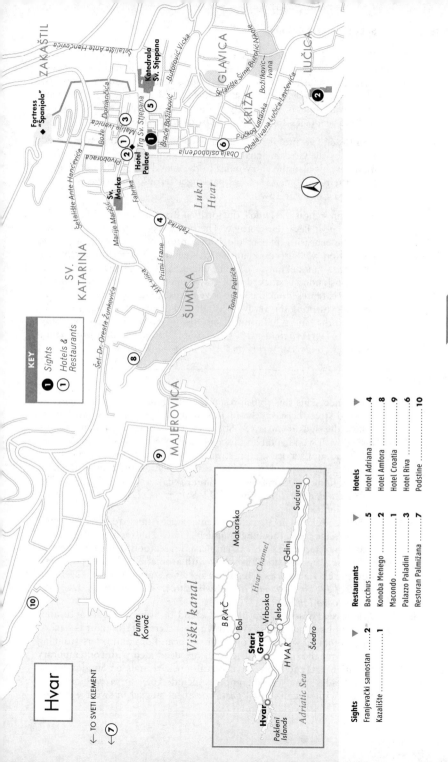

Hvar

← TO SVETI KLEMENT

KEY

1️⃣ Sights

① Hotels & Restaurants

Sights

<table>
<tr><td>Franjevački samostan</td><td>2</td></tr>
<tr><td>Kazalište</td><td>1</td></tr>
</table>

Restaurants

<table>
<tr><td>Bacchus</td><td>5</td></tr>
<tr><td>Konoba Menego</td><td>2</td></tr>
<tr><td>Macondo</td><td>1</td></tr>
<tr><td>Palazzo Paladini</td><td>3</td></tr>
<tr><td>Restoran Palmižana</td><td>7</td></tr>
</table>

Hotels

<table>
<tr><td>Hotel Adriana</td><td>4</td></tr>
<tr><td>Hotel Amfora</td><td>8</td></tr>
<tr><td>Hotel Croatia</td><td>9</td></tr>
<tr><td>Hotel Riva</td><td>6</td></tr>
<tr><td>Podstine</td><td>10</td></tr>
</table>

6

Galešnik, which now stands in ruins. The small town is an alternative to the busier Hvar Town and is surrounded by swimmable beaches—including the island's most popular nude beaches—and some resorts. It's surrounded by thick forests of pine trees. Jelsa's one real advantage over Hvar Town is a very early-morning catamaran to take you to Bol on Brač island. ⊠*20 km (13 mi) east of Hvar Town.*

Stari Grad. The site of the original Greek settlement on Hvar, called Pharos by the Greeks, Stari Grad is a conglomeration of smaller communities; it's also the entry-point to the island for bus transportation from the mainland, as well as passenger ferries. The town is 10 km (6 mi) east of Hvar Town.

The main sight is the **Tvrdalj,** the fortified Renaissance villa of the 16th-century poet Petar Hektorović. The home has been renovated twice over the centuries, first in the 18th-century baroque style; a partial restoration was also done in the 19th century. Hektorović attempted to create a "model universe" to be embodied in his home. To that end, a large fish pond is stocked with gray mullet, as they were in the poet's own time, representing the sea; above the fish pond in a tower is a dovecote, representing the air. Ivy was allowed to cover the walls to tie the home to the land. Quotations from his poetry are inscribed on many walls. ⊠*Trg Tvrdalj bb* ☎*021/765–068* ⊠*10 Kn* ⊙*May, June, Sept., and Oct., daily 10–1; July and Aug. daily 10–1 and 5–9.*

WHERE TO EAT

$$–$$$$
Fodor'sChoice
★

✕**Macondo.** This superb fish restaurant lies hidden away on a narrow, cobbled street between the main square and the fortress—to find it, follow the signs from Trg Sv Stjepana. The dining room is simply furnished with wooden tables, discreet modern art, and a large open fire. The food and service are practically faultless. Begin with the delicate scampi pâté, followed by a mixed seafood platter, and round off with a glass of homemade *orahovica* (walnut rakija). ⊠*2 blocks north of Trg Sv Stjepana, Hvar Town* ☎*021/742–850* ⊟*AE, DC, MC, V* ⊙*Closed Dec.–Mar.*

$$–$$$$

✕**Palazzo Paladini.** In a beautiful Renaissance courtyard garden planted with orange trees, this long-standing, family-run restaurant serves up Dalmatian specialties with an emphasis on seafood. The signature dish is *hvarska gregada* (local fish stew with aromatic herbs and potatoes), and the chef also does a highly praised vegetarian platter. ⊠*1 block north of Trg Sv Stjepana, Hvar Town* ☎*021/742–104* ⊟*AE, DC, MC, V* ⊙*Closed Jan.–Apr.*

$$–$$$$
★

✕**Restoran Palmižana.** On the tiny island of Sveti Klement, a 20-minute taxi-boat ride from Hvar Town, this terrace restaurant is backed by a romantic wilderness of Mediterranean flora and offers stunning views over the open sea. The walls are decorated with contemporary Croatian art, and there are classical-music recitals on Sunday morning. Besides fresh seafood, goodies include *kožji sir sa rukolom* (goat cheese with arugula), and *pašticada* (beef stewed in sweet wine and prunes). ⊠*Vinogradišće Uvala, Sveti Klement* ☎*021/717–270* ☰*AE, DC, MC, V* ⊘*Closed Nov.–Mar.*

$$–$$$ ✕**Bacchus.** With outdoor tables on the main square, this small and sometimes chaotic eatery is popular with locals for its *merenda* (inexpensive prix-fixe lunch), and is reputed to prepare the best *ramsteak* (rump steak) in town. It stays open year-round. ⊠*Trg Sv Stjepana, Hvar Town* ☎*021/742–698* ☰*AE, DC, MC, V.*

$–$$ ✕**Konoba Menego.** On the steps between the main square and the castle, this authentic stone-walled konoba has candlelit tables and whole *pršut* (prosciutto) hanging from the wooden beamed ceiling. Come here to snack on small platters of locally produced, cold Dalmatian specialties such as *kožji sir* (goat cheese), pršut, *salata od hobotnice* (octopus salad) and *masline* (olives), accompanied by a carafe of homemade wine. Before leaving, round off your meal with *pijane smokve* (figs marinated in brandy), and be sure to check out the world atlas where guests sign on the pages of their home towns. ⊠*Groda bb, Hvar Town* ☎*021/742–036* ☰*No credit cards* ⊘*Closed Dec.–Mar.*

WHERE TO STAY

$$$$ 🏨**Hotel Adriana.** On the seafront, looking across the busy harbor toward the Old Town, the Adriana reopened in June 2007 after total renovation. The rooms are decorated in minimalist style in subtle earthy shades with dark wooden floors, flat-screen TV, and bathrooms with glass partitions. There is a rooftop pool and sophisticated cocktail bar affording stunning views onto the sea and Old Town, and a chic ground-floor restaurant serving Mediterranean cuisine on the harbor front. The luxurious Sensori Spa offers seven types of massage, beauty treatments, yoga and Pilates. Pros: prime location on seafront promenade, beautifully designed interior, luxurious spa. Cons: very expensive, most bathrooms have a big shower but no tub, some guests complain that breakfast is below par for a hotel of this price range. ⊠*Fabrika bb, Hvar Town 21450* ☎*021/750–200* 🖷*021/750–201* ⊕*www.sun canihvar.hr* ⬳*50 rooms, 9 suites* ♿*In-room: safe, refrigerator, Wi-Fi. In-hotel: restaurant, room service, bars, pool, spa, public Wi-Fi, some pets allowed, no-smoking rooms* ☰*AE, DC, MC, V* ⏺❘*BP.*

$$$$ 🏨**Hotel Riva.** Reopened in 2006 after total renovation, the Riva is a
★   particularly lovely small luxury hotel. Occupying a 100-year-old stone building on the palm-lined waterfront, opposite the ferry landing station, it is now considered Hvar's hippest hideaway. The rooms are rather small but funky, each decorated in pale gray with splashes of red, and a large black-and-white portrait of a film icon such as Anita Ekberg or James Dean. The prudish may not approve of the bathrooms, since the shower cubicle is visible from the bedroom through a large clear-glass window. Out front there is a delightful open-air terrace decorated with potted olive trees, where the Roots Restaurant serves innovative Mediterranean cuisine and the B.B. Club cocktail bar works into the early hours. If you object to late-night noise, forfeit the sea view and ask for a room at the back. Pros: prime location on seafront promenade, beautifully designed interior, excellent bar and restaurant. Cons:

very expensive, rooms in front can be noisy at night (bars) and in the early morning (ferry), rooms are rather small. ✉ *Riva bb, Hvar Town 21450* 🖳 *021/750–100* 🖷 *021/750–101* ⊕ *www.suncanihvar.hr* ☎*46 rooms, 8 suites ♿ In-room: safe, refrigerator, Wi-Fi. In-hotel: restaurant, room service, bar, public Wi-Fi, some pets allowed, no-smoking rooms* ▤ *AE, DC, MC, V* ❘◯❘*BP.*

$$–$$$ 🖳**Hotel Amfora.** Reopened in July 2007 after a major renovation, this
♻   colossal white, modern structure sits in its own bay, backed by pine-woods, a pleasant 10-minute walk along the coastal path from the center of town. The chic rooms are decorated in warm hues of cream, beige, and chocolate brown and have flat-screen TVs and spacious bathrooms. Free Wi-Fi is available throughout the building. The seafront is rimmed by a 1930s stone colonnade, offering easy access to the water and equipped with private cabanas. At this writing, the hotel was closed for a second winter; summer 2008 will see the opening of new Sensori Spa wellness center, the romantic Sunset restaurant, plus a large, free-form, cascading pool set in gardens out front. The excellent recreation facilities make this an ideal choice for families with kids on longer stays. Pros: location in newly landscaped grounds overlooking the sea, chic modern design, private beach cabins. Cons: vast 1970s building lacks charm even after renovation, large and somewhat impersonal, poor signage within the complex (some guests complain they get lost). ✉ *Majerovica bb, Hvar Town 21450* 🖳 *021/750–300* 🖷 *021/750–301* ⊕ *www.suncanihvar.hr* ☎ *246 rooms, 78 suites ♿ In-room: safe, refrigerator, Wi-Fi. In-hotel: 2 restaurants, room service, bars, room service, pools, spa, beachfront, public Wi-Fi* ▤ *AE, DC, MC, V* ⊗ *Closed for final renovation work in late 2007, reopening Apr. 2008* ❘◯❘*BP.*

$$–$$$ 🖳**Podstine.** This peaceful, family-run hotel lies on the coast, a 20-minute walk west of the town center. It's set in lush gardens planted with palms and lemon trees that step down to the seafront in a series of terraces, with outdoor tables for dining and romantic subtle lighting by night. The garden fronts on a pebble beach complete with sun beds, parasols, a shower, and even a berth for a yacht, if you are coming in by sea. The rooms are cool and peaceful, and have spacious marble bathrooms; most have sea views and balconies. Pros: peaceful seafront location, beautiful gardens, small beach out front with sun beds and umbrellas. Cons: far from Old Town, absolutely no nightlife nearby (the hotel's bar shuts at 11 PM even in summer), standard rooms are rather dark and gloomy and have no views. ✉ *Hvar Town 21450* 🖳 *021/740–400* 🖷 *021/740–499* ⊕ *www.podstine.com* ☎ *40 rooms ♿ In-room: dial-up, refrigerator. In-hotel: restaurant, room service, bar, gym, beachfront, diving, public Internet* ▤ *AE, DC, MC, V* ⊗ *Closed Nov.–Mar.* ❘◯❘*BP.*

$$ 🖳**Hotel Croatia.** A family-run hotel surrounded by a pine-scented garden overlooks the sea and is a lovely 10-minute seafront walk southeast of the main square. The building dates back to 1936, and the rooms are peaceful even though the furnishings are basic (but comfortable). All meals, including breakfast, are served on a garden terrace offering glorious views over the sea to the Pakleni Islands. Pros: most rooms

have sea views, breakfast served on open-air terrace in garden, slightly out of the town center and more peaceful (no noisy bars, no noise from ferries). Cons: rooms rather basic, poor service (reception sometimes left unattended). ⊠ *Majerovica bb, Hvar Town 21450* ☎ *021/742– 400* 🖷 *021/741–707* ⊕ *www.hotelcroatia.net* ⇌ *22 rooms* ♿ *In-hotel: restaurant, bar, beachfront, no elevator* ⊟ *AE, DC, MC, V* ⊗ *Closed Oct.–Mar.* ⦿ *BP.*

NIGHTLIFE & THE ARTS

Croatia is generally not a hot spot for nightlife, but the island of Hvar may be starting a renaissance on the party front. Several stylish cocktail bars and clubs have opened in the past few years to cater to the annual influx of summer visitors.

Classical-music recitals in the cloisters of the Franciscan monastery have long been the highlight of the **Hvar Summer Festival.** Also look out for theater, folklore, and jazz at various open-air locations around town. The annual festival runs from mid-June to late September.

Carpe Diem (⊠ *Riva, Hvar Town* ☎ *021/717–234*), a harborside cocktail bar with a summer terrace decked out with Oriental furniture and potted plants and two burly bouncers at the gate, is where Hvar's richest and most glamorous visitors come to see and be seen. Stop in to see why Hvar has been labeled the next Ibiza. It's open late. **Kiva** (⊠ *Riva, Hvar Town* ☎ *No phone*), in total contrast to most of the newer hot spots, is a down-to-earth wine bar popular with locals and visitors in search of a friendly, laid-back, late-night drinking den. You'll find it hidden away in a narrow side street off the harbor, behind Nautica bar. **Veneranda** (⊠ *Sv Veneranda, Hvar Town* ☎ *No phone*) offers open-air drinking and dancing by a pool in the grounds of a former Greek Orthodox monastery. Most evenings begin with a film projection after dusk: the crowds arrive after midnight. It is a 10-minute walk west of town. Follow the seafront promenade, then head for the lights in the pine woods.

SPORTS & THE OUTDOORS

BEACHES

Although there are several decent beaches within walking distance of town—the best-equipped being the Hotel Amfora's pebble beach, 10 minutes west of the main square—sun worshippers in the know head for the nearby Pakleni Otoci (Pakleni Islands), which can be reached by taxi boats that depart regularly (in peak season, every hour, from 8 to 8) from in front of the Arsenal in the town harbor. The best known and best served are **Sveti Jerolim** (on the island of the same name, predominantly a nudist beach), **Stipanska** (on the island of Marinkovac, a clothing-optional beach), and **Palmižana** (on the island of Sveti Klement, also clothing-optional).

DIVING

Those with a taste for underwater adventure might have a go at scuba diving. The seabed is scattered with pieces of broken Greek amphorae, while the area's biggest underwater attraction is the Stambedar seawall, home to red and violet gorgonians (a type of coral), which is close to the Pakleni Islands. For courses at all levels, try **Diving Center Viking** (✉ *Podstine, Hvar Town* ☎ *021/742–529* ⊕ *www.viking-diving.com*).

SAILING

Hvar Town is a popular port of call for those sailing on the Adriatic; the town harbor is packed with flashy yachts through peak season. **ACI Marina** (✉ *Palmižana Bay, Sveti Klement* ☎ *021/744–995* ⊕ *www. aci-club.hr*) in Palmižana Bay on the island of Sveti Klement, one of the Pakleni Otoci, lies just 2.4 nautical mi from Hvar Town. This 160-berth marina is open from April through October, and is served by regular taxi boats from Hvar Town through peak season.

YOGA

Trendy Hvar even offers yoga. **Suncokret** (✉ *Palmižana Bay, Dol* ☎ *091/739–2526* ⊕ *www.suncokretdream.net*) was founded by a New Yorker and her Dalmatia-born partner. Their holistic wellness retreats combine yoga, nature walks, Reiki, life path workshops, and painting. Guests are accommodated in private cottages in the village, and typical Dalmatian meals are provided. Most courses last one week, but visitors are also welcome to drop in for a session. Dol lies 4 mi (6 km) from Starigrad and 16 mi (26 km) from Hvar Town.

VIS

34 nautical mi southwest of Split by ferry.

Closed to foreigners until 1989, the distant island of Vis is relatively wild and unexploited. To get here from Split, you can either take the SEM Marina fast catamaran service, or a 2½-hour Jadrolinija ferry ride to arrive in Vis Town. Built around a wide harbor, the town is popular with yachters, who appreciate its rugged nature, unpretentious fish restaurants, and excellent locally produced wine. The pretty fishing village of Komiža is 11 km (7 mi) from Vis Town. Here you're just a 40-minute boat ride away from the Modra Spilja (Blue Cave), often compared to the Blue Grotto on Italy's Capri.

Throughout the summer, local fishermen will take tourists from both Vis Town and Komiža into the **Modra Spilja** *(Blue Cave)* by boat. Some of these trips are done on a regular basis. Hidden away on the small island of Biševo (5 nautical mi southwest of Komiža), the cave is 78 feet long and 39 feet wide. Sunlight enters through the water, reflects off the seabed, and casts the interior in a fantastic shade of blue. If you're lucky, you'll have time for a quick swim. Ask at the marina or at the tourist-information office to see who is offering trips. ✉ *Boševo.*

WHERE TO EAT

$$–$$$$ ✕**Jastožera.** The former lobster house, built in 1883, was cleverly converted to make an impressive restaurant in 2002. Tables are set on wooden platforms above the water, and it's even possible to enter the central dining area in a small boat. The house specialty is *jastog sa spagetima* (lobster with spaghetti). ⊠*Gunduličeva 6, Komiža* ☎*021/713–859* ✉*AE, DC, MC, V* ⊗*Closed Oct.–Apr.*

$$–$$$$ ✕**Villa Kaliopa.** With tables set under the trees in the romantic walled
Fodor'sChoice garden of a 16th-century villa, dinner at this restaurant in Vis Town
★ is an unforgettable experience. The menu changes daily depending on what fresh fish and shellfish have come in. Your server will bring a platter to the table so you can choose your own fish before it's cooked. ⊠*V Nazora 32, Vis Town* ☎*021/711–755* ✉*AE, DC, MC, V* ⊗*Closed Nov.–Mar.*

$$–$$$ ✕**Konoba Bako.** Popular with locals and visitors alike, this excellent fish restaurant overlooks a tiny bay in Komiža. Outdoors, tables are set right up to the water's edge, and inside there's a small pool with lobsters and amphoras. The *salata od hobotnice* (octopus salad), *škampi rižot* (scampi risotto), and barbecued fish are all delicious. ⊠*Gunduliceva 1, Komiža* ☎*021/713–742* ✉*AE, DC, MC, V* ⊗*Closed mid-Nov.–mid-Feb.*

$$–$$$ ✕**Pojoda.** A modern glass-and-wood conservatory looks onto a courtyard garden planted with orange and lemon trees, accessed through an archway off a narrow side street. Dishes are named in local dialect: check out the *manistra na brudet* (bean and pasta soup) and *luc u verudi* (tuna stewed with vegetables). An amusing extra: from November though February, when the restaurant is closed, the owner offers two-day Dalmatian cooking classes for men only. ⊠*Don Cvjetka Marasovića 8, Vis Town* ☎*021/711–575* ✉*AE, DC, MC, V* ⊗*Closed Nov.–Mar.*

WHERE TO STAY

$ ⊡**Hotel Paula.** In Vis Town, east of the ferry quay, this friendly, family-run hotel is hidden away between stone cottages in a quiet, cobbled side street. All the rooms are smartly furnished and modern; on the top floor there's a honeymoon suite with a Jacuzzi and a large terrace with a sea view. Downstairs there's a good fish restaurant with tables on a walled summer terrace; it stays open year-round. Pros: nice traditional stone building in Old Town, modern and comfortable rooms, friendly staff. Cons: a couple of blocks in from the seafront (only the top-floor suite has a sea view), often fully booked, 20-minute walk from ferry landing can be difficult for visitors with heavy luggage. ⊠*Petra Hektorovića 2, Vis Town 21480* ☎*021/711–362* ⊕*www.paula-hotel.t-com.hr* ⊅*10 rooms, 1 suite* △*In-room: kitchen (some). In-hotel: restaurant, bar, bicycles, no elevator* ✉*AE, DC, MC, V* ⊚|*BP.*

$ ⊡**Tamaris.** Overlooking the harbor and seafront promenade in Vis Town, Tamaris occupies a late-19th-century building. The location is perfect, the rooms basic but comfortable, and it stays open all year. Pros: on seafront promenade in center of town, most rooms have sea views, cheerful café terrace out front. Cons: interior badly in need of refurbishment, rooms very basic, service rather indifferent. ⊠ *Šetalište Apolonija Zanelle 5, Vis Town 21480* ☎🛏021/711–350 ⤳*27 rooms* ♿*In-hotel: restaurant, bar, no elevator* ▭*AE, DC, MC, V* ⟨◯⟩*BP.*

SPORTS & THE OUTDOORS

DIVING

Scuba-diving enthusiasts will find underwater attractions including several underwater caves, at least half a dozen shipwrecks, and some spectacular coral reefs. Beginners and those with previous experience should contact **Issa Diving Centre** (⊠*Ribarska 91, Komiža* ☎*021/713–651* ⊕*www.scubadiving.hr*) for organized diving trips and training at all levels.

MAKARSKA

67 km (42 mi) southeast of Split.

The seafront promenade, lined with palms and cheerful open-air cafés, looks onto a protected bay dotted with wooden fishing boats. From here one enters the Old Town, a warren of stone buildings and cobbled streets surrounding the main square, which is backed by the parish church and a small open-air market off to one side. The atmosphere is relaxed and easygoing. The only drama you'll likely see is created by the limestone heights of Biokovo Mountain, which seems to alternate between protecting and threatening the town, depending on the color of the sky and the cloud formations that ride over its rugged peaks.

Makarska has developed an unpretentious, relatively cheap brand of tourism, popular with East Europeans. It does get very busy through peak season; the ideal time to visit is either late spring or early autumn, when the weather is perfect for hiking on Biokovo.

Behind Makarska, a large area of the rocky heights that form Biokovo Mountain has been designated as **Park Prirode Biokovo** (*Biokovo Nature Park* ⊠*Trg Tina Ujevića 1/I, Makarska* ☎*021/616–924*). Part of the Dinaric Alps, which run from Slovenia down to Montenegro, Biokovo abounds in rare indigenous plant species. It's possible to reach the highest peak, Sveti Jure (5,781 feet) in five-and-a-half hours from Makarska. However, this is a strenuous hike, for which you will need good boots and plenty of water. Few staff in the park's office speak English; it's usually much easier to organize an excursion through Biokovo Active Holidays *(see* ⇨Sports & the Outdoors, *below)*, a company that offers organized trips up the mountain, traveling part of the way by jeep.

WHERE TO EAT

$$–$$$$ ✕**Stari Mlin.** Ethnic music, incense, and colorful canvases set the mood
★ inside this old stone building, and the internal garden is draped with
vines and decorated with pots of herbs and cherry tomatoes. Barbe-
cued seafood tops the menu, but there is an extra surprise here, a
select choice of authentic Thai dishes. The owner worked for several
years aboard a cruise ship before returning home to run the family
restaurant. It stays open all year. ✉ *Prvosvibanska 43* ☎ *021/611–509*
▭ *AE, DC, MC, V.*

$$–$$$ ✕**Hrpina.** This long-standing, family-run restaurant overlooks a small
piazza just off the main square. Dalmatian seafood dishes such as
školjke na buzaru (shellfish in garlic, white wine, and parsley) and *crni
rižot* (black risotto made from cuttlefish) are served at heavy wooden
tables on a terrace lined with potted geraniums. It stays open all year.
✉ *Trg Hrpina 2* ☎ *021/611–619* ▭ *No credit cards.*

WHERE TO STAY

$ ☷**Hotel Biokovo.** In the center of Makarska, on the palm-lined sea-
front promenade, this old-fashioned hotel was renovated in 2004. All
rooms have pine floors; fabrics are either royal blue or Bordeaux red.
The ground-floor terrace café is popular with locals all year long. Pros:
location on seafront promenade in the Old Town, friendly and helpful
staff, pleasant café terrace out front. Cons: limited facilities, parking
can be a problem. ✉ *Obala Kralja Tomislava, 21300* ☎ *021/615–244*
🖷 *021/615–081* ⊕ *www.hotelbiokovo.hr* ⤳ *55 rooms, 5 suites* ⚐ *In-
room: refrigerator, dial-up. In-hotel: restaurant, bar, public Internet*
▭ *AE, DC, MC, V* ⊺⊙⊺*BP.*

$ ☷**Hotel Porin.** This 19th-century building stands on the seafront prome-
nade and was refurbished to form a small hotel, which opened in 2002.
There's a small roof terrace for hotel guests, a restaurant overlooking
the sea that caters weddings and seminars, and a café accessed from
the cobbled street one block back from the seafront. Pros: location on
seafront promenade in the Old Town, front rooms have lovely views
onto the bay, small (so guests receive individual attention from the
staff). Cons: often fully booked, limited facilities. ✉ *Marineta 2, 21300*
☎ *021/613–744* 🖷 *021/613–688* ⊕ *www.hotel-porin.hr* ⤳ *7 rooms,
1 suite* ⚐ *In-room: refrigerator. In-hotel: restaurant, bar, no elevator*
▭ *AE, DC, MC, V* ⊺⊙⊺*BP.*

SPORTS & THE OUTDOORS

BEACHES
The main town beach, a 1½-km (1-mi) stretch of pebbles backed by
pine woods, lies northwest of the center and close to a string of big
modern hotels. Alternatively, walk along the narrow coastal path
southeast of town to find rocks and a series of secluded coves. Farther
afield, the so-called Makarska Rivjera is a 40-km (25-mi) stretch of
coast running from Brela to Gradac, dotted with fishing villages that

have developed into seaside resorts, each with its own shingle beach or concrete bathing area.

DIVING

Local underwater attractions include a nearby reef, known as Kraljev Gaj, which is populated by sponges, coral, octopi, and scorpion fish, while farther out from the coast you can visit the *Dubrovnik,* an old steam boat that sank in 1917. Scuba-diving enthusiasts, as well as complete beginners, can try **More Sub** (⊠ *Krešimira 43, Makarska* ☎ *021/611–727* ⊕ *www.more-sub-makarska.hr*) for organized diving trips and training at all levels.

HIKING

For sound information about hiking, your best bet is to contact **Biokovo Active Holidays** (⊠ *Kralja Petra Krešimira IV 7B* ☎ *021/679–655* ⊕ *www.biokovo.net*). This agency started out by specializing in one-day guided hiking trips up Biokovo Mountain, but it has now expanded its program to include a range of one-week and two-week hiking-and-boating options throughout the country. You can also make unusual "sunrise" and "sunset" visits to Biokovo, entailing a jeep ride, a short walk, and a stop for food and drinks while you enjoy the mountaintop views. Tours are available April through October.

LASTOVO

Lastovo Island is 80 km (50 nautical mi) west of Dubrovnik (no direct ferry) and 80 km (50 nautical mi) southeast of Split (daily direct ferry connection).

Very few Croatians have visited Lastovo, though they will all tell you that it's beautiful. Like Vis, Lastovo was a Yugoslav military naval base during the Tito years, and was therefore closed to foreigners, so commercial tourism never developed. Today there is still just one hotel.

Lying far out to sea, Lastovo is an island of green, fertile valleys and is practically self-sufficient: locally caught seafood, not least the delicious lobster, and homegrown vegetables are the staple diet. The main settlement, Lastovo Town, is made up of stone houses built amphitheater-style into a hillside, crisscrossed by cobbled alleys and flights of steps; they're renowned for tall chimneys resembling minarets. The only other settlement on the island is the small port of Ubli, which is 10 km (6 mi) from Lastovo Town.

Although it is officially in Southern Dalmatia, locals chose to have direct transport links with Split in Central Dalmatia rather than Dubrovnik. To get there, take the Jadrolinija daily ferry service from Split to Ubli, stopping at Hvar Town and Vela Luka en route. Jadrolinija also runs a daily catamaran from Split covering the same route; it's faster but a little more expensive.

WHERE TO EAT

$$–$$$$ ✕**Konoba Triton.** Triton is widely acknowledged to be the best restaurant on island, and it's particularly popular with those traveling by sailboat, who can moor up on a small quay out front. The owner catches and cooks the fish himself; he also produces the wine, olive oil, and vegetables. You'll find it in Zaklopatica, a north-facing bay 3 km (2 mi) west of Lastovo Town. There are several apartments to rent upstairs. ✉*Zaklopatica* ☎*020/801–161* 🖃*No credit cards* ⊘*Closed Nov.–Mar.*

$$–$$$ ✕**Konoba Bačvara.** Traditional home-cooked Dalmatian fare is served at this family-run eatery in an old stone building in Lastovo Town. Barbecued seafood predominates, and you'll also have the chance to try homegrown vegetables and local wine. ✉*Počival, Lastovo Town* ☎*020/801–131* 🖃*No credit cards* ⊘*Closed Nov.–May.*

WHERE TO STAY

$ ⌂**Hotel Solitudo.** The only hotel on the island, Hotel Solitudo (confusingly sometimes referred to as Hotel Ladesta) is a modern white building on a peaceful bay backed by pines, 3 km (2 mi) north of Ubli. All rooms have a balcony and sea view, and sports facilities include a beach, diving club, and 50-berth marina. The hotel rents out bicycles, boats, and surfboards. Renovation work began in 2001 and has yet to be completed, though several new rooms have opened. It stays open all year. Pros: lovely seafront location, peaceful off-the-beaten-path island, on-site dive shop. Cons: renovation work still incomplete, basic rooms. ✉*Pasadur, 3 km (2 mi) from Ubli, 20290* ☎*020/802–100* 🖷*020/802–444* ⌕*73 rooms* ♿*In-hotel: 2 restaurants, bar, beachfront, diving, no elevator* 🖃*AE, DC, MC, V* ⊙*BP.*

SPORTS & THE OUTDOORS

BEACHES

The best beaches lie on **Saplun,** one of the tiny, unpopulated **Lastovnjaci Islands,** which are a short distance northeast of Lastovo and are served by taxi-boats through high season.

DIVING

Paradise Diving Center (✉*Pasadur, 3 km [2 mi] from Ubli* ☎*020/805–179* ⊕*www.diving-paradise.net*) is a scuba-diving center based in the Hotel Solitudo. Just a five-minute boat ride from the diving center and at a depth of 49 feet lies a reef of red, yellow, and violet gorgonias. Farther afield, experienced divers can expect to explore sea caves and sunken ships.

SAILING

Hotel Solitudo Marina (✉*Pasadur, 3 km [2 mi] from Ubli* ☎*020/802–100*) is a 50-berth marina attached to Hotel Solitudo.

SPLIT & CENTRAL DALMATIA ESSENTIALS

AIR TRAVEL

The national carrier, Croatia Airlines, operates domestic flights from Split to Zagreb, Dubrovnik, Pula, and Osijek. During the summer high season you can fly directly to Split from Amsterdam, Bari, Brussels, Catania, Copenhagen, Frankfurt, Gothenburg, Hamburg, Helsinki, Istanbul, Lisbon, London, Lyon, Manchester, Milan, Munich, Oslo, Palermo, Paris, Prague, Rome, Sarajevo, Skopje, Stockholm, Tel Aviv, Turin, Vienna, Warsaw, and Zurich. Also through summer, Croatia Airlines flies nonstop from the island of Brač to Zagreb, Munich, and Frankfurt. Adria, British Airways, ČSA and Malev also fly to Split. In addition, through the summer the low-cost airlines EasyJet and Wizzair operate between London and Split.

Information **Adria Airways** (⊠ *Obala kneza Domagoja, Gradska Luka, Split* ☎ *021/338–445*). **British Airways** (⊠ *Split Airport, Kaštela* ☎ *021/797–303*). **Croatia Airlines** (⊠ *Obala Hrvatskog Narodnog Preporoda 9, Grad, Split* ☎ *021/362–997*). **ČSA** (⊠ *Dominisova 10, Grad, Split* ☎ *021/343–422*). **Malev** (⊠ *Split Airport, Kaštela* ☎ *021/895–274*).

AIRPORTS & TRANSFERS

Split is served by Split Airport (SPU) at Kaštela, 25 km (16 mi) northwest of the city center. The island of Brač is served by Brač Airport at Veško Polje, 14 km (8¾ mi) northeast of Bol.

Information **Split Airport** (⊠ *Kaštela* ☎ *021/203–171 general information, 021/203–218 lost and found* ⊕ *www.split-airport.hr*). **Brač Airport** (⊠ *Veško Polje* ☎ *021/559–711 general information* ⊕ *www.airport-brac.hr*).

AIRPORT TRANSFERS
You can take an airport bus to obala Lazereta, near the Split Bus Station. For your return, the airport bus leaves Split 90 minutes before each flight. A one-way ticket costs 30 Kn, and the travel time is 40 minutes. Brač airport is not served by bus but taxis are available.

Information **Split airport bus** (☎ *021/203–171*).

BANKS & EXCHANGE SERVICES

There are banks in all the destinations mentioned in this chapter. ATMs are now widespread, and you will find at least one even in small towns on the islands. It is possible to exchange currency in banks and also in most local travel agencies.

BOAT & FERRY TRAVEL

From June through September, Jadrolinija and Blue Line both run regular services to Ancona (Italy), departing at 9 PM from Split and arriving in Ancona at 7 AM the following day. The same vessels depart at 9 PM from Ancona to arrive in Split at 7 AM. Journey time is approximately 10 hours in either direction. In peak season only, Blue Line also runs day crossings departing from Ancona at 11 AM on Saturday, Sunday, and Monday. Through winter these services are reduced slightly.

From June to September the Italian company SNAV runs Croazia Jet, a daily catamaran service between Ancona (Italy) and Split, departing at 5 PM from Split and arriving in Ancona at 9:30 PM. The same vessel departs at 11 AM from Ancona to arrive in Split at 3:30 PM. The journey time is 4½ hours in either direction. The same company runs Pescara Jet, a daily catamaran service between Pescara (Italy) and Split, stopping at Stari Grad (island of Hvar) en route. The vessel departs at 5 PM from Split and arrives in Pescara at 11 PM, then leaves Pescara the following morning at 10:30, arriving in Split at 4:15 PM. On Saturdays only, a corresponding catamaran connects from Stari Grad (Hvar) to Bol (Brač). Jadrolinija operates coastal ferries that run from Rijeka to Dubrovnik. Ferries depart from Rijeka twice a week in the evening, and arrive in Split in the early morning on the following day (journey time is approximately 10 hours) and then continue down the coast to Dubrovnik (journey time is approximately 9 hours), stopping at Stari Grad (island of Hvar) and Korčula en route. From Dubrovnik, they then cover an overnight stretch to Bari in Italy. Jadrolinija runs daily ferries to Supetar (island of Brač), Stari Grad (island of Hvar), and Vis from Split. Jadrolinija runs a daily catamaran from Split to Hvar Town (island of Hvar), which then continues to Vela Luka (island of Korčula) and Ubli (island of Lastovo). A separate service runs to Bol (island of Brač) and then continues to Jelsa (island of Hvar).

Information **Jadrolinija** (☎ 021/338–333 ⊕ www.jadrolinija.hr). **Blue Line** (☎ 021/352–533 ⊕ www.blueline-ferries.com). **SNAV** (☎ 021/322–252 ⊕ www. snav.it).

BUS TRAVEL

International buses arrive daily from Trieste, Ljubljana, Belgrade, Sarajevo, Munich, and Stuttgart. There are buses once a week from Vienna, and London via Paris.

There are good bus connections to destinations all over Croatia. There are approximately 30 buses per day to Zagreb, 12 to Dubrovnik (in Southern Dalmatia), 14 to Zadar (in Northern Dalmatia) and 12 to Rijeka (in Kvarner). Buses traveling south to Dubrovnik stop at Makarska en route, while those going north to Zadar stop at Šibenik. In addition, regular local buses run every 30 minutes up the coast to Trogir and down the coast to Omiš. Timetable information is available from the Split Bus Station, or from their Web site (see below).

Information **Split Bus Station** (✉ Obala Kneza Domogoja 12, Split ☎ 060/327–777 ⊕ www.ak-split.hr).

CAR TRAVEL

While visiting Split and the nearby islands of Brač, Hvar, and Vis, you are certainly better off without a car. However, you may wish to rent a vehicle to drive up the coast to Šibenik and Krka National Park, or down the coast to Omiš and Makarska, although these destinations are also well served by buses.

Information **Budget** (✉ Trubićeva Obala 12, Split ☎ 021/399–214 ✉ Split Airport, Kaštela ☎ 021/203–151). **Dollar Thrifty** (✉ Hotel Marjan, Obala K Branimira 8, Split ☎ 021/399–000 ✉ Split Airport, Kaštela ☎ 021/895–320). **Hertz** (✉ Trubićeva Obala 2, Split ☎ 021/360–455 ✉ Split Airport, Kaštela ☎ 021/895–230).

INTERNET, MAIL & SHIPPING

During the summer, small, temporary Internet cafés spring up in the main resorts; some may be nothing more than a regular café with a PC in the corner. Even on the islands you will find somewhere to check e-mail. However, very few well-established, fully-equipped Internet cafés exist in the region.

Information **Split Main Post Office** (⊠ *Obala Kneza Domagoja, Split*) lies on the road leading along the seafront from the center of town to the ferry port. It is open daily 7 AM–8 PM.

TAXI TRAVEL

In Split the main taxi ranks lie at each end of the *Riva* (Obala Hrvatskog Preporoda), in front of the *pazar* (open-air market), and in front of Hotel Bellevue. You will also find taxis waiting outside the train station (Obala Kneza Domagoja). Or you can call for a taxi in Split.

Information **Radio Taxi** (☎ *970 in Split*).

TOUR OPTIONS

Atlas organizes one-day excursions departing from Split (by bus) to the pilgrimage site of Međugorje, where the Virgin Mary is said to have appeared in 1981 (in Bosnia-Herzegovina, passports required).

Information **Atlas** (⊠ *Nepotova 4, Split* ☎ *021/343–055* ⊕ *www.atlas-croatia.com*).

TRAIN TRAVEL

There are three day trains and two night trains (with sleeping cars) daily between Split and Zagreb (journey time 5½ hours daytime; 8½ hours nighttime). In addition, there are three day trains daily between Split and Šibenik (journey time approximately 3½ hours, with a change at Perković).

Information **Split Train Station** (⊠ *Obala Kneza Domogoja 9, Split* ☎ *060/333–444* ⊕ *www.hznet.hr*).

VISITOR INFORMATION

Information **Split & Dalmatia County Tourist Board** (⊠ *Prilaz brace Kaliterna 10/I, Split* ☎ *021/490–032* ⊕ *www.dalmatia-cen.com*). **Bol Tourist Information Center** (⊠ *Porat Bolskih Pomoraca, Bol* ☎ *021/635–638* ⊕ *www.bol.hr*). **Hvar Town Tourist Information Center** (⊠ *Trg Sv Stjepana 16, Hvar Town* ☎ *021/741–059* ⊕ *www.hvar.hr*). **Lastovo Tourist Office** (⊠ *Pjevor bb, Lastovo* ☎ *020/801–018* ⊕ *www.lastovo-tz.net*). **Makarska Tourist Information Centre** (⊠ *Obala Kralja Tomislava 16, Makarska* ☎ *021/612–002* ⊕ *www.makarska.hr*). **Omiš Tourist Information Centre** (⊠ *Trg Sv Stjepana 16, Omiš* ☎ *021/861–350* ⊕ *www.tz-omis.hr*). **Skradin Tourist Information Center** (⊠ *Trg Male Gospe 3, Skradin* ☎ *022/771–306* ⊕ *www.skradin.hr*). **Split Tourist Information Center** (⊠ *Peristil, Split* ☎ *021/345–606* ⊕ *www.visitsplit.com*). **Šibenik Tourist Information Center** (⊠ *Obala Dr. Franje Tuđmana 5, Šibenik* ☎ *022/214–411* ⊕ *www.sibenik-tourism.hr*). **Trogir Tourist Information Center** (⊠ *Trg Ivana Pavla II 1, Trogir* ☎ *021/881–412* ⊕ *www.trogir.hr*). **Vis Tourist Information Center** (⊠ *Šetalište Stare Isse 5, Vis Town* ☎ *021/717–017* ⊕ *www.tz-vis.hr*).

Dubrovnik & Southern Dalmatia

WORD OF MOUTH

"We took the overnight ferry from Bari, Italy, to Dubrovnik, which was such a fun way to travel! We woke (very rested) about an hour before the ferry pulled into port, and had a light breakfast and enjoyed the beautiful scenery as the ferry arrived in Dubrovnik."

—EmilyMB

"I would recommend cycling on Korčula, though the little towns are not that much. . . . Nonetheless, [there are] lots of spots to stop for a dip in the crystal clear waters. . . . We were there for 2 nights, a total of 48 hours. But it felt like forever because it was so good in Korčula."

—4everywhere

By Jane Foster **THE HIGHLIGHT OF SOUTHERN DALMATIA** is undoubtedly the majestic walled city of Dubrovnik, from 1358 to 1808 a rich and powerful independent republic, which exerted its economic and cultural influence over almost the entire region. Jutting out to sea and backed by rugged mountains, it's an unforgettable sight and now Croatia's most upmarket and glamorous destination.

From Dubrovnik a ferry runs all the way up the coast to Rijeka in the Kvarner region, making several stops along the way, and occasionally extending its itinerary to include an overnight lap from Dubrovnik to Bari, Italy. There are also regular local ferry and catamaran services from Dubrovnik to outlying islands. The nearest and most accessible of these are the tiny car-free Elafitis, ideal as a day trip for someone on a short stay who still wants a brief taste of island life.

Moving down the mainland coast, Cavtat was founded by the ancient Greeks. Today a sleepy fishing town through winter, it turns into a cheerful holiday resort come summer, with a palm-lined seaside promenade, several sights of cultural note, and a handful of reasonably priced hotels.

Back up the coast, northwest of Dubrovnik, lies the village of Trsteno, with its delightful Renaissance arboretum stepping down toward the sea in a series of terraces. Proceeding northwest one arrives at Ston, known for its oysters and mussels, and its 14th-century walls forming the gateway to Pelješac Peninsula. Pelješac is of particular note for its excellent red wines: several families open their vineyards and cellars to the public for wine tastings. The main destination here is Orebić, a low-key resort with a good beach and water-sports facilities, backed by a majestic hillside monastery. From Orebić there are regular ferry crossings to Korčula Town, on the island of Korčula, one of the most sophisticated settlements on the Croatian islands, with its fine Gothic and Renaissance stone buildings bearing witness to almost 800 years of Venetian rule. Nearby Lumbarda provides a good stretch of sand beach, plus a delicate white wine known as Grk. In contrast to Korčula, the sparsely populated island of Mljet offers little in the way of architectural beauty but has preserved its indigenous coniferous forests, which rim the shores of two emerald-green saltwater lakes. They are contained within the borders of Mljet National Park, a haven for hiking, mountain biking, swimming, and kayaking. If you're traveling from Central to Southern Dalmatia by road, you'll pass through a narrow coastal strip given over to Bosnia-Herzegovina, so have your passport at hand for the border checkpoint. Most Croatian buses have a 20-minute stop here so people can jump off and shop, since many things—notably cigarettes—are much cheaper in Bosnia.

EXPLORING SOUTHERN DALMATIA

ABOUT THE RESTAURANTS
Seafood predominates throughout the region. Restaurants in Dubrovnik are the most expensive, and tend to cater to upmarket international tastes, with expensive "white" fish topping most menus and multilingual waiters pampering diners. The region's top venue for shellfish is

Southern
Dalmatia

KEY
━━ Rail Lines
🚢 Ferry

Sarajevo
Ilidza
Vrbas R.
Foča
Pljevlja
E762
Tjentište
Konjic
Jablanica
BOSNA I HERCEGOVINA
(BOSNIA - HERCEGOVINA)
Avtovac
CRNA GORA
(MONTENEGRO)
Posušje
Mostar
Nevesinje
Nikšić
Imotski
← TO SPLIT
Zagvozd
Ljubuški
Počitelj
Bileća
HRVATSKA
(CROATIA)
Stolac
Makarska   E65   Zaostrog   Gradac
Metković
Trebinje
Trebišnjica
Crkvice   Risan   Perast
Brač
Drvenik
Ploče
Doli
Kotor
Sućuraj
Trpanj
Ston
Slano
Trsteno
Hercegnovi
E73 E80
Orebić   Pelješac Peninsula
Šipan
Gulf of
Kotor
Hvar
Lopud
Cavtat   Ćilipi
Mljet
Dubrovik
see detail
map
TO BAR →
Korčula
Korčula
see detail
map
Adriatic Sea
0   30 miles
Lastovo
0   30 kilometers

Neretva
E73

the village of Mali Ston on the Pelješac Peninsula, where locally grown
ostrige (oysters, at their best from February through May) and *dagnje*
(mussels, at their best from May through September) attract diners
from far and wide. Similarly, the island of Mljet is noted for its *jastog*
(lobster), a culinary luxury that is highly appreciated by the sailing
crowd. If you are lucky enough to find food prepared *ispod peke,* be
sure to try it. A terra-cotta casserole dish, usually containing either
lamb or octopus, is buried in white embers over which the *peka* (a
metal dome) is placed to ensure a long, slow cooking process. Such
dishes often need to be ordered one day in advance. Regarding desserts, the region's specialty is *rožata,* an egg-based pudding similar to
French crème caramel.

ABOUT THE HOTELS

Southern Dalmatia's (and indeed Croatia's) best and most expensive
hotels are in Dubrovnik. The top-notch establishments lie in and near
the Old Town, whereas in nearby Lapad you'll find around 20 large,
modern socialist-era hotels, many of which have been purchased by
foreign investors and renovated to include 21st-century luxuries such
as wellness centers. Outside Dubrovnik standards drop, with some
hotels still without air-conditioning or Internet service. Many visitors

prefer to rent a private room or apartment: it's cheaper, more homey, and gives you a chance to live as the locals do.

Many hotels in Dubrovnik stay open all year. For the rest of the region, the season runs from Easter through late October, peaking during July and August, when prices rise significantly and it may be difficult to find a place to sleep if you have not booked in advance.

WHAT IT COSTS IN EUROS (€) AND CROATIAN KUNA (KN)				
	¢	$	$$	$$$	$$$$
RESTAURANTS	under 20 Kn	20 Kn–35 Kn	35 Kn–60 Kn	60 Kn–80 Kn	over 80 Kn
HOTELS In euros	under €75	€75–€125	€125–€175	€175–€225	over €225
HOTELS In kuna	under 550 Kn	550 Kn–925 Kn	925 Kn–1,300 Kn	1,300 Kn–1,650 Kn	over 1,650 Kn

Restaurant prices are for a main course at dinner. Hotel prices are for two people in a double room in high season, excluding taxes and service charges.

TIMING

Dubrovnik receives visitors all year. Although some stay in town for several nights, many others arrive by cruise ship (en route from Venice to the Greek islands), flooding the streets during daylight hours but disappearing come sunset. The city is exceptionally crowded during the Summer Festival (mid-July to mid-August), with everyone from international performers to backpackers scrambling to find a room in the Old Town. Some hotels offer Easter and New Year packages, so you can expect Dubrovnik to be surprisingly busy at these times, too.

The rest of the region is more easygoing, with seasonal fluctuations similar to the rest of the Croatian coast. The July and August high season brings an influx of foreign visitors, the majority of whom are from Europe. Prices rise significantly during this period, as do temperatures, and accommodation can be difficult to find: as compensation, the long summer evenings offer cultural performances and late-night drinking under the stars.

Low season runs from November through April, a period when many hotels and restaurants close completely. That said, through winter you may be lucky enough to find bargain-priced accommodation and blissful days of sunshine and deep blue sky, albeit with a bracing chill in the air. For most people the best time to visit is the shoulder season, May through June and September through October. You'll find no crowds, decent weather, and a chance to tune into the local way of life.

DUBROVNIK

Lying 216 km (135 mi) southeast of Split and commanding a splendid coastal location, Dubrovnik is one of the world's most beautiful fortified cities. Its massive stone ramparts and splendid fortress towers curve around a tiny harbor, enclosing graduated ridges of sun-bleached orange-tiled roofs, copper domes, and elegant bell towers.

SOUTHERN DALMATIA TOP 5

- Walk the entire circuit of Dubrovnik's medieval city walls—which date back to the 13th century—for splendid views.

- Eat fresh mussels at a waterside restaurant in the Pelješac peninsula's Mali Ston. They're justifiably famous and served year-round. The most famous restaurant in the area is Kapitanova Kuća.

- Attend a tasting in an old-fashioned stone konoba at a vineyard on Pelješac Peninsula. Either Bartulović Vina or Matuško Vina is a good choice.

- Swim in Mljet's pristine Veliko Jezero surrounded by dense pine forests; you can also take a boat to the Benedictine monastery on an island in Veliko Jezero.

- Head out from Dubrovnik in a sea kayak to the scattered Elafiti islands.

In the 7th century AD, residents of the Roman city Epidaurum (now Cavtat) fled the Avars and Slavs of the north and founded a new settlement on a small rocky island, which they named Laus, and later Ragusa. On the mainland hillside opposite the island, the Slav settlement called Dubrovnik grew up. In the 12th century the narrow channel separating the two settlements was filled in, and Ragusa and Dubrovnik became one. The city was surrounded by defensive walls during the 13th century, and these were reinforced with towers and bastions in the late 15th century.

From 1358 to 1808 the city thrived as a powerful and remarkably sophisticated independent republic, reaching its golden age during the 16th century. In 1667 many of its splendid Gothic and Renaissance buildings were destroyed by an earthquake. The defensive walls survived the disaster, and the city was rebuilt in baroque style.

Dubrovnik lost its independence to Napoléon in 1808, and in 1815 passed to Austria-Hungary. During the 20th century, as part of Yugoslavia, the city became a popular tourist destination, and in 1979 it was listed as a UNESCO World Heritage Site. During the war for independence, it came under heavy siege, though thanks to careful restoration work few traces of damage remain. Today Dubrovnik is once again a fashionable, high-class destination, drawing not a few celebrities.

EXPLORING DUBROVNIK

All of the main sites lie in Stari Grad (Old Town) within the city walls, an area which is compact and car-free.

WHAT TO SEE

12 **Akvarij** *(Aquarium)*. This dark, cavernous space houses several small pools and 27 well-lit tanks containing a variety of fish from rays to small sharks, as well as other underwater denizens such as sponges and sea urchins. Children will find the octopus, in his glass tank either very

GREAT ITINERARIES

Southern Dalmatia is more than just Dubrovnik. The itineraries below aim to give you some idea of what to see in a limited time.

IF YOU HAVE 3 DAYS

Devote Day 1 to **Dubrovnik,** walking a full circuit of the city walls, exploring the historic monuments in the Old Town, and attending an open-air concert or theatrical performance if the Dubrovnik Summer Festival is in progress. On Day 2 make an early start to visit the arboretum at **Trsteno,** a green wilderness of exotic plantings on the grounds of a Renaissance villa. Return to Dubrovnik to take the midday ferry to **Lopud,** one of the car-free Elafiti Islands, and walk across the island for an afternoon of swimming on the Šunj sand beach. If Lopud's romantic escapism appeals, stay overnight; otherwise, return to Dubrovnik for the bright lights. Next morning, splash out on a taxi-boat ride along the coast from Dubrovnik's old harbor to **Cavtat.** Return either by taxi-boat or local bus to Dubrovnik for your final night.

IF YOU HAVE 5 DAYS

Spend your first day in Dubrovnik, as outlined above. Next morning, take a taxi-boat to Cavtat as outlined in the previous itinerary, returning to Dubrovnik in time for the early evening bus to **Korčula Town,** where you should sleep. Next day check out Korčula's Venetian-style architecture in the morning, then spend the afternoon either on the beach at Lumbarda or rent a motorboat and visit the tiny scattered islets of the Korčula archipelago. Stay a second night in Korčula; if you're lucky you might catch an evening performance of the Moreška sword dance. On the

next morning take a ferry to **Orebić** on the Pelješac Peninsula. First walk up to the Franciscan monastery, then devote the afternoon to exploring the local vineyards and wine cellars, either independently by car or as part of an organized tour group. Stay the night in Orebić. The following day catch the early morning bus for Dubrovnik. En route you could jump off at **Ston** to explore the 15th-century defensive walls and walk over to Mali Ston to sample the local oysters. **Trsteno** is another possible stop en route. Return to Dubrovnik in the afternoon to prepare for your final night.

IF YOU HAVE 7 DAYS

Spend your first four days as on the itinerary above. On Day 5, wake up in Orebić, then travel southeast along the Pelješac Peninsula to Trstenik to catch the morning ferry to Polače on the island of **Mljet.** Proceed to Pomena, where you will stay the night. Now you are already within the confines of **Mljet National Park,** a paradise of dense pinewoods centering on two interconnected saltwater lakes. Here you can either hike or rent a mountain bike to cycle the perimeter of the lakes, or take time out to swim. Alternatively, Odissej Hotel in Pomena can arrange a half-day sailing or diving trip. In the evening take a national park boat to St. Mary's Islet on Veliko Jezero, occupied by a former monastery, which now hosts a restaurant, making a romantic venue for dinner. On the next morning, drive the length of Mljet to spend a few hours on the sand beach of Saplunara. Leave the island via the port of Sobra aboard the midafternoon ferry for Dubrovnik, where you should spend your final evening.

IF YOU LIKE

HISTORY

The region's most magnificent historic monument has to be Dubrovnik's Old Town, a UNESCO World Heritage Site. Northwest along the coast, tiny Ston is noteworthy for its 14th-century walls, which formed a unique defense system, controlling land access onto Pelješac Peninsula. Korčula Town, a compact settlement of medieval stone buildings on a small peninsula, owes its ingenious "herring-bone" urban plan and elegant Gothic and Renaissance architecture to Dubrovnik's archrival, Venice. Fortunately, each of these historic centers has been protected from the threat of development.

ISLANDS

The region's islands offer the perfect opportunity to escape modern-day life. The tiny, car-free Elafiti Islands, which can be visited as a day trip from Dubrovnik, make a fine introduction to Dalmatia as it once was. Farther out to sea, Mljet remains wild and relatively free of commercial development. One-third of Mljet has been declared a national park to protect its indigenous pinewoods and two saltwater lakes.

WINE

Southern Dalmatia produces some excellent wines, notably the reds from the Pelješac Peninsula and the whites from the island of Korčula. On Pelješac, just one grape variety, Plavac Mali (closely related to California zinfandel) produces three sorts of red—Dingač, Postup, and Plavac—depending on the soil and topography of the vineyards it grows in. Here several wine cellars offer tastings, the best known being Grgić in Trstenik, Bartulović in Prizdrina, and Matuško in Potomje. On Korčula

the grape variety Pošip produces a crisp dry white wine, the best coming from the interior villages of Čara and Smokvica. The golden-colored Grk is highly esteemed and said to date back to the ancient Greeks. The Dubrovnik-based travel agency Atlas runs wine-tasting trips to both Pelješac and Korčula.

BEACHES

The best beaches and the cleanest water for swimming are on the islands. Sand is rare in Croatia, but in Southern Dalmatia you'll find blissful, back-to-nature, sandy beaches at Lumbarda (on Korčula), Saplunara (on Mljet), and Šunj (on Lopud). Trstenica in Orebić is a 1-km-long (½-mi-long) stretch of mixed sand and pebble. Nudism is popular, and official nudist beaches are marked FKK (from the German *Freikörperkultur,* meaning "free body culture"). Eastwest in Dubrovnik is a fully equipped, see-and-be-seen beach club just outside the city walls, where you'll spot international celebrities and would-bes in designer swimwear.

SAILING

Southern Dalmatia is a paradise for yachting enthusiasts, thanks to its myriad islands and well-equipped marinas. Dubrovnik ACI marina is the region's main charter base, with around a dozen companies there. Other marinas include the Korčula ACI marina on Korčula, and the Hotel Odisej marina on Mljet. Each year the ANA Sailing School, based in Cavtat near Dubrovnik, offers one-week sailing courses at various levels through summer. If you take a typical one-week charter departing from Dubrovnik, you can expect to visit the Elafitis, Mljet, and Korčula.

7

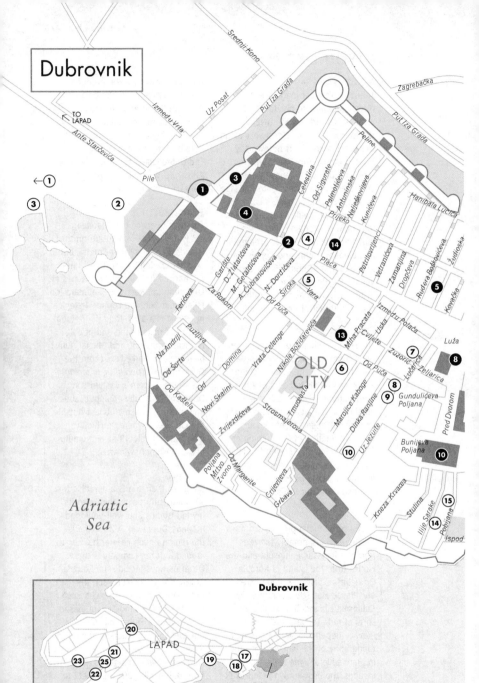

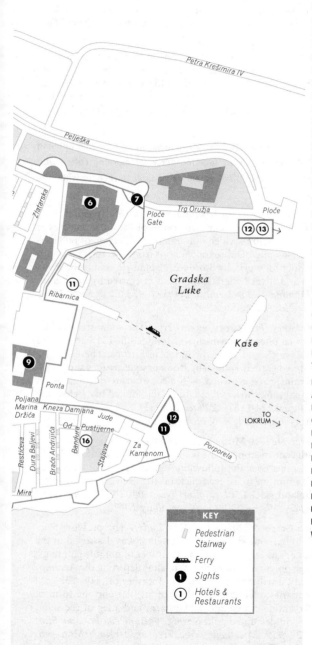

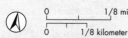

amusing or horribly scary. ⊠*Damjana Jude 2, Stari Grad* ☏*020/323–978* ⏍*30 Kn* ⏱*June–Sept., daily 9–8; Apr., May, Oct., and Nov., daily 9–6; Dec.–Mar., daily 9–1.*

❽ Crkva Svetog Vlaha *(Church of St. Blaise).* This 18th-century baroque church replaced an earlier one destroyed by fire. Of particular note is the silver statue on the high altar of St. Blaise holding a model of Dubrovnik, which is paraded around town each year on February 3, the Day of St. Blaise. ⊠*Luža, Stari Grad* ⏍*Free* ⏱*Daily 8–noon and 4:30–7.*

■■■■■■■
NEED A BREAK?

Gradska Kavarna (⊠*Placa, Stari Grad*) occupies the old Arsenal building and remains Dubrovnik's favorite meeting place for morning coffee with cakes or an evening aperitif. It has an ample summer terrace for when the weather is nice.

❻ Dominikanski samostan *(Dominican monastery).* With a splendid, late-15th-century floral Gothic cloister as its centerpiece, the monastery is best known for its museum, which houses a rich collection of religious paintings by the so-called Dubrovnik School from the 15th and 16th centuries. Look out for works by Božidarević, Hamzić, and Dobričević, as well as gold and silver ecclesiastical artifacts crafted by local goldsmiths. ⊠*Sv Domina 4, Stari Grad* ☏*020/321–423* ⏍*15 Kn* ⏱*May–Oct., daily 9–6; Nov.–Apr., daily 9–5.*

❹ Franjevačka samostan *(Franciscan monastery).* The monastery's chief claim to fame is its pharmacy, which was founded in 1318 and is still in existence today; it's said to be the oldest in Europe. There's also a delightful cloistered garden, framed by Romanesque arcades supported by double columns, each crowned with a set of grotesque figures. In the Treasury a painting shows what Dubrovnik looked like before the disastrous earthquake of 1667. ⊠*Placa 2, Stari Grad* ☏*020/321–410* ⏍*20 Kn* ⏱*May–Oct., daily 9–6; Nov.–Apr., daily 9–5.*

❸ Gradske Zidine *(city walls).* Most of the original construction took place during the 13th century, though the walls were further reinforced with towers and bastions over the following 400 years. On average they are 80 feet high and up to 10 feet thick on the seaward side, 20 feet thick on the inland side. ⊠*Placa, Stari Grad* ☏*020/324–641* ⏍*50 Kn* ⏱*May–Sept., daily 8–7:30; Oct.–Apr., daily 10–3.*

Fodor'sChoice
★

❿ Katedrala Velika Gospa *(Cathedral of Our Lady).* The present structure was built in baroque style after the original was destroyed in the 1667 earthquake. The interior contains a number of notable paintings, including a large polyptych above the main altar depicting the *Assumption of Our Lady,* attributed to Titian. The Treasury displays 138 gold and silver reliquaries, including the skull of St. Blaise in the form of a bejeweled Byzantine crown and also an arm and a leg of the saint, likewise encased in decorated gold plating. ⊠*Bunićeva Poljana, Stari Grad* ☏*020/323–459* ⏍*Cathedral free, Treasury 10 Kn* ⏱*Mon.–Sat. 9–5:30, Sun. 11–5:30.*

9 **Knežev Dvor** *(Bishop's Palace).* Originally created in the 15th century but reconstructed several times through the following years, this exquisite building with an arcaded loggia and an internal courtyard shows a combination of late-Gothic and early Renaissance styles. On the ground floor there are large rooms where, in the days of the republic, the Great Council and Senate held their meetings. Over the entrance to the meeting halls a plaque reads: OBLITI PRIVATORUM PUBLICA CURATE (Forget private affairs, and get on with public matters). Upstairs, the rector's living quarters now accommodate the Gradski Muzej (City Museum), containing exhibits that give a picture of life in Dubrovnik from early days until the fall of the republic. ✉*Pred Dvorom 3, Stari Grad* ☎*020/321–497* 💰*35 Kn* 🕙*May–Oct., daily 9–6; Nov.–Apr., daily 9–2.*

13 **Muzej Pravoslavne Crkve** *(Orthodox Church Museum).* Next door to the Orthodox church, this small museum displays religious icons from the Balkan region and Russia, as well as several portraits of eminent early-20th-century Dubrovnik personalities by local artist Vlaho Bukovac. ✉*Od Puca 8, Stari Grad* ☎*020/323–283* 💰*10 Kn* 🕙*May–Oct., daily 9–2; Nov.–Apr., Mon.–Sat. 9–2.*

2 **Placa.** This was once the shallow sea channel separating the island of Laus from the mainland. Although it was filled in during the 12th century, it continued to divide the city socially for several centuries, the nobility living in the area south of Placa and the commoners living on the hillside to the north. Today it forms the venue for the *korzo*, an evening promenade where locals meet to chat, maybe have a drink, and generally size one another up. ✉*Stari Grad.*

11 **Pomorski Muzej** *(Maritime Museum).* Above the aquarium, on the first floor of St. John's Fortress, this museum's exhibits illustrate how rich and powerful Dubrovnik became as one of the world's most important seafaring nations. On display are intricately detailed models of ships as well as engine-room equipment, sailors' uniforms, paintings, and maps. ✉*Damjana Jude 2, Stari Grad* ☎*020/323–904* 💰*35 Kn* 🕙*May–Oct., daily 9–6; Nov.–Apr., Tues.–Sun. 9–2.*

NEED A BREAK? **Buža** (✉*Od Margarita, Stari Grad*) Through a small doorway (signed COLD DRINKS) in the south side of the city walls, off the narrow street of Od Margarita, this informal bar serves cold drinks and coffee at tables arranged on a series of terraces set into the rocks affording stunning views over the open sea.

5 **Sinagoga** *(Synagogue).* This tiny 15th-century synagogue, the second-oldest in Europe (after Prague's) bears testament to Dubrovnik's once thriving Jewish community, made up largely of Jews who were expelled from Spain and Italy during the medieval period. ✉*Žudioska 5, Stari Grad* ☎*020/321–028* 💰*10 Kn* 🕙*Weekdays 10–8.*

1 **Vrata od Pila** *(Pile Gate).* Built in 1537 and combining a Renaissance arch with a wooden drawbridge on chains, this has always been the main entrance to the city walls. A niche above the portal contains a

CLOSE UP

Dubrovnik under Siege

From November 1991 to May 1992 Dubrovnik was intermittently shelled by the Yugoslav army and Serb and Montenegrin irregulars, who were stationed on the rugged hills behind the city. Electricity and water supplies were cut off, and the local population took refuge in basements, surviving on a slowly diminishing quantity of food-stuffs, fuel, and medical supplies. The city's massive medieval fortifications stood up well to the assault, though none of Dubrovnik's main monuments was targeted—apparently the Yugoslav army wanted to capture the city intact. Extensive media coverage whipped up a storm of international criticism over the wanton bombing of this historic city, which effectively turned world opinion against Belgrade and in favor of granting Croatia diplomatic recognition. Once hostilities ceased, the cleanup and rebuilding began. During the second half of the 1990s, money poured in from all over the world for the restoration of the shrapnel-scarred facades and the shattered terra-cotta rooftops. Today, thanks to the work of highly skilled craftsmen, barely any traces of war damage remain.

statue of Sveti Vlah (St. Blaise), the city's patron saint, holding a replica of Dubrovnik in his left hand. From May to October, guards in deep-red period-costume uniforms stand vigilant by the gate through daylight hours, just as they would have done when the city was a republic. ⊠ *Pile, Stari Grad.*

➐ **Vrata od Ploča** *(Ploče Gate).* One of two gates in the town walls, Ploče comprises a stone bridge and wooden drawbridge plus a 15th-century stone arch bearing a statue of Sveti Vlah (St. Blaise). As at Pile Gate, guards in period costume stand vigilant here through the summer season. ⊠ *Ploče, Stari Grad.*

➓ **War Photo Limited.** Shocking but impressive, this modern gallery
Fodor'sChoice devotes two entire floors to war photojournalism. Past exhibitions
★ include images from conflicts in Afghanistan, Iraq, the former Yugoslavia, Israel, Palestine, and Lebanon. Refreshingly impartial by Croatian standards, the message—that war is physically and emotionally destructive whichever side you are on—comes through loudly and clearly. You'll find it in a narrow side street running between Placa and Prijeko. ⊠ *Antuninska 6, Stari Grad* ☎ *020/322–166* ⊕ *www.warphotoltd.com* 🎫 *30 Kn* ⊗ *May and Oct., Tues.–Sat. 10–4, Sun. 10–2; June–Sept., daily 9–9.*

WHERE TO EAT

As elsewhere along the coast, seafood dominates restaurant menus. The narrow, cobbled street Prijeko, which runs parallel to Placa, is packed with touristy restaurants and waiters touting for customers. Less commercial and infinitely more agreeable eateries are scattered throughout the town.

$$$-$$$$ ✕**Proto.** A reliable choice for dinner, Proto is on a side street off Stradun, with tables arranged on a vine-covered, upper-level, open-air terrace. The menu features a good selection of traditional Dalmatian seafood dishes—including oysters from nearby Ston—and barbecued meats, notably succulent steaks. The restaurant dates back to 1886. Recent guests have included U.S. actor Richard Gere, and Irish singer Bono. ✉*Široka 1, Stari Grad* ☎*020/323–234* 🚫*AE, DC, MC, V.*

$$$-$$$$ ✕**Restaurant Atlas Club Nautika.** Probably Dubrovnik's most exclusive restaurant, Nautika lies close to Pile Gate, just outside the city walls. It occupies the former Nautical Academy building, dating from 1881, and has two terraces overlooking the sea. Although some people feel that it is overpriced, it remains a sound choice for business lunches and formal celebrations. The restaurant serves shellfish, lobster, and fresh fish, as well as meat dishes, and has an excellent wine list. ✉*Brsalje 3, Pile* ☎*020/442–526* 🚫*AE, DC, MC, V.*

$$$ ✕**Levanat.** In Lapad, on a seafront walkway offering splendid views over the calm waters of Lapad Bay, Levanat opened in 2002 and quickly established itself as a firm favorite among locals and visitors alike. The menu offers a good selection of Dalmatian cuisine, with an emphasis on seafood. ✉*Šetalište Nika i Meda Pučića 15, Lapad* ☎*020/435–352* 🚫*AE, DC, MC, V* ⊙*Closed mid-Nov.–mid-Mar.*

$$-$$$ ✕**Konoba Ekvinocijo.** In the Old Town, in a quiet residential area close to the cathedral, this highly regarded family-run eatery serves up tasty Croatian favorites, including a delicious lobster soup, freshly caught seafood, locally produced sausages, and charcoal-grilled steaks. Tables and wicker chairs are arranged on a small outdoor terrace, and the service is warm and friendly. In case you were wondering, *ekvinocijo* means equinox. ✉*Ilije Sarake 10, Stari Grad* ☎*020/323–633* 🚫*AE, DC, MC, V* ⊙*Closed mid-Nov.–mid-Mar.*

$$-$$$ ✕**Konoba Penatur.** With outdoor tables next to the Church of St. Blaise, ★ this informal restaurant offers a bargain prix-fixe menu at lunchtime and romantic candlelit dining in the evening. Look out for excellent Croatian seafood specialties such as *salata od hobotnice* (octopus salad), *girice* (small fish deep fried, similar to British whitebait), and *škampi* (scampi). There's also a reasonable choice of vegetarian pasta dishes. ✉*Lučarica 2, Stari Grad* ☎*020/323–700* 🚫*AE, DC, MC, V.*

$$-$$$ ✕**Lokanda Peškarija.** Just outside the town walls—and affording unfor-
Fodor's Choice gettable views over the old harbor—this seafood restaurant is a particularly good value. The seafood on offer is guaranteed fresh each

---

ST. BLAISE

The bearded figure of St. Blaise, Dubrovnik's patron saint, was featured on the Republic's coins and flags. The former Bishop of Sebaste in Turkey, Blaise lost his life in AD 316 during a Roman-led anti-Christian campaign. Also a doctor, he once miraculously saved a child who was choking on a fish bone, and still today, those ailing from throat problems pray to him for healing. He was made Dubrovnik's protector in 972, having appeared to the rector in a dream warning of an imminent Venetian attack and thus saving the city.

7

day, not least because the restaurant stands next door to Dubrovnik's covered fish market. It has a beautifully designed, split-level interior with exposed stone walls and wooden beams, plus romantic outdoor candlelit tables by the water. Definitely not only for tourists, locals love eating here as well, so reservations are recommended, especially for dinner. ⊠*Na Ponti, Stari Grad* ☎*020/324–750* ☐*AE, DC, MC, V* ☻*Closed Jan. and Feb.*

$$–$$$ ✕**Marco Polo.** This favorite haunt of actors and musicians during the Summer Festival is in the Old Town, close to Crkva Sv Vlaha. The minuscule dining room is only big enough for four tables, but there's a summer terrace in the courtyard. Choose from a range of excellent seafood dishes, including shellfish, risottos, and fresh fish. ⊠*Lučarica 6, Stari Grad* ☎*020/323–719* ☐*AE, DC, MC, V* ☻*Closed Nov.–Mar.*

$$–$$$ ✕**Mimosa.** Located between the Old Town and Lapad, Mimosa makes a perfect choice for a light lunch. The menu offers a decent selection of meat, fish, pasta, and vegetarian dishes, with pizza as a cheap option. Outside, you dine at wooden tables and benches on a large, vine-covered terrace. Indoors, the dining room is decorated in minimalist style, in white, red, and black. There's live Dalmatian klapa music on Monday, Wednesday, and Friday evenings. ⊠*Branitelja Dubrovnika 9, Pile* ☎*020/411–157* ☐*AE, DC, MC, V.*

$$–$$$ ✕**Orhan.** With tables on a small quay close to the water's edge, this
★ highly regarded but friendly and easygoing restaurant specializes in seafood, while also offering a range of typical Dalmatian meat dishes. You'll find it just outside Pile Gate, at the foot of Lovrijenac fortress. ⊠*Od Tabakarije 1, Pile* ☎*020/414–183* ☐*AE, DC, MC, V.*

$$–$$$ ✕**Tovjerna Sesame.** Just outside the city walls and close to Pile Gate, this romantic eatery occupies a vaulted, candlelit space with bohemian decor. It's popular with locals, and the menu is adventurous by Dalmatian standards: beef carpaccio with Parmesan, rocket (arugula), and capers; pasta truffle dishes; and a range of beautifully presented, creative salads. It's ideal for a light supper accompanied by a good bottle of wine. ⊠*Dante Alighieria, Pile* ☎*020/412–910* ☐*AE, DC, MC, V.*

$$ ✕**Orsan.** With a pretty, leafy terrace overlooking the Yacht Club Orsan
Fodor'sChoice marina, opposite Gruž Harbor, on the edge of the Lapad Peninsula,
★ this informal, family-run restaurant is known for its reasonably priced, fresh seafood dishes, just as Croatians would eat at home. Firm favorites include *salata od hobotnice* (octopus salad), *svježa morska riba* (fresh fish) and *rozata* (a Dubrovnik desert similar to crème caramel). It's a good restaurant to remember if visiting Dubrovnik in winter, when many of the city's more touristy restaurants are closed. ⊠*Ivana Zajca 2, Lapad* ☎*020/435–933* ☐*AE, DC, MC, V.*

$–$$ ✕**Kamenica.** Overlooking the morning market in the Old Town, Kame-
★ nica remains popular for its fresh oysters and generous platters of *girice* (small fried fish) and *pržene ligne* (fried squid). It's cheap and cheerful, and if you don't like seafood, you can always get a cheese omelet. ⊠*Gundulićeva Poljana 8, Stari Grad* ☎*No phone* ☐*No credit cards* ☻*No dinner Nov.–Mar.*

$–$$ ✕**Mea Culpa.** Within the city walls and open until midnight year-round, Mea Culpa is said to make the best pizza in town. The dining room is a bit cramped, and you may find the music unreasonably loud, but from spring to autumn there are large wooden tables outside on the cobbled street. ✉*Za Rokom 3, Stari Grad* ☏*020/323–430* ▭*No credit cards.*

WHERE TO STAY

There are only two small but extremely desirable hotels within the city walls. The most exclusive establishments line the coastal road east of the center, offering stunning views of the Old Town and the sea, whereas modern hotels with cheaper rooms and decent sports facilities can be found in Lapad, 3 km (2 mi) west of the center. The only way to save money in Dubrovnik is to rent a private room, but, like the hotels, even these can be up to double the price of those elsewhere in Croatia.

$$$$ 🏨**Dubrovnik Palace.** Located in Lapad, this vast but undeniably chic, 10-story design hotel reopened in 2006 following a complete renovation. The rooms are decorated in subtle shades of beige and gray, and all have a sea view and balcony affording stunning sunsets, flat-screen TV, and bathroom stocked with Gharani Štrok toiletries. Facilities include the Wren's Spa & Beauty Centre, an outdoor pool complex, and a dive shop. Pros: chic interior design, excellent sports facilities (including a luxurious spa), seafront location with private beach. Cons: expensive, vast with somewhat impersonal service, feels more like a business than a luxury hotel. ✉*Masarykov put 20, Lapad 20000* ☏*020/430–000* ⊕*www.dubrovnikpalace.hr* ⤴*271 rooms, 37 suites* ♿*In-room: safe, refrigerator, Ethernet. In-hotel: 4 restaurants, room service, bars, tennis court, pools, gym, spa, beachfront, diving, laundry service* ▭*AE, DC, MC, V* ⊙*BP.*

$$$$ 🏨**Hotel Bellevue.** Built into a spectacular rocky cliff overlooking the sea, this design hotel lies between the Old Town and Gruž harbor. Reopened in November 2006, following a total renovation, it now has a smart minimalist look. Guest rooms have wooden floors, modern furnishings, and textiles in warm hues, while the suites have the added luxury of a bathroom with Jacuzzi tub. The hotel has its own beach (accessible by elevator) with sun beds and towels free for hotel guests. The new Spa & Wellness center offers sauna, massage, an indoor pool, Jacuzzi, and a gym. Some guests lament that the hotel restaurants are overpriced and, therefore, often virtually empty. Pros: cliff-top location overlooking the sea, chic interiors, luxurious spa. Cons: expensive, not in Old Town, service rather impersonal

GHARANI ŠTROK

If you stay in the Dubrovnik Palace, Hotel Bellevue, or Hotel Excelsior, your bathroom will be stocked with luxurious Gharani Štrok toiletries. The company is best known for its bohemian dresses, which are much loved by Keira Knightley, Nicole Kidman, and Madonna and sold in top stores around the world. Gharani Štrok was founded in London in 1995 by two friends, Croatian-born Vanja Štrok and Iranian-born Nargess Gharani. Vanja's father, Goran Štrok, is chairman of GS Hotels & Resorts, which owns several prominent Dubrovnik hotels, hence the connection.

and sometimes indifferent. ✉*Pera Čingrije 7, 20000* ☎*020/330–000* ⊕*www.hotel-bellevue.hr* ☞*81 rooms, 12 suites* ♿*In-room: safe, refrigerator, Wi-Fi. In-hotel: 2 restaurants, room service, bars, pool, gym, spa, beachfront, laundry service* ⊟*AE, DC, MC, V* ⦿❘*BP.*

$$$$ 📷 **Hotel Excelsior.** On the coastal road east of the center, this prestigious, modern hotel offers well-furnished rooms with balconies overlooking the sea and Old Town. Each of the luxury suites has a jetted tub. The hotel has excellent sports, health and beauty, and business facilities. Of special note is the Taverna Rustica, a highly regarded restaurant with romantic nighttime views across the water to the city walls; it's popular with residents and nonresidents alike. Pros: seafront location with great views of the Old Town, spacious rooms, lovely restaurant terrace. Cons: big with somewhat impersonal service, modern but slightly lacking in charm, poor sound insulation between neighboring rooms. ✉*Put Frane Supila 12, Ploče 20000* ☎*020/353–300* ⊕*www.hotel-excelsior. hr* ☞*146 rooms, 18 suites* ♿*In-room: refrigerator, dial-up. In-hotel: 2 restaurants, room service, bar, pool, gym, laundry service, public Internet* ⊟*AE, DC, MC, V* ⦿❘*BP.*

$$$$

Fodor's Choice
★

📷 **Pučić Palace.** In the heart of the Old Town, occupying a beautifully restored 18th-century baroque palace, this small luxury boutique hotel offers the sort of aristocratic delights that its location suggests: rooms with dark oak parquet floors and wood-beam ceilings, antique furnishings, and Italian mosaic-tile bathrooms supplied with Bulgari toiletries. Fine wining and dining are also possible here, with the Defne restaurant serving eastern Mediterranean cuisine on a romantic upper-level terrace lined with potted lemon trees. The ground-floor Café Royal is a popular meeting point for morning coffee and pastries, with tables outside on the piazza on warm days. In the evening, head for the adjoining Razonoda wine bar, where you can sample some of Croatia's most sought-after wines and spirits. Pros: located in Old Town, beautifully furnished interior, small and guests receive individual attention from staff. Cons: expensive, often fully booked, lacks many facilities. ✉*Ul od Puča 1, Stari Grad, 20000* ☎*020/326–200* ⊕*www.thepucicpalace. com* ☞*19 rooms* ♿*In-room: safe, refrigerator, dial-up. In-hotel: restaurant, room service, bar, no elevator, laundry service* ⊟*AE, DC, MC, V* ⦿❘*BP.*

$$$$ 📷 **Villa Dubrovnik.** At this writing, the hotel was scheduled to reopen in late summer 2008 following a complete renovation. This romantic retreat lies a 20-minute walk east of the center and comprises a white modernist structure built into the rocks, as well as a series of terraces and a garden coming down to a hideaway cove with a small beach. The rooms are light and airy, and all have balconies and views across the water to Lokrum Island and the Old Town. There are two restaurants with open-air terraces, plus a rooftop lounge affording a stunning vista. The hotel boat offers a water-taxi service to and from the Old Town and the islands of Lokrum and Lopud; airport transfers by private car are available on request. Pros: hillside location with a view of the Old Town, chic design (and new in 2008), sophisticated restaurants and rooftop lounge. Cons: very expensive, 20-minute walk from Old Town. ✉*V Bukovca 6, Ploče 20000* ☎*020/422–933* ⊕*www.villa-dubrovnik.*

br ⟿*56 rooms, 10 suites* ⌂*In-room: refrigerator, dial-up. In-hotel: 2 restaurants, room service, bars, pool, gym, spa, beachfront, public Internet* ▭*AE, DC, MC, V* ⊘*Closed Dec.–Mar.* ❙⊙❙*MAP.*

$$$ ▦**Hotel Stari Grad.** One of only two hotels in the Old Town, this refined and intimate establishment occupies a renovated palace that once belonged to the Drašković family, giving you some idea of how the local aristocracy once lived. The rooms are furnished with reproduction antiques, and in summer breakfast is served on a lovely roof terrace with views over the surrounding buildings. You'll find it in a quiet side street close to Pile Gate. Pros: Old Town location, small and intimate, so guests receive individual attention from staff, breakfast served on wonderful roof terrace. Cons: often fully booked, small bathrooms, parking difficult. ✉*Od Sigurate 4, Stari Grad, 20000* ☎*020/322–244* ⊕*www.hotelstarigrad.com* ⟿*8 rooms* ⌂*In-room: refrigerator, dial-up. In-hotel: bar, no elevator, laundry service* ▭*AE, DC, MC, V* ❙⊙❙*BP.*

$$ ▦**Grand Hotel Park.** This modern hotel in Lapad is surrounded by a green, leafy park and is close to the sea. Rooms are simple, modern, and comfortable, with views of either the sea or gardens; 71 rooms in an annex are more basic but have the advantage of being in a renovated, though older, building. The main restaurant offers live music on an open-air terrace throughout the summer, and there's a good range of sports and business facilities. Maybe a little far from the Old Town for sightseeing enthusiasts (it's 4½ km [3 mi] to the city walls) this hotel is recommended for those on longer stays who want to take things slowly and relax. Pros: good location for swimming on Lapad's beaches, friendly and helpful staff, good sunset views. Cons: distance from Old Town, big and rather impersonal, food somewhat disappointing. ✉*Šetalište Kralja Zvonimira 39, Lapad 20000* ☎*020/434–444* ⊕*www.grandhotel-park.hr* ⟿*156 rooms, 71 annex rooms, 6 suites* ⌂*In-room: refrigerator, dial-up. In-hotel: 2 restaurants, room service, bar, pools, public Internet* ▭*AE, DC, MC, V* ❙⊙❙*BP.*

$$ ▦**Hotel Komodor.** Affording spectacular sunsets views over Lapad Bay, just a five-minute walk from the beach and a 20-minute bus ride to Dubrovnik's Old Town, this midrange hotel offers 63 comfortable rooms, an outdoor pool, and a restaurant with an open-air terrace. It's noted especially for its helpful and friendly staff and generous buffet breakfasts. It's ideal for families with young children as well as couples. Pros: seafront location, friendly and helpful staff, good views of the sunset. Cons: distance from Old Town, small bathrooms, pool area close to busy road. ✉*Masarykov put 5, Lapad 20000* ☎*020/433–500* ⊕*www.hotelimaestralcom* ⟿*63 rooms* ⌂*In-room: refrigerator. In-hotel: restaurant, room service, bar, pool, beachfront, laundry service, public Internet* ▭*AE, DC, MC, V* ⊘*Closed Nov.–Mar.* ❙⊙❙*BP.*

$$ ▦**Hotel Lapad.** Occupying a 19th-century building with a garden and an outdoor pool, Hotel Lapad overlooks Gruž harbor, just a 15-minute walk west of the Old Town, making it a good midrange option. A boat service to nearby beaches is at your disposal. Rooms in the new wing are somewhat more spacious than those in the old wing and, therefore, a little more expensive. The hotel offers good discounts off-season.

7

Pros: near harbor (ideal for early morning ferries), friendly and helpful staff. Cons: distance from Old Town, big and rather impersonal, some guests complain about noisy plumbing. ⊠*Lapadska obala 37, Lapad 20000* ☎*020/432–922* ⊕*www.hotel-lapad.hr* ⬦*194 rooms* ⬥*In-room: refrigerator. In-hotel: restaurant, room service, bar, pool,* ▤*AE, DC, MC, V* ☉*Closed Nov.–Mar.* ⏀*BP.*

$$ **Hotel Zagreb.** Set in a small garden with palms, close to a pleasant pebble beach, this red 19th-century villa is right on the pedestrian-only seafront promenade in Lapad. Renovated in 2005, it offers one of the best low-cost options in Dubrovnik. There's a restaurant with a terrace where breakfast is served, and comfortable air-conditioned rooms with en suite bathrooms, but no extras. There's not even a pool, which is a consideration if you're not into pebbly beaches. A convenient bus stop is nearby if you don't fancy the 4-km (2½-mi) walk to the Old Town. Pros: located on pedestrian-only seafront promenade, close to the beach, breakfast served on pleasant open-air terrace. Cons: distance from Old Town, food rather disappointing. ⊠*Šetalište Kralja Zvonimira 27, Lapad 20000* ☎*020/436–146* ⊕*www.hotels-sumratin. com* ⬦*23 rooms* ⬥*In-hotel: restaurant, room service, bar, no elevator, public Internet* ▤*AE, DC, MC, V* ☉*Closed Nov.–Mar.* ⏀*BP.*

$ **Amoret Apartments.** In the heart of the Old Town, these delightful two-person studio apartments occupy two carefully restored 16th-century stone buildings, one on Restićeva (a narrow street behind the cathedral) and the other on Dinka Ranjine (a narrow street behind the Church of St. Blaise). Each unit consists of a single room, a bathroom, and a full kitchen. All are tastefully furnished with antiques and beds with wrought-iron bedsteads. The owner is an extremely friendly and helpful Croatian lady called Dinka. Pros: located in Old Town, homey and atmospheric rooms with antique furniture, inexpensive by Dubrovnik standards. Cons: often fully booked, rooms can be noisy at night (nearby restaurants and neighbors). ⊠*Restićeva 2, Stari Grad, 20000* ☎*020/324–005* ⊕*www.dubrovnik-amoret.com* ⬦*6 apartments* ⬥*In-room: no phone, kitchen, refrigerator. In-hotel: no elevator* ▤*No credit cards.*

$ **Karmen Apartments.** An excellent budget choice in the Old Town, these homey, light, and airy apartments look directly onto the fishing boats in the old harbor. Each unit has two or three beds, a bathroom, and a kitchen. Expect high ceilings, wooden floors, colorful painted-wood furniture, and handmade bedspreads. It's run by the Van Bloemen family, who arrived here from London in 1972 and founded the Hard Jazz Cafe Troubadour. Former guests include Goran Višnjić, the Croatian-born actor who played ER's Dr. Luka Kovac. You'll find the entrance in a narrow side street between the Rector's Palace and the aquarium. Pros: location in Old Town, homey and atmospheric rooms with bohemian decor, great views of the old harbor. Cons: often fully booked, can be noisy at night (harborside restaurants). ⊠*Bandureva 1, Stari Grad, 20000* ☎*020/323–423* ⊕*www.karmendu.com* ⬦*4 apartments* ⬥*In-room: no phone, kitchen, refrigerator, DVD. In-hotel: no elevator* ▤*No credit cards.*

The Republic of Dubrovnik

As an independent republic from 1358 to 1808, Dubrovnik kept its freedom not through military power, but thanks to diplomatic cunning. Would-be aggressors, including Hungary and the Ottoman Turks, were paid an annual fee in return for peaceful relations, and Dubrovnik avoided involvement in international conflicts between Christians and Muslims, preferring to remain neutral.

The republic's economy was based on shipping and trading goods between Europe and the Middle East, and by the 16th century the republic had consulates in some 50 foreign ports, along with a merchant fleet of 200 ships on the Mediterranean. By this time its territory had also extended to include 120 km (75 mi) of mainland coast (from Neum to the Bay of Kotor) plus the islands of Lastovo and Mljet.

The chief citizen was the Rector, who had to be over 50; he was elected for only a month at a time to share management of the republic's business with the Grand Council (composed of members of the local nobility) and the Senate (a consultative body made up of 45 "wise men," all over the age of 40). Most of the military and naval commands were held by members of the nobility, while lower-ranking soldiers were mercenaries from the regions that are now Germany and the Czech Republic. The increasingly prosperous middle class carried on trade. The Archbishop of Dubrovnik had to be a foreigner (usually an Italian), a law intended to keep politics and religion apart.

Outstandingly sophisticated for its time, Dubrovnik was very conscious of social values: the first pharmacy opened in 1317; the first nursing home was founded in 1347; slave trading was abolished in 1418, and the first orphanage opened in 1432.

NIGHTLIFE & THE ARTS

Restrained through winter, aristocratic Dubrovnik wakes up with a vengeance come summer. Most nightlife takes place under the stars, as bars set up outdoor seating, discos take place by the sea, and even the cinema is open-air. The world-renowned Dubrovnik Summer Festival offers quality theatrical performances and classical-music concerts with international performers. An after-dinner drink at an outdoor table in the Old Town makes a romantic way to round of the evening. Those in search of more lively pursuits should visit one of several chic nightclubs with music and open-air bars, which cater to the city's tanned and glamorous summer visitors.

NIGHTLIFE

BARS **Arsenal** (⌧*Pred Dvorom 1, Stari Grad* ☏*020/321–065*), a trendy wine bar, is adorned with heavy wooden furniture and much red velvet. It occupies the former Arsenal, where Dubrovnik's old-fashioned galleys were once repaired. Most people come here to drink fine wine, enjoy live music, and dance, though there is also an excellent terrace restaurant affording fine views over the harbor if you need something other than liquid sustenance. **Buža** (⌧*Od Margarite bb, Stari Grad* ☏*No phone*), with tables arranged on a series of terraces built into the rocks, overlooks the sea just outside the south-facing city walls. The informal bar makes a romantic venue for an evening drink. Don't expect high style—drinks are served in plastic cups—but the mellow music, crashing waves, and nighttime candles make it a memorable experience. Open daily until 3 AM. **Hard Jazz Cafe Troubadour** (⊠ *Bunićeva Poljana 2, Stari Grad* ☎ *020/323–476*) is a long-standing Dubrovnik institution with occasional impromptu jazz concerts. Well-worn antiques and memorabilia fill the cozy, candlelit interior, and through summer tables spill outside onto the piazza. **Hemingway** (⊠ *Pred Dvoram, Stari Grad* ☎ *no phone*) is a see-and-be-seen cocktail bar with outdoor tables and cushioned wicker chairs, perfect for people-watching.

DANCE CLUBS **Eastwest Beach Club** (⊠ *Frana Supila, Banje Beach* ☎ *020/412–220*) is one of several chic establishments where you might spot well-known actors and sports celebrities. Eastwest combines a daytime café overlooking a well-equipped pebble beach and a nighttime restaurant with an Italian-inspired menu and a cocktail bar and rooftop VIP open-air lounge open until 5 AM. You'll find it a five-minute walk east of the Old Town. **Labarint** (⊠ *Dominika 2, Stari Grad* ☎ *020/322–222*) opened in 2003 and is still attracting a moneyed, fortysomething clientele. The club combines a late-night terrace bar with live music and views over the old harbor, a black-and-red nightclub with live cabaret and jazz, and a smart restaurant in a cozy, ancient-walled dining space.

THE ARTS

Dubrovnik's cultural highlight is the annual **Dubrovnik Summer Festival** (⌂ *Poljana P Miličevića 1* ☎ *020/323–400* ⊕ *www.dubrovnik-festival. hr*), which runs from early July to late August. The world-renowned festival includes a variety of open-air classical concerts and theatrical performances, notably Shakespeare's *Hamlet*, at various venues within the city walls. **Kino Slavica** (⊠ *Dr. A. Starčevića 42, Pile*) is an open-air summer cinema in a walled garden between the Old Town and Lapad. Predominantly English-language films are shown in their original versions with subtitles. The six-day **Libertas Film Festival** (⊕ *www. libertasfilmfestival.com*) takes place each year in the Old Town from late June into early July. Guests have included actors Woody Harrelson and Owen Wilson.

SPORTS & THE OUTDOORS

BEACHES

The more upmarket hotels, such as the Excelsior and Villa Dubrovnik, have their own beaches that are exclusively for the use of hotel guests. The most natural and peaceful beaches lie on the tiny island of **Lokrum**, a short distance south of the Old Town. Through high season boats leave from the Old Harbor, ferrying visitors back and forth from morning to early evening. Ferries run every half hour from 9 AM to 7:30 PM. Tickets cost 35 Kn.

The **Eastwest Beach Club** (⊠ *Frana Supila, Banje Beach* ☎ *020/412–220*), just a short distance from Ploče Gate, is a fashionable spot with a small pebble beach complete with chaise longues and parasols, waterskiing and jet-skiing facilities, and a chic café.

SAILING

The 450-berth **ACI marina** (⊠*Mokošica* ☎*020/455–020*) is 2 nautical mi from Gruž harbor and 6 km (3½ mi) from the city walls. The marina is open year-round, and a number of charter companies are based there.

SEA KAYAKING

Fodor'sChoice ★ Besides introductory half-day sea-kayaking tours from Dubrovnik to Lokrum, **Adriatic Kayak Tours** (⊠*Zrnsko Frankopanska 6, Ploče* ☎*020/312–770* ⊕*www.adriatickayaktours.com*) offers a one-week island-hopping itinerary by kayak around the Elafiti Islands, as well as cycling and snorkeling trips.

SHOPPING

Despite its role as an important tourist destination, Dubrovnik offers little in the way of shopping or souvenir hunting. If you're in search of gifts, your best bet is a bottle of good Dalmatian wine or *rakija*.

Croata (⊠*Put Frane Supila 12, Ploče* ☎*020/353–279*), a small boutique in the Hotel Excelsior, specializes in "original Croatian ties" in presentation boxes. **Dubrovačka Kuća** (⊠*Svetog Dominika, Stari Grad* ☎*020/322–092*), a tastefully decorated wineshop, stocks a fine selection of regional Croatian wines, *rakija,* olive oil, and truffle products, plus works of art by contemporary artists on the upper two levels; it's close to Ploče Gate. **Ronchi** (⊠*Lučarica 2, Stari Grad* ☎*020/323–699*), a long-standing Dubrovnik institution, is a delightful hat shop dating back to 1858, when the present owner's great-great-grandfather arrived here from Milan, Italy. Expect an amusing array of stylish, if somewhat eccentric, reasonably priced handmade bonnets.

LOPUD

Lopud is 7 nautical mi northwest of Dubrovnik by ferry.

Thirteen tiny islets make up the Elafiti Islands, which are less than a one-hour ferry ride from Dubrovnik. Historically, they have always been under Dubrovnik's control, first when monks from the Franciscan monastery used to visit the islands to gather herbs for use in their pharmacy; later, the local aristocracy kept summer villas here. Today there are still no cars on the islands, and only the three larger ones—Koločep, Lopud, and Šipan—are inhabited, with a total population of less than 900. There are regular ferry services between Dubrovnik and Koločep, Lopud, and Šipan. Any of the three can be comfortably visited as a day trip, but if you intend to stay a night, Lopud is best equipped to deal with visitors. In fact, an increasing number of visitors who wish to escape the chaos of urban life choose to base themselves on Lopud and visit Dubrovnik from the island, rather than vice versa. With a year-round population of approximately 300, tiny Lopud has just one settlement, Lopud Town, made up of old stone houses built around a sheltered bay, plus a handful of seasonal eateries, a large 1970s hotel, several small family-run hotels occupying restored villas, and a tourist office, which is open only from May through October. From town, a concrete footpath leads through pinewoods and herb-scented olive groves: follow the signs, and in 15 minutes you will have crossed the island to arrive at Šunj, a glorious 1-km-long (½-mi-long) sand beach curving around a southeast-facing cove.

WHERE TO EAT

$$$–$$$$ ✕**Restoran Obala.** This surprisingly smart eatery offers fine dining on the seafront promenade, with idyllic sunset views across the bay and waiters dressed in traditional Dalmatian waistcoats. The house specialty is *školjke na buzaru* (mixed shellfish cooked in wine and garlic), and if you're lucky you'll also be treated to live music. ⊠ *Obala Iva Kuljevana* 🕾 *020/759–170* 🖃 *AE, DC, MC, V* ⊗ *Closed Nov.–Mar.*

$$ ✕**Konoba Peggy.** Guests at this informal konoba sit at heavy wooden tables and benches on a pretty terrace with lemon trees and a view onto Lopud's elegant church bell tower. The menu features typical Dalmatian fare, including fresh fish which the owner cooks over an open fire. You'll find it in a narrow side street above the ferry landing. ⊠ *Narikla 22* 🕾 *020/759–036* 🖃 *No credit cards* ⊗ *Closed Nov.–Mar.*

WHERE TO STAY

$$ 🏨 **Hotel Villa Vilina.** This old stone villa, with palms out front overlooking the sea, has been carefully restored as a boutique hotel with a small pool. The restaurant serves dishes made from homegrown produce. Rooms with a sea view are slightly more expensive, but worth it. Pros: traffic-free island with regular ferries to Dubrovnik, location in a raised garden overlooking the harbor, breakfast and dinner served on lovely outdoor terrace. Cons: often fully booked, far from urban glamour (no nightlife, shopping). ⊠ *Obala Iva Kuljevana 5, 20222* 🕾 *020/759–333* ⊕ *www.villa-vilina.hr* 🖅 *14 rooms, 3 suites* ♿ *In-room: refrigerator. In-hotel: restaurant, room service, pool, no elevator* 🖃 *AE, DC, MC, V* ⊗ *Closed Nov.–Apr.* ⑩*BP.*

$ 🏨 **Hotel Glavović.** Lopud's first hotel when it opened in 1927, Hotel Glavovic was last renovated in 2004. The rooms are very basic and rather lacking in character, but the restaurant has a lovely seaside terrace. It's recommended for those wishing to escape the hustle and bustle of modern-day life, not for those looking for full resort comforts. Pros: traffic-free island with regular ferries to Dubrovnik, location overlooking the harbor. Cons: often fully booked, far from urban glamour, rooms rather basic. ⊠ *Obala Iva Kuljevana, 20222* 🕾 *020/759–359* ⊕ *www.hotel-glavovic.hr* 🖅 *12 rooms, 2 suites* ♿ *In-room: dial-up. In-hotel: restaurant, room service, no elevator* 🖃 *No credit cards* ⊗ *Closed Nov.–Apr.* ⑩*BP.*

$ 🏨 **La Villa.** In a 19th-century villa with romantic gardens overlooking Lopud Bay, this small hotel is run by a friendly young Croatian couple. The six guest rooms have minimalist modern furniture and primary-colored fabrics, mosaic-tile bathrooms, and either look onto the open sea or the back garden, which is planted with a giant magnolia tree, orange trees, and lavender bushes. Pros: traffic-free island with regular ferries to Dubrovnik, energetic and friendly management, simple but tasteful modern decor. Cons: often fully booked, far from urban glamour, no restaurant or bar. ⊠ *Obala Iva Kuljevana 33, 20222* 🕾 *020/759–259* ⊕ *www.lavilla.com.hr* ⇆ *6 rooms* ⚲ *In-room: no phone, refrigerator, no TV. In-hotel: no elevator, public Internet* ⊟ *No credit cards* ☾ *Closed Dec.–Mar.* ⏐◎⏐ *BP.*

CAVTAT

17 km (10½ mi) southeast of Dubrovnik.

Founded by the ancient Greeks as Epidauros, then taken by the Romans and renamed Epidaurum, the original settlement on the site of Cavtat was subsequently destroyed by tribes of Avars and Slavs in the early 7th century. It was the Romans who fled Epidaurum who founded Dubrovnik.

Today's Cavtat, which developed during the 15th century under the Republic of Dubrovnik, is an easygoing fishing town and small-scale seaside resort. The medieval stone buildings of the Old Town occupy a small peninsula with a natural bay to each side. A palm-lined seaside promenade with open-air cafés and restaurants curves around the main bay, while the second bay is overlooked by a beach backed by several socialist-era hotels.

Cavtat can be visited as a half-day trip from Dubrovnik. The easiest way to get there is by bus. Much more fun, but also more expensive, is a taxi-boat ride along the coast from Dubrovnik's Old Harbor (7 nautical mi); the journey time is approximately one hour.

In the cemetery, on the highest point of a pine-scented peninsula, **Mauzolej Obitelji Račić** *(Račić Mausoleum)* was created by Croatian sculptor Ivan Meštrović for the Račić family in 1921. Made from white marble and capped with a cupola, it is octagonal in plan, and the main entrance is guarded by two art nouveau caryatids. It was closed for restoration in summer 2007, but can still be visited upon request. ⊠ *Rat* 🕾 *020/478–646* 💳 *5 Kn* ☾ *By appointment only.*

The former home of local artist Vlaho Bukovac (1855–1922) has been renovated to become **Galerija Vlaho Bukovac** *(Vlaho Bukovac Gallery)*, which provides a space for contemporary art exhibitions on the ground floor. Upstairs, around 30 of Bukovac's oil paintings, tracing the periods he spent in Paris, Prague, and Cavtat, are on display in his former studio, along with pieces of period furniture. ⊠ *Bukovćeva* 🕾 *020/478–646* 💳 *20 Kn* ☾ *Tues.–Sat. 9–1 and 2–5; Sun. 2–5.*

WHERE TO EAT

$$$–$$$$ ✕ **Leut.** Considered by many to be the best restaurant in Cavtat, Leut has an open-air terrace on the seafront promenade, with outdoor heaters so you can still eat out in winter. Favorite dishes include a delicious *rižot od škampi* (scampi cream risotto) and the local sweet specialty, *dubrovačka rožata* (Dubrovnik crème caramel). ✉ *Trumbićev put 11* ☎ *020/478–477* ▭ *AE, DC, MC, V.*

$$–$$$ ✕ **Taverna Galija.** Barbecued fish tops the bill here, along with seafood risotto and pasta dishes, colorful salads, and a welcome but limited choice of vegetarian platters. You'll find it in a narrow alleyway leading uphill from the harbor, close to Hotel Supetar. ✉ *Vuličevićeva 1* ☎ *020/478–566* ▭ *AE, DC, MC, V* ⏲ *Closed Nov.–Mar.*

WHERE TO STAY

$$$–$$$$ **Hotel Croatia.** Occupying its own rocky, pine-studded peninsula, just a 10-minute walk west of the center, this vast 1970s hotel offers modern, luxurious rooms decorated in pastel shades, plus excellent sports facilities including three seawater pools and two beaches equipped with sun beds and umbrellas. Pros: good sports facilities including private beach, some (but not all) rooms have fine sea views. Cons: modern concrete building slightly lacking in atmosphere, large with somewhat impersonal service, food rather disappointing. ✉ *Frankopanska 10, 20210* ☎ *020/475–555* 🌐 *www.hoteli-croatia.hr* *480 rooms, 7 suites* *In-room: safe, refrigerator, dial-up. In-hotel: 5 restaurants, room service, bars, pool, gym, spa, beachfront, public Internet* ▭ *AE, DC, MC, V* ⏲ *Closed mid-Nov.–mid-Mar.* 🍽 *BP.*

$$$ **Villa Pattiera.** This family-run boutique hotel on the seafront promenade in the center of Cavtat is a little gem. The 12 rooms all have wooden floors and are decorated in tones of beige, rust, peach, and salmon. Most rooms have balconies; the standard rooms look onto a courtyard garden out back (and are therefore slightly quieter), while the deluxe and superior rooms afford sea views. Breakfast is served in the adjoining restaurant Dalmacija, a highly regarded eatery popular with residents and nonresidents alike. Pros: location on the seafront promenade in the Old Town, friendly and helpful staff, excellent breakfast served on pleasant terrace. Cons: often fully booked, front rooms can be noisy. ✉ *Trumbićev put 9, 20210* ☎ *020/478–800* 🌐 *www.villa-pattiera.hr* *12 rooms* *In-room: refrigerator, Ethernet. In-hotel: restaurant, room service, no elevator, some pets allowed* ▭ *AE, DC, MC, V* ⏲ *Closed mid-Nov.–mid-Mar.* 🍽 *BP.*

$$ **Hotel Supetar.** On the seafront promenade overlooking the harbor, this old stone building has been renovated to provide basic but comfortable rooms, and an upper-level restaurant with a terrace where breakfast is served through summer. Pros: location, on the seafront promenade in the Old Town, front rooms have good views of harbor, friendly staff gives guests individual attention. Cons: front rooms can be noisy, rooms are basic and rather small, decor needs updating. ✉ *Dr Ante Starčević 27, 20210* ☎ *020/479–833* 🌐 *www.hoteli-croatia.hr* *28 rooms* *In-hotel: restaurant, no elevator* ▭ *AE, DC, MC, V* ⏲ *Closed Nov.–Mar.* 🍽 *BP.*

SPORTS & THE OUTDOORS

The best beaches lie east of the center, overlooking **Uvala Tiha** (Tiha Bay) where most of the large modern hotels are located.

The **ANA Sailing School** (✉ *Cavtat* ☎*051/711–814* ⊕*www.sailing-ana. hr*), which has its head office in Rijeka and its main base on the island of Murter near Šibenik, offers one-week sailing courses at various levels in Cavtat through summer. If you are interested in scuba diving, **Diving Centre Cavtat** (✉*Frankopanska bb, Cavtat* ☎*020/478–365* ⊕*www. divingcentercavtat.hr*) organizes certification and diving trips.

TRSTENO

24 km (15 mi) northwest of Dubrovnik.

A small village on the coastal road between Split and Dubrovnik (E65), Trsteno, an otherwise insignificant place, has been put on the map by its arboretum. There's nowhere particularly memorable to eat in the village, but the small Trsteno café, which lies to the right of the arboretum's main entrance, has tables in the garden making a pleasant setting for coffee or a cold drink.

Within the grounds of a small Renaissance villa, **Trsteno Arboretum** was set up during the 16th century by the Gucetić family. Laid out on a geometric plan, it is filled with exotic trees and shrubs grown from seeds and saplings collected by local sailors on distant voyages. The site itself is breathtaking, the grounds running down toward a cliff over-looking the sea. The baroque fountain of Neptune and two nymphs dates from 1736. The best time to visit is spring or fall, when the leaves are changing color. ✉*Magistrala Trsteno* ☎*020/751–019* ☑*15 Kn* ⊙*May–Oct., daily 8–8; Nov.–Apr., daily 8–3.*

STON

54 km (34 mi) northwest of Dubrovnik; 67 km (42 mi) plus 2 nautical mi from Korčula.

Today Ston is best known for its fresh oysters and mussels, grown in Mali Ston Channel and served in a handful of year-round waterside restaurants in Mali Ston. Historically, the town dates back to 1333, when it was founded by the Republic of Dubrovnik. It's made up of two separate settlements, Ston (on the main Dubrovnik–Orebić road) and Mali Ston (just off the main road), which were each individually fortified; a system of defensive walls was then built to connect the two, effectively controlling land access onto the peninsula. Dubrovnik's chief interest in Ston was its salt pans, out of which the republic made a considerable profit. Of the original 5½ km (3 mi) of walls, 3 km (2 mi) remain intact. Begin your visit in Ston, then follow the walls on foot to arrive in Mali Ston, about 15 minutes away on foot.

WHERE TO EAT

$$$–$$$$ ✕ **Bota.** Occupying a 14th-century salt warehouse, Bota is known for its menu of outstanding, locally caught seafood. If raw oysters make you squeamish, try the *pohane oštrige* (oysters deep-fried in bread crumbs). Also look out for the extraordinary *stonski makaruli,* a pudding made from pasta, nuts, sugar, and cinnamon, unique to Ston but said to have originated in Spain. ⊠ *Mali Ston* ☎ *020/754–482* ⊟ *AE, DC, MC, V.*

$$$–$$$$ ✕ **Kapitanova Kuća.** Known throughout Croatia, the name of this res-
★   taurant is synonymous with Ston and fresh oysters. Most people come here exclusively to eat shellfish grown in Mali Ston Channel, but you'll also find a limited choice of meat dishes. The owner and cook, Lidija Kralj, has been presented a cooking award by Croatian national television. The Kralj family also runs the nearby Hotel Ostrea. ⊠ *Mali Ston* ☎ *020/754–264* ⊟ *AE, DC, MC, V.*

WHERE TO STAY

$$ 🏨 **Hotel Ostrea.** A former mill, this old stone building has been renovated to make a small upscale hotel complete with wood floors and antique furniture. There's a ground-floor restaurant with a terrace shaded by awnings, where breakfast is served through summer. It stays open all year. Pros: location overlooking the sea in the Old Town, atmospheric homey rooms are furnished with antiques, excellent seafood restaurants nearby. Cons: often fully booked, no elevator (some guests might have problems with the stairs). ⊠ *Mali Ston, 20230* ☎ *020/754–555* ⊕ *www.ostrea.hr* ↴ *9 rooms, 1 suite* ⅙ *In-room: refrigerator. In-hotel: restaurant, room service, no elevator* ⊟ *AE, DC, MC, V* ⊠|*BP.*

SPORTS & THE OUTDOORS

The best beach for swimming lies in **Prapratna Uvala** (Prapratna Bay), 3 km (2 mi) south of Ston.

OREBIĆ

Orebić is 110 km (69 mi) northwest of Dubrovnik and 2 nautical mi northeast of Korčula.

Backed by the rocky heights of Sveti Ilija (3,153 feet), Orebić straggles along the coast, facing across a narrow sea channel to the island of Korčula. Historically, the town spent several centuries under the Republic of Dubrovnik, supplying many able seamen to the republic's merchant navy. From 1865 to 1887 the town even had its own shipping company: today you can see a string of villas and their gardens overlooking the coastal promenade, built by wealthy local sea captains. Today tourism is the chief source of income. Attractions include a decent sand beach, a delightful hillside monastery, and the proximity of the Pelješac Peninsula's vineyards, which produce highly esteemed red wines. A regular ferry service links Orebić to Korčula, with approximately 10 crossings per day through peak season; journey time is 20 minutes. Visitors on a tight budget often opt to stay in Orebić and visit Korčula, rather than vice versa, as the former is notably cheaper.

A 20-minute walk along a pleasant country road that winds its way up through pinewoods brings you to the delightful 15th-century hillside **Franjevački samostan** *(Franciscan Monastery)*, perched 492 feet above sea level. The view across the sea channel to the island of Korčula is most impressive, and the view, in fact, explains the monastery's prime location. During the days of the Republic of Dubrovnik, Pelješac was under Dubrovnik's control, while Korčula was ruled by her archrival, Venice. From this privileged vantage point, the Franciscan monks would spy upon their island neighbors, under strict orders to send a messenger to Dubrovnik if trouble looked likely. In its heyday, the monastery was home to twenty-some monks; now only two remain. However, it is a most welcoming retreat, with a lovely cloister and a fascinating museum, displaying scale models of the ships that local sea captains sailed across the oceans, and an array of votive pictures dedicated to the Virgin, commissioned and donated by sailors who had been saved from trouble on the high seas. Before leaving, check out the cemetery, where gray marble tombstones shaded by cypress trees mark the final resting places of many a local seafarer. ⊠ *Orebić* ☎ *020/713–075* ⊠ *15 Kn* ⊙ *Mon.–Sat. 9–noon and 4–7, Sun. 4–7.*

WHERE TO EAT

$$–$$$ ✕ **Mlinica.** Set in a garden, with a footpath running down to the seafront, this old stone building was formerly an olive mill. The flagstone floor and a wooden beamed ceiling have been kept, and wooden tables and benches have also been added to create a rustic eatery serving delicious octopus and lamb dishes prepared under a *peka* (a metal dome used for slow cooking over embers). It's open from May through October for dinner only. ⊠ *Štalište Kneza Domagoja* ☎ *020/713–886* ⊟ *AE, DC, MC, V* ⊙ *Closed Nov.–Apr. No lunch.*

$$–$$$ ✕ **Pelješki Dvor.** Heavy wooden furniture fills a series of small, interconnected dining rooms at this informal restaurant, recommended for barbecued meat and fish dishes. There's also a sunny, walled garden with outdoor tables. ⊠ *Obala Pomoraca 28* ☎ *020/713–329* ⊟ *AE, DC, MC, V* ⊙ *Closed Nov.–Mar.*

WHERE TO STAY

$$ 🏨 **Grand Hotel Orebić.** Formerly known as the Hotel Rathaneum, this 1970s socialist-era hotel reopened in May 2007 following total renovation. Overlooking the sea and backed by pinewoods, it lies a 10-minute walk along the coastal path from town. The rooms are smartly furnished and have dark blue carpets and beige bedspreads and curtains; most have balconies and a sea view. Sports options include bicycles, canoes, and surfboards for rent. There's a small beach out front. Pros: seafront location with views across channel to Korčula, refurbished for 2007 so everything is new. Cons: big and rather impersonal, food

rather disappointing, small bathrooms. ⊠*Kralja Petra Krešimira IV 107, 20250* ☎*020/798–000* ⊕*www.grandhotelorebic.com* ➩*203 rooms* ⚕*In-room: safe, refrigerator. In-hotel: restaurant, room service, bar, pool, gym, beachfront, water sports, bicycles, public Internet* ☰*AE, DC, MC, V* ☉*Closed Nov.–Mar.* ⍭❘*BP.*

$ ⍰**Hotel Orsan.** A pleasant 15-minute walk along the coastal path from the center of town brings you to this 1970s building with terraced grounds filled with palms, cypresses, and a pool, which also fronts a pebble beach. All rooms have balconies, looking onto either the sea or the park. Pros: seafront location with small beach, outdoor pool. Cons: often fully booked, popular with large tour groups. ⊠*Kralja Petra Krešimira IV 119, 20250* ☎*020/713–193* ⊕*www.orebic-htp. hr* ➩*94 rooms, 3 suites* ⚕*In-room: refrigerator. In-hotel: restaurant, room service, bar, pool, beachfront* ☰*AE, DC, MC, V* ☉*Closed Nov.– Mar.* ⍭❘*BP.*

SPORTS & THE OUTDOORS

BEACHES

Orebić's best beach, **Trstenica** is a 1½-km (1-mi) stretch of sand and pebble lying on the east side of the island. Through summer it is equipped with showers, sun beds, and umbrellas for hire, and a snack bar.

DIVING

Diving instruction and dive trips are available from **Adriatic** (⊠*Mokalo 6* ☎*020/714–328* ⊕*www.adriatic-mikulic.com*), which lies a 15-minute drive east of Orebić. It's open from early May through late October.

WINDSURFING

The Korčula Channel, between Pelješac and the island of Korčula, offers perfect conditions for windsurfing. You can receive instruction and rent boards from **Perna Centar Surf & Kite** (⊠*Orebić* ☎*098/395– 807* ⊕*www.perna-surf.com*) from early May through late October.

WINE TASTING

Several family-run vineyards and wine cellars in Orebič are open to the public for wine tasting and purchases. Tasting sessions usually include a selection of three or four different wines and maybe some rakija, and are accompanied by bread and cheese. Sessions last between 30 minutes and 1 hour. You need private transport to reach the vineyards, and it is best to call one day in advance, as vineyards are often busy with large tour groups. **Bartulović Vina** (⊠*Prizdrina* ✛*13 km [8 mi] southeast of Orebić* ☎*020/742–346*) is a friendly, family-run vineyard especially popular with visitors thanks to its authentic Dalmatian konoba with exposed stone walls and rustic wooden tables and benches. It's the best choice if you want to combine wine tasting with a full-blown meal, as the proprietors will prepare lunch or dinner if you call one day in advance. If you do not opt for a full meal, your wine-tasting session will be accompanied by homemade bread, *pršut*, sheeps' cheese, and olives. The Bartulović family has been making wine on Pelješac for some 470 years, and they now produce around 25,000 bottles per year. As everywhere on Pelješac, red predominates, but this vineyard is unique in that it also produces small quantities of rosé. **Matuško Vina** (✉ *Potomje* ⚓*15 km [9 mi] southeast of Orebić* ☎*020/742–393*) has a recently built a shop where visitors can taste and buy wines. On the shelves you will find Dingač (top-quality red wine), Plavac Mali (quality red wine), Rukatac (quality dry white wine from Korčula), and Stolno Vino (red and white table wines). The shop is open daily (summer 7 AM–8 PM; winter 7 AM–5 PM). A typical tasting session consists of two red wines (Plavac and Dingać), plus prošek (a sweet wine similar to sherry), loza (rakija made from grapes), and višnjevača (rakija made from cherries), accompanied by bread and cheese.

KORČULA

Korčula island is 49 nautical mi northwest of Dubrovnik and 57 nautical mi southeast of Split by ferry.

Southern Dalmatia's largest, most sophisticated, and most visited island, Korčula was known to the ancient Greeks, who named it *Kerkyra Melaina,* or "Black Corfu." Between the 10th and 18th centuries it spent several periods under Venetian rule, much to the frustration of Dubrovnik, which considered the Italian city-state its archrival. Today most Croatians know it for its traditional sword dances and its excellent white wines. **Korčula** is also the name of the capital, which is near the island's eastern tip. At first view, it seems like a much smaller version of Dubrovnik: the same high walls, the circular corner fortresses, and the church tower projecting from within an expanse of red roofs. The main difference lies in the town plan, as narrow side streets run off the main thoroughfare at odd angles to form a herringbone pattern, preventing cold winter winds from whistling unimpeded through town. The eight centuries under Venetian rule bequeathed the town a treasure trove of Gothic and Renaissance churches, palaces, and piazzas, all built from fine local stone, upon which the island's early wealth was based. Korčula's main claim to fame, though one still disputed by historians, is that it was the birthplace of Marco Polo (1254–1324). The center is small and compact and can be explored in an hour. The most impressive way to arrive in Korčula Town is by Jadrolinija coastal ferry from Dubrovnik, which stops here en route to Rijeka. Less pleasurable but faster is the daily bus service connecting Dubrovnik and Korčula Town, which follows the regional road along Pelješac Peninsula, then boards a ferry at Orebić for a short crossing to Korčula. Alternatively, the island is also served by the port of Vela Luka, close to its western tip, with daily ferry and catamaran services running between Split (Central Dalmatia) and the island of Lastovo, stopping at Vela Luka en route. From Vela Luka, a bus runs the length of the island to Korčula Town.

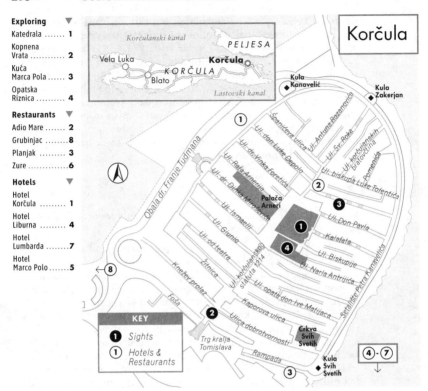

WHAT TO SEE

❶ **Katedrala** *(Cathedral).* On the main square, the splendid Gothic-Renaissance cathedral is built from a wheat-colored stone that turns pale gold in sunlight, amber at sunset. Enter through the beautifully carved Romanesque main portal, which is guarded by Adam and Eve standing upon twin lions. Inside, check out the elegant 15th-century ciborium; within, two paintings are attributed to the Venetian master Tintoretto. ✉*Trg Sv Marka* 🎫*Free* 🕑*May–Oct., daily 9–3 and 5–8; Nov.–Apr., by appointment.*

❷ **Kopnena Vrata** *(Land Gate).* The main entrance into the Old Town is topped by the 15th-century Revelin Tower, housing an exhibition connected with the *Moreška* sword dance, and offering panoramic views over the Old Town. ✉*Kopnena Vrata* 🎫*15 Kn* 🕑*July and Aug., daily 9–9; May, June, Sept., and Oct., daily 9–7; Nov.–Apr., by appointment only.*

❸ **Kuća Marca Pola** *(Marco Polo House).* A couple of blocks east of the main square is the place where the legendary 13th-century discoverer is said to have been born, when Korčula was part of the Venetian Empire. At present only the tower is open, with a modest exhibition about Polo's life on the first floor and a belvedere up top offering panoramic views. There are plans to restore the entire house and garden to form an educational museum, though this project is unlikely to be completed before summer 2009. ⊠ *Ul Marka Pola* ⌨*15 Kn* ⊙*July and Aug., daily 9–9; May, June, Sept., and Oct., daily 9–7; Nov.–Apr., by appointment only.*

❹ **Opatska Riznica** *(Abbot's Treasury).* Next to the cathedral, the treasury museum occupies the 17th-century Renaissance bishop's palace. This collection of sacred art includes Italian and Croatian Renaissance paintings, the most precious being a 15th-centruy triptych, *Our Lady with Saints,* by the Dalmatian master Blaž Jurjev Trogiranin, plus gold and silver ecclesiastical artifacts and ceremonial vestments. ⊠*Trg Sv Marka* ⌨*15 Kn* ⊙*May–Oct., daily 9–3 and 5–8; Nov.–Apr., by appointment only.*

WHERE TO EAT

$$-$$$$ ✕**Adio Mare.** A long-standing favorite with locals and visitors alike,
Fodor'sChoice Adio Mare occupies a Gothic-Renaissance building in the Old Town,
★ close to Kuća Marca Pola. There's a high-ceiling dining room as well as an open-plan kitchen, so you can watch the cooks while they work. The menu has not changed since the restaurant opened in 1974: expect Dalmatian classics such as *pašta-fažol* (beans with pasta) and *pašticada* (beef stewed in wine and prunes), as well as fresh fish and seafood. The local wine, *pošip,* is excellent. This restaurant is particularly popular, so reservations are strongly recommended, especially in August. ⊠*Sv. Roka 2* ☎*020/711–253* ⊟*AE, DC, MC, V* ⊙*Closed Nov.–Mar. No lunch.*

$$-$$$ ✕**Zure.** In the village of Lumbarda, this friendly, family-run eatery offers a delicious selection of authentic Dalmatian seafood dishes served at wooden tables in a walled garden. There's no fixed menu; what's on offer varies depending on the day's catch. But you can expect goodies such as octopus stew and lobster with spaghetti. Be sure to round off with a glass of homemade *šipak* (pomegranate) rakija. ⊠*Lumbarda 239* ☎*020/712–008* ⊟*No credit cards* ⊙*Closed Jan.–Mar., but may open on request.*

$$ ✕**Planjak.** This down-to-earth eatery harks back to the former socialist era. Expect hearty Balkan home cooking such as *sarma* (cabbage leaves stuffed with rice and meat) and *gulaš* (goulash). Locals tend to sit inside, while visitors eat out on the terrace. You'll find it on a small piazza, one block back from the ferry landing. It's open year-round. ⊠*Plokata 19 Travanja 1914* ☎*020/711–015* ⊟*AE, DC, MC, V.*

$-$$ ✕**Grubinjac.** On the hill above Korčula Town, on the road to Žrnovo, this rustic eatery occupies an old-fashioned stone farmhouse. Guests tuck into local specialties such as Dalmatian *pršut* (prosciutto), cheeses, and homemade wine on a terrace surrounded by olive trees. Keen walkers might hike up from Korčula Town. ⊠*Grubinjac bb* ☎*020/711–410* ⊟*No credit cards* ⊙*Closed Oct.–May., but may open on request.*

WHERE TO STAY

$$$ 🖼**Hotel Marco Polo.** This hotel reopened in summer 2007 following a renovation and the addition of a wellness center and an outdoor pool. The low-rise, 1970s-built Marco Polo is now Korčula's most luxurious hotel. Its 94 rooms have dark blue carpets, cream bedcovers and upholstery, and orange curtains, and most afford sea views. It stays open year-round. Pros: seafront location with small beach, refurbished in 2007 so everything is new, good sports facilities. Cons: not in Old Town, modern building slightly lacking in atmosphere, food slightly disappointing. *⊠Korčula bb, 20260* 🕾*020/726–100* ⊕*www.korcula-hotels.com* ⊠*94 rooms* ⌂*In-room: safe, refrigerator. In-hotel: 2 restaurants, bar, pools, gym, spa, beachfront, water sports, bicycles* ▤*AE, DC, MC, V* ⦿*BP.*

$$ 🖼**Hotel Korčula.** Built in 1871, when the area was a part of Austria-Hungary, the building was converted to become the island's first hotel in 1912. Exuding old-fashioned charm, it offers a delightful seafront café terrace, ideal for watching the sunset over the water, but no other extras. It's the only hotel in the Old Town; all the others are a short distance east of the center. Pros: best location of all Korčula's hotels (on the seafront in the Old Town), pleasant terrace overlooking sea, attractive older building. Cons: basic and decor very dated, front rooms can be noisy (restaurant and ferry landing), limited facilities. *⊠Obala Dr Franje Tuđmana 5, 20260* 🕾*020/711–078* ⊕*www.korcula-hotels. com* ⊠*20 rooms, 4 suites* ⌂*In-room: no a/c. In-hotel: restaurant, room service, no elevator* ▤*AE, DC, MC, V* ⦿*BP.*

$$ 🖼**Hotel Liburna.** On a small peninsula that is just a 10-minute walk east of the center, this modern, low-rise hotel has views back across the water to the Old Town. Its basic but comfortable rooms and good sports facilities make it worth considering. Rooms with a sea view have a small surcharge. Pros: seafront location with small beach, good sports facilities, friendly and helpful staff. Cons: not in Old Town, modern building slightly lacking in atmosphere, basic rooms. *⊠Put od Luke 17, 20260* 🕾*020/726–006* ⊕*www.korcula-hotels.com* ⊠*83 rooms, 26 suites* ⌂*In-room: no a/c, refrigerator. In-hotel: 2 restaurants, room service, tennis courts, pool, beachfront* ▤*AE, DC, MC, V* ⊘*Closed Nov.–Feb.* ⦿*BP.*

$ 🖼**Hotel Lumbarda.** Located 6 km (4 mi) from Korčula Town, in the village of Lumbarda, this white, modern, three-story hotel overlooks the seafront promenade of Lumbarda Bay and is backed by pinewoods. It offers basic but comfortable accommodations, a pleasant terrace with a pool and restaurant out front, and a scuba-diving center. Pros: seafront location, good sports facilities, inexpensive by Dalmatian Coast standards. Cons: far from Korčula Old Town (4 mi), modern building slightly lacking in charm. *⊠Prvi Žal, Lumbarda 20263* 🕾*020/712–700* ⊕*www.lumbardahotel.com* ⊠*44 rooms* ⌂*In-room: refrigerator. In-hotel: restaurant, bar, pool, beachfront, diving, no elevator, public Internet, some pets allowed* ▤*AE, DC, MC, V* ⊘*Closed Oct.–May* ⦿*BP.*

NIGHTLIFE & THE ARTS

On the tip of the peninsula, inside the Tiepolo Tower, part of the town fortification system, **Cocktail Bar Massimo** (✉ *Šetalište Petra Kanavelića* ☎ *020/715–073*) offers wonderful sunset views. It's open from May through October. The **Moreška** (✉ *Kopnena Vrata* ☎ *100 Kn*) is a colorful sword dance performed at 9 PM each Monday and Thursday evening from May to October just outside the city walls, next to the Kopnena Vrata (Land Gate). Discounted tickets are available for 80 Kn at hotel receptions and travel agencies throughout town.

THE MOREŠKA

The Moreška is traditionally performed each year on July 29 (the feast day of Korčula's protector, St. Theodore). The word *Moreška* means "Moorish" and is said to celebrate the victory of the Christians over the Moors in Spain. The dance itself is not native to Croatia and was performed in many different Mediterranean countries, including Spain, Italy, and Malta. The story of the dance is a clash between the Black (Moorish) King and the White (Christian) King over a young maiden. The dance is done with real swords.

SPORTS & THE OUTDOORS

In addition to the activities described below, see ⇨ Tour Options *in* Southern Dalmatia Essentials, at the end of this chapter for more activities, including wine-tasting tours, which can be organized by Atlas Travel.

BEACHES

The closest spot for a quick swim is **Banje,** a small pebble beach about 10 minutes on foot east of the town walls, close to Hotel Liburna. For more leisurely bathing, the best beaches lie near the village of **Lumbarda,** which is 6 km (4 mi) southeast of Korčula Town. The most popular of these is the sandy south-facing **Przina,** 2 km (1 mi) south of Lumbarda, while the smooth-white-stoned **Bili Žal** lies a short distance east of Lumbarda. If you don't like the local beach options, rent a speedboat from **Rent-a-Djir** (✉ *Obala Hrvatskih Mornara* ☎ *020/715–120* ⊕ *www.korcula-rent.com*) and take to the open sea to explore the tiny scattered islets of the nearby Korčula archipelago, which has many secluded bays for swimming.

DIVING

MM Sub (✉ *Lumbarda* ☎ *020/712–288* ⊕ *www.mm-sub.hr*) is a diving center based in Lumbarda offering diving instruction and trips for those with some experience. Nearby diving destinations include an underwater archaeological site, as well as several sea caves and shipwrecks.

SAILING

The 159-berth **ACI marina** (✉ *Korčula* ☎ *020/711–661*) remains open all year.

7

SHOPPING

Cukarin (⊠*Hrvatska Bratske Zajednice* ☎*020/711–055*), is a family-run store renowned for its four different types of delicious handmade biscuits, as well as homemade *rakija* flavored with local herbs.

MLJET

Polače is 18 nautical mi west of Dubrovnik by ferry.

Mljet is a long, thin island of steep, rocky slopes and dense pine forests, more than a third of which is contained within Mljet National Park. The Kings of Bosnia, who ruled the island during medieval times, gave it to Benedictine monks from Puglia in Italy during the 12th century, who in turn passed it on to the Republic of Dubrovnik in 1410. No great towns ever grew up here, and today it is home to half a dozen small villages, with a total population of about 1,100 people. Lovers of ancient Greek literature will be interested to know that Mljet has been identified as Homer's lost island Ogygia, where Ulysses met the nymph Calypso.

The most convenient and speedy ferry service is the high-speed cata-maran *Nona Ana*, operated by the Rijeka-based company Alpex. The service runs daily, leaving Dubrovnik at 9 AM, and departing from Polače at 7 PM to return to the city. Tickets are available through the Dubrovnik-based agency **Atlantagent** (⊠*Stjepana Radića 26, Dubrovnik* ☎*020/419–044*).

Nacionalni Park Mljeta *(Mljet National Park).* A local bus runs from the port of Sobra to the national park at the west end of the island. If you arrive on Mljet through Polače, you are within walking distance of the park. Upon arrival, pay the entrance fee at one of several wooden kiosks (if you stay overnight, this fee is included in the price of your accommodation). Within the densely forested park lie two intercon-nected saltwater lakes, Malo Jezero (Little Lake) and Veliko Jezero (Big Lake), ideal for swimming from spring to autumn. Boats run to the charming 12th-century Benedictine monastery on Otočić Svete Marije (St. Mary's Islet), in the middle of Veliko Jezero, and a series of foot-paths and bike paths traverse the park. Mountain bikes and kayaks are available for hire at Mali Most, the bridge between the two lakes, and at Hotel Odisej in Pomena. ⊠*Pristanište 2, Govedjari* ☎*020/744–041* ⊕*www.np-mljet.hr* ⊠*90 Kn.*

★ One of Croatia's few sandy beaches, **Saplunara,** lies at the southeastern tip of the island, outside the confines of the national park. Happily, it remains relatively wild and untended, so there are no facilities as such, but you will find several seasonal eateries in the tiny nearby settlement of the same name. ⊠*Saplunara* ✛*15 km (10 mi) southeast of Sobra.*

WHERE TO EAT

$$$–$$$$ ✕**Taverna Melita.** On St. Mary's Islet, in Veliko Jezero, dining tables are arranged on the waterside terrace in front of the monastery. The menu includes a good range of meat and fish dishes, with lobster, the local specialty, taking pride of place. The restaurant runs a boat to and from Pristanište after 8:30 PM, when the national park's ferry service stops. ⊠ *Otočić Svete Marije* ☎*020/744–145* ☰*AE, DC, MC, V* ⊘*Closed mid-Oct.–mid-Mar.*

$$–$$$ ✕**Villa Mirosa.** Overlooking the sea near Saplunara beach, on the east end of the island, this informal, family-run eatery serves barbecued meat and fish dishes on a lovely terrace lined with potted geraniums. The olive oil, wine, and rakija are all homemade, and the seafood on offer is caught by the owners. ⊠*Saplunara 26* ☎*020/746–133* ☰*No credit cards* ⊘*Closed Oct.–May.*

WHERE TO STAY

$$ ▦**Hotel Odisej.** The only hotel on the island, Odisej is a large, white, modern structure overlooking the sea in the village of Pomena, a 15-minute walk from Malo Jezero. The rooms are basic but comfortable, and there are excellent sports facilities, including a scuba-diving school, a small marina, as well as bicycles, surfboards, kayaks, and canoes to rent. The hotel lies 30 km (20 mi) from Sobra and 5 km (3 mi) from Polače, and can arrange transfers to and from these ports. Pros: seafront location in the national park, good sports facilities, friendly and helpful staff. Cons: slightly lacking in charm, large and rather impersonal, food disappointing. ⊠*Pomena, 20226* ☎*020/744–022* ⊕*www.hotelodisej.hr* ⥱*157 rooms, 2 suites* ⚷*In-room: refrigerator. In-hotel: 2 restaurants, room service, bar, pool, beachfront, diving, water sports, bicycles* ☰*AE, DC, MC, V* ⊘*Closed Nov.–Mar.* ⎁*BP.*

SPORTS & THE OUTDOORS

BEACHES

The best beach, **Saplunara,** is sandy and backed by pinewoods. It lies on the southeastern tip of the island, outside of the national park. Within the park, the water in Malo Jezero (Little Lake) and Veliko Jezero (Big Lake) tends to be several degrees warmer than that in the sea, so the swimming season is somewhat extended.

DIVING

For scuba diving, try the **Freaky Diving Center** (⊠*Hotel Odisej, Pomena* ☎*020/362–111* ⊕*www.freaky-diving.com*) at Hotel Odisej. Advanced divers can ask to explore the *S57,* a well-preserved German torpedo boat that sank in 1944, and now lies just 6 nautical mi from the dive center.

DUBROVNIK & SOUTHERN DALMATIA ESSENTIALS

AIR TRAVEL

The national carrier, Croatia Airlines, operates year-round internal flights between Dubrovnik, Zagreb, and Split, plus summer flights to Pula. Through summer, it also flies regularly between Dubrovnik and Amsterdam, Brussels, Catania, Copenhagen, Frankfurt, Glasgow, Gothenberg, Helsinki, Istanbul, Lisbon, London, Manchester, Nottingham, Milan, Munich, Oslo, Palermo, Paris, Prague, Rome, Sarajevo, Skopje, Stockholm, Tel Aviv, Turin, Vienna, Warsaw, and Zurich.

Austrian Airways, British Airways, Lufthansa, and Malev all operate scheduled flights to Dubrovnik. Austrian Airways and Lufthansa do not have local offices, but are represented by Croatia Airlines. Through summer, many other European carriers offer seasonal or charter service to Dubrovnik, including Sky Europe, German Wings, and Aer Lingus.

Information **Austrian Airlines** (✉ *Brsalje 9, Pile, Dubrovnik* ☎ *020/413–776*). **British Airways** (✉ *Dubrovnik Airport, Pile, Dubrovnik* ☎ *020/773–212*). **Croatia Airlines** (✉ *Brsalje 9, Pile, Dubrovnik* ☎ *020/413–776*) and (✉ *Dubrovnik Airport, Čilipi, Dubrovnik* ☎ *020/773–224*). **Lufthansa** (✉ *Brsalje 9, Pile, Dubrovnik* ☎ *020/413–776*). **Malev** (✉ *Dubrovnik Airport, Pile, Dubrovnik* ☎ *020/773–208 May–Oct. only*).

AIRPORTS & TRANSFERS

Dubrovnik is served by Dubrovnik Airport (DBV) at Čilipi, 18 km (11 mi) southeast of the city.

Information **Dubrovnik Airport** (☎ *020/773–377 general information, 020/773–328 lost and found* ⊕ *www.airport-dubrovnik.hr*).

AIRPORT TRANSFERS   The airport bus leaves the Dubrovnik Bus Station 90 minutes before each flight and meets all incoming flights. A one-way ticket costs 25 Kn. Journey time is approximately 20 minutes.

Contacts **Airport bus** (☎ *020/773–232*). **Dubrovnik Bus Station** (✉ *Obala Pape Ivana Pavla II 44A, Gruž, Dubrovnik* ☎ *060/305–070*).

BANKS & EXCHANGE SERVICES

You'll find banks in all the destinations in the region (including the island of Lopud) mentioned in this chapter. ATMs are now widespread, and you will find at least one even in small towns on the islands. It is possible to exchange currency in banks and also in most local travel agencies.

BOAT & FERRY TRAVEL

Jadrolinija runs a twice-weekly ferry service between Dubrovnik and Bari (Italy). Ferries depart from Bari late in the evening, arriving in Dubrovnik early the next morning, with a similar schedule from Dubrovnik to Bari (journey time approximately eight hours either direction). The Italian company Azzurra Lines runs a similar service, also from June to September.

The same Jadrolinija vessel covers the coastal route, departing from Rijeka twice weekly in the evening to arrive in Dubrovnik early the following afternoon. From Dubrovnik the ferries depart midmorning to arrive in Rijeka early the following morning (journey time approximately 20 hours in either direction). Coming and going, these ferries stop at Korčula, Stari Grad (island of Hvar), and Split. From Dubrovnik, Jadrolinija runs daily car ferries to the Elafiti Islands (Koločep, Lopud, and Šipan) and Sobra (island of Mljet). Through summer (June–Sept.), Nova runs high-speed boats between Dubrovnik and Cavtat, and between Dubrovnik and the Elafiti Islands (Koločep, Lopud, and Šipan) for foot passengers only. If you are traveling as a foot passenger, a faster (but more expensive) way to reach Mljet is to take *Nona Ana*, a high-speed catamaran running daily from Dubrovnik to Sobra and Polače (island of Mljet); tickets are available through the Dubrovnik-based agency Atlantagent. It is also possible to visit Mljet as part of an organized day trip by catamaran from Dubrovnik or Korčula Town, operated by the Atlas travel agency. Last, but not least, the island of Korčula is connected to the Pelješac Peninsula by a Jadrolinija car-ferry service operating several times a day between Orebić and Dominče (2 km [1 mi] from Korčula Town). A Mediteranska Plovidba ferry runs a frequent passenger service between Orebić and Korčula Town (foot passengers only).

Information Atlantagent (⊠ *Stjepana Radića 26, Dubrovnik* ☎ *020/313–355*). **Azzurra Lines** (☎ *020/313–178* ⊕ *www.azzurraline.com*). **Jadrolinija** (⊠ *Stjepana Radića 40, Dubrovnik* ☎ *020/418–000* ⊕ *www.jadrolinija.hr*). **Mediteranska Plovidba** (☎ *020/711–156*). **Nova** (⊠ *Sv. Križa 3, Dubrovnik* ☎ *020/313–599* ⊕ *www.nova-dubrovnik.com*).

BUS TRAVEL

There are daily bus services from Dubrovnik to Ljubljana (Slovenia); Medjugorje, Mostar, and Sarajevo (Bosnia-Herzegovina); and Trieste (Italy); plus a twice-weekly service to Frankfurt and a once-weekly service to Zurich. There are regular bus routes between Dubrovnik and destinations all over mainland Croatia, with approximately 12 buses per day to Split (Central Dalmatia), eight to Zagreb and three to Rijeka (Kvarner). Within the Southern Dalmatia region, there are four buses daily to Ston and two to Orebić on Peljesac Peninsula, one of which continues to Korčula. Regular local buses run every hour up the coast to Trstenik, and every 30 minutes down the coast to Cavtat. Timetable information is available from Dubrovnik Bus Station, which moved in 2006 and now lies close to the ferry harbor in Gruž.

Information Dubrovnik Bus Station (⊠ *Obala Pape Ivana Pavla II 44A, Gruž, Dubrovnik* ☎ *060/305–070*).

CAR TRAVEL

While visiting Dubrovnik and the nearby islands of Mljet and Korčula, you are certainly better off without a car. However, as the city is not linked to the rest of Croatia by train, you may wish to rent a car if you are traveling on to Split or Zagreb, rather than taking the plane or bus.

A car can also be handy if you wish to drive up to Međugorje, Mostar, or Sarajevo, in Bosnia-Herzegovina.

Car Rental Agencies Best Buy Rent (⊠ *V Nazora 9, Pile, Dubrovnik* ☎ *020/422–043* ✉ *Dubrovnik Airport, Čilipi* ☎ *020/773-373*). **Budget** (⊠ *Obala Stjepana Radića 24, Gruž, Dubrovnik* ☎ *020/418-998* ✉ *Dubrovnik Airport, Čilipi* ☎ *020/773-290*). **Hertz** (⊠ *F Supila 9, Ploče, Dubrovnik* ☎ *020/425-000* ✉ *Dubrovnik Airport, Čilipi* ☎ *020/771-568*). **Mack** (⊠ *F Supila 3, Ploče, Dubrovnik* ☎ *020/423-747* ⊕ *www.mack-concord.hr*). **Milenium Rent** (⊠ *Put Iva Vojnovića 5, Lapad, Dubrovnik* ☎ *020/333-176* ⊕ *www.milenium-rent.com*).

INTERNET, MAIL & SHIPPING

The one well-established, fully equipped Internet café of note in the region is Dubrovnik Internet Centar, in Dubrovnik.

The Dubrovnik main post office lies a 15-minute walk northwest of the Old Town. It is open Monday to Friday, from 7 AM to 8 PM, Saturday from 8 to 4.

Information Dubrovnik Internet Centar (⊠ *Ante Starčevic'ca 7, Pile, Dubrovnik* ☎ *020/416-307*). **Dubrovnik Main Post Office** (⊠ *Put republike 32, Dubrovnik*).

TAXI TRAVEL

In Dubrovnik there are taxi ranks just outside the city walls at Pile Gate and Ploče Gate, and in front of Gruž harbor.

Information Taxi Station Gruž (☎ *020/418-112*). **Taxi Station Pile** (☎ *020/424-343*). **Taxi Station Ploče** (☎ *020/416-158*).

TOUR OPTIONS

Atlas organizes one-day excursions from Dubrovnik to neighboring countries (passports required), including the pilgrimage site of Medjugorje, Bosnia-Herzegovina, where the Virgin Mary is said to have appeared in 1981; Mostar, Bosnia-Herzegovina, with its Turkish-inspired Old Town and reconstructed bridge; and the Bay of Kotor, Budva, and the jet-setters' retreat of Sveti Stefan, Montenegro.

Information Atlas (⊠ *Vukovarska 19, Dubrovnik* ☎ *020/422-222* ✉ *Trg 19 Travanja, Korčula* ☎ *020/711-060* ⊕ *www.atlas-croatia.com*).

VISITOR INFORMATION

Information Dubrovnik & Nertva County Tourist Board (⊠ *Cvijete Zuzorić 1/1, Stari Grad, Dubrovnik* ☎ *020/324-999* ⊕ *www.visitdubrovnik.hr*). **Cavtat Tourist Office** (⊠ *Tiha 3, Cavtat* ☎ *020/478-025* ⊕ *www.tzcavtat-konavle.hr*). **Dubrovnik Tourist Office** (⊠ *Stradun, Stari Grad, Dubrovnik* ☎ *020/323-350* ⊕ *www.tzdubrovnik.hr*). **Korčula Tourist Office** (⊠ *Obala Dr Franje Tuđmana, Korčula* ☎ *020/715-701* ⊕ *www.korcula.net*). **Lopud Tourist Office** (⊠ *Lopud* ☎ *020/759-086*). **Mljet Tourist Office** (⊠ *Polače* ☎ *020/744-086*). **Orebić Tourist Office** (⊠ *Trg Mimbeli, Orebić* ☎ *020/713-718* ⊕ *www.tz-orebic.com*). **Ston Tourist Office** (⊠ *Ston* ☎ *020/754-452*).

Slovenia

WORD OF MOUTH

"Don't let Slovenia's small size deter you because there are plenty of fun things to do and see. Slovenia has a small coastline on the Adriatic, but we choose to spend our 16 days touring the interior, from bases in the east, center, and west regions of Slovenia. It may sound like a lot of driving, but to cross the whole country on their modern autobahn takes only a few hours."

—LuvToRoam

"We enjoyed our walking tour of the Old Town and were fortunate to go into City Hall and have a private audience with the Mayor of Ljubljana. There was a large Saturday market . . . and the Church of St. Nicholas was worth a visit."

—fun4all4

By Mark Baker
Updated by
Evan Rail

SLOVENIA MAY BE THE BEST-KEPT SECRET in Europe. Just half the size of Switzerland, the country is often treated as fly-over—or drive-through—territory by travelers heading to better-known places in Croatia or Italy. That's good news for anyone choosing Slovenia as a destination in its own right. It means fewer crowds—even in the peak summer touring months—fewer hassles, and in many ways a more authentic travel experience.

And Slovenia's sights are no less outstanding than those of its neighbors. Admittedly, Slovenia's small Adriatic coastline—not even 30 mi end to end—can't match Croatia for sheer natural beauty. But the coastal towns, especially the intact Venetian jewel of Piran, are lovely in their own right. The Julian Alps northwest of the capital are every bit as spectacular as their sister Alpine ranges in Austria and Switzerland. The electric-blue-turquoise waters of the Soča River, rushing out of the mountains, must be seen—or better, rafted—to be believed. And that's just a start. The extensive cave systems, unspoiled countryside, and even the funky charm of Ljubljana await those with the imagination to choose a destination that is more off the beaten path.

Slovenia's relative obscurity owes much to its history. From Roman times to nearly the present day, Slovenian territory was incorporated into far-larger empires, relegating Slovenia through the ages to the role of rustic, if charming, hinterland.

The territory of Slovenia has been inhabited for tens of thousands of years, but the country's modern history begins with the arrival of the Romans in the 1st century BC. They built villas along the coast and founded the inland urban centers of Emona (Ljubljana) and Poetovio (Ptuj), which today still retain traces of their Roman past. The 6th century AD saw the first influx of Slav migrants, the ancestors of present-day Slovenes, who set up an early Slav state. During the 8th century, the region came under the control of the Franks, and in the 9th century it was passed to the dukes of Bavaria.

In 1335 the Habsburgs took control of inland Slovenia, dividing it into the Austrian crown lands of Carinthia, Carniola, and Styria. Meanwhile, the coastal towns had requested Venetian protection, and they remained under *la serenissima* until 1797, after which they, too, were taken by Austria. During the 15th and 16th centuries, the Turks, eager to extend the Ottoman Empire across the Balkans and north to Vienna, made repeated attacks on the region. However, Slovenia remained under the Habsburgs until 1918, with the exception of a brief period from 1809 to 1813, when it became part of Napoléon's Illyrian Provinces.

In the aftermath of World War I, Italy seized control of the coastal towns, whereas inland Slovenia became part of the Kingdom of Serbs, Croats, and Slovenes; in 1929, the name of the kingdom was changed to Yugoslavia (Land of the Southern Slavs).

Hitler declared war on Yugoslavia in 1941, and shortly afterward Axis forces occupied the country. Slovenia was divided between Germany,

Italy, and Hungary. Josip Broz, better known as Tito, set up the anti-Fascist Partisan movement, and many Slovenes took part in resistance activities. When the war ended in 1945, Slovenia became one of the six constituent republics of Yugoslavia, with Tito as president. Slovenes today are proud of their Partisan past, and traveling through the country you see monuments and wall plaques bearing the red star, a symbol of the Partisans and of communist ideology; many squares and roads are still named after Tito.

Half Slovene and half Croat, Tito was undeniably an astute leader. He governed Yugoslavia under communist ideology, but the system was far more liberal than that of the Soviet-bloc countries: Yugoslavs enjoyed freedom of movement, and foreigners could enter the country without visas. During the cold war, Tito never took sides but dealt cleverly with both East and West, thus procuring massive loans from both.

However, when Tito died in 1980, the system he left behind began to crumble. The false nature of the economy, based on borrowing, became apparent. During the 1980s, an economic crisis set in and inflation soared. Slovenia, accounting for only 8% of Yugoslavia's population, was producing almost a third of the nation's exports. This hard-earned foreign currency ended up in Belgrade and was used in part to subsidize the poorer republics. It was time for change.

In early 1990, buoyed by the recent revolutions across Eastern Europe, Slovenia introduced a multiparty system and elected a non-communist government. Demands for increased autonomy from Yugoslavia were stepped up, with the threat of secession. A referendum was held, and nearly 90% of the electorate voted for independence. Unlike the other Yugoslav republics, Slovenia was made up almost exclusively of a single ethnic group: Slovenes. Thus, the potential status of ethnic minorities, should the republic secede, was never an issue. Slovenia proclaimed independence on June 25, 1991, and the so-called 10-Day War followed. Yugoslav federal troops moved in, but there was little violence to compare with the heavy fighting in nearby Croatia and Bosnia. Belgrade had already agreed to let Slovenia go.

In 1992, Slovenia gained international recognition as an independent state and began the painstaking process of legal, political, and economic reform needed to join the European Union. That effort bore fruit in May 2004, when Slovenia, along with seven other Central and Eastern European countries, was admitted into the EU; it adopted the euro as its official currency in 2007. Today, Slovenia's future looks bright. It's simply a matter of time before the country's charms are fully discovered.

EXPLORING SLOVENIA

The principal areas of interest to tourists include the lively and very likable capital Ljubljana, the Julian Alps and Triglav National Park, to the northwest, the alpine lakes of Bled and Bohinj, and the Adriatic coast and the Karst region to the southwest. The region to the east,

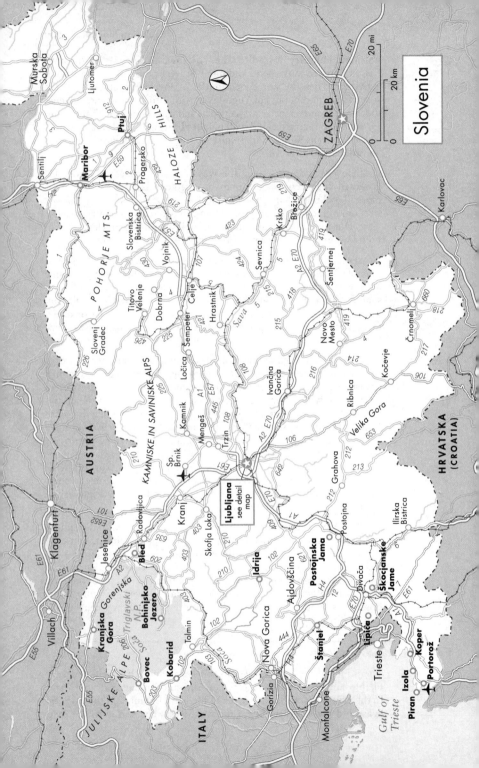

SLOVENIA TOP 5

■ Tripping out on the amazing archi-tecture of Ljubljana, courtesy of Jože Plečnik, the chief architect in the renovation of Prague Castle.

■ Hiking through the forests and trenches on the Kobarid Historical Walk, at the World War I battle-ground-cum–nature reserve near Kobarid, after putting the event in some context at the Kobariški muzej.

■ Relaxing on the marble-laden Trg Tartini, just steps from the Adriatic in Piran, a medieval walled Venetian

town and the jewel of Slovenia's Adriatic coast.

■ Traveling through the rolling hills of the wine country around the old Roman town of Ptuj; after you roam, you can enjoy a wine-tasting session at the Vinska Klet.

■ Taking a refreshing dip in Slove-nia's magnificent alpine Lake Bled, just below the watchful eye of Bled Castle.

centering on Maribor, Ptuj, and the Haloze Hills, has several vineyards and excellent wine cellars.

ABOUT THE RESTAURANTS

Slovenia's prime contribution to dining has got to be the *gostilna*, essentially an inn or tavern but cleaner, warmer, and more inviting than the English translation suggests. These are frequently family-run, especially in the smaller towns and villages, with Mom in the kitchen and Pop out front pouring beers and taking orders. The staff is usually happy to suggest local or regional specialties. Some of the better ones are situated alongside vineyards or farms.

Meal times follow the Continental norm for lunch and dinner. Even if a restaurant posts earlier opening times, the kitchen won't normally start operating until noon. Dinners typically start around 7 PM. It can be tough finding a breakfast place, so it's best to take the standard hotel or pension offering of sliced meats and cheeses when available.

Restaurants usually close one day a week. In larger towns like Lju-bljana that's likely to be Sunday. In resort areas that cater to a weekend crowd, Monday is the usual day off. If in doubt, phone ahead.

ABOUT THE HOTELS

Don't expect Slovenia to be a cheap option; lodging prices are similar to what you see in Western Europe, and with the euro soaring in value, prices will be particularly painful for Americans. During peak season (July and August), many hotels—particularly those on the coast—are fully booked. Hotels are generally clean, smartly furnished, and well run. Establishments built under communism are often equipped with extras such as saunas and sports facilities but tend to be gargantuan structures lacking in soul. Hotels dating from the turn of the 20th cen-tury are more romantic, as are the castle hotels. Over the last decade many hotels have been refurbished and upgraded.

Slovenian Cuisine

At first glance, Slovenian cuisine looks a little like fusion food since it melds elements of Italian, Hungarian, Austrian, and Balkan cooking—often to good effect. Italy's contribution stands out most clearly in the full range of pastas and risottos you'll see on many menus. Pizza is ubiquitous and generally of high quality. From Austria come the many pork and other meat dishes and schnitzels, though they are often served with local—and sometimes unusual—sides like spinach *njoki* (gnocchi) or even *ajda* (buckwheat) dumplings. The Balkan influence is seen in the profusion of grilled meats and in one of the most common street foods: *burek*, an oily phyllo pastry stuffed with salty cheese or meat.

Typical local dishes include *krvavice* (black pudding) served with *žganci* (polenta) or Kraški pršut (air-dried Karst ham). Another favorite is *jota*, a filling soup of sauerkraut, beans, and smoked pork. Look too for regional specialties, such as the easier-to-

eat-than-pronounce *žlikrofi*—tiny tortellini stuffed with minced potato, onion, and bacon that are the pride of cooks throughout the Idrija region but are nearly impossible to find anywhere else.

With the Adriatic close at hand, you can find excellent seafood. Look for mouthwatering *škampi rižot* (scampi risotto), followed by fresh fish prepared *na žaru* (grilled). Fresh trout with *tržaška* (garlic and parsley) sauce is a staple on any menu near the Soča River. The first-rate fish—usually priced on menus per kilogram (2.2 pounds)—are expensive, so don't be surprised when the bill comes.

For an extra boost stop at a *kavarna* (coffee shop) for a scrumptious, calorie-laden *prekmurska gibanica*, a layered cake combining curd cheese, walnuts, and poppy seeds. Another national favorite is *potica*, a rolled cake filled with either walnuts, chocolate, poppy seeds, or raisins.

Private lodgings are a cheaper alternative to hotels, and standards are generally excellent. Prices vary depending on region and season. Look for signs proclaiming *sobe* (room to let) or *apartma* (apartments), alongside roads or in towns. Local tourist information centers, or in resorts like Bled or Piran private travel agencies, will often maintain lists of local rooms for rent.

Many hotels will offer better rates for stays of more than three days. Hotel rates frequently include breakfast—usually a mix of breads, cheeses, and cold cuts served buffet-style. Pensions and private rooms may include lunch or dinner—be sure to ask what's included in the price and whether you can opt out if you choose.

Between April and October camping is a reasonable alternative. Most campgrounds are small but well equipped. On the coast, campsites are found at Izola and Ankaran. In Triglav National Park and the Soča Valley there are sites at Bled, Bohinj, Bovec, Kobarid, Soča, and Trenta. Camping outside of organized campsites is not permitted.

To really experience day-to-day life in the countryside you should stay on a working farm. Agritourism is rapidly growing in popularity, and at most farms you can experience an idyllic rural setting, delicious home cooking, plus a warm family welcome. A brochure, *Tourist Farms in Slovenia,* is available from the tourist board. More information is available on the board's Web site.

WHAT IT COSTS IN EUROS (€)	¢	$	$$	$$$	$$$$
RESTAURANTS	under €8	€8–€12	€12–€20	€20–€30	over €30
HOTELS	under €75	€75–€125	€125–€175	€175–€225	over €225

Restaurant prices are for a main course at dinner. Hotel prices are for two people in a double room in high season, excluding taxes and service charges.

TIMING

The countryside is at its most beautiful in spring and fall, though the best period to visit depends on what you plan to do during your stay. Ljubljana is vibrant the whole year through. Many visitors want to head straight for the coast. Those in search of sea, sun, and all-night parties will find what they're looking for in peak season (July and August), including cultural events, open-air dancing, busy restaurants, and crowded beaches. If you want to avoid the crowds, hit the Adriatic in June or September, when it should be warm enough to swim and easier to find a place to put your beach towel.

In the mountains there are two distinct seasons: winter is dedicated to skiing, summer to hiking and biking. Some hotels close in November and March to mark a break between the two periods. Conditions for more strenuous walking and biking are optimal in April, May, September, and October.

Lovers of fine food and wine should visit Slovenia during fall. The grape harvest concludes with the blessing of the season's young wine on St. Martin's Day, preceded by three weeks of festivities. In rural areas autumn is the time to make provisions for the hard winter ahead: wild mushrooms are gathered, firewood is chopped, and *koline* (sausages and other pork products) are prepared by hand.

LJUBLJANA

Slovenia's small but exceedingly charming capital is enjoying a tourism renaissance. The advent of low-cost flights from the United Kingdom and increased air service from other European countries have led to a dramatic influx of visitors in recent years and elevated the city's profile abroad. Tourism officials now talk of Ljubljana proudly in the same breath as Prague or Budapest as one of the top urban destinations in Central Europe. That may be wishful thinking, but there's no denying a sense of excitement as new hotels and restaurants open their doors, and each month seems to bring another admiring article in a prestigious newspaper or magazine abroad. Unfortunately, there is still no nonstop service from the United States.

IF YOU LIKE

HIKING

Slovenes love their mountains, and when you reach the northwest of the country you will understand why. The most popular alpine hiking route runs from Maribor, near the Austrian border, to Ankaran on the Adriatic coast. It crosses Triglav National Park and can be walked in 30 days. For less devoted walkers, a day or two of backpacking from one of the alpine resorts is an invigorating way to explore the landscape. Bovec, Bohinj, and Krajnska Gora are all excellent hiking bases. Mountain paths are usually well marked, and mountain lodges have dormitory-style accommodations. Detailed maps are available at local tourist-information centers.

HORSEBACK RIDING

The country's most famous equestrian center is the Lipica Stud Farm, home of the splendid Lipizzaner white stallions. Riding lessons are available, though the farm is geared more toward experienced riders than beginners. It also offers summer riding sessions lasting several days to several weeks. For beginners, a better option might be the Mrcina Ranč at Studor, near Lake Bohinj. Visitors to the Krka Valley can ride at the Struga Equestrian Center at a 12th-century medieval manor near Otočec Castle. The brochure *Riding in Slovenia, Home of the Lipizzaner,* is available from the Slovenian Tourist Board.

KAYAKING, CANOEING & RAFTING

The Soča River has ideal conditions for white-water rafting, kayaking, hydrospeeding (a small board for bodysurfing waves), and canyoning. The season lasts from April to October. The best rapids lie between Bovec and Kobarid. Numerous outfitters in Bovec rent boats and equipment and also offer instruction and guided rafting and kayaking trips. Less exhilarating—though still very fun—river rafting is available near Bled and Bohinj.

WINE & SPIRITS

Slovenes enjoy drinking and produce some excellent wines, but very little of the total output is exported. You can tour the three main wine regions following a series of established "wine roads" (*vinska cesta*). These routes pass through rolling hills, woodlands, and villages and lead directly to vineyards and wine stores. The best white wines, *sivi pinot* (pinot grigio) and *beli pinot* (pinot blanc), are produced in the Podravje region in northeast Slovenia. A notable red is Teran, a varietal made from the refosk grape and produced in the Karst region to the southwest. There has been a recent drive to introduce more sparkling wines: look for the excellent Penina, made using the classic Champagne method from chardonnay and pinot blanc grapes. The favorite national spirit is the potent *rakija*. The base is alcohol distilled from fruit; a variety of wild herbs are added later to give it a more distinct flavor.

The tiny city center is immediately captivating. Part of the charm is doubtless the emerald green Llubljanica River that winds its way slowly through the Old Town, providing a focal point and the perfect backdrop to the cafés and restaurants that line the banks. Partly, too, it's the aesthetic tension between the stately baroque houses along the river and the white neoclassical, modern, and Secessionist set pieces that dot the streets and bridges everywhere. Meticulously designed pillars, orbs, and obelisks lend the city an element of whimsy, a feeling of good cheer that's immediately infectious. And part of the credit goes to the Ljubljaners themselves, who on a warm summer evening can be counted on to come out and party in force. It's a place that's meant to be enjoyed.

In truth, Ljubljana has always viewed itself as something special. Even when it was part of the former Yugoslavia, the city was considered a center of alternative music and arts. This was especially true during the 1980s, when it became the center of the Yugoslav punk movement. The band Laibach, noted for mocking nationalist sentiments, and the absurdist conceptual-art group Neue Slowenische Kunst (NSK) both have their roots here.

The romantic heart of the Old Town dates back centuries. The earliest settlement was founded by the Romans and called Emona. Much of it was destroyed by the Huns under Attila, though a section of the walls and a complex of foundations—complete with mosaics—can still be seen today. In the 12th century, a new settlement, Laibach, was built on the right bank of the river, below Castle Hill, by the dukes of Carniola. In 1335, the Habsburgs gained control of the region, and it was they who constructed the existing castle fortification system.

The 17th century saw a period of baroque building, strongly influenced by currents in Austria and Italy. Walk along the cobblestones of the *Mestni trg* (Town Square) and the *Stari trg* (Old Square) to see Ljubljana at its best, from the colored baroque town houses with their steeply pitched tile roofs to Francesco Robba's delightful *Fountain of the Three Carniolan Rivers*.

For a brief period, from 1809 to 1813, Ljubljana was the capital of Napoléon's Illyrian Provinces. In 1849, once again under the Habsburgs, Ljubljana was linked to Vienna and Trieste by rail. The city developed into a major center of commerce, industry, and culture, and the opera house, national theater, national museum, and the first hotels came into existence.

In 1895 much of the city was devastated by an earthquake. The reconstruction work that followed was carried out in florid Viennese Secessionist style. Many of the palatial four-story buildings that line Miklošičeva, such as the Grand Hotel Union, date from this period.

After World War I, with the birth of the Kingdom of Serbs, Croats, and Slovenes, Ljubljana became the administrative center of Slovenia. Various national cultural institutes were founded, and the University of Ljubljana opened in 1919. If you have been to Prague, you will already

GREAT ITINERARIES

Slovenia's small size can be an advantage. From the centrally located capital, Ljubljana, you can drive to any point in the country in three or four hours.

IF YOU HAVE 3 DAYS

If you have limited time, take one day to discover the Old Town of **Ljubljana**. For the next two days, choose between the mountains or the coast. If you're looking for natural beauty and/or adventure, head for the mountains and lakes of Triglav National Park. Base yourself in **Bled** or **Bohinj**. For the third day, get an early start and head for **Bovec**, via **Kranjska Gora**, for hiking or white-water rafting on the Soča River. If you seek sun and sea instead, go southwest toward the Karst and coast. Stop off at the Škocjan Caves en route, and spend your nights in the beautiful Venetian port of **Piran**.

IF YOU HAVE 5 DAYS

For a longer stay, combine the two optional itineraries listed above. Spend the first day and night exploring Ljubljana's Old Town before making your way northwest to the mountains. After nights in Bled and/ or Bohinj and exploring the Soča River valley, continue southwest to the coast. Use Piran as your base for visiting the coastal towns of **Izola** and **Portorož**.

IF YOU HAVE 7 DAYS

If you have a full week, spend a day and night in Ljubljana and then make your way east for a night to the wine-making area around **Maribor** and **Ptuj**. Return to the capital, and then head north for the beauty of the Alps, as outlined in the five-day itinerary. Wrap up the week with a couple of days relaxing on the coast. In hot weather, you can go for a swim at the beaches around Portorož.

have seen some of the work of Jože Plečnik (1872–1957). Born in Ljubljana, Plečnik studied architecture in Vienna under Otto Wagner, then went on to lecture at the Prague School of Applied Arts and served as the chief architect for the renovation of Prague Castle. It was Plečnik who added many of the decorator touches to the city's parks, squares, and bridges. Some of his finest projects include the Triple Bridge, the open-air market on Vodnik Square, and the plans for the Križanke Summer Theater.

The Tito years saw increased industrialization. The population of Ljubljana tripled, and vast factory complexes, high-rise apartments, and modern office buildings extended into the suburbs.

EXPLORING LJUBLJANA

The city center is concentrated within a small area, so you can cover all the sights on foot.

WHAT TO SEE

13 **Cankarjevo nabrežje.** Numerous cafés line this pretty riverside walkway. When the weather is good, tables are placed outside overlooking the water. ⊠ *Between Tromostovje and Čevljarski most.*

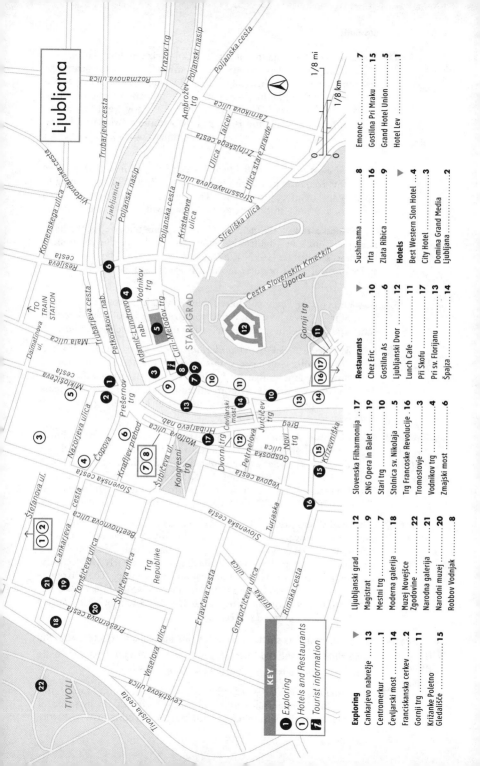

Ljubljana

KEY

- ① Exploring
- ① Hotels and Restaurants
- 🛈 Tourist information

Exploring ▶

Cankarjevo nabrežje	**13**
Centromerkur	**1**
Čevljarski most	**14**
Franciskanska cerkev	**2**
Gornji trg	**11**
Križanke Poletno Gledališče	**15**

Ljubljanski grad	**12**
Magistrat	**9**
Mestni trg	**7**
Moderna galerija	**18**
Muzej Novejše Zgodovine	**22**
Narodna galerija	**21**
Narodni muzej	**20**
Robbov Vodnjak	**8**

Slovenska Filharmonija	**17**
SNG Opera in Balet	**19**
Stari trg	**10**
Stolnica sv. Nikolaja	**5**
Trg Francoske Revolucije	**16**
Tromostovje	**3**
Vodnikov trg	**4**
Zmajski most	**6**

Restaurants ▶

Chez Eric	**10**
Gostilna As	**6**
Ljubljanski Dvor	**12**
Lunch Cafe	**11**
Pri Skofu	**17**
Pri sv. Florijanu	**13**
Špajza	**14**

Sushimama	**8**
Trta	**16**
Zlata Ribica	**9**

Hotels ▶

Best Western Slon Hotel	**4**
City Hotel	**3**
Domina Grand Media Ljubljana	**2**

Emonec	**7**
Gostilna Pri Mraku	**15**
Grand Hotel Union	**5**
Hotel Lev	**1**

0   1/8 mi

0   1/8 km

❶ Centromerkur. This magnificent art nouveau–style building, dating from 1903, is the oldest department store in town. Most of the structures in Ljubljana built at this time borrowed from the Viennese Secession, making this building—which draws its inspiration more from Paris—a relative rarity. The entrance, off Prešernov trg, bears a flaring iron butterfly wing and is topped by a statue of Mercury. Inside, graceful wrought-iron stairways lead to upper floors. ✉ *Trubarjeva 1* ☎ *01/426–3170.*

⓮ Čevljarski most *(Cobblers' Bridge).* Linking the old and new sides of town, this romantic pedestrian bridge was built in 1931 according to plans by the architect Jože Plečnik. The name is derived from a wooden structure that once stood here and was lined with shoemakers' huts.

❷ Franciskanska cerkev *(Franciscan Church).* This massive, pink, high-baroque church was built between 1646 and 1660. The main altar, by Francesco Robba (1698–1757), dates from 1736. The three sets of stairs in front are a popular meeting place for students. ✉ *Prešernov trg 4* ⊙ *Daily 8–6.*

⓫ Gornji trg *(Upper Square).* This cobbled street, just around the corner from Stari trg, is where you'll find some of the capital's finest restaurants and a small but growing collection of design and art studios.

⓯ Križanke Poletno Gledališče *(Križanke Summer Theater).* In the courtyard of an 18th-century monastery, this open-air theater was constructed according to plans drawn up by Jože Plečnik. It was completed in 1976, nearly two decades after the architect's death. The theater seats 1,400, and there's a movable roof in case of rain. ✉ *Trg Francoske Revolucije.*

OFF THE BEATEN PATH **Plečnik's House.** Architecture enthusiasts will enjoy a visit to architect Jože Plečnik's house, still as he left it, to see his studio, home, and garden. The only drawback is the limited opening times: just four hours a day, two days a week. From the Križanke Summer Theater, cross Zoisova cesta, and then follow Emonska to Karunova. ✉ *Karunova 4, Trnovo* ☎ *01/280–1600* 💶 *€5* ⊙ *Tues. and Thurs. 10–2.*

⓬ Ljubljanski grad *(Ljubljana Castle).* Ljubljana's hilltop castle affords magnificent views over the river and the Old Town's terra-cotta rooftops, spires, and green cupolas. On a clear day, the distant Julian Alps are a dramatic backdrop. The castle walls date from the early 16th century, although the tower was added in the mid-19th century. The surrounding park was landscaped by Plečnik in the 1930s. ✉ *Studentovska ul, uphill from Vodnikov trg* ☎ *01/432–7216* 💶 *€3* ⊙ *Apr.–Oct., daily 9 AM–11 PM; Nov.–Mar., daily 10–7.*

NEED A BREAK? The castle ramparts shelter a pleasant café and summer garden. After the steep climb from the Old Town, stop in for a refreshing drink at the Castle Terrace (✉ *Ljubljanski grad* ☎ *01/439–4140*).

❾ Magistrat *(Town Hall).* Guarded by an austere 18th-century facade, this building hides delightful secrets within. In the internal courtyard, for example, the walls are animated with murals depicting historic battles for the city, and a statue of Hercules keeps company with a fountain bearing a figure of Narcissus. ⊠ *Mestni trg 1* ☎ *Free* ⊙ *Weekdays 9–3, weekends as part of guided tour of city.*

❼ Mestni trg *(Town Square).* This cobbled square extends into the oldest part of the city. Baroque town houses, now divided into functional apartments, present marvelously ornate facades: carved oak doors with great brass handles are framed within columns, and upper floors are decorated with balustrades, statuary, and intricate ironwork. Narrow passageways connect with inner courtyards in one direction and run to the riverfront in the other. The street-level floors contain boutiques, antiques shops, and art galleries.

NEED A BREAK?

If you plan to dine in the Old Town, stop first at Movia (⊠ *Mestni trg 2* ☎ *01/ 425–5448*) for an aperitif. This elegant little wine bar stocks a selection of first-rate Slovenian wines, for consumption both on and off the premises. It is closed Sunday.

⓲ Moderna galerija *(Modern Gallery).* The strikingly modern one-story structure contains a selection of paintings, sculpture, and prints by Slovenian 20th-century artists. In odd-number years it also hosts the International Biennial of Graphic Art, an exhibition of prints and installations by artists from around the world. Works by Robert Rauschenberg, Susan Rothenburg, and Max Bill have been shown. The gallery was renovated in 2007. ⊠ *Cankarjeva 15* ☎ *01/241–6800* ⊕ *www. mg-lj.si* ☎ *Free* ⊙ *Tues.–Sat. 10–6, Sun. 10–1.*

㉒ Muzej Novejše Zgodovine *(Museum of Modern History).* The permanent exhibition on Slovenes in the 20th century takes you from the days of Austria-Hungary, through World War II, the victory of the Partisan liberation movement and the ensuing Tito period, and up to the present day. Relics and memorabilia are combined with a dramatic sound-and-video presentation (scenes from World War II are projected on the walls and ceiling, accompanied by thundering gunfire, screams, and singing). You'll find the museum in a pink-and-white baroque villa in Tivoli Park. ⊠ *Celovška 23* ☎ *01/300–9610* ⊕ *www.muzej-nz.si* ☎ *€4* ⊙ *Tues.–Sun. 10–6.*

㉑ Narodna galerija *(National Gallery).* This imposing turn-of-the-20th-century building houses the greatest collection of Slovenian art from the 13th through the early 20th century, and a smaller but impressive collection of European paintings. ⊠ *Cankarjeva 20* ☎ *01/241–5418* ⊕ *www.ng-slo.si* ☎ *€5* ⊙ *Tues.–Sun. 10–6.*

⓴ Narodni muzej *(National Museum).* The centerpiece here is a bronze urn from the 5th century BC known as the Vace Situle. Discovered in Vace, Slovenia, it is a striking example of Illyrian workmanship. ⊠ *Muzejska 1* ☎ *01/241–4400* ⊕ *www.narmuz-lj.si* ☎ *€3* ⊙ *Tues., Wed., and Fri.– Sun. 10–6, Thurs. 10–8.*

❽ Robbov Vodnjak *(Robba's Fountain).* When the Slovene sculptor Francesco Robba saw Bernini's *Fountain of the Four Rivers* on Piazza Navona during a visit to Rome, he was inspired to create this allegorical representation of the three main Kranjska rivers—the Sava, the Krka, and the Ljubljanica—that flow through Slovenia. ✉ *Mestni trg.*

⑰ Slovenska Filharmonija *(Slovenian Philharmonic Hall).* This hall was built in 1891 for one of the oldest music societies in the world, established in 1701. Haydn, Brahms, Beethoven, and Paganini were honorary members of the orchestra, and Mahler was resident conductor for the 1881–82 season. ✉ *Kongresni trg 10* ☎ *01/241–0800.*

NEED A BREAK? From the Philharmonic Hall, head to the other side of Kongresni trg to find **Zvezda** (✉ *Kongresni trg 4* ☎ *01/421–9090*). This popular café has comfortable chairs and minimalist lighting, making it a perfect spot for an afternoon *kava smetana* (coffee with whipped cream). The ice cream and cakes are made on the premises and the staff never hurries you.

⑲ SNG Opera in Balet *(Slovenian National Opera and Ballet Theater).* This neo-Renaissance palace, with an ornate facade topped by an allegorical sculpture group, was erected in 1892. When visiting ballet and opera companies come to Ljubljana, they perform here. At this writing, the opera house was closed for a major renovation and was not expected to reopen until mid-2008. ✉ *Župančičeva 1* ☎ *01/241–1764* ⊕ *www.opera.si* ☉ *Weekdays 11–1 and one hour before performances.*

⑩ Stari trg *(Old Square).* More a narrow street than a square, the Old Square is lined with cafés and small restaurants. In agreeable weather, tables are set out on the cobblestones.

NEED A BREAK? The best cup of tea in Ljubljana—as well as great coffees—and one of the few breakfast places in town can be found at **Čajna Hiša** (✉ *Stari trg 3* ☎ *01/439–4140*).

❺ Stolnica sveti Nikolaja *(Cathedral of St. Nicholas).* This proud baroque cathedral overshadows the daily market on Vodnikov trg. Building took place between 1701 and 1708, and in 1836 the cupola was erected. In 1996, in honor of Pope John Paul II's visit, new bronze doors were added. The main door tells the story of Christianity in Slovenia, whereas the side door shows the history of the Ljubljana diocese. ✉ *Dolničarjeva 1* ☎ *01/234–2690* ⊕ *lj-stolnica.rkc.si* 🎟 *Free* ☉ *Daily 7–noon and 3–7.*

⑯ Trg Francoske Revolucije *(French Revolution Square).* When Napoléon took Slovenia, he made Ljubljana the capital of his Illyrian Provinces. This square is dominated by Plečnik's **Ilirski Steber** (Illyrian Column), which was erected in 1929 to commemorate that time.

❸ Tromostovje *(Triple Bridge).* This striking structure spans the River Ljubljanica from Prešernov trg to the Old Town. The three bridges started as a single span, and in 1931 the two graceful outer arched bridges, designed by Plečnik, were added.

❹ Vodnikov trg *(Vodnik Square).* This square hosts a big and bustling flower, fruit, and vegetable market. An elegant riverside colonnade designed by Plečnik runs the length of the market, and a bronze statue of the Slovene poet Valentin Vodnik, after whom the square is named, overlooks the scene. ⊙ *Market Mon.–Sat. 7–3.*

❻ Zmajski most *(Dragon's Bridge).* Four fire-breathing winged dragons crown the corners of this locally cherished concrete-and-iron structure.

OFF THE BEATEN PATH

Žale. To see one of Plečnik's most dramatic structures, ride bus No. 2, 7, or 22 from the post office out to Žale, a cemetery and memorial designed by the architect in the 1930s. The entrance colonnade and adjoining promenades reflect the Secessionist influence, creating a tranquil resting place inside. ⊠ *Tomačevska cesta, Novo Jarse.*

WHERE TO EAT

Central European food is often considered bland and stodgy, but in Ljubljana you can eat exceptionally well. Fresh fish arrives daily from the Adriatic, and the surrounding hills supply the capital with first-class meat and game, dairy produce, and fruit and vegetables. Ljubljana's relative diversity also affords an opportunity to dabble in international cuisines like Mexican, Japanese, and Chinese if you've already spent some time in the countryside and are looking for a change of pace. At some of the better restaurants the menus may verge on nouvelle cuisine, featuring imaginative and beautifully presented dishes. Complement your meal with a bottle of good Slovenian wine; the waiter can help you choose an appropriate one. For a lunchtime snack visit the market in Vodnik Square. Choose from tasty fried squid and whitebait in the riverside arcade or freshly baked pies and *kròf* (jelly-filled doughnuts) at the square's bakeries.

$$$–$$$$ ✕**Chez Eric.** The cuisine here shows a happy marriage of French and Slovenian cooking. The small number of entrées—four meat and four fish—ensure that each item gets the attention it deserves. Eat on the terrace in warmer months. The restaurant occupies the former site of the Rotovž, next to the town hall on Mestni trg. ⊠ *Mestni trg 3* ☎ *01/251– 2839* ⊟ *AE, DC, MC, V* ⊙ *Closed Sun.*

★ $$$–$$$$ ✕**Gostilna As.** This refined restaurant—not to be confused with the on-premises beer garden and after-hours club of the same name—is tucked away in a courtyard just off Wolfova ulica. As—or "Ace"—is *the* place to try innovative fish dishes (priced by the dekagram) and pasta specialties, all complemented by a first-rate wine list. The ambience is old-fashioned, but the dishes are creative and modern. ⊠ *Knafljev prehod 5a* ☎ *01/425–8822* ⌂ *Reservations essential* ⊟ *AE, DC, MC, V.*

$$$ ✕**Pri sv. Florijanu.** On Gornji trg, on the way to the castle, this upscale eatery serves a new generation of Slovenian cuisine with an international touch, borrowing from French and Asian influences. In every season the chef seems to have the right touch with Slovenia's bounty; porcini mushroom risotto and pumpkin ravioli in the fall, asparagus soup and *motovílec* (lamb's lettuce) salad in the spring. The service is both inviting and discreet. ⊠ *Gornji trg 20* ☎ *01/251–2214* ⊟ *AE, DC, MC, V.*

$$$ ✕**Špajza.** A few doors away from Pri sv. Florijanu, you'll find a restaurant with a series of romantic candlelit rooms and bohemian decor.

8

The menu has local specialties like *Kraški pršut* (Karst air-dried ham) and scampi tails, as well as an inspired selection of salads. They do a great tiramisu. ⊠ *Gornji trg 28* ☎ *01/425–3094* 🖃 *AE, DC, MC, V* ⊙ *Closed Sun.*

$$$ ✕ **Zlata Ribica.** Although there is a good range of Slovenian and Italian specialties, it's not the food that's the main draw here—it's the riverside location near the Triple Bridge. On a warm summer evening, there's not a better table in town. Despite the name, which translates as "goldfish," there's not much in the way of seafood here—instead the focus is on salads, grilled meats, and game. ⊠ *Cankarjevo nab 5* ☎ *01/241–2680* 🖃 *AE, DC, MC, V.*

$$–$$$ ✕ **Ljubljanski Dvor.** Situated close to Čevljarski most, overlooking the river, this restaurant doubles as a pizzeria (which remains open on Sunday, when the restaurant is closed). The summer terrace makes it an ideal stopping point for lunch. ⊠ *Dvorni trg 1* ☎ *01/251–6555* 🖃 *AE, DC, MC, V* ⊙ *Closed Sun.*

$$–$$$ ✕ **Lunch Cafe.** As the name implies, the perfect spot for a quick and easy soup-and-salad lunch, or a light pasta dinner. The focus here is simple food done well. The affable staff is knowledgeable about wines, and the low prices make it a good place to sample a couple of glasses. ⊠ *Stari trg 9* ☎ *01/425–0118* 🖃 *AE, DC, MC, V.*

$$–$$$ ✕ **Při Skofu.** This tiny, eclectic neighborhood place serves as a kind of temple for foodies in the suburb of Trnovo. The emphasis is on traditional Slovenian cooking, but not the sort that makes it onto many standard menus. The gnocchi, risotto, and buckwheat dumplings come highly recommended. Most ingredients are purchased daily at Ljubljana's open-air market. The menu changes daily, so ask the server what looks good that day. ⊠ *Rečna 8, Trnovo* ☎ *01/426–4508* 🖃 *AE, DC, MC, V.*

$$–$$$ ✕ **Sushimama.** A light sushi dinner paired with a crisp white wine can be a welcome antidote to the heavy meat and starch offered on most Slovenian menus. This new arrival boasts a Japanese chef, fresh fish, and a spare, minimalist decor that focuses your attention on the food. Reservations are essential on weekend nights. ⊠ *Wolfova 12* ☎ *040/70–20–70* 🖃 *AE, DC, MC, V* ⊙ *Closed Sun.*

★ $–$$ ✕ **Trta.** In a country filled with pizza joints, this may be Slovenia's best. It offers supersize pies, fresh and inventive ingredients, and a small garden for warm evenings. Walk south along the river (on the same side as the Old Town), cross over busy Zoisova cesta, and continue along Grudnovo nabrežje. ⊠ *Grudnovo nab 23* ☎ *01/426–5066* 🖃 *AE, DC, MC, V* ⊙ *Closed Sun.*

WHERE TO STAY

Most of the listed hotels are clustered conveniently around Miklošičeva cesta, the main axis running from the train station down to Tromostovje (Triple Bridge). Ljubljana is expensive by Central and Eastern European standards (comparable to those in Western Europe), but hotel standards are high. In summer you can get better deals through private accommodations or university dorms. Ask about these options at the tourist-information center kiosk in the train station.

★ $$$–$$$$ ⊞**Grand Hotel Union.** The pricier "Executive" section of this bustling hotel complex in central Ljubljana occupies a magnificent Secessionist-style building; the interior and furnishings remain typically turn-of-the-20th-century Vienna. The "Business" section is in an attached modern building overlooking a pleasant courtyard with a fountain; all the rooms in this section have broadband Internet connections. All hotel facilities are shared by both sections of the hotel and have been modernized with great care. ✉ *Miklošičeva 1–3, 1000* ☎ *01/308–1270* ⊕ *www.gh-union.si* ↩ *297 rooms, 12 suites* ♿ *In-room: safe, kitchen (some), Ethernet (some), dial-up (some). In-hotel: 2 restaurants, pool, gym, public Internet, no-smoking rooms* ▭ *AE, DC, MC, V* ⦿*BP.*

$$–$$$$ ⊞**Hotel Lev.** A series of renovations since 1997 have transformed a nondescript modern building into the country's leading hotel. The Lev makes up for its location—about a 10-minute walk from the city center—with stunning views of Tivoli Park and the Julian Alps outside of Ljubljana. Parking is free, and you'll find easy access to all major highways; soundproof windows keep traffic from spoiling the comfort. Rooms are decorated in soothing pastel tones. Check the Web site for occasional summer discounts. ✉ *Vošnjakova 1, 1000* ☎ *01/433–2155* ⊕ *www.hotel-lev.si* ↩ *170 rooms* ♿ *In-room: safe (some), dial-up. In-hotel: restaurant, room service, bar, gym, laundry service, public Internet, parking (no fee), no-smoking rooms* ▭ *AE, DC, MC, V* ⦿*BP.*

$$–$$$ ⊞**Best Western Slon Hotel.** Close to the river, this high-rise hotel stands on the site of a famous 16th-century inn and maintains an atmosphere of traditional hospitality. The breakfast is among the finest in the city. The run-of-the-mill rooms are comfortable, and the wood floors are a nice alternative to wall-to-wall carpeting. ✉ *Slovenska 34, 1000* ☎ *01/470–1131* ⊕ *www.hotelslon.com* ↩ *185 rooms* ♿ *In-room: no a/c (some), safe, Ethernet, Wi-Fi. In-hotel: 2 restaurants, room service, no-smoking rooms, parking (no fee)* ▭ *AE, DC, MC, V* ⦿*BP.*

$$–$$$ ⊞**Domina Grand Media Ljubljana.** It's the hotel of the future. At least that's what the owners of this—the city's newest addition to the upscale lodging class—would have us believe. Some of the high-concept amenities include plasma screens in all the rooms, total Internet connectivity, a fully equipped wellness center, and retro-modern furniture straight out of the Jetsons. The location is a bit out of the way, but the hotel offers free shuttle service to the center. ✉ *Dunajska cesta 154* ☎ *01/588–2500* ⊕ *www.dominagmljubljana.com* ↩ *160 rooms, 57 suites* ♿ *In-room: safe, Ethernet, dial-up, Wi-Fi. In-hotel: 2 restaurants, no-smoking rooms* ▭ *AE, DC, MC, V* ⦿*BP.*

$$ ⊞**City Hotel.** The former Turist Hotel has undergone a makeover. The result has been enhanced services, such as wider Internet access for guests, but at a higher price. The basic rooms are clean and the location is excellent. ✉ *Dalmatinova 15, 1000* ☎ *01/239–0000* ⊕ *www.cityhotel.si* ↩ *123 rooms* ♿ *In-room: kitchen (some), Wi-Fi (some). In-hotel: 2 restaurants, bicycles, public Internet* ▭ *AE, DC, MC, V.*

★ $ ⊞**Emonec.** One of the city's newest two-star hotels, Emonec fills a longtime gap in the market for a clean, affordable hotel in the center.

8

Don't expect much in the way of frills or services, but the simple modern rooms are tastefully furnished, the breakfast is fine, and the staff is helpful. At this price level in Ljubljana, that's a considerable bargain. ⊠ *Wolfova 12, 1000* ☎*01/200–1520* ⊕*www.hotel-emonec.com* ⟿*26 rooms* ♿*In-room: no a/c, Ethernet. In-hotel: bicycles, public Internet, parking (no fee), no elevator* ⊟*AE, DC, MC, V* ⊚|*BP.*

$ 🍴**Gostilna Pri Mraku.** This friendly pension offers good value with simple but comfortable rooms and a decent restaurant. It is situated on a quiet side street, close to the Križanke Summer Theater. ⊠ *Rimska 4, 1000* ☎*01/421–9600* ⊕*www.daj-dam.si* ⟿*30 rooms* ♿*In-room: no a/c (some), safe. In-hotel: restaurant, public Internet, no elevator* ⊟*AE, DC, MC, V.*

NIGHTLIFE & THE ARTS

Although they were considered the workaholics of Yugoslavia, Slovenes do know how to enjoy themselves. One in 10 of the capital's inhabitants is a student, hence the proliferation of trendy cafés and small art galleries. Each year the International Summer Festival breathes new life into the Ljubljana cultural scene, sparking off a lively program of concerts and experimental theater. For information about forthcoming cultural events, check *Events in Ljubljana,* a monthly pamphlet published by the Ljubljana Promotion Center, and the English-language magazine *Ljubljana Life,* both available in major hotels and tourist offices.

NIGHTLIFE

The listed bars and clubs are all situated within walking distance of the center. However, during summer the all-night party scene moves to the Adriatic coast, where open-air dancing and rave parties abound.

CAFÉS

The most idyllic way to close a summer evening is with a nightcap on the terrace of one of the riverside cafés in the Old Town.

Hip **Cafe Galerija** (⊠ *Mestni trg 5* ☎*01/426–0327*) serves stylish cocktails by candlelight in a North Africa–inspired hideout. With a large terrace and glamorous clientele, **Cafe Maček** (⊠ *Krojaška 5* ☎*01/425–3791*) is the place to be seen down by the river. **Caffe Boheme** (⊠ *Mestni trg 19* ☎*01/548–1342*) in the heart of the Old Town is spacious inside and has a terrace with tables and umbrellas outside.

MUSIC

For Latin music or a pick-me-up breakfast in the early hours, visit **Casa del Papa** (⊠ *Celovška 54A* ☎*01/434–3158*): three floors of exotic food, drinks, and entertainment in tribute to Ernest Hemingway. For live jazz visit **Jazz Club Gajo** (⊠ *Beethovnova 8* ☎*01/425–3206*), which attracts stars from home and abroad. Clark Terry, Sheila Jordan, and Woody Shaw have all performed here. The student-run club **K4** (⊠ *Kersnikova 4* ☎*01/431–7010*) hosts visiting DJs and plays a mix of musical styles—house, hip-hop, surf—throughout the week. It attracts a young and alternative crowd; Sunday is gay night.

BARS & CLUBS

If it's rowdy beer-drinking and shot-downing you're looking for, the epicenter for this is the courtyard just off Wolfova ulica 6, or in nice weather just follow the crowds—and the noise—to the Knafljev prehod. **As Lounge** (⊠*Knafljev prehod* ☎*01/425–8822*). **Cutty Sark** (⊠*Knafijev prehod* ☎*01/425–1477*). **Bar Minimal** (⊠*Mestni trg 4* ☎*01/426–0138*), as the name suggests, is a spare, all-white space for Ljubljana's beautiful people. One place that is definitely not chic is the shabby former squat **Metelkova** (⊠*Metelkova, Tabor* ☎*01/432–3378*). At one time this was an army barracks that was occupied by students and transformed into a multipurpose venue for shows and happenings. It's constantly under threat of demolition by city authorities. If you get hunger pangs after a night in the bars in the Old Town, head to **Romeo** (⊠*Stari trg 6* ☎*No phone*) for great sandwiches and quesadillas. It's open until midnight. For great cocktails, head over to **Salon** (⊠*Trubarjeva 23* ☎*01/433–2006*) on a funky street just north of the main Old Town cluster. The gold lamé and leopard-skin interior lend a cool, East Village–like vibe.

THE ARTS

ANNUAL EVENTS

Each year in June, the International Jazz Festival and the Druga Godba (a festival of alternative and ethnic music) are staged at the Križanke Summer Theater. For schedules and tickets contact the box office at Cankarjev dom. Ljubljana's **International Summer Festival** (⊠*Trg Francoske Revolucije 1–2* ☎*01/241–6026* ⊕*www.festival-lj.si*) is held each July and August in the open-air Križanke Summer Theater. Musical, theatrical, and dance performances attract acclaimed artists from all over the world.

PERFORMANCE HALLS

Cankarjev dom (*Cankar House* ⊠*Prešernova 10* ☎*01/241–7100* ⊕*www. cd-cc.si*) opened in 1980 as a modern, rather characterless venue. As a cultural center, however, it is the driving force behind the city's artistic activities, offering up-to-date general information and tickets. A progressive film festival takes place here every November.

CLASSICAL MUSIC

Ljubljana has plenty of events for classical-music lovers. The season, which runs from September through June, includes weekly concerts by the Slovenian Philharmonic Orchestra and the RTV Slovenia Orchestra, as well as performances by guest soloists, chamber musicians, and foreign symphony orchestras. The 19th-century performance hall housing concerts by the **Slovenska Filharmonija** (*Slovenian Philharmonic* ⊠*Kongresni trg 10* ☎*01/241–0800* ⊕*www.filharmonija.si*) is a traditional classical-music venue. The orchestra dates to 1908, but its predecessors have roots in the early 18th century.

FILM

Cinemas generally screen the original versions of films, with Slovenian subtitles. **Kinoteka** (⊠*Miklošičeva 28* ☎*01/434–2520* ⊕*www. kinoteka.si*) runs some great retrospectives.

THEATER, DANCE & OPERA

Ljubljana has a long tradition of experimental and alternative theater, with dance often thrown into the mix. Contemporary dance plays by the internationally recognized choreographers Matjaz Faric and Iztok Kovac and performances by the dance troupes Betontanc and En Knap are ideal for English speakers.

From September through June the **SNG Opera in Balet** (*Slovene National Opera & Ballet Theater* ⊠*Župančičeva 1* ☎*01/241–1764* ⊕*www.opera.si*) stages everything from classical to modern and alternative productions.

> ### GIFT IDEAS
>
> The most interesting gifts to buy in Slovenia are the homemade products you come across in your travels: wine from Ptuj, *rakija* (a potent spirit distilled from fruit) from Pleterje Monastery, herbal teas from Stična Monastery, and honey from Radovljica. The Slovenian products best known abroad are connected with outdoor sports. If you'd like some Planika walking boots or Elan skis, you can get a good deal on them here.

SHOPPING

Although you wouldn't come to Slovenia to do much serious shopping, fashionable shoe stores abound in Ljubljana; for the latest selection head to shops on Stari trg in the Old Town. If you want to do some hiking but have come unprepared, **Anappurna** (⊠*Krakovski Nasip 10* ☎*01/426–3428*) has a good selection of mountaineering equipment. You can pick up antiques and memorabilia at the **Ljubljana Flea Market** (⊠*Cankarjevo nab*), held near Tromostovje (Triple Bridge) each Sunday morning. The most interesting shopping experience is undoubtedly a visit to the **open-air market** (⊠*Vodnikov trg*), where besides fresh fruit and vegetables you can find dried herbs and locally produced honey. **Skrina** (⊠*Breg 8* ☎*01/425–5161*) has some unusual local crafts.

SIDE TRIP TO THE KRKA VALLEY

A drive through the Krka Valley makes a perfect day trip from Ljubljana. The monasteries of Stična and Pleterje offer insight into contemporary monastic life, and there are two castles, Otočec and Mokrice, where you can stop for lunch—or a romantic overnight stay in exquisite surroundings.

Take the E70 highway east out of Ljubljana, and then turn right at Ivančna Gorica to follow a secondary road along the Krka Valley. For a more direct journey home, return to the E70 just north of Šentjernej. There are also buses from Ljubljana to Ivančna Gorica and Šentjernej, but these are practical only if you don't mind walking the final stretch to the monasteries.

★ The **Stična Samostan** (*Stična Monastery*) lies 2 km (1 mi) north of Ivančna Gorica. Founded by the Cistercians in 1135, the monastery was fortified in the 15th century to protect against Turkish invasion.

The Krka Valley

E57
Celje
Trbovlje
Hrastnik
Domzale
Zagorje
HRVATSKA
(CROATIA)
A1
424
423
219
LJUBLJANA
108
417
Sava
Sevnica
Stična
Samostan
215
Krško
29
Ivančna
Gorica
Trbnje
418
A2
Brežice
106
Zagradec
E70
Mokrice
Otočec
Šentjernej
Žužemberk
216
419
0   10 mi
Krka
Ribnica
Novo
Mesto
Pleterje
Samostan
Velika
Gora
216
105
0   10 km

Today there are only 10 monks, plus three nuns who attend to the cooking. The monks produce excellent herbal teas that work (allegedly) against cellulite, insomnia, poor memory, and practically every other problem you can think of, on sale in the monastery shop. The early-Gothic cloisters, the baroque church, and the adjoining **Slovenian Religious Museum** are open to the public. The museum's collections include archives dedicated to the work of Bishop Friderik Baraga, a 19th-century missionary to the United States who compiled the first dictionary of the Native American Otchipwe language. Call first to arrange a visit. ⊠ *Stična 17, Ivančna Gorica* ☎ *01/787-7100* ⌖€4 ⊙ *Tues.–Sat. 8–11 and 2–5, Sun. 2–5.*

★ The Carthusian monks of **Pleterje Samostan** *(Pleterje Monastery)* aim "to find God in silence and solitude." Therefore, you can't enter the monastery proper, but you are welcome to view the magnificent 15th-century Gothic church and to watch a fascinating audiovisual presentation (in English) about the way the monks live. The walled monastery is nestled in a lonely valley surrounded by woods. Once a week the monks take a 45-minute walk around the perimeter of the complex. The route is marked with a blue circle and yellow cross, so you can follow the trail independently. A small shop sells rakija, honey, wine, and cheese made by the monks. To reach the monastery from Stična Monastery follow the Krka River through Zagradec, Žužemberk, and Novo Mesto. At Šentjernej, turn south and travel for 6 km (4 mi) to reach Pleterje. ⊠ *Drča 1, Šentjernej* ☎ *07/308-1225* ⌖ *Free* ⊙ *Daily 7:30–5:30.*

WHERE TO STAY

$$ Hotel Grad Otočec. About 8 km (5 mi) west of Šentjernej, on the road to Novo Mesto, you will find the entrance to the medieval Otočec castle, dating from the 13th century. Now a luxury hotel, complete with period furniture, Otočec sits on an island in the Krka River and is accessible by a wooden bridge. You can also camp on the castle grounds. Nonguests are welcome to dine in the restaurant, where the house specialty is locally caught game. Or just stop by for a drink in the courtyard café. Equestrian and tennis centers are close by. ⊠ *Grajska*

8

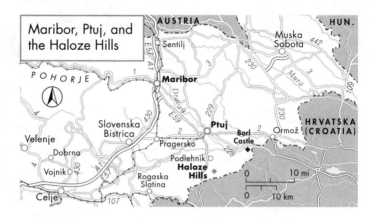

1, *Otočec ob Krki, 8222* 📠*07/384–8900* ⊕*www.terme-krka.si* ➷*16 rooms* ♨*In-hotel: restaurant* ▭*AE, DC, MC, V* ⦿❙*BP.*

♨ $$ 🔳**Hotel Toplice.** With 11 springs supplying thermal water, Terme Čatež is the largest natural spa in Slovenia. Hotel Toplice—the newest of the four hotels connected to the spa—is the ultimate destination for recharging your batteries. It houses expansive indoor thermal baths as well as a fully loaded sports center. ⊠*Topliska 35, Čatež ob Savi, 8251* 📠*07/493–5023* ⊕*www.terme-catez.si* ➷*140 rooms* ♨*In-room: refrigerator, safe. In-hotel: restaurant, tennis courts, pool, gym, spa, public Internet* ▭*AE, DC, MC, V* ⦿❙*BP.*

SPORTS & THE OUTDOORS

For horse lovers the **Struga Equestrian Center** (⊠*Otočec* 📠*07/307– 5627*), at a 12th-century medieval manor, is a 20-minute walk from Otočec Castle. The center offers riding lessons and rents horses.

MARIBOR, PTUJ & HALOZE HILLS

During the 1st century AD, Poetovio, now known as Ptuj, was the largest Roman settlement in the area that is now Slovenia. Much later, in the 13th century, Maribor was founded. Originally given the German name Marchburg, the city took its Slavic name in 1836. For centuries the two towns competed for economic and cultural prominence within the region, and Maribor finally gained the upper hand in 1846, when a new railway line connected the city to Vienna and Trieste. The area between Maribor and Ptuj is a flat, fertile floodplain formed by the Drava River. South of Ptuj lie the hills of Haloze, famous for quality white wines.

MARIBOR

128 km (80 mi) northeast of Ljubljana on the E57.

The presence of thousands of university students gives Maribor— Slovenia's second-largest city—a youthful vibe. You'll find plenty of pubs and cafés, especially in the Lent district along the Drava River. The Old Town has retained a core of ornate 18th- and 19th-century town houses, typical of imperial Austria, and much of it is off-limits to cars.

The heart of the Old Town is **Rotovški trg** with the **Kužno Znamenje** (Plague Memorial) at its center and overlooked by the proud 16th-century Renaissance **Rotovž** (town hall).

From Rotovški trg, a number of traffic-free streets lead down to a riverside promenade, known as **Lent.** It is lined with bars, terrace cafés, restaurants, and boutiques.

Below the streets of Maribor lies one of Europe's largest wine cellars. The **Vinag wine cellar** has some 3½ km (2 mi) of underground tunnels, holding almost 6 million liters of wine. Tours and tastings can be arranged in advance by phone. ⊠ *Trg Svobode 3* ☎ *02/220–8111* ⊕ *www.vinag.si.*

The Vodni Stolp (Water Tower), a former defense tower, houses the **Vinoteka Slovenskih Vin** *(Slovenian Wine Shop).* Here you can sample and purchase more than 500 different Slovenian vintage wines. ⊠ *Usnjarska 10* ☎ *02/251–7743.*

WHERE TO STAY & EAT

In summer, Maribor University dorms are open to visitors, providing a cheap alternative to hotels. For details ask at the Maribor tourist-information center.

\$–\$\$ ✕ **Toti Rotovž.** Close to the town hall, this building has been carefully restored to reveal vaulted brick ceilings and terra-cotta floors. The restaurant serves an eclectic mix of Slovene and international dishes, whereas the *klet* (wine cellar) in the basement cooks up barbecued steaks. ⊠ *Glavni trg 14* ☎ *02/228–7650* ⊟ *AE, DC, MC, V.*

\$ 🖾 **Hotel Orel.** The modern Orel offers the best accommodations in the city center—an easy stroll down the pedestrian zone to the river. There is a pleasant restaurant at street level, the rooms are comfortable, and the service is friendly. Guests are granted access to the sauna and swimming pools at the Fontana Recreation Center, which is about 220 yards away from the hotel. ⊠ *Grajski trg 3A, 2000* ☎ *02/250–6700* ⊕ *www. termemb.si* ⤺ *80 rooms* ♿ *In room: Ethernet, refrigerator. In-hotel: restaurant, parking (no fee)* ⊟ *AE, DC, MC, V* ⦾ *BP.*

SPORTS & THE OUTDOORS

In winter in the Pohorje Mountains, just 6 km (4 mi) southwest of Maribor, you'll find alpine ski runs and cross-country trails. A **cable car** takes you from the south side of town up to the winter resort.

Two well-established bike paths pass through the region. The 95-km (59-mi) **Drava Trail** follows the course of the Drava River through the Kozjak Hills to Maribor and then proceeds to Ptuj. The 56-km (35-mi) **Jantara Trail** runs from Šentilj on the Austrian border to Maribor and continues to Slovenska Bistrica. However, finding a place to rent a bike can be somewhat problematic. Inquire at the Maribor tourist-information center for assistance and information.

PTUJ

25 km (16 mi) southeast of Maribor, 130 km (81 mi) east of Ljubljana.

Ptuj, built beside the Drava River and crowned by a hilltop castle, hits the national news each year in February with its extraordinary Carnival celebration, known as Kurentovanje. During the 10-day festival the town's boys and men dress in the bizarre Kurent costume: a horned mask decorated with ribbons and flowers, a sheepskin cloak, and a set of heavy bells around the waist. The task of the Kurent is to drive away the winter and welcome in the spring. You can see Kurent figures on 18th-century building facades in the center of Ptuj, on Jadranska ulica No. 4 and No. 6. It's a charming place and worth an overnight stay.

Ptujski Grad *(Ptuj Castle)* stands at the top of a steep hill in the center of town. Planned around a baroque courtyard, the castle houses a museum that exhibits musical instruments, an armory, 15th-century church paintings, and period furniture. ⊠ *Grajska Raven* ☎ *02/787–9230* ⊕ *www.pok-muzej-ptuj.si* ⊠ *€4* ⊙ *Mid-Apr.–mid-Oct., daily 9–6; mid-Oct.–mid-Apr., daily 9–4.*

The **Ptuj Regional Museum,** in a former Dominican monastery, has an outstanding collection of ancient artifacts and coins, as well as Roman statuary and tombstones. The museum offers guided tours in English. ⊠ *Muzejski trg 1* ☎ *02/787–9230* ⊠ *€4* ⊙ *Sept.–June, daily 9–6; July and Aug., weekdays 9–6, weekends 9–8.*

Vinska Klet *(Ptuj Wine Cellars)* offers a tasting session with five different wines, bread, and cheese, plus a bottle to take home. You are also given a tour of the underground cellars. A sound-and-video presentation takes you through the seasons of wine making at the vineyards. The wines stocked here come predominantly from the Haloze Hills. One of the best wines is Šipon, a dry white that pairs nicely with pork dishes and rich sauces. ⊠ *Vinarski trg 1* ☎ *02/787–9810* ⊠ *€6–€8* ⊙ *Weekdays 7–7, Sat. 7–noon.*

WHERE TO EAT

★ $-$$$ ✕ **Ribič.** This lovely riverside restaurant is arguably the city's best. Though the menu offers seafood such as crab and lobster, the real treats here are the river fish, such as trout. The interior is simple, and the walls are hung with fishing nets. In warmer months, sit on the terrace with a view over the Drava. ⊠ *Dravska 9* ☎ *02/749–0653* ▭ *AE, DC, MC, V.*

WHERE TO STAY

★ $ ▦ **Garni Hotel Mitra.** If you stay overnight in Ptuj, you'll do fine in this popular, three-story, old-fashioned inn. The 19th-century facade suits the street just perfectly. Note that the rooms can get hot in summer—it's best to request a room on the cooler second floor, away from the roof.

✉*Prešernovo 6* ⌨*02/787–7455* ⊕*www.hotelptuj.com* ⛏*21 rooms, 2 apts.* ♿*In-room: no a/c. In-hotel: restaurant, refrigerator (some), no elevator* ▭*AE, DC, MC, V* ⏋⊙⏐*BP.*

SPORTS & THE OUTDOORS

If you have access to a bike, you'll find a great run to the east of Ptuj along the 20-km (12-mi) Jeruzalem-Ljutomer *Vinska cesta* (wine road). Rent a bike at the Terme Ptuj, or ask at the Ptuj tourist-information center for other possible options.

🕓 **Terme Ptuj** (✉*Pot v Toplice 9* ⌨*02/782–7821* ⊕*www.terme-ptuj.si*) is more a family fun center than a serious spa, with a big pool and water park. You can also rent bikes here.

THE HALOZE HILLS

Borl Castle is 11 km (7 mi) southeast of Ptuj, 140 km (87 mi) east of Ljubljana.

The Haloze Hills lie south of Ptuj, close to the Croatian border. Grapes are generally planted on the steeper, south-facing slopes, to take full advantage of the sunshine, whereas the cooler, north-facing slopes are covered with trees and pastures. The best way to explore the region is to pick up the Haloze wine route near **Borl Castle,** through an undulating landscape of vineyards and woodlands. For a map of the route plus a comprehensive list of vineyards and wine stores open to the public, inquire at the Ptuj tourist-information center.

On the road between Podlehnik and Poljčane, keep an eye out for the sign for Štatenberg Castle; you can't stay there, but it has a good restaurant. Built between 1720 and 1740, Štatenberg is a typical example of the baroque style favored by the local aristocracy during the 18th century.

8

WHERE TO EAT

$ ✗**Štatenberg Castle.** This restaurant serves traditional dishes, such as roast meats, accompanied by excellent local wines. Throughout summer you can sit at tables outside in the courtyard. ✉*Štatenberg 86, Makole* ⌨*02/803–0216* ▭*No credit cards* ⊙*Closed Mon.*

MARIBOR, PTUJ & HALOZE HILLS ESSENTIALS

AIR TRAVEL

In mid-2007, Ryanair became the first low-cost airline with connections to Maribor, flying three times a week from London Stansted.

BUS TRAVEL

Regular buses link Maribor and Ptuj to Ljubljana. However, the train is cheaper and more comfortable. An hourly bus service connects Maribor and Ptuj; the 45-minute journey costs around €5.

Information Maribor Bus Station (✉*Mlinska 1, Maribor* ⌨*02/235–0212*).

CAR TRAVEL

To reach Maribor from Ljubljana take the E57; for Ptuj turn off at Slovenska Bistrica. A car is almost essential for exploring the Haloze Hills wine route. Some of the country roads are narrow and winding. Although there is snow in winter, it is extremely rare to find roads closed.

TRAIN TRAVEL

Regular train service links Ljubljana and Maribor; several international trains continue to Graz and Vienna. It is also possible to reach Ptuj by train from Ljubljana, though you may have to change at Pragersko. For information contact Ljubljana's train station (⇨ *Train Travel in Ljubljana Essentials*). Several trains daily connect Maribor and Ptuj, with a change at Pragersko; the 45-minute journey costs around €8.

Information **Maribor Train Station** (⊠ *Partizanska 50, Maribor* ☎ *02/292–2100*).

VISITOR INFORMATION

Information **Maribor Tourist Information** (⊠ *Partizanska 47, Maribor* ☎ *02/234–6611* ⊕ *www.maribor-tourism.si*). **Ptuj Tourist Information** (⊠ *Slovenski trg 3, Ptuj* ☎ *02/771–0173* ⊕ *www.ptuj-tourism.si*).

THE ALPS & THE SOČA VALLEY

Northwest of Ljubljana lies an unspoiled region of breathtakingly beautiful mountains, alpine lakes, and fast-running rivers. Much of the region is part of the protected Triglavski Narodni Park (Triglav National Park), and it's the perfect jumping-off spot for adventure pursuits of all sorts. Superior skiing, hiking, rafting, biking, and fly-fishing draw people here from around the world.

Each of the major towns and resorts in the region—Bled, Bohinj, Kranjska Gora, and Bovec—offers something a little different. At Bled the focus is on comfort and excellent facilities, poised against a fairy-tale backdrop of an island church in a green-blue lake. Bohinj's charms are more rustic—a pristine deep-green alpine sea, bordered by mountains on three sides. Kranjska Gora and Bovec offer more immediate access to high-octane adventure. The former is Slovenia's leading ski resort. In summer it opens its lifts to mountain bikers and free-riders seeking the adrenaline rush of a dash down the slopes. Bovec, on the Soča River, offers world-class rafting and canyoning—or gentler floats—down what must be one of the world's most beautiful mountain streams.

These regional centers can be approached individually or, in summer, by car or bus as part of a large loop running northwest from Ljubljana. Proceed first to Bled and on to Bohinj, then push on farther north to Kranjska Gora, over the impossibly high Vršic pass, and down to Bovec. The return to Ljubljana is via the World War I battle town of Kobarid and Idrija.

EN ROUTE

On the road to Bled from Ljubljana you pass a junction for Radovljica. Turn off here to see the lovingly preserved 17th-century town center and visit the intriguing **Čebelarski muzej** (*Beekeeping Museum*

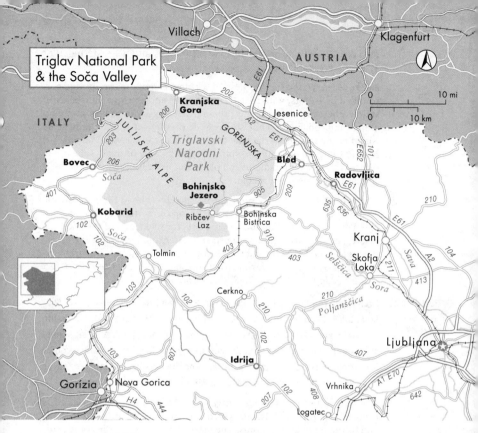

Triglav National Park
& the Soča Valley

Villach
Klagenfurt
AUSTRIA
ITALY
JULIJSKE ALPE
Kranjska Gora
Jesenice
Triglavski Narodni Park
GORENJSKA
Bled
Bovec
Soča
Radovljica
Kobarid
Bohinjsko Jezero
Ribčev Laz
Bohinska Bistrica
Kranj
Tolmin
Škofja Loka
Cerkno
Selščica
Sora
Poljanščica
Ljubljana
Gorízia
Nova Gorica
Idrija
Vrhnika
Logatec

0   10 mi
0   10 km

⊠ *Linhartov trg 1, Radovljica* ☎ *04/532–0520).* The museum charges
an admission fee of €3.50. It's open from May through August, Tuesday to Sunday from 10 to 1 and 4 to 6; in September and October, it's
open Tuesday to Sunday from 10 to noon and 3 to 5; in March, April,
November, and December, it's open only on Wednesday and weekends
from 10 to noon and 3 to 5.

BLED

50 km (31 mi) northwest of Ljubljana on the E61.

Bled is among the most magnificently situated mountain resorts in
Europe. The healing powers of its thermal springs were known during the 17th century. In the early 19th century the aristocracy arrived
to bask in Bled's tranquil alpine setting. Even today—when Bled can
swell to overflowing in the high season of July and August—it retains
something of the refined feel of a *fin de siècle* spa town.

Recent years have brought a string of improvements to Bled's tourist
facilities. New resorts and wellness centers, arguably the country's best
golf course, and a clutch of new adventure-oriented travel agencies
mean there is now much more to do than simply stroll the banks of

the lake. Bled is also an excellent base for hikes into the eastern half of Triglav National Park.

Blejsko Jezero *(Lake Bled)* is nestled within a rim of mountains and surrounded by forests, with a castle on one side and a promenade beneath stately chestnut trees on the other. Horse-drawn carriages clip-clop along the promenade while swans glide on the water. On a minuscule island in the middle of the lake the lovely **Cerkov svetega Martina** (St. Martin's Pilgrimage Church) stands within a circle of trees. Take a ride over to the island on a *pletna*, an old-fashioned canopied wooden boat similar to a Venetian gondola.

☾ The stately 16th-century **grad** *(castle)* perches above the lake on the summit of a steep cliff, against a backdrop of the Julian Alps and Triglav Peak. You can climb up to the castle for fine views of the lake, the resort, and the surrounding countryside. An exhibition traces the development of the castle through the centuries, with objects from archaeological finds to period furniture on display. ⊠*Bled* ☎*04/578–0525* ⌨*€6* ⊙*May–Sept., daily 8–8; Oct.–Apr., daily 9–5.*

NEED A
BREAK?

Even if you're not staying at the illustrious Grand Hotel Toplice (⊠ *C. Svobode 12* ☎*04/579-1000)*, you're welcome to use its sauna and soak in the thermal waters (28°C [83°F]) of the indoor swimming pool. A small admission fee includes a towel and locker. Or try the Toplice's wellness center for various massage treatments, facials, and the tantalizingly labeled "citrus body sensation" (a full-body massage with orange and lemon balm).

☾ The **Soteska Vintgar** *(Vintgar Gorge)* was cut between precipitous cliffs by the clear Radovna River, which flows down numerous waterfalls and through pools and rapids. The marked trail through the gorge leads over bridges and along wooden walkways and galleries. ⊠*Zgornje Gorje Rd., 5 km (3 mi) northwest of Bled.*

WHERE TO EAT

★ $$$–$$$$ ✕**Gostilna Lectar.** This warm country-style inn serves an impressive selection of traditional dishes. For a cross section of the local cuisine, try the pumpkin soup, the Peasant's Plate (buckwheat dumplings, mixed smoked meats, potatoes, and fresh steamed vegetables), and the apple strudel. The restaurant is 10 km (6 mi) south of Bled on the E61 highway. ⊠*Linhartov trg 2, Radovljica* ☎*04/537–4800* ⊟*AE, DC, MC, V.*

☾ $–$$$ ✕**Mlino.** Follow the footpath along the south side of the lake 20 minutes from the center of Bled to reach this informal family restaurant with a lovely garden terrace. Try the Mlino Plate, a mixed platter of barbecued meats served with *djevec* (rice cooked with vegetables). There is a special menu for children, and boats are for hire on the lake. ⊠*C. Svobode 45* ☎*04/574–1404* ⊟*AE, DC, MC, V.*

$–$$ ✕**Gostilna pri Planincu.** This friendly place is busy year-round. Locals meet here for morning coffee or a bargain prix-fixe lunch—or just to drink the cheapest beer in town. While rowdy farmers occupy the front bar, lovers share a candlelit supper in the dining room. Portions are "for people who work all day": roast chicken and fries, steak and mushrooms, black pudding, and turnips. For dessert, walnut *štrukli* (dumplings) are served with cream. ⊠ *Grajska 8* ☎ *04/574–1613* ⊟ *AE, DC, MC, V.*

$–$$ ✕ **Pletna.** An informal pizzeria not far from Mlino has excellent pizzas, very good grilled meats, and a second-story terrace with a lovely view over the lake. Follow the footpath along the south side of the lake about 15 minutes from the center of Bled. ⊠ *C. Svobode 37* ☎ *04/576– 7211* ⊟ *AE, DC, MC, V.*

WHERE TO STAY

$$$ ⊞ **Vila Bled.** Late Yugoslav president Tito was the gracious host to numerous 20th-century statesmen at this former royal residence, amid 13 acres of gardens overlooking the lake. It was converted into a luxurious hotel in 1984 and became part of the Relais & Châteaux group in 1987. After a renovation in 2004, the managers wisely chose to retain many of the original furnishings from the 1950s—giving the rooms and public areas a formal but still retro-chic feel. It's unique. ⊠ *C. Svobode 26, 4260* ☎ *04/579–1500* ⊕ *www.vila-bled.com* ↔ *10 rooms, 20 suites* ↻ *In-hotel: restaurant, bar, tennis court, spa* ⊟ *AE, DC, MC, V* ⦿ *BP.*

★ **$$–$$$** ⊞ **Grand Hotel Toplice.** This old-fashioned, ivy-covered resort hotel has been favored by British travelers since the 1920s. Directly on the lake, the main building has balconies and big windows from which you can take in dramatic views of the castle and the Julian Alps. The rooms, lounges, and bar are all furnished with antiques and heirloom rugs. It's worth the splurge for a lakeside room. ⊠ *C. Svobode 12, 4260* ☎ *04/579–1000* ⊕ *www.hotel-toplice.com* ↔ *206 rooms* ↻ *In-room: Ethernet. In-hotel: 3 restaurants, bar, pools, gym, spa, public Wi-Fi* ⊟ *AE, DC, MC, V* ⦿ *BP.*

$ ⊞ **Penzion Bledec Youth Hostel.** Just five minutes from the lake and 10 minutes from the castle, Bledec is one of the cleanest and most comfortable youth hostels in Europe. Rooms have mostly three or four beds with shared bath; there are also a few private double rooms. ⊠ *Grajska 17, 4260* ☎ *05/574–5250* ⊕ *www.mlino.si* ↔ *13 rooms with shared bath* ↻ *In-room: no a/c. In-hotel: restaurant, bar, public Internet, no elevator* ⊟ *MC* ⦿ *BP.*

SPORTS & THE OUTDOORS

During summer, the lake turns into a family playground, with swimming, rowing, sailing, and windsurfing. The main swimming area lies below the castle along the northern shore. In winter on Straža Hill, immediately above town, you can ski day and night, thanks to floodlighting. Just 10 km (6 mi) west of Bled, a larger ski area, Zatrnik, has 7 km (4½ mi) of alpine trails. The area's two golf courses—the 18-hole "Kings" course and the 9-hole "Lake" course—are located 4 km (2½ mi) outside of town at the Golf & Country Club Bled. For information on winter and summer sports, contact Bled's tourist-information center or one of the many private travel and activity agencies around town.

Bled Rafting (⊠ *Hrastova 2, Bled* ☎ *041/678–008* ⊕ *www.bled-rafting. si*) specializes in rafting, kayaking, and canyoning trips on area rivers. **Golf & Country Club Bled** (⊠ *Kidričeva 10c, Bled* ☎ *04/537–7711* ⊕ *www.golf.bled.si*) runs the area's two golf courses (18 holes, the

8

other 9 holes); rents clubs, caddies and carts; provides instruction; and sanctions golf events. **3glav Adventures** (⊠*Ljubljanska 1, Bohinj* ☏*041/683–184* ⊕*www.explore-more.com*) is a great young outfit that can put together hiking and rafting outings, or organize more extreme activities like parachuting and paragliding.

BOHINJSKO JEZERO

25 km (16 mi) southwest of Bled, 75 km (47 mi) from Ljubljana.

Bohinjsko Jezero (Lake Bohinj) lies to the south and west of Bled along a crowded two-lane highway that thins out the farther you travel from Bled. If you're driving, follow the signs to "jezero" (lake). The lake area proper begins in the small lakeside village of Ribčev Laz. Lake Bohinj is quieter, wilder, and in many ways prettier than Bled, its sister lake to the east.

Unlike Bled, Bohinj lies entirely within the Triglav National Park. This has greatly inhibited development of the shore and surrounding areas. The entire length of the north shore is wild and accessible only by foot. The lake, at an altitude of 1,715 feet, is surrounded on three sides by the steep walls of the Julian Alps. The altitude means the temperature of the water—even in August—rarely rises above a brisk but still swim-mable 74°F.

There is no town called "Bohinj" as such. The small village of Ribčev Laz, on the eastern end of the lake functions as the de facto town center, where you'll find a grocery store, post office, currency exchange, an ATM, and the tourist-information center. On the western shore lies the remote village of Ukanc, anchored by the Hotel Zlatorog, a campsite, and a few small shops. Just to the north and east of Ribčev Laz are the tiny hamlets of Stara Fužina, Studor, and Srednja Vas. Addresses are simple enough when you figure out what they mean: the name of the village is first, followed by the house or building number; administra-tively, "Bohinjsko Jezero" is treated as the "town."

On the eastern bank of Lake Bohinj in Ribčev Laz, you'll find the 15th-century Gothic church of **Sveti Janez** *(St. John)*. The small church has a fine bell tower and contains a number of notable 15th- and 16th-century frescoes. ⊠*Ribčev Laz.*

At the west end of Lake Bohinj near Ukanc a cable car leads up **Mt. Vogel** to a height of 5,035 feet. From here, you have spectacular views of the Julian Alps massif and the Bohinj valley and lake. From the cable-car base, the road continues 5 km (3 mi) beyond the lake to the point where the Savica River makes a tremendous leap over a 194-foot waterfall. The cable car runs year-round from 8 AM until 6 PM (until 7 PM in July and August). A round-trip ticket costs €8. Gasoline-powered engines are not allowed on Lake Bohinj because of the danger of pol-lution. The super-quiet **Turistična Ladja** *(Tourist Boat)* runs on electrical power. The boat makes hourly runs during daylight hours from June to mid-September from the boat dock just below Ribčev Laz to Camp

Zlatorog on the western side of the lake and back. A ticket costs €6.50 one way, or €8 round-trip.

WHERE TO EAT

Most of the hotels and pensions in the area offer full or least half-board, reducing the number of independent restaurants. That's not to say there aren't places worth searching out. Because pension food can sometimes become monotonous, there may be afternoons or evenings when you want to strike out on your own anyway.

$$ ✕ **Pizzerija Center.** About the only option in the main commercial center, Ribčev Laz, for a quick lunch or dinner, this place serves agreeable enough pizzas, but try the grilled lake fish (*charr*) if you see it on the menu—it's a local treat. ⊠ *Ribčev Laz 50* ☎ *04/572–3170* ⊟ *AE, DC, MC, V.*

★ $–$$ ✕ **Gostilna Rupa.** Excellent home-cooked meals and a breathtaking view off the terrace toward the valley and the mountains beyond are your reward for an easy 5-km (3-mi) drive or bike ride from Ribičev Laz to the tiny hamlet of Srednja Vas. If you're really hungry, order the house specialty *mavželj* (essentially spiced ground beef and pork, breaded and fried); it comes served with buckwheat dumplings, sauerkraut, and potatoes. You won't need dessert. On Thursday in warm weather there's a pig roast. ⊠ *Srednja Vas 87* ☎ *04/572–3401* ⊟ *AE, DC, MC, V.*

$–$$ ✕ **Planšar.** This tiny, informal eatery in the tiny village of Stara Fužina—just down from Ribčev Laz—is something of a local institution and one of the few places to sample the area's cheeses—hard and soft. Mix and match cheese and dumpling plates, or go for a hot, filling soup. For dessert, it's *štrukli* (dumplings) served with cream. ⊠ *Stara Fužina 179* ☎ *04/572–3095* ⊟ *AE, DC, MC, V.*

WHERE TO STAY

The Bohinj area is the perfect place to bypass the hotels and stay in a private home or pension. The tourist-information center in Ribčev Laz maintains an extensive list. Pensions are usually priced per person and often include lunch or dinner. Some of the nicest properties are in the outlying villages of Ukanc, Stara Fužina, and Srednja Vas—though you'll need your own transportation (bike or car) to get there.

☺ $$ 🏨 **Hotel Zlatorog.** A very likable, guest-friendly alpine-style hotel stands on the far western edge of the lake. The facilities—including an indoor pool and sauna—and proximity to the ski lifts make it a great winter choice. The large lawn and on-site playground are perfect for families with young children. Even if you're not staying here, you can rent bikes or use the hotel's two tennis courts (€3–€8 an hour). Rooms are divided between the main hotel and an adjoining villa. ⊠ *Ukanc 65, 4265* ☎ *04/572–3381* ⊕ *www.alpinum.net* ⇆ *43 rooms, 31 villa rooms* ₺ *In-room: refrigerator. In-hotel: restaurant, bar, tennis courts, pool, bicycles* ⊟ *AE, DC, MC, V* ⊚*BP.*

$ 🏨 **Hotel Bellevue.** Off the beaten track, high above Ribčev Laz, this 1930s-era alpine lodge nevertheless affords wonderful views of the lake. Be sure to request a lakeside room. Agatha Christie apparently fell in love with the hotel and stayed here for a month in 1967 on a working holiday. The hotel has set up an Agatha Christie reading room,

8

complete with mini-library and typewriter. ⊠*Ribčev Laz 65, 4265* ☏*04/572–3331* ⊕*www.alpinum.net* ↘*76 rooms* ⟐*In-hotel: restaurant, bar, tennis court, no elevator* ⊟*AE, DC, MC, V* ⵔ*BP.*

$ ⊡ **Pension Stare.** This delightful family-run pension is on the far western end of the lake in the tiny hamlet of Ukanc. To find it, continue beyond the Hotel Zlatorog, down a tiny lane and over a plank bridge. The young couple who own it will greet you with a glass of wine or beer on the terrace. It's very popular, so book in advance. ⊠*Ukanc 128, 4265* ☏*04/574– 6400* ⊕*www.national-park-hotel.com* ↘*10 rooms* ⟐*In-room: no a/c, no TV. In-hotel: restaurant, no elevator* ⊟*AE, DC, MC, V* ⵔ*BP.*

$ ⊡ **Vila Park.** A luxurious little A-frame pension sits astride an impossibly gorgeous alpine meadow and just beside the bright-green Savica stream that feeds Lake Bohinj. Hardwood floors, tasteful furnishings, and full modern conveniences put this head and shoulders above the typical offerings. The entrance is down a tiny road just beyond the Zlatorog Hotel in Ukanc. ⊠*Ukanc 129, 4265* ☏*04/572–3300* ⊕*www. vila-park.com* ↘*10 rooms* ⟐*In-room: safe, dial-up. In-hotel: restaurant, bar, no elevator* ⊟*AE, DC, MC, V* ⵔ*BP.*

SPORTS & THE OUTDOORS

Bohinj is a natural base for exploring the trails of the Triglav National Park. Before heading out, pick up a good trail map from the tourist-information center. The cable car to Vogel is an excellent starting point for many of the walks. Just remember to get an early start, wear proper hiking boots, take plenty of water, and protect yourself against the sun. Other popular warm-weather pursuits include swimming, biking, rafting, canyoning, and horseback riding. In winter you can ski at the ski areas of Vogel and Kobla.

Ⓒ **Alpinsport** (⊠*Ribčev Laz 53* ☏*04/572–3486* ⊕*www.alpinsport.si*), in the village of Studor, rents mountain bikes and organizes raft, kayak, hydrospeed (a small board for bodysurfing rapids), and canyoning trips. **Perfect Adventure Choice/PAC Sports** (⊠*Ribčev Laz 50* ☏*04/574–6511* ⊕*www.pac-sports.com*) is another local outfitter offering river trips and rafting, as well as bike rental and caving expeditions. **Mrcina Ranč** (⊠*Studor, Bohinj* ☏*041/790–297* ⊕*www.ranc-mrcina.com*) organizes horseback rides in and around Bohinj and the Triglav National Park to suit all skill levels. It's open year-round.

KRANJSKA GORA

39 km (24 mi) northwest of Bled, 85 km (53 mi) from Ljubljana.

Kranjska Gora, amid Slovenia's highest and most dramatic peaks, is the country's largest ski resort. In summer, the area attracts hiking and mountaineering enthusiasts. It's a pleasant town in any season. The resorts spread out along the perimeter, leaving the surprisingly charming core intact.

WHERE TO EAT

$–$$ ✕**Bar Pristavec.** The cute, laid-back place is just off the main square, and it's perfect for a morning coffee and a light roll or sandwich. ⊠*Borovška 77* ☎*No phone* ⊟*No credit cards.*

★ **$–$$** ✕**Gostilna pri Martinu.** This beautifully appointed traditional gostilna has excellent home cooking. Try the homemade sausages or a local favorite, *telecja obara* (veal stew). ⊠*Borovška 61* ☎*04/582–0300* ⊟*AE, DC, MC, V.*

$–$$ ✕**Papa Joe.** *The* place to party during ski season serves excellent drinks and decent pizzas and sandwiches. The real draw is the late-night closing time; in season, Papa Joe doesn't close its doors until 5 AM. ⊠*Borovška 86* ☎*04/588–1526* ⊟*AE, DC, MC, V.*

WHERE TO STAY

Most of Kranjska Gora's hotels are relatively large and were built during the 1970s and '80s to accommodate ski groups. The tourist-information center can help you find smaller properties, pensions, and private rooms if you are looking for something simpler and cheaper.

$$ ⬚**Hotel Larix.** A large, modern hotel, similar in price and appearance to the Hotel Kompass across the street, the Larix is cheerier and offers better facilities. These include a large indoor pool, sauna, and wellness center. The location is right next to the main ski lifts on the slopes. Even if you're not staying here, you can pay to use the pool and sauna. ⊠*Borovška 99, 4280 Kranjska Gora* ☎*04/588–4100* ⊕*www.htp-gorenjka.si* ⌂*120 rooms* ⌂*In-hotel: 3 restaurants, bar, pool, gym, spa* ⊟*AE, DC, MC, V* ⎮⊙⎮*BP.*

★ **$** ⬚**Hotel Kotnik.** This charming little pastel-yellow inn is just a few minutes' stroll from the central square and has a well-informed reception desk. Traditionally furnished rooms are simple but fine for a short stay. Oven-fired pizzas are served in the adjoining restaurant. ⊠*Borovška 75, 4280 Kranjska Gora* ☎*04/588–1564* ⊕*www.hotel-kotnik.si* ⌂*15 rooms* ⌂*In-hotel: restaurant, room service, no elevator* ⊟*AE, DC, MC, V* ⎮⊙⎮*BP.*

SPORTS & THE OUTDOORS

Skiing is the number-one sport in Kranjska Gora. There are more than 30 km (19 mi) of downhill runs, 20 ski lifts, and 40 km (25 mi) of groomed cross-country trails open during the winter ski season, which typically runs from mid-December through mid-March. During summer, from late May through mid-September, mountain biking is big, and you'll find plenty of places to rent bikes, as well as 12 marked trails covering 150 km (93 mi) to take you through scented pine forests and spectacular alpine scenery. An unused railway track, tracing the south edge of the Karavanke Alps, brings hikers and bikers all the way to the village of Jesenice, about 20 km (12 mi) away. The Kranjska Gora Bike Park is oriented more toward experienced free-riders and thrill seekers—those who like to take their bikes to the top of the hill and careen back down. There are also numerous hiking trails; you can pick up a good local trail map from the tourist-information center or at kiosks around town.

8

Fun Bike Park Kranjska Gora (✉ *Borovška 103, Kranjska Gora* ☎ *031/ 499–499* ⊕ *www.kranjskagora.mtbpark.si*) rents full- and front-suspension mountain bikes for use along downhill mountain and forest trails. The emphasis here is on fast, adrenaline-filled rides. Lifts are open from May through the third week of September.

Kranjska Gora Recreational Ski Center (✉ *Borovška 103, Kranjska Gora* ☎ *04/588–1414* ⊕ *www.kr-gora.si*) runs the lifts and is the main center for skiing information. The Web site—though mostly in Slovenian—lists prices in English and has a live Web cam so that you can see the conditions.

Sport Bernik (✉ *Borovška 88a, Kranjska Gora* ☎ *04/588–1470*) is a full-service sports-equipment rental center, with both skis and mountain bikes in their respective seasons. It's located close to the ski center.

EN ROUTE
From Kranjska Gora, head south over the breathtaking **Vršič Pass,** some 5,253 feet above sea level. You'll then descend into the beautiful Soča Valley, winding through the foothills to the west of Triglav Peak and occasionally plunging through tunnels. From Trenta, continue west for about 20 km (12 mi) to reach the mountain adventure resort of Bovec.

In Trenta, you'll find the Triglav National Park Information Center at **Dom Trenta** (✉ *Na Logu v Trenti, Trenta* ☎ *05/388–9330*). Here, you can watch a presentation about the history and geography of the region and tour the small museum. It's also a good access point to the 20-km (12-mi) Soča Trail that winds its way along the river's banks. The center is open from April through October, daily from 10 to 6.

BOVEC

35 km (22 mi) south of Kranjska Gora, 124 km (77 mi) from Ljubljana.

Bovec is a friendly, relaxed, youth-oriented town that owes its modern existence largely to the adventure tourism possibilities afforded by the Soča River. The center is filled with private travel agencies, all offering a similar array of white-water rafting, kayaking, canoeing, hydrospeeding, and canyoning trips. The Soča—by the time it reaches Bovec—is a world-class river that regularly plays host to international rafting events. The main tour operators are experienced, and the rafting trips are aimed at all levels of experience. The river is at its best in spring, swelled by the melting snowcaps. But it is raftable throughout the summer. Even if you don't decide to ride, plan a walk along the Soča's banks—the emerald green or electric blue (depending on the glint of the sun) color of the water must be seen to be believed.

WHERE TO EAT
With its emphasis on sport, Bovec is not exactly teeming with great places to eat. Nevertheless there are a couple of central gostilnas that serve basic food, and the hotel restaurants are decent as well.

$$–$$$ ✕**Martinov Hram.** Fresh grilled trout in four variations and excellent local wines by the liter make the terrace of this fun, family restaurant one of Bovec's best evening destinations. The multilingual waiters and international clientele create a worldly, cosmopolitan feel in an otherwise quiet burg. ✉*Trg Golobarskih Žrtev 28* ☎*05/388–6214* ▤*AE, DC, MC, V.*

$$ **Gostilna Sovdat.** A clean and family-run inn serves basic pork and other meat dishes, Wiener schnitzel, and several pasta entrées. Open-air seating is in the back. ✉*Trg Golobarskih Žrtev 24* ☎*05/388–6027* ▤*AE, DC, MC, V* ⊘*Closed Thurs.*

$–$$ ✕**Gostišče Vančar.** This charmingly rustic guesthouse about 3 km (2 mi) outside of Bovec is in the small village of Čezsoča. The restaurant is very popular with locals from the neighborhood, and the portions are huge. The house also has six very clean and comfortable rooms to let. ✉*Čezsoča 43, Čezsoča* ☎*05/389–6076* ▤*No credit cards.*

WHERE TO STAY

$ ▦**Alp.** This 1970s-era hotel has been modernized and remains in good shape. The rooms are clean and functional. The location is central, just a couple of steps away from the main activities agencies and tourist office. Guests can use the Hotel Kanin swimming pool. ✉*Trg Golobarskih Žrtev 48, 5230 Bovec* ☎*05/388–4000* ⊕*www.alp-chandler.si* ↴*103 rooms* ♿*In-hotel: restaurant, bar, pool* ▤*AE, DC, MC, V* ⑩*BP.*

$ ▦**Hotel Dobra Vila.** A welcome high-end addition to the local lodging scene is a lovingly restored, early-20th-century telephone exchange building. The owners added a wine cellar, a top-class restaurant, a reading room, and lovely public areas. The rooms and bath facilities have period fittings. ✉*Mala vas 112, 5230 Bovec* ☎*05/389–6400* ⊕*www.dobra-vila-bovec.com* ↴*12 rooms* ♿*In-hotel: restaurant, bar, laundry service, public Internet. In-room: refrigerator* ▤*AE, DC, MC, V* ⑩*BP.*

SPORTS & THE OUTDOORS

White-water rafting is not the only game in town. Bovec is a great base for leisurely cycling trips or more aggressive mountain-bike climbs. Private bike outfitters or the tourist-information center can provide maps and advice. It's also a great base for hiking the western regions of the Triglav National Park. The map *Bovec z Okolico* is available at the tourist-information center and kiosks around town; it marks out several good walks and bike trips of varying degrees of difficulty.

Alpe Šport Vančar (✉*Trg Golobarskih Žrtev 28* ☎*05/389–6350* ⊕*www. bovecsport.com*) arranges rafting, kayaking, and canyoning trips of all types, as well as paragliding. It is well regarded locally. **Outdoor Freaks** (✉*Klanc 9a* ☎*041/553–675* ⊕*www.freakoutdoor.com*) rents high-quality Cult mountain bikes and is a good source for local riding and trail information. **Soča Rafting** (✉*Trg Golobarskih Žrtev 48* ☎*05/389–6200* ⊕*www.socarafting.si*) is one of the better-known rafting and kayaking outfitters.

8

KOBARID

21 km (13 mi) from Bovec, 115 km (71 mi) from Ljubljana.

From Bovec the road follows the Soča River south, running parallel with the Italian border, to pass through the pretty market town of Kobarid.

It's hard to believe now that this idyllic scene was home to some of the bloodiest mountain battles ever fought. In 1917—toward the end of World War I—the combined forces of the Austrian and German armies launched a surprise offensive to try to dislodge Italian forces holding Kobarid and the surrounding Soča Valley. The battle raged on as hundreds of thousands were killed under appalling conditions on both sides. In the end, the Italians retreated and were almost knocked out of the war. "Caporetto"—Kobarid's Italian name—became synonymous throughout Italy with shame and defeat.

Fodor'sChoice
★
In the center of Kobarid, the **Kobariški muzej** *(Kobarid Museum)* has a fascinating exhibition of the fighting, including diaries of the soldiers involved. The museum also gives a 20-minute video presentation—with projections, sound effects, and narration in English. The **Kobarid Historical Walk** takes you on a 5-km (3-mi) hike through lovely countryside, over a hair-raising bridge, and up to a spectacular waterfall. You'll follow the former front line and visit various sites related to World War I along the way. The path is clearly marked, and a self-guiding pamphlet and map are available at the Kobarid Museum. ⊠*Gregorčičeva 10* ☎*05/389–0000* ⊕*www.kobariski-muzej.si* ☞*€4* ☉*Daily 9–7.*

WHERE TO STAY & EAT

$–$$$
Fodor'sChoice
★
✗ **Hotel Hvala.** This delightful family-run hotel is possibly one of the most welcoming places you'll ever stay. The excellent hotel restaurant, Restauracija Topli Val—easily the best in the area—serves local trout and freshwater crayfish, as well as mushrooms and truffles in season. Italians drive over the border just to eat here. ⊠*Trg Svobode 1, 5222* ☎*05/389–9300* ⊕*www.topli-val-sp.si* ⇆*28 rooms, 4 suites* ⎙*In-hotel: restaurant* ═*AE, DC, MC, V* ⎀*BP.*

SPORTS & THE OUTDOORS

The Soča is a prime fishing spot. The river is well stocked with marble trout, rainbow trout, and grayling. However, if you want to fish, bring your own equipment—or be prepared to buy it here—as it is almost impossible to rent. You also need to buy a day permit; for details inquire at Hotel Hvala. The season runs from April through October.

X Point (⊠*Trg Svobode 6* ☎*05/388–5308*) organizes kayaking, rafting, and canyoning trips and also rents out mountain bikes. In Srpenica, 13 km (8 mi) northwest of Kobarid, **Alpine Action** (⊠*Trnovo ob Soči, Srpenica* ☎*05/388–5022*) arranges river trips and rents bikes.

IDRIJA

50 km (31 mi) from Kobarid, 60 km (37 mi) from Ljubljana.

Proceed south from Kobarid, passing through the town of Tolmin and on to Idrija, a former mercury-mining town with some interesting sites, excellent food, and one of the country's most beautiful old hotels. Idrija is also known for its handmade lace.

Head to **Anthony's Shaft** to see the oldest part of the mercury mine, the miners' chapel dating back to the 18th century, and a video about the way the miners once lived. ⊠ *Kosovelova 3* ☎ *05/377–1142* ☉ *Tours weekdays at 10 and 4; weekends at 10, 3, and 4.*

WHERE TO STAY & EAT

★ $$ ✕ **Gostilna Kos.** This old-fashioned inn reputedly serves some of the best *Idrija žlikrofi* (tortellini filled with potato, onion, and bacon) around. You can have yours served as a side with roast pork or goulash, or as a main course served plain or topped with sauce. ⊠ *Tomšičeva 4* ☎ *05/372–2030* ☐ *AE, DC, MC, V.*

$$–$$$$ ☷ **Kendov Dvorec.** This exclusive 14th-century manor house is in Spod-
Fodor'sChoice nje Idrija, 4 km (2½ mi) from Idrija. Each bedroom is individually dec-
★ orated with 19th-century antiques and details such as bed linens edged with local handmade lace. Reserve a room well in advance because the reputation of this hotel keeps it full. The restaurant is not open to the public, but the owners will prepare a special meal if you phone ahead. ⊠ *Spodnje Idrija, 5280* ☎ *05/372–5100* ⊕ *www.kendov-dvorec.com* ⇗ *11 rooms* ⚘ *In-room: dial-up. In-hotel: restaurant, no elevator* ☐ *AE, DC, MC, V* ❑ *BP.*

SHOPPING

Numerous boutiques sell *Idrijska čipka* (Idrija lace). For the most original designs try **Studio Irma Vončina** (⊠ *Mestni trg 17* ☎ *05/377–1584*). It's open weekdays 10 to noon and 1 to 4, Saturday 10 to noon.

ALPS & THE SOČA VALLEY ESSENTIALS

BUS TRAVEL

Hourly buses link Ljubljana to Bled, Bohinj, and Kranjska Gora. There are also several buses daily from Ljubljana through Idrija to Kobarid and on to Bovec. The resorts are linked by local buses; their frequency depends on the season. For schedule and fare information ask at a local tourist-information center.

CAR TRAVEL

From Ljubljana a four-lane highway (E61) runs northwest past Kranj and continues—occasionally reverting to a two-lane highway on some stretches—to the resorts of Bled and Kranjska Gora. Lake Bohinj lies 25 km (16 mi) southwest of Bled along local highway 209. The Vrsic Pass, which connects Kranjska Gora and Bovec, is closed during the winter. If you want to go to Idrija, Kobarid, or Bovec from November to April, you will have to approach them via the south.

8

The Karst Region &
the Adriatic Coast

TRAIN TRAVEL

In theory it is possible to reach the area from Ljubljana by train, but because Bled Jezero station lies some distance from Lake Bled, and Bohinjska Bistrica station lies even farther from Lake Bohinj, it is simpler and quicker to take the bus.

From mid-June to mid-September ABC Rent-a-Car in Ljubljana arranges trips on an old-fashioned steam locomotive, following the Bohinj line, through the Soča Valley. The trip begins from Jesenice, stops in Bled and Bohinjska Bistrica, and finally brings you to Most na Soči. This is a very family-friendly excursion.

Information **ABC Rent-a-Car** (⌧ *Ulica Jožeta Jame 16, Ljubljana* ☎ *01/510–4320*).

VISITOR INFORMATION

Information **Bled Tourist Information** (⌧ *C. Svobode 15, Bled* ☎ *04/574–1122* ⊕ *www.bled.si*). **Bohinj Tourist Information** (⌧ *Ribčev Laz 48, Bohinj* ☎ *04/574–6010* ⊕ *www.bohinj.si*). **Idrija Tourist Information** (⌧ *Lapajnetova 7, Idrija* ☎ *05/377–3898* ⊕ *www.rzs-idrija.si*). **Kobarid Tourist Information** (⌧ *Gregorčičeva 10, Kobarid* ☎ *05/389–9200* ⊕ *www.kobarid.si*). **Kranjska Gora Tourist Information** (⌧ *Tičarjeva 2, Kranjska Gora* ☎ *04/588–1768* ⊕ *www. kranjska-gora.si*).

THE KARST & ADRIATIC COAST

As you move south and west from Ljubljana toward the Adriatic, the breeze feels warmer, the air smells fresher, and the landscape looks less and less like Austria and more and more like Italy.

The word "karst," or in Slovenian *Kras,* is both a geological and geographic term referring to the large limestone plateau stretching roughly from Nova Gorica in the north to well beyond Divača in the south. It is bordered on the west by the Italian frontier and on the east by the fertile, wine-growing Vipava valley. The Karst is typified by sinkholes, underground caves, and streams. The region is dotted by caves, including two—Postojna and especially Škocjan—of jaw-dropping beauty and size.

To most Slovenians, the word "karst," conjures up two things: *pršut* (air-dried ham) and blood-red Teran wine. The two pair beautifully, especially with a plate of cheese and a basket of homemade bread, taken at a traditional *osmica*, a small farmhouse restaurant. Teran is a strong wine made from the refosk grape that you will either love or loathe from the first sip. It takes its name from the *terra rossa*, or red soil, that typifies the Karst.

For visitors, the Karst is ideal for low-key exploration. The gentle terrain and the many wine roads (look for the sign that reads *vinska cesta*) are perfect for leisurely walks or bike rides. Several wine roads can be found in the area around the town of Komen and along the main road from Komen to Dutovlje. The pretty towns—with their old stone churches and red-tiled roofs—are a delight. If you have wheels, visit Stanjel to the east of Komen. It's a nearly abandoned hilltop village that's found new life as a haven for artists. The Lipica stud farm—the original breeding ground of the famed Lipizzaner horses of Vienna's Spanish Riding School—is an excellent base.

A little farther on, Slovenia's tiny piece of the Adriatic coast gives tourists a welcome chance to swim and sunbathe. Backed by hills planted with olive groves and vineyards, the small strip is only 47 km (29 mi) long and dominated by the towns of Koper, Izola, Piran, and Portorož.

Following centuries of Venetian rule, the coast remains culturally and spiritually connected to Italy, and Italian is still widely spoken. The medieval port of Piran is a gem and a must-see. Its Venetian core is nearly perfectly preserved. Portorož is a classic fun-and-sun resort. Koper, Slovenia's largest port, and Izola, its biggest fishery, are workaday towns that nevertheless retain a lot of historical charm. For beachgoers the best-equipped beach is at Bernadin, between Piran and Portorož. The most unspoiled stretch of coast is at the Strunjan Nature Reserve—which also has an area reserved for nudists—between Piran and Izola.

Piran and Portorož are very different in character, but either can serve as an excellent base depending on what you plan to do. Choose Portorož if your primary interest is swimming and sunbathing, or if you're seeking a modern hotel with all of the amenities. Pick Piran if you're looking for something quainter, quieter, and more starkly beautiful. Whatever you choose, you can travel easily between the two. Buses make the 10-minute trip at least once an hour in season.

Both Piran and Portorož fill to capacity in July and August, so try to arrange accommodation in advance. If you show up without a room, inquire at one of the privately run travel agencies. Along the coast, these are likely to be more helpful than the local tourist-information centers.

POSTOJNSKA JAMA

44 km (27 mi) southwest of Ljubljana.

☾ **Postojnska Jama** *(Postojna Cave)* conceals one of the largest networks of caves in the world, with 23 km (14 mi) of underground passageways. A miniature train takes you through the first 7 km (4½ mi), to reveal a succession of well-lighted rock formations. This strange underground world is home of the snakelike "human fish" on view in an aquarium in the Great Hall. Eyeless and colorless because of countless millennia of life in total darkness, these amphibians can live for up to 60 years. Temperatures average 8°C (46°F) year-round, so bring a sweater, even in summer. Tours leave every hour on the hour throughout the year. ✉ *Jamska 30, Postojna* ☎ *05/700–0163* ⊕ *www.postojna-cave. com* ☞ *€18* ☽ *May–Sept., daily 8:30–6; Apr. and Oct., daily 8:30–5; Nov.–Mar., weekdays 9:30–1:30, weekends 9:30–3.*

ŠKOCJANSKE JAMA

26 km (16 mi) from Postojna, 76 km (47 mi) from Ljubljana.

Fodor'sChoice
★
☾

The 11 interconnected chambers that make up the **Škocjan Jama** *(Škocjanske Caves)* stretch for almost 6 km (about 4 mi) through a dramatic, subterranean landscape so unique that UNESCO has named them a World Heritage Site. The 90-minute walking tour of the two chilly main chambers—the Silent Cave and the Murmuring Cave—winds past otherworldly dripstone sculptures, massive sinkholes, and stalactites and stalagmites that resemble the horns of some mythic creature. The highlight is Europe's largest cave hall, a gorge 479 feet high, 404 feet wide, and 984 feet long, spanned by a narrow bridge lighted with footlights. Far below, the brilliant jade waters of the Reka River rush by on their underground journey. The view is nothing short of mesmerizing. ✉ *Škocjan 2, Divača* ☎ *05/763–2840* ⊕ *www.park-skocjanske-jame.si* ☞ *€11* ☽ *June–Sept., daily at 10, 11:30, and 1–5 (tours leave hourly); Apr., May, and Oct., tours daily at 10, 1, and 3:30; Nov.–Mar., tours at 10 and 1.*

LIPICA

5 km (3 mi) west of Divača, 30 km (19 mi) south of Stanjel, 80 km (50 mi) from Ljubljana.

Lipica is best known as the home of the *Kobilarna Lipica*, the Lipica Stud farm, where the fabled white Lipizzaner horses were first bred. The horse farm is still the primary reason most people come here, though the area has developed into a modern sports complex, with two hotels, a popular casino, an indoor pool, tennis courts, and an excellent 9-hole golf course. It makes a pleasant, hassle-free base for exploring the nearby Škocjan caves and Karst region. The horses, the large areas of green, and the facilities of the Hotel Maestoso—including a pool—are all great for families with children.

☾ The **Kobilarna Lipica** *(Lipica Stud Farm)* was founded in 1580 by the Austrian archduke Karl II. It's where the white Lipizzaners—the majestic horses of the famed Spanish Riding School in Vienna—originated. Today the farm no longer sends its horses to Vienna, but breeds them for its own performances and riding instruction. The impressive stables and grounds are open to the public. Riding classes are available, but lessons are geared toward experienced riders and must be booked in advance. ⊠*Lipica 5, Sežana, 6210* ☎*05/739–1708* ⊕*www.lipica.org* ⊙*Dressage performances June–Oct., Tues., Fri., and Sun. at 3. Stable tours July and Aug., daily 9–6; Apr.–June and Sept. and Oct., daily 10–5; Nov.–Mar., daily 11–3.*

WHERE TO EAT

$$–$$$ ✕**Gostilna Muha.** A friendly, family-run tavern in the village of Lokev is about 4 km (2 mi) from the Lipica stud farm. Sit back and allow the proprietor to suggest the day's specialties. A good starter is *jota* (bean and sauerkraut soup) followed by slow-roasted pork and a green salad topped with a spoonful of beans. ⊠*Lokev 138, Lokev* ☎*05/767–0055* ⊟*No credit cards.*

$$ ✕**Gostilna Gombač.** Just down the street from the similar Muha, the only obvious difference between these two gostilnas is a pleasant terrace here for dining outdoors on a warm evening. The kitchen is most proud of its game—try the roast hare served with a plate of *njoki* (gnocchi) and a glass of Union beer. ⊠*Lokev 165, Lokev* ☎*05/767–0466* ⊟*No credit cards.*

WHERE TO STAY

$ 🛏**Hotel Maestoso.** The modern building dates from the 1970s, but nevertheless it's well-maintained and comfortable. The rooms are clean, all with modern bath facilities; some even have a terrace. The reception desk can help you get your bearings. The equipment room on the side of the hotel will rent golf clubs and carts. The Hotel Klub—behind the Maestoso—rents bikes. ⊠*Lipica 5, 6210 Sežana* ☎*05/739–1580* ⊕*www.lipica.org* ⇆*65 rooms* ⑂*In-room: refrigerator (some). In-hotel: restaurant, bar, golf course, tennis courts, pool, public Internet* ⊟*AE, DC, MC, V* ⧠*BP.*

KOPER

50 km (31 mi) southwest of Divača (Lipica), 105 km (65 mi) southwest of Ljubljana.

Today a port town surrounded by industrial suburbs, Koper nevertheless warrants a visit. The Republic of Venice made Koper the regional capital during the 15th and 16th centuries, and the magnificent architecture of the Old Town bears witness to the spirit of those times.

The most important buildings are clustered around **Titov trg,** the central town square. Here stands the **Cathedral,** which can be visited daily from 7 to noon and 3 to 7, with its fine Venetian Gothic facade and bell tower dating back to 1664. Across the square the splendid **Praetor's Palace,** formerly the seat of the Venetian Grand Council, combines Gothic and Renaissance styles. From the west side of Titov trg, the narrow, cobbled **Kidriceva ulica** brings you down to the seafront.

Stop for coffee or a glass of wine at Loggia Cafe, housed within the 15th-century Venetian Gothic loggia. In summer there are tables out on the terrace overlooking the town square. ⊠ *Titov trg 1* ☎ *05/627–3213*.

Hrastovlje. Hidden behind the 16th-century defensive walls of this small town is the tiny Romanesque **Cerkev sveti Trojice** (Church of the Holy Trinity). The interior is decorated with a remarkable series of frescoes, including the bizarre *Dance Macabre*, completed in 1490. The church is locked, but if you ask in the village the locals will be glad to open it for you. From Koper take the main road toward Ljubljana; then follow the signs for Hrastovlje (22 km [14 mi] from Koper).

WHERE TO EAT

$$$–$$$$ ✕ **Skipper.** Noted for its vast summer terrace overlooking the marina, Skipper is popular with the yachting fraternity. The menu includes pasta dishes, risottos, grilled meats, and fish. ⊠ *Kopališko nab 3* ☎ *05/626–1810* ⊟ *AE, DC, MC, V.*

$–$$ ✕ **Marina.** This popular pizza place is just across from the Skipper on the port. Try the house specialty, pizza "Koper," a salty but irresistible mix of goat cheese, capers, and *pršut* ham. ⊠ *Kopališko nab 2* ☎ *05/627–1982* ⊟ *No credit cards.*

IZOLA

6 km (4 mi) from Koper, 112 km (70 mi) from Ljubljana.

Izola is a normally placid fishing town that lets its hair down in summer. DJs decamp from Ljubljana for parties on the coast, artists set up their studios, and the city adopts the relaxed persona of a shaggy beach town. Less industrial than Koper and less self-consciously pretty than Piran, Izola makes a perfect day outing.

It's also a great place to eat. Unlike Piran, where the seafront restaurants cater almost exclusively to tourists, Izola's harbor restaurants are the real deal. The fish is fresh and the customers—many of them local Slovenes—are demanding.

Like that of its immediate neighbor, Koper, the city's history goes back hundreds of years. Izola rose to prominence in the Middle Ages and then declined in the 16th and 17th centuries with the rise of the port of Trieste in present-day Italy. The name "Izola" comes from the Italian word for "island" and describes a time when the walled city in fact was an island. The city walls were knocked down by the French occupation at the start of the 19th century. The bricks were then used to connect the city to the mainland.

WHERE TO EAT

The best restaurants are situated along the marina. The restaurants fill quickly in the evenings, so go early to be assured of a table.

$$-$$$$ ✕**Ribič.** This is the local favorite. The day's catch and prices are listed on a chalkboard out front. If in doubt, ask the server what looks good that day. You can be sure the fish is fresh, but watch the prices. The fish are sold by weight, and you may end up paying more than you intended. ⊠*Veliki trg 3* 🕾*05/641–8313* ⊟*AE, DC, MC, V.*

NIGHTLIFE

During summer, the Adriatic coast becomes a haven for all-night parties. **Ambasada Gavioli** (⊠*Izola* 🕾*05/641–8212* ⊕*www.ambasada-gavioli.com*) remains one of the coast's—and the country's—best dance clubs. Gavioli regularly brings in DJs from around the world to play techno, trance, funk, and fusion. You'll find it southwest of the port in the city's industrial area.

SPORTS & THE OUTDOORS

You can rent yachts at the Izola marina from **Jonathan Yachting** (⊠*Izola* 🕾*05/677–8930* ⊕*www.jonathan.si*). Prices vary depending on the season and the size of the yacht.

PORTOROŽ

7 km (4 mi) from Izola, 124 km (77 mi) from Ljubljana.

Portorož is the most popular of Slovenia's seaside resorts. The name—Port of Roses—recalls the time, a hundred years ago, when it was an exclusive haunt for Austro-Hungarian aristocrats. Those days, however, are long gone. Portorož today definitely caters to the everyman. Here you'll find chock-a-block hotels, restaurants, bars, casinos, and nightclubs—all of the things you associate with a modern package-vacation destination.

Portorož is difficult to grasp at first. The central area is small, although hotels and resorts spread out in all directions along the coast and the surrounding hills. Most of the action takes place along a small stretch of seacoast. Here you'll find the public beaches (which charge a small fee to swim), a pool, and a string of shops and low-priced eateries.

WHERE TO STAY & EAT

Staying in Portorož is expensive, but the hotel standards are high. Many hotels offer cheaper package deals when booked in advance. If you are looking for a cheaper option on accommodations, book a room through **Maona** (⊠*Obala 14b, Portorož* 🕾*05/674–0363* ⊕*www.maona.si*), a local travel agency.

$$–$$$$ ✕**Ribič.** Enjoy good fresh fish in a relaxed garden setting, 2 km (1 mi) down the coast from Portorož at Seča. ⊠*Seča 143, Seča* 🕾*05/677–0790* ⊟*AE, DC, MC, V* ⊗*Closed Tues.*

$$$$ 🏨**Grand Hotel Palace.** This modern seaside hotel is connected to the thermal-spa recreation center, which offers massages and medicinal treatments. Rooms are comfortable, and the service is professional. Three other hotels are adjacent in the same complex and interconnected, offering a similar level of service. This is the most expensive of the four. ⊠*Obala 43, 6320* 🕾*05/696–1025* ⊕*www.hoteli-palace.si*

8

⊊189 rooms, 7 suites ᴌIn-hotel: 2 restaurants, bar, pools, spa, parking (fee) ⊟AE, DC, MC, V ¶⊘IBP.

$$$ ⊞Grand hotel Bernardin. In a complex of three large, modern hotels, the Bernardin occupies a pretty and secluded bluff above the seashore. All modern amenities are here, including the area's only on-site convention center. The affiliated Hotel Histrion has a full-service wellness center and offers special packages. There's an attached water park. ⊠Obala 2, 6320 ☎05/695–0000 ⊕www.h-bernardin.si ⊊230 rooms, 19 suites ᴌIn-room: refrigerator. In-hotel: 2 restaurants, room service, bar, pool, gym, spa, beachfront, public Internet, parking (no fee) ⊟AE, DC, MC, V ¶⊘IBP.

SPORTS & THE OUTDOORS
You can rent bikes at **Atlas Express** (⊠Obala 55 ☎05/674–8821).

PIRAN

3 km (2 mi) from Portorož, 126 km (78 mi) from Ljubljana.

The jewel of the Slovenian coast, the medieval walled Venetian town of Piran stands compact on a small peninsula, capped by a neo-Gothic lighthouse and presided over by a hilltop Romanesque cathedral. Narrow, winding, cobbled streets lead to the main square, Trg Tartini, which in turn opens out onto a charming harbor. Historically, Piran's wealth was based on salt making. Culturally, the town is known as the birthplace of the 17th-century violinist and composer Giuseppe Tartini.

If you are arriving by car, don't even try to negotiate the tiny lanes around the harbor. Instead leave the car in the lot outside of town; the lot farthest out has the cheapest long-term rates. A shuttle bus will then take you into town.

☺ The **Sergej Mašera Pomorski muzej** *(Sergej Mašera Maritime Museum)* tells the story of Piran's connections with the sea. There is a beautiful collection of model ships, sailors' uniforms, and shipping instruments, and a fascinating historical section on the town's changing affiliations over the centuries. ⊠Cankarjevo nab 3 ☎05/671–0040 ☎€3.50 ⊘Maritime Museum Apr.–June and Nov.–Mar., Tues.–Sun. 9–noon and 3–6; July and Aug., Tues.–Sun. 9–noon and 6–9.

WHERE TO STAY & EAT
Piran's waterfront is filled with romantic, open-air restaurants. The quality of the food and the relatively high prices are pretty much uniform. The best advice is to stroll the walk and see which one appeals. Better food at better prices can be found away from the shore, although then you sacrifice the view.

Piran has only a small number of hotels, and most visitors opt to stay in private rooms or pensions. In season, it's easiest and cheapest to book through the centrally located private travel agency **Maona** (⊠Cankarjevo nab 7, Piran ☎05/673–4520 ⊕www.maona.si), which offers doubles in private homes starting at around €50–€60 a night. The rate will be higher for stays of fewer than three nights. Ask for something central and look at the room before accepting; some rooms can be charming, but others are just basic.

$$-$$$ ✗**Gostilnica.** The most intimate of the seafront restaurants is situated toward the end of the promenade. It's a good place to try the *škampi rižot* (scampi risotto), or another favorite, *njoki s skampi in gorgonzola* (shrimp gnocchi with Gorgonzola sauce). ⊠*Prešernovo nab* ☎*05/673–2226* ▭*AE, DC, MC, V.*

★ **$$-$$$** ✗**Neptun.** Highly regarded by the locals, this tiny, family-run place focuses on all manner of fish, grilled or fried. Try the grilled shrimp or calamari. In summer you can dine at tables along the quiet street. ⊠*Županičeva 7* ☎*05/673–4111* ▭*No credit cards.*

$-$$ ⌂**Hotel Piran.** A modern building on a quiet patch of coastline close to the seaside restaurants, Hotel Piran is the best place to stay if a sea view is what you're after. Breakfast is served on a rooftop terrace, where you can enjoy stunning views of the Adriatic. ⊠*Kidričevo nab 4, 6330* ☎*05/676–2502* ⊕*www.hoteli-piran.si* ⇥*80 rooms, 10 suites* ⌂*In-room: no a/c, refrigerator (some). In-hotel: bar, public Internet, some pets allowed* ▭*AE, MC, V* ⫶⧉*BP.*

★ **$** ⌂**Hotel Tartini.** An old facade hides a modern interior with a spacious central atrium. Most rooms have terraces that open out to views of the surrounding red-tiled roofs or the harbor. The location, overlooking Trg Tartini, is out of this world. If you can live without being on the seafront, this is your best option in town. ⊠*Trg Tartini 15, 6330* ☎*05/671–1000* ⊕*www.hotel-tartini-piran.com* ⇥*43 rooms, 2 suites* ⌂*In-room: refrigerator. In-hotel: restaurant* ▭*AE, DC, MC, V* ⫶⧉*BP.*

THE ARTS
Piran Musical Evenings are held in the cloisters of the Minorite Monastery every Friday in July and August. The **Primorski Summer Festival** of open-air theater and dance is staged in Piran, Koper, Portorož, and Izola.

THE KARST & ADRIATIC COAST ESSENTIALS

BUS TRAVEL
Several buses a day connect Ljubljana to Koper, Piran, and Portorož, passing through Postojna and Divača on the way. There is also a daily service connecting the coastal towns to Trieste, Italy.

A network of local buses connects all listed sights, with the exception of those in Štanjel and Lipica. Schedules vary depending on the time of year, so contact a local bus station for information.

CAR TRAVEL
A car is advisable for touring the Karst region. However, parking can be a problem along the coast during summer, when town centers are closed to traffic. The E63 highway connects Ljubljana to the coast, passing through the Karst region en route.

TRAIN TRAVEL

Four trains daily link Ljubljana and Koper, passing through Postojna and Divača en route.

VISITOR INFORMATION

Information **Štanjel Tourist Information** (✉ Štanjel Grad, Štanjel ☎ 05/769–0056 ⊕ www.komen.si). **Koper Tourist Information** (✉ Ukmarjev trg 7, Koper ☎ 05/664–6230 ⊕ www.koper.si). **Izola Tourist Information** (✉ Sončno nab. 4, Izola ☎ 05/640–1050 ⊕ www.izola.si). **Lipica Tourist Information** (✉ Lipica 5, Lipica ☎ 05/739–1580 ⊕ www.lipica.org). **Piran Tourist Information** (✉ Trg Tartini 2, Piran ☎ 05/673–4440 ⊕ www.piran.com). **Portorož Tourist Information** (✉ Obala 16, Portorož ☎ 05/674–0220 ⊕ www.portoroz.si). **Postojna Tourist Information** (✉ Jamska 30, Postojna ☎ 05/700–0100 ⊕ www.postojna-cave.com).

SLOVENIA ESSENTIALS

To research prices, get advice from other travelers, and book travel arrangements, visit www.fodors.com.

TRANSPORTATION

BY AIR

There are no direct flights between the United States and Slovenia. The Slovenian national carrier, Adria Airways, flies from many Western European cities to Ljubljana Airport. Adria also has flights to the capitals of other ex-Yugoslav republics from Ljubljana. Adria is a regional carrier of the Star Alliance, linking it with the extensive networks of Austrian Airways, United Airlines, Lufthansa, Air Canada, and LOT, among others. In Slovenia, tickets can be purchased by phone and delivered anywhere in the country in 24 hours.

Aeroflot, Air France, Austrian Airways, Finnair, Hungary's Malev, Serbia's JAT, Turkish Airlines, Ukraine Airlines, Czech Airlines, and Poland's LOT all now offer regular connections to Ljubljana from their respective capital cities. Low-cost airlines have added flights from London's Stansted airport (easyJet, flying to Ljubljana, and Ryanair, flying to Maribor) and Brussels (Wizz Air).

Information **Adria Airways** (✉ Kuzmičeva 7, Ljubljana ☎ 01/369–1010 ⊕ www.adria-airways.com). **Aeroflot** (✉ Dunajska cesta 21, Ljubljana ☎ 01/230–7560 ⊕ www.aeroflot.ru). **Air France** (✉ Kuzmičeva 5, Ljubljana ☎ 01/244–3447 ⊕ www.airfrance.com). **Austrian Airlines** (✉ Čopova 11, Ljubljana ☎ 01/244–3060 ⊕ www.aua.com). **Czech Airlines/CSA** (✉ Brnik Airport Terminal, Brnik ☎ 04/206–1750 ⊕ www.czechairlines.cz). **EasyJet** (☎ 04/206–1677 ⊕ www.easyjet.com). **Finnair** (☎ 08/01300 ⊕ www.finnair.com). **JAT** (✉ Slomškova 1, Ljubljana ☎ 01/231–4340 ⊕ www.jat.com). **LOT** (✉ Brnik airport terminal, Brnik ☎ 04/259–4252 ⊕ www.lot.com). **Lufthansa** (✉ Gosposvetska 6, Ljubljana ☎ 01/239–1900 ⊕ www.lufthansa.com). **Malev** (✉ Brnik airport terminal, Brnik ☎ 04/206–1665 ⊕ www.malev.hu). **Ryanair** (⊕ www.ryanair.com). **Turkish Airlines** (☎ 04/206–1680 ⊕ www.turkishairlines.com). **Ukraine International Airlines** (⊕ www.flyuia.com).

AIRPORTS & TRANSFERS

The Ljubljana Airport is at Brnik, 25 km (16 mi) north of the city. The Maribor airport is at Slivnica, 9 km (6 mi) to the south.

Information **Ljubljana Airport** (✉ *Brnik* ☎ *04/206–1981* ⊕ *www.lju-airport.si*). **Maribor Airport** (✉ *Slivnica* ☎ *02/629–1553* ⊕ *www.maribor-airport.si*).

TRANSFERS

Public bus service runs regularly between the airport and Ljubljana's main bus station in the city center. Buses depart from the airport every hour on the hour weekdays and slightly less frequently on weekends. Tickets cost around €4. A private airport shuttle makes the same run in slightly less time. Departures average every 90 minutes or so and the cost is €20. A taxi costs approximately €30. The ride takes about 30 minutes.

Information **Ljubljana Airport Shuttle** (☎ *040/887–766*).

BY BOAT & FERRY

From early March to late October the *Prince of Venice* high-speed catamaran makes regularly scheduled trips between Venice and Izola, with connecting bus service to Piran and Potorož. Kompas Travel in Potorož can make the booking. The trip takes 2½ hours.

Venezia Lines offers similar runs between Venice and Piran in season, and offers overnight hotel packages in Venice. Maona Travel in Piran can arrange this.

Information **Kompas** (✉ *Obala 41, Portorož* ☎ *05/617–8000* ⊕ *www.kompas-online.net*). **Maona** (✉ *Cankarjevo nab 7, Piran* ☎ *05/673–4520* ⊕ *www.maona.si*).

BY BUS

International and domestic bus lines and the Ljubljana municipal bus service all operate conveniently from the city's main bus terminal, not far from the center.

Private coach companies operate to and from Trieste in Italy and Zagreb in Croatia, as well as other European destinations farther afield. Domestic bus service is frequent from the capital to most Slovenian cities and towns (including most of the destinations in this guide). Outside of a car, the bus remains the only practical option to Bled and Bohinj and mountain destinations west and north of the capital. Except during peak travel periods, you can simply buy your ticket on the bus when you board. Otherwise, purchase tickets a day in advance with a reserved seat. Many buses do not run on Sunday.

Within Ljubljana, the municipal bus network is extensive, and service is frequent during weekdays. Service continues but is less frequent on Saturday, Sunday, and holidays. Buses on most lines stop running around 11 PM. To ride the bus, buy plastic bus tokens (*žetoni*) at kiosks and post offices, or simply pay the €1 fare in exact change to the driver.

Information **Llubl-jana Bus Station** (✉ *Trg OF 5, Ljubljana* ☎ *01/090–4230* ⊕ *www.ap-ljubljana.si*).

BY CAR

From Budapest and Vienna the Slovenian border is no more than a two-hour drive; from Prague it's eight hours. A tunnel speeds traffic through the Karavanke Alps between Slovenia and Austria. From Vienna the passage is by way of Maribor to Ljubljana, with a four-lane highway most of the way. Slovenia's roads also connect with Italy's *autostrada*.

You don't need a car if you are not planning to leave Ljubljana; however, traveling by car undoubtedly gives you the chance to reach remote areas of the country when and as you wish. Main roads between large towns are comparable to those in Western Europe. Toll plazas are frequent, so have small bills and change handy.

Gas stations on border crossings and main roads leading to larger towns are open 24 hours a day; others are open Monday through Saturday from 7 AM to 8 PM.

To rent a car you must have a license that is valid in the issuing country. A midsize car costs about €100 for 24 hours, with unlimited mileage—but much better rates are available for longer periods or if the car is booked in advance over the Internet. You'll also need a valid credit card. Rental agencies can be found in all major towns and at the Ljubljana Airport. *See Car Rentals in Llubljana Essentials.*

Information **AMZS-Hertz** (⊠ *Dunajska 122, Ljubljana* ☏ *01/530–5380* ⊕ *www. hertz.si).* **Avis** (⊠ *Čufarjeva 2, Ljubljana* ☏ *01/430–8010* ⊕ *www.avis.si).* **Budget** (⊠ *Miklošičeva 3, Ljubljana* ☏ *01/421–7340* ⊕ *www.budget.si).* **Dollar/Thrifty Car Rental** (⊠ *Brnik air terminal, Brnik* ☏ *04/236–5750* ⊕ *www.subrosa.hr).* **National Rent a Car** (⊠ *Baragova 5, Ljubljana* ☏ *01/588–4450* ⊕ *www.nation alcar-slovenia.com).*

RULES OF THE ROAD

Slovenes drive on the right and are obliged to keep their headlights on at all times. Speed limits are 50 kph (31 mph) in urban areas and 130 kph (81 mph) on highways. Local drivers are courteous by European standards. The permitted blood-alcohol level is 0.05%; drivers caught exceeding this level can expect penalties similar to those of other European countries.

BY TAXI

Private taxis operate 24 hours a day. Phone from your hotel or hail one in the street. Drivers are bound by law to display and run a meter.

BY TRAIN

There are several trains daily to Venice (five hours), Vienna (six hours), and Budapest (eight hours). There is an overnight service to Prague (12 hours) and a rapid daytime EuroCity connection to Berlin (15 hours). The train station is just north of the city center.

Information **Ljubljana Train station** (⊠ *Trg OF 6, Ljubljana* ☏ *01/291–3332* ⊕ *www.slo-zeleznice.si).*

CONTACTS & RESOURCES

BANKS & EXCHANGE SERVICES

In major cities banks and ATMs are easy to find. Since Slovenia has adopted the euro as its official currency, you don't need to change money again if you are coming from another euro-zone country. Still, you may see that many prices are still listed in the former currency, the tolar (SIT), which traded at a rate of about 240 to the euro. Prices quoted in this chapter are in euros, unless otherwise noted.

EMBASSIES & CONSULATES

Information **U.S. Embassy** (⊠ *Prešernova 31, Ljubljana* ☎ *01/200–5500* 🖷 *01/200–5555*).

EMERGENCIES

Information **Ambulance & Fire** (☎ *112*). **Emergency Road Assistance** (☎ *987*). **Police** (☎ *113*). **Lekarna Miklošič Pharmacy** (⊠ *Miklošičeva 24, Ljubljana* ☎ *01/231–4558*). **Ljubljana Emergency Medical Services** (☎ *01/232–3060*).

INTERNET, MAIL & SHIPPING

Many hotels now set aside at least one terminal for guests to access the Internet—and some of the better places are now adding wireless Wi-Fi networks. Ljubljana has several Internet cafés (known locally as cybercafés), though these are harder to find in outlying cities and towns. Frequently cafés and bars will maintain a computer terminal or two and allow access for a fee—usually around €5 an hour.

Postage is assessed according to weight. The standard international letter rate, including airmail, is €.70 for very light letters, and €1.17 for standard size. Postcards sent abroad cost €.60. Post offices are open weekdays from 8 to 6 and Saturday from 8 to noon. Stamps are also sold at hotels, newsstands, and kiosks.

Information **Xplorer CyberCafe** (⊠ *Petkovškovo nab 23, Ljubljana* ☎ *01/430–1991*) is the best in town, centrally located and with long opening hours. **Val Hostel** (⊠ *Gregorčičeva 38a, Piran* ☎ *05/673–2555*), a charming hostel in the center of Piran, offers Internet access to nonguests for a nominal fee.

LANGUAGE

Slovene is the country's chief language. In the east, signs are posted in Slovene and Hungarian; on the Adriatic coast both Slovene and Italian are officially used. English, German, and Italian are spoken in many places. In Slovene the words for street (*ulica*) and drive (*cesta*) are abbreviated to ul and c. *Nabrežje* (abbreviated to nab) means "embankment." The word for square is *trg*.

TAXES

Visitors who buy goods worth more than €50 (about $70) at any one store on a single day are entitled to a refund of taxes, which can be as much as 16.67% in Slovenia. When you make a purchase, ask for a Request for V.A.T. Refund form, *Zahtevek za vracilo DDV*. A customs officer will certify the form when you leave the country. To obtain the refund, go to the Global Refund office at the border crossing point or the airport. Exporting historic artifacts is forbidden.

8

TELEPHONES

COUNTRY CODE
The country code for Slovenia is 386. When dialing from outside the country, drop any initial "0" from the area code.

INTERNATIONAL CALLS
To make international calls, dial "00" and then the appropriate country code (calls to the United States and Canada, for example, are preceded by "001"). International calls can be made from local telephones or post offices. For collect calls dial the operator. For international inquiries, dial international directory assistance.

Information **International Directory Assistance** (☎1180). **Operator** (☎115).

LOCAL CALLS
Pay phones take magnetic telephone cards, available from post offices and kiosks. Lower rates apply from 10 PM to 7 AM and all day Sunday.

Information **Local Directory Assistance** (☎1188).

TIPPING
Although tax is already included in listed prices, tips are not included in restaurant bills, and a 10% tip is considered customary. If the service is especially good, tip 15%.

TRAVEL AGENCIES
Local travel agencies often supplement the work of the official tourist-information centers and can frequently help in booking excursions and finding rooms. In Bled and on the Adriatic coast, the local private agencies are the main source for finding private accommodations.

Information **Emona Globtour** (✉ *Baragova 5, Llubljana* ☎ *01/588–4400* 🖷 *01/588–4455*). **Kompas Turizem Ljubljana** (✉ *Pražakova 4, Llubljana* ☎ *01/200–6100* 🖷 *01/200–6434* ⊕ *www.kompas.si*). **Promet T & T** (✉ *Celovška 23, Llubljana* ☎ *01/519–3511* 🖷 *01/519–5345*). **Tirtur Ljubljana** (✉ *Majorja Lavriča 12, Llubljana* ☎ *01/519–8802* 🖷 *01/519–8809*).

VISITOR INFORMATION
Ljubljana's Turistično Informacijski Center (Tourist Information Center) is next to the Triple Bridge on the Old Town side. It's an excellent resource for maps, brochures, advice, and small souvenirs like postcards and T-shirts. It's open weekdays from 8 to 7, Saturday 9 to 5, and Sunday 10 to 6. If you are arriving by train, the TIC kiosk in the train station can help you find accommodations. It's open daily from 8 AM to 9 PM from June through September and 10 to 6 from October through May.

Information **Slovenian Tourist Information Center** (✉ *Krekov trg 10, Ljubljana, 1000* ☎ *01/306–4575* ⊕ *www.slovenia.info*). **Turistično Informacijski Center** (*Tourist Information Center [TIC]* ✉ *Stritarjeva, Ljubljana* ☎ *01/306–1215* ⊕ *www. ljubljana.si*). **TIC kiosk** (✉ *Trg OF 6, Ljubljana* ☎ *01/433–9475*).

UNDERSTANDING CROATIA & SLOVENIA

A SHORT HISTORY OF CROATIA

Croatia sits astride the geographical boundary between the Balkans and Central Europe. Croats, who speak a Slavic language, are related—linguistically and ethnically—to many of the other Slavic peoples of Europe, including their neighbors the Serbs, Slovenes, and Bosnians. Croatia and its peoples have also been heavily influenced over the centuries by the Romans, Turks, Italians, and Austrians. An essay such as this can provide only a brief overview of developments, but it is worth mentioning three themes that will assist travelers in understanding a great deal of Croatia's past. The first theme is that history has left an important physical legacy in architecture from Roman times to the wars of the 1990s. The second theme pertains to Croatia's human landscape, which evinces considerable diversity in ethnicity, culture, and language. The third theme is the strained political scene in 20th-century Croatia, hotly contested by radical political movements on both the right and the left.

THE EARLY HISTORY OF THE CROATIAN LANDS

The three main regions that form Croatia today are known as Slavonia, Dalmatia, and Croatia proper (the inland region also known as Civil Croatia). These have also been called the "Triune Kingdom." In addition, the ethnically mixed Istrian peninsula is now considered Croatian territory. Bosnia-Herzegovina has a mixed population and once had a pronounced regional identity, but some Croat nationalists consider it their territory.

Even before the influx of the Slavs between AD 500 and 800, the region of Croatia had a long history. The Illyrians and Thracians were originally at home there, and traces of Hellenistic and Celtic influences can also be seen. From the 3rd century BC to the 1st century AD, Rome controlled the Balkans; indeed, at times Croatian history was closely tied to Roman politics, even though it was hardly a central province of the far-flung empire. For instance, the well-known Emperor Diocletian (AD 284–305) was from Dalmatia, as were four other emperors. After his reign, Diocletian returned to his native Split, where he built a large palace. The city of Pula also contains many important Roman sites dating from this time.

Rome's influence on the Croatian lands has been far-reaching. The Romans developed the region's basic infrastructure and industries related to mining and metallurgy. The Croatian coast was established as an outpost of European high culture; this connection was soon strengthened by the Croats' conversion to Christianity and later by ties to the Renaissance city-states of Italy, especially Venice. The Italian influence can be felt even today, particularly in the Istrian peninsula and on some of the islands.

As the Empire was divided into its eastern and western halves, the internal frontier came to symbolize for many the "fault line" between Latin culture and Roman Catholicism, on the one hand, and Greek culture and Orthodox Christianity, on the other. The division was actually always quite porous and inexact, but its nature changed during the Ottoman Turkish invasions starting in the 14th century. Islam again became one of the major religions of Europe, and new ethnic groups arrived or were created in the former Byzantine lands.

Despite the fact that the Croatian lands clearly belonged to Rome's sphere of influence, the Croatian culture went through some complicated developments after the fall of the western portion of the Roman Empire in AD 476. First, many Croats—like their neighbors, the Slovenes—had been converted to Christianity by Frankish (or "German") missionaries from Charlemagne's Holy Roman Empire. Second, Croatian monks working in Dalmatia developed a unique alphabet, known as Glagolitic, from contact with Orthodox missionaries. Croatia remained Catholic after the official religious break between Rome and Constantinople in 1054, but the Glagolitic alphabet was used in some places into the 19th century, serving to reinforce Croatian identity amidst various political and ethnic rivalries. Finally, the Ottoman occupation of the Balkans made much of Croatia into a contested region of population flux and the new cultural norms associated with being a "bulwark of Christendom."

The first independent Croatian state was formed by the leader Tomislav. In 924 he was crowned king of Croatia and recognized by the pope. Although historians disagree over the exact extent of his territory, Tomislav did set another important precedent as well: he united many regions of the former Roman provinces of Dalmatia and Pannonia (central Croatia and Slavonia). The national symbols of the kuna (currency denomination) and šahovnica (red-and-white checkerboard coat of arms) originated at this time.

CROATIA IN THE HIGH MIDDLE AGES

By 1102 the royal line had died out, and the Sabor (assembly of nobles) accepted Hungarian rule. Croatia preserved its own laws and customs through the Pacta Conventa, which seems to have been essentially a personal union between the countries, not an annexation. Medieval Croatia also achieved considerable cultural heights. The first known writing in Croatian dates from around 1100, on a stone tablet from the island of Krk, known as the Bašćanska Ploča. In the 16th century, Dubrovnik dramatist and poet Ivan Gundulić (1555–1638) wrote *Osman* in the Croatian language to inspire resistance to the Turks. Croatia's unique literary history had begun. Dubrovnik also boasted major scientists and composers. Soon there were three major outside forces contending for Croatian territory: the Ottoman Empire, the Kingdom of Hungary, and the Venetian Republic. The Venetians quickly displaced rivals such as the Byzantine Empire and the kingdoms of Serbia and Bosnia. A major blow came in 1202, when Venice directed the Fourth Crusade to sack the important port of Zadar.

The Ottoman expansion into Europe reached Hungary in 1526; Sultan Suleiman defeated Hungary's King Lajos at Mohacs. The Croatian nobles had already been defeated at Udbina in 1493. Ottoman rule would last for 150 years, but the Hungarian and Croatian nobility quickly opted for personal union with the royal Habsburg family in Vienna. In 1593 the Croats stemmed the tide of Turkish invasion by the successful defense of the fortress-city of Sisak, but intense fighting in the area continued until the Treaty of Karlowitz in 1699. That momentous agreement removed most of Croatia and Hungary from Ottoman sovereignty, and Habsburg rule continued.

The wealthy city-state of Dubrovnik retained its independence until Napoléon's invasion of 1797. Bosnia-Herzegovina, home to many Croats and other groups, would remain under Ottoman rule until 1878. As central Croatia was liberated by the crusading Habsburgs, they created a military frontier zone that is often known by its Croatian (and Serbian) name of Vojna Krajina. The frontier included the Lika region south of Zagreb and stretched all along the southern periphery of the Empire from Italy to Romania. The Austrians recruited Serbs and other groups into the area, adding new minority groups to the Croatian lands.

The nobility, or landowning class, of Croatia played the key role in developments over the next several centuries. Croatia's basic feudal structure was preserved by the Habsburgs, although some nobles from the Zrinski and Frankapan families were executed for plotting against Vienna.

The country also remained overwhelmingly Catholic; Catholic scholars working in Venice and Rome also produced the earliest dictionaries and grammars of the Croatian language. These trends stand in sharp contrast to the neighboring Serb lands, where Ottoman rule removed nearly all traces of the traditional elites. The Croat nobles resented Vienna for its attempts at centralization and its territorial compromises with the Ottomans. At times the Croats gravitated, culturally and politically, toward outside powers that could provide leverage in their struggle against Vienna: Russia, France, and even at times their own erstwhile foes the Venetians and the Ottomans.

THE CROATIAN NATIONAL REVIVAL

The remaining Croatian nobility was revived as a political "nation" by the enlightened despotism of one of the most iconoclastic of the Habsburg emperors, Joseph II (r. 1780–90). Joseph's modernizing vision involved centralization of power in Vienna and, to some extent, Germanization. Both of these processes elicited strong negative reactions around the Empire, where traditional autonomy existed in many areas. In Croatia it was the nobility who responded with alarm both to Joseph and to the excesses of the French Revolution. Many in the Croatian elite chose to strengthen ties with Hungary, forming a political party known as the Unionists, or Magyarones, a term corresponding basically to "Hungarophiles."

In 1809 the invading Napoléon created a short-lived satellite state out of conquered Habsburg lands called the Illyrian Provinces. This state abolished feudalism and turned local administration, including language policy, over to the Croats and Slovenes. These actions increased popular awareness of Croatian nationality. It was from these two starting points—both of them reactions to external events—that the tortured development of modern, mass nationalism in Croatia began.

The Magyarone solution soon became problematic as Hungary gradually increased its control over the Croatian lands decade by decade. Croats, now alienated from both Vienna and Budapest, began to react in various new ways. Of considerable importance was the Illyrian Movement, which was at once a Croatian national movement and a kind of supra-national forerunner of Yugoslavism. Its chief exponent was the writer and editor Ljudevit Gaj, who helped establish the basis for the modern Croatian language. The Illyrians espoused political cooperation among the Slovenes, Serbs, and Croats within the framework of the Habsburg Empire; they were basically federalists and did not seek an independent nation-state just for Croats. The National Party, led by Bishop Josip Strossmayer, revived Illyrianism in the form of Yugoslavism and also greatly enriched Croatian cultural life by founding the Yugoslav Academy of Sciences and the modern University of Zagreb.

Croatia, like many other societies, was part of a multiethnic empire when the ideas of Romantic nationalism reached it; it also lacked a strong middle class that understood liberal government. Croatian nationalism is complex, involving both political (or civic) and ethnic considerations. As in other Balkan states, the necessity for Croats to distinguish themselves from their closely related neighbors, and to compete with them for shared territory, sometimes fostered the growth of exclusionist mindsets.

In 1848, nationalism and liberalism brought major insurrections across Europe. Although Hungary rebelled, the Croats remained loyal to Vienna. In the middle of the 19th century, the Croatian political scene was dominated by an important figure named Josip Jelačić (1801–59), an Austrian military officer and a convinced Illyrianist. In 1848 the Habsburgs turned to him to help defeat the nationalist uprising in Hungary. He succeeded and managed to unite nearly all Croatian territory under Austrian rule. He also abolished feudalism and promoted Croatian interests on major cultural issues. Although Jelačić is a Croatian hero today, he also propounded a progressive version of nationality based on regional rather than ethnic identity. The long-reigning Emperor Franz Josef tried to placate the Hungarians by issuing the Ausgleich (Compromise) in 1867, breaking the empire in two and renaming it "Austria-Hungary." The Croats wisely negotiated their own version of the Ausgleich, known as the Nagodba, in 1868.

INTO THE GREAT WAR: FROM HABSBURGS TO YUGOSLAVS

This arrangement gave the Croats, at last, a considerable degree of internal autonomy, and Croatia even had representatives in the Hungarian parliament and cabinet and also in Vienna. But it also provided for the Croatian territories to be split up again, with control over Dalmatia and Istria going to Vienna while Slavonia and central Croatia were under the Hungarian crown. In addition, the major port of Rijeka was run as a separate entity by Budapest.

These final Habsburg decades were turbulent. Territorial divisions wounded Croatian pride and hindered economic development. Hungarian manipulation of the political scene and attempts at Magyarization continued. Count Károly Khuen-Héderváry ruled from 1883 to 1903 and became notorious for setting Croatia's Serbian and ethnic Croatian populations against each other. Despite his tactics and the turmoil of World War I, the Serbs and Croats of Croatia actually achieved a considerable level of political cooperation. They succeeded in forming coalitions to push for reunification of the Croatian lands and to oppose misrule from both Budapest and Vienna.

In 1918, with the Habsburg Empire vanquished, a combination of factors induced Croatian politicians to lead their country into the new Kingdom of Serbs, Croats, and Slovenes (called Yugoslavia after 1929). By 1921 many Croats grew suspicious of the new state, run from Belgrade by the Serbian king. Many political parties, as well as the ban (viceroys) and the Sabor, were suppressed. Royal legitimacy was shaky: Serbs dominated the police, military, and economy; agriculture, the mainstay of the economy, languished; and Italy retained possession of large amounts of Croatian territory in Istria and Dalmatia. Stjepan Radić, the leader of the powerful Croatian Peasant Party, alternately boycotted and negotiated with the central government; his murder in 1928 fueled radicalism in Croatia.

As World War II approached, Belgrade grew more willing to compromise with Croatia. A 1939 arrangement known as the Sporazum restored the ban and Sabor and combined many Croatian lands into one autonomous unit. But war broke out just weeks later.

WORLD WAR II & THE SECOND YUGOSLAVIA

The darkest chapter in Croatian history took place amidst the chaos of World War II. An interwar political agitator on the fascist right, Ante Pavelić (1889–1959) rose to power and ruled the "Independent State of Croatia" for 49 bloody months.

Pavelić, who founded the Ustaša (insurrectionist) movement in 1929, originally developed his ideas within the tradition of the Croatian Party of Right. This group, founded by Ante Starčević (1823–96) in 1861, advocated the creation of a greater Croatia, including Bosnia-Herzegovina. They believed that Bosnian Muslims (today's Bosniaks) and Serbs were ethnic Croats who had been forced to adopt other faiths. Pavelić developed ties with similar movements in Nazi Germany, Bulgaria, Hungary, and especially Mussolini's Italy. The Ustaša helped assassinate King Aleksandar in 1934. The most revolutionary aspects of the Ustaša movement were their willingness to use terror and genocide against minorities in order to form an ethnically "pure" Croatian state and their desire to create a mass political movement that displaced the established elites in the country. Mussolini's army installed Pavelić's government in Zagreb after the Axis invasion of 1941, and the Nazis agreed to let Pavelić rule. Croatia was immediately split into two spheres of influence. The Ustǎe were unpopular, but they ruled by terror over a population that included vast numbers of non-Croatians, especially Serbs. The Germans were increasingly disconcerted by the Ustaša's murderous policies, which spawned significant resistance movements. The main German goal in the region was simply the extraction of mineral and agricultural wealth. In all, the Ustaša government killed over 300,000 Serbs, along with tens of thousands of Jews and Roma (Gypsies). In addition to a number of concentration camps like the notorious Jasenovac east

of Zagreb—where about 85,000 people, mostly Serbs, were killed—many horrific rural massacres occurred. Pavelić's state was a failure; the communist Partisans and the Chetniks (Serbian royalists) actually controlled much of its territory. Yugoslavia was reconstituted after World War II, this time under the rule of Josip Broz Tito (1892–1980), a communist born in Croatia. The trauma of World War II was the main reason for decades of "Croatian silence" in Yugoslavia. In 1967, leading cultural and academic figures broke ranks with the party and publicly asserted the distinctiveness and legitimacy of the Croatian language. This was divisive, because it ran counter to the official embrace of a common "Croato-Serbian" or "Serbo-Croatian" language and culture.

A period of dissent and crackdown known as the "Croatian Spring" followed. There were demonstrations, strikes, and many debates in print about Yugoslavia's political discrimination and economic exploitation. This lasted until 1972, and resulted in Tito's sidelining numerous prominent Croatian communists, including many who could have provided cosmopolitan, intelligent alternatives to both communism and what came after. The repression belies the fact that Tito's regime became, after 1952, the most liberal socialist state in Eastern Europe; in addition, the LCY (League of Communists of Yugoslavia) was not averse to using the nationalism of some Yugoslav peoples (such as the Bosnians, the Macedonians, and the Albanians of Kosovo) to further its agenda—just not Croatian nationalism.

Famous political figures in Croatia in the postwar period included Tito, of course, but also his close ally Vladimir Bakarić, who held a number of important governmental posts. Franjo Tuđman, a communist Partisan officer during World War II and then a historian, was jailed several times for questioning centralist orthodoxy on national issues. The poet Vlado Gotovac, who again became a pro-democracy dissident under President Tuđman in the 1990s, was purged in the Croatian Spring, and the philosophers Milan Kangrga and Rudi Supek of the countrywide Praxis movement attracted attention and official disfavor with their alternative analyses of Marx.

Despite significant grievances, Croatia underwent considerable modernization under communist rule. There were increases in industrialization, urbanization, life expectancy, standard of living, and literacy. New universities were founded in Split, Rijeka, and Osijek. Croatia's beaches became famous across Europe. The economy was also helped by the large numbers of Croats who worked abroad as *Gastarbeiter* (guest workers), but heavy immigration and low birth rates left many worried about the country's demographic future.

Both Serbia and Croatia felt the heavy hand of Tito's rule; as the most powerful traditional nations in Yugoslavia, Tito neutralized their ability to rock the federal boat. The LCY encouraged nation-building, however, in Bosnia, Macedonia, Montenegro, and among the Albanians of Kosovo both as a counterweight to Croatian and Serbian ambitions and as a developmental strategy.

FROM TITO TO TUĐMAN & BEYOND: SOVEREIGN CROATIA

Historians disagree over when Yugoslavia passed the point of no return. At some point in the decade between Tito's death in 1980 and the momentous political changes in Slovenia and Croatia by 1991, the breakup actually began. In 1990, Slovenia and Croatia held free, multiparty elections, declared their sovereignty, and held referenda in which they overwhelmingly approved the idea of independence. But even then the eventual violence was not inevitable. Two highly regarded Croatian reformist politicians, Ante Marković and Stjepan Mesić,

were stymied in their efforts to place the Yugoslav federation on a new foundation. What soon exploded were not the so-called "ancient ethnic hatreds" but rather the aggressive and conflicting aims of various political factions competing in a superheated environment. This violence was furthered by the egoism of conniving politicians, sensationalism in the media, and mixed signals from Western Europe and the United States.

The 1980s had been extremely tense across the country. Serbs and Albanians clashed in Kosovo; hyperinflation, unemployment, public debt, and strikes characterized a ruined economy; and the fall of the Berlin Wall marked the end of other European socialist states. The rise of the dictator Slobodan Milošević in Serbia brought new levels of confrontation to politics and revealed gross Serbian manipulation of the economy. Croats and Slovenes gradually realized that Yugoslavia was unworkable as a country. The Serbian population, incited by ambitious politicians, lashed out at Croat police in the spring of 1991. Thus, even before Croatia's declaration of independence on June 25, 1991, the villages of Pakrac and Borovo Selo became scenes of bitter bloodshed, as did the famed Plitvice Lakes National Park and other areas in central Croatia. There were about 600,000 Serbs living in Croatia, comprising over 12% of the population. The new Croatian government, led by the now-nationalist Tuđman, was brash in its treatment of minorities and irresponsible in its handling of the legacy of World War II, and these approaches greatly increased Serbs' anxiety.

After secession, full-scale fighting broke out. The autumn of 1991 saw two shocking sieges: the bloody street-fighting and massacres at Vukovar in Slavonia and the weeks-long shelling of venerable Dubrovnik for no legitimate military purpose. The contemporary Croatian poet Slavko Mihalić described this era

364 < Understanding Croatia & Slovenia

as one in which the Serbian leader—"the one who sends the bombs"—grimly and accurately promised to turn Croatia into a "national park of death." In fact Milošević was willing to let Croatia secede but without its Serb-inhabited regions; later, he and Tuđman agreed on how to partition Bosnia-Herzegovina as well. In May 1992 the war spread to independence-minded Bosnia, where 200,000 people died, many of them civilians, and 2 million were made homeless. In Croatia, 10,000 people were killed and over a fourth of the country fell to the Serbs. Large numbers of Croats and Bosnians were driven from their homes with terror campaigns of "ethnic cleansing." With American aid, Croatian forces rallied in the summer of 1995 and recaptured Slavonia and the Krajina region. Many thousands of Serbs fled and property issues remain unresolved. Croatian forces also committed atrocities in Bosnia-Herzegovina, but most of the international community finally recognized that the lion's share of guilt for the wars themselves belonged to the Serbian government. The Dayton peace accords of late 1995, backed by NATO's military might, paved the way for Serbian withdrawal from Croatia and Bosnia.

President Tuđman was roundly criticized internationally for his authoritarian tendencies and over-zealous nationalism. Internal opposition grew as well, especially over his censorship and policies in Bosnia. Tuđman allowed political parties other than the HDZ (Croatian Democratic Union), but they were weak until his death in December 1999. Since then, Mesić has been president, and the prime ministership has been held by both the Social Democrats of Ivica Račan and the revived HDZ of Ivo Šanader. Since Tuđman's death, Croatia has begun serious cooperation with The Hague war-crimes tribunal. Many other reforms have also succeeded, but open questions include the quest for autonomy by the ethnically and historically distinct region of Istria and Croatia's ability to cooperate on a variety of issues with its neighbors. Most Croats still look forward to joining the European Union in the next several years.

—*John K. Cox, Associate Professor of History, Wheeling Jesuit University*

WINE IN CROATIA

The Croats, the first of the invading Slavs to take up the cult of the vine, arrived in their viticulturally blessed homeland as recently as the 7th century BC and can today lay claim to some of the world's richest wine-making resources. A wine renaissance is occurring in Croatia today.

The early 20th century was bad for the wine business—phylloxera, war, crippling economic policies, all of which ravaged wineries here and led to the mass emigration of many vintners who fled to the United States, New Zealand, Australia, South Africa, and South America. Bringing their knowledge of vine cultivation and wine production with them, they left Croatia's vineyards virtually deserted.

More recently, the 1990–95 war for Croatian independence, which cast a global spotlight on the tiny country, nearly wiped out a viticulture two millennia in the making. It appears, however, that the land itself cannot forget its heritage. Blessed with unique geography, so crucially ideal for wine, Croatia currently hosts more than 100 indigenous grapes—second only to Italy. As Croatian vintners are rushing to expand before the country enters the European Union, the country's wines are once again finding a special place in the hearts of oenophiles everywhere. Perhaps it's a pleasant coincidence that zinfandel, the backbone and darling of California's wine industry, has been traced back recently to its reputed place of origin—Kaštel Novi, near Split, on the Dalmatian coast. Millions of years ago during the Eucene period, plate tectonics created the distinctive coastal landscapes of Dalmatia and Istria, the most important wine-producing regions. In the steep limestone bluffs of the Dalmatian karst, several indigenous varieties have proven themselves exceptionally suited to the environment. To the casual observer, prominent layers of limestone belie the existence of buried layers of rich, ancient soil and ample moisture from underground drainage systems. Steep, rocky cliffs, hills, valleys, caves, and 1,185 islands that were created during the shifting of the Earth's plates created an area known as the "golden corridor" of the Adriatic. This Mediterranean landscape is particularly suited to *Vitus vinifera L* (the cultivated grapevine), a hearty and prolific, yet temperamental plant that requires precise combinations of climate, geography, and soil to flourish. In Croatia, with her numerous, diverse microclimates, the grape has had the necessary conditions to proliferate and adapt to isolated environments.

WINE MAKING & ITS DEEP ROOTS

The Delmati, an Illyrian tribe, were the first to cultivate the vine in modern-day Croatia, as early as the 11th century BC. When the Romans invaded the Dalmatian Coast in the 3rd century BC, they discovered that wine production had preceded them; they found, in fact, an entire wine industry. The Greeks, who'd been sharing the region with the Illyrians, had not failed to exploit *Vitus sylvestris* (the wild grapevine), which was plentiful there, merging it with the strains of the cultivated vines they brought from their own country. The conquering Roman soldiers also brought new varietals with them as a way of expanding their culture; the vine itself was a symbol of their power.

By the 9th century, Croatian princes had a cup bearer as part of their court staff, whose duties involved wine-cellar maintenance and the selection and serving of wines within the court. When Venice subjugated much of Dalmatia in the 14th century, the planting of new vineyards was restricted to the areas around Split. It was in this period that noble families, after building their vineyards, built fortresses in the middle of their estates for protection, perhaps anticipating the destruction of the coming Venetian-Turkish wars. In Slavonia and Dalmatia, a large number of the vineyards, then documented at more than 7,000, were destroyed during these wars. By the time the Habsburgs had ousted the Ottomans, the Austrians were already well on their way to introducing new varietals to the area, capitalizing on the superior wine-producing capacity of their newly acquired resources.

Modern developments in cloning techniques and the use of industrial machinery brought wine making in Croatia to the economic position it occupies today, where 10% of the population derives income from the industry. By the end of Marshall Tito's reign, however, only a tenth of Croatia's then-extant 180,000 hectares survived the farm mechanization of communism, and many of those fields were burned in the war of the early 1990s. The government plans to free up state-owned land to plant ew vineyards. Nevertheless, things are moving slowly.

THE NAPA VALLEY CONNECTION

Croatia has had some world-class help in reestablishing its wine-making industry. Miljenko "Mike" Grgič of Napa Valley fame is at the forefront of the race to expand and realize the potential of Croatia's indigenous varietals. Grgič left Croatia in 1954, feeling stifled by the communist government. In California, he became renowned as a winemaker when his 1973 Chateau Montelena Chardonnay won a blind tasting in Paris. Afterward, the top-quality wine market opened its mind and wallet to wines from the world over. Mr. Grgič then established Grgich Hills Cellar in Napa Valley, and it is now one of California's most respected producers. When Croatia won its independence in 1995, Mike Grgič went back to establish **Grgič Vina** (✉ *Trstenik 78, Trstenik* ☎*020/748–090*) in a tiny town of some 100 residents on the Pelješac Peninsula in Central Dalmatia. Croatia's first international winery surprised everyone by turning a profit within two years (5 to 10 years is typical). The winery produces high-end boutique wines: a flavorful,

fruity white from the indigenous pošip; and a ruby-red, from the hearty plavac mali, the "little blue" grape that is widely considered the highest-quality Croatian varietal. These bottles range between $20 and $50 a bottle. Grgič hopes to support the local wine communes by using their grapes as well.

LABELS, REGIONS & WINERIES

A bit of wine label terminology is sure to enhance your sampling experience: red wine is called either *crno vino* or *crveno vino,* whereas white wine is *bijelo vino*; *ruzica* may label a rosé. Dessert wine (*desertno vino*) is an easy one. *Jenusavo vino* (sparkling wine) is a bit more difficult to remember. As for descriptive terminology, *suho vino* indicates a dry wine, and *polosuh vino* means medium-dry. *Slatko vino* is sweet; *prirodno* is organic. The highest-quality wines are labeled *vrhunsko* (literally, top quality). *Geografsko porijelko* (geographical origin) precedes the name of the grape: *Primoštenski Babić* means Babić grown in Primošten. Croatia is split into two main wine-growing regions: the arid continental part and the coastal region, much of which shares the same latitude as Bordeaux, Provence, Tuscany, and Oregon. The continental region produces 90% of the country's whites, whereas the coastal almost 70% of the reds. There are 12 subregions in Croatia, the most important of which are: **Central and Southern Dalmatia** (Sjeverna and Južna Dalmacija), where the hearty plavac mali flourishes on the Pelejesic Peninsula, and the Dubrovačka malvasia (served as a delicacy in the 14th century) was once produced; **Middle Dalmatia** (Sredja Dalmacija), where the famous babič grape is grown near Primošten; and the **Northern Coastal Belt** (Hrvatsko Primorje), which includes the islands of Cres, Lošinj, Rab, Pag, and Krk—famous for the Žlatina varietal, which is produced by the Katunar winery. These are breathtaking regions, as is **Istria** (Istra), known for its *malvasia Istriana* (white) and *teran* (red).

The region of **Meddjimurje,** situated in continental Croatia along the Slovenian and Hungarian border, also has some fine wineries specializing in white wines made from *graševina* grapes, better known as Welschriesling, as well as tramina, chardonnay, and sauvignon blanc. Although a work in progress at this writing, a general **Web site** (⊕*www.hrvatska-vina.com*) on Croatian wines and winemakers is being set up to facilitate vineyard visitations and schedule wine tastings.

ISTRIAN WINERIES

At **AgroLaguna Winery** (✉*Vukovarska 19, Poreč* ☎*052/432–203 or 052/432–111*) it is possible to taste a number of high-quality Istrian wines. One varietal, malvazija, is well known throughout the Adriatic, dating back to the days of the Venetian city-states. Muškat ottonal is another high-quality native variety. Small, lovingly produced batches of barrique provide high-quality (red) wine. Gran teran, from **Moreno Coronica** (✉*Koreniki 86, Koreniki* ☎☎*052/730–196*), in the northeast corner of the peninsula, has been a gold-medal winner at international wine competitions.

NORTHERN COASTAL BELT WINERIES

At **Katunar winery** (✉*Sv. Nedilija, Vrbnik, Krk* ☎*051/857–393* ⊕*www.katunar.com*), in the Kvarner Gulf, you can sample the žlatina varietal, which is indigenous to the island. Individual visits and group tours can be arranged to sample the dry white *žhlatina Katunar* or the *černo Katunar* (a dry red), or the "pearl wine" *biser mora,* a dessert wine produced from 100% zlahtina grapes. This dry white wine is famous among Croatians around the world.

CENTRAL & SOUTHERN DALMATIAN WINERIES

The rich bouquet of the ruby-red *Dingač,* the current darling of Croatia's export market, goes perfectly with a traditional meal of roast *janjetina* (lamb) or a plate of grilled *lignje* (baby squid). The *plavac*

mali grapes grown on the steep hillsides of Dingač produce a full-bodied, slightly dry wine. These particular 168 acres, along with some areas of Hvar, have the highest average temperatures in Croatia, the reason why Dingač's alcohol content may reach as high as 17.6%, the highest of Croatian wines. The seaside slopes upon which the grapes are grown are so steep that donkeys are the only possible helpmates (machine harvesting is impossible). The donkey found on some bottles of Dingač is a symbol of the hearty, stubborn vine that reaches its full potential in this very limited region. At one of Croatia's best-known wineries, **Vinarija Dingač Cooperative** (*Dingač Cooperative* ✉*Potomje* ☎*020/742–010*) it is possible to sample several excellent wines. Each year, Vinarija Dingač produces 12,500 cases of a deep-red wine that is fruity without being sweet. In a market flooded with low-priced good-quality wines from South Africa and Australia, many in the Croatian wine industry believe that the future of Croatian wine depends on these superior products. This boutique-style varietal is widely available abroad. In Southern Dalmatia's Pelješac Peninsula, visitors are welcome at **Vinarija Ivo Skaramucha** (✉*Rijavichno, Kina Peljeshka* ☎*020/742–211*) to sample the indigenous plavac mali varietals. **Frano Miloš Winery** (✉*Ponikve 15, Ston* ☎*020/753–098*) is north of Dubrovnik. Visitors may have the opportunity to sample obscure small-batch wines of unique geographic origins. Be ready to try such wines as plavac ponikve, nadhanuche, and stagnum. The stagnum here is of a particularly high quality. **Villa Coruna** (✉*Ston* ☎*020/833–126 or 020/833–146*) is a small, country restaurant perched over a bay where you can sample delicious white wines made in small batches from the pošip grape by the owner Andres Vuković, who delights in pairing his lovingly crafted wine with oysters freshly plucked from the sea. On the beautiful lavender-scented island of Hvar you can visit **Plančić Winery** (✉*21462 Vrbanj Svirče, Stari Grad, Hvar* ☎☎*21/768–030* ⊕*www.plancic. com*), where Antun Plančić has been producing a variety of top-quality wines, including rosé and dessert wines, as well as some local rakija since 1919. Look out for *bogdanuša* (dry white wine) or *Ivan Dolac[sc]* (a select red). **The Plenković Winery** (✉*Sveta Nedilja, Hvar* ☎*021/745–725*), along with its restaurant and hotel, are also well worth a visit. In fact, in the past few years the *zlatan plavac* (a dry red) made by Zlatan Plenković has continually won prestigious awards at local and international wine fairs. Plenković may soon become the largest single-family producer in Croatia.

NORTHERN DALMATIA WINERIES
The vineyards that surround Primošten Bay have been compared to a honeycomb, and are an impressive sight to behold. A photograph of the region even hangs in the lobby of the United Nations building in New York. The stone walls, so carefully built by human hands centuries ago, have the UN-administered status of a monument to human effort. The fields of babić grapes surrounding Primošten Bay were built upon layers of rock—an unlikely success story—but the vines adapted to the karst landscape, their roots going deep into the soil. Since replanting from American rootstock, babić has spread throughout Dalmatia, but the best babić wines are still produced on Primošten, in the town of Šibenik. The **Bibič Winery** (✉*Plastovo* ☎*023/329–260*), which operates a wine boutique in Zadar, produces wine both from native Dalmatian varieties, including babić, plavina, lašina, and debit, and non-native grapes, including grenache and shiraz. The winery is just outside of Skradin. **Vinoplod-Vinarija** (✉*Velimira Škorpika 2, Šibenik* ☎*022/333–671 or 022/334–011*), the award-winning makers of primoštenski babić, can be contacted for tours and tastings.

CONTINENTAL WINERIES
Jakopič Winery (✉*Železna Gora 92, Orehovčak Štrigova* ☎☎*040/851–300*), near the spa town of Sveti Martin in the Varaždin region, is operated by brothers Martin and Branimir Jakopič, who offer superb dining as well as scenic tours of the lush vineyards situated on the borders of Slovenia, Hungary, and Austria. A 20-minute drive northwest of the town of Čakovec brings you close to the Slovenian border in the heart of lush, green vineyard country. Here, at the **Lovreč Winery** (✉*Sveti Urban* ☎*40/830–171*), four generations have been cultivating the vines; the winery is known for high-quality, award-winning wines made from chardonnay, sauvignon blanc, pinot gris, Johannesburg riesling, white riesling, and gewürztraminer. Wine-tasting sessions are available in English. If you call ahead, you may also arrange to attend seminars and lectures about vine cultivation.

THE ZINQUEST: FINDING ZINFANDEL IN CROATIA
Much excitement has been generated in recent years around California's ubiquitous zinfandel grape, whose origin had long been guessed at, but which remained shrouded in mystery. Until recently, that is. In 1998 Professor Carole Meredith of the University of California at Davis, a renowned grapevine geneticist who had previously uncovered the origins of chardonnay, cabernet sauvignon, and petit syrah, began a similar search for zinfandel's origin. The exciting four-year project, which entailed the collection of leaf samples from indigenous varieties of southern Dalmatia, DNA fingerprinting analyses of samples cultivars, and comparisons with zinfandel cuttings from California, shed new light on the origins of the state's most popular grape.

In the spring of 1998, assisted by Jasenka Piljač, a former student at the University of California at Davis, and two Croatian scientists, Ivan Pejić and Edi Maletić, Professor Meredith collected leaf samples from 148 individual plavac mali vines in Southern Dalmatia. Thirty-one samples were collected on the island of Hvar, and 105 from the Peljesac Peninsula. Twelve samples were also taken on the island of Korčula. Although the initial search in 1998 gave no positive matches with zinfandel, the expeditions that followed led the team of scientists to an old vineyard in Kaštel Novi, where a few additional "suspects" were discovered. The DNA analyses performed at Davis confirmed that a wine locally known as crljenak kaštelanski—completely forgotten and virtually eradicated from Dalmatian vineyards—is the long-sought Croatian corollary of zinfandel. The small vineyard where crljenak kaštelanski

was found belongs to a local firefighter, Ivica Radunić, who owns **Radunić Winery** (✉ *Narodnog Preporoda 46-Brce, Kaštel Novi* ☎ *021/231–138* ✎ *ivicaradunic@ vip.hr web*). His family's wine-growing tradition goes back several generations, and the winery is conveniently located near the Split Airport. Ivica is happy to accommodate visitors. Jasenka Piljač's book, *Zinfandel: A Croatian-American Wine Story* (🌐 *www.crozinfandel.com*) chronicles her work as a part of the Meredith Zinquest team and includes in-depth information about Croatia's viticultural past, present, and future. Hers is the only serious book on Croatian viticulture available in English.

—*Marijana Oroz*

SAILING & CRUISING THE CROATIAN COAST

The Croatian Adriatic has over 2,000 km (1,242 mi) of mainland coast, with more than 1,000 islands and islets (67 of which are inhabited). Unlike Greece, where the islands are dispersed, the Croatian islands run parallel to and close to the mainland coast, which, for the most part, means easy island-hopping in protected waters.

Besides the picturesque coastal towns, Croatia has three national parks on the sea: Brijuni National Park (a cluster of 14 small green islands just off Istria), Kornati National Park (an archipelago of 89 arid, rocky islands, islets, and reefs off North Dalmatia), and Mljet National Park (a large, fertile island, one-third of which is covered with coniferous forest, in South Dalmatia). In addition, Krka National Park (a spectacular series of waterfalls in a canyon in Central Dalmatia), can even be approached by sailboat, if you sail up the Šibenik Channel as far as Skradin.

SAILING

Often considered a glamorous and expensive way to travel, a holiday aboard a sailboat is now an affordable alternative to a land-bound vacation. In fact, it is the ultimate way to explore Croatia's stunningly beautiful mainland coast and islands. No other form of transport gives you such flexibility and such close contact with the sea: aboard a yacht you can sunbathe on the deck, put down anchor and swim wherever you choose, and discover isolated coves accessible only from the water, some of which have idyllic beaches and informal restaurants serving the very freshest seafood. And, surprisingly, a week aboard a sailing boat can be cheaper than staying in a mid-range hotel.

If you are already an experienced sailor, you can charter a so-called bareboat yacht, meaning that you rent just the boat and sail independently. By Croatian law, at least one of the crew needs to have an internationally recognized sailing license, plus a radio certificate (available from all port authorities).

If you have never sailed before, or have little experience, then you will need a skipper. Generally skippers do more than just guide the boat: most are from the region and, therefore, know the local waters and weather conditions, the history and culture, the protected coves for putting down anchor, the local gastronomic hideouts, and the best diving spots. Most charter companies have their own skippers (who generally speak at least two foreign languages, including English).

The third option is sailing in a flotilla. A flotilla is a group of yachts (typically between 5 and 10), with people of mixed levels of sailing experience, led by a qualified expert. You gain the privacy of your own sailboat but also the security of knowing that help is always close at hand should you need it. Of course, you also get to meet new people.

A typical one-week sailing itinerary in Central Dalmatia could run as follows. Day 1: Set sail from Split to Maslinica on the island of Šolta. Day 2: Maslinica to Vis Town on the island of Vis. Day 3: Sail round the island, from Vis Town to Komiža, calling at Biševo en route. Day 4: Komiža to Hvar Town on the island of Hvar. Day 5: Hvar Town to Bol on the island of Brač. Day 6: Bol to Milna on the island of Brač. Day 7: Early morning departure from Milna to Split. The Croatian Adriatic has 50 well-equipped marinas providing 13,500 sea berths and 4,500 dry berths. All berths are equipped with water and power supplies, and most marinas also have at least one restaurant, a grocery store, a nautical-gear store, a repair shop, a gas station, and toilets and showers. Some, but not all, have laundry facilities. The leading nautical-tourism company, Adriatic Croatian International (known as ACI, pronounced "Atsi"), runs 21 marinas. Twenty Croatian marinas have been awarded the European "Blue Flag" for safety, cleanliness, and respect for the environment. Most marinas stay open all year.

Last but not least, remember that Croatia recently introduced a law declaring zero-alcohol tolerance for those in charge of a boat. If you are caught sailing in a state of inebriation you could face steep fines.

CHARTER COMPANIES

On the Croatian Adriatic there are over 140 charter companies operating tens of thousands of boats of all sizes, making this one of the busiest charter areas in Europe. As a rough guide to prices, in summer 2007 high season, Sail Croatia offered an eight-berth Beneteau 411 Celebration sailing boat for €3,838 per week, working out to €480 per person per week, though this price does not include food, fuel, or mooring fees.

The most popular way to research and book charter yachts is via the Internet. Most sites include photos and layout schemes of the boats, lists of onboard equipment, and even sample itineraries. Once you have selected your boat, all you need to do is confirm the availability of the date with the charter company and pay a nonrefundable deposit equal to 30% to 50% of the charter price. The remaining 50% to 70% of the charter fee is usually paid four weeks before the commencement of the charter.

The season runs from May through October, with the best winds for sailing in May and June. Demand and prices peak in July and August, when you can expect calmer sea and less wind, making conditions ideal for motorboats but less fun for true sailors. During peak season, charter rentals generally begin at 5 PM Saturday and end at 9 AM the following Saturday.

Some companies offer extra activities, which can be combined with sailing, such as scuba diving, kayaking, surfing, hiking, mountain biking, or vineyard tours. Another popular option is "sail and stay," which gives you a week aboard a yacht followed by a week in a hotel or villa. There are even special sailing packages for weddings and honeymoons. As tourism is developing rapidly in Croatia, you should check with individual companies to see what the new season has to offer.

INTERNATIONAL COMPANIES

Most of the international companies are headquartered in the United Kingdom, but there are a couple of worldwide operations that have offices in the United States as well.

Activity Yachting (☎[44] 1243/641–304 ⊕www.activityyachting.com) offers sailing programs that operate along the 161 km (100-mi) stretch of coastline between Split and Zadar. Flotilla holidays (with or without tuition) are available, sharing a five-berth boat. Bareboat rental can also be arranged, or you can take a tailor-made program combining a week's sailing with a week in a villa or hotel.

Dalmatian Destinations (☎[44]20/7730–8007 ⊕www.dalmatiandestinations.com) is an upmarket travel company that provides fully crewed sailing boats, motorboats, and gulets in Croatia. Their itineraries include an "Organic Route" tracking down Dalmatia's best seasonal and regional cuisine and a "Cultural Route" taking in architecture, art, and music along the coast.

LateSail (☎[44] 1227/479–900 ⊕www.latesail.com) acts as a clearinghouse for the world's leading charter operators and offers a wide range of yachts at cut-rate prices in over 50 destinations, including Croatia.

Nautilus (☎[44]1732/867–445 ⊕www.nautilus-yachting.com) keeps yachts, catamarans, and motorboats at bases in Pula, Zadar, Biograd, Murter (close to Kornati National Park), Split, and Dubrovnik. Flotilla sailing is also available.

Neilson (☎*[44]870/333–3356* ⊕*www. neilson.co.uk*) is based in Lumbarda on Korčula. It offers one-week flotilla sailing (generally from Lumbarda to Dubrovnik and back), and a two-week villa-and-flotilla combination, with the first week ashore learning sailing basics, and the second week aboard a boat. It is also possible to combine surfing, cycling, and scuba diving with sailing.

SailCroatia(☎*[44]8717/338–686* ⊕*www. sailcroatia.net*) offers a fleet of 15 yachts of various sizes up to 56 feet, sleeping between two and 10 people; or you can book one of a couple of larger crewed yachts measuring up to 100 feet with 12 berths. Boats can be chartered on a bareboat basis or with a skipper who will provide guidance and tuition. Itineraries are flexible, but departures are generally from Split. It's also possible to opt for sail-and-stay, including time on land.

Sailing Holidays (☎*[44]20/8459–8787* ⊕*www.sailingholidays.com*) is a flotilla specialist, offering both informal flotillas and bareboat sailing, or a combination of the two (a couple of days with a flotilla then the rest of the week alone). If you set off from their base in Kremik (Primošten, near Šibenik) you will visit Kornati National Park, and if you start from Tučepi (near Makarska) you will sail down to Dubrovnik.

The Moorings (☎*[33]15/300–3030* ⊕*www. moorings.com*) is an international sailing specialist with bases in Dubrovnik and Kremik (Primošten, near Šibenik) in Croatia. The company offers bareboat, skippered, and flotilla sailing in yachts and catamarans with anything from two to five double cabins.

CROATIAN COMPANIES

If you want to simply rent a boat and chose your own skipper, you can contact the **Adriatic Skipper Association** (⊕*www. usj.hr*). Expect to pay €100–€150 per day for his or her services, and remember that you are also responsible for the skip-

per's food. For a full list of charter companies, the **Croatian National Tourist Board** (⊕*www.croatia.hr*) publishes a list on its Web site. Go to "Tourism Plus" then "Nautics," where you will find region-by-region listings.

ACI (⌂*Maršala Tita 151, Opatija, Croatia 51410* ☎*[385] 51/271–288* ⊕*www. aci-club.hr*) is Croatia's largest marine management company. It runs charters from its base in Trogir (Central Dalmatia), either bareboat or with a skipper. **Euromarine** (☎*[385]1/2325–237* ⊕*www. euromarine.hr*) has bases in Pula, Biograd, Split, and Dubrovnik, chartering more than 90 sailing boats, motorboats and catamarans.

Club Adriatic (☎*[385]1/463–7512, 800/673–9592 in the U.S.* ⊕*www.charter.hr*) is an online charter service with over 1,300 bareboat, crewed, and luxury yachts along the coast. The site is particularly recommended when you are searching for special low-season offers and last-minute discounts.

Pivatus (☎*[385]52/215–155* ⊕*www. pivatus.hr*) has bases in Pula and Split, chartering sailing boats and motorboats of various sizes, both bareboat or with a skipper.

Ultra Sailing (☎*[385] 21/398–980* ⊕*www. ultra-sailing.hr*) has a total of 30 sailing boats in three bases in Dalmatia: Kaštel (near Split), Split, and Dubrovnik.

SAILING SCHOOLS

Adriatic Nautical Academy (*ANA* ⊕*www. sailing-ana.hr*) is an annual sailing school held at Jezera on the island of Murter in Central Dalmatia, offering one-week courses (late March to early November). The school also has a summer base in Cavtat, near Dubrovnik in Southern Dalmatia (late April to late October). In 2007 a one-week Level 1 Beginner's Course at Jezera cost €485, while the same course in Cavtat cost €680.

Ultra Sailing (☎ *[385] 21/398–980* ⊕ *www. ultra-sailing.hr*) was founded by former members of the Croatian Olympic Team who now work as instructors, offering one-week courses (March through October) in Milna on the island of Brač (in Central Dalmatia). In 2007 the one-week Basic Course cost €600.

CRUISING

A visitor with limited time in Croatia will find that traveling down the Adriatic aboard a cruiser is an ideal way to see the country's mainland ports and islands. Although it is tempting to try using the Jadrolinija coastal ferry, which runs from Rijeka to Dubrovnik with several stops en route, it's not really an ideal solution. The timetable is complicated and inconsistent, with different arrival and departure times each day, and some days there's no boat at all. At best, the ferry makes a fine way to travel overnight from Rijeka to Split, or through the day from Split to Korčula or Dubrovnik. Many of the well-known international cruise lines (notably Carnival, Celebrity, Costa, Crystal, Cunard, Holland America, Norwegian, Oceania, Princess, Seabourn, Silversea, Star Clippers, and Windstar) now include Croatia on their Mediterranean itineraries, mainly en route from Venice to the Greek islands. Croatia is also included in some "Eastern Mediterranean" cruises, which might include Greece, Turkey, North Africa, and the Middle East. The favorite port of call is undoubtedly Dubrovnik, but Korčula Town, Hvar Town, Split, Šibenik, Rab Town, Opatija, Pula, and Rovinj also show up on some itineraries. An alternative to cruising on a large ship is traveling aboard a medium-sized old-timer. Several Croatian companies now offer informal one-week cruises on beautifully restored wooden gulets, generally taking between 12 to 40 passengers.

Adriatic Cruises (⊕ *www.adriaticcruises. hr*) runs just one ship, the MS *Dalmacija,* whose claim to fame is having been used in the film *The Talented Mr. Ripley.* The *Dalmacija* has been renovated to preserve her old-fashioned charm, retaining the teakwood promenade and sundeck, and details such as brass handrails. Each year from mid-April to early November, she runs one-week cruises along the Adriatic, departing from Venice and visiting Zadar, Ploče, Korčula, Kotor (Montenegro), Dubrovnik, Pula, and Koper (Slovenia), before returning to Venice. The crew is Croatian, and there are 140 cabins accommodating a total of 300 passengers.

Dubrovnik Travel (☎ *[385]20/313–555* ⊕ *www.dubrovniktravel.hr*) operates 12 boats with capacities ranging from 12 to 300 passengers. Its largest boat, the MS *Arion,* runs one-week cruises from Koper (Slovenia), calling at Pula, Zadar, Split, Korčula, Dubrovnik, Kotor (Montenegro), and Ploče.

Elite Travel (☎ *[385]20/358–200* ⊕ *www. elite.hr*) offers one-week motor-sail cruises aboard old-timers running Saturday to Saturday. The "Dalmatian Highlights Cruise," for up to 26 passengers, starts and ends in Dubrovnik, visiting the Elafiti, Mljet, Vela Luka (Korčula), and Hvar islands. Alternatively, the "Adriatic Paradise Cruise" has a capacity of 40 passengers, beginning and ending in Trogir, taking in Split, Vis, Korčula, Dubrovnik, Mljet, and Hvar. **Katarina Line** (☎ *[385] 51/603–400* ⊕ *www.katarina-line.hr*) offers one-week cruises aboard 21 vintage sailing ships from mid-May to mid-October, for groups of between 22 and 40 passengers. Departures are from Opatija (covering Kvarner and North Dalmatia) and Split and Dubrovnik (covering Central and South Dalmatia). Itineraries are variable but include visits to the islands and plenty of time for swimming.

—Jane Foster

CROATIAN VOCABULARY

ENGLISH	CROATIAN	PRONUNCIATION

BASICS

Yes/no	Da/ne	dah/neh
Please	Molim (vas)	**moh**-leem (vahs)
Thank you (very much)	Hvala (lijepo)	**hvah**-lah (lyeh-poh)
Excuse me	Oprostite	oh-proh-stee-teh
Hello	Zdravo	**zdrah**-voh
I'm sorry.	Žao mi je.	**zhah**-oh mee yeh
Do you speak English?	Da li govorite engleski?teh	Dah lee **goh**-voh-ree-**ehn**-glehs-kee
I don't understand.	Ne razumijem.	neh rah-**zoo**-myehm
Please show me . . .	Molim vas, moh-leem vahs, pokažite mi . . .	**poh**-kah-zhee-teh mee
I am American (m/f).	Ja sam yah sahm Amerikanac (Amerikanka).	**ah**-meh-ree-kah-nahts **ah**-meh-ree-kahn-kah
My name is . . .	Zovem se . . .	**zoh**-vehm seh
Right/left	Desno/Lijevo	**dehs**-noh/**lyeh**-voh
Open/closed	Otvoreno/zatvoreno	**oh**-tvoh-reh-noh/ **zah**-tvoh-reh-noh
Where is . . . ?	Gdje je . . . ?	gdyeh yeh
. . . the train station?	. . železnička?	**zheh**-lehz-neech-kah
. . . the bus stop?. . .	autobusna	**ahoo**-toh-boos-nah
. . . the airport?. . .	aerodrom?	**ah**-eh-roh-drohm
. . . the post office?	. . . pošta?	**posh**-tah
. . . the bank?	. . . banka?	**bahn**-kah
Here/there	Ovdje/tamo	**ohv**-dyeh/**tah**-moh
I would like. . .	Molim (vas). . . htjela bih. . .	**moh**-leem (vahs)/Htio/ hteeoh/htyeh-lah beeh (m/f)
How much does it cost?	Koliko košta?	**koh**-lee-koh **kosh**-tah
Postcard	Razglednica	**rahz**-gleh-dnee-tsah
Help!	Upomoć!	**oo**-poh-moch

NUMBERS

One	Jedan	**yeh**-dahn
Two	Dvad	vah
Three	Tri	tree
Four	Četiri	**cheh**-tee-ree
Five	Pet	peht
Six	Šest	shest
Seven	Sedam	**seh**-dahm
Eight	Osam	**oh**-sahm
Nine	Devet	**deh**-veht
Ten	Deset	**deh**-seht
One hundred	Sto	stoh
One thousand	Tisuća	**tee**-soo-chah

DAYS OF THE WEEK

Sunday	Nedjelja	**neh**-dyeh-lyah
Monday	Ponedjeljak	**poh**-neh-dyeh-lyahk
Tuesday	Utorak	**oo**-toh-rahk
Wednesday	Srijeda	**sryeh**-dah
Thursday	Četvrtak	**cheht**-vruh-tahk
Friday	Petak	**peh**-tahk
Saturday	Subota	**soo**-boh-tah

WHERE TO SLEEP

A room	Soba	**soh**-bah
The key	Ključ	klyooch
With bath/shower	S kupaonicom/tušem	suh koo-pah-**oh**-nee-tsohm/**too**-shehm

FOOD

A restaurant	Restoran	rehs-**toh**-rahn
The menu	Jelovnik	yeh-**lohv**-neek
The check, please.	Molim, račun.	**moh**-leem, **rah**-choon
Can I order, please?	Mogu li naručiti, molim vas?	**moh**-goo lee nah-**roo**-chee tee, **moh**-leem vahs

Breakfast	Doručak	**doh**-roo-chahk
Lunch	Ručak	**roo**-chahk
Dinner	Večera	**veh**-cheh-rah
Bread	Kruh	krooh
Butter	Putar/maslac	**poo**-tahr/mahs-lahts
Salt/pepper	Sol/papar	sohl/**pah**-pahr
Wine	Vino	**vee**-noh
Beer	Pivo	**pee**-voh
Water/mineral water	Voda/mineralna voda	**voh**-dah/**mee**-neh-rahl-nah **voh**-dah
Milk	Mlijeko	**mlyeh**-koh
Coffee	Kava	**kah**-vah
Tea	Čaj	chay

SLOVENIAN VOCABULARY

ENGLISH	SLOVENIAN	PRONUNCIATION

BASICS

ENGLISH	SLOVENIAN	PRONUNCIATION
Yes/no	Da/ne	dah/nay
Please	Prosim	**proh**-seem
Thank you (very much)	Hvala (lepa)	**hvah**-lah (**lay**-pah)
Excuse me	Oprostite	oh-pros-**tee**-tay
I'm sorry	Žal mi	jezh-**ow** mee yay
Hello/how do you do	Dober dan	**doh**-boo dan
Do you speak English?	Govorite angleško?	goh-vor-**ee**-tay ang-**lay**-shkoh
I don't speak Slovenian.	Ne govorim slovensko	nay goh-vor-**eem** sloh-**ven**-skoh
I don't understand.	Ne razumem	nay raz-**oom**-em
Please speak slowly.	Prosim, govorite	**proh**-seem goh-vor-počasi.
Please write it down.	Prosim, napišite.	**proh**-seem, nah-**pee**-shee-tay
Please show me.	Prosim, pokažite.	**proh**-seem, poh-**kah**-zhee-tay
I am American	Jaz sem američan	yoo sum ah-mer-ee-**chan**
I am English	Jaz sem anglež	yoo sum ang-**lezh**
My name is . . .	Ime mi je . . .	ee-**may** mee yay . . .
Right/left	Desno/levo	**des**-noh/ **lee**-voh
Open/closed	Odprt/zaprt	**od**-prt/ **za**-prt
Arrival/departure	Prihod/odhod	pree-**hod**/ od-**hod**
Where is . . . ?	Kje je . . . ?	k-**yay** yay . . . ?
. . . the train station?	. . . železniška	zheh-**lay**-zneesh-kah
. . . the bus stop?	. . . avtobusna	aw-toh-**boos**-nah
. . . the airport?	. . . letališče?	let-al-**ee**-shuh-cheh
. . . the post office?	. . . pošta?	**poh**-shtah
. . . the bank?	. . . banka?	**ban**-kah
Stop here	Vstavi tuka	juh-**stah**-vee **took**-ay
I would like . . .	Hotel bi . . .	hot-**ay**-oo bee . . .

How much does it cost?	Koliko stane?	**koh**-lee-koh **stah**-nay
Letter/postcard	Pismo/dopisnica	**pee**-smoh/doh-**pee**-snee-tsah
By airmail	Zračna pošta	**zrah**-chnah **poh**-shtah
Help!	Na pomoč!	nah poh-**moch**

NUMBERS

One	Ena	enah
Two	Dva	dvah
Three	Tr	itree
Four	Štiri	**shtee**-ree
Five	Pet	pit
Six	Šest	shest
Seven	Sedem	**sed**-em
Eight	Osem	**oh**-sem
Nine	Devet	deh-**vit**
Ten	Deset	deh-**sit**
One hundred	Sto	toh
Two hundred	Dve sto	dvee stoh

DAYS OF THE WEEK

Monday	Ponedeljek	poh-neh-**dee**-lyek
Tuesday	Torek	**tor**-ek
Wednesday	Sreda	**sree**-dah
Thursday	Četrtek	**chet**-rtek
Friday	Petek	**pee**-tek
Saturday	Sobota	soh-**boh**-tah
Sunday	Nedelja	nay-**dee**-lyah

WHERE TO SLEEP

A room	Soba	**soh**-bah
The key	Ključ	kluh-**yooch**
With bath/a shower	s kopanicu	s prhoskoh-pan-**ee**-tsoo/**spruh**-hoh

FOOD

Restaurant	Restavracija	rest-aw-**rats**-ee-yah
The menu	Jedilnik	yed-**eel**-nik
The check, please.	Prosim, račun.	**proh**-seem, rach-**oon**
Breakfast	Zajtrk	**zay**-trik
Lunch	Kosilo	kos-**eel**-oh
Dinner	Obed	oh-**bed**
Bread	Kruh	kroo
Butter	Maslo	**mas**-loh
Salt/pepper	Sol/poper	sol/**poh**-per
Bottle	Steklenica	stek-len-**ee**-tsah
Red/white wine	Črno/belo vino	chur-noh/bel-oh**vee**-noh
Beer	Pivo	**pee**-voh
Water/mineral water	Voda/mineralna	**voh**-dah/min-er-**al**-vodanah **voh**-dah
Milk	Mleko	**mlih**-koh
Coffee (with milk)	Kava z mlekom	**kah**-vah **zmlih**-kom
Tea (with lemon)	Čaj z limono	chay zleem-**on**-oh

Croatia & Slovenia Essentials

PLANNING TOOLS, EXPERT INSIGHT, GREAT CONTACTS

There are planners and there are those who, excuse the pun, fly by the seat of their pants. We happily place ourselves among the planners. Our writers and editors try to anticipate all the issues you may face before and during any journey, and then they do their research. This section is the product of their efforts. Use it to get excited about your trip to Croatia & Slovenia, to inform your travel planning, or to guide you on the road should the seat of your pants start to feel threadbare.

GETTING STARTED

We're really proud of our Web site: Fodors.com is a great place to begin any journey. Scan Travel Wire for suggested itineraries, travel deals, restaurant and hotel openings, and other up-to-the-minute info. Check out Booking to research prices and book plane tickets, hotel rooms, rental cars, and vacation packages. Head to Talk for on-the-ground pointers from travelers who frequent our message boards. You can also link to loads of other travel-related resources.

∎ RESOURCES

ONLINE TRAVEL TOOLS

The first place to start to plan a trip to Croatia is the Croatian National Tourist Board's Web site. In addition to a general overview of the culture and history of the country, it has lots of practical information on accommodations, travel agencies, and events all listed with phone numbers. Then consult Regional Tourist Board sites (for Kvarner, Istria, and Dalmatia) to narrow the focus even further. Plitvice National Park has a comprehensive Web site with local accommodations links.

The Slovenia National Tourist Board's Web site gives a similar overview of the country with links to highlighted destinations such as Triglav National Park and regional tourist offices.

All About Croatia Croatia National Tourist Board (⊕ *www.croatia.hr*) **Dalmatia Region** (⊕ *www.dalmatia.hr*) **Istria Region** (⊕ *www.istria.hr*) **Kvarner Region** (⊕ *www.kvarner.hr*) **Plitvice National Park** (⊕ *www.np-plitvicka-jezera.hr*)

All About Slovenia Slovenian National Tourist Board (⊕ *www.slovenia-tourism.si*) **Slovenian Times** (⊕ *www.sloveniatimes.com*) has news in English. **Slovenian Traffic Information Center** (⊕ *www.promet.si*) **Triglav National Park** (⊕ *www.tnp.si*)

Currency Conversion Google (⊕ *www.google.com*) does currency conversion. Just type in the amount you want to convert and an explanation of how you want it converted (e.g., "14 Swiss francs in dollars"), and then voilà. **Oanda.com** (⊕ *www.oanda.com*) also allows you to print out a handy table with the current day's conversion rates. **XE.com** (⊕ *www.xe.com*) is a good currency conversion Web site.

Safety Transportation Security Administration (*TSA*; ⊕ *www.tsa.gov*)

Time Zones Timeanddate.com (⊕ *www.timeanddate.com/worldclock*) can help you figure out the correct time anywhere.

Weather Accuweather.com (⊕ *www.accuweather.com*) is an independent weather-forecasting service with good coverage of hurricanes. **Weather.com** (⊕ *www.weather.com*) is the Web site for the Weather Channel.

Other Resources CIA World Factbook (⊕ *www.odci.gov/cia/publications/factbook/index.html*) has profiles of every country in the world. It's a good source if you need some quick facts and figures.

INSPIRATION

Rebecca West's 1941 travelogue *Black Lamb and Grey Falcon: A Journey through Yugoslavia* is recommended reading for anyone traveling through Croatia. Completely subjective and opinionated, many of West's observations about the Balkans ring true to this day. (Although the title suggests there were travels through Slovenia, she seemed to begin her trip in Zagreb.) *How We Learned to Survive Communism and Even Laughed* and *Café Europa: Life After*

Communism by Rijekan-born Slavenka Drakulić are ironic looks at Croatia under Tito. *April Fool's Day* by Josip Novakovich is a novel set in absurd postwar Croatia.

Twilight of the Idols: Recollections of a Lost Yugoslavia by Aleš Debeljak is a moving account of the breakup of Yugoslavia told from a Slovenian perspective. Miha Mazzini's funny tale of coming of age in 1970s Slovenia is the subject of *The King of the Rattling Spirits*.

VISITOR INFORMATION

Before You Leave **Croatian Tourist Board** (☎ 212/829-4416 ⊕ www.croatia.hr). **Slovenian Tourist Office** (☎ 954/491-0112 ⊕ www.slovenia-tourism.si).

In Croatia **Croatian Tourist Board** (☎ 01/455-6455).

In Slovenia **Slovenian Tourist Board** (☎ 01/189-1840).

▌ THINGS TO CONSIDER

PASSPORTS & VISAS

U.S. citizens do not need visas to enter either Croatia or Slovenia for a typical vacation visit.

U.S. Passport Information **U.S. Department of State** (☎ 877/487-2778 ⊕ http://travel.state.gov/passport).

U.S. Passport Expediters **A. Briggs Passport & Visa Expeditors** (☎ 800/806-0581 or 202/338-0111 ⊕ www.abriggs.com). **American Passport Express** (☎ 800/455-5166 or 800/841-6778 ⊕ www.americanpassport.com). **Passport Express** (☎ 800/362-8196 ⊕ www.passportexpress.com). **Travel Document Systems** (☎ 800/874-5100 or 202/638-3800 ⊕ www.traveldocs.com). **Travel the World Visas** (☎ 866/886-8472 or 301/495-7700 ⊕ www.world-visa.com).

SHOTS & MEDICATIONS

For more information see Health under On the Ground in Croatia and Slovenia, below.

If you travel a lot internationally—particularly to developing nations—refer to the CDC's *Health Information for International Travel* (aka Traveler's Health Yellow Book). Info from it is posted on the CDC Web site (www.cdc.gov/travel/yb), or you can buy a copy from your local bookstore for $24.95.

Health Warnings **National Centers for Disease Control & Prevention** (*CDC* ☎ 877/394-8747 *international travelers' health line* ⊕ www.cdc.gov/travel). **World Health Organization** (*WHO* ⊕ www.who.int).

TRIP INSURANCE

What kind of coverage do you honestly need? Do you even need trip insurance at all? Take a deep breath and read on.

We believe that comprehensive trip insurance is especially valuable if you're booking a very expensive or complicated trip (particularly to an isolated region) or if you're booking far in advance. Who knows what could happen six months down the road? But whether or not you get insurance has more to do with how comfortable you are assuming all that risk yourself.

Comprehensive travel policies typically cover trip-cancellation and interruption, letting you cancel or cut your trip short because of a personal emergency, illness, or, in some cases, acts of terrorism in your destination. Such policies also cover evacuation and medical care. Some also cover you for trip delays because of bad weather or mechanical problems as well as for lost or delayed baggage. Another type of coverage to look for is financial default—that is, when your trip is disrupted because a tour operator, airline, or cruise line goes out of business. Generally you must buy this when you book your trip or shortly thereafter, and it's only available to you if your operator isn't on a list of excluded companies.

If you're going abroad, consider buying medical-only coverage at the very least. Neither Medicare nor some private insur-

Trip Insurance Resources

INSURANCE COMPARISON SITES

Insure My Trip.com	800/487-4722	www.insuremytrip.com
Square Mouth.com	800/240-0369	www.quotetravelinsurance.com

COMPREHENSIVE TRAVEL INSURERS

Access America	866/807-3982	www.accessamerica.com
CSA Travel Protection	800/873-9855	www.csatravelprotection.com
HTH Worldwide	610/254-8700 or 888/243-2358	www.hthworldwide.com
Travelex Insurance	888/457-4602	www.travelex-insurance.com
Travel Guard International	715/345-0505 or 800/826-4919	www.travelguard.com
Travel Insured International	800/243-3174	www.travelinsured.com

MEDICAL-ONLY INSURERS

International Medical Group	800/628-4664	www.imglobal.com
International SOS	215/942-8000 or 713/521-7611	www.internationalsos.com
Wallach & Company	800/237-6615 or 504/687-3166	www.wallach.com

ers cover medical expenses anywhere outside of the United States (including time aboard a cruise ship, even if it leaves from a U.S. port). Medical-only policies typically reimburse you for medical care (excluding that related to pre-existing conditions) and hospitalization abroad, and provide for evacuation. You still have to pay the bills and await reimbursement from the insurer, though.

Expect comprehensive travel insurance policies to cost about 4% to 7% or 8% of the total price of your trip (it's more like 8%–12% if you're over age 70). A medical-only policy may or may not be cheaper than a comprehensive policy. Always read the fine print of your policy to make sure that you are covered for the risks that are of most concern to you. Compare several policies to make sure you're getting the best price and range of coverage available.

OK. You know you can save a bundle on trips to warm-weather destinations by traveling in rainy season. But there's also a chance that a severe storm will disrupt your plans. The solution? Look for hotels and resorts that offer storm/hurricane guarantees. Although they rarely allow refunds, most guarantees do let you rebook later if a storm strikes.

BOOKING YOUR TRIP

Online Booking Resources

AGGREGATORS		
Kayak	www.kayak.com	also looks at cruises and vacation packages.
Mobissimo	www.mobissimo.com	
Qixo	www.qixo.com	also compares cruises, vacation packages, and even travel insurance.
Sidestep	www.sidestep.com	also compares vacation packages and lists travel deals.
Travelgrove	www.travelgrove.com	also compares cruises and packages.
BOOKING ENGINES		
Cheap Tickets	www.cheaptickets.com	a discounter.
Expedia	www.expedia.com	a large online agency that charges a booking fee for airline tickets.
Hotwire	www.hotwire.com	a discounter.
lastminute.com	www.lastminute.com	specializes in last-minute travel the main site is for the U.K., but it has a link to a U.S. site.
Luxury Link	www.luxurylink.com	has auctions (surprisingly good deals) as well as offers on the high-end side of travel.
Onetravel.com	www.onetravel.com	a discounter for hotels, car rentals, airfares, and packages.
Orbitz	www.orbitz.com	charges a booking fee for airline tickets, but gives a clear breakdown of fees and taxes before you book.
Priceline.com	www.priceline.com	a discounter that also allows bidding.
Travel.com	www.travel.com	allows you to compare its rates with those of other booking engines.
Travelocity	www.travelocity.com	charges a booking fee for airline tickets, but promises good problem resolution.
ONLINE ACCOMMODATIONS		
Hotelbook.com	www.hotelbook.com	focuses on independent hotels worldwide.
Hotel Club	www.hotelclub.net	good for major cities worldwide.
Hotels.com	www.hotels.com	a big Expedia-owned wholesaler that offers rooms in hotels all over the world.
Quikbook	www.quikbook.com	offers "pay when you stay" reservations that let you settle your bill at checkout, not when you book.
OTHER RESOURCES		
Bidding For Travel	www.biddingfortravel.com	a good place to figure out what you can get and for how much before you start bidding on, say, Priceline.

Unless your cousin is a travel agent, you're probably among the millions of people who make most of their travel arrangements online.

But have you ever wondered just what the differences are between an online travel agent (a Web site through which you make reservations instead of going directly to the airline, hotel, or car-rental company), a discounter (a firm that does a high volume of business with a hotel chain or airline and accordingly gets good prices), a wholesaler (one that makes cheap reservations in bulk and then re-sells them to people like you), and an aggregator (one that compares all the offerings so you don't have to)?

Is it truly better to book directly on an airline or hotel Web site? And when does a real live travel agent come in handy?

▌ ONLINE

You really have to shop around. A travel wholesaler such as Hotels.com or Hotel-Club.net can be a source of good rates, as can discounters such as Hotwire or Priceline, particularly if you can bid for your hotel room or airfare. Indeed, such sites sometimes have deals that are unavailable elsewhere. They do, however, tend to work only with hotel chains (which makes them just plain useless for getting hotel reservations outside of major cities) or big airlines (so that often leaves out upstarts like jetBlue and some foreign carriers like Air India).

Also, with discounters and wholesalers you must generally prepay, and everything is nonrefundable. And before you fork over the dough, be sure to check the terms and conditions, so you know what a given company will do for you if there's a problem and what you'll have to deal with on your own.

To be absolutely sure everything was processed correctly, confirm reservations made through online travel agents, discounters,

and wholesalers directly with your hotel before leaving home.

Booking engines like Expedia, Travelocity, and Orbitz are actually travel agents, albeit high-volume, online ones. And airline travel packagers like American Airlines Vacations and Virgin Vacations—well, they're travel agents, too. But they may still not work with all the world's hotels.

An aggregator site will search many sites and pull the best prices for airfares, hotels, and rental cars from them. Most aggregators compare the major travel-booking sites such as Expedia, Travelocity, and Orbitz; some also look at airline Web sites, though rarely the sites of smaller budget airlines. Some aggregators also compare other travel products, including complex packages—a good thing, as you can sometimes get the best overall deal by booking an air-and-hotel package.

▌ WITH A TRAVEL AGENT

If you use an agent—brick-and-mortar or virtual—you'll pay a fee for the service. And know that the service you get from some online agents isn't comprehensive. For example Expedia and Travelocity don't search for prices on budget airlines like jetBlue, Southwest, or small foreign carriers. That said, some agents (online or not) *do* have access to fares that are difficult to find otherwise, and the savings can more than make up for any surcharge.

A knowledgeable brick-and-mortar travel agent can be a godsend if you're booking a cruise, a package trip that's not available to you directly, an air pass, or a complicated itinerary including several overseas flights. What's more, travel agents that specialize in a destination may have exclusive access to certain deals and insider information on things such as charter flights. Agents who specialize in types of travelers (senior citizens, gays and lesbians, naturists) or types of trips (cruises, luxury travel, safaris) can also be invaluable.

Remember that Expedia, Travelocity, and Orbitz are travel agents, not just booking engines. To resolve any problems with a reservation made through these companies, contact them first.

A top-notch agent planning your trip to Russia will make sure you get the correct visa application and complete it on time; the one booking your cruise may get you a cabin upgrade or arrange to have bottle of champagne chilling in your cabin when you embark. And complain about the surcharges all you like, but when things don't work out the way you'd hoped, it's nice to have an agent to put things right.

A travel agent may be helpful in planning a trip to Croatia if your itinerary will take you to more than two or three places and will require car rentals, ferry tickets, or domestic flights. The tourism infrastructure in Croatia is user-friendly, however, and with a little legwork of your own you can easily book a multi-destination trip yourself. Slovenia's major attractions are easily organized and reached from Ljubljana. Both countries have excellent free information from the local tourism offices.

Agent Resources American Society of Travel Agents (☎ 703/739–2782 ⊕ www. travelsense.org).

Croatia and Slovenia Travel Agents Association of Croatian Travel Agencies (⊕ www. uhpa.hr) lists every possible excursion you can have (organized by region) in Croatia. **JayWay Travel** (⊕ www.jaywaytravel.com) is a U.S.-based Croatia travel specialist.

▌ ACCOMMODATIONS

If your experience of Slovenia and Croatia is limited to Zagreb and Ljubljana, you may be pleasantly surprised by hotel standards, which in most cases are as high as those in Western Europe. Many properties are new or recently renovated, so most rooms are equipped with mod-

ern amenities like broadband Internet and cable TV.

Outside major cities, hotels and inns are a bit more hit or miss. Sometimes countryside hotels can be rustic but chic, sometimes they can be downright grim, with 30-year-old bathroom fixtures. Checking out a property's Web site will usually give you some idea. Sadly, you'll still find huge, impersonal Yugoslavia-era concrete boxes in both Slovenia and Croatia, although most have been renovated thoroughly on the inside. In Croatia a room in a private home will almost always be the cheapest option; acceptable rooms are fairly easy to find.

In Ljubljana and Zagreb, expect to pay high prices for hotels, on par with those of Western Europe. Ljubljana can be unreasonably expensive in the summer months, mostly due to lack of beds. Reservations are vital if you plan to visit the capitals, Piran, Istria, Dalmatia, or Plitvice National Park during the summer season. Elsewhere in the Croatian and Slovenian countryside, reservations can be made a day or two in advance.

The lodgings we list are the cream of the crop in each price category. We always list the facilities that are available, but we don't specify whether they cost extra; when pricing accommodations, always ask what's included and what costs extra. Properties are assigned price categories based on the range from their least-expensive standard double room at high season (excluding holidays) to the most expensive. Properties marked ✕▦ are lodging establishments whose restaurants warrant a special trip.

CATEGORY	COST IN KUNA	COST IN EUROS
$$$$	over 1,650 Kn	over €225
$$$	1,300 Kn– 1,650 Kn	€175–€225
$$	925 Kn–1,300 Kn	€125–€175
$	550 Kn–925 Kn	€75–€125
¢	under 550 Kn	Under €75

Hotel prices are for two people in a double room in high season, excluding taxes and service charges.

Most hotels and other lodgings require you to give your credit-card details before they will confirm your reservation. If you don't feel comfortable e-mailing this information, ask if you can fax it (some places even prefer faxes). However you book, get confirmation in writing and have a copy of it handy when you check in.

Be sure you understand the hotel's cancellation policy. Some places allow you to cancel without any kind of penalty— even if you prepaid to secure a discounted rate—if you cancel at least 24 hours in advance. Others require you to cancel a week in advance or penalize you the cost of one night. Small inns and B&Bs are most likely to require you to cancel far in advance. Most hotels allow children under a certain age to stay in their parents' room at no extra charge, but others charge for them as extra adults; find out the cutoff age for discounts.

Assume that hotels operate on the European Plan (**EP**, no meals) unless we specify that they use the Breakfast Plan (**BP**, with full breakfast), Continental Plan (**CP**, Continental breakfast), Full American Plan (**FAP**, all meals), Modified American Plan (**MAP**, breakfast and dinner) or are **all-inclusive** (**AI**, all meals and most activities).

APARTMENT & HOUSE RENTALS

In Croatia, villa rentals are becoming more popular, particularly in Istria, where some pretty medieval stone houses have been converted into high-end rental properties. Apartment rentals of mixed quality are common all over the coast. Croatia has a well-organized network of independent apartment owners who rent their properties. Often the owners live in a nearby dwelling, so are on hand to get involved if a problem arises. Apartments can be found both in popular destinations like Dubrovnik and Hvar as well as remote islands such as Vis. It's always best to see photos before renting a property for a week or longer. Aside from apartment rentals in Kranjska Gora, the country's major ski destination, there are few villa rentals in Slovenia.

Croatia Specialists Adriatica.net (☎ 01/241–5611 ⊕ www.adriatica.net), a Web-based agent, rents villas as well as converted lighthouses in Croatia. **Broker** (☎ 021/547–004 ⊕ www.croatia-tourism.com). **Vintage Travel** (⊕ www.vintagetravel.co.uk), a U.K.-based company, specializes in Croatian villa rentals, particularly in Istria.

Slovenia Specialists Kranjska Gora Tourism office (☎ 04/588–5020 ⊕ www.kranjska-gora. si) rents condos and villas in the Slovenian ski area.

▌ AIRLINE TICKETS

Most domestic airline tickets are electronic; international tickets may be either electronic or paper. With an e-ticket the only thing you receive is an e-mailed receipt citing your itinerary and reservation and ticket numbers.

The greatest advantage of an e-ticket is that if you lose your receipt, you can simply print out another copy or ask the airline to do it for you at check-in. You usually pay a surcharge (up to $50) to get a paper ticket, if you can get one at all.

The sole advantage of a paper ticket is that it may be easier to endorse over to another airline if your flight is canceled and the airline with which you booked can't accommodate you on another flight.

Discount air passes that let you travel economically in a country or region must often be purchased before you leave home. In some cases you can only get them through a travel agent.

CHARTER FLIGHTS

Charter companies rent aircraft and offer regularly scheduled flights (usually nonstops). Charter flights are generally cheaper than flights on regular airlines, and they often leave from and travel to a wider variety of airports. For example, you could have a nonstop flight from Columbus, Ohio, to Punta Cana, Dominican Republic, or from Chicago to Dubrovnik, Croatia.

You don't, however, have the same protections as with regular airlines. If a char-

---

WORD OF MOUTH

Did the resort look as good in real life as it did in the photos? Did you sleep like a baby, or were the walls paper thin? Did you get your money's worth? Rate hotels and write your own reviews in Travel Ratings or start a discussion about your favorite places in Travel Talk on www.fodors.com. Your comments might even appear in our books. Yes, you too can be a correspondent!

Online Booking Resources

APARTMENT & HOUSE RENTALS		
At Home Abroad	212/421–9165	⊕ www.athomeabroadinc.com
Barclay International Group	516/364–0064 or 800/845–6636	⊕ www.barclayweb.com
Drawbridge to Europe	541/482–7778 or 888/268–1148	⊕ www.drawbridgetoeurope.com
Homes Away	416/920–1873 or 800/374–6637	⊕ www.homesaway.com
Hometours International	865/690–8484	⊕ thor.he.net/~hometour
Interhome	954/791–8282 or 800/882–6864	⊕ www.interhome.us
Suzanne B. Cohen & Associate	207/622–0743	⊕ www.villaeurope.com
Vacation Home Rentals Worldwide	201/767–9393 or 800/633–3284	⊕ www.vhrww.com
Villanet	206/417–3444 or 800/964–18	⊕ www.rentavilla.com
Villas & Apartments Abroad	212/213–6435 or 800/433–3020	⊕ www.vaanyc.com
Villas International	415/499–9490 or 800/221–2260	⊕ www.villasintl.com
Villas of Distinction	707/778–1800 or 800/289–0900	⊕ www.villasofdistinction.com
Wimco	800/449–1553	⊕ www.wimco.com

ter can't take off for mechanical or other reasons, there usually isn't another plane to take its place. If not enough seats are sold, the flight may be canceled. And if a company goes out of business, you're out of luck (unless, of course, you have insurance with financial default coverage; ⇨ *Trip Insurance under Things to Consider in Getting Started, above*).

▌ RENTAL CARS

When you reserve a car, ask about cancellation penalties, taxes, drop-off charges (if you're planning to pick up the car in one city and leave it in another), and surcharges (for being under or over a certain age, for additional drivers, or for driving across state or country borders or beyond a specific distance from your point of rental). All these things can add substantially to your costs. Request car seats and extras such as GPS when you book.

Rates are sometimes—but not always—better if you book in advance or reserve through a rental agency's Web site. There are other reasons to book ahead, though: for popular destinations, during busy times of the year, or to ensure that you get certain types of cars (vans, SUVs, exotic sports cars).

Make sure that a confirmed reservation guarantees you a car. Agencies sometimes overbook, particularly for busy weekends and holiday periods.

Traveling by car is a good way to see Croatia and Slovenia, giving you the freedom to flee a crowded seaside beach and take refuge in the relatively unpopulated interior if the mood strikes you. In both Slovenia and Croatia, excursions to the national parks are best done by car so that you can take in all the sites, not just the ones the tour bus shows you. Highways in both countries are well maintained and tolls frequent, so have some small change with you when on the road.

Slovenia uses the euro, Croatia the kuna. Toll roads in Croatia will accept both euros and kuna but not U.S. dollars, so make sure you have cash on hand before you get on the highway. Tolls on Croatia's new highways can add up. The quality of interior roads varies; in Slovenia they're better than you'd expect, and in Croatia they can be surprisingly poor. The main artery along the Croatian coast—the Magistrala—can come to a standstill on summer weekends, so traveling between popular coastal destinations is best done on weekdays when there's less turnover in package vacations. A new highway from Zagreb to Zadar and Split was completed in 2005; there are plans to continue it down the coast to Dubrovnik. This should ease the summer traffic considerably.

Unfortunately, rental cars in Croatia and Slovenia are expensive. Even if you rent locally, companies charge a daily and weekly rate that is generally higher than in most American cities. For an economy car (Opel Corsa or Renault Twingo) you're likely to pay upwards of $50 per day in Croatia (slightly less from local rental agencies), even more if you need an automatic transmission. Most companies are represented in the main tourist areas and airports. The easiest way to book a rental car from abroad is on the Internet.

In Croatia and Slovenia an International Driver's Permit is not necessary to rent a car from a major agency; a valid driver's license is all you'll need. If you intend to drive across a border (as you must do if you drive from Dubrovnik to southern Dalmatia, stopping briefly in Bosnia-Herzegovina) ask about **restrictions on driving into other countries.** The minimum age required for renting is usually 21 or older, and some companies also have maximum ages; be sure to inquire when making your arrangements.

Car Rental Resources

AUTOMOBILE ASSOCIATIONS		
American Automobile Association	315/797–5000	www.aaa.com;
		most contact with the organization is through state and regional members.
National Automobile Club	650/294–7000	www.thenac.com; membership open to CA residents only.
CROATIA		
Hrvatski Autiklub	*1/661–1-999*	*www.hak.hr*
LOCAL AGENCIES		
Autorent	*In Slovenia 051/601–804*	*www.rentacarslo.com*
Mack Car Rental	*In Croatia ☎01/369–4555*	*www.mack-concord.hr*
Europcar	*091/430–3038 in Rijeka Airport; 04/206–1684 in Ljubljana Airport*	*www.europcar.com*

CAR-RENTAL INSURANCE

Everyone who rents a car wonders whether the insurance that the rental companies offer is worth the expense. No one—including us—has a simple answer. It all depends on how much regular insurance you have, how comfortable you are with risk, and whether or not money is an issue.

If you own a car, your personal auto insurance may cover a rental to some degree, though not all policies protect you abroad; always read your policy's fine print. If you don't have auto insurance, then seriously consider buying the collision- or loss-damage waiver (CDW or LDW) from the car-rental company, which eliminates your liability for damage to the car. Some credit cards offer CDW coverage, but it's usually supplemental to your own insurance and rarely covers SUVs, minivans, luxury models, and the like. If your coverage is secondary, you may still be liable for loss-of-use costs from the car-rental company. But no credit-card insurance is valid unless you use that card for *all* transactions, from reserving to paying the final bill. All companies exclude car rental in some countries, so be sure to find out about the destination to which you are traveling.

Diners Club offers primary CDW coverage on all rentals reserved and paid for with the card. This means that Diners Club's company—not your own car insurance—pays in case of an accident. It doesn't mean your car-insurance company won't raise your rates once it discovers you had an accident.

Some rental agencies require you to purchase CDW coverage; many will even include it in quoted rates. All will strongly encourage you to buy CDW—possibly implying that it's required—so be sure to ask about such things before renting. In most cases it's cheaper to add a supplemental CDW plan to your comprehensive travel-insurance policy (⇨ *Trip Insurance under Things to Consider in Getting Started, above*) than to purchase it from a rental company. That said, you don't want to pay for a supplement if you're required to buy insurance from the rental company.

In Slovenia, quoted rates will include both CDW and theft insurance. A compact car often costs as much as €99 for

24 hours, with unlimited mileage. You'll need a credit card to rent. Agencies can be found in all major towns and at the Brnik Airport, north of Ljubljana.

In Croatia, quotes also include CDW and theft insurance, but expect to prices to be even higher than in Slovenia. A compact car with both CDW and theft insurance costs about €105 for 24 hours in Croatia, with mileage 2.08 Kn per km (½ mi). Car-rental agencies can be found at airports and major tourist destinations.

You can decline the insurance from the rental company and purchase it through a third-party provider such as Travel Guard (www.travelguard.com)—$9 per day for $35,000 of coverage. That's sometimes just under half the price of the CDW offered by some car-rental companies.

▌ VACATION PACKAGES

Packages *are not* guided excursions. Packages combine airfare, accommodations, and perhaps a rental car or other extras (theater tickets, guided excursions, boat trips, reserved entry to popular museums, transit passes), but they let you do your own thing. During busy periods packages may be your only option, as flights and rooms may be sold out otherwise.

Packages will definitely save you time. They can also save you money, particularly in peak seasons, but—and this is a really big "but"—you should price each part of the package separately to be sure. And be aware that prices advertised on Web sites and in newspapers rarely include service charges or taxes, which can up your costs by hundreds of dollars.

Some packages and cruises are sold only through travel agents. Don't always assume that you can get the best deal by booking everything yourself.

Each year consumers are stranded or lose their money when packagers—even large ones with excellent reputations—

go out of business. How can you protect yourself?

First, always pay with a credit card; if you have a problem, your credit-card company may help you resolve it. Second, buy trip insurance that covers default. Third, choose a company that belongs to the United States Tour Operators Association, whose members must set aside funds to cover defaults. Finally, choose a company that also participates in the Tour Operator Program of the American Society of Travel Agents (ASTA), which will act as mediator in any disputes.

You can also check on the tour operator's reputation among travelers by posting an inquiry on one of the Fodors.com forums.

Croatia is a popular European package-tour destination, so there are loads of tours heading there every week throughout the summer season from all the major European capitals, but especially from London. Packages including flights booked from the United States are less common, and you may have to look long and hard to find one. If a package is what you're looking for, you can combine a low-cost flight to the United Kingdom with one of the following tours and in the end make out fairly well on price. The following companies have package tours originating in the United Kingdom.

Packagers Bond Tours (✉ *2 Upper High St., Epsom, Surrey KT17 4QJ U.K.* ☎ *01372/745–300* ⊕ *www.bondtours.com).* **Inghams** (☎ *020/8780–4400* ⊕ *www.inghams.co.uk*) **Simply Travel** (☎ *0870/166–4979* ⊕ *www. simply-travel.co.uk).* **Tapestry Holidays** (☎ *020/8235–7800* ⊕ *www.tapestryholidays. com).* **Thomson** (☎ *0870/165–0079* ⊕ *www. thomson.co.uk).*

Organizations American Society of Travel Agents (*ASTA* ☎ *703/739–2782 or 800/965–2782* ⊕ *www.astanet.com).* **United States Tour Operators Association** (*USTOA* ☎ *212/599–6599* ⊕ *www.ustoa.com).*

Local tourism boards can provide information about lesser-known and small-niche operators that sell packages to only a few destinations.

▌ GUIDED TOURS

Guided tours are a good option when you don't want to do it all yourself. You travel along with a group (sometimes large, sometimes small), stay in prebooked hotels, eat with your fellow travelers (the cost of meals sometimes included in the price of your tour, sometimes not), and follow a schedule.

But not all guided tours are an if-it's-Tuesday-this-must-be-Belgium experience. A knowledgeable guide can take you places that you might never discover on your own, and you may be pushed to see more than you would have otherwise. Tours aren't for everyone, but they can be just the thing for trips to places where making travel arrangements is difficult or time-consuming (particularly when you don't speak the language).

Whenever you book a guided tour, find out what's included and what isn't. A "land-only" tour includes all your travel (by bus, in most cases) in the destination, but not necessarily your flights to and from or even within it. Also, in most cases prices in tour brochures don't include fees and taxes. And remember that you'll be expected to tip your guide (in cash) at the end of the tour.

Super-Deluxe Abercrombie & Kent (☎ 800/554–7016 ⊕ www.abercrombiekent. com).

Deluxe Brendan Vacations (☎ 800/421–8446 ⊕ www.brendanvacations.com). **Globus** (☎ 866/276–1241 ⊕ www.cosmos.com). **Overseas Adventure Travel** (☎ 800/493–6824 ⊕ www.oattravel.com). **Tauck Tours** (☎ 800/788–7885 ⊕ www.tauck.com).

SPECIAL-INTEREST TOURS

BICYCLING & HIKING

Most airlines accommodate bikes as luggage, provided they're dismantled and boxed.

Contacts Backroads (☎ 800/462–2848 ⊕ www.backroads.com). **Butterfield & Robinson** (☎ 800/678–1147 ⊕ www.butterfield. com).**Saddle Skedaddle** (☎ 0191/265–1110 in the U.K. ⊕ www.skedaddle.co.uk).

FOOD & WINE TOURS

Contacts Adriatic Holidays (☎ 0186/551–6577 in the U.K. ⊕ www.adriaticholidaysonline. com). **My Croatia Ltd.** (☎ 0870/7622–842 in the U.K. ⊕ www.mycroatia.co.uk).

Arblaster & Clarke Wine Tours Ltd. (☎ 0173/026–3111 in the U.K. ⊕ www. winetours.co.uk).

HISTORY & ART

Contacts Smithsonian Study Tours and Seminars (☎ 202/357–4700 ⊕ www. smithsonianjourneys.org).

SKIING

Contacts Inghams (☎ 020/8780–4400 in the U.K. ⊕ www.inghams.co.uk).

YACHTING & SAILING

Contacts Adriatic Holidays (☎ 0186/551–6577 in the U.K. ⊕ www.adriaticholidaysonline.com). **The Moorings** (☎ 800/952–8420 ⊕ www.the moorings.com). **Sail Croatia** (☎ 020/8459–8787 in the U.K. ⊕ www.sailcroatia.com). **Sailing Holidays Ltd.** (☎ 020/8459–8787 in the U.K. ⊕ www. sailingholidays.com). **Sunsail** (⊕ www.sunsail. com). **Unique World Cruises** (☎ 800/669–0757 ⊕ www.uniqueworldcruises.com).

▌ CRUISES

Several Croatian ports, including Dubrovnik, Split, Hvar, Korčula, and Zadar, are common port calls for Eastern Mediterranean cruises. Small ships cruise up and down the country's coastline. *For more information on cruising in Croatia, see the essay "Sailing and Cruising Croa-*

TRANSPORTATION

If your goal is to spend time in Zagreb and then head to the coast, traveling by car is the most efficient way to travel in Croatia. However, if your coastal city of choice is Split, Pula, Rijeka, or Dubrovnik, then a flight to the local airport will save time. The new E65 highway connecting Zagreb to Rijeka, Zadar, and Split is the fastest route to Kvarner and Central Dalmatia. Zagreb is not yet linked with Dubrovnik by highway, so part of that drive will be on the single-lane *Magistrala* which can be choked with traffic in high season. The bus system is the second-best option, as there is bus service to just about every seaside town (and remote village) in the Croatia. Train travel to the coast is the poorest option, since there is very little service to southern Dalmatia at all; however, if your trip to Croatia is mostly inland, then train travel is a reasonably good option.

Trains are a better bet in Slovenia, although the country is also well served by buses. A car is the easiest option if you have a short time in the country, since you can drive it from top to bottom in one day and take in many of the major sights in two days traveling by car. From Ljubljana there's good rail service to Pula in Istria.

TRAVEL TIMES FROM ZAGREB BY CAR		
Zadar	3 hours	285 km (177 mi)
Pula	3.5 hours	264 km (164 mi)
Rijeka	2 hours	160 km (99 mi)
Split	4 hours	408 km (253 mi)
Dubrovnik	7.5 hours	550 km (341 mi)
Ljubljana	1.75 hours	140 km (87 mi)
Maribor	1.75 hours	115 km (71 mi)

Ask the local tourist board about hotel and local transportation packages that include tickets to major museum exhibits or other special events.

▌ BY AIR

Flying time from London to Zagreb is 2 hours 30 minutes, from Prague to Zagreb it is 90 minutes, and from Warsaw it is 1 hour 40 minutes.

Flying time from London to Ljubljana is 80 minutes, from Bratislava to Dubrovnik is 85 minutes, from Budapest to Dubrovnik is 75 minutes, from London to Venice is 2 hours 10 minutes.

Domestic air tickets in Slovenia and Croatia are best purchased through travel agents or airport offices in city locations. Airports in both countries have offices for the national airlines (Croatian Airlines in Croatia and Adria Airlines in Slovenia) but their opening hours are unreliable, and attempting to purchase a ticket at the airport may backfire. Both the national airlines have usable Web sites where e-tickets can be purchased.

Airlines & Airports Airline and Airport Links.com (⊕ *www.airlineandairportlinks.com*) has links to many of the world's airlines and airports.

Airline Security Issues Transportation Security Administration (⊕ *www.tsa.gov*) has answers for almost every question that might come up.

AIRPORTS

In Croatia most international flights arrive at Zagreb (ZAG); however, there are also many connecting flights from various European airports to Split (SPU) and Dubrovnik (DBV), and even a few to Pula (PUY), Rijeka (RJK), and Zadar (ZAD). Almost all flights into Slovenia arrive at Ljubljana (LJU). Trieste, Italy (TRS), is a good alternate destination for both Slovenia and Croatia (particularly Istria).

Croatia **Dubrovnik Airport** (☎ 020/773–377 ⊕ www.airport-dubrovnik.hr). **Pula Airport** (☎ 052/530–105 ⊕ www.airport-pula.hr). **Rijeka Airport** (☎ 051/842–132 ⊕ www.rijeka-airport.hr). **Split Airport** (☎ 021/203–171 ⊕ www.split-airport.hr). **Zadar Airport** (☎ 023/313–311 ⊕ www.zadar-airport.hr). **Zagreb Airport** (☎ 01/626–5222 ⊕ www.zagreb-airport.hr).

Slovenia **Brnik Airport** (✉ Ljubljana ☎ 04/206–1981 ⊕ www.lju-airport.si). **Maribor Airport** (☎ 02/629–1175 ⊕ www.maribor-airport.si). **Portorož Airport** (☎ 05/672–2525 ⊕ www.portoroz-airport.si).

GROUND TRANSPORTATION

Ground transportation to major cities from airports in Croatia and Slovenia is well organized and reasonably user-friendly. Both shuttle buses and metered taxis operate at most airports all year long.

FLIGHTS

There are no direct air connections between the United States and either Croatia or Slovenia, though some U.S.–based airlines offer codeshare flights through their European travel partners. Travelers from the United States must fly into a major European hub such as Amsterdam, London, Frankfurt, Budapest, Prague, Vienna, or Warsaw and then transfer to a flight to Zagreb, Split, or Dubrovnik. Connections are on national carriers (Croatia Airlines or Adria Airways) or another European-based carrier. Several European airlines offer connections to Slovenia and Croatia.

Traveling to Slovenia or Croatia using a combination of a major airline and a low-cost European airline is a good idea. If you are traveling to Istria or Slovenia, a budget flight to nearby Venice (2½ hours to Ljubljana by car or train) or Trieste (1½ hours to Ljubljana or Rijeka by car or train) is an option. Most of these discount airlines sell tickets only on the Internet. Just be aware that so-called London-based discount airlines rarely fly from Heathrow (more often it's Gatwick or Stansted). All these airlines have stringent baggage limits, and offer few free in-flight services, if any. And if you transfer from a major airline to a discounter, you may need to reclaim your bags and re-check them, so make sure you leave plenty of time between your flights.

EasyJet flies from London to Ljubljana, Split, Rijeka, and Venice. German Wings flies to Split and Zagreb from Cologne-Bonn and Stuttgart, and to Zagreb from Hamburg. Ryanair flies from London to Zadar and Pula in Croatia, Trieste and Venice in Italy, and Maribor in Slovenia. Sky Europe flies to Dubrovnik, Split, and Zadar from Bratislava or Budapest. Wizzair flies from London to Split and Zagreb, and from Brussels to Ljubljana.

Airline Contacts **Adria Airways** (☎ 020/7734–4630 in the U.K., 01/369–1010 in Slovenia ⊕ www.adria-airways.com). **Aer Lingus** (☎ 800/474–7424 ⊕ www.flyaerlingus.com). **Air France** (☎ 800/237–2747 ⊕ www.airfrance.com). **Alitalia** (☎ 800/223–5730 ⊕ www.alitaliausa.com). **American Airlines** (☎ 800/433–7300 ⊕ www.aa.com). **Austrian Airlines** (☎ 800/843–0002 ⊕ www.aua.com). **British Airways** (☎ 800/247–9297 ⊕ www.britishairways.com). **Continental Airlines** (☎ 800/231–0856 ⊕ www.continental.com). **Croatia Airlines** (☎ 020/8563–0022 in the U.K., 02/413–776 in Croatia ⊕ www.croatiaairlines.hr). **Czech Airlines** (CSA ☎ 212/223–2365 ⊕ www.csa.cz). **Delta Airlines** (☎ 800/241–4141 ⊕ www.delta.com). **KLM Royal Dutch Airlines** (☎ 800/225–2525 ⊕ www.klm.com). **LOT Polish Airlines** (☎ 800/223–0593 ⊕ www.lot.com). **Lufthansa** (☎ 800/645–3880 ⊕ www.lufthansa.com). **Malév Hungarian Airlines** (☎ 212/566–9944 ⊕ www.malev.hu). **Northwest Airlines** (☎ 800/225–2525 ⊕ www.nwa.com). **United Airlines** (☎ 800/538–2929 ⊕ www.united.com). **USAirways** (☎ 800/622–1015 ⊕ www.usairways.com).

EUROPE-BASED DISCOUNT AIRLINES

Information **EasyJet** (🕾 *No phone* ⊕ *www.easyjet.com*). **German Wings** (🕾 *870/252-1250* ⊕ *www.germanwings.com*). **Ryanair** (🕾 *090/6270-5656 in the U.K., 353/1-249-7791 worldwide* ⊕ *www.ryanair.com*). **Sky Europe Airlines** (🕾 *090/5722-2747 in the U.K., 421/4850-4850 worldwide* ⊕ *www.skyeurope.com*). **Wizzair** (🕾 *(48) 22/351-9499 in Poland* ⊕ *www.wizzair.com*).

❚ BY BOAT

Several companies run ferries from Italy to Croatia. The most popular route, which is offered by all ferry services, is Ancona to Split. Jadrolinija also runs services from Bari to Dubrovnik and from Ancona to Zadar. From June to September, SNAV runs a daily high-speed catamaran service between Ancona and Split. Jadrolinija and SEM are based in Rijeka and Split, respectively. Adriatica is based in Venice, and SNAV is based in Ancona.

From early March to late October the *Prince of Venice* hydrofoil makes regularly scheduled trips between Venice and Portorož. From mid-July to mid-September, the Italian firm Adriatica runs a round-trip service from Trieste, calling at Piran and stopping at several towns on the Croatian Adriatic coast.

Information **Adriatica** (🕾 *041/781-611 in Venice, Italy* ⊕ *www.adriatica.it* ✉ *Cankarjevo nab 7, Piran, Slovenia* 🕾 *05/674-6508*). **Jadrolinija** (🕾 *051/211-444* ⊕ *www.jadrolinija.hr*). **Prince of Venice** (*Kompas Turizem,* ✉ *Obala 41, Portorož* 🕾 *05/617-8000*). **SEM** (🕾 *021/338-292* ⊕ *www.sem-marina.hr*). **SNAV** (🕾 *071/207-6116 in Ancona, Italy*).

❚ BY BUS

Bus travel in both Slovenia and Croatia is inexpensive and efficient. During the high season the worst you'll have to put up with is crowded buses. Most buses heading out to tourist sites like Škojanske Jama or Plitvice National Park will be air-conditioned, but ask before you buy your ticket, especially if it's a blistering hot day. Buses from Zagreb to the coast get booked up quickly in the summer, so once you know your travel dates you should purchase your ticket. The bus is the best option if you are traveling from Zagreb to Slavonia and don't wish to rent a car. Slovenian timetables can be found online in English; Croatian timetables can be found online, but the Web site is mostly in Croatian.

Bus Information Croatia: **Autobusni kolodvor Zagreb** (⊕ *www.akz.hr*). Slovenia: **Avtobusna postaja Ljubljana** (⊕ *www.ap-ljubljana.si*).

❚ BY CAR

In Croatia having a car certainly gives you greater mobility in rural areas on the mainland but causes endless complications if you plan to go island-hopping. In high season cars can wait for hours to board ferries even if you have made reservations. In addition, parking in coastal resorts is very restricted, and there are tolls on a number of highways throughout the country. Depending on where you plan to go, it might be a better idea to rent a car only on those days when you need one.

In Slovenia, traveling by car undoubtedly gives you the chance to reach remote areas of the country when and as you wish. Main roads between large towns are comparable to those in Western Europe. Highways charge a toll depending on the route and distance traveled. But you won't need a car if you plan to stay only in Ljubljana.

GASOLINE

In Croatia, gas stations are open daily from 7 to 7; from June through September, many stations are open until 10. In the bigger cities and on main international roads some stations offer 24-hour service. All pumps sell Eurosuper 95, Super 98, Normal, and Eurodiesel.

In Slovenia, gas stations on border crossings and main roads leading to larger towns are open 24 hours a day, whereas others are open Monday to Saturday from 7 AM to 8 PM.

Croatian Fuel Prices INA (⊕ *www.ina.hr*).

PARKING

In Croatia the historic centers of walled medieval towns along the coast (Split, Trogir, Hvar, Korčula, and Dubrovnik) are completely closed to traffic, putting heavy pressure on the number of parking spaces outside the fortifications. In Slovenia's major towns parking spaces are marked with a blue line and a sign denoting time restrictions. Buy a ticket, obtainable from gas stations and newsstands; write down the time you parked; and attach it to your windshield.

ROAD CONDITIONS

In Croatia the coastal route from Rijeka to Dubrovnik is scenic but tiring; it can be notoriously slippery when wet. The new E65 highway that links Zagreb with Rijeka, Zadar, and Split is fast and has frequent, well-maintained rest stops. During winter, driving through the inland regions of Gorski Kotar and Lika is occasionally made hazardous by heavy snow. It's advisable not to take a car to the islands, but if you do decide to drive, remember that the roads are narrow, twisty, and unevenly maintained.

Road conditions in Slovenia are generally good, with well-maintained and cleared roads in all seasons. In the mountains, where snowfall can be heavy, it's best to drive with snow tires in the winter months. Make sure your rental car has these if you rent during this period.

ROADSIDE EMERGENCIES

In case of a breakdown, your best friend is the telephone. Try contacting your rental agency or the appropriate national breakdown service.

Emergency Services Croatia (☎ *987*). **Slovenia** (*Automobile Association of Slovenia* ☎ *1987*).

RULES OF THE ROAD

Croatians drive on the right and follow rules similar to those in other European countries. Speed limits are 50 kph (30 mph) in urban areas, 80 kph (50 mph) on main roads, and 130 kph (80 mph) on motorways. Seatbelts are compulsory. The permitted blood-alcohol limit is 0.05%; drunken driving is punishable and can lead to severe fines.

Slovenes drive on the right and are obliged to keep their headlights on at all times. Speed limits are 60 kph (37 mph) in urban areas and 120 kph (74 mph) on highways. Local drivers are courteous by European standards. The permitted blood-alcohol level is 0.05%; drivers caught exceeding this level can expect penalties similar to those of other European countries.

▌ BY TRAIN

In Croatia, Zagreb is connected to Rijeka and Split by rail, but there is no line south of Split to Dubrovnik. International services run from Zagreb to the European cities of Ljubljana, Budapest, Belgrade, Vienna, Munich, Berlin, and Venice.

In Slovenia, daily trains link Ljubljana with Austria, Italy, Hungary, and Croatia. Many are overnight trains with sleeping compartments. The internal rail network is limited, but trains are cheap and efficient.

The "Zone D" Interail pass is valid for Croatia for EU residents, but Eurail is not.

ON THE GROUND

▮ COMMUNICATIONS

INTERNET

Internet cafés are a common sight along the coast in Croatia and in Zagreb. In Slovenia, Ljubljana has an abundance of Internet cafés, but they are much harder to find in the countryside. Wi-Fi connections are being pitched as the new thing, with modern hotels like the Domina Grand Media in Ljubljana using their connectivity as a major selling point in brochures. Wi-Fi service varies from place to place: some hotels and cafés offer it for free, although usually there's an hourly fee—anywhere from 40 Kn to 60 Kn in Croatia—to use your laptop in most places. Internet cafés charge about the same hourly rate. In Zagreb, there are a handful of Internet cafés along Preradovićeva ulica.

Contacts Cybercafes (⊕ *www.cybercafes. com*) lists over 4,000 Internet cafés worldwide.

PHONES

The good news is that you can now make a direct-dial telephone call from virtually any point on earth. The bad news? You can't always do so cheaply. Calling from a hotel is almost always the most expensive option; hotels usually add huge surcharges to all calls, particularly international ones. In some countries you can phone from call centers or even the post office. Calling cards usually keep costs to a minimum, but only if you purchase them locally. And then there are mobile phones (⇨ *below*), which are sometimes more prevalent—particularly in the developing world—than landlines; as expensive as mobile phone calls can be, they are still usually a much cheaper option than calling from your hotel.

In both Slovenia and Croatia you can make calls from the *pošta* (post office), where you enter a kiosk and pay when you have finished, or from a public tele-phone booth on the street, where magnetic phone cards are necessary. Phone cards can be purchased at the post office or newsstands. Area and country codes are as follows: Croatia (385), Dubrovnik (20), Split (21), Zagreb (1); Slovenia (386), Ljubljana (1).

When dialing a number from abroad, drop the initial 0 from the local area code.

CALLING WITHIN CROATIA AND SLOVENIA

To make a local call in Croatia, dial the area code (if you are not already in that area) followed by the number you wish to reach.

In Slovenia, pay phones take magnetic telephone cards, available from post offices and kiosks. Lower rates apply from 10 PM to 7 AM and all day Sunday.

Contacts Local Directory Assistance (☎ *988*).

CALLING OUTSIDE CROATIA & SLOVENIA

To make an international call in Croatia, dial "00," then the appropriate country code (Australia 61; Canada 1; United States 1; and United Kingdom 44).

The country code for the United States is 1.

Contacts Croatia International Directory Assistance (☎ *902*). **Slovenia International Directory Assistance** (☎ *989*).

Access Codes AT&T Direct (☎ *0800/220–111 in Croatia, 800/435–0812 in Slovenia* ⊕ *www.att.com*). **MCI WorldPhone** (☎ *0800/220–112 in Croatia, 080–8808 in Slovenia* ⊕ *www.mci.com*). **Sprint International Access** (☎ *0800/220–113 in Croatia, 800/877–4646 in Slovenia* ⊕ *www.sprint.com*).

MOBILE PHONES

If you have a multiband phone (some countries use different frequencies than what's used in the United States) and your service provider uses the world-standard GSM network (as do T-Mobile, Cingular, and Verizon), you can probably use your phone abroad. Roaming fees can be steep, however: 99¢ a minute is considered reasonable. And overseas you normally pay the toll charges for incoming calls. It's almost always cheaper to send a text message than to make a call, since text messages have a very low set fee (often less than 5¢).

If you just want to make local calls, consider buying a new SIM card (note that your provider may have to unlock your phone for you to use a different SIM card) and a prepaid service plan in the destination. You'll then have a local number and can make local calls at local rates. If your trip is extensive, you could also simply buy a new cell phone in your destination, as the initial cost will be offset over time.

If you travel internationally frequently, save one of your old mobile phones or buy a cheap one on the Internet; ask your cell phone company to unlock it for you, and take it with you as a travel phone, buying a new SIM card with pay-as-you-go service in each destination.

In Slovenia, Mobitel, the biggest mobile-phone provider, has roaming contracts with several overseas cellular-phone companies. Check the company's Web site to see if you can use your service with a prepaid phone card for calling in Slovenia. T-Mobile owns Hrvatska Telekom and has contracts with other T-Mobile worldwide providers. Check the company's Web site for local roaming rates.

Contacts Cellular Abroad (☎ *800/287-5072* ⊕ *www.cellularabroad.com*) rents and sells GMS phones and sells SIM cards that work in many countries. **Hrvatska Telekom** (⊕ *www. tportal.hr*). **Mobal** (☎ *888/888-9162* ⊕ *www. mobalrental.com*) rents mobiles and sells GSM

phones (starting at $49) that will operate in 140 countries. Per-call rates vary throughout the world. **Mobitel** (⊕ *www.mobitel.si*). **Planet Fone** (☎ *888/988-4777* ⊕ *www.planetfone. com*) rents cell phones, but the per-minute rates are expensive.

■ CUSTOMS & DUTIES

You're always allowed to bring goods of a certain value back home without having to pay any duty or import tax. But there's a limit on the amount of tobacco and liquor you can bring back duty-free, and some countries have separate limits for perfumes; for exact figures, check with your customs department. The values of so-called "duty-free" goods are included in these amounts. When you shop abroad, save all your receipts, as customs inspectors may ask to see them as well as the items you purchased. If the total value of your goods is more than the duty-free limit, you'll have to pay a tax (most often a flat percentage) on the value of everything beyond that limit.

As with most European countries, you can import duty-free 200 cigarettes, 1 liter of spirits, and 2 liters of wine into both Croatia and Slovenia. Foreign citizens can bring personal items into the country without paying customs taxes.

U.S. Information U.S. Customs and Border Protection (⊕ *www.cbp.gov*).

■ EATING OUT

The standard of food in Slovenia is very high, with restaurants serving fresh fish, pasta, and vegetable dishes even in the dead of winter. There's a definite preference for seasonal foods, so if you come in October you'll find mushroom dishes everywhere; in April it's hard to find a menu in the country that doesn't feature asparagus. There are regional specialties, of course, but since the country is so small you can usually find these outside of the specific region, and certainly in Ljubljana.

Food in Croatia varies by region. You'll find some very good restaurants in Zagreb and the coast and some mediocre ones in the interior. Fish is always a good bet here, local calamari and sea bass being real treats for the visitor. Truffle season in Istria is in late October, and that delicacy can be found on virtually every Istrian menu then.

Pizza, in both Slovenia and Croatia, is available in just about every city, town, or village. This is most often served at a sit-down restaurant making it a good choice for both families and vegetarians. It's usually served one pie per person, not by the slice. In general, pizza in Slovenia and Croatia is freshly baked, thin-crusted, and delicious. They come with toppings like local ham and mushrooms, but expect more exotic things like pineapple, tuna, and frozen peas as well. The classic *margherita* (plain cheese) is always available. *For information on food-related health issues, see Health below.*

MEALS & MEALTIMES
As the working day begins early here (with some offices opening as early as 7:30 AM on weekdays), you'll find cafés open early as well. Lunch is usually served between noon and 3 in restaurants, and dinner is most often served after 7 or so. In the height of the tourist season at the coast, restaurants may stay open later (after 10) to handle the volume. *Bifes* (stand-up take-out places) are open most of the day and serve both hot and cold food. Around 4 PM in Ljubljana and Zagreb you'll notice people filling up coffee shops for an afternoon fix of caffeine and perhaps some cake.

Even most basic lodgings in Croatia and Slovenia include some kind of breakfast (*zajtrk* in Slovene; *doručak* in Croatian) in the room rate. Savor it; breakfast outside your hotel may be limited to a small melted ham and cheese sandwich (known as a *toast*) in a café. Later in the morning, you can wander into a cake shop (*slaščičarna* in Slovene; *slastičarna* in

Croatian) for a coffee and slice of cake. You may also find a *burek* (savory meat- or cheese-filled pastry) for breakfast at one of the street-side vendors near high traffic areas. Lunch (*kosilo* in Slovene; *ručak* in Croatian) is the main meal for many locals; it usually includes hot food and perhaps a soup. In major cities there are now such lighter offerings as salads and pastas; you can sometimes find a few sandwich shops. On the coast you find grilled meats available throughout the day at snack bars near the beaches. Dinner (*večerja* in Slovene; *večera* in Croatian) is usually taken in a restaurant (*restavracija* in Slovene, *restoran* in Croatian) and tends to be a bit more formal than in the United States. Meals often begin with soup, followed by grilled meat or fish, and dessert. The exception is at the coast, where lively, outdoor casual restaurants are the norm.

Unless otherwise noted, the restaurants listed in this guide are open daily for lunch and dinner.

PAYING
Credit cards are becoming more and more accepted, but it's a good idea to ask before you order, just in case. ATM machines are found in abundance on the Croatian coast, as well as in Zagreb and Ljubljana, so you can usually ensure that dinner goes on as planned. Tips should not be included in the bill, so scrutinize any bill that appears to add one. If service has been good, a 10% to 15% gratuity will be appreciated by the waitstaff.

CATEGORY	COST
$$$$	Over 80 Kn
$$$	60–80 Kn
$$	35–60 Kn
$	20–35 Kn
¢	Under 20 Kn

Restaurant prices are for a main course at dinner.

RESERVATIONS & DRESS

Regardless of where you are, it's a good idea to make a reservation if you can. In some places (Hong Kong, for example), it's expected. We only mention them specifically when reservations are essential (there's no other way you'll ever get a table) or when they are not accepted. For popular restaurants, book as far ahead as you can (often 30 days), and reconfirm as soon as you arrive. (Large parties should always call ahead to check the reservations policy.) We mention dress only when men are required to wear a jacket or a jacket and tie.

WINES, BEER & SPIRITS

Wine is produced in both Slovenia and Croatia and enjoyed regularly with meals. Both countries consume more than they produce, so tasting some vintages here is a good idea since you're unlikely to find them at home. White wines from the Vipava Valley in Western Slovenia are on par with Italian whites from just across the border: dry, fruity, and full-bodied. Croatia produces wine in Istria and in certain regions along the coast, and it, too, is quite drinkable.

Cocktails are becoming popular as an aperitif but only in trendy places catering to a stylish and perhaps foreign crowd. The traditional aperitif in this part of the world is *rakija*, a fruit or herbal spirit made in abundance in both countries. It's fairly cheap to buy and varies greatly in quality. The fruit varieties (pear, blueberry) are drinkable enough as an aperitif; the herbals are a bit rough going down. Many establishments brew their own with great pride. If you're staying in a family-run pension, trying some of the home brew is an instant icebreaker.

▌ELECTRICITY

Electricity in Slovenia and Croatia is 220 volts; both countries use standard European plugs with two round prongs.

Consider making a small investment in a universal adapter, which has several types of plugs in one lightweight, compact unit. Most laptops and mobile phone chargers are dual voltage (i.e., they operate equally well on 110 and 220 volts), so require only an adapter. These days the same is true of small appliances such as hair dryers. Always check labels and manufacturer instructions to be sure. Don't use 110-volt outlets marked FOR SHAVERS ONLY for high-wattage appliances such as hair dryers.

Contacts Steve Kropla's Help for World Traveler's (⊕ *www.kropla.com*) has information on electrical and telephone plugs around the world. **Walkabout Travel Gear** (⊕ *www.walkabouttravelgear.com*) has a good coverage of electricity under "adapters."

▌EMERGENCIES

Embassy in Croatia U.S. Embassy (⊠ *Hebrangova 2, Zagreb* ☎ *01/661–2200* ⊕ *www.usembassy.hr*).

Embassy in Slovenia U.S. Embassy (⊠ *Prešernova 31, Ljubljana* ☎ *01/200–5500*).

General Emergency Contacts

Croatia Ambulance (☎ *94*). **Fire Emergencies** (☎ *93*). **Police Emergencies** (☎ *92*).

Slovenia Ambulance & Fire (☎ *112*). **Automobile Association of Slovenia** (*AMZS* ☎ *987 for 24-hour emergency roadside assistance*). **Police** (☎ *113*).

▌ HEALTH

The most common types of illnesses are caused by contaminated food and water. Especially in developing countries, drink only bottled, boiled, or purified water and drinks; don't drink from public fountains or use ice. You should even consider using bottled water to brush your teeth. Make sure food has been thoroughly cooked and is served to you fresh and hot; avoid vegetables and fruits that you haven't washed (in bottled or purified water) or peeled yourself. If you have problems, mild cases of traveler's diarrhea may respond to Imodium (known generically as loperamide) or Pepto-Bismol. Be sure to drink plenty of fluids; if you can't keep fluids down, seek medical help immediately.

Infectious diseases can be airborne or passed via mosquitoes and ticks and through direct or indirect physical contact with animals or people. Some, including Norwalk-like viruses that affect your digestive tract, can be passed along through contaminated food. If you are traveling in an area where malaria is prevalent, use a repellant containing DEET and take malaria-prevention medication before, during, and after your trip as directed by your physician. Condoms can help prevent most sexually transmitted diseases, but they aren't absolutely reliable and their quality varies from country to country. Speak with your physician and/or check the CDC or World Health Organization Web sites for health alerts, particularly if you're pregnant, traveling with children, or have a chronic illness.

For information on travel insurance, shots and medications, and medical-assistance companies see Shots & Medications under Things to Consider in Before You Go, above.

SPECIFIC ISSUES IN CROATIA AND SLOVENIA

Water is safe for drinking throughout Croatia. EU countries have reciprocal health-care agreements with Croatia, entitling those nationals to medical consultation for a basic minimum fee. Citizens from outside the EU have to pay in accordance with listed prices. Most doctors speak some English.

Drinking water is safe in Slovenia as well, although there is a national preference for bottled mineral water in restaurants. Slovenia has reciprocal health-care agreements with the rest of the EU, but citizens from outside the euro zone will have to pay doctor's and hospital fees directly. In Ljubljana the private Barsos Clinic deals primarily with expatriate patients.

Do not fly within 24 hours of scuba diving.

OVER-THE-COUNTER REMEDIES

In Croatia and Slovenia, over-the-counter medications are sold in pharmacies, which are open until 6 or 7 PM on weekdays and 1 or 2 PM on Saturdays. In each town there is usually a 24-hour pharmacy for emergencies. Most European pharmacists speak a word or two of English or German, but you're better off asking for a remedy by its medical name (ibuprofen) than its brand name (Advil). Pharmacies don't have a lot of open shelf space for goods, so you will have to ask the pharmacist for what you want. In both countries paracetemol (and its brand name Panadol) is more recognized than acetaminophen (and the brand name Tylenol) for basic pain relief. Claritin, the allergy relief medication, is sold in Slovenia and Croatia at the pharmacy by that name. Many products that Americans would normally find in their local drugstore—cough syrup, diaper cream, cough drops, muscle cream, and vitamins, to name a few—must be bought in the pharmacy in Croatia and Slovenia. While this system is inconvenient if you get an allergy attack in the middle of the night, the upside is that prices are kept down by the government, so many things will be a fraction of the cost at home. The word for pharmacy in Slovenia is *lekarna* and in Croatia *lijekarna.*

▌ HOURS OF OPERATION

In Croatia business hours are from 8:30 to 4. Banks are open in all the main cities weekdays from 7 to 7, and on Saturday from 7 AM to 11 AM; in smaller towns banks have shorter hours and are often closed during lunchtime. Post offices are open weekdays 7 to 7, and on Saturday from 7 to noon; in smaller towns post offices are open shorter hours, sometimes only in the morning. During the high tourist season (June through September), post offices are generally open until 9 PM, including Saturday. In Zagreb shops and department stores are open weekdays 8 to 8, and on Saturday from 8 to 1. Along the coast most shops are open weekdays from 8 to 1 and 5 to 8, Saturday from 8 to 1. On the islands hours vary greatly from place to place, but usually at least one general store will be open Monday through Saturday for essentials.

In Slovenia most banks are open weekdays from 9 to noon and 2 to 4:30, and Saturday from 9 to 11. The main museums are open Tuesday through Sunday 10 to 6. Larger shops are open Monday through Saturday from 10 to 6, whereas smaller ones may open mornings only from 10 to 2. Most stores are closed Sunday.

HOLIDAYS

In Croatia, national holidays include the following: January 1 (New Year's Day); January 6 (Epiphany); Easter Sunday and Monday; May 1 (May Day); Corpus Christi (40 days after Easter); June 22 (Anti-fascist Day); August 5 (National Thanksgiving Day); August 15 (Assumption), October 8 (Independence Day), November 1 (All Saints' Day), December 25 and 26 (Christmas).

In Slovenia, national holidays include the following: January 1 and 2 (New Year's Day); February 8 (Prešeren Day, Slovene cultural day); Easter Sunday and Monday (usually March or April); April 27 (National Resistance Day); May 1 and 2 (Labor Day); June 25 (Slovenia National Day); August 15 (Assumption); October 31 (Reformation Day); November 1 (All Saints' Day); December 25 and 26 (Christmas).

▌ MAIL

From Croatia, airmail letters and postcards take about five days to reach other European countries and two weeks to get to Australia, Canada, and the United States. To send a post card costs 3.50 Kn to Europe, 5 Kn to the United States. A letter costs 5 Kn to Europe, 6.50 Kn to the United States.

From Slovenia, airmail postage to the United States is €.76 for a letter, €.29 for a postcard. Post offices are open weekdays 8 to 6 and Saturday 8 to noon. Stamps are also sold at hotels, newsstands, and kiosks.

▌ MONEY

Costs for goods and services are on a par with those of Western Europe. Notable exceptions are public transportation, alcohol, and cigarettes, all of which are cheaper in both Croatia and Slovenia than elsewhere in Europe. Groceries can be expensive at shops by the coast, so if you've rented an apartment for a week or more, consider buying some staples at one of the hypermarkets on your way out of Zagreb.

ITEM	AVERAGE COST
Cup of Coffee	$1.00
Glass of Wine	$4.00
Glass of Beer	$2.25
Sandwich	$3.00
One-Mile Taxi Ride in Capital City	$3.00
Museum Admission	$1.50–$2.50

Based on an exchange rate of 4.9 Kn to US$1, effective at the time of writing.

Prices throughout this guide are given for adults. Substantially reduced fees are almost always available for children, students, and senior citizens.

Banks never have every foreign currency on hand, and it may take as long as a week to order. If you're planning to exchange funds before leaving home, don't wait till the last minute.

ATMS & BANKS

Your own bank will probably charge a fee for using ATMs abroad; the foreign bank you use may also charge a fee. Nevertheless, you'll usually get a better rate of exchange at an ATM than you will at a currency-exchange office or even when changing money in a bank. And extracting funds as you need them is a safer option than carrying around a large amount of cash.

PIN numbers with more than four digits are not recognized at ATMs in many countries. If yours has five or more, remember to change it before you leave.

In Croatia ATMs are now found throughout the country, even on the islands. In Slovenia ATMs are less common in small towns and villages, although there are quite a few in Ljubljana.

CREDIT CARDS

Throughout this guide, the following abbreviations are used: **AE**, American Express; **DC**, Diners Club; **MC**, MasterCard; and **V**, Visa.

It's a good idea to inform your credit-card company before you travel, especially if you're going abroad and don't travel internationally very often. Otherwise, the credit-card company might put a hold on your card owing to unusual activity—not a good thing halfway through your trip. Record all your credit-card numbers—as well as the phone numbers to call if your cards are lost or stolen—in a safe place, so you're prepared should something go wrong. Both MasterCard and Visa have general numbers you can call (collect if you're abroad) if your card is lost, but you're better off calling the number of your issuing bank, since MasterCard and Visa usually just transfer you to your bank; your bank's number is usually printed on your card.

If you plan to use your credit card for cash advances, you'll need to apply for a PIN at least two weeks before your trip. Although it's usually cheaper (and safer) to use a credit card abroad for large purchases (so you can cancel payments or be reimbursed if there's a problem), note that some credit-card companies *and* the banks that issue them add substantial percentages to all foreign transactions, whether they're in a foreign currency or not. Check on these fees before leaving home, so there won't be any surprises when you get the bill.

Before you charge something, ask the merchant whether or not he or she plans to do a dynamic currency conversion (DCC). In such a transaction the credit-card *processor* (shop, restaurant, or hotel, not Visa or MasterCard) converts the currency and charges you in dollars. In most cases you'll pay the merchant a 3% fee for this service in addition to any credit-card company and issuing-bank foreign-transaction surcharges.

Dynamic currency conversion programs are becoming increasingly widespread. Merchants who participate in them are supposed to ask whether you want to be charged in dollars or the local currency, but they don't always do so. And even if they do offer you a choice, they may well avoid mentioning the additional surcharges. The good news is that you *do* have a choice. And if this practice really gets your goat, you can avoid it entirely thanks to American Express; with its cards, DCC simply isn't an option.

Major credit cards are accepted in most hotels, and some shops and restaurants.

Reporting Lost Cards American Express (☎ 800/528–4800 in the U.S. or 336/393–1111 collect from abroad ⊕ www.american-express.com). **Diners Club** (☎ 800/234–6377 in the U.S. or 303/799–1504 collect from abroad ⊕ www.dinersclub.com). **MasterCard** (☎ 800/627–8372 in the U.S. or 636/722–7111 collect from abroad ⊕ www.mastercard.com). **Visa** (☎ 800/847–2911 in the U.S. or 410/581–9994 collect from abroad ⊕ www.visa.com).

CURRENCY & EXCHANGE
The Croatian currency is called the kuna (Kn), which is made up of 100 lipa. The kuna is not yet fully convertible, so you cannot buy the currency outside of Croatia or exchange it once outside the country.

As of January 2007, the euro (€) became the monetary unit in Slovenia. Most hotels in both Slovenia and Croatia are already priced in euros, but in Croatia they also accept kuna as payment.

For the most favorable rates, change money through banks. Although ATM transaction fees may be higher abroad than at home, ATM rates are excellent because they are based on wholesale rates offered only by major banks. You won't do as well at exchange booths in airports or rail and bus stations, in hotels, in restaurants, or in stores.

In Slovenia you can exchange money and traveler's checks in a *banka* (bank) or *mjenjačnica* (exchange office). Rates for changing currency and traveler's checks are usually about the same.

Even if a currency-exchange booth has a sign promising no commission, rest assured that there's some kind of huge, hidden fee. (Oh … that's right. The sign didn't say no *fee*.). And as for rates, you're almost always better off getting foreign currency at an ATM or exchanging money at a bank.

TRAVELER'S CHECKS & CARDS
Some consider this the currency of the cave man, and it's true that fewer establishments accept traveler's checks these days. Nevertheless, they're a cheap and secure way to carry extra money, particularly on trips to urban areas. Both Citibank (under the Visa brand) and American Express issue traveler's checks in the United States, but Amex is better known and more widely accepted; you can also avoid hefty surcharges by cashing Amex checks at Amex offices. Whatever you do, keep track of all the serial numbers in case the checks are lost or stolen.

Traveler's checks are not necessary to travel anymore, particularly in countries like Slovenia and Croatia, where theft is unusual, ATMs are readily available, and credit cards are widely accepted. The main advantage of traveler's checks is that they are replaceable, so if they are lost or stolen, your whole vacation can be quickly recovered. In most cases replacement is guaranteed within 24 hours. When traveling in the countryside, cash is usually the best bet, especially when attempting to book a private room or get a meal at a simple restaurant.

American Express now offers a stored-value card called a Travelers Cheque Card, which you can use wherever American Express credit cards are accepted, including ATMs. The card can carry a minimum of $300 and a maximum of $2,700, and it's a very safe way to carry your funds. Although you can get replacement funds in 24 hours if your card is lost or stolen, it doesn't really strike us as a very good deal. In addition to a high initial cost ($14.95 to set up the card, plus $5 each time you "reload"), you still have to pay a 2% fee for each purchase in a foreign currency (similar to that of any credit card). Further, each time you use the card in an ATM you pay a transaction fee of $2.50 on top of the 2% transaction fee for the conversion—add it all up and it can be considerably more than you would pay when simply using your own ATM card. Regular traveler's checks are just as secure and cost less.

Contacts American Express (☎*888/412–6945 in the U.S., 801/945–9450 collect outside of the U.S. to add value or speak to customer service* ⊕*www.americanexpress.com*).

▌ RESTROOMS

Public restrooms can be found in some cities in Slovenia and Croatia, usually near high traffic areas like markets or beaches. Where there are permanent facilities, a price is usually posted outside, and an attendant is on hand to accept payment. At some places by the seaside, coin-operated portable toilets are common, especially in the busy summer season.

Find a Loo The Bathroom Diaries (⊕*www. thebathroomdiaries.com*) *is flush with unsanitized info on restrooms the world over—each one located, reviewed, and rated.*

▌ SAFETY

Croatia and Slovenia are both relatively safe by Western standards (Slovenia claims to have one of the lowest crime rates in Europe), and there are no particular local scams that visitors should be aware of. Violent crime is rare. Be on guard for pickpockets in crowded markets, and don't wander alone down dark streets at night.

In Croatia the exceptional danger from land mines has been greatly reduced by government programs; however, care should be taken in eastern Slavonia, the former area of conflict; all deserted and unreconstructed areas should be considered still potentially hazardous. Nevertheless, even in this region the main roads are guaranteed to be safe.

Distribute your cash, credit cards, I.D.s, and other valuables between a deep front pocket, an inside jacket or vest pocket, and a hidden money pouch. Don't reach for the money pouch once you're in public.

▌ TAXES

In Croatia foreigners who spend over 500 Kn in one store on a single day can reclaim PDV (tax) return upon leaving the country. To do this, you need to present the receipts and the goods bought at the *carina* (customs) desk at the airport, ferry port, or border crossing on your way out of the country.

In Slovenia any visitor who buys goods worth more than €50 at any one store is entitled to a refund of taxes. When you make a purchase ask for a Request for VAT Refund form, *Zahtevek za vracilo DDV*. A customs officer will certify the form when you leave the country. To obtain the refund, go to the Kompas MTS office at the border crossing point or the airport. Exporting historic artifacts is forbidden.

When making a purchase, ask for a V.A.T. refund form and find out whether the merchant gives refunds—not all stores do, nor are they required to. Have the form stamped like any customs form by customs officials when you leave the country or, if you're visiting several European Union countries, when you leave the EU. After you're through passport control, take the form to a refund-service counter for an on-the-spot refund (which is usually the quickest and easiest option), or mail it to the address on the form (or the envelope with it) after you arrive home. You receive the total refund stated on the form, but the processing time can be long, especially if you request a credit-card adjustment.

Global Refund is a Europe-wide service with 225,000 affiliated stores and more than 700 refund counters at major airports and border crossings. Its refund form, called a Tax Free Check, is the most common across the European continent. The service issues refunds in the form of cash, check, or credit-card adjustment.

V.A.T. Refunds Global Refund (800/566–9828 www.globalrefund.com).

TIME

Croatia and Slovenia are on Central European Time (CET), one hour ahead of Greenwich Mean Time and six hours ahead of the Eastern time zone of the United States.

TIPPING

When eating out in Croatia, if you have enjoyed your meal and are satisfied with the service, it is customary to leave a 10% to 15% tip. It is not usual to tip in cafés or bars. Maids and taxi drivers are not usually tipped. Tour guides do receive a tip, especially if they are particularly good. For porters on trains and bellhops at hotels, 5-10 Kn per bag will be appreciated.

In Slovenia the tax is already included in listed prices. Tips are not included in bills, however, and a 10% tip is customary. If the service is especially good, tip 15%. In hotels, tip bellhops €1–€2 per bag and room service waiters €1–€2 for a room delivery. In taxis, round up to the nearest euro amount.

INDEX

NOTES

George Cell

MONTENEGRO

069 221 107

= (+382)

Home

435 TRG OROZIA   042 304 268
85330 KOTOR

ABOUT OUR WRITERS

Although there's no substitute for travel advice from a good friend who knows your style, our contributors are the next best thing—the kind of people you would poll for travel advice if you knew them.

John K. Cox is associate professor and chair of history at Wheeling Jesuit University. His other publications include *The History of Serbia* (Greenwood, 2002) and *Slovenia: Evolving Loyalties* (Routledge, 2005). He specializes in 20th-century Balkan intellectual history and is currently writing a study of the works of Ismail Kadare. He wrote the Croatia history essay for the first edition of *Fodor's Croatia & Slovenia*.

Jane Foster is a freelance writer who hails from the Yorkshire Dales in the United Kingdom. She studied for a degree in architecture before moving to Rome in 1990, where travel, art, and culture became her main interests. In 1996 she made a brief visit to Croatia and was immediately captivated by the countries of the former Yugoslavia. She lived in Split for six years, where she learned to speak Croatian and cook Dalmatian-style, and also fell prey to the pleasures of sailing and nudism. Although she is now based in Athens, she makes frequent trips back to Croatia for both work and pleasure.

Betsy Maury, a former senior editor at Bantam, Doubleday, Dell, lived in Slovenia for four years, traveling widely in that country and in neighboring Croatia. Since 1999 she has made her home in Budapest. Her enthusiasm for Hungarian cuisine—as well as a love of Hungarian food—keeps her busy exploring the cosmopolitan city in search of interesting restaurants, and her love of wine has brought her to Croatia on several occasions. She travels widely throughout Central Europe, working as a freelance writer.

A contributor to previous Fodor's guides to Eastern & Central Europe and Budapest, **Paul Olchváry** lived in Hungary from 1990 to 2000 and has thoroughly explored not only that country but also neighboring Croatia over the years. Translator of nine books from the Hungarian and a writer of short stories and novels, he was a copywriter at Princeton University Press from 2000 to 2005, when he absconded with his wife Dorottya to a cabin in the woods of Kismaros, Hungary, to pursue his own writing.

Marijana Oroz graduated with a degree in English from Ohio State University and still contributes to *Columbus Alive,* a major weekly publication in the area. Her parents hail from Croatia, and her visits to the country and exposure to her sister's wine-importing business have familiarized her with the beauty of the Croatian landscape and its viticultural treasures. Because of her family's roots, Croatian wine is as close to her heart as it is to her palate. She wrote the Croatia wine essay for the first edition of Fodor's Croatia & Slovenia.

Evan Rail moved to Prague in 2000, and stayed there primarily because of the kvasnicové pivo. For many years he reviewed restaurants and covered food and drink for the *Prague Post* until he left to write the *Good Beer Guide to Prague and the Czech Republic* for CAMRA, a U.K. beer consumers' organization. His stories have been included in *Best Food Writing* and *Travelers' Tales* anthologies and appear frequently in the *New York Times* travel section.